Dùn Èistean, Ness

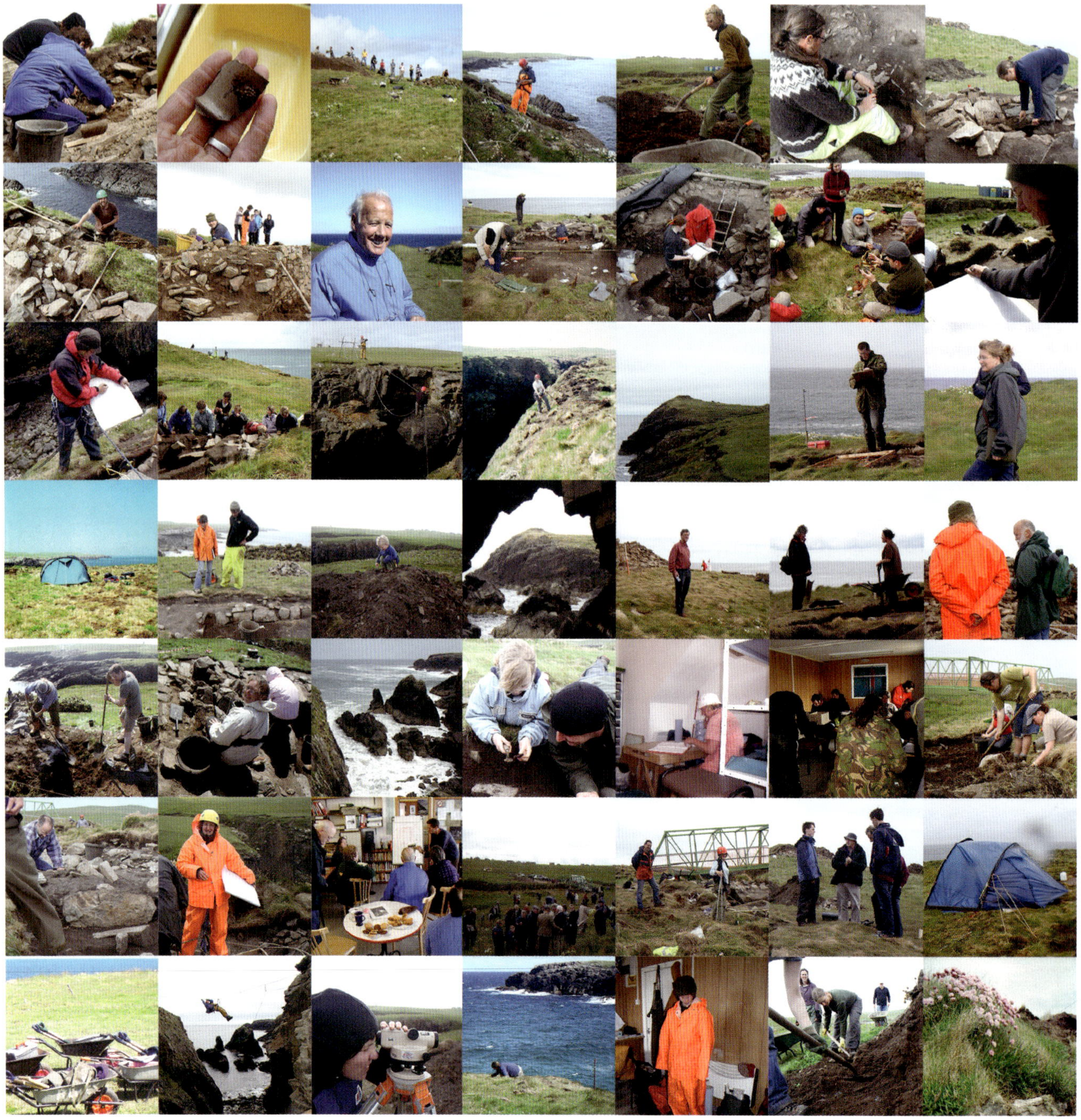

Dùn Èistean, Ness
The excavation of a clan stronghold

by

Rachel C Barrowman

With contributions from
T B Ballin, C Barrowman, J D Bateson, C E Batey, C M Batt, A Becket, E Campbell,
R Cerón-Carrasco, C Dalglish, S Driscoll, N Ferguson, A MacCoinnich, I McHardy, L E
McKenna, J McKenzie, D Maguire, E Masson-MacLean, R Murdoch, Z Outram, T Poller,
S Ramsay, I A Simpson, D Sneddon, D U Stiùbhart and R Will

Illustrations by
C Francoz, G McSwan, J Arthur, J Bacon, C Barrowman, C Evans,
A O'Donnell, I Shearer and J Sievewright

Supported by
Heritage Lottery Fund, Historic Scotland, Comhairle nan Eilean Siar, Comunn na Gàidhlig,
Clan Morrison Society, Comunn Eachdraidh Nis and the University of Glasgow

acair

In memory of Mark Elliot

*The Dùn Èistean Project, including
this publication, was supported by:*

Heritage Lottery Fund

Historic Scotland

Comhairle nan Eilean Siar

Comunn na Gàidhlig

The Clan Morrison Society

Commun Eachdraidh Nis

The University of Glasgow

First published in 2015 by Acair Ltd., An Tosgan
Seaforth Road, Stornoway, Isle of Lewis HS1 2SD

info@acairbooks.com
www.acairbooks.com

Page ii: Composition of images from fieldwork, by Chris Barrowman

contents

summary

Dùn Èistean is a small, tidal cliff-bound island situated just off the east coast of Ness, at the northern tip of the Isle of Lewis in the Western Isles of Scotland. It is separated from the Ness mainland by a 15m-wide gap bounded by sheer cliffs 16m high, and in local tradition is considered to be the stronghold of the Clan Morrison. A steel footbridge that was erected by the Clan Morrison Society in time for a Clan gathering in Ness in 2002 means that the site can now easily be accessed. With the setting up of the Dùn Èistean Archaeology Project (DEAP) by the Western Isles Council archaeologist, local Morrisons and the Ness Historical Society, funding was secured from the Heritage Lottery Fund, Historic Scotland and the Western Isles Council for archaeological fieldwork at the site by Glasgow University between 2000 and 2007.

These excavations revealed the remains of a defended settlement on the stack that was similar to a castle in its layout. It was in repeated use for short bursts of time, with a defensive perimeter wall, a lookout tower, communal quarters and ancillary buildings, a corn-drying kiln and a pond dug to collect rainwater. The rare assemblage of environmental material includes evidence that the drying and processing of oats and barley was a major part of life, meat was consumed, mainly from sheep and cattle, and the wild resources of fish and shellfish were exploited. The main fuel used was peat, although wood and domestic rubbish were also burnt. The buildings on the site were all constructed from turf and stone walls with turf roofing supported on driftwood timbers, reflecting the knowledge and resources available in the local environment. Even the small lookout tower was built in the local tradition, from stone and turf walls with an earthen core, and probably a turf roof. The artefactual assemblages hint at external contacts through imported pottery sherds and coins, and at conflict in the form of lead artillery and a unique assemblage of gunflints, both of which were manufactured and used on the site.

The location of Dùn Èistean may draw the modern observer to conclude that it was situated in a remote rural backwater, but the excavations have shown that is part of a long tradition of clan strongholds seen in the MacLeod lordship on the western seaboard of north-west Scotland, and was caught up in the political turmoil experienced between the islands and the mainland governmental authorities in Scotland in the 1500s and early 1600s AD. Set in the context of the historical evidence and oral traditions from these troubled centuries in Lewis, the location of Dùn Èistean on the coast of the Ness peninsula thrust out into the North Atlantic, meant that it was situated in the busy sea routes around northern Britain and Europe. With views along the Lewis coast and across to the Scottish mainland, it would have been highly visible in a maritime world, and ideally placed to potentially control or monitor passing sea traffic. Whilst the excavations have demonstrated that the stack was therefore far from being on the edge, unaffected by political troubles, the material evidence also testifies to a way of life that had developed a unique local response to wider threats, maintaining the self-sufficiency of a people with a strong local identity.

Is e eilean-tràghaidh beag, cuairtichte le creagan, a tha ann an Dùn Èistean a tha air a shuidheachadh far costa an ear sgìre Nis, aig fìor cheann a tuath Eilean Leòdhais sna h-Eileanan an Iar an Alba. Tha caolas a tha 15m a leud eadar fearann Nis agus an dùn, cuairtichte le creagan a tha 16m a dh'àirde, agus air aithneachadh san dualchas ionadail mar dhaingneach Chlann Mhic Ghille Mhoire. Tha drochaid stàilinn a chaidh a togail ann an 2002 le Comann Chlann Mhic Ghille Mhoire an uair a bha cruinneachadh aca, a' ciallachadh gu bheil e a-nis furasta faighinn chun làraich. An uair a chaidh Pròiseact Arc-eòlas Dhùn Èistein (DEAP) a stèidheachadh le arc-eòlaiche Chomhairle nan Eilean Siar, Moireastanaich a bha a' fuireach gu h-ionadail agus Comunn Eachdraidh Nis, chaidh maoineachadh fhaighinn bho Maoin Dualchais a' Chrannchuir, Alba Aosmhor agus Comhairle nan Eilean Siar airson obair sgrùdaidh arc-eòlais a rinneadh le Oilthigh Ghlaschu eadar 2000 agus 2007.

Sheall an obair cladhachaidh a rinneadh gun robh ionad tuineachaidh a bha air a dhìon air an stac a bha air a chur a-mach coltach ri caisteal. Bha e air a bhith air a chleachdadh bho àm gu àm airson greisean goirid, agus bha balla dìon mun cuairt air, tùr faire, cairtealan coitcheann agus fo-thoglaichean, àth airson gràn a thiormachadh agus sloc a chaidh a dhèanamh gus am biodh fìor-uisge aca. Tha na stuthan a chaidh a lorg mar fhianais gun robh a bhith a' tiormachadh agus ag obrachadh coirce agus eòrna na phàirt mhòr den obair aca. Bhiodh iad ag ithe feòil chaorach agus mhart agus a' dèanamh feum den iasg agus maorach a bha ri fhaighinn. B' e mòine am prìomh stuth connaidh a bha aca ged a bhiodh iad cuideachd a' losgadh fiodh agus sgudal bho na taighean. Bha na toglaichean air fad air an dèanamh de bhallaichean sgrath agus clach le mullach de sgrath air muin fiodh cladaich a tha mar chomharr air an eòlas agus na stòrasan a bha rim faotainn san àrainn ionadail. Chaidh eadhoin an tùr faire beag a thogail ann an dòigh a bha traidiseanta gu h-ionadail, le ballaichean cloiche agus sgrath le ùir sa mheadhan, agus dh'fhaodadh e a bhith le sgrath air a' mhullach. Tha an stuth a chaidh a lorg a' seallltainn gur dòcha gun robh ceanglaichean ann ris an t-saoghal mhòr leis gun robh pìosan crèadhadaireachd agus buinn air an lorg, agus gun robh strì a' dol oir chaidh urchairean luaidhe agus cruinneachadh iongantach de sporran gunna a lorg a chaidh an saothrachadh agus an cleachdadh air an làrach.

Dh'fhaodadh duine a bhith dhan bheachd an-diugh gun

robh Dùn Èistean air a shuidheachadh ann an àite a bha air leth
iomallach, aonranach, ach tha na cladhachaidhean air dearbhadh
gun robh an làrach seo mar phàirt de thraidisean fada de dhaingni-
chean a bha aig sliochd nan Leòdach sìos taobh siar iar thuath na
h-Alba, agus gun robh e an teis mheadhan na strì phoilitigeach a bha
eadar na h-eileanan agus ùghdarrasan an riaghaltais air tìr mòr na
h-Alba sna 1500an agus tràth sna 1600an AC. Stèidhichte ann an
co-theacsa fianais eachdraidheil agus traidiseanan beul-aithris bho
na linntean buaireasach sin ann an Leòdhas, tha suidheachadh Dhùn
Èistein far costa Nis sa Chuan Shiar a' ciallachadh gun robh e ann
an tèis mheadhan slighean mara tranga mun cuairt air ceann a tuath
Bhreatainn agus an Roinn Eòrpa. Le deagh shealladh sìos costa
Leòdhais agus a-null gu Tìr Mòr na h-Alba, bhiodh e furasta fhaicinn
bho thaobh na mara, agus ann an deagh shuidheachadh gus sùil a
chumail air bàtaichean a bha a' seòladh seachad no airson smachd a
chumail orra. Ged mar sin a tha na cladhachaidhean air sealltainn
gun robh an stac fada bho bhith iomallach, agus air falbh bho strì
phoilitigeach, tha an stuth a chaidh a lorg a' comharrachadh dòigh
beatha a chaidh a leasachadh mar fhreagairt ionadail sònraichte a
thaobh bhagraidhean na b' fharsaing, a bha a' gleidheadh diongaltas
dhaoine aig an robh fèin-aithne làidir ionadail.

illustrations

Photographs and figures are all copyright Glasgow University and GUARD/GAL unless otherwise acknowledged:

Chris Barrowman (CB)
Hector Barrowman (HB)
Rachel Barrowman (RB)
Calum Iain Bartlett (CIB)
Severe Terrain Archaeological Campaign (STAC)
Judy Harry (JH)
Angus Mackintosh (AM)
Comunn Eachdraidh Nis (CEN)
Susan Ramsay (SR)
Historic Scotland (HS)
Royal Commission on the Ancient and Historical Monuments of Scotland (RCAHMS)

Survey and line drawings by John Arthur, Charlotte Francoz, Gillian McSwan and Ingrid Shearer unless otherwise acknowledged. Finds drawings by J Bacon, Jill Sievewright, Caitlin Evans and Anne-Marie O'Donnell. Reconstruction drawings by Gillian McSwan.

* = On CD in the back of the book

tables

acknowledgements

The author would like to thank the following for making the Dùn Èistean Archaeological Project a success, and helping with all aspects of this book.

The supporters of the project were the Heritage Lottery Fund, Historic Scotland, Comhairle nan Eilean Siar, Comunn na Gàidhlig, the Clan Morrison Society, Comunn Eachdraidh Nis and the University of Glasgow. All provided either financial support or help in kind. Thanks also to the many small, private donors. A huge debt of gratitude is owed to those who initiated the project over 15 years ago, and supported it throughout, Angus and Dolina Morrison, Knockaird, the late John William Morrison, Lord Lieutenant of the Isles, his son, Andrew, Viscount Dunrossil, the late Ian Morrison, former Chief of the Clan Morrison, and the Clan Morrisons Society of North America, Mary MacLeod and Stephen Driscoll (the then Director of GUARD at Glasgow University).

Thanks to the many individuals in Ness who visited the excavations, shared information and gave a warm welcome to the archaeologists who invaded the district every summer, all of whom have fond memories of their time in Ness as a result. Many thanks especially to all at the Comunn Eachdraidh Nis over the years who have helped and supported the archaeologists in so many ways, in particular Joan Morrison, Katie Mary MacKenzie, Annie MacSween, Anne MacLeod, Alison Brown, Wilma Patterson, Mairi MacKenzie, Kenny Don MacLean, Donnie Campbell and Hugh MacInnes. Moran taing.

Many have been involved with the project since the first season of archaeological work in 2000, either on or off site. Thanks go to those who worked with Chris Barrowman during the early years of the project; Gary Tompsett, John Duncan, John Arthur, Ian McHardy, Andrew Baines, Donna Maguire, Alastair Becket and Scott Coulter, and to those stalwart excavation supervisors who I had the pleasure of working with in the later years; Chris Dalglish, Tessa Poller, Ian McHardy and Alastair Becket. In no particular order, thanks also to Hector Maclean, Knockaird Grazings Committee, the late Margaret Macaulay, the late Norman Smith, Calum MacKenzie, Willie Taylor, Carol Knott, Lewis and Harris Young Archaeologists Club, Philomena Kennedy, Scott Macleod, Emily Walker, Gavin Smart, Ian Henderson, Murdo Macleod, Saria Steyl, Murdo McSween, Jim Crawford, Maureen Kilpatrick, Christine Rennie, Lauren Bick, Juanita Hunter, Jamie Hynd, Edouard Masson-MacLean, Donna Maguire, Laura McMeekin, Julie Masson-MacLean, Gail Scobie, Eilidh Sinclair, Rebecca Younger, Rob MacCafferty, Christine Maxwell, Richard Sangster, Mairi MacIver, Calum Iain Bartlett, Julie Candy, Tom Crowley, Catherine Lamont, Anne-Marie O'Donnell, Heather Rand, Maggie, Richard and Phil Davidson, Yancy Moore, Jennifer Morrison and Wayne Morrison, Mairi Alice Bartlett, Jen Cochrane, Pauline McLachlan, Aileen Maule, Joan O'Donnell, Elizabeth FitzPatrick (University of Galway) Rod McCullagh, John Raven and Steven Watt (Historic Scotland) and Anna Ritchie (Heritage Lottery Fund). Thanks to Comhairle nan Eilean Siar and the University of Glasgow/GUARD (now GUARD Archaeology Ltd) who project managed DEAP: Mary MacLeod, Deboarah Anderson, John Atkinson, Beverley Ballin-Smith and Bob Will.

Ewan Campbell: would like to thank Charlotte Douglas, Anne-Marie O'Donnell and Mariana Silva Porto for cataloguing the local pottery assemblage and Anne-Marie for the painstaking work of reconstructing vessels 28 and 29. Thanks also to George Haggerty for identifying the Rhenish stoneware sherd.

Aonghas MacCoinnich: would like to acknowledge the support of the AHRC funded project, 'Living on the Edge? Plantation and politics in the north Atlantic archipelago, 1493-1637' led by Alison Cathcart at the University of Strathclyde, and is grateful to Mr W David H Sellar (University of Edinburgh), colleagues Allan Macinnes and Alison Cathcart (University of Strathclyde) and Alasdair Ross (University of Stirling) for taking time from busy schedules to read and discuss points in this paper. He also benefited from a spirited e-mail exchange with Andy Morrison, from the writings of Dòmhnall Uilleam Stiùbhart and from discussions with the editor, Rachel Barrowman. All of these exchanges saved him from many errors. Any remaining mistakes are, of course, all entirely of his own making. Mo thaing cuideachd gu mo phàrantan ris an robh mi a' bruidhinn mura seo thar iomadach bliadhna agus aig a bheil, mar a th'agam fhìn, suim mhòr nar cuid sgìre is nar cuid eachdraidh.

Domhnall Uilleam Stiùbhart: would like special thanks to go to Mary Macleod; Chris and Rachel Barrowman, and other members of GUARD; Aonghas MacCoinnich, who made perspicacious and detailed comments on earlier drafts of this paper; Michael Robson; Annie MacSween; John Randall of the Islands Book Trust; and the two remarkably gifted fieldworkers with whom he was privileged enough to work, Christina Smith and Màiri Maciver. They have compiled an exceptionally valuable collection of the place-names of the district, and their associated traditions and memories, which add substantially to our knowledge of the history of Sgìre Nis. He would also like to thank staff and archivists at Edinburgh University Library, Museum nan Eilean, the National Library of Scotland, the National Museums of Scotland, the National Records of Scotland, the School of Scottish Studies Archives, and not least the now disgracefully broken up Scottish Catholic Archives. He would particularly like to acknowledge the expertise, generous assistance, hospitality - and patience - which everyone at Comunn Eachdraidh Nis showed over several years while he carried out research. Mìle taing dhuibh uile bhon Bhacach bhochd seo.

The author is especially beholden to historians Finlay MacLeod, Dòmhnall Uilleam Stiùbhart and Aonghas MacCoinnich, who gave freely of their time and patiently answered my many, often obvious, questions, and to the late Mark Elliot, Museum nan Eilean. Thanks also to Agnes Rennie and Margaret Anne MacLeod at Acair Books Ltd, Beverley Ballin-Smith, Chris Dalglish, Aonghas MacCoinnich, Mary MacLeod and Chris Barrowman who read through the text, and Annie MacSween who proofed the Gàidhlig. Charlotte Francoz and Gillian McSwan worked over and above on many of the lovely illustrations. Finally I would like to thank my long suffering husband, Chris, who took my vague sketches and ideas, and made them a reality in his fantastic graphic design of the book, our children Martha and Hector for their patience and above all, Almighty God, with whom all thing are possible. To Him be all the glory.

one

This book describes the results of six seasons of archaeological work managed by Glasgow University Archaeological Research Division (GUARD) on Dùn Èistean between 2000 and 2007. GUARD was first commissioned by the Dùn Èistean Committee at the Comunn Eachdraidh Nis to undertake an archaeological survey in 2000, with geophysical survey and small-scale trial excavations following in 2001 and 2002. From the results of these investigations it was obvious that Dùn Èistean was an exceptional site both in its fine state of preservation and its medieval date. This period of history in Lewis and Harris is not well documented and had been subject to little archaeological research.

In 2004 Comhairle nan Eilean Siar archaeologist, Mary MacLeod, and the Dùn Èistean committee moved the project to a new phase of extensive survey, excavations and research in Ness, with the aim of promoting the scholarly investigation and public interpretation of Dùn Èistean and the surrounding Ness landscape. The site became the heart of a multi-disciplinary project funded by the Heritage Lottery Fund, Historic Scotland and Comunn na Gàidhlig, with help in kind from project partners Comunn Eachdraidh Nis, Comhairle nan Eilean Siar and Glasgow University. From the start one of the fundamental principles of the project was to integrate archaeological and historical research, and to work through the medium of Gaelic where possible in Ness, which is still a strong Gaelic-speaking area. As well as three seasons of extensive excavations on Dùn Èistean, directed by the author and managed by GUARD, the project included research and recording of the place-names, history and oral traditions of the Ness area through the medium of Gaelic (the Dùn Èistean History Project; see Stiùbhart 2006a; 2006b; chapter 3, below), and a survey of the Ness district (the Ness Archaeological Landscape Survey, see Barrowman, C S 2015).

The book is split into four sections: The first (Background) consists of two chapters that give the archaeological and historical background to the site, and provide an overview of what was known about Dùn Èistean before the excavations began, including research into the history and oral traditions of Ness. The second section (Groundwork) contains six chapters that describe, with excavation plans, the evidence for buildings and other features found in each excavation 'area' on the site. The third section (Analyses) gives the results of the specialist analyses of the material found in the excavations, including the artefacts, environmental material, soils analysis and radiocarbon dating, and what they can tell us about the daily life of the inhabitants of Dùn Èistean. Finally, an overview is provided in the last section of the book (Conclusions), which attempts to pull together and discuss all the different strands of evidence, provide a story of the development and use of the stronghold, and explore the wider implications for the archaeology of the late medieval period in Ness and further afield.

As this book is an excavation report it by necessity contains a lot of detailed evidence and analyses. However it has been designed so that the reader can choose how much detail to plunge into. For those wishing to get an overall view of the main findings, summaries in larger type are provided at the beginning of each chapter, with interpretative plans and illustrations. If more detail is required the remainder of each chapter describes the findings in full, with accompanying data on a CD in the back of the book.

Gaelic conventions used in this publication

Throughout this book the English form of the main village names in Ness is used, for example Knockaird, Habost. Gaelic forms are used where there is no established English usage, for example Dun Othail or Dùn Èistean. As far as possible the recommendations of *Ainmean Aitean Alba* (AAA) are adhered to.[1] Unfamiliar Gaelic words are in italics, especially if an English equivalent is also cited. English equivalents of Gaelic village-names used in the text are as follows:

Barabhas	Barvas
Carlabhagh	Carloway
Cnoc Àrd	Knockaird
Cros	Cross
Dail bho Dheas	South Dell
Eòradal	Eorodale
Eòropaidh	Eoropie
Lìonal	Lionel
Port Nis	Port of Ness
Suainebost	Swainbost
Tàbost	Habost

Endnotes

[1] *Ainmean-Àite na h-Alba* (Gaelic Place-Names of Scotland) is the national advisory partnership for Gaelic place-names in Scotland. Its purpose is to agree correct forms of Gaelic place-names for maps, signs and general use. It draws on the expertise of its member organisations, local knowledge, and historical sources to agree authoritative forms of Gaelic place-names. To ensure consistent spelling it uses established principles such as the Gaelic Orthographic Conventions and the guidance it has produced on Gaelic place-names. The partnership has been working with the Ordnance Survey, local councils, roads authorities and other public bodies since 2000 to provide Gaelic names for maps and signs. To meet the growing demand for reliable information on Gaelic place-names, it is setting up the national Gaelic place-name gazetteer referred to in the National Plan for Gaelic. For more information, please visit www.gaelicplacenames.org.

backg

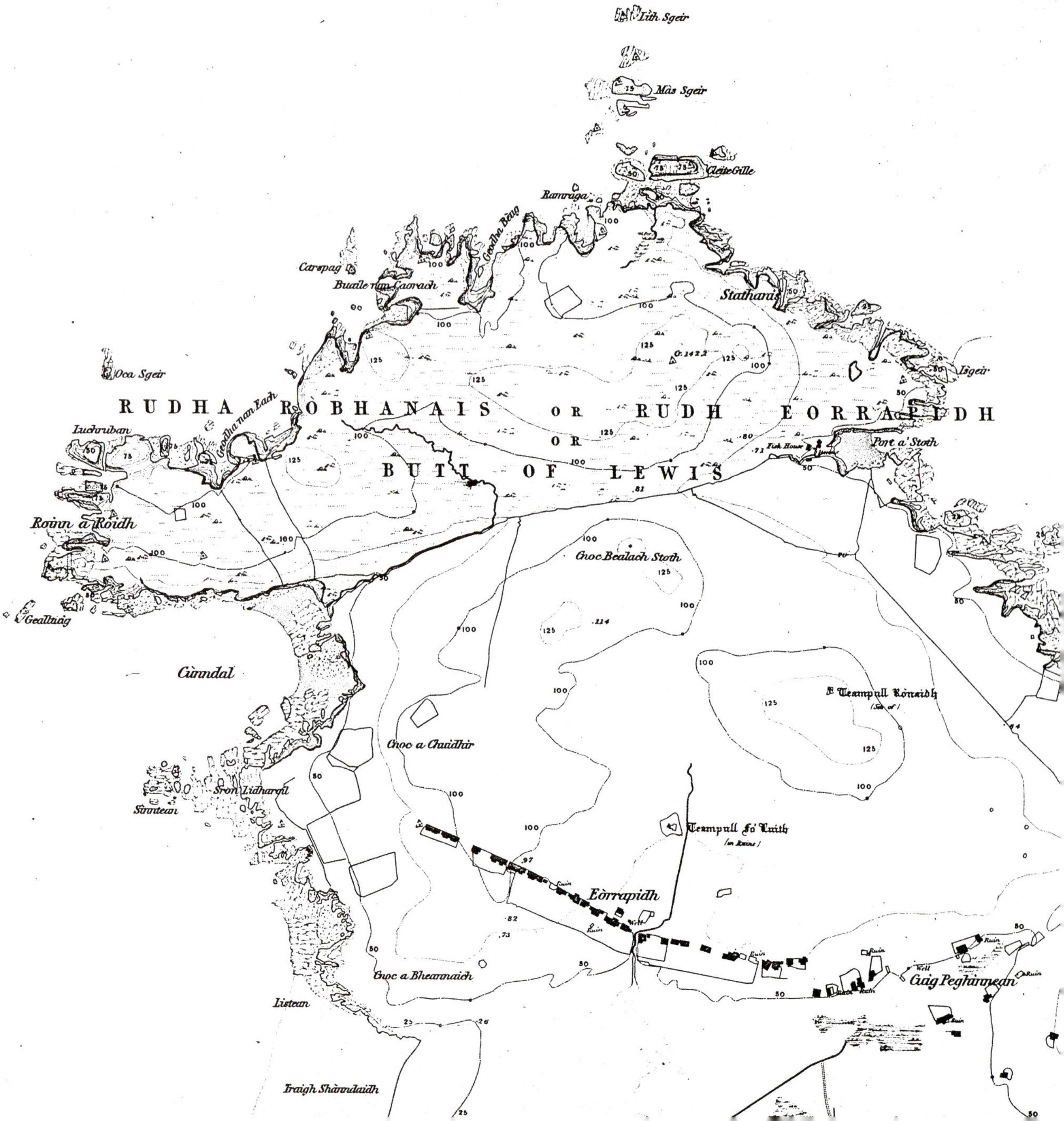

Lith Sgeir

Màs Sgeir

Cleite Gille

Ramraiga

Carspag

Buaile nan Caorach

Stathanais

Oca Sgeir

R U D H A   R O B H A N A I S   O R   R U D H   E O R R A P I D H

Isgeir

Luchruban

B U T T   O F   L E W I S

Port a' Stoth

Fish House

Roinn a' Roidh

Gealtraig

Cnoc Bealach Stoth

Cùnndal

Cnoc a Chaidhir

Teampull Rònaidh

Cnoc a Chaidhir

Sròn Lidharol

Sirinnean

Teampull Mo' Luith
(in Ruins)

Eòrrapidh

Ruin

Cnoc a Bhearnaich

Cnag Peghinnean

Listean

Traigh Shànndaidh

round

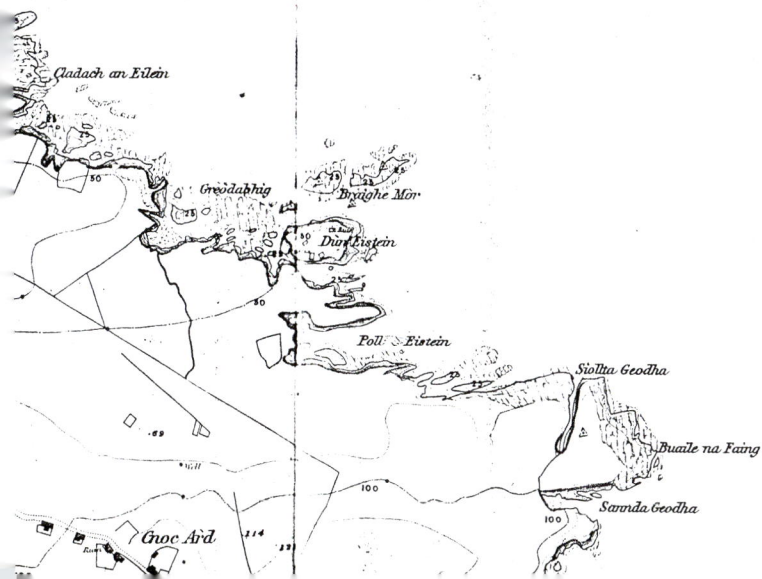

Cladach an Eilein

Greòdabhig   Braighe Mòr

Dun Eistein

Poll Eistein

Siollta Geodha

Buaile na Faing

Sannda Geodha

Cnoc Àrd

two

This chapter tracks the development of Dùn Èistean as an archaeological site, and the history of archaeological work there since the nineteenth century. Although Martin Martin describes Dùn Èistean as being a fort in 1703, it was keen antiquarian, Captain F W L Thomas who first recorded the oral traditions linking the Morrisons (Morisons) with Dùn Èistean in an article published in 1878, and so brought the archaeological remains on the island to the attention of the scholarly world. There are no references to Dùn Èistean in any surviving documentary records earlier than the early 1850s, and so since then archaeology has held the best potential to find out more about the island. Thomas' friend and fellow antiquarian, Malcolm MacPhail, dug a small trench into the main structure on Dùn Èistean in 1867, and Thomas reported his scant findings in his 1878 article. Over 50 years later surveyors from the Royal Commission for Archaeological and Historical Monuments in Scotland (RCAHMS) in the early 1920s, and the Ordnance Survey in 1969 confirmed the archaeological importance of the site. It was not until the launching of the Dùn Èistean project in 2000 however that archaeological fieldwork began on the site. The project grew into a multi-disciplinary research project with initial survey and then excavations carried out on the island every year bar one between 2000 and 2007, and the survey results and excavation methodology from this work are outlined in this chapter.

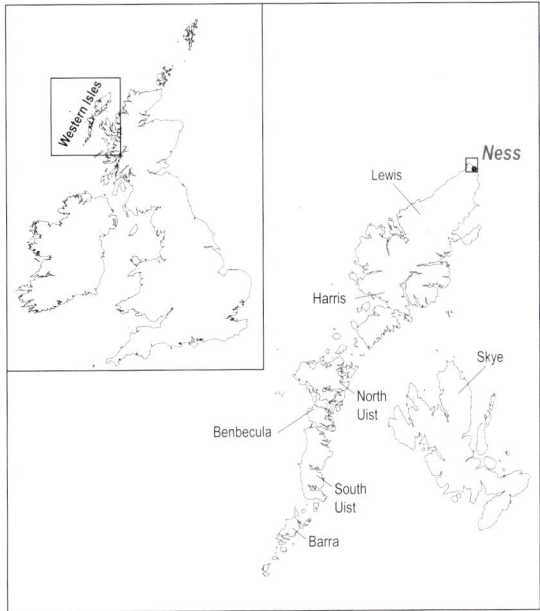

Illus 2.2 Location of Dùn Èistean

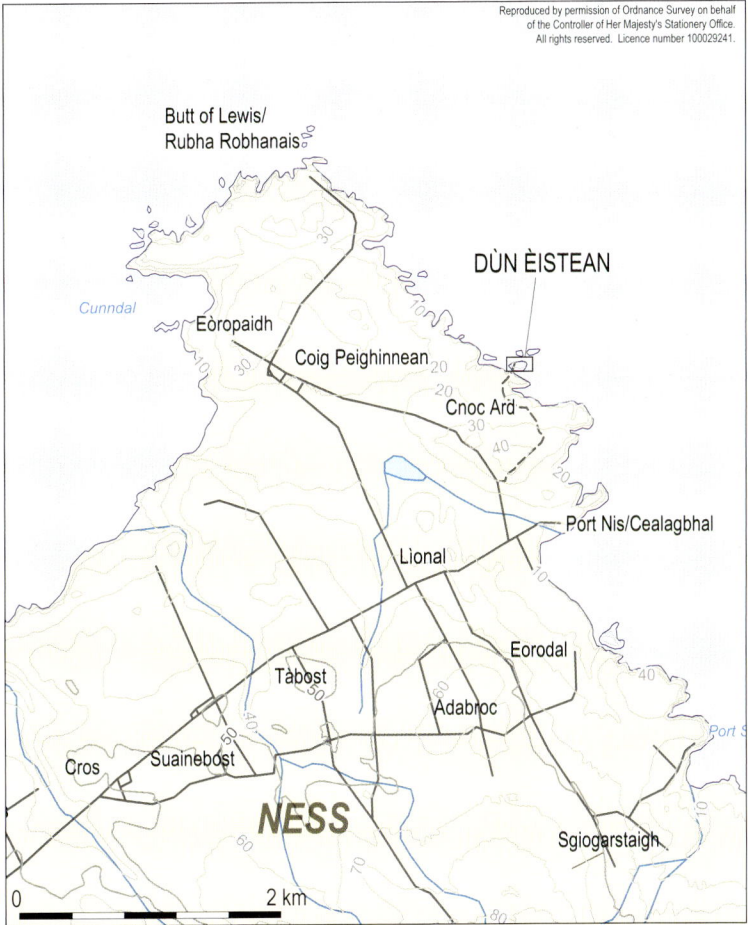

Topography and geology

Dùn Èistean (or Dun Eisdean) is situated in Knockaird in Ness, at the north end of the Isle of Lewis. A small tidal island or stack, it covers an area of 120m x 70m, and is separated from the Ness mainland by sheer cliffs 16m high, either side of a 15m-wide gap. The name derives from the Norse *stein,* meaning 'stone, boulder, standing stone', which may apply to the whole rocky island, or from the Old Norse *Eiðsstein,* 'the steinn of the isthmus' (Cox 2006). The rock that underpins Dùn Èistean can be given the general name of 'Lewisian Gneiss', often described as the oldest rock in the world (although it would be more accurate to say that it is *one of the oldest* rocks in the world; Angus 1997, 13[1]). It is made up of both 'metasediments' and 'metavolcanic' rocks, ie those formed by intense heat and/or pressure on sedimentary rocks deep in the Earth's crust, namely Anchorite and basic igneous (volcanic) rocks that were heated/pressured to form 'Meta-anchorite' and 'Metabasic' rocks. Within these rocks there are faults or intrusions called 'lines of weakness' and over time the sea has eroded the coastline along these fault lines to form caves, geos (narrow inlets), promontories (small headlands) and small stacks or islands such as Dùn Èistean. The erosion is an ongoing process and can be seen in the slumps and rock falls along the cliffs near the Dùn.

The top of Dùn Èistean is relatively flat, with a gently sloping rise to the highest point on the north-east side. It is covered in rough grazing, Sea Daisies (Sea Mayweed, *Tripleurospermum maritimum*) and Sea Pinks (Sea Thrift, *Armeria maritima*), which grow on the acid, nutritionally-deficient soils of the island. The Dùn is part of the common grazings and until the last thirty years or so, was regularly grazed by sheep in the summer or when rams were put on to the island to separate them from the rest of the flock outside the breeding season. To get sheep on to the Dùn or get access to the fishing off the rocks on the seaward sides, it was necessary to scramble down the cliff on the mainland side, cross the gap at low tide and climb the precipitous cliffs on the other side.

Unlike the majority of Ness, Dùn Èistean is not owned by the local estate (now a community owned estate, the *Urras Oighreachd Ghabhsainn* (Galson Estate Trust), but by the Clan Morrison Society, who bought the site in 1967. Antiquarians recorded a local oral tradition in the nineteenth century that Dùn Èistean was the stronghold of the Clan, and since then it has been considered the Morrison ancestral home by many Morrisons throughout the Diaspora. When the Clan Morrison Society was formed in 1909, the Clan crest featured the war cry of 'Dun Uisdein', and later, a tower with a defiant fist extending from the castellated wall heads.[2]

Early references

The oldest surviving written reference to Dùn Èistean by name is Martin Martin, who writes:

'There are several natural and artificial Forts in the Coast of this Island,

which are call'd Dun, from the *Irish* word *Dain*, which signifies a Fort: The natural Forts here are *Dun-owle, Dun-eoradil, Dun-eisten.*'

Martin Martin 1703, 8

Martin classed Dùn Èistean as one of several 'natural' forts on the coast of Lewis, that is, easily defended due to its natural features (cliff-bound, tidal), rather than an 'artificial' fort, where the built structure itself was the defence eg *Dùn Bhuirgh* (Dun Borve), on the west coast of Ness, or *Dùn Chàrlabhaigh* (Dun Carloway) further inland to the south (Barrowman, R C 2007, 58). He also noted that there are many Dun sites around the coast of Lewis, so it is interesting that he chose to mention Dùn Èistean, *Dùn Eòradail* (Dun Eorodale) and Dùn Othail in particular. These three duns have many things in common, not least that they are all on the north-east coast of Lewis, and all considered in local tradition to date to the late medieval/post-medieval period. Perhaps Martin picked these three duns out because he visited them, or was in the district and had them described to him (Burgess 2003, 41-2). The fact that he singles them out by name suggests that they were still accorded some importance locally at the end of the seventeenth century, only two or three generations after tradition records they were occupied.

The next mention of Dùn Èistean occurs 150 years later in 1852, when the Ordnance Survey surveyors visited Knockaird, in Ness, and spoke to local man, John Morison, recording:

'This is a small round Island which is arable on the Sea Shore and Isolated only at high water. There is the ruins of some kind of building on the highest point of it which appears more at present like a heap of stones thrown together than the ruin of a castle as the name Signifies. Nothing regarding it can be collected from the neighbouring people. There are other ruins on the Island beside that considered as the castle.'

OS Name Book 3A

Despite the informant being a Morrison, no traditions relating to Dùn Èistean were collected by the Ordnance Survey. Within two decades however this was all to change when F W L Thomas published a paper 'On the Traditions of the Morrisons' in which he identified Dùn Èistean in local tradition as the fort of the Morrisons of Ness (Thomas 1878).

Dun Eystein, Ancient Fortress of the Clan Morison, near the Butt of Lewis

Captain F W L Thomas and Malcolm MacPhail

Frederick W L Thomas, RN, FSA (Scot) was a Captain in the Royal Navy who worked for the Admiralty Hydrographic Office. In 1857 he was sent to join Captain Henry C Otter, director of the Scottish Survey, who since 1846 had been charting the waters around the Western Isles (MacLean and MacLeod 1989). Thomas, who was a keen photographer and antiquarian, developed an enthusiasm for the antiquities and traditions of the Western Isles. In the 1860s he published papers on the 'beehive' houses of Lewis and Harris and the tradition of the *Each-Uisge* or 'water-horse' (Thomas 1862; 1870), as well as a notes on several 'articles' that he had found whilst investigating the antiquities on the islands (eg Thomas 1863). In the following decade he was to publish, amongst other papers, an account of the traditions of the Morrisons and the MacAulays respectively (1878; 1880). Throughout this period he worked on an extensive paper 'On the Duns of the Outer Hebrides', which was finally published in 1890, after his death.

During his explorations, Thomas met Malcolm MacPhail, a Free Church student from Shawbost, who worked as a teacher in Lionel school in Ness (see Stiùbhart in Chapter 3, below; Robson 2004, 17-34). The two developed an enthusiasm for archaeological sites in Ness, particularly the duns, which Thomas was busy researching. MacPhail, on Thomas' behalf, began conducting detailed surveys and collecting local traditions relating to the duns, and the two gentlemen corresponded about his investigations, which included Dùn Èistean[3].

On 11 Dec 1866 MacPhail wrote:

> 'I visited Duneistin two days ago and found that without some labour I could not see much of the walls, or where the entrance was. I however endeavoured to measure it as correctly as I could. The enclosed sketch plan may perhaps enable you to form some idea of the kind of building it was. Its construction is quite different, I think, from either Dun Charlabhagh or Dunbhragar.'

Two months later, MacPhail had returned to the site and conducted a more detailed survey, writing in February 1867:

> 'At the time I sent you a sketch-plan of Duneistin it was very little of the walls I could see. I have since explored the central circle so far that I have reached the foundations and can now see all that is to be seen of it, viz. four and a half feet. It is very strange that there is nothing like a doorway to be seen about it. Unless it was below what is to be seen of the walls, I do now know where it was. While exploring it I saw nothing except small bits of charcoal – a very small bit [of] flint and a bit of leather used for making the brogues which could not endure handling. The Dun is square (outer walls dimensions of 23 feet by 18) but the central circle is of an oval shape (dimensions 6½ feet by 4 feet 2 inches).'
> 'There are the ruins of other houses to be seen on the island. The Dun is sometimes called 'Tigh nan arm'.

The findings from MacPhail's 'detailed surveys' and collection of local oral traditions from Ness, were used extensively by Thomas in both his articles 'Duns of the Outer Hebrides' (1890) and 'Traditions of the Morrisons (Clan MacGhillemhuire), hereditary judges of Lewis' (1878). Despite the assurance by the Ordnance Survey in 1852 that 'Nothing regarding it can be collected from the neighbouring people', by 1878 Thomas claims that at the end of the sixteenth century; '…the Morrisons fortified themselves in Dun Eystein, at Ness', going on to say:

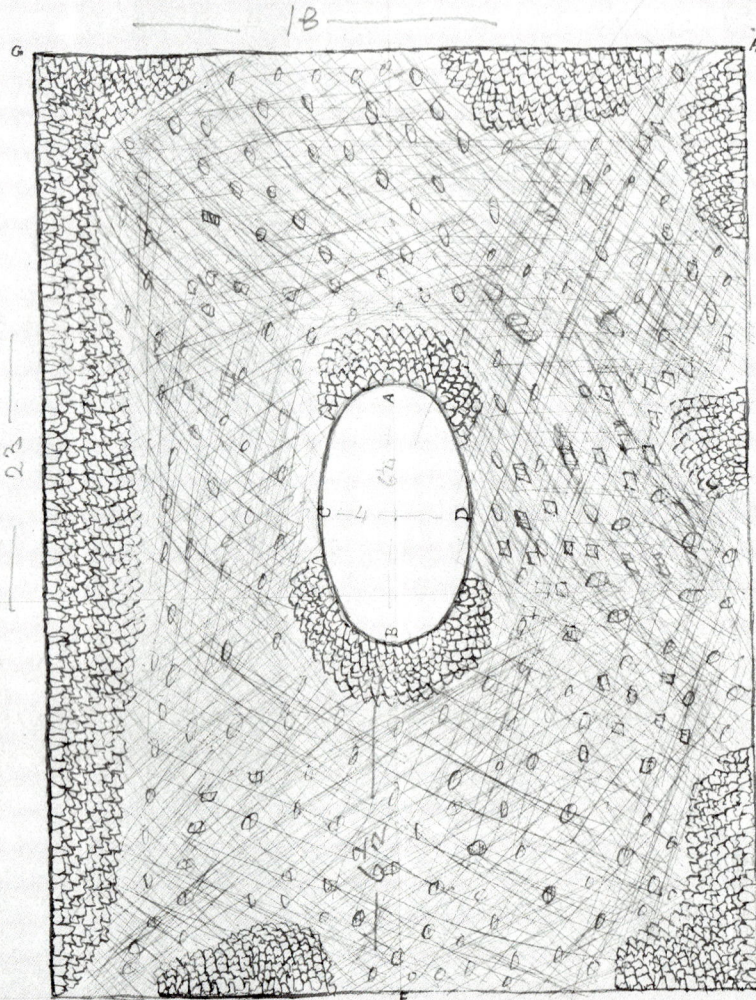

Tigh nan Arm.

Dun Eystein

House of Arms

Represents the parts of the wall to be seen.

Distance from A to B six feet three inches – from C to D 4 feet.

From B to E five and a half feet.

— F to G twenty three feet. From G to H is eighteen feet.

Scale – ¼ inch : one foot.

Illus 2.5 MacPhail's 1866 sketch plan of 'Tigh nan Arm', Dùn Èistean. Reproduced by kind permission of the RCAHMS, Society of Antiquaries of Scotland Collection (SAS 27)

'Dun Eystein is a natural stronghold at the north end of Ness, of Lewis, in the townland of Cnoc Aird, to which the Morrisons were want to retire when hard pressed or in times of war. It is a flat, cliffy island, of a somewhat oval shape, about 75 yards long and 50 yards broad, and is separated from the mainland by a narrow, perpendicular ravine, through which the sea flows at high water. The ravine is between 30 and 40 feet broad, and the same in height. The remains of a strong wall follow the edge of the cliff on the landward side of the island, and through the wall there are said to have been squints or loopholes for observation and defence.

Towards the north-east corner of the island is a dûn or castle, sometimes called Tigh nam Arm; or the House of Arms, now but 4½ feet high. The outside of the dun is an oblong square, 23 by 18 feet; and this basement is nearly solid, for the central area, which is of an oval shape, is only 6½ by 4½ feet, and there is no appearance of any doorway. The entrance or doorway was no doubt at the height of the first floor, similar to a dun in Taransay. The walls are of dry-stone masonry, but that is no proof of age in this part of the country. When exploring the ruins, the Rev. M Macphail, who made the above measurements, found a small piece of flint, fragments of charcoal, and a strip of leather such as was used for making brogues.

There are the remains of huts upon the island; and on the south sides is a flat ledge, called *Palla na Biorlinn*, or the Ledge of the Galley or Birlin, whereon tradition tells that the Morrisons used to haul up their boat. There is no tradition of the Eysteinn who gave his name to the dun; it is a common Norse name.'

(Thomas 1878, 516)[4]

Thomas states that 'These legends, along with most of the foregoing tales, have been selected either from the MS "Traditions of Lewis" by Donald Morison of Stornoway [died 1834, see MacCoinnich, below], or from the Rev. M MacPhail's "Traditions of Ness", which were obligingly collected by him in answer to my request for information concerning the "Brieve of Lewis"' (Thomas 1878, 541)[5]. Thomas' statement that '…the Morrisons fortified themselves in Dun Eystein, at Ness', is probably taken from one of two almost identical documents written some time around the 1630s, and discussed by MacCoinnich in Chapter 3 (below). One of these sources is by Sir Robert Gordon, and is cited by Thomas later in his article. Both sources state '…the breiwe and his kinn … strengthened themselfe within a fort in the Iland called ness'. Perhaps Thomas had access to an oral tradition recorded by Macphail that identified the un-named 'fort in the Iland called neise' as being Dùn Èistean[6]. Certainly Dùn Èistean would be an obvious candidate for the fort in Ness given the remains that are on the island.

Following the visit by the Ordnance Survey in the 1850s, and Thomas' articles, Dùn Èistean was firmly put on the map as an archaeological site worthy

The Hero's Leap

In Lewis, the traditions of those times have taken a romantic form.......Many a wild and impossible story has been invented from the shadowy remembrance of the tragedies of the 17th century, but the only one relating to Dun Eystein is the following, which has a narrow foundation in fact.

Neil Macleod, called in the legend Odhar, ie, dun, the bastard uncle of Torquil Dubh Chief of Lewis, attacked the Morrisons on the Habost moor, but was defeated. Neil sent to Harris for assistance, and came again to Habost; but the Morrisons had taken shelter in Dun Eystein. The Macleods arrived at night and marched to Dun Eystein, when one of the Morrisons, unaware of the presence of an enemy, came out of the hut. An Uig man shot an arrow – Baobh an Dorlaich, literally, the Fury of the Quiver, the last arrow of the eighteen that should be used – at him, and he was struck by the arrow, which passed through his body. The wounded Morrison cried for help; the rest came out, and Allan, the eldest, and by far the bravest, of them sprang across the ravine which separated Dun Eystein from the adjacent cliff, and loudly demanded that the assassin should be given up to him. The Macleods denied all knowledge of the deed; but Allan reproached them with cowardice, and said "If you have come to fight you ought, according to the laws of war from the creation of the world, to have waited till there was light enough to see each other." He then asked Neil for his Leigh, ie, Doctor, to attend the wounded man. Neil, after some hesitation, consented; Allan took the Leigh under his arm and leaped back across the ravine with him into the dun. The wounded man died, however. The Morrisons fled from Dun Eystein to the mainland, whither Neil pursued; but the Morrisons had seen Neil crossing the Minch, and, slipping out from among the islands, tried to get back to Lewis. The Macleods ascended a hill, espied the brieve's birlinn, and gave chase. There were only Allan Morrison and his two brothers in the boat; so Allan Mor, who was very strong, set his two brothers to row against himself, and composed and sang this iorram or boat song, with which the Ness fishermen still lighten their toil.

The chorus "Nailibh i's na-ho-ro", is repeated after every line:

Iomair a Choinnaich fhir mo chridhe;	Row, Kenneth, man of my heart;
Iomair I gu laidair righinn;	Row with vehement might;
Gaol nam ban og's gradh nighean.	The darling of damsels, and the beloved of girls.
Dh'iomrain fein fear mu dhithis,	I myself could row against two;
'S nam eiginn e fear mu thri.	And may be against three.
Tha eagal mor air mo chridhe	There is great fear on my heart
Gur I biorlinn Neill tha' tighinn,	That it is Neill's barge that is coming,
No eathair Mhic Thormaid Idhir.	Or the boat of the son of dun Thormod.
'S truagh namch robh mi fein 's Nial Odhar	It is a pity that I and dun Neil were not
An' lagan beag os ceann Dhun Othail;	In a small hollow above Dun Oo-ail;
Biodag namn laimh, is e bhi fodham,-	A dirk in my hand and he beneath.
Dhearbhinn feinn gun teidheach i domhain;	I would be sure it should go deep,
'S gun biodh fuil a chleibh 'na ghabhail.	And that the blood of his breast should flow down his reins.

Neil overtook the Morrisons a short time after they had passed Dun Othail (pro. Dun Oo-ail), where they fought desperately. Neil attacked them on one side, and the Harris men, in a second boat, on the other. Allan engaged Neil's party and killed nearly all his men, when Neil exclaimed ' My men, something must be done, or the monster (biast) will not leave a head on the shoulders of any one of us'. They fastened a sword to the end of an oar, therewith to stab Allan, who, when he saw it coming, made such a desperate blow as to cut the oar in two, but striking into the gunnel of the boat his sword stuck fast, and before he could extricate it the Macleods closed round him, and both himself and his two brothers were killed. They were buried in a small hollow a little above Dun Othail.

Taken from Rev. Malcolm Macphail's 'Traditions of Ness', MS; Thomas 1878, 545-6

of attention. Fifty years later, the Royal Commission for the Archaeological and Historical Monuments of Scotland visited and described the remains there as 'the foundations of a group of small huts impinging on one another and an oval enclosure, 29ft x 13ft internally, containing a hut circle, 6½ft in diameter, and three other small oval compartments', and 'an artificial pond' to the south of the 'tigh', 'banked on the E and excavated on the W, still showing moisture' (RCAHMS 1928). By 1969, when the Ordnance Survey revisited the site in the summer in June, they described it as a settlement, 'probably medieval, comprising a complex of small rectangular stone built huts with rounded corners, now heavily turfed'. The artificial pond was dry at this time and the enclosure that had been described by the Commission as 'oval' was noted as 'actually a rectangular hut with rounded ends, with settings of stones within, suggesting oval compartments'. The 'tigh' was described as oval, but with 'no trace of built walling'. Overall the OS found this structure 'Impossible to classify' (NMRS; visited by OS (RL) 16 June 1969).

These surveys led to the site being scheduled at the same time as many others in the Western Isles as a monument of national importance in 1992, and in 1997 it was subsequently recognised as being potentially under threat from coastal erosion during the Lewis Coastal Erosion Survey (Burgess and Church 1997, 281-2).

The early years fieldwork on Dùn Èistean 2000-2002

with Chris Barrowman, Stephen Driscoll and Donna Maguire

The Dùn Èistean project first came about when the late John William Morrison, Viscount Dunrossil, Lord Lieutenant of the Isles, set events in motion to build a bridge across to the site. At the prompting of the North America Clan society, the late Dr Iain Morrison, who had become chief of the clan in 1974 and could trace his lineage back fourteen generations to the Morrisons of Harris, contacted the newly-appointed Western Isles Council Archaeologist, Dr Mary MacLeod. In 1999 a Dùn Èistean Committee was formed based in the *Comunn Eachdraidh Nis* (Ness Historical Society) with the Clan Morrison Society and Dr MacLeod, to launch a project to investigate the archaeology of Dùn Èistean. Archaeologists at Glasgow University Archaeological Research Division (GUARD), now GUARD Archaeology Ltd (GAL) were approached by the committee and asked to tender for a project to survey and record the remains on the site, and the Dùn Èistean Project was initiated to raise the funds to survey and excavate the site in advance of plans to build a footbridge over to the site. GUARD were commissioned to undertake the archaeological work, which included a detailed topographical survey in 2000, and geophysical surveys and evaluation excavations in 2001. Mary described her excitement, and the beginnings of the project, in a special issue of Criomagan, published by the Comunn Eachdraidh Nis in 2001.

At the turn of the millennium Chris and I, tired of city life and at looking at run-down houses in the countryside around Glasgow with mortgages way out of our league, decided that after all our summer fieldwork was over we would give island life a go and move with our two year old daughter to

Illus 2.6 and 2.7 Criomagan June 2001 (with kind permission of Comunn Eachdraidh Nis)

Illus 2.8 Aerial photograph, date unknown: This superb unsourced oblique aerial photograph was taken in excellent light conditions when the island was still being regularly grazed. It probably dates to the 1970s as it featured in an exhibition mounted by the Lewis and Harris Museum Society in c 1980. It shows the structures on Dùn Èistean in amazing clarity, including remains of buildings, a large circular mound of rubble on the highest point, a pond in the centre of the island, and a long, low grassy bank atop the cliff edges on the landward sides

my family's holiday home in Eorodale, Ness. A few weeks later, Dr, now Professor, Steve Driscoll, the then Research Director with GUARD called Chris into his office to discuss a project proposal from the Western Isles Council Archaeologist, and the Clan Morrison Society in America and the Isle of Lewis. Chris was a keen climber and this project was going to involve climbing onto and camping on a sea stack. Strangely enough, the stack was only a couple of miles from our new home in Ness. We had the feeling that it was all meant to be.

Working on a challenging site like Dùn Èistean needed a plan, so before embarking on the archaeological survey, Steve and Chris travelled to Ness on a reconnaissance mission in March 2000 to plan the survey and resolve the various logistical questions concerning how best to access and work on the site safely. The coast at Dùn Èistean is some 2 km from a paved road and at that time there was no track across the uneven boggy ground down to the island so survey equipment would have to be carried across crofts and common grazing, down to the coast.

Angus Morrison (*Angus a' Phab*), Knockaird resident and member of the Clan Morrison Society, took Steve and Chris to the site and showed them three known routes onto the island. He showed them a copy of a map drawn by Angus MacLean (*Aonghas Dho'll Tinkar*), aged 88, of Knockaird,[7] which marked the local names for the caves, geos, rocks and ledges on and around Dùn Èistean. It was fascinating, with names such as '*Geodha na Sean Daoine*' (Geo of the Old Men) and '*Barra na Birlinn*' (spit, or bar, of rock of the galley). There were also notes written by Aonghas, deposited in the Comunn Eachdraidh Nis

Illus 2.9 Place names map by Angus MacLean, Cnoc Àrd, reproduced by kind permission of Hector and Kenneth Donald MacLean and above, Illus 2.10 Angus Morrison (Angus a' Phab) and Chris on Dùn Èistean, June 2000

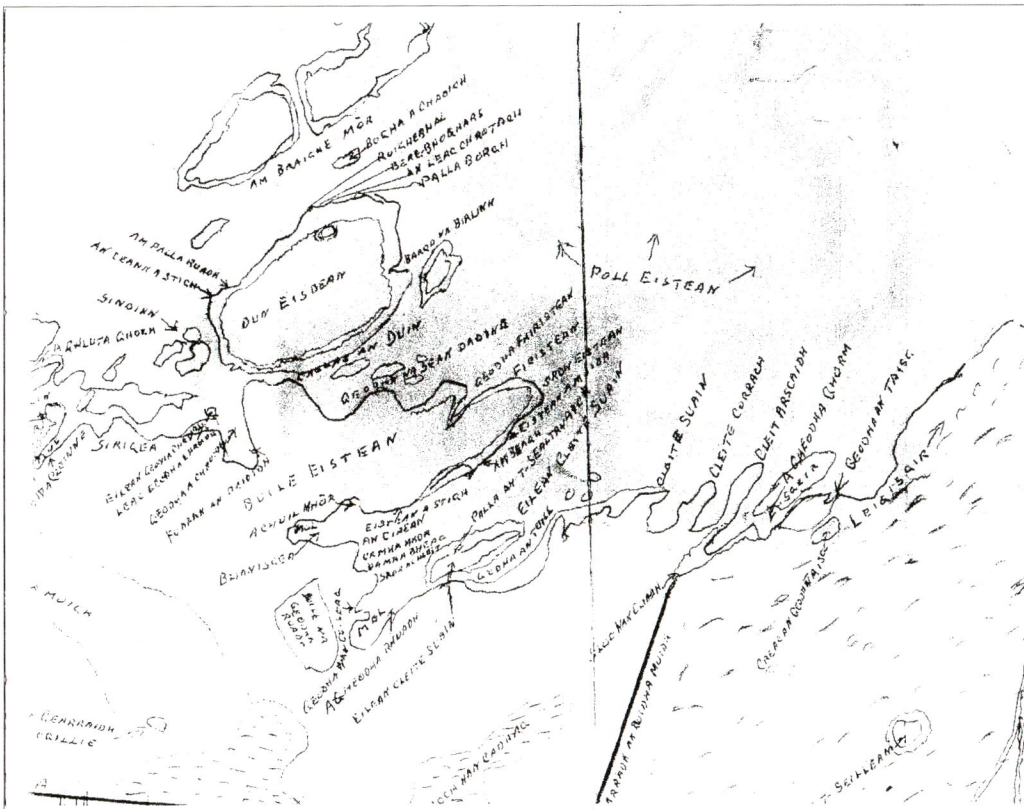

by the late Norman Smith (*Tormod Sguigs*), 10 Lionel, in which *Barra na Birlinn*, a small cove at the east end of the island, was said to have been used by *Niall Odhar MacLeod* as an anchorage for his galley. This was an alternative local name for '*Palla na Birlinn*' or '*Palla na Biorlinn*', as recorded by Thomas (1878, 516; see above) as being the traditional access to the island from the sea. However, no-one could be identified who remembered using it and it wasn't considered to be a viable route onto the island for the survey.

Angus then took Steve and Chris onto the island up a second route that followed a steep slope up the south-west corner of the island, up a rock face well-provided with steps and handholds for most of its length. This approach was only accessible at the lowest tide for a few hours, but was the easiest approach and could be climbed without ropes. A third route, directly up the cliffs where the gap between the island and the mainland was narrowest, required ropes. Angus pointed out a post in a gap in the wall at the top of the cliff on the island side, which had been used by residents for this purpose when hauling sheep onto the island. The position of this route was further up the beach of boulders at the base of the gap between the island and the mainland, and so it stayed drier for longer and may have been the preferred route in antiquity and for hauling provisions up to the island.

Steve and Chris chose the second route with the easiest approach, and decided that a survey team of three should be used to ensure that all work was conducted safely - the third person acting as a rope anchor when it was necessary to survey around the cliff edges. Chris chose the remaining members of the team, Gary Tompsett and John Arthur, in part for their rock climbing experience and fitness, as well as for their archaeological survey expertise. They flew up to Lewis in April to begin the survey, but stormy weather prevented them getting onto the stack at low tide. This was very frustrating for them, but the team used the time instead to survey the mainland adjacent to the island. Six weeks later,

Illus 2.11 Gap at low tide and Illus 2.12 Camping on the island June 2000

on 1ˢᵗ June, with Gary unable to go and replaced by climber and archaeologist, John Duncan, the survey team tried again. This time they were successful. With sunny weather and a calm sea, they were able to climb the cliffs onto the site at a suitable low tide and then camp overnight on the island for two nights in order to complete the survey. Working on the site during this time gave them a unique opportunity to experience Dùn Èistean in complete isolation – as people had experienced it in history, truly cut off from the mainland of Lewis if only for a short time.

A topographic survey records changes in height on the ground and locates natural and manmade features to produce a map of a specific area. The aims of the topographic survey on Dùn Èistean were to make a detailed record of the remains on the summit of the island (120 x 70m) and a similar-sized area of the mainland opposite, provide a preliminary statement regarding their age, function and condition and produce maps and plans that could be readily used for education and interpretation of the site. The survey was carried out using an Electronic Total Station, with a series of survey 'stations' set up on the headland and on the island to allow as complete a coverage of the area as possible. Each structure was measured and described during the survey, and theories were made as to when the buildings were occupied and what they were used for. These theories were to be tested later through excavation, and are included in each of the relevant chapters below.

Illus 2.13 Gary and John surveying

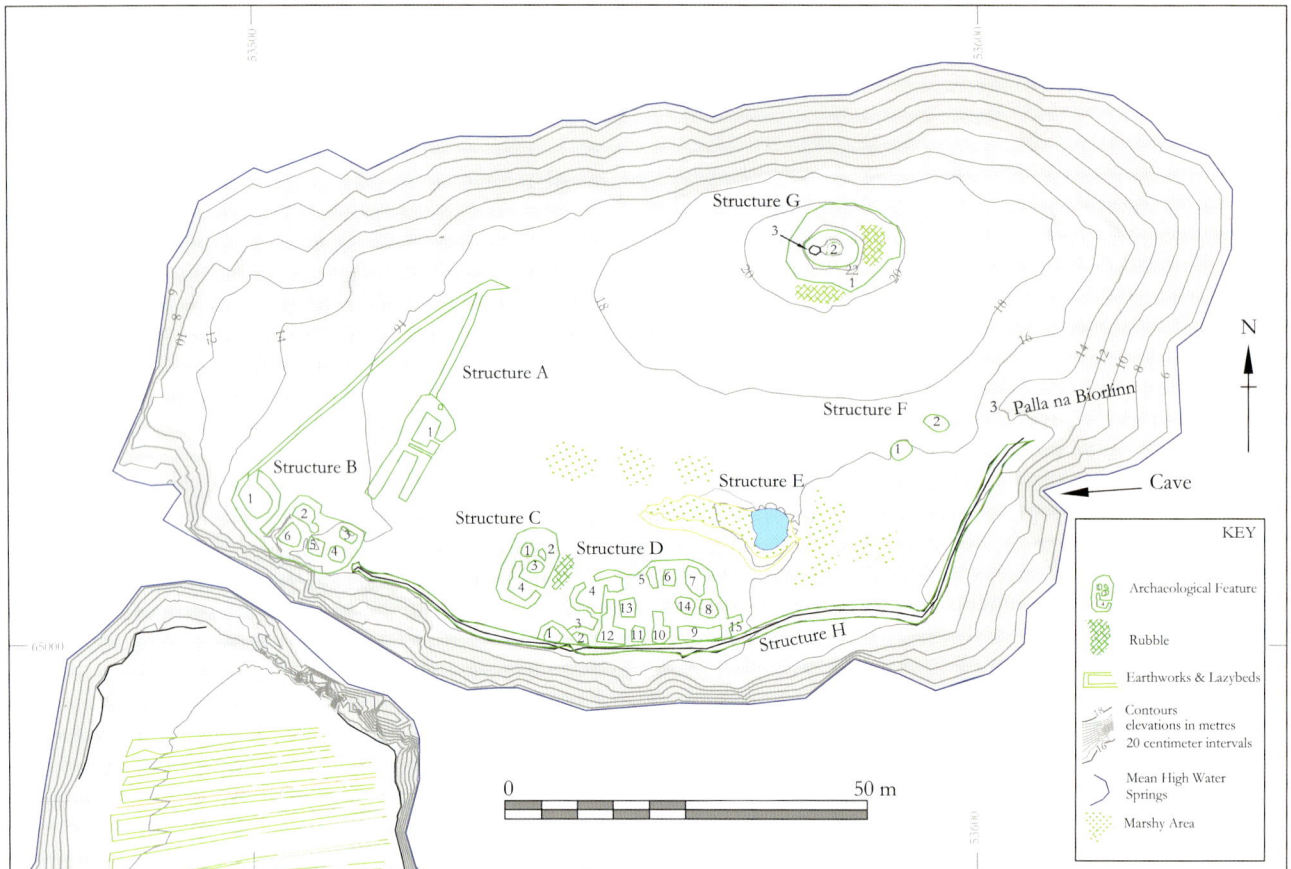

Illus 2.14 Topographic survey of Dùn Èistean. On the map: Structure G, Structure A, Structure F, Palla na Biorlinn, Structure B, Structure E, Structure C, Structure D, Cave, Structure H.

KEY

	Archaeological Feature
	Rubble
	Earthworks & Lazybeds
	Contours elevations in metres 20 centimeter intervals
	Mean High Water Springs
	Marshy Area

0   50 m

The survey recorded seven groups of features on the island (Barrowman and Driscoll 2000):

A: Two rectangular buildings, A1 and A2, linked by a common west wall with a gap of about 0.5m between the south wall of A1 and the north wall of A2. A1 4m x 2.5m with walls approximately 1m wide and 0.25m high, and a possible entrance in the middle of the east wall. A2 less well-preserved with walls 1m wide and 0.25m high but no south wall or entrance visible. A stretch of wall, 1m wide and 0.25m high, joined the west wall of A at the north-west corner of A1, then extended about 15m to the north where it joined the perimeter wall (Structure H).

B: An irregular conglomeration of six dry-stone cells that shared a common south wall on the extreme south-west of the island hard on the edge of the cliff at the narrowest point across the gap. The largest cell (B1) 5m by 3m with an almost circular interior set apart to the west of a tight cluster of five roughly oval cells, between *c* 2m – 5m in internal diameter with walls approximately 0.5m wide standing 0.5m high. There were no obvious entrances, but the collapse and tumble could easily obscure any original gaps. Structure B1 was more substantial (walls 1m wide by 0.5m high) and had a possible entrance to the north-west.

C: A substantial sub-rectangular building, 11m by 6m, aligned north-south, set back from the cliff on the west side of Structure D, with well-

Illus 2.14 Topographic survey of Dùn Èistean, Illus 2.15 Structure A from the south-west and Illus 2.16 Structure B4 from the west

preserved walls stand up to 1.5m in places. The building was divided into three or four internal compartments, but these may have been the consequence of tumbled rubble. None of the three small cells at the north end of the building (C1, 2 and 3) had obvious entrances, and were relatively small, measuring between *c* 2m by 2m and 2m by 1m. The fourth, C4, was larger and more regular, measuring 3m by 2m. It appeared to have an entrance from the east and a linking passage leading towards the three small compartments. Immediately to the east of the structure was a mass of tumbled rubble, but no coherent form could be identified, and it was interpreted as tumble.

D: The largest and most complicated group of buildings on the island, similar to Structure B, being composed of small cells and set against a wall running along the cliff edge. At least 15 individual cells identified. Overall the structure measured approximately 30m by 12m; the walls generally between 0.25m and 1m high and between 0.5 and 1m wide. On the west was a circular cell (D1) against the perimeter wall, *c* 2.5m by 2.5m internally, and independent of the other cells with no common walls or obvious entrance. D2 and D3 on the west of the structure were rectilinear, open ended to the west and shared a central wall. North of these a larger cell (D4), 3m by 3m, appeared to have an additional element (2m by 1m) adjoining it to the north-east. Cells D5 - 8 around the north edge of the structure had internal diameters of 2m by 2m to 4m by 3m. D14 was of a similar size and situated in the middle towards the east. D9 was a long, rectilinear (6m by 2m) cell on the south side of the structure adjacent to the perimeter wall, and the best-preserved cell in the complex. D10 - 13 were situated in the middle of the structure and had rectilinear elements with the largest of these, D12, 5m by 3m. At the east end of the complex a tiny, open-ended cell, D15, 2.2m by 1.4m, was formed by a stretch of wall jutting out from the main structure and the perimeter wall.

E: An artificial pond in the centre of the island dug into the turf and contained by a low earthen bank. At the time of the survey, ie in the summer, the pond contained fresh water approximately 0.3m deep, and was circular, up to 7m in diameter. However, judging from the bank and the extent of the marshy ground around it, its original size may have been about 7m x 20m. A channel or runnel cut through the east edge, presumably to allow excess water to drain away. Overspill has formed irregular terraces and a marshier area below the pond to the east.

F: F1 and F2 were two slight hollows adjacent to each other, quarried into the foot of the slope occupied by the dun, 4m by 2m and 3.5m by 2m respectively. An upright slab of rock was situated to the back (north) of the east hollow (F2). Directly to the north-east of these hollows was a natural gully, running straight down to the sea (F3) is known as *Palla na Birlinn* (Ledge of the Galley) in oral tradition (Thomas 1878, 516) used to haul boats up onto the island, or *Barra na Birlinn* in local tradition ('Spit/bar/rock of the Galley', see Illus 2.9, above).

G: This irregular mass of masonry on the highest part of the island could be seen for considerable distances along the north Lewis coast and

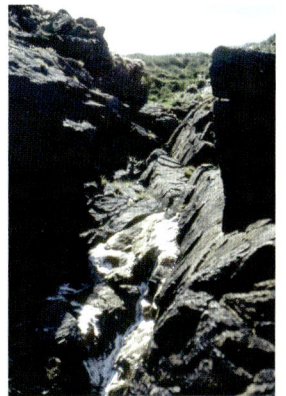

Illus 2.17 Chris taking photographs of features, Illus 2.18 Structure D9 from the west, Illus 2.19 Structure E, and Illus 2.20 *Palla na Birlinn*, looking up towards the island

Illus 2.21 Structure G from the east, Illus 2.22 Structure H at the south-east corner of the island, Illus 2.23 Surveying on the mainland and Illus 2.24 Cultivation remains on the mainland

stood on a natural terrace around the south side of the dun that extended approximately 3m beyond the edge of the rubble spread before sloping down to the pond 25m to the south. On the north side the structure stands on the edge of a relatively steep slope that drops onto the cliff edge. Three different parts of the structure were identified. A large oval spread of rubble, labelled G1, *c* 8m by 15m, was very ruinous and the substantial amount of tumble obscured all structural detail. A smaller walled structure, G2, 2m by 2m was built on top of the rubble with walls standing *c* 1m high and 1m wide. The original form of this structure had been modified through the construction of a modern cairn, G3. The form of this structure did not reveal anything about its original function. It seemed too small and exposed to have been a dwelling. It could conceivably have been some sort of watch-post.

H: A low wall along the cliff edge on the landward side of the island. Where an exterior wall face could be seen it was of coursed rubble construction with no sign of mortar. The wall stood 0.7m high and 1.5m wide and was not accompanied by large amounts of tumble, suggesting it was never very substantial. On the east it emerges from natural outcrops adjacent to Palla na Birlinn (F3) and runs south along the south side of the stack for about 85m to the south-east corner of the island. A stretch of the wall runs from the north-west corner of cell B1, 38m along the north-west side of the island, before hooking east towards Structure G and disappearing after 2-3m. From here it forms a dog-leg, turning south and extending for a further 15m and becoming incorporated as the west side of Structure A. The wall Structure H defines a triangular area on the west side of the island, with Structure B on the south side and Structure A on the east, with a possible entrance into the area between the two. Particular care was taken to survey the inaccessible cliff edges, on either side of the ravine, where any ancient bridge would have been located. No sign of a deliberate gap in the cliff-edge wall wide enough to accommodate a bridge was identified, nor was there a sign of a base or platform on the island. A break occurs in the wall just to the east of Structure B, at the narrowest gap between the island and the mainland and has been utilised in the recent past.

I, J, K and L: A heavily eroded feature of two concentric banks with a slight internal ditch, 1m wide and 0.2m deep, interpreted as possibly a natural geological feature or old sheep tracks, a low mound, 0.9m high, only well-defined on the south side and so eroded that it was difficult to be certain that this is not a natural mound, and two low mounds, possibly of stone clearance, measuring 5m by 4m by 0.5m high and 4m by 4m by 0.5m high respectively, both at the head of cultivation ridges.

The geophysical survey and trial trench evaluation, which took place the year after the topographic survey, required a longer season of three weeks work and also more equipment. The access route used by the survey teams in the spring and summer of 2000 could only be used for short periods and by properly equipped and qualified teams, and the surveyors realised in 2001 that sustained fieldwork would require a permanent, dependable means of access. Camping on the island for this length of time was also no longer a practical

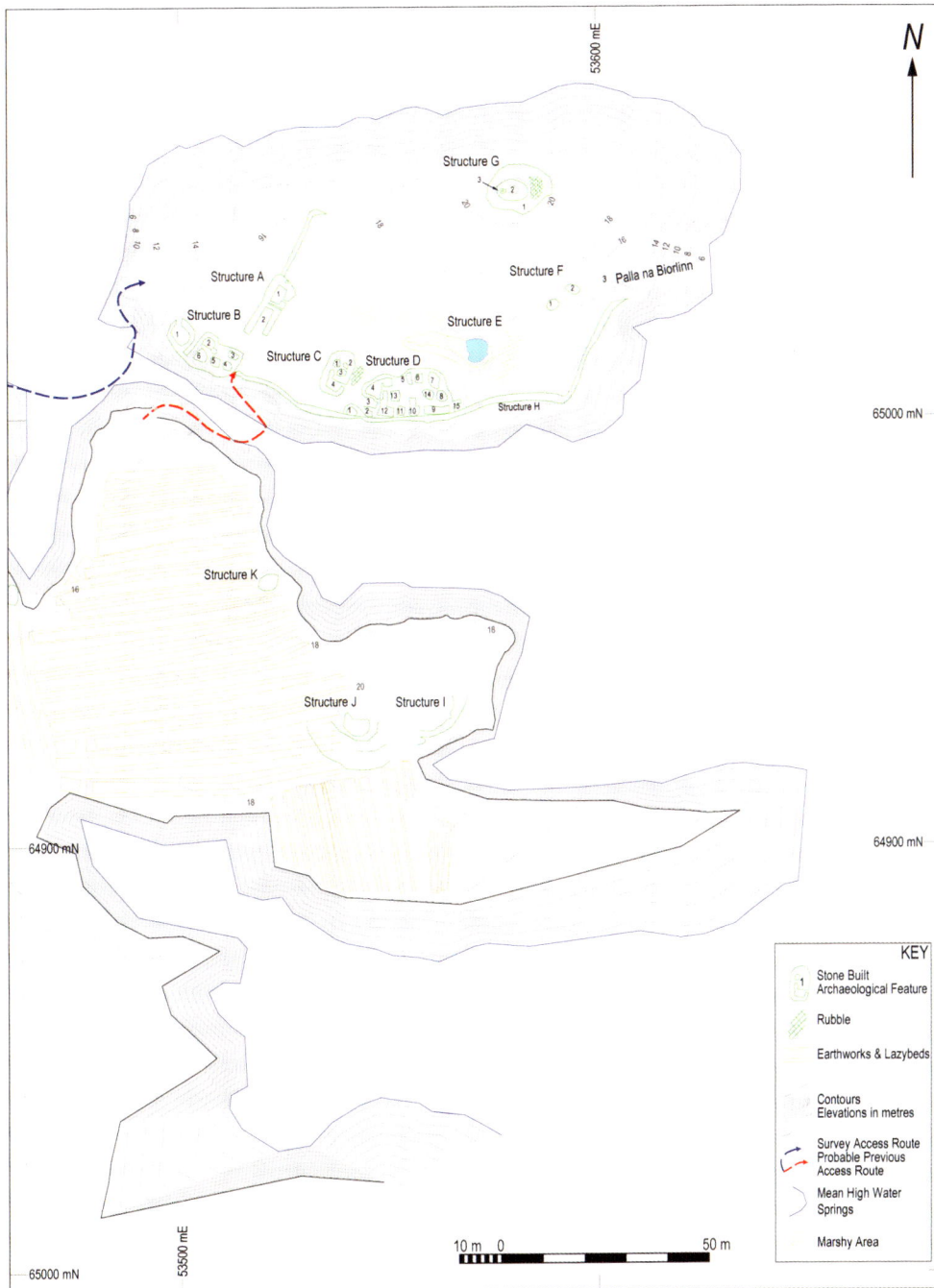

Illus 2.25 Topographic survey plan of Dùn Èistean and features on mainland

Structure G

Structure A

Structure F

Palla na Biorlinn

Structure B

Structure E

Structure C

Structure D

Structure H

Structure K

Structure J

Structure I

53600 mE

65000 mN

64900 mN

64900 mN

65000 mN

53500 mE

N

KEY

Stone Built Archaeological Feature

Rubble

Earthworks & Lazybeds

Contours Elevations in metres

Survey Access Route Probable Previous Access Route

Mean High Water Springs

Marshy Area

10 m 0   50 m

solution and moving equipment backwards and forwards would have been very time consuming. Ropes and climbing harnesses had already been used as a back-up when accessing the site in the previous year, but in 2001 this was taken one step further with the designing of a 'Tyrolean traverse' by rope access expert and archaeologist Ian McHardy. Personnel were able to clip a rope harness onto the traverse and pull themselves, equipment or soil samples backwards and forwards on the rope across the gap.

Access using the traverse was much safer than scrambling down and over slippery rocks. The team no longer had to consider the tides, and normal

Illus 2.26 to 2.30 Setting up the Tyrolean Traverse

working hours were now possible without staying overnight on the island. However, bad weather still made things more difficult. The weather was very changeable in the first week of the survey, with bands of rain blowing in from the south-west throughout the day. The site 'tent' on the island had to be rebuilt due to severe wind damage, which ripped the flysheet into shreds, and the team had to resort to creating a bivouac using one of the upstanding structures on the island as the main shelter in inclement weather.

Despite these challenges, the geophysical survey and trial trench excavation was completed (Barrowman 2002). The aims of the geophysical survey were to identify any further archaeological structures not visible on the surface and clarify the extent and form of the visible structures to help determine where to locate trial excavation trenches. Two types of geophysical survey were used: magnetometry using a Geoscan FM36 fluxgate gradiometer, with manual timer and resistivity using a Geoscan RM15 resistivity meter with twin probe electrodes, spaced 0.5m apart, with two fixed remote probes. Magnetometry essentially measures the difference in the magnetic susceptibility between topsoil and rocks, which also affect the Earth's field locally. This makes it possible to detect ditches, pits and other silted-up excavated features. Because topsoil is *normally* more magnetic than the underlying subsoil or bedrock, excavated features that have silted or backfilled with topsoil will produce a positive magnetic signal. Less magnetic material intruding into the topsoil will produce the opposite affect, a negative signal.

Resistivity measures the difference in resistance to the electrical current. While most rocks are resistant to current flow and so have a high resistivity, soils are less resistant. This is mainly due to the liquid content of soils, particularly if they are acidic. Soils and clays will tend to hold ground water, so will have a lower resistivity than rock or stone. Therefore resistivity measurement is really a measure of the amount of water held in the ground at a particular point. Different soils lose their water content by drainage faster than others (for example, sand drains quicker than clay). Therefore soil compaction and type will also affect the rate of water absorption.

The overgrown grass and vegetation on Dùn Èistean presented some problems, as did the weather conditions. The low winter rainfall in the area had caused the soil on the island to dry out and areas that had been marshy during the topographic survey in 2000 had dried significantly since then. This resulted in problems with contact and flow of electrical currents across the probes during the resistance survey. Although the resistivity survey was successful and all the archaeological features shown on the topographic survey were detected, the resistance signals were weak and discontinuities between grids presented problems for the interpretation and identification of anomalies that were not related to the visible structures.

After the geophysics were finished, four small trial trenches (Trenches 1 to 4) were excavated in June 2001 in the areas of Structures A, D and G, and a 'blank' area in the centre of the site to assess the results of the surveys and to help decide how further work should be targeted on the site. Excavation is an

Illus 2.31 Donna undertaking the geophysical survey

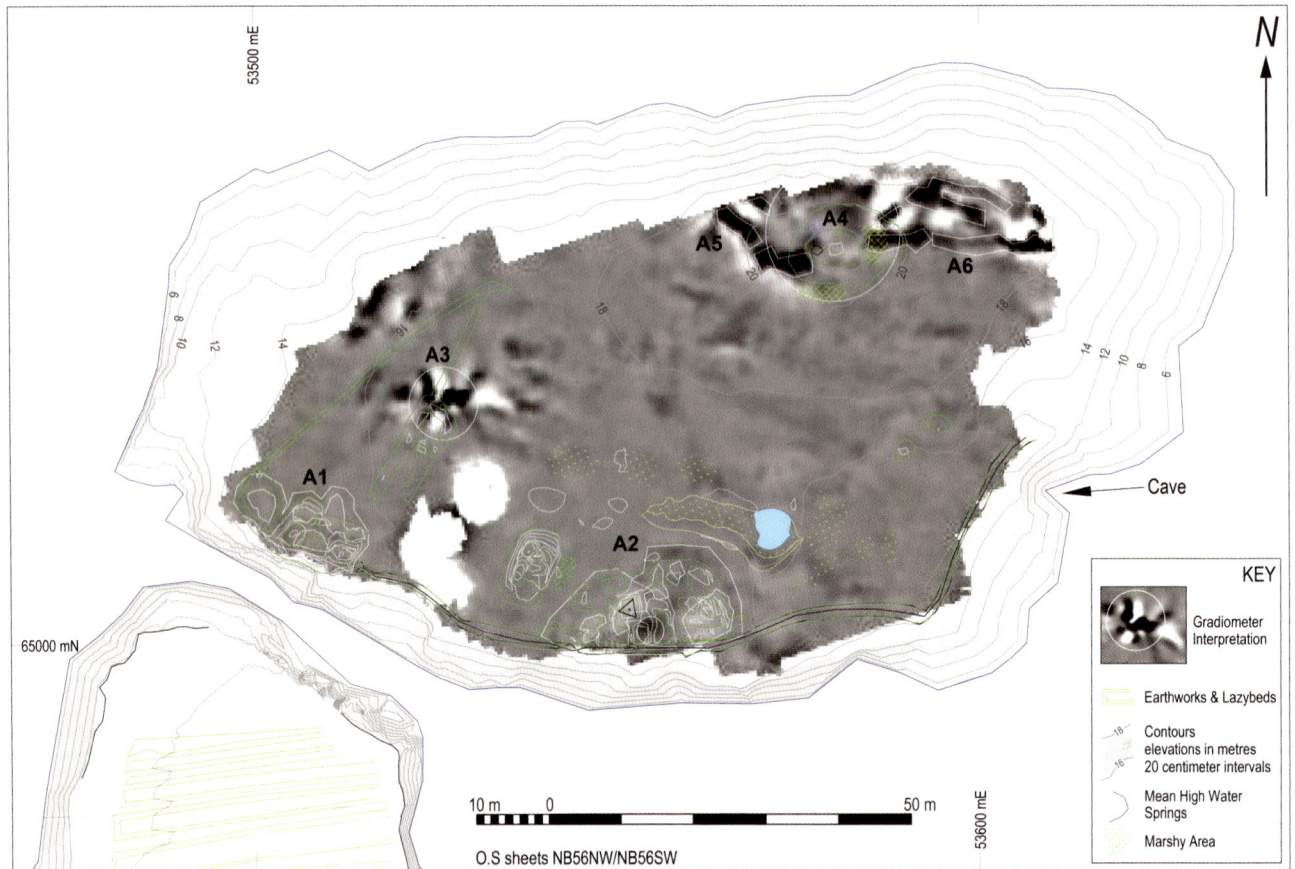

Illus 2.32 Gradiometer survey 2001. Dark areas indicate positive anomalies and the lighter areas indicate negative anomalies

Gradiometry results

A1: Several positive linear anomalies within an area measuring 15 x 10m, which correspond to Structure B, and indicate the approximate shape of six cells.

A2: Several positive linear anomalies corresponding to Structure D. A stronger positive anomaly within this area (A2a) may represent burning within either cell 10 or 11 in Structure D and indicates a possible hearth.

A3: One of the strongest positive magnetic anomalies, and may indicate an area of burning situated directly to the E of Structure A.

A4: An area of slight positive and negative anomalies indicating soil disturbance in the area of Structure G.

A5: A series of linear positive and negative readings. The positive anomalies (shown in black) take the form of two parallel lines, each approximately 3m wide, separated by a negative anomaly approximately 1 - 1.5m wide. Although the northernmost positive line stops after c 3m, the positive anomaly to the S runs for c 7m along the SW of Structure G, and has a 1m wide break half way along its length. After a break of 7m to the immediate S of Structure G, the anomaly continues again around the SE corner of the structure, and runs off for approximately 25m down slope to the E of the island. These features may represent a foundation trench or ditch.

A6: This part of the feature is less clear and harder to follow. The N part of the anomaly is very amorphous at this point. It is possible that these anomalies may indicate a ditch, which has been cut into the solid geology and has filled with a higher magnetic material. The gap between the anomalies may indicate the presence of a causeway or entrance.

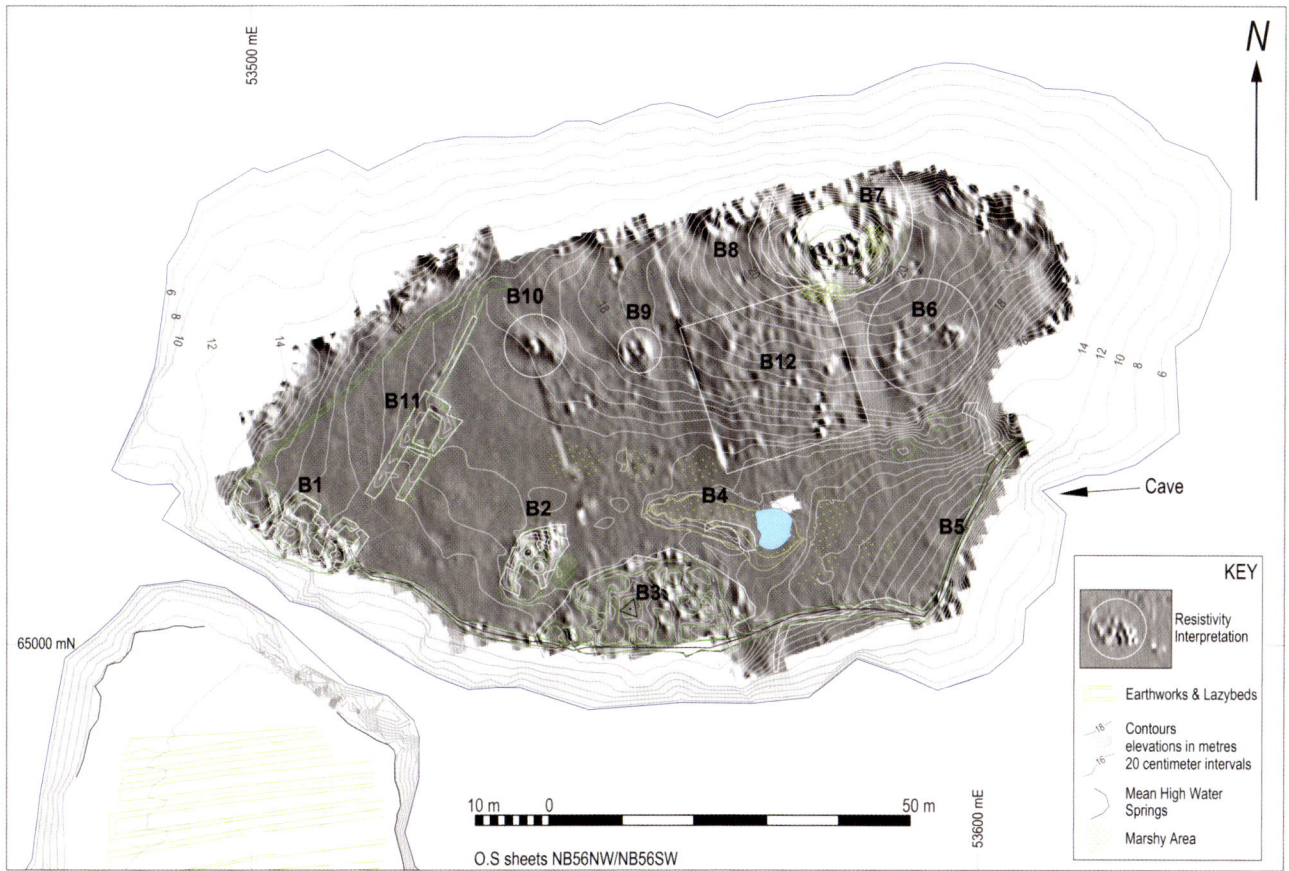

Illus 2.33 Resistivity survey 2001. Dark areas indicate high resistance readings and lighter areas indicate low resistance readings

Resistivity results

B1: A complex of high resistance signals clearly indicating stone structures, which correspond with the small group of cells, structure B.

B2: Anomalies indicating high resistance signals that correspond with the oval building, Structure C.

B3: A complex of high resistance anomalies corresponding to the large group of cells, Structure D.

B4: A high resistance anomaly, possibly a retaining wall of the pond, Structure E. The weakness of the high resistance signals suggest that this feature may be constructed of earth with little stone.

B5: A high resistance anomaly corresponding with the line of the perimeter wall, Structure H, where it follows the edge of the island to the SE.

B6: These anomalies appear to indicate a small group of high resistance features similar in signal to those observed at B1, B2 and B3. It is possible that these may represent small cellular structures of similar makeup, which were identified as structure F.

B7: These anomalies correspond with the most prominent feature on the island, Structure G. The high resistance signal may reasonably be considered to be due to rubble spread around the small structure in the centre.

B8: This weak high resistance anomaly would suggest either a turf wall or a robbed out stone wall; there is no indication of this anomaly on the surface.

B9 and B10: Anomalies similar to that of B6, which may again indicate cellular buildings.

B11: A strong, high resistance feature, characteristic of a stone building, which corresponds with the rectangular building Structure A.

The square indicated by B12 shows an area where the data was corrupted due to poor contact of probes during survey, as discussed previously.

Illus 2.34 Aerial photograph of Dùn Èistean. Reproduced with kind permission of the RCAHMS

expensive and time-consuming business, so it was worth getting it right. This was followed by further excavations in 2002 when the Clan Morrison Society in the USA, UK and further afield succeeded in raising enough money to commission the building of a steel footbridge across the gap to the island from the mainland side. With joint funding from Historic Scotland, two trenches (Trenches 1 and 2) were excavated either side of the gap where the bridge footings were to go to help decide where best to put the bridge, and where the least damage would be done to the archaeology on the site (Barrowman 2004a). These were completed just in time for the International Clan Morrison Gathering in Ness in July 2002 when hundreds of Morrisons walked onto Dùn Èistean for the first time. The publicity led to a small excavation being undertaken in the north end of Structure A for the BBC Time Fliers television series the following summer in 2003.

The Dùn Èistean project excavations 2005-7

After a break of two years, the multi-disciplinary Dùn Èistean Archaeology Project began in 2005 with the result of the earlier excavations used to decide where and how to excavate. Three seasons of large-scale excavations followed in 2005-7. Hypotheses made from the early work could now be tested through excavation (see Barrowman 2002; Maguire 2002). These included that Structure G1, rather than being the earliest structure on the island, was medieval or later in date, that Structure A1 was a later, post-medieval dwelling house, and A2 a shed or outbuilding, Structure B was a 'gatehouse' to the island, and Structure C was a dwelling house, possibly of Norse architectural tradition due to the slightly bow-shaped side walls. It had been suggested that Structure C was occupied later than B or D, perhaps at the same time as A, as suggested by the degree of preservation of the building. Structure D was considered the main residential component of the site and it was suggested that the hollows F1 and F2 could have been used as boat noosts. The bridge footing excavations in 2002 had confirmed that Structure H was a breastwork, probably of late medieval date if Thomas' reference to gun loops or squints was taken at face value. The results of the geophysical survey also identified a strong series of linear positive and negative anomalies around Structure G, interpreted as a possible rock-cut ditch on the west side of the structure, and strong positive magnetic anomalies near Structure A indicating that burning may be present and that some form of working area may exist to the east of the structure. The magnetometer survey also indicated a hearth or area of possible burning was to be found within D10 or D11 in Structure D. These suggestions were all tested by excavation and the results are laid out in Chapters 4-9 below.

The excavations on Dùn Èistean were based on an underlying principle of minimal intervention to investigate these research questions whilst at the same time ensuring the sustainable development of the site. It was tempting with such a fascinating site to dig everything up and explore as much as possible, but this would have left nothing for future generations to enjoy. Unless an archaeological site is to be destroyed by development, in which case all the archaeology needs to be excavated and recorded before it is damaged, there is an understanding that a part of it should always be left in tact and untouched for posterity. Once the archaeology is dug away it has gone forever, and who knows what improved techniques will be available to us in 20, 30 or a 100 years time.

Dùn Èistean is such a special site that it is protected by law as a Scheduled Ancient Monument. An application had to be made to Historic Scotland for Ancient Monument Consent to undertake excavation on the site. Scottish Natural Heritage also suggested that the timing of fieldwork should take the ground-nesting birds into account to make sure that the majority of the Artic Tern chicks had fledged before the excavations began. In addition to these concerns the Clan Morrison as owners of the site, wanted the site to be left in such a way after the end of the excavations that the remains were still visible and could be understood. The local Dùn Èistean committee were keen that the future management and development of the monument should be considered from the start for its protection, and that there should be some social, educational and economic benefit to the community and to visitors. It was hard not to feel a little anxious in the face of so many competing expectations!

The plan of campaign for the large-scale excavations in 2005-7 had to take all of these concerns into account. No more than 50% of any unthreatened structure was excavated[8], and when sections were cut through walls in order to look at earlier phases and to clarify the way buildings were put together, the walls were reinstated afterwards. This was particularly hard with the ruined tower, Structure G. Here excavation was carried out with care inside and out so as to limit additional stresses on the walls of the structure and to leave all walls

Illus 2.35 Structure F 2007, 50% of Structure F2 excavated

Illus 2.36 Flotation tank processing environmental soil samples behind the Comunn Eachdraidh Nis, Habost

intact. At the end of every season of excavation all trenches were filled back in and re-turfed, with a permeable membrane laid over the base of the trench to protect the archaeology. In addition to this, no areas where ground-nesting birds were present were excavated, and if birds were present, disturbance was kept to a minimum by roping off the areas concerned, making sure that visitors and personnel stuck to designated paths, and coming off site three times a day for breaks.

As much as possible of the field project was also located in Ness. Environmental samples were taken from site to the Comunn Eachdraidh Nis in Habost, where they were processed through a Siraf flotation tank. There was also a 'DEAP' room here where finds and sample residues were laid out to dry and the project computer was kept for work on the website and Gaelic translation, and a small exhibition of finds from the excavation. Much of the project was bilingual, and employed a Gaelic student placement locally as part of the fieldwork team in 2005-7, joint-funded with Comunn na Gàidhlig through

---

mu dheidhinn

'S e stac eadar-chuanach a th' ann an Dùn Èistean a tha suidhichte air costa taobh an ear-thuath Eilean Leòdhais. A rèir beul-aithris, 'S e daingneach meadhan aoiseach Chlann Mhoireasdan (eadar 350 agus 600 bliadhna air ais) a bh' ann. Sna linntean eadar 800 gu 1300 AD bha na h-Eileanan an Iar fo smachd nan Gall Lochlannach, 's ann mar seo a fhuair iad an t-ainm 'Innse Gall'. Le crìonadh cumhachd nan Gall mun 13mh linn thòisich comhstrì agus sabaid eadar na diofar chinnidhean is teaghlaich is iad a' coimhead airson cumhachd fhaighinn thairis air a chèile. Tha sean sgeulachdan sa choimhearsnachd co-cheangailte ri Dùn Èistean agus clann Mhoireasdan a' tighinn bhon àm chaochlaideach seo ann an eachdraidh Leòdhais. Tha sean dhaigneachdan eile coltach ri Dùn Èistean sgapte tro na h-Eileanan an Iar agus tòrr dhiubh a' beantainn ris an linn seo. Tha cuideachd fianais bho na làraich seo a' sealltainn gun deach an cleachdadh cho fada air ais ri 'Aois an Iarainn' no fiùs - nas tràithe- dh'fhaodadh gu bheil fianais nas aosta aig Dùn Èistean fo na clachan is na toglaichean a bhuineas do na linntean sin nach eil air a thighinn am follais fhathast.

deap

'S e Pròiseact Airceòlas Dhùn Èistein pròiseact dèantach eadar-fhoghlamach, ioma-chuspaireach, le taic bho Maoin Dualchais a' Chrannchur Nàiseanta (HLF), Alba Eachdraidheil, Comunn Chlann Mhoireasdan, Comunn Eachdraidh Nis, Comhairle nan Eilean Siar agus Oilthigh Ghlaschu. Tha am pròiseact a' gabhail a-steach rannsachadh arc-eòlach de cheann a tuath Nis (Sgrùdadh Arc-eòlas Sgìre Nis, NALS) agus an cladhachadh aig Dùn Èistean – gach cuid fo Bhuidheann Rannsachadh Arc-eòlas Oilthigh Ghlaschu (GUARD sa

Bheurla). 'S e amas GUARD ar tuigse de Dhùn Èistean agus ceann a tuath sgìre Nis adhartachadh; bhon tuineachadh is tràithe gu nam Meadhan Aoisean agus na linntean a leanas. Tha am pròiseact a' leantainn nam builean aig pròiseactan eile, eisimeileach agus neo-eisimeileach, a ghabh a-steach rannsachadh aithriseach, mìneachadh ainmean-àite agus cruinneachadh beul-aithris.

Tha pròiseact DEAP a' leantainn airson trì sèasanan de chladhachadh aig Dùn Èistean (eadar 2005-07) le dà shèasan de dh'obair, an dèidh a' chladhachaidh, a' dèanamh mìneachaidh air na chaidh a lorg. Tha cothroman ann airson saor-thagraichean cuideachadh a dhèanamh leis a h-uile pàirt dhen phròiseact, fiùs an cladhachadh thairis air an t-samhradh.

Tha cladhachadh 2006 a' dol air adhart eadar 3 Iuchar agus 12 Lùnastal. Tha trì àrainnean mòra airson an cladhachadh fosgailte gus an urrainn do rannsachadh a bhith air a dhèanamh de dhà bhuidheann mòr de thobhtaichean air an taobh den làrach a tha air taobh a' Chnuic Àrd den dùn (Togalach B agus D) agus an tùr air taobh an ear-thuath.

cladhachadh

Tha DEAP air cladhachan a chuir air dòigh sna bliadhnachan 2001-02 is 2005 aig Toglaichean A, D agus G. Chaidh dà thogalach a lorg taobh ri taobh ri taobh aig A le teallaich annta, pìosan crèadhadaireachd briste agus ball-peileir musgaid – a' sealltainn gu bheil e coltach gun robh iad air an cleachdadh eadar an 16mh is an 18mh linn. Bha na rudan seo suidhichte aig oir an làraich far am b' urrainn do na creagan a bhith air an sreap an uair a bha an làn a-muigh. Chaidh crèadhadaireachd briste agus stuth eile mar pigean bho thìr-mòr 's bhon Ghearmailt a bhuineadh don 16mh linn a lorg ann an togalach D nuair a chaidh dìg fhosgladh. Tha daoine dhan bheachd gur e togalach G, a tha fhathast 2m a dh'àird, sean tùr a chaidh a thogail san 16mh linn agus chaidh ball-musgaid agus tuilleadh crèadhadaireachd briste a lorg na bhroinn ann an 2005.

Tha ballaichean cip a tha air tuiteam agus stèidhean cloiche aig toglaichean B agus D. Tha iad furasta am faicinn air taobh sear 's taobh siar na drochaid nuair a bhios tu a' coiseachd chun an Dùin. Tha cill mar pàirt dhen bhalla a tha a' dol timcheall na làraich. Tha àrc-eòlaichean a'

smaoineachadh gur dòcha gun robh na toglaichean seo air an cleachdadh mar stòran no àitean-còmhnaidh airson greisean goirid.

'S e an tùr am pàirt as àirde den stac agus mar seo bhiodh e gu math fradharcach airson mìltean mun cuairt, na sheasamh a-mach mar shamhla chumhachdach. Tha deagh shealladh à seo a-mach gu cuan chun iar gu Rubha Robhanais a-null chun Charbh agus gu deas 's an ear thairis air a' Chuan Sgìth agus sìos cho fada ri mòr-thìr Alba.

suidheach

Lean na soidhnichean bho chòrnair a' Chnuic Àird faisg air Port Nis agus tionndaidh chun taobh cheart faisg air mullach a' chnuic. Bheir an rathad sin thu chun na làraich. Faodaidh tu faighinn a-steach le càr ach chan eil an rathad uabhasach math. Cuimhnich gun dùin thu na geataichean ma bha iad dùinte. ma's e ur toil e.

fios

Airson cothrom bruidhinn ri cuideigin bho DEAP, no ma tha thu airson d' ainm a chuir air adhart airson cuideachadh le pàirt sam bith den phròiseact, faodaidh tu post-dealain a chuir gu deap2005@tiscali.co.uk agus gheibh thu fios air ais cho luath 's a ghabhas. No faodaidh tu fònadh 01851 810377. Tha barrachd fiosrachadh ri fhaighinn air an làrach-lìn againn www.duneistean.org.

Illus 2.37 Gaelic leaflet translation from 2006

their *Sgeama Greis Gnoìmhachais nan Oileaneach* to translate text for the exhibition and website, and provide Gaelic tours of the site to visitors if requested.

As well as samples taken for environmental analysis, Kubiena tin soil micromorphology samples were taken on site of hearths, floor layers, turf walls and wall core material[9], and pollen core samples were taken from the basal deposits in the pond Structure E using a Russian corer. Excavators were also required to wear safety harnesses and ropes when working close to the edge of the island in some of the trenches, and in 2005-7, with a larger team, two portacabins were set up temporarily off site, and used as a finds shed/tool store, and a tea hut when the weather conditions were unfavourable. Every member of the excavation team, staff, students and volunteers were asked to contribute a daily site diary which was uploaded onto the project website. With the end of the final season of excavation mid-August 2007, the site was backfilled for the last time and work began on the post-excavation analyses of all the material excavated, the results of which are reported below.

Illus 2.38 Soil micromorphology Kubiena tins in wall section in Trench C in 2007, Illus 2.39 De-turfing, Illus 2.40 Planning down the back of Structure G required ropes and a safety harness in 2007 and Illus 2.41 Inside the site portacabin

Endnotes

[1] The geological observations in this paragraph are taken from Stewart Angus' book 'The Outer Hebrides: The Shaping of the Islands', published by the White Horse Press, Strond, Harris, 1997. Reference was also made to Fettes et al 1992, and the British Geological Survey, Lewis and Harris (North), 1:100 000 Solid Geology map, National Environmental Research Council, 1981.

[2] See 'The Clan Morrison', in *The Celtic Monthly*, Vol 18, Glasgow 1910, pp168-169; 'The Clan Morrison Society', in The Celtic Monthly, Vol 19, Glasgow 1911, p77; Dùn Èistean appears as 'Dun Uisdean', or 'Hugh's Castle', in clan tradition but it is unlikely that Èistean derives from Uisdean; Dr Finlay MacLeod pers comm; Richard Cox 2006.

[3] See Robson 2004 17-45, particularly 18, 36 and Appendix, 53-58.

[4] The 'On the Duns of the Outer Hebrides' article contains the same information, except that the flint find is identified as 'probably a strike-a-light' (Thomas 1890, 365-369) and Thomas describes the 'tigh' as having the appearance of "an incipient peel", probably from the twelfth century, by comparison with Cubbie Roo's castle in Orkney (Thomas 1890, 366).

[5] This is now published: The Morrison Manuscript: Traditions of the Western Isles, 1975, Stornoway, Isle of Lewis: National Society Daughters of Founders and Patriots of America, Edited by Norman Macdonald.

[6] I am grateful to Aonghas MacCoinnich for drawing attention to the fact that although the manuscript of Donald Morison (died *c* 1830) is often cited, Morison actually specifically refers in his manuscript to the recently newly published (1813) Sir Robert Gordon's manuscript history of the Earldom of Sutherland (from 1630), with its fort on Neise and tales of feud. Thus even the Morison seanchaidh's accounts were fed by the Gordon source. MacCoinnich raises the question as to whether there would have been ANY local knowledge at all of Dùn Èistean without the fortuitous publication of Gordon's manuscript from 1630 in 1813.

[7] Angus MacLean passed away in 2005, aged 93.

[8] With the exception of Structure C where 75% was excavated, and total excavation of the interior of Structure G was necessary because 50% excavation would have left too confined and too unsafe an area in which to work.

[9] In 2007 Dr Joanne McKenzie (Stirling University) attended the excavations to collect soil micromorphological samples and was able to advise on site on the soil sampling strategy and prioritising of features for sampling. She reports her results in Chapter 12, below.

three

historical background

The majority of the archaeological material from Dùn Èistean can be dated to the late medieval/post-medieval period through finds analysis and radiocarbon dating. In this chapter, Aonghas MacCoinnich provides a detailed historical background relevant to specific aspects of the period evidenced in the archaeology at the site, such as the political background in the MacLeod territories at this time, the use of artillery, the dates of sieges and the cultural and trade contacts resulting from fishing, piracy and warfare in the North Sea and the western Scottish seaboard at this time. He also explores the Morrison tradition, and the evidence for the hereditary *britheamhan* or judges in the historical record in the later sixteenth century. In particular he describes the part they played in the turbulent and chaotic period described in the history of Lewis as the '*Linn nan Creach*', or Age of Raids, from the forfeiture of the Macdonald Lords of the Isles in 1493 to the eventual MacKenzie takeover of Lewis in 1610. In the second part of the chapter an overview is given by Domhnall Uilleam Stiùbhart of the results of the Dùn Èistean History project, the historical 'arm' of the Dùn Èistean project, which researched the local oral traditions and place-names of Ness. He focuses on those aspects relevant to Dùn Èistean and the district of Ness in the late medieval period, and highlights the traditions held in the Ness community itself such as those relating to a sanctuary at the north end of Ness, the 'MacLeods of Eoropie' and 'MacLeod's law'. His work demonstrates the value of local traditions within a multi-disciplinary research framework in an area such as Ness.[1]

Illus 3.2 Extract from Blaeu Atlas (Willem Blaeu 1634) detail of Dutch shipping in waters around the Western Isles. By permission of the National Library of Scotland

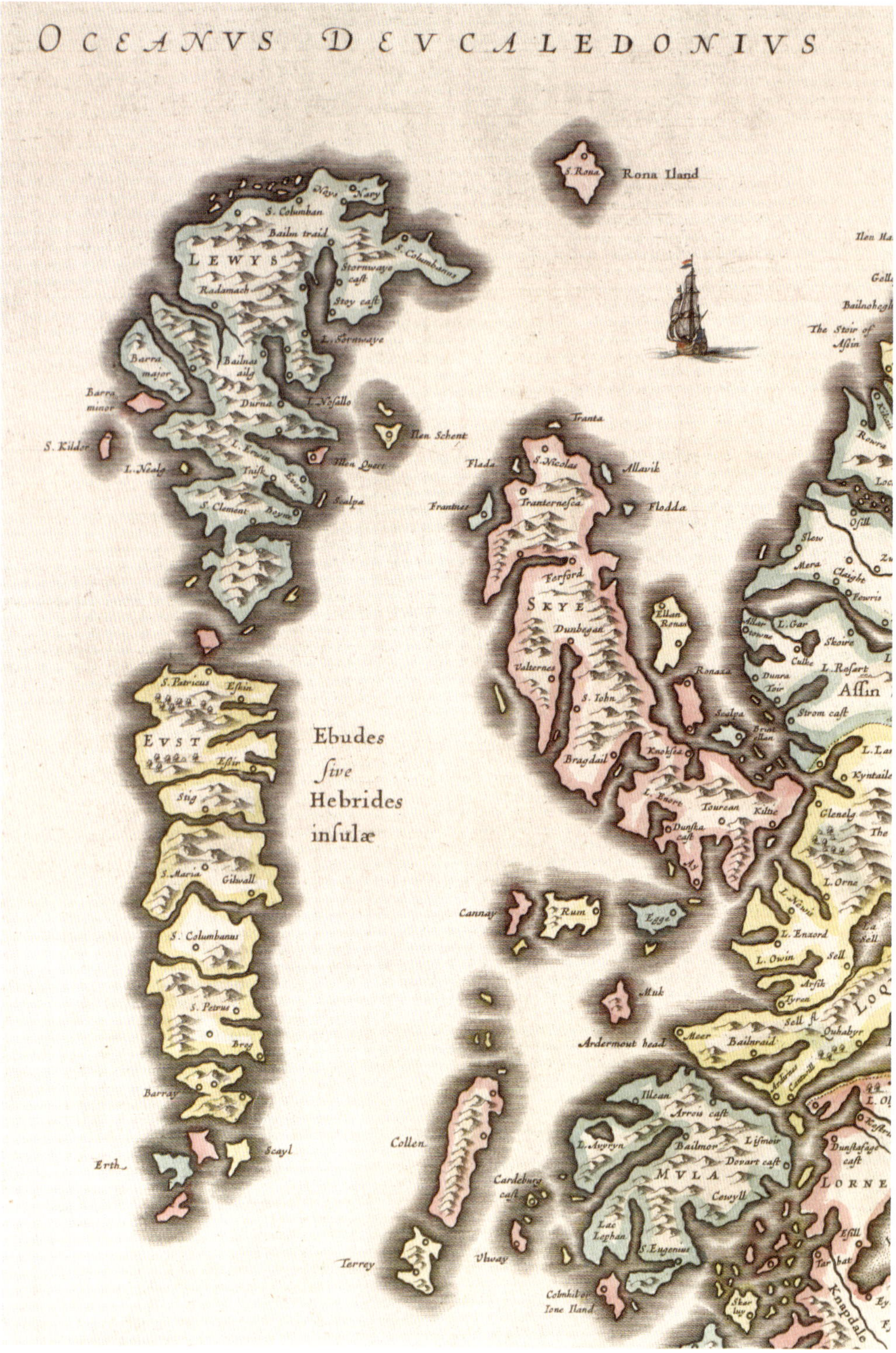

OCEANVS DEVCALEDONIVS
Rona Iland
LEWYS
SKYE
EVST
Ebudes
ſive
Hebrides
inſulæ
MVLA
Rum
Egge
Cannay
Muk
Collen
Flodda
Ardermout head
Terrey

Dùn Èistean and the 'Morisons' of Ness in the lordship of Lewis. The historical background, *c* 1493 – *c* 1700[2]

by Aonghas MacCoinnich

Introduction and the nature of the historical sources

Dùn Èistean and Habost in Ness, Lewis, are areas strongly associated with the 'Clan Morison' from the fourteenth century through until the seventeenth century (Matheson 1979, 60-1, 63; Mackenzie 1903, 61-3; Cameron 1937, 193-5). Tradition has it that they lived in *An Taigh Mòr*, or The Big House, on Habost machair, Ness, and that they were hereditary judges or *britheamhan*, a word meaning 'judges' often anglicised as 'brieves.' They seem to have been tenants of the MacLeods of Lewis, possibly from the fourteenth century onwards (Thomas 1878, 506, 542). As longstanding occupants of land in Ness, and followers of the MacLeod of Lewis chiefs, the Morisons would also have had *dùthchas,* a 'kindly' or hereditary right to hold their lands in Ness, based on the length of their family's possession of these lands over several generations (Macinnes 1996, 16; Sanderson 1982, 58-60). Morisons, rather than their MacLeod chiefs, are usually associated with Ness in this period but the MacLeods themselves may well have had a physical presence in Ness itself too, in Eoropie, according to local traditions of '*Taigh MhicLeòid*' somewhere close by *Teampall Mholuaidh* just over a mile from Dùn Èistean (see Stiùbhart, this volume; Barrowman 2005, 10-13, 15; Stiùbhart 2006a, 211-17).

There are no firm documentary fixes surviving which explicitly link the Morisons to the structure of Dùn Èistean, but there is no doubt that the kindred were well established in the area during the sixteenth and seventeenth centuries when they first appear on the historical record. They were referred to in writings from the sixteenth century under the name '*britheamh*' rather than Morison. The *britheamhan* occupied a part of the MacLeod of Lewis lordship and this is the wider context in which they should be considered rather than solely in the Ness area. The MacLeods of Lewis not only controlled Lewis but also had title to or occupied Vaternish in Skye, Raasay, Gairloch, Còigeach, Assynt and Eddrachilles in the fifteenth and sixteenth centuries and one could reasonably expect their *britheamhan* to operate in this wider area (MacCoinnich 2007, 19-21). MacLeod connections with the Macdonalds of Sleat brought them into contact frequently during the sixteenth century, especially in Trotternish, the Macdonald territory closest to Lewis. Indeed, the MacLeods themselves had answered to the Macdonald Lords of the Isles prior to their forfeiture in 1493 and directly to the sovereign after that date as the Scottish monarchs increasingly, although not always effectively, sought more direct control of the region. The period between 1493 and 1610, known in Gaelic as '*Linn nan Creach*' (Age of Raids), saw considerable unrest across the whole region due to the collapse of the Lordship and spasmodic, often ineffective, royal attempts to control the western seaboard. The MacLeods of Lewis, in particular, were frequently in rebellion against the crown at this time, often supporting insurrections connected to the restoration of the Macdonald Lordship of the Isles for reasons that are not clearly understood (see MacCoinnich forthcoming).

The late Reverend William Matheson has written on the Morisons of Ness prior to 1600 augmenting the sketchy contemporary historical source material with traditions and linguistic evidence: the latter forming the basis for much of his investigation (Matheson 1970, 186-90, 245; 1979). While the reader is referred to Matheson's discussion, 'The Morrisons of Ness' (1979), that of Captain Thomas (1878), and more recently Dr Dòmhnall Uilleam Stiùbhart (2006a and b and also in this volume), all of which rely to a great extent on tradition-based evidence, the emphasis in this present piece is somewhat different, privileging contemporaneously generated primary source material wherever this is possible. These materials were generated in or around the lifetime of the protagonists by writers who had direct first hand knowledge of the people, places and events in question. Such sources have usually preserved names, dates and places accurately and whilst they have their own problems of interpretation, are more reliable in terms of detail than tradition committed to paper sometimes centuries later.

The most useful types of such contemporary materials available to us are family or clan histories, produced by powerful neighbouring mainland dynasties such as the Mackenzies of Kintail and Seaforth and the Gordons of Sutherland, and estate papers, and paperwork generated by or for the authorities in Edinburgh such as the *Register of the Privy Council of Scotland*. None of these sources were generated by people from Ness or Lewis, and they must be read with an awareness that the writers all had their own agenda, which differed considerably from those of the inhabitants of the Ness (or Lewis) area. However, although these documents are often fragmentary they do give us a contemporary voice albeit often an unsympathetic one. An exception to this is the 'Ewill Trowbles of the Lewis,' probably written for Robert Gordon by an exiled member of the MacLeods of Lewis sometime between 1610 and 1630 (MacCoinnich 2006a, 215-28, 221, and below).

Tradition and later Morison histories on the other hand from the nineteenth century and later, while they do give a valuable 'local' view, and will contain a kernel of truth, should be treated with the greatest of caution due to the distortions inherent in tradition and oral history. Once oral history is divorced from any written record it can become unreliable especially when it moves beyond a historical horizon of three to four generations: the unreliability and lack of accurate detail increasing the less reciters have any personal knowledge of the people or events in their narrative. This may still preserve valuable information, as the Morison traditions recorded in the early 1800s do, but the greater the distance in time between the event and the reciter the less likely it will be that accurate details of names, dates, places and sequences of events will be retained.

The reciters of oral tradition, or poets who had no recourse to writing, had different priorities to modern historians: the stories or various aspects of the story, often taking precedence over 'fact'. Other less interesting details could of course be omitted. Details of incidents beyond living memory can lose definition in this manner and can be reshaped and recounted with 'considerable artistic style.' Such recitations are, according to John Macinnes, often 'concerned with individuals with only a passing reference to the wider historical framework' (Macinnes 2006, 48-56, 61-2 and at 52; Clanchy 1970, 165-73). In Lewis the lack of written record or historical framework for this period is felt particularly keenly due to the seizure and disappearance of the family papers of the MacLeods of Lewis in the late sixteenth century and subsequent plantations of the island by various outside parties.[3] Some of the meagre surviving traditions from the same period, notably the traditions related by Donald Morison, cooper and *seanchaidh* of Stornoway (d. 1834), written down over two hundred years after the event are fluid in terms of their treatment of time and the identities of *dramatis personae*. They also show some evidence of the stories having been re-shaped over succeeding generations in their journey through oral tradition.[4] Nevertheless they do seem to preserve information that, although a little confused at times, can be tentatively matched with the documentary record for the late sixteenth century. Song, on the other hand, due to its need to retain rhyme and metre, seems to have been a little more effective than tales as a device for remembering the past. One song associated with the exploits of *Dòmhnall Càm* of Uig in sixteenth century Ireland seems to have survived until the opening decades of the nineteenth century but was subsequently lost (Macdonald 1975, 24). Another such song, *an t-Iorram Niseach* (see Chapter 2, above), seems to be a unique survival from Lewis related to this period, *c* 1600, addressing the conflict between the MacLeods and the *britheamhan* of Ness. Although much of the detail surrounding the composition and survival of this song are unclear, some of the main protagonists remain readily identifiable giving a unique local perspective on the action.

Both the Rev. William Matheson in his study on the Morison family, *An Clàrsair Dall*, and Dr Dòmhnall Uilleam Stiùbhart have shown what can be done in terms of assessing traditions in their studies related to north Lewis in the later seventeenth and early eighteenth century when such traditions can be linked to or tested against a credible contemporaneous documentary base (Matheson 1970; Stiùbhart 2006a; see Stiùbhart, below). Prior to the mid-seventeenth century, however, such contemporaneous sources are less plentiful and tradition, where it can be compared against surviving fragmentary contemporary material, is often highly unreliable. What follows is an attempt to build a picture of the 'Morisons' or '*britheamhan*' in the Dùn Èistean area between 1493 and *c* 1700 from contemporaneous sources inasmuch as these sources will allow. The dearth of detailed documentary materials relating to the people and the place means that such a discussion must of necessity be less narrowly focused on the Dùn Èistean and Ness area, but concentrate instead on the 'Morisons' or '*britheamhan*' within the wider framework of the Lewis estate possessed by the MacLeods of Lewis between the fourteenth century and 1598, the Fife Adventurers between 1598 and 1609, and the Mackenzies of Kintail and Seaforth between 1609 and 1844, with an eye to the connections of the people of Lewis (and Ness) with other island groups and the wider world in the late medieval and Early Modern period.

Names: Morison, McBref or MacGillevorie?

The name 'Morison' or 'Morrison' (one 'r' is favoured in this paper and seems to have been preferred from the mid-seventeenth to nineteenth century although spellings were not consistent) was known and used widely in Ness certainly from the mid-seventeenth century up until the present day and historical narrative, genealogy and tradition tie these Morisons back in time to the earlier period of the Lordship of the Isles.[5] Families of the same name appear in Harris, Mull and other areas of the Highlands and Islands who either may or may not be related.[6] There were 'Morisons', in Eadar a' Chaolais and Durness in Sutherland that, by the nineteenth century, claimed kinship to the Morisons of Ness (Mackenzie 1903, 63). A group bearing the name 'Morison' also claimed protection from the Bishop of Caithness in 1576 (Wormald 1985, 249). However, this was nearly seventy years earlier than the 'Morisons' of Lewis who were identified using 'Breif,' 'mac Breif' and variants thereof at this time in the 1570s and not 'Morison' or its variants. While it is possible that they may indeed have been 'related' the fact that both groups were calling themselves by different names in the 1570s, 'Mcbrief' in Ness and 'Morison' in Caithness, suggests that caution should be exercised in relation to later claims of biological kinship. Only the family associated with the MacLeods of Lewis, however, to my knowledge, were known as '*britheamhan*' during the sixteenth century.

The earliest known usage of the name 'Morison' for this family in Lewis dates from as late as 1640-1643, when Mr Donald Morison appears in the documentary sources as minister in Ness (see below, and Matheson, 1970, 245-6). The name given to members of this family in contemporary Scots and Latin documents *prior* to 1640 x 1643 was 'MacGilleVorie' and 'McBreif' and variants thereof rather than 'Morison.' These names are clearly attempts at rendering the Gaelic forms '*MacGilleMhoire*' and *Mac a' Bhritheimh* into Scots and Latin dress. Sir Robert Gordon, writing around 1630, referred to an incident around 1600 involving 'Gilcalme moir mac Iain (chieff of the clan wic Gill woir efter the death of the *breive*)...' (Weber 1813, 272). Another record relating to members of this family from 1598 named them as 'Angus m'Keane Bref, Jhone Dow McBreif, Angus Mc Bref' (*RPCS xiv*, p. cxxiii).

The hereditary judges and royal reform of legal systems after 1493

While the family were clearly identified by the '*britheamh*' (judge) label, little is known of the nature of the law. We are told by a contemporary writer, Donald Monro, in 1549, less than five years after the last serious attempt to reinstate the Lordship of the Isles (which had also involved Lewismen), that the 'lawis of Renald McSomharkle' had been practiced in this lordship. This seemingly refers to laws made by Raghnall mac Somhairle, fl. *c* 1140-1192, one of the progenitors of the Macdonald clan. Such laws should in theory have been abolished under the terms of the treaty by which Scotland acquired the Western Isles at Perth in

1266. In practice, however, these laws seem to have continued in use in the isles following the annexation of the Hebrides by the Scottish crown (Monro 1549, 310; McDonald 1997, 73-9; MacQueen 1995, 10). The laws of the lordship of the Isles are long lost but they were seemingly still very attractive to west coast clans in 1545 (including the MacLeods of Lewis and the 'brief' kindred) who raised a major rising in an attempt at reinstating the Lordship of the Isles in preference to the rule of law being imposed by Edinburgh. It was also noted by Monro, rector of 'Y' or *Braigh na h-Aoidhe* near Stornoway, who had, on the face of it, no reason to praise the overthrown Macdonalds, that in the time of the Lords of the Isles 'thair was great peace and welth in the Iles throw the ministration of justice' (Monro 1549, 310; MacInnes 1940, no. 61, p. 18). Such a reference may hint at the continuing appeal of the old systems within the isles in contrast with that on offer from the increasingly acquisitive Stewart monarchy.

According to a late seventeenth century Macdonald clan historian, probably Captain Uisdean Macdonald of Paiblesgearraidh, North Uist, the *britheamhan* in the old Lordship of the Isles had been entitled to a fee of one eleventh of the value of the cases they considered (MacPhail 1914, 24-5; MacGregor 2008, 366; 2002, 201, 212 note 115). Macdonald's source of information about the practices of these *britheamhan* may well have been his local clergyman. The parish minister in North Uist, 1688-92 was none other than the Rev. Allan Morison, of *Sliochd a' Bhritheimh* (the 'Brieve' kindred), who succeeded his father, Mr Donald Morison, as minister in Ness in 1695. That Morison was an informant for the Macdonald historian is further suggested by the Macdonald history's unhistoric use of the name 'Morison' rather than 'brieve' in a scene involving the MacLeods of Lewis set in the early sixteenth century (MacPhail 1914, 58; Matheson 1970, 246; FES vii, 135, 146). This account apart, there is little that sheds light on the nature of the *britheamhan*'s legal practice. The role of the *britheamhan* was suggested by William Matheson to be quite different from our understanding of a judge's role, being 'not to pronounce judgement and sentence, but to state what the law was in its bearing on any particular case – not so much a judge, more of a juriconsult and arbiter.' Matheson's understanding seems, in turn, to have been influenced by John Cameron, who drew heavily on better-known Irish examples in his exposition of the practice of Gaelic law in Scotland (Matheson 1979, 61; Cameron 1937, 193-5).

An abundance of ancient law texts survive from Ireland, and several families are known to have practiced the old Gaelic style of law there over a number of generations in the late medieval and Early Modern periods (see Kelly 1988, 250-62; 2005, 263-6; Simms 1990, 51-76). There is some evidence of *britheamhan* in mainland lowland Scotland in the twelfth and thirteenth centuries prior to the retreat of Gaelic from the area.[7] However, although there may have been *britheamhan* in Islay and Skye, almost nothing is known of such families in Gaelic Scotland during the period under consideration here, *c* 1400-1700, with the sole exception of the Morisons of Ness (Black 1946 [1993], 107, 459-60; Matheson 1979, 61; Bannerman 1998: 19 at note 96; Sellar 1989, 19, 22 at note 32; Munro and Munro 1986, xliii, 22-3). Although the native Gaelic legal traditions in both Scotland and Ireland may have had much in common, the political and legal environments in both countries were very different, something which may well have impacted on the practice of the *britheamhan* in Scotland. Nevertheless, the reported tradition that the Hebridean *britheamhan* extracted a judicial fee of one-eleventh of the value of each case under review seems to echo practice in Gaelic Ireland (MacPhail 1914, 24-5; Kelly 1988, 250-62; 2005, 263-6; Simms 1990, 51-76). Following the first rebellion against the Crown, led by Torcaill MacLeod in 1504-6, parliamentary legislation enacted in March 1504 made their intentions clear regarding the practice of law in the isles:

> '…it is statute and ordanit that all oure soverane lord liegis beande under his obeysance, and in speciale the Ilis, be reulit be oure soverane lordis aune lawis and the commoune lawis of the realme ande be nain uther lawis'*
>
> *Translated from Scots to English as: 'Item, it is decreed and ordained that all our sovereign lord's lieges who are under his rule, and in particular the Isles, [are to] be governed by our sovereign lord's own laws and the common laws of the realm and by no other laws'[8]

The intention clearly seems to have been to harmonise the legal system in the isles with practice elsewhere in Scotland (Pitcairn 1833, i, 107-8; MacQueen 1995, 13; Mackenzie 1903).

One document survives which may give us a glimpse of the way in which Scottish kings directly tried to influence the practice of law in the area from 1493 onwards: a grant by James IV to a Highland student of law, Coinneach mac Uilleim (Kanoch Wilyameson) of the income from the lands of 'Baramosmor' and 'Kilmartine' in Trotternish in 1508 to support his education '…at the skolis, and for to lern the kingis lawis of Scotland and to exercyse the samin within the boundis of the ilis…' ('Gift, King James IV to a Highland Student of Law,' in *Collectanea de Rebus Albanacis, 22*; see Bannerman 1988, 13-14). The location of Kilmartine in Trotternish is clear but 'Baramosmor' is more difficult. It is tempting to see this as a form of the placename of Barvas/Barabhas in north Lewis associated with the *britheamh* kindred, which would fit neatly with the *britheamh* kindred, although it may also have been Gearos 'Mòr' in the Staffin area. This Coinneach probably belonged to a hereditary family of lawmen and may well have been connected to the *britheamh* family associated with Lewis. In 1485 there is also a record of a William 'archiudex' or high *britheamh*, presumably Coinneach's father, witnessing a deed of Angus Macdonald, master of the Isles, on 14 November 1485 (Munro and Munro 1986, 186; Bannerman 1988, 13). It may be that this William accompanying the Macdonald, Master of the Isles in 1585, was the last of this family to hold office in the Lordship of the Isles, and that his kin and descendants, like their former Macdonald masters (and MacLeod of Lewis supporters), aspired towards a restoration of the old order during the sixteenth century. Trotternish, in north Skye, was a contested land for much of the sixteenth century between the Macdonalds, the MacLeods of Harris, and the MacLeods of Lewis. The Macdonalds, however, dominated it for much of the period. The Macdonalds of Sleat had close ties of kinship and affinity with the lordship of the MacLeods of Lewis during much of the sixteenth century and certainly kept company with the tenants of the lordship of Lewis on occasion, such as the *britheamhan* (MacCoinnich 2007, 18). The *britheamh* kindred, as followers of the MacLeods of Lewis, thus had a clear, if little understood, connection with the lands of Trotternish at this time, and several of the *britheamh* kindred were specifically associated with the area.

Another intriguing connection which may hint at older ecclesiastical links between Lewis and north Skye, is suggested by the place names Kilmoluaig in Trotternish, and *Teampall Mholuaidh* in Pabaigh, Raasay and Ness, the latter close by *Dùn Èistean* (see discussion by Stiùbhart, below). The latter two dedications were in *Sìol Torcaill* territory. There were, however, clearly connections of some kind, as outlined above, between the *britheamh* kindred in Lewis and north Skye in the historic era. *Pàdraig mac Mhaighistir Mhàrtainn*, a name strongly associated with Trotternish, was the minister of the parish of Barvas and Ness in the 1560s, again, perhaps, hinting at a link between north Lewis and north Skye (MacPhail 1916, 280-281; Martin 1999, 4).

While the nature of the ecclesiastical or personal connections between Trotternish and Lewis of the *britheamh* kindred and others is uncertain at the beginning of the sixteenth century, it seems clear that the king wanted to take a much more proactive role in the secular lordship of the area. James IV, keen to win supporters in the region following the suppression of a serious rising designed to reinstate the Macdonald Lordship of the Isles, 1503-1507, wanted to train the next generation of hereditary lawmen in the isles along the lines followed elsewhere in his kingdom, and the 'skolis' that James had in mind were almost certainly in the lowlands, thus anticipating the better known Statutes of Iona by 100 years (Goodare 1998, 52). This coincided with a major re-shuffling in landholding patterns by James, 1493-1509, who placed a series of magnates such as the Mackenzies, Macleans and others within former Macdonald lands, thus giving them a vested interest in preventing a Macdonald return (MacCoinnich 2004, 130, 133-135, 147-148).

Coinneach mac Uilleim, discussed above, may not have been the only member of the *britheamh* family to avail himself of a university education. William Matheson also spotted a 'Eugenius Makbrehin' as a student matriculating at St Andrews in 1525 (Matheson 1979, 71; Anderson 1926, 220). If this person was one and the same as the person known to history as *Uisdean mac a' Bhritheimh*, or Hugh the brieve who died *c* 1566, then a pattern may have been established of the education of 'learned families' in lowland universities from the more 'remote' parts of Gaelic Scotland somewhat earlier than is usually assumed (Matheson 1979, 71). This would seem to be supported by the pattern of extant writings from the area in this period, largely in Latin and in Scots rather than Gaelic, with growing Scots literacy among the elites in the Highlands and Islands from the end of the fifteenth century onwards (MacCoinnich 2008, 319-320). The implication of this, as noted by William Matheson, was that while this family of 'brieves' seem to have retained their reputation and standing until the advent of the seventeenth century, the old legal mores of 'Renald mc Sorle,' referred to by

Dean Monro in 1549, were likely to have been in decline following the collapse of the Lordship of the Isles (Matheson 1979, 71, 73). The abrupt death of James IV at Flodden in 1514 followed by a succession of short personal reigns and royal minorities (until James VI's initiatives of 1587) robbed these plans of momentum (Macinnes 1993; Cathcart 2009). Although we know little about their activities, there is no doubt that 'lawmen' (whatever the nature of the law) survived and flourished during the sixteenth century in Lewis. This is supported by the evidence of personal names and by-names such as 'breif' and the evidence of a well-informed key witness, Sir Robert Gordon of Sutherland, who sheltered some of the few surviving members of the family of the MacLeods of Lewis following the Mackenzie conquest and plantation, 1609-13, and was thus informed by people who were in a position to know (MacCoinnich 2006a, 221-2). According to Sir Robert, writing around 1630, the role of the brieve in Lewis was as follows:

> 'The Breive is a kind of judge amongst the islanders, who hath ane absolute judicatorie, unto whose authoritie and censure they willinglie submitt themselves, when he determineth any debatable question betuin partie and partie' (Weber 1813, 268).

By 1630, however, when Sir Robert wrote his manuscript, it was clear that any such native institutions had disappeared, as was the case in Shetland, where growing royal authority abolished the similar office of 'foud' and other local law and custom at much the same time (Ballantyne and Smith 1994, xiv-xv; also see Donaldson 1984, 26-34). Records of a witchcraft case in Stornoway in 1631 make this clear. Here, the justiciars were not named *McBreif*, *MacGille Mhoire* or even *Morisons*, but Mackenzies, members of the new elite in charge of Lewis (Yeoman 2004, 242, 243; see also MacPhail 1916, 60-4; Mackenzie 1903, 242-65).

The britheamhan in historical sources

Hard and fast historical fixes are difficult to find for the earlier periods in surviving documents. The 'brief' family do appear to have held a prominent place within the Lordship of the MacLeods of Lewis (and the Isles) for a long time, almost always seen at the side of their chief. A Dòmhnall 'Breif', active within the Lordship of the isles, 1447-57, and in the company of MacLeod of Lewis was almost certainly a member of the Lewis *britheamhan* (Sellar 1989, 3-4). A 'Donaldo Brehiff' appears in the company of Torcaill MacLeod of Lewis in a document dated 1456 (Munro and Munro 1986, no 62-4, 90-6). He also, however, appears as a witness to a deed by Eoin Macdonald, Lord of the Isles and Earl of Ross, at Dingwall in 1457, named as 'Donald McGillemore, iudex insularum,' suggesting, perhaps, a wider role in the Lordship of the Isles (Munro and Munro 1986, 205).[9]

William the archiudex or high brieve from the 1480s, and Coinneach son of William the law student a generation later, have been noted above. An 'Alexander McBreif' together with MacLeods and Macdonalds, was involved in a rebellion against the Mackenzies of Kintail and king James V in 1540, and a 'Hugo McBreif' (*Uisdean son of the Brieve*) was given a pardon in August 1556

Table 3.1 Some documentary references to the extended 'brieve' family, known from the mid 17th century as 'Morrison', from surviving contemporary sources. On CD at back of book.

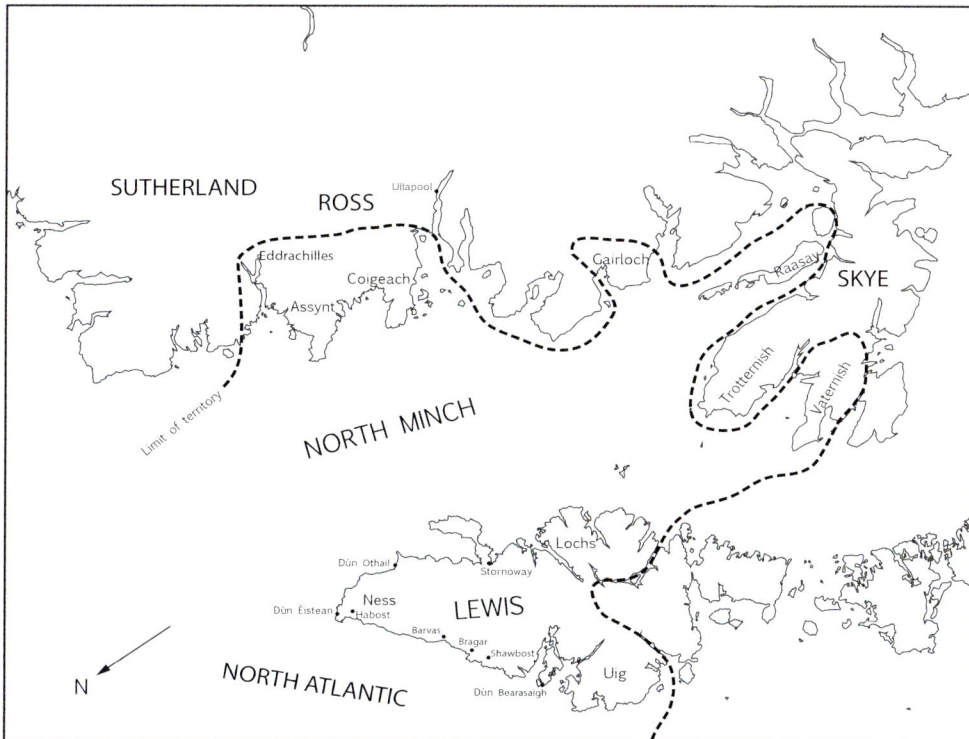

by the king for killings, burning and destruction of grain, goods and houses in Shetland and Orkney (*RSS iv*, 3307, p. 589). William Matheson has made the persuasive suggestion, noted above, that this Uisdean was one and the same as the "Eugenius Makbrehin" matriculated at St Andrew in 1525 (Matheson 1979, 70). Eugenius / Hugo / Uisdean ('Hugonis Breif') was also involved in raiding in Mull, Tiree and Coll with the Macdonalds of Sleat, probably in the 1540s, and he received a remission (or pardon) for this in 1562 (*RSS v*, no. 1160, p. 307).

This Uisdean, named in the remission obtained by Dòmhnall Gormson Macdonald of Sleat, 7 December 1562, was almost certainly the same '*Hucheon breve of Lewes*,' who allegedly admitted adultery with Seònaid Mackenzie, the wife of Ruairidh MacLeod of Lewis (*RSS ii*, no 3943, 597-8; MacPhail 1916, 280-1). This 'admission' of adultery was gained from the pre- and post-Reformation (1560) parson of Barvas, S[i]r Patrik mcMaister Mairtin (Pàdraig mac Mhaighistir Màrtainn), to whom Uidean had allegedly confessed while suffering from a life threatening illness, when he was 'on the poynt of dethe.' Uisdean may have survived that illness and lived to the early 1560s, although he had probably died by the time of the report of his former 'confession' in 1566 (and thus could not gainsay it). Pàdraig mac Mhaighstir Màrtainn, his erstwhile confessor, must have converted to Protestantism soon after the Reformation of 1560 and continued in his charge as minister of Barvas (a parish which included Ness), suggested by his naming as parson there in 1566, and by the witnessing of his deed by the Protestant Bishop of the Isles, John Carswell (MacPhail 1916, 280-1). Pàdraig alleged that Uisdean, Brieve of Lewis, had, through his adultery with Seònaid Mackenzie, lady of Lewis, fathered a child and that the child resulting from this adultery was Torcaill 'Conanach' MacLeod, ostensible heir

Table 3.2 Family tree: Macleod relationships. On CD at back of book

to the Lordship of Lewis (Matheson 1979, 69). This may have been an attempt by Ruairidh MacLeod of Lewis to disown his eldest surviving son and heir, Torcaill Conanach, and disentangle himself from the Mackenzies, who supported Torcaill.

There are several problems with the interpretation of this document of 1566 (printed in MacPhail 1916, 280-1) which has Uisdean the brieve and the parson of Barvas (and Ness) at its centre, not least the fact that it appears to have been engineered to support Macdonald of Sleat and Campbell designs (suggested by the presence of Bishop Carswell on the witness list), and that it was subsequently ignored by those who should have refuted it: Torcaill Conanach, the Mackenzies and even by Ruairidh MacLeod of Lewis himself some years later. Trouble between Ruairidh MacLeod and his son Torcaill continued although Ruairidh made no subsequent attempts at disowning Torcaill on the grounds of paternity (MacPhail 1916, 281-4; MacCoinnich 2007, 13). Whatever the truth of these allegations, Ruairidh MacLeod's repudiation of his first wife, Seònaid (a sister of Mackenzie of Kintail), and attempt at disowning her son, Torcaill Conanach, caused a feud within the MacLeod clan (and trouble with the Mackenzies) that would last for forty years and result ultimately in the destruction of the MacLeod clan in Lewis.

The MacLeods, under pressure from the Regent Mar, made an attempt to patch up the feud over the succession in 1572 (Mackenzie 1903, 152). Ruairidh granted Torcaill lands in a charter and part of this transaction involved a sasine, the document by which the transaction was enacted on the ground, witnessed by the leading men in the lordship. This sasine from 1572 survives. Members of the *britheamh* kindred, together with other followers of the MacLeod chief, and men from districts throughout the lordship of Lewis: Point, Uig, Raasay, Gairloch, Còigeach, Vaternish and Assynt lent their names to this document giving a snapshot of some of the most prominent men in various locales in the lordship at that time. Three members of the brieve's family are explicitly mentioned including (*'Alane filio A[n]gusi Bref in Abost Nyss in Lewis'* in April 1572, *NAS RH 6/2247*), a successor, perhaps, and a probable kinsman of 'Hugonis' (Uisdean) Brief. This is the earliest surviving mention of Habost or a 'Brefe' of which I am aware that explicitly places the *britheamhan* in the Ness/Dùn Èistean area, although there is no reason to doubt their presence there long before this (MacCoinnich 2007, 20-1, 31).

The 'Evil Troubles' of the Lewis and the Fife Adventurers

The legal proceedings, brought by Ruairidh MacLeod of Lewis against his son, Torcaill Conanach, in 1566 in an attempt to disinherit him had thus involved *Sliochd a' Bhritheimh*, closely associated with Ness (and thus probably Dùn Èistean), from the very start. Although the feud relating to the MacLeod succession was papered over in 1572, with the sasine referred to above, this proved to be a temporary settlement. Trouble flared up again in earnest in 1595 with the death of old Ruairidh MacLeod (Mackenzie 1903, 148-58; 164-70; MacCoinnich 2007, 12-13). Ruairidh's son from his third marriage,

This wasx the first stap mead easie for the Mckenzies who neverthelse heated the Breiwe and his trybe so hat[e]full ar[e]
wyces ewer quhen they are profitable bot now the breive and his kin perceaveing
th[a]t they were hated of all men begane (though too lat[e]) to repent this excreable and unnatural fact wch they had committed againgst ther m[aste]r.

After the death of Torq[uil] Dow the Breiwe and his kinn returned into
The Lewes and strengthened themselves
Within a fort in the lland called ness
Bot Neall McLe[o]d the bastard brother of
Torq[uil] Dow persewed them[,] killed divers[e]
Of them and constrained them to leave
The fort of Neise.

Torcaill Dubh, became chief. Torcaill Dubh was opposed by the Mackenzies who strongly supported their own kinsman, Torcaill Conanach, in his claim to be the rightful heir of Lewis. Most of the MacLeods of Lewis disagreed. The Brieve's kindred were split on the matter, and some supported the other sons of MacLeod of Lewis to the bitter end. However, most of the *britheamh* kindred at this time seem to have taken the side of the Mackenzies and their pretender. They seized a Dutch ship, lured Torcaill Dubh on board, and then seized and bound him in the early summer of 1597 and handing him over to the Mackenzies who then executed MacLeod (see the discussion below under the heading 'raiding, piracy and the *britheamhan*').

The result of this, according to a near-contemporary source, was that: 'the briewe and his tribe were heated *[i.e. 'hated']* by all men' and that they fled to their stronghold in Ness, possibly Dùn Èistean, soon after their betrayal of their chief, pursued by Niall 'Odhar' MacLeod (see below; MacPhail 1916, 269), who emerged as the leader of the MacLeods of Lewis. Niall had not forgiven *Sliochd a' Bhritheimh* for their role in the capture and murder of his brother Torcaill Dubh. The *britheamhan*, knowing that Niall and others would be gunning for them made an effort to protect themselves. The writer of 'Ewill Trowbles' describes their actions as follows: 'After the death of Torq[uill] Dow the brieve and his kinn returned to the Lewes and strenthened themselfes within a fort in the iland called Ness' (MacPhail 1916, 269).

However, Niall MacLeod apparently besieged them there, and made

Illus 3.4 Scanned excerpt from 'The Evill Troubles'. By permission of the National Library of Scotland, Adv MS. MS 22.7.11.

them, 'leave the fort of Neise'. This source, *The Evill Troubles of the Lewis*, was probably written at the end of the 1620s by a member of the MacLeods of Lewis, who, if not an eyewitness would have personally known those who were. It is one of two, related, almost identical early-seventeenth century sources that mention a fort in Ness, probably Dùn Èistean. The other is by Sir Robert Gordon, tutor of the earldom of Sutherland, who sheltered some surviving members of the MacLeod of Lewis family, 1610-20. Gordon's narrative on the MacLeods of Lewis is almost identical to the 'Ewill Trowbles of the Lewis.' The textual similarity together with the known association between Gordon and the MacLeods suggests that Gordon's description of these same troubles drew on the writing of one of those to whom he granted sanctuary (MacCoinnich 2006a, 221).

The Mackenzies were not the only people from the outside who were interested in Lewis. Lewis sat in the middle of what were at the time regarded by people as the richest fishing grounds in Europe, frequented by Dutch, English, and Lowland Scots fishermen, merchants and pirates (MacCoinnich 2002, 138, 143-6). King James, to the dismay of both the Mackenzies and the MacLeods of Lewis, took advantage of the discord between the clans and granted the forfeited MacLeod lands to a consortium of merchants and nobles mainly from Fife in 1598. The 'portioners of Lewis' (as they called themselves) or the 'Fife Adventurers' hoped to establish a model new town and develop the lucrative fishery in the area. James VI hoped the settlement would bring stability and prosperity to the area and bring in much needed revenue, and that the establishment of a civilised model town would be seen as a good example to the locals who would follow the lead set by southern settlers (see Mackenzie 1903; MacCoinnich forthcoming).

It was clear, though, that there would be resistance from the locals who stood to lose their lands. The Fife colonists were soon to learn the hard way that while they could consider the locals 'uncivilised' and call them 'barbarous' as Mackenzie put it: 'the primitive instinct of self-defence still flourished in Lewis with undiminished vigour…' (Mackenzie 1903, 179). The initial force of 500-600 men for the 'conquessing of the Lewis' at the start of November 1598 was led by Colonel William Stewart of Houston, the Commendator of Pittenweem, an experienced soldier who had fought in the Dutch Brigades against the Spanish in the 1570s and risen up through the ranks on the basis of his ability. He was a favourite of King James who tended to despatch Stewart to various trouble spots. Stewart was also familiar with the Highlands and Islands, having led several expeditions to the area in the previous decade (Calderwood 1849, iv, 448; Pitcairn 1862, 233, 143; Dunthorne 2004). While the Fife Adventurers quickly captured Lewis in November 1598, the speed of their apparent victory was deceptive and they experienced considerable resistance over the months and years that followed, losing many men from conflict and disease (MacCoinnich, forthcoming).

The MacLeods responded by fighting back against these adventurers and some of them were able to forgive the brieve's kindred for the betrayal of

Torcaill Dubh making common cause against the incoming colonists. Murchadh MacLeod of '*Sebuste*' [Siabost] captured, 7 December 1598, and successfully ransomed one of the leading adventurers, James Leirmonth of Balcomie, having intercepted his ship at sea. The unfortunate Learmonth, kept in captivity in the Còigeach area for over a month, died at Orkney shortly after his release (*RPCS xiv*, cxxiii; Mackenzie 1903, 183-4, 189; NAS CC 8/8/34, ff. 486-9). Murchadh's accomplices were named by the Scottish Privy Council as Angus mKeane Bref, Jhone Dow mcBreif, Angus mcBreif (*Aonghas mac Iain a' Bhritheimh, Iain Dubh mac a' Bhritheimh, Aonghas mac a' Bhritheimh*). Torcaill Dubh's other brother Niall, however, had been unable to forgive the treachery of the *britheamhan* or his own brother Murchadh for joining them. Niall ambushed Murchadh and the *britheamh* kindred, captured them and handed them over to the Fife Adventurers who executed Murchadh MacLeod's followers, sending a dozen heads (presumably of leading members of the *britheamh* kindred) 'in a poke' to Edinburgh. Murchadh of '*Sebust*' (Siabost) the erstwhile leader of the executed *McBreifs* was taken for a 'trial' to St Andrews and executed (Mackenzie 1903, 190-1). The reference to heads of Lewismen being sent to Edinburgh in a 'poke' is corroborated by two independent contemporary accounts from Fife, that of David Calderwood, *c* 1575-1650, and that of David Moysie, fl. 1570 x 1614 (Calderwood 1849, v, 736; Dennistoun 1830, 165).

The colonists, although they based themselves in Stornoway, pursued and slew those natives who resisted them in the surrounding area. Some excerpts from a surviving account of the colony follow, below, written by a minister, Mr John Ross, who accompanied the Fife Adventurers when he arrived in Stornoway in 1605, which gives a description of the type of violence which accompanied the foundation of the colony:[10]

> [in 1599] '....and out of that *[i.e., the colonists' base in Stornoway]* they [*the colonists' soldiers*] had many out breaks upon the hieland men, persewit them, until the maist pairt of the countrie people wer movit to yeild thamselvis unto them to be ther servantis & tennents, vowing unto tham obedience...'
>
> (*NLS Wod Qu. Vol. XX*, fol. 352-7: Transcribed in full in MacCoinnich 2004, 447-55).

When the colonists (1605) tried to remove the 'country people' and replace them with their own tenants, some refused to move, and:

> '[...] 2 companies at Starnewall goes fowrth to persew them, and first apprehends twel[f] of the principalls of them, and brings them into the campe... ... and slew them all except thrie, whom they broght w[t] them to Crail And being put to ane assiss[e] into Craill they ar condemit & hangit [...]'*
>
> *'…Two companies from Stornoway went forth and pursued them, and firstly apprehended twelve of the principal men and brought them back into their camp… …and they slew all of them except three, who they brought with them back to Crail in Fife, where they were given a trial and condemned and hanged…'

For those not initially killed the prospects were equally grim, incarceration and execution. In the words of the minister:

> '[...] And that thei had many of them in fast prisone who after the arywall of the laird of A[i]rdr[i]e wer all put to ane assyss & wer condemit & execut[ed]. Thir Lewes men, then, that refusit to goe out of the countrie being put out of the warld for the maist part [...]'

> *'And they had many of them (ie Lewis men) in a secure prison. And, after the arrival of the laird of Airdrie (Robert Lumsden, one of the principal planters), all of them (the imprisoned Leòdhasaich) were given a trial, and condemned and executed.'

The MacLeods of Lewis mounted a sustained attack and laid siege to Stornoway for three weeks in 1605. According to the colonists' minister, they set all the 'peitstacks in fyre' (thus depriving the colonists of winter fuel). The siege was finally raised by forces led by Ruairidh Mackenzie (brother of Kintail) and Ruairidh Mòr MacLeod of Harris.

> '[...] heirupon, the Lewes men flees. And, ther companie persewes them, sets fyr in some of ther houses, & burnes ther cornes and spoiles ther goods [...]'

Such pursuit of Lewis men by armed forces in 1605 and the firing of not only houses but the reference to the burning of their 'cornes' or food supplies and the spoiling of their goods suggest that repairing to an inaccessible location with good natural defences might be a prudent tactic for the population of rural Lewis. Unfortunately, while this source is more detailed for the Stornoway settlement, it is vague in terms of the rest of the island. It is clear from this, though, that the natives practised guerrilla warfare against the settlers and that the settlers' soldiers attempted to chase these natives back to their home communities. Although no documents have, as yet, been discovered explicitly linking the Fife colonists or 'adventurers' with the structure of Dùn Èistean it is almost certain that the colonists' soldiers would have paid such a structure close attention if it were intact at this time. The frequency of references in the Morison traditions of the Lewis from the early 1800s to locals resorting to different *dùin* in various locales throughout Lewis might repay further attention (Macdonald 1975, 15-18, 22; see also below).

A commission granted to the Fife adventurers in 1605 gave them permission to carry hagbuts [large bore portable muskets] and pistols and kill anyone who defied them without fear of legal retribution. The colonists were also reinforced, periodically, by neighbouring clans (who were not well trusted by the colonists) and by levies from lowland Scotland. By 1607, however, Niall MacLeod had proved a match for the colonists, and had expelled them, occupying and fortifying their 'prettie' town of Stornoway and then holding it against them (Macphail 1916, 59-63, 270-277). The Privy Council granted a commission of fire and sword to the Mackenzies in September 1607. This gave them power to pursue anyone who ran to 'any strenths and housses' (or forts) in Lewis and surrounding islands and 'asseidge the said strenths and housses, raise fyre and all other kinds of force and warlike ingyne [siege engines] that can be had for the wynning [capturing] therof…', permitting them to: imploy and bestow his majesties ordinance, powlder and bullet to that effect.' (RPCS, vii, 84-7, 435). Even if the fort at Ness, probably Dùn Èistean, survived Niall's attentions, *c* 1597, then it is likely that it may have been slighted or deliberately destroyed in the early 1600s on the orders of the Privy Council (*RPCS vii*, 84-92). The Mackenzies who took over Lewis following the failure of the Fife Adventurers' schemes were themselves no strangers to the use of force, and resistance in Lewis seems to have subsided soon after their arrival in 1609, with the exception of some elements of the MacLeods who held out for several years (Mackenzie 1903, 246, 248-52, 254-5).

Trained for war: the MacLeods of Lewis and the Irish Wars

Niall 'Odhar' MacLeod referred to by Macdonald of Sleat, as 'tutor of Lewis' in 1598, was a formidable warrior and was one of the main leaders of the resistance to lowland plantation (1598-1607) and Mackenzie plantation (1607-1613). His indictment when the authorities in Edinburgh finally caught up with him in 1613 stated that he had been bred and trained and raised in 'wickedness.' (*NAS JC 2/5/81*). The reference to 'trained' was probably not loose usage of language. We know that other contemporary clans, such as the Frasers and Gordons, kept their men trained for war during the sixteenth century, drilled by veterans of continental warfare, and certainly Niall MacLeod of Lewis fits this pattern (Mackay 1905, xxxix, 129, 150, 165, 171, 255, 257; MacCoinnich 2002, 155; Martin 1999, 72). Niall seems to have been armed to the teeth and knew how to handle his weapons. His charge sheet when he finally appeared before a court in Edinburgh in 1613 states that he had boarded a vessel in Loch Broom thirteen years earlier with 'bowis, darlochis, muskettis and tua handit suordis' (Pitcairn 1833, iii, 247-7). As one of the leading members of the MacLeod of Lewis family he may well have had a significant hand in MacLeod participation in the Irish wars in the 1580s and 1590s.

While reports of Hebrideans abound in the 1580s in English reportage of their conflict in Ulster, they tend not to single out the individual clans too often, often using 'Macdonald' as a catchall (Macinnes 1993, 33). The MacLeods, it is not certain exactly which branch, certainly made an impact on the Burkes of Mayo in 1591. Some 700 islesmen arrived in thirteen birlinns and had a pitched battle with the locals. The sons of the chiefs of the MacNeils of Barra and the son of a chief of MacLeod were among the slain. Gráinne Ní Mháille, the famous Irish pirate chief went in pursuit of the MacLeods and MacNeils with a fleet of twenty of her ships although it is unknown if she caught up with them (*CSP Ireland iv*, 396-7; O' Dowd 2000). While the exact identity of the Scots involved in that incident is not specified, it is clear that the MacLeods of Lewis, and by implication tenants from throughout their estates, were heavily involved in the Irish wars in the final decades of the sixteenth century. The umbrella terms 'Macdonald' and 'MacLeod of Harris' appear more frequently, and one suspects that Gaels from all around the western seaboard tended to be lumped together in the English sources. The MacLeods of Lewis are specifically

Although the wealthier elements of society all possessed horses, cavalry does not often feature in the record of conflict in the west Highlands and Islands (although it does to a greater extent in the eastern Highlands) and the birlinn, galley or long fada (longship) seems to have been a more practical mode of transport whether in peace or war. The continual unrest in Ireland prior to the English conquest of 1601 provided employment opportunities for up to 6,600 from the west Highlands and Island according to one English estimate from the 1590s. The crown struggled to exercise control of the Highlands and Islands which remained a militarised society in the following decades (Macinnes 2006, 57-61). Reports of conflict from the area abound. In terms of the descriptions of their equipment habergeons (mail coats) feature regularly as do dirks, axes of various kinds, spears and targes. Swords whether one handed or 'tua handit' were an ever present, both before during and well after the period in question. Bows and arrows (and darlochs or quivers) continued to be favoured among Highland clans until the end of the seventeenth century due to rapidity of fire and accuracy of skilled bowmen in comparison with more clumsy and expensive hagbutt, culverin or musket. Despite the apparent conservatism in the weaponry used in the Gaidhealtachd, however, firearms were, nevertheless, present on a fairly widespread basis (Caldwell 2007; Macinnes 1996, 65-66).

The firearms in use in this period seem to have been cannon, and portable firearms known variously as hackbuts, hagbuts or harquebus, culverins, muskets and pistols (or pistolettes). While firearms were present in the kingdom of Scotland from the end of the fifteenth century, it was in the mid sixteenth century that they seemed to become more commonplace according to Maxwell-Irving's study of the effects of firearms on for-tifications in the Borders (Maxwell-Irving 1971, 193-202). A similar pattern can be seen in the records relating to the north of the kingdom. A list of examples has been compiled to illustrate the growth in the usage of firearms in the Highlands and Islands / Gaelic Scotland during the latter half of the sixteenth century and is included on the CD in the back of this volume. This is not exhaustive, nor is it intended to be, and could be greatly expanded on, but it should serve to illustrate the point that while older weapons such as bows and swords remained commonplace the newer weapons were gaining ground in the Highlands and Islands much as they were in the rest of the kingdom during the course of the sixteenth century. The following is just a selection of examples extracted from this list:

1506 Sept Cannon was present at Stornoway from as early as 1506 when it was used at the siege of Stornoway castle. The ship, the Raven, and gunners and armourers are known to have been present in the royally sanctioned expedition to Lewis at this time (TA iii, 340, 347-351. TA iv, 90).

1545-6 Dòmhnall Dubh rebellion. An English observer noted that the Highlanders had 'few guns.' He did not say that they had no guns. Clearly they had some in 1545-6, but not a significant number (Gregory 1881, 171).

1595 22 July Letter John Auchinross, Dumbarton, to George Nicolson, Edinburgh. Reports that Macleod of Lewis (and Harris) with Donald Gorm with 2500 men passed by Mull, that the Macleods parleyed with Maclean... ...they were joined by 500 men from Angus Macdonald in Islay. Significantly Auchinross had noted that they had no lead or powder (CSP Scot xi, 650). He did not say there were no guns, indicating that

Table 3.3 Weapons and firearms in Gaelic Scotland, c 1500-1630. On CD at back of book

Illus 3.5 'The English solders return in triumph, carrying severed Irish heads and leading a captive by a halter', from 'The Image of Irelande', by John Derrick (London, 1581). By permission of Edinburgh University Library

B And though the pray recouer'd be, yet are not all things ended:
For why: the souldiours doe pursue, the Roges that haue offended.
Who neuer ceace till in the bloud, of these light fing'red theeues:
A To see a souldiour toze a Karne, O Lord it is a wonder:
And eke what care he taketh to part, the head from neck a sonder.

To see another leade a theefe, with such a lordly grace:
And for marke how loth the knaue, doth follow in that case.
C To see how trimme their glibbed heades, are borne by valiant men,
D And gard'd with a royall route, of worthy souldiours then.
All these thinges sufficient, to moue a subjects minde:
To part the souldiours, which reward, the woodkerne in their kinde.

guns may have been anticipated. What he did say was that they had no ammunition.

1599 '[you, Neil Macleod of Lewis, your brother Norman Macleod and your followers attack the colony at Stornoway...] ...come all bodin in feir of weir with bowis durloches tua handit sword[i]s, hagbuttis, pistolettis & utheris wappones invasive in oppin and hosteill maner about fourtene yeir synce or th[er] by to the said lleand of the Lewis...' And, Neil was also accused of having attacked the merchant/fishing ship of John Blair a merchant of Perth who was anchored in Loch Broom: '...and th[er] as pirattis, thevis and sea robberis eftir dischargeing of dyv[er]ss muscattis hagbuttis & utheris ingynes of fyre worke at the said schip and companie...' Excerpt from the Trial of Neil Macleod of Lewis in 1613 (NAS JC 2/5 fol. 80r-84r).

1603 8 Mar 'Caution fund for the portioners of the Lewis' Instructions for the Fife adventurers or colonists of Lewis to go and recover the island from the native rebels: 'That everie ane of thame, betuix and midsommer nixt, sall levie and tak up threttie men of weir, weill provydit and weill furneissed with armour, powder and bullet, and thrie scoir bollis meill...' (RPCS vi, 545-6).

c.1605-1607 Account of the Fife Adventurers being besieged by the natives at Stornoway. Mentions of gunshots and references to musketeers, and the settlers defending themselves by building 'rounds' of timber at each corner of their fortified dwellings in Stornoway, where 'hagbut[t]ers might stand and defend the howss...' And, in a description of when the colonists' fort in Stornoway came under attack from Lewismen, 'the sowlders wer busie schooting ther guns...' (NLS Wod Qu. xx, fol. 356r-357r;

MacCoinnich 2004, 452-454).

1607 April [You, Neil Macleod of Lewis...] '...yo[u]r complices to the nu[m]ber of thrie hundrethe persones or th[er]by all bodin in feir of weir wt suordis durkis bowis darloches hagbutis muscattis and pistolettis resolveing wt y[ou]r selff to put thei hailll Lawland gentilmen being than w[i]thin thei said lleand of the Lewis to the suord q[uhai]rby...' Excerpt from the Trial of Neil Macleod of Lewis in 1613 (NAS JC 2/5 fol. 80r-84r).

1608 27 June Burgh of Glasgow supplied and furnished a contingent of men from the burgh to assist in the suppression of rebels in the isles. 'xx hagbitteris [Hagbutters]...   ...appointit for the furnsing of the armie and his men to wait upone the leivtennent, and he hes nominat and chosen John Sterling, deakin of hammermen, to be thair captain...' [29 July. Men sent to the isles on the king's service] '...xxv men of weir with James Stirling thair commander to pas to the Ilis on the kingis service' All the soldiers were to be supplied by the burgh with hagbuts, bandoliers, and 'flassis' (Marwick 1876, 283, 286-7, 294, 297).

1612 A surviving official price list from Scotland in 1612 shows how widespread guns had become by then. This has a list of the prices current in Scotland at the time, including arrows, axes, crossbows, dagger blades sword hilts together with firearms. Arrows, the groce, containing tuelf dozen, £4; Schooting arrows [crossbows ?], the groce, £24; Axes, the dozen, £3; Dagger blades, the dozen, £4. Guns: Hagbuttis £3, Muskets £6, Pair pistols £6. Hilts for swords or daggers starting at £8 for the dozen; Hunderweight of powder, 40 Shillings. Swords, the dozen, starting at £12' (Innes 1867).

mentioned in relation to their participation in Ireland and Irish warfare on several occasions: in February 1575 (O' Dowd 2000, no. 1312.3, p. 781); in April 1581 (*CSP Ireland* ii, 301); and in July 1595 (*CSP Scot xi*, 629, 636, 638, 644-5, 650, 654-5, 684-5).

Although individuals are seldom named in reports of the MacLeods of Lewis being active in Ireland, it is almost certain that Niall like many of his followers (including the *britheamh* in Ness and his kin prior to 1597) would have been veterans of the Irish wars. The report in traditional history of the *britheamh* taking an Irish wife home to Ness, while completely unverifiable, nevertheless, fits very well with the circumstantial evidence (Matheson 1970, 187). The fact that a significant section of the MacLeods of Lewis (and almost certainly their followers such as the brieve kindred) had first hand knowledge of the Irish theatre of war not only in terms of weaponry and tactics but also in terms, presumably, of defensive structures, may have implications for our understanding of Dùn Èistean.

Raiding, piracy and the britheamhan

The MacLeods of Lewis were also raiding the lands on the mainland and a *Hucheoun Breiff* and an *Allane Breiff* are described as the 'household men' or followers of 'Torquill McCleud' (Torcaill Conanach, the Mackenzie claimant) in a raid on the Munros in 1599 (*RPCS* vi, 84). The Munros of Foulis in Easter Ross had an interest in Loch Broom in the second half of the sixteenth century, when they had a tack of the assize herring of Loch Broom and the north Isles, from the 1540s through to the 1580s (McInnes 1940, no 51, 88, 15, 28; *RSS vi*, no 1800, 342). This meant that the Munros too were neighbours of the Lordship of Lewis, in Còigeach, and had a vested interest in the region. This may also have been an additional front in the intermittent open warfare being waged between the Mackenzies and the Munros in Easter as well as Wester Ross at this time (McInnes 1940, no 85, 24-5). This is all the more intriguing as a Munro genealogy written in 1734 claims that there had also been a marital link between the Munros and the brieves: with a marriage between the son of Uilleam Munro of Meikle Allan (fl. 1565) and a daughter of *Ailean the Britheamh* of Habost, Ness (fl. 1572-1600).[11]

The reputation enjoyed by Hebridean clans for preying on the busy shipping routes of Dutch and Baltic merchantmen, Lowland Scottish fishermen and English pirates plying these waters at the time is also well attested. A near contemporary narrative source states that the *britheamh* was not averse to piracy and captured a Dutch ship in the early summer of 1597. The Dutch ship captured by the *britheamh* and handed over to Mackenzie with its captive was almost certainly *the Eger id est the Hunter* of Emden, a ship of 40-55 tons burthen with four artillery pieces, captained by Omne Deirikson and owned by Tobias Boull and Stais Orene (NAS RD 1/64 fol. 216; MacCoinnich forthcoming). The *britheamh* then used this ship to lure Torcaill Dubh MacLeod of Lewis on board in 1597 under the pretext of sharing the cargo (MacPhail 1916, 268-9; cf. Weber 1813, 269-70 and MacPhail 1916, 56-7). No sooner was Torcaill Dubh on board than they bound him and carried him as a captive to his enemy Coinneach Òg Mackenzie of Kintail. Mackenzie, presented with an unexpected windfall of both a captive enemy and a valuable foreign ship was not one to pass up on such opportunities. The ship, with the assent (either willing or unwilling) of the original skipper and owners, was sold to James Crombie, a burgess of Perth, 17 June 1597, for 2000 merks. Mackenzie, nothing if not ruthless, executed Torcaill Dubh in July 1597 and then abandoned the *britheamh* and his followers leaving them to face the wrath of the remaining MacLeods led by Torcaill Dubh's illegitimate half-brother, Niall MacLeod. While tradition has the Macaulays of Uig as the main protagonists of the Morisons of Ness, it would seem that it was the MacLeods, led by Niall, who are the best attested historical enemy of most of *sliochd a' Bhritheimh* from 1597 onwards once the lordship of Lewis sank into factional fighting – conflict that intensified in November 1598 when the colonists arrived from Fife (Mackenzie 1903, 63-4, 189-90; Macphail 1916, 269-76).

Niall is also associated with the *britheamh* kindred in the well-known

Gaelic song that would seem to date from this time, '*an t-Iorram Niseach*.' This places Niall and the *britheamhan* in the vicinity of another Dùn, Dùn Othail (see Chapter 2, above; Ó Baoill and Bateman 1994, 48-9, 217; sung by *Màiri Nic a' Ghobhainn* (Mary Smith) of Ness on her CD, 'Sgiath Airgid' (Macmeanmna, Skye, 2004).

Illus 3.6 Dun Othail

The exact circumstances related to the composition of this song have become half-forgotten due to its long transmission in oral tradition. It is, nevertheless, a remarkable survival, which gives us a snapshot of the depth of enmity engendered between the *britheamh* family and Niall 'Odhar' after 1597 that both corroborates and amplifies the story emerging from surviving documentary sources. This song also clearly pinpoints another defensive structure, Dùn Othail, some eight miles down the coast from Dùn Èistean, albeit a site whose physical remains are very slight (Barrowman 2004b, 133-4; McHardy et al 2009). Niall MacLeod of Lewis, was himself eventually forced by the Mackenzies to retreat to another fortified sea stack: Dùn Bearasaigh at the entrance to Loch Roag, 1609-13 (Mackenzie 1903, 254-5). Such unsettled and dangerous conditions at the time throughout the island, may have encouraged the building of strongholds and *dùin* and, according to tradition, the recycling of much older structures such as Dùn Chàrlabhaigh (Mackenzie 1903, 167-8). The recourse to such dùin was still remembered by tradition in the early nineteenth century although the details are, understandably, a little vague (Macdonald 1975, 15-16, 17, 18, 22). The existence of other, frustratingly un-named, strongholds is made clear in a document from August 1607 that clearly states that Ruairidh Mòr MacLeod of Harris had captured Stornoway castle and 'other fortalices' on the island (*RPCS vii*, 430). Elsewhere in the Highlands and Islands there are traditional associations of dùin with particular clans, such as Dùn Ringill in Skye, associated with the Mackinnon clan, Dùn Raghnaill in South Uist, associated with the Clanranald, and An Dùn, Clashnessie, Assynt. Other sites with less clear associations proliferate in the area and many of them may well have been used in the late medieval/Early Modern period.[12]

Niall 'Odhar' MacLeod, together with tenants (including the *britheamh* kindred) drawn from all of the Lewis estate, were steeped in a culture of raiding and fighting and ranged far and wide. There had been heavy raiding on Orkney in 1461-2 by men of Eoin Lord of the Isles, almost certainly including a Lewis contingent (Storer-Clouston 1914, xliv, xlvi, xlviii, 54). By the 1540s and 1550s there seems to have been a long running violent dispute between the '*foud*' of Shetland (a Shetlandic law officer) and the men of Lewis with reciprocal raiding. Ola Sinclair, sometime *foud* of Shetland, was given a respite (a reprieve or a royal pardon) in October 1555 for killing an Uilleam 'Lewis' and others, possibly members of the brieve's family, who were in Shetland in 1543 (*RSS iv*, 3071. This Remission to Sinclair was re-issued in 17 October 1564. *RSS v*, 1794, p. 500). The following year Uisdean the Brieve 'Hugo McBreif' from 'Trouternes' was given a pardon by the king for killings and plunder in Shetland and Orkney and feuding and killing with the Sinclairs there in 1556, burning houses, provisions and goods only 6 years after Hugh had been summoned to see the regent at Inverness (*RSS iv*, no 3307, p. 589).

It is unlikely that all the violence was one way and it is almost certain

In solchem Habit Gehen die 800 In Stettin angekommen Irrländer oder Irren.

Es ist ein Starckes dauerhafftigs Volck behilfft sich mit geringer speiß hatt es nicht brodt so Essen sie Würtzeln, Wans auch die Notturfft erfordert Können sie des Tages Uber die 20 Teütscher meilweges lauffen, haben neben Musqueten Ihre Bogen vnd Köcher vnd lange Messer.

Illus 3.7 Stettin-Mackay image of Highland Soldiers in German c 1630. By permission of the British Library

that reciprocal raids may have been undertaken by Shetlanders and Orcadians who were far from soft targets, whether for marauding Lewismen or raiding English forces. English raiding in the north and on Orkney was not, apparently, uncommon during the sixteenth century. However, a party of Orcadians led by Edward Sinclair routed a 500-strong English raiding party at Papdale in Orkney in 1557 (Anderson 1982, 32) and traditions from Orkney and Shetland point to other occasions when the locals in both island groups saw off Lewismen (Mackenzie 1903, 104-6). It seems too that the killing of the son of the *foud* by a Lewisman, mentioned above, was not an isolated event. When Uisdean the brieve gained his remission for the murder of Henry Sinclair (30 August 1556), his kinsman Iain 'Breif' managed to obtain a royal protection for himself and his kin the very next day (*RSS iv,* no 3308, p. 589). Again although there is no surviving explicit evidence to support any hostile activity from Orkney or Shetland in a Lewis context, the difficult relations that the MacLeods occasionally had with the islands to the north (and the implication of the timing of the remission and the protection) means that Dùn Èistean was probably in the front line of any retaliatory action from the north.

Such raiding by *Leòdhasaich* (Lewis folk), and no doubt the *Nisich* (Ness folk), could wreak widespread devastation on the northern Isles. In 1559 the parish of Westray in Orkney said they were unable to pay ecclesiastical taxes as their lands had been 'wastit be Lewis men' (Kirk 1995, 666-7). Even allowing for some exaggeration from a desire to minimise tax exposure there is likely to have been some substance to the claim. The MacLeods of Lewis were connected to the Orcadian politics through the marriage of the chief, Ruairidh to Barbara Stewart (probably at some time in the 1540s). Barbara Stewart had been a wealthy widow prior to her marriage to Ruairidh and had property in Orkney in her own right.[13] This marriage may have been the reason that the MacLeods of Lewis were involved in Orkney and Shetland where another Stewart, Patrick, Lord of Orkney and Shetland, a kinsman of Barbara, was accused of encouraging the raiding of 'wild Irish' (possibly meaning the MacLeods of Lewis and their followers) to teach his tenants a lesson (Anderson 1982, 32, 94). 'Irish' was simply the English word used for 'Gaelic' in this period (Horsburgh 2002, 234-9).

Fishing and commercial trading routes in the north Minch

Lowland Scots fishers were frequent visitors to the north Minch or the 'North Yllis' (as the Outer Hebrides were known) from the 1570s onwards, in increasingly large numbers. It is significant that the number of complaints from these fishermen increased exponentially as they gave vent to their displeasure at their treatment at the hands of locals who sought to exploit these incoming fishers. From the point of view of the local chiefs (and probably the community) these fishermen were coming to their seas and sea lochs and exploiting their resources. Clearly, local chiefs (as groups like the O' Driscolls and others did in Ireland) saw this as an opportunity to raise revenue (Breen 2001, 424, 429; Naessens 2007, 220-6; Kelleher 2007). The problem was that whereas the chiefs in the Hebrides did have a right in law to charge fishers for coming ashore ('ground leave') and for packing and curing their fish, they were increasingly in dispute with lowland fishers who resented their exactions. Furthermore it was claimed (probably with some truth) that the locals in the isles often resorted to force or intimidation to extract these dues. This was one of the underlying causes of tension that occasionally exploded into violence and which helped build the pressure among the Fife fishermen (and their noble patrons) for plantation in the island (Mackenzie 1903, 153-4; MacCoinnich forthcoming).

The presence of such shipping, international as well as Scottish, on the sea lanes around Lewis was not ignored by the islanders. The rhetoric emanating from Edinburgh and London, concerned with protecting and enforcing their trading monopolies in Lewis during the period, showed a great deal of concern with the presence of foreigners, particularly Dutch merchants and fishermen in the area. Several of the writings from burgh sources for the period demonstrate the worry felt by burgesses that locals would trade directly with the Dutch. It may be that the burgesses' fears were well founded and the Dutch certainly had a presence in the area (Wood 1936, 55, 66, 77, 264; *RCRBS ii*, 323, 350, 354, 405; *RCRBS iii*, 142, 257-323; MacCoinnich 2002, 135, 146). A lively diplomatic debate raged between the Netherlands and the British state over fishing rights and national waters in this period. In fact one of the earliest detailed maps of Scotland, from 1634, printed in Amsterdam (Blaeu 1635), makes this point well by showing a ship carrying the Dutch flag in the north Minch, emphasising the importance of the area as well as the Dutch right to traffic there (see Illus 3.2). What may well have been a Dutch vessel from the period was recently discovered on the seabed off the coast of Kinlochbervie.[14]

Commercial transactions and contacts probably went on all the time, usually not leaving a paper trail (thus no 'history') and only making historical 'headlines' when matters went wrong. The real and ready availability of wine in the household of island chiefs and Edinburgh's attempts to control (and thus tax) the flow of wine (probably of Spanish or French origin) to the isles in 1609, whether via Dutch, English, or Scots middlemen underlines this (Macgregor 2006, 141-4; Gregory 1881, 332; MacLeod 1938, 110; Mijers 2006) and references to wine can be found in surviving late medieval and Early Modern Gaelic poetry from the area (McLeod and Bateman 2007, 366, 370, 388; Ó Baoill and Bateman 1994, 64-6, 72; MacPhàrlain 1923, 143-8; Clancy 2010, 111-12). The attempts by the government to regulate the consumption of wine by island chiefs and their followers was simply one of the more conspicuous items in the famous programme for reform touted by the government on 1609, known as the Statutes of Iona. For most of the islands this meant in effect that King James VI and I and his government was prepared to work with Hebridean chiefs. This did not include the MacLeods of Lewis who were not included in the new royal highland policy (Macinnes 1996, 65-6; Goodare 1998; MacGregor 2006; Cathcart 2009; MacCoinnich, forthcoming).

Implications of the historical background for interpretation of Dùn Èistean 1493-1610

As discussed above, little is known of Dùn Èistean from the historical record and it is not mentioned by name in any surviving documents. However, the nature of the remains on the island and its situation is suggestive of a strategically important place. How far the local stronghold of Dùn Èistean was involved in the rebellions of 1504-6, 1530 and 1540-55 is unknown from the historical record. Insurrection and the royal reaction to it, was one context that may have had an impact on Dùn Èistean although there is no documentary evidence one way or another. For instance, Torcaill MacLeod of Lewis held out in Stornoway castle in 1505-6, supporting Dòmhnall Dubh the Macdonald claimant to the Lordship of the Isles, in defiance of James IV. The Treasurers' Accounts from this time reveal some details about the logistics of the royal expedition to crush Torcaill's rising and point to some of the mechanisms at work during the siege. Payments were made in October 1506 to Thomas Hathoway to furnish the ship, the *Raven*, for the expedition to Lewis, with details of the crew including gunners, wrights, masons and an armourer. The Bishop of Caithness was also reimbursed in 1507 for his payments to William Duncan, master of David Logan's ship that was in 'the Lewis,' and also for workmen, wrights, and masons wages from the previous year (TA iii, 347-51, 383-4; TA iv, 90; MacCoinnich 2007, 9-10). The expedition led by the Earl of Huntly also besieged and captured Stornoway castle using cannon, emphasising Steve Boardman's point that the advent of gunpowder and advances in artillery meant that stone castles were no longer impregnable, even in the parts of the kingdom which had been remote from royal power, by the end of the fifteenth century (Boardman 2006, 268). It seems unlikely that such royal expeditions to subdue the lordship of Lewis, while focused on Stornoway, would have ignored strongholds on other parts of the island such as Dùn Èistean.

Dùn Èistean, although admittedly poorly provided in terms of an anchorage or for launching shipping, was ideally placed at the entrance to the north Minch to be able to monitor if not intercept shipping. As we have seen, the north Atlantic was a busy place in the sixteenth and seventeenth centuries and its rich fishing grounds were a prized and a disputed resource. It sat beside the main sea road used by the Baltic States and the Netherlands to reach the outside world whenever the English were hostile and closed what they called the 'narrow seas' (the Straits of Dover) to continental traffic (MacCoinnich 2004, 334; MacCoinnich 2002, 143).

The Mackenzies take over

The MacLeods, despite their own disunity, had managed to fight off the Lowland planters between 1598 and 1609 but at a great cost to themselves. By 1609, the last principal colonists Sir George Hay of Nether Liff (later Chancellor of Scotland) and Sir James Spens of Wolmerston (later James VI's envoy in Sweden) having wearied of the continual opposition and the overt and covert hostility of the neighbouring Mackenzies and others sold out their rights to Mackenzie of Kintail. The MacLeods, weakened by nearly ten years of conflict, were no match for the MacKenzies of Kintail (later known as Seaforth) who then conquered the island (1609-11) and kept a hold of it until 1844.

What of the McBrefs in Ness and elsewhere? Many would have been killed during the intense conflict of 1597-1610, and some at least continued fighting on the side of the MacLeods. The leader of the invading Mackenzie forces was Ruairidh Mackenzie of Còigeach, known as the Tutor of Kintail. He received a commission in 1613 to track down and capture surviving elements of the MacLeods of Lewis and their supporters who refused to surrender, including a Dòmhnall "McIndowie Breiff." This Dòmhnall was still on the run in August 1616, when he was involved in a rebellion led by Gillecalum (Malcolm) MacLeod (*RPCS x*, 609-11, 622). After that little is heard of him or of any other 'Breif' in the records. There are indications, however, discussed below, that most of the kindred had sided with the Mackenzies in the years after 1597 (when they betrayed Torcaill Dubh), although details are hard to come by.

Niall MacLeod continued to resist the Mackenzies until 1613. He had, however, been marginalised by the Mackenzies relatively quickly and the newcomers had a firm grip of most of Lewis from 1611 onwards. It is unlikely that any structure in north Lewis such as Dùn Èistean would have been used to defy the Mackenzies, especially given that most of the local *britheamh* kindred seem to have sided, as far as can be seen, with the Mackenzies. The earliest surviving detailed map of Lewis, probably drawn by a Captain Dymes for the British fishery company around 1630, shows a church (*Teampall Mholuaidh*) and the 'Pigmies Isle' (*Luchruban*) close to where Dùn Èistean should be. There is no indication, however, of any fortification (Macleod 1989, 9). There is, similarly, no indication of a defensive structure either on Blaeu's map of 1634. Although the absence of the structure of Dùn Èistean from the map is not conclusive proof of its abandonment or slighting by this date (Stornoway castle, which we know survived at this date was not on this map either), it would be surprising if such a building had survived the chaotic conditions of 1598-1610.

From judges to ministers

Thereafter we see nor hear no more of the 'McBreifs,' or *britheamhan*. Those that survived did not continue in rebellion and had clearly made terms with the incoming Mackenzie regime. Whatever the exact role of the *britheamhan* had been as 'lawmen' under the MacLeods, this did not continue under the new Mackenzie administration. This becomes clear when records relating to surviving witchcraft trials in Stornoway in the 1630s show that they were presided over not by *britheamhan* or Morisons, but by leading members of the Mackenzie family (Yeoman 2004, 242-3). The family of the *britheamhan* had switched professions by this time away from being lawmen to being ministers, and their name had altered to the form we know today - Morison.

The 'brief' kindred had, like their MacLeod chiefs, not been able to retain any semblance of unity during what chroniclers called the 'Ewill trowbles of the Lewis' where the rule of the MacLeods had ended amidst dissension and violence within and invasion from without. Some members of the brieve dynasty had remained loyal to ailing MacLeod of Lewis cause as late as 1614. Others had, as discussed above, leagued with the Mackenzies of Kintail from the beginning of the 'trowbles of the Lewes' (1598-1611), and this was probably the key to the survival and re-emergence of at least one branch of the family as the turmoil of plantation subsided by the mid seventeenth century. While the Fife adventurers had stipulated that there was to be a clear differentiation between themselves and the colonised, with restrictions on marriages and friendships between the planters and 'hieland men', the Mackenzies took a different approach. Those who opposed the Mackenzie takeover were eradicated in short order, but the Mackenzies, culturally identical and Gaelic speakers like the tenants of their new lands, sought to build bridges with their new tenants using the mechanics of clanship. The Macaulays of Uig, for example, were summarily evicted by the Fife adventurers in 1605 but, like the Macbreifs or Morisons, were drawn into the sphere of the Mackenzie polity from 1609- a process probably helped by ties of marriage and fosterage (*RPCS xiv*, p. cxxx; *NAS RD 1/119* fol. 13v-14r; Macdonald 1967, 28-31, 130-1; Macdonald 1975, 28-9; Maciver 2003, 57; Matheson 1970, 206, 245-6).

The next sighting of the 'Breif' kindred in Ness, some 25 years later, in 1640-3, sees a Mr Donald Morison, minister in the kirk of Ness being given a life-rent tack of the lands of Habost from the Mackenzies of Seaforth (Matheson 1970, 245-6; 'Information, Mr Alan Morisoune agt the Laird of Assint,' (*c* 1716) *AUL MS 2787/3/3/7/4*). This Donald Morison was clearly related to, and a direct descendant of, the family who had previously been known in records as 'MacGilleVorie' (*MacGilleMhoire*) or 'McBref' (*mac a' Bhritheimh*) or variants thereof. John Morisone, indweller of Lewis claimed, sometime between 1678 and 1688, that 'all the Morisones in Scotland' were descended from 'Mores the son of Kenannus' which, given the climate of pedigree faking among his contemporaries, has to be taken with a large pinch of salt (Mitchell and Clark 1906-1908, ii, 214); see also Matheson 1970, 186-7; Matheson 1979, 62; Maciver 2003, 56-64. See also the discussion below).

'MacGilleMhoire' was not only clearly a Gaelic (thus barbarous) name but also one that may well have had pre-Reformation overtones. A letter from John Morison of Bragar to Mr Allan Morison of Ness, dated 1700 which was discovered recently by Dr Dòmhnall Uilleam Stiùbhart may provide another clue. This letter discusses Rev. Donald Morison's efforts at stamping out pre-Reformation religious practices in Ness some fifty years earlier. This suggest there might also be a connection between the name change to Morison and the Rev. Donald Morison's efforts, also around the same time in the mid seventeenth century, at persuading his congregation (and kinsmen) to drop old religious practices connected to Teampall Mholuaidh, such as the annual offering to 'a sea god called Shony' and processions with the cross 'Mulruy' (Stiùbhart 2006a, 205-6, 210-13; Martin 1999, 29). It is unlikely to be a coincidence that the name

'Morison' appears in the surviving written record at the same time as some of the leading members of the family switched from being 'brieves' to being ministers. Religious reform was accompanied by a change of name.

From McBref/MacGilleMhuire to Morison

The adoption of the name 'Morison' at some point during the first half of the seventeenth century was probably a matter of convenience in an increasingly anglophone world. It bore some similarity to MacGilleMhoire, anglicising it as 'Moire-son', in much the same pattern, perhaps, as names of neighbouring kindreds such as MacMhathain and MacMhurchaidh became Scotticised or anglicised as Matheson and Murchison respectively. Moreover, the form 'Morison' was free of overtones of a barbarous Gaelic past in a way that 'McBref', Mac Gille Mhoire and their variations were not (MacCoinnich 2006a, 218). *Sliochd a' Bhritheimh* were not the only clan to rebrand their names at this time. Those bearing the names 'MacNeacail' and 'MacBeatha' in the records from neighbouring Skye prior to the 1620s, for example, became Nicolsons and Beatons, respectively, although they had no connection to their namesakes in the south who bore these well-established lowland names. Elsewhere Clann MhicDhùn Leibhe in Lismore became Livingstones and the MacCallums of Argyll became the Malcolms of Poltalloch. Not only were names re-packaged, but the past itself could be re-invented and the parallel practice of pedigree faking was widespread in the highlands at this time (Bannerman 1998, 3-5. Sellar et al 1999, 13-15. Sellar 1981, 108-113. Black 1946; 1993, 463). Given this adoption of the name 'Morison' sometime in the early seventeenth century it is worth considering, briefly, who else in Scotland called themselves this name.

W C Mackenzie floated the possibility of the Morrisons of Dairsie near St Andrews in Fife as catalysts of the name change by means of the Fife adventurers. This cannot be ruled out, but this particular Morison family gained these lands of Dairsie later than the plantation (Dairsie was held at the time of plantation by the Leirmonth family), and this Morison family may not have been particularly prominent at this time (1610-43). The attendance of Eugenius Makbrehin at St Andrews University in the 1520s (above), and Mr Donald Morison at the same university a century later (below), throws up another intriguing link, however, between the brieve kindred and the East Neuk of Fife. Mackenzie also draws our attention to a family from Caithness who in his own day claimed kinship with the Lewis 'Morisons'. This link should be treated with caution as the usage by the Caithness group of 'Morison' pre-dates that of the Lewis family by some eighty years to the 1570s – while the Lewis family were still by that time using other names such as 'breif' and its variants (see above). An Alexander Morison of Prestongrange (Lothian) was, ironically, a prominent lawman in Scotland at this time: a connection, perhaps, that may not have been lost on *Sliochd a' Bhritheimh* (Young 1993, 509-10).

One Morison, however, that most people in the Highlands and Islands as well as those connected to the world of the Mackenzies would be familiar with was Mr Andrew Morison, *c* 1552-1633, the chief collector of customs north of the Forth, based at Chanonry (now Fortrose) and Avoch, (Adam 1991, 200-1, 241; *NAS RS 37/4* fol. 325). The Chanonry and Avoch area, where Andrew Morison was based, was the centre of Mackenzie operations in Lewis and Ross at this time. Mr Andrew Morison can be demonstrated to have had a longstanding and close acquaintance with Mr William Lauder, Donald Morison's father in law. Andrew Morison and Lauder are on record as witnessing the same deed or conducting business together on several occasions and no doubt knew each other extremely well.[17] In fact one of our first sightings of a 'Morison' in Lewis (as mentioned briefly above) dates to between 1640 and 1643 when this Donald 'Morison' minister of Barvas married Lauder's daughter (Matheson 1970, 246). This may prove nothing in itself but it is a striking co-incidence. We may never know exactly how, when and why the *Brieve* kindred stopped calling themselves *Mc Breif* in English/Scots and adopted the name 'Morison,' but the name change coincided with a career change, with Donald and one of his cousins, being the first of several generations of this family to embark on a career in the clergy.

Another member of the same kindred, 'Murdoch mc Huistone' also a minister in Barvas and possibly Mr Donald's predecessor, appears on record in 1642-3 and he too, according to William Matheson, was a Morison. Significantly, however, Mr Murdoch, a slightly older contemporary of Mr Donald was known by his patronymic rather than by 'Morison.' Together with Mr Donald Morison, Mr Murdoch was the first of many of these Morison ministers who appear on record in the later seventeenth and early eighteenth century and who were descended from the '*britheamhan*'. Mr Donald Morison graduated from St Andrews in 1640 and married, as noted above, Jean Lauder from the Black Isle in 1643 (MacTavish 1943, i, 33, 64, 78; FES vii, 199; Matheson 1979, 187, 196-7, 245-51). Although resident at Habost, this couple retained a landed interest in the Avoch area until at least 1665 (NAS RS 38/2 fol 244r).

Jean's father, Mr William Lauder, in addition to his connections to Andrew Morison, was one of the busiest lawmen on behalf of the Mackenzies of Kintail and Seaforth in the first third of the seventeenth century. This marriage between a daughter of the most prominent notary in the Mackenzie regime and one of the old families in Lewis was another indication of the bridges built between the Mackenzies and their new tenants in Lewis. Donald, who was an informant for Martin Martin in 1695, died in 1698, and was succeeded as minister in Ness by his son, Mr Allan Morison (Martin 1999, 19, 24, 26; Matheson 1970, 191n, 245-6). The link between these Morisons and the earlier 'McBrefs' or *Sliochd a' Bhritheimh*, is confirmed by a complaint in a recently discovered document made by Mr Allan Morison. It is addressed to his lawyer, Alexander MacLeod, in 1712, at a time when the Mackenzies were trying to remove him from his tack in Habost, while Morison, on the other hand, was trying to get Mackenzie to pay him his stipend. Allan Morison referred to;

> '...the lands of Habost which I possessed as a kindly tenant, my
> predecessors for many genera[tio]ns being possessors therof, of w[hi]
> c[h] they had liferent Tack the last of w[hi]c[h] expired att the time of

my father & mothers decease, anno 1698. And if I would dispense with the lands of Habost I had no place to goe to - not haveing manss or Gleib, nor any house to reside inn, except such as I had on this tack of Habost...'

('Information, Mr Alan Morison agt, the Laird of Assint... ...to Mr Alex[ande]r McLeod, advocat (c. 1705)'. Aberdeen University Library, Seton of Mounie papers: AUL MS 2787/3/3/7/4).

In other words, Morison's argument was that he had a hereditary right (known as *dùthchas* in Gaelic or *kindness* in English) to the lands of Habost as his family had been there for 'many generations' prior to 1698. Morison also said that he had no house apart from the one that he had at Habost. In order to credibly claim such a right to dùthchas, or kindly tenancy, Morison's family had to have continuous occupation of the site for at least three or four generations. This directly links these Morisons with the 'Allan breiff in Abostnys' of 1572. (Macinnes 1996, 16; Coutts 2003, 172-3; Sanderson 1982, 58-62; Sanderson 2002, 49-50). This statement by Mr Allan Morison not only provides solid documentary evidence for '*an taigh mòr Thàboist*' traditionally associated with the brieve family (big house in Habost; see Barrowman, C S 2007b, 35-8; Barrowman, C S 2015, 180-3) but provides incontrovertible documentary evidence (if it were needed) supporting the tradition that these Morison ministers were directly descended from the line of the brieves. Mr Allan Morison remained as minister in Habost until his death in 1723, when he was succeeded in turn by his son Murdo who was minister of Barvas (including Ness) until 1767 (Matheson 1970, 246-7).

Aberdeen University Library
AUL MS 2787, Seton of Mounie papers.

British Library, London
BL Add. Ch 69218 Additional Charters (Mackenzie collection).
BL Add MS 39210 Mackenzie Manuscripts.

Court of the Lord Lyon, Edinburgh
Court of the Lord Lyon, Edinburgh. Funeral Escutcheons, Vol. 34

Department of Scottish History, University of Glasgow
Argyll Transcripts. Photostat copies of extracts of original documents made by Niall Campbell, 10th Duke of Argyll. In the Department of Scottish History, University of Glasgow.

ICA Inveraray Castle Archive
Bundle 592.

National Archives of Scotland, Edinburgh
NAS CC 17 Orkney and Shetland Commissary Court.
NAS GD 1/665 Seaforth Papers.
NAS GD 1/1149 Mackenzie of Coul Papers.
NAS GD 46 Seaforth Muniments.
NAS GD 160 Drummond Castle Papers (Earls of Perth).
NAS JC 2/5 High Court Book of Adjournal - Jul 1611-7 Oct 1619.
NAS RD 1 Register of Deeds.
NAS RH 6 Register House charters.
NAS RS 36/1 Register of Sasines, Inverness, Ross, Sutherland & Cromarty (Secretary's Register) 1606-1608.
NAS RS 37/1-6. Register of Sasines, Inverness, Ross, Sutherland and Cromarty, 1617-1643.
NAS SC 11 Sheriff Court Records, Orkney.

National Library of Scotland, Edinburgh
NLS Adv MS 22.7.1 The Ewill Trowbles of the Lewis.
NLS MS 1018 Mey and Tarbat Charters.
NLS Wod. Qu. Vol. XX Wodrow quarto manuscripts (vol. 20).

AM references to unpublished manuscripts

Local traditions concerning the late medieval history and topography of Sgìre Nis

by Domhnall Uilleam Stiùbhart

Introduction

The following brief paper[18] offers a review and tentative analysis of a selection of oral and orally-derived sources, mainly recorded over the past 150 years, from the local tradition of the district of Ness, Lewis: *Sgìre Nis*. This material relates primarily to the late medieval history and topography of the locality, and to the various kindreds who inhabited it. Very few contemporary documents relate to the district during this era, the time before the internecine feuds that convulsed the island from the mid-sixteenth century. This makes traditional perspectives on the past drawn from local oral tradition a potentially valuable resource. Treated with care and rigour, these sources offer us opportunities to develop new methodologies and frames of reference that complement disciplinary perspectives derived from archaeological fieldwork and excavations on the one hand, and analysis of later historical documents on the other.

This discussion will concentrate upon the evidence for a large-scale, possibly chartered, sanctuary in the district, and examine the history of the monumental church at its core and its possible associations with other neighbouring sites of power. It is intended as a complement to Aonghas

Illus 3.8 Location map of places mentioned in the text

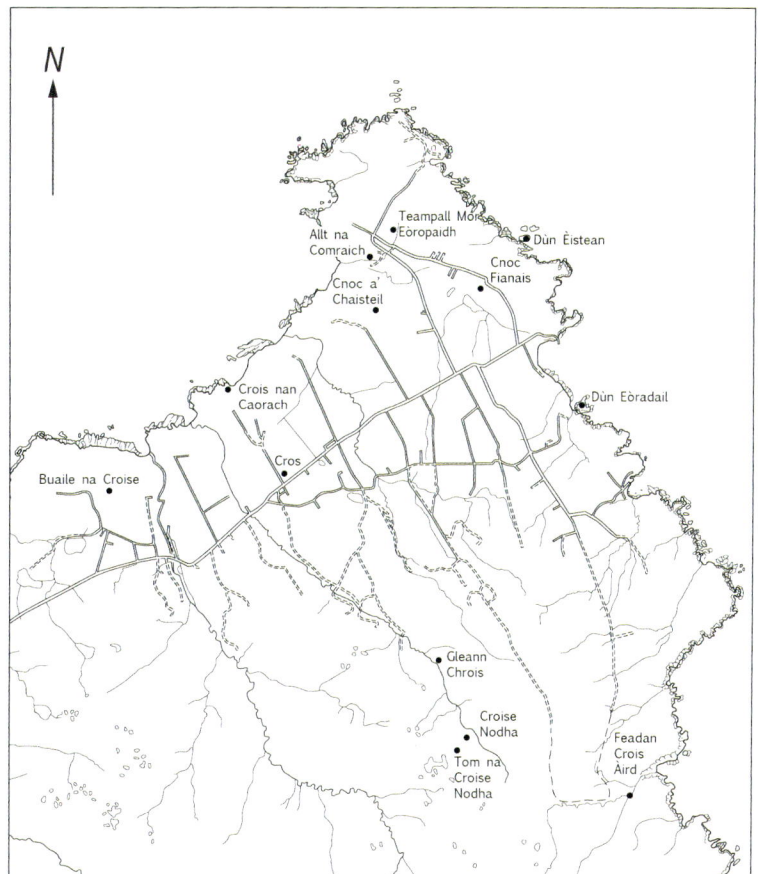

MacCoinnich's invaluable assessment of the documentary evidence relating to the history of the Morisons of Ness during the sixteenth and seventeenth centuries; to other published papers examining the origins of the MacLeod and Morison kindreds; and to the archaeological excavations and fieldwork which have been carried out as part of the Dùn Èistean project.

The conclusions drawn from my analysis are of course even more speculative and provisional than is the norm in Scottish medieval historiography, and it is anticipated that they will be subjected to more rigorous testing, insofar as this is possible, through ongoing archaeological groundwork on the one hand, and more detailed contextual comparisons by late medieval historians, archaeologists, and place-name scholars on the other. It is hoped that this investigation into one particular locality might be of use in indicating potentially productive methodologies for interrogating other historical and pseudo-historical traditions from the Scottish *Gàidhealtachd*, and in suggesting what such sources might and might not divulge to interested historians and archaeologists.

Any historian intending to research the history of *Sgìre Nis* before the mid-sixteenth century immediately runs up against a fundamental obstacle: the lack of conventional primary written sources. What we do have is a plethora of local traditions and historical anecdotes ostensibly relating to this period, generally embedded in local topography, relating to sites and spaces of erstwhile ecclesiastical and secular power, and to supposed historical personages connected with them. This material has been recorded from the people of Ness themselves by a succession of local scholars, travellers, and, latterly, fieldworkers, from the late seventeenth century up to the present day. The material is in Gaelic, in English, and, in one exceptional case, in Latin. It is preserved in the form of letters, reports, accounts, memoirs, speeches, place-name notebooks, field notebooks, stray scraps of paper, and tape recordings: some published, some not. These sources are scattered between Comunn Eachdraidh Nis in Habost; Museum nan Eilean, Stornoway; Dunvegan Castle, Skye; and in Edinburgh, the National Records of Scotland; the National Library of Scotland; the National Museums of Scotland; the School of Scottish Studies; Edinburgh University Library; and the Scottish Catholic Archives.

Taken as historical sources, oral and orally-derived traditions purporting to relate to any particular event in the past are of course of a rather different currency from contemporary documents. Their messages are inflected by the process of transmission and the varying perspectives, understandings, and misunderstandings of the informants and recorders, not to mention the immediate circumstances of recording itself. Traditions are abridged, simplified, circumscribed, and personalised, sometimes within a remarkably brief period of time, as the complexities of an original event fall out of living memory, or are no longer regarded as relevant. Traditions undergo alteration because the new generation no longer entirely comprehends, or for that matter is interested in, deeper structural contexts of the events being referred to. As traditions migrate from district to district, they are constantly reapplied to different places, different kindreds, and different peoples. They can be recast, or indeed totally reinvented, under the influence of folk motifs, the distinctive and familiar elements of a tale that recur in different stories, in different cultures. Traditions can be modified or indeed created afresh through the effect of written and printed sources, whether manuscripts, printed books, periodicals, or newspapers. In this respect, it should be remembered that oral traditions and the written word have coexisted and exerted a mutual influence upon each other throughout the Gàidhealtachd for many centuries. Traditions can be altered to make a better and more entertaining story. In sum, just like any other story, a historical tradition is more likely to survive in *beul-aithris* (folklore) if it is easily memorised, if it is patterned, if it is entertaining, well-stocked with bones of contention to be discussed and debated in the céilidh-house, and above all if it offers a vivid and personalised explanation of how things came to be the way they are. Oral traditions explain why particular families came to reside in a district, why unusual landmarks or noteworthy place-names came into being, why remarkable buildings and monuments were constructed, indeed why a community lives the way it does (Stiùbhart 2007).

There are few written documentary sources before the sixteenth century that might illuminate the history of *Sgìre Nis*. Nevertheless, by treating oral and orally-derived traditions with the same care and prudence as we would any other historical textual source, and, crucially, by drawing upon the insights of archaeologists who have worked in the district, we can begin cautiously to compile a rough outline of certain aspects of the district's more distant past, a provisional interpretation of some features of the history of Ness during the centuries before extant written sources. The oral material under discussion here has been selected from a much wider pool of historical tradition in *Sgìre Nis* for its relative ease of interpretability. Other narratives circulating in the district, for instance those relating to internecine strife among the Morisons or to the downfall of the MacLeods, have been too affected by the vagaries of transmission and the reshaping of imaginative seanchaidhean in search of a good story to be of immediate historical value. Such stories, focusing upon individual personalities and events, have to be read against the grain in an attempt to uncover evidence for wider socio-economic structures, processes, and trends: reflexive and interpretive analysis as much ethnographic or anthropological in nature as purely historical.

Sgìre Nis as sanctuary

There are two major boundaries in the Ness area. One is physical, dividing townland pasture from common moorland. The other, the principal focus of this paper, is - at least in the present day - rather more conceptual in nature, delineating sacred from secular space. The physical boundary is immediately apparent to anyone rambling over *Mòinteach Nis* (the Ness moorland), or for that matter over any other moorland on the west side of the island. Several miles in from the coast, stretching south-west from *Sgìre Nis* to *Carlabhagh* (Carloway), stands what remains of *An Gàradh Dubh*, the great, and, judging from how more recent boundaries cut across it, clearly very old 'black' turf dyke dividing township lands from common grazings. 'Bha na bailtean gu lèir ga chumail an-àirde' ('All the townships kept it standing'), as John Smith (1909-68) ('Cheocaidh') from Cros remarked when recorded by the School of Scottish Studies Place-Names Survey (SSS, PN1966/16, no. 21).

The township of Cros forms part of the second boundary, a number of place-names containing *cros* or *crois* - elements absent elsewhere in the district - apparently dividing *Sgìre Nis* from the rest of the island. From the west, in Dail bho Dheas there is *Buaile na Croise*, 'the Fold, or Enclosure, of the Cross', and, though maybe irrelevant, *Crois a' Mhargaidh*, 'the Market Cross';[19] in Cros, as well as the village itself and *Gleann Chrois*, we have *Crois nan Caorach*, 'the Cross of the Sheep' and, on the moorland, *Crois Nodha*, 'New Cross', and nearby *Tom na Croise Nodha*, 'Hill of the New Cross';[20] while near Cuidhsiadar on the east coast there is *Feadan Crois Àird*, 'High Cross Stream'.[21] There is also a *Sgeir Chrois* in Port Nis, which probably refers to its position athwart the beach.[22] Note also that in the entire *Carlabhagh* register there are only two related place-names containing *crois*, an element which Richard Cox interprets as referring not to a cross, but to a projecting spit of land (Cox 2002, 70, 234, 302). Modern tradition understands some of the sites in *Sgìre Nis* not so much as erstwhile physical markers than as places where pilgrims would cross themselves. According to John Smith, speaking of travellers from the other side of the island (that is, the east side) arriving at *Tom na Croise Nodha*: 'Bha iad ri cur a' chrois orra fhéin 'nuair a chitheadh iad an Teampall' ('They would cross themselves when they'd see the Teampall'), while Angus Campbell states of the same place: 'Bha trì croisean ann anns na seann làithean - bhiodh tu a' faicinn trì dhiubh bho mhullach an tuim seo, agus 'gad chroiseadh fhéin' ('There were three crosses in the old days - you'd see [the] three of them from the top of this hill, and cross yourself'). In a 1949 recording for the Scottish Dialect Survey, Angus Campbell (1903-82), '*Am Puilean*', states:

> 'Bha cuibhreann den talamh air a dhèanamh 'na thalamh naomh no comraich mar a theireadh iad, agus bha e 'na àite-fasgadh aig daoine bha dèanamh olc no droch ghnìomh. Nam faigheadh iad a-steach a dh' ionnsaidh an talaimh naoimh a bh' ann a-seo, cha b'urrainn dhan a' lagh gréim a chur orra gos an tigeadh iad a-mach às an àite sin.'[23]
> *A portion of the land was made sacred, into a sanctuary as they called it, and it was a place of refuge for evildoers or wrongdoers. If they could get into this sacred territory, the law couldn't seize them until they left the place.

Nearly a century beforehand, in 1867, the young *Siarach* William Watson wrote down a similar account while recording local folklore during his university holidays. The description was probably translated from the narration of the well-known seanchaidh Angus Gunn (*c* 1788-1875), '*An Guinneach*':

> 'Buaile na Croise was built at Dell by MacLeod of Eoropie. …
> MacLeod's law was that anyone from whencesoever he came & whatsoever his crime was to be considered as under his protection as soon as he entered Buaile na Croise, & it was unlawful for the pursuer

to follow the delinquent any further or to do him any harm till at least he left Ness. MacLeod's policy in establishing this law seems to have been to increase the number of his people & hence of his power and importance. He was afterwards compelled to remove his Buaile from Dell to Tràigh Shanndaigh - Uisge na Coimirich - a place quite near to his own residence at Eoropie.'

Those who took advantage of MacLeod's law and received his protection were said to have come to Ness 'Am freasdail làmh dhearg' ie in consequence of a red hand (EUL Carmichael Watson MS 95 fos.27–8).

It is significant that MacLeod of Lewis was referred to in nineteenth-century local tradition as 'MacLeod of Eòropaidh'. The same title appears in a similar account recorded by the Rev. Malcolm Macphail, a boyhood friend of Watson probably drawing on the same informant, Angus Gunn:

'MacLeod of Eoropie (MacLeod of Lewis), tradition asserts, erected a cross in an enclosed space in South Dell, Ness, known to this day as 'Buaile na Crois' - the cross enclosure - and enacted a law to the effect that the whole of the Ness district to the north of 'Buaile na Crois' was to be a sanctuary. He was obliged, says our legend, to remove the cross to 'Uisge na Comhraiche' near his own mansion-house' (Macphail 1898).

Interestingly, Macphail's ancestors may themselves have arrived in Lewis as fugitives to the sanctuary (Matheson 1974, 400, 402-8, 416-27; Lawson 2008, 34-5, 46-7).

The nineteenth-century tradition concerning the later sanctuary boundary is echoed in the well-known local anecdote purporting to explain the place-name *Bruga Frangais*: 'MacLeòid' (or, alternatively, the pygmies of *Luchruban*!) condemned a man to death on *Cnoc Fianais* within the sanctuary, then had him removed outwith the refuge to the hillock in order to carry out the sentence (Mackenzie 1905, 255).[24] In reality, however, the original name form is likely to have been *Bruga a' Bhrangais*, the hillock of the branks: the fetters or pillory used to punish local miscreants.

After enumerating the places of worship in Lewis, Martin Martin states that 'all these Churches and Chapels were, before the Reformation, Sanctuaries, and if a Man had committed Murder, he was then secure and safe when once within their Precincts': the usual state of affairs, at least in theory, according to mainstream canon law (Martin 1703, 28). Even among the plethora of *asyla* throughout the islands, however, the sanctuary in the north of the island stood out, embracing as it did an entire district. The sanctuary in *Sgìre Nis* was quantitatively different from any others in the Western Isles, with the possible exceptions of *Teampall Chàirinis* in North Uist and *Stadhlaigearraidh* in South Uist (EUL Carmichael Watson MS 95, fos.27-8; Martin 1703, 28; Matheson 1974, 398-9; Robertson 1976, 256-62).[25] Technically, as opposed to the general sanctuaries in the rest of Lewis, it may have possessed the status of a chartered or special refuge in which fugitives could settle permanently (Jordan 2008; McSheffrey 2009).

Accounts in local folklore concerning the refuge receive unexpected corroboration in Joan Blaeu's mid-seventeenth century map of the island, in which the area referred to today as '*An Taobh Thall*', the apex of *Sgìre Nis*, is labelled '*Ard*

Chombrick': '*Àird Chomraich*', the height, or better peninsula, of the sanctuary. It is of course hardly a coincidence that this major sanctuary was immediately adjacent to *An Taigh Mòr*, the seat of the Morison brieves of Tàbost, who must have pursued a relatively lucrative practice as mediators or legal brokers, employing their legal knowledge in order to negotiate agreements between fugitives and would-be avengers (see Hyams 2001, 26-30). In his late seventeenth-century *History of the MacDonalds*, Captain Hugh MacDonald states that judges were awarded 'the eleventh part of every action decided' (Macphail 1914, 24-5). Note also Martin Martin (1703, 115) who writes: 'The Orators, in their Language call'd *Is-Dane*, were in high esteem both in these Islands and the Continent, until within these forty Years, they sat always among the Nobles and Chiefs of Families in the *Streah* or Circle. Their Houses and little Villages were Sanctuaries, as well as Churches, and they took place before Doctors of Physick.' This might explain why the most prominent family of the Gaelic learned orders, the MacMhuirichs, were latterly domiciled in the major sanctuary of Stadhlaigearraidh in South Uist (EUL Carmichael Watson MS 119 fo.65[v]).

The reputation of the sanctuary, and its administrators, was not just confined to Lewis, if it is indeed the case, as family tradition avers, that the ancestors of the Gunns - *Na Guinnich*; the Murrays - the family of *An Gobha Gorm* or the Blue Smith; and the MacPhails fled to Ness across the Minch from

Sutherland. It might be suggested that their flight was the result of factional feuds, either with the chiefs of Mackay or the earls of Sutherland, but lack of documentary evidence means that this must remain pure speculation (Grimble 1965 (1993), 43-4; Gunn 1897, 46, 50-2; Mackay 1897, 20-8, 30-1; Mackay 1906, 54, 83-3).

An Teampall Mòr

The focus of the sanctuary of *Sgìre Nis* was the church known as *Teampall Mór Eòropaidh*, the outstanding extant example of monumental architecture dating from the late medieval period in the entire island (see Robson 1997). Its traditional importance is pointed up in an official report on Lewis composed by Capt. John Dymes in 1630:

> 'In theire religion they are very ignorant and have been given to the idolatrous worshipp of divers Sts. as doth appeare by theire Chappells w[ch] are yett to be seene, but they are now most espetially devoted to one of their Sts. called St. Mallonuy whose Chappell is seated in the north part of the Ile, whome they have in great veneration to this daie and keepe the Chappell in good repair. This St. was for cure of all theire wounds and soares and therefore those that were not able to come vnto the Chappell in person they were wont to cutt out the proporcion of their lame armes or leggs in wood wth the forme of their sores and wounds thereof and send them to the St. where I have seene them lyinge vpon the Altar in the Chappell. Within the Chappell there is a Sanctum Sanctorum w[ch] is soe holy in theire estimation that not anie of their weomen are suffered to enter therein. Anie woman w[th] child dareth not to enter within the doores of the Chappell, but there are certaine places without where they go to theire devotions. They had two gen[er]all meetings in the yeare at this Chappell, the one at Candlemas, and the other at Alhollautide where theire custome was to eat and drincke vntill they were druncke. And then after much dancing and dalliance togeather they entred the chappell at night with lights in their hands where they continued till next morninge in theire devotions. The last tyme of theire meeting was at Candlemas last. They were prevented of theire Idolatrous worpp by a gent. whoe is a Minister in the Ile, who albeit the place was farre from his aboade and out of his Cure, hee mett them at theire Assembly in the Chappell where he began first to reason wth them, then to admonish them and afterwards to threaten them with God His Judgm[ts] and the Lawes of the Realme, in somuch as divers of the better sort of them promised to forsake that wonted Idolatry of theirs' (Mackenzie 1903, 592).[26]

Whoever the gentleman minister was, his strictures mostly went unheeded; it would be another generation before the custom was - apparently - 'quyt abolyshed' by the episcopalian minister, and descendant of the brieves, the Rev. Donald Morison *c* 1620-?1695) (EUL 3097.12). Mackenzie suggests that the earlier minister might have been Farquhar Clerk, recorded as minister of Ui in

1642 (Mackenzie 1903, 524-5).

The original intention of such celebrations can be seen in a papal letter of 1403: 'To all the Christian faithful. Indult granting an indulgence to visitors to the church of St. Mary in Barwas in the isle of Lewis, Sodor diocese, on certain feast days and those who contribute to its reparation' (McGurk 1976, 103; also Barrell 2000, 254; cf. Watkins 2004). In other words, the visiting - and indeed the upkeep - of the chapels in Lewis was not just a matter of 'superstitious rites', but closely tied in with patterns of belief, 'official' as well as 'unofficial', of the old pre-reformation religion which remain as perfectly conventional Catholic ritual elsewhere up to the present day. The letter suggests that the twenty-four chapels on the island were at the very least culpably neglected by the established church, not just in an attempt to keep social order - and, in the absence of parish clergy, the feast days certainly seem to have degenerated - but also in an effort to abolish the cults of their saints, and indeed to efface the remaining traces of the Catholic church in Lewis.

The dedication of the *Teampall Mór* has caused some perplexity over the years. In the copy of a letter written originally by John Morison of Bragar (*c* 1630-1708), *Iain mac Mhurch' 'ic Ailein*, grandson of the last brieve of Lewis, to his first cousin the Rev. Allan Morison of Barvas (*c* 1655-1723), the Rev. Colin Campbell of Achnaba (1644-1726) transcribed:

> 'I have been a boy travelling in yor parish and at four miles distance from the kerk Molruy, when wee came in view of it, all the company fell on there knees discovered there heads, saying there Pater noster, Praying the saint Molruy to blesse them. I have seen oxen sent 12 miles off to that kerk to be slane and given to the poor.' (*EUL MS* 3097.12*; see Stiùbhart 2006a*).

Campbell's 'Molruy' suggests that the minister misread as the more familiar Maol-rubha the original letter's 'Molvey'. The dedication confused nineteenth-century visitors too: Second Corporal Michael Hayes of the Ordnance Survey recorded it in May 1852 as 'Fo'luith', while in the brief notes Alexander Carmichael jotted down on 27 October 1873 from the then bed-ridden Angus Gunn, it appears as 'Bholai'ey', 'Phollaiy', 'Pholley' and 'Phol Aoi'. In other words the temple was consecrated to 'Moluaidh', a name derived through the variant 'Moloch' from Moluag, the saint of Carmichael's native Lismore (EUL Carmichael Watson MS 115, fos.2ᵛ, 3; NRS RH4/23/148; cf. Carmichael 1900 i: 126-7; Robson 1991, 2, 99-103; also Mackenzie 1792, 290). It is interesting to note that the alternative form of the saint's name - 'Molonachus' - appearing as Dyme's 'St. Mallonuy', as 'templa St Molonochi' in a fragmentary list of island chapels from *c* 1700 preserved in the Scottish Catholic Archives, and as '*Tiample Maloni*' in Colin Mackenzie's 1792 account of Lewis antiquities, certainly persisted - possibly under the influence of the clergy - into the mid-nineteenth century, being recorded by Arthur Mitchell as 'Maolonfhadh' (SCA SM3/14, '75'; Mackenzie 1792, 291; Mitchell 1862, 267; for St Moluag, see Clancy 2003 219-23, 225-6; Dransart 2003, 234-40; Watson 1926, 292-3).

Nevertheless, Angus Gunn averred that 'Bhol. came fr[om] Baile na

Neirv where the King lived', *Baile na Nirribhidh* evidently being a rationalisation of *Baile na Beirbhe*, Bergen, an entrepôt whose name was as familiar to nineteenth-century *Leòdhasaich* as it was to their Viking ancestors. After a peculiar and apparently counterintuitive aside that 'Phollaiy built his temple put coal [?charcoal] under the (Steigh) to put an echo in[i]t', Gunn told Carmichael how, after the walls were built, the saint prayed for a roof: 'thainic gu[th] thuige 'n dei dhan choil[each] gairm e dhol a thearnadh gu trai Sheannta [i.e. Tràigh Shanndaidh]. gu ro an ceann eir tin [tighinn].' The roof magically fitted the new church: 'Rinn i n ceann's cha ro bior a chor s cha ro bior as ionais. No nails in it. Spars & couples fitting into one another so ingenously that it wld never move.' This may or may not be a distant memory that the original church had a keel-shaped roof; it certainly suggests the importance of recycling timber cast ashore in a wood-scarce island. Reused timbers from it apparently still survive in the district cf. SSS PN1966/17 [Angus Campbell, 'Am Puilean', Suaineabost], no.23; Robson 1997, 71. Carmichael possibly misunderstood Angus Gunn's explanation of how the mortar for the temple wall was made: cf. SSS SA1949/9/A5 (Angus Campbell, 'Am Puilean', Suaineabost).[27]

Given Carmichael's own statement in his manuscript memoir of Gunn that 'My limited time and imperfect understanding of the kind courtesy old mans impaired enunciation prevented me writing down much of his highly interesting old lore', (EUL Carmichael Watson MS 230(a), fo.26) the more detailed version of the legend he appended thereto may be somewhat embroidered, probably with information gleaned from other Ness seanchaidhean:

> 'A son of the King of Scandinavia became a good man and wishing to perform good deeds for the evil deeds he had done he built a church down at Rudh Eorapaidh and called it Teampull Maoluag, Saint Maoluag's or Saint Malachie's Temple the walls of which are still entire. When the walls of the temple were built the King's son had no roof to put on and he was in great straits. He did not know in all the living world what to do for a roof for the weather was so stormy that his fathers galleys could not go to Lochlan for wood to make a roof. The prince prayed and prayed and when he prayed his best a voice came to him in a dream of the night and told him to go to the Stoth and that he would find a roof there. The Prince arose and went down to the Stoth and there he found a roof floating in the Port prepared and of the size required for his temple. The roof was taken up and placed on the walls of the building which it fitted' (EUL Carmichael Watson MS 230(a), fos.27-8).[28]

Teampall Mholuaidh was unquestionably one of the most important centres of worship in Lewis during the late medieval period, the focus of a complex of temporal and ecclesiastical power alike. For some centuries both Morisons and MacLeods possessed power bases there; indeed, the residual but insistent evidence of local tradition might be interpreted to suggest that we are not so much dealing with two closely allied families as two branches of the same original kindred. Donald Murray (1859-1921), drawing upon information supplied by his namesake the Eòropaidh seanchaidh, describes the Teampall as 'the Laird's Church. The

MacLeod Chiefs of Lewis had a mansion house in Eorobie in close proximity to the Temple and no one could find access to it but through a gateway which went through the mansion house'. This particular 'mansion house', of course, would have been one of several residences used by the MacLeods of Lewis while perambulating their *dùthchas*. A related site somewhat to the south, a small hillock now known as *Cnoc a' Chaisteil*, is described by the Rev. Donald Macdonald in the Old Statistical Account as once occupied by '*Caistel Olgre (i. e.)* Olaus his Castle'. His contemporary Colin Mackenzie ascribes the Teampall's construction to 'one of the first MᶜLeods of Lewis', while William Cook Mackenzie recounts a tradition that it was built by 'King Olaf of Norway.' The last ascription clearly derives from a misconstrual of *Teampall Naomh Mholuaidh* as 'Teampall Naomh Oluaidh', with additional confusion of Olaf with Olghair, ancestor of the MacLeods - and possibly the Morisons as well (Murray: n.p.; Macdonald 1797: 270; Mackenzie 1792: 291; Mackenzie 1919, 141; the ancestry of the MacLeods is discussed in Halford-MacLeod 1994; MacLeod 2000; Matheson 1980a and b; Morrison 1986, 120; Sellar 1998; also Abernethy 2004; Matheson 1979).

There may already have been a *Teampall Mholuaidh* in Eòropaidh before the coming of the dominant kindreds of the late medieval era. It is remarkable that the older of the two chapels on the once exceptionally fertile and strategically significant island of Pabaigh in the Sound of Harris is also dedicated to Moluag. According to the traditional account of the MacLeods retailed in the early nineteenth-century Bannatyne Manuscript, both *Sgìre Nis* and *Pabaigh* appertained to the mysterious 'Clan Igaa [Clann a' Ghobha] or the descendants of the Armourer' whose heiress is supposed to have married GilleMhoire, the progenitor of the Morisons. Although for a single kindred to occupy the opposite extremities of an island might appear somewhat unusual, a similar situation obtained in North Uist, where the Macleans held both Boraraigh (the 'fort island') and Griomasaigh (Lawson 2004, 147).[29] Perhaps tellingly, the later, larger temple in Pabaigh is dedicated to Moire or Mary, as is the chapel in Barvas, the erstwhile parish church of Ness and the West Side. It might tentatively be inferred that in order to underline their ascendancy the incoming Morisons, *Clann MhicGilleMhoire*, built a *Teampall Mhoire* in both of the territories they had recently acquired. Although the new church in Pabaigh superseded its smaller neighbour, this was not the case with the Teampall Mhoire in Barvas. Despite the grant of parochial status and, as has been seen, the favourable papal indult of 1403, the church never eclipsed the preeminence of the illustrious Teampall Mór, and today lies drowned in the sands (Martin 1703, 48; Lawson 1994, 12-14; Robson 1997, 55; 2004, 18).

The MacLeod gateway, 'a zigzag covered walk' or causeway leading up to a rampart before the church, was apparently finally choked by sand in the first half of the nineteenth century; much of the stonework of both the stronghold and rampart had already been plundered for local use, particularly - as part of a wider and seemingly deliberately systematic reuse of the material of local historic structures to construct new institutional foci for church and education - in the building of Lionail Schoolhouse. A number of traditional accounts refer to a great iron gate in the rampart, probably the iron-grated door or yett common in late medieval strongholds throughout the country (Christison 1883; 1888). Mention of the iron gate might recall the original possessors of the district, the Clann a' Ghobha referred to above. The yett remained celebrated in local tradition for at least two centuries after its removal, with William Watson recording a description of how Torcail Conanach, the Mackenzie claimant for the MacLeod chieftaincy, 'was not so anxious about getting the island of Lews as about getting the (iron) Gate of McLeod at Eoropie'.[30]

The fame of *Teampall Mholuaidh* outlasted that of its sanctuary. Around 1700 it is recorded:

> 'In Levissa variæ erant celiæ, quarum una no[min]e Sᵗ Molonochi in hanc usque die[m] miraculis clara'.[31]

A century later 'a great deal of superstitious veneration' was still paid to the church, some of the people still retaining 'a few of the Popish superstitions' (Macdonald 1797, 270):

> 'The country people send their friends that are long lingering in sickness, to sleep here for a night, where they believe the Saint grants them a cure, or relief by death'. (Mackenzie 1792, 291).

Further details were recorded by the Rev. John Downie, recently transferred from Stornoway to Urray, in a letter of 14 April 1789 for the ecclesiastical antiquary Lieutenant-General George Henry Hutton:

> 'There are several Chapels up & down the Island, which still bear the name of the Saints to whom they were dedicated, as John Peter Mary Bridget &c., the walls of them in general are pretty entire, & surrounded by a Cemetery. Ignorance & Superstition have created & to this day propagated a perswasion that cures are performed by addressing the tutelar Saints of these Solitary mansions. One in particular in the district of Ness is larger & more entire than any of the rest. Patients of disordered intellects are freq[uen]tly bro[ugh]t thither, a bed of straw & blankets is made up for them within the walls, where they are left till morning alone. The Saint is expected to appear to them in person, to cure them. I know not his name in English or Latin, but in Gallic Mo Lài is the name. Mo is only a term of endearment used by his Votaries'.[32]

This raises the interesting possibility that the cure was effected with the covert participation of the locals themselves, maybe through the *cléireach* or clerk of the *Teampall*. Writing in May 1833, George Clayton Atkinson records that 'St Malachi's':

> has much celebrity throughout the Western Islands, for the power it possesses of curing insane persons, and those afflicted with a variety of diseases. (Quine 2001, 127).

That the prestige of the *Teampall* endured so long might be ascribed to the increased isolation of *Sgìre Nis* from the island authorities, temporal and spiritual alike, during the eighteenth century. It seems that following the death of the Rev. Allan Morison in 1723 his cousin Donald, grandson of Iain mac Mhurch' 'c Ailein, took over the tack of Tàbost. Barvas appears to have become the centre of worship in the parish, with ministers, perhaps understandably, neglecting the 'remote and ignorant' district of Ness 'owing to the distance the want of Roads and the number of rapid waters which intervine particularly in the winter Season'.[33] Although the Ordnance Survey name-books record that *Teampall Pheadair* at Suaineabost was said to have been rebuilt in 1756, it was towards the end of the century, and particularly with the accession of Rev. Donald Macdonald to Barvas parish in 1790, that the church initiated a more active approach to the district. The process of spreading ecclesiastical authority may have already been underway before Macdonald arrived from Applecross. Writing in 1813 of *Teampall na Crò Naoimh* in Galson, William Daniell recounts and comments:

> 'It was visited till within these last few years by many of the peasantry, who would assemble here at stated periods to feast and dance for two or three successive nights. At one of these merry meetings it was ascertained that a man had taken an indecorous liberty with a female; the hallowed purity of the temple was in consequence destroyed and it has not since been resorted to. As a proof of the high offence taken at this indignity by the genius of the place, it is asserted, and firmly believed by the islanders that a taper lighted within the walls is immediately extinguished. The fable affords a pleasing exemplification of their simple and guileless manners, and this is not the only instance in which popular superstition has been converted to moral purpose. The removal of such delusions is a natural consequence of social improvement, but it is highly important that the dissemination of sound and rational improvements should immediately supplant them and establish restraints of superior efficacy' (Daniell 1820, v: 63).

If Daniell's account is to be trusted, it may be connected with the Barvas kirk session's hounding in the early 1780s of 'Murdo Clairach Tenant in Galson' - seemingly the cléireach or clerk of the teampall - for 'keeping as a Domestic in his family a woman with whom he had been guilty of Adultery, to which it was notour he had paid no regard'.[34]

Writing in the middle of the following decade, Macdonald tells of how the place of worship in Ness, 'an old Popish church, called St Peter's, was enlarged and rebuilt last year; it is thatched with heath.' (Macdonald 1797, 268). The rebuilding involved the destruction of other chapels in the district. Angus Gunn, probably referring to the second of these reconstructions, told Carmichael that 'When Eaglais Phead was built the roof was taken off [Teampall Mholuaidh] & put on'; Teampall Pheadair was extended using the 'stones of [nearby] Temple Tomais' (EUL Carmichael Watson MS 115, fos.2ᵛ, 4ᵛ). The evangelical revival begun by the schoolmaster John MacLeod in Galson in 1820, culminating in the erection of the government church at Cross nine years later, brought the era of community worship in the teampaill to an end (Macfarlane 1924, 13-18, 47-9, 88-90; MacGilliosa 1981, 13-15; MacLeod 1965, 107, 113-14; Mac-Neacail 1894, 8).[35]

Nevertheless, roofless as it was, *Teampall Mholuaidh* retained a residual sanctity even after the evangelical ascendancy took hold in the district. In 1873

Angus Gunn told Carmichael that until forty or fifty years previously: 'When peop[le] came ashore (say fr[om] Rona) Clann ic ill Mhoire) [sic] they went deisail an Teample & gail [gabhail] an Urni – before going to the sermon of the min[i] st[er]' (EUL Carmichael Watson MS 115, fo.3). At the end of the nineteenth century, the Rev. Malcolm Macphail states:

> 'Such was the veneration the Eoropie Fane was held within living memory, even sixty years ago, by the people of the Eoropie district, that they would pass on the north side of the ruined temple when leaving the stackyard, but return from the field on the south side – thus completing the tour of the temple 'Deiseil''(Macphail 1898; also idem 1895, 168).

According to Donald Murray:

> 'When I was a boy it was believed by some that if one afflicted with insanity could be coaxed to sleep within the precincts of the Temple he was sure to be at least partially restored. The rites and ceremonies after arriving at the Temple were in the key days of the shrine particular and minute. After arriving at dusk the patient was made to walk round the Temple seven times sunwise (deiseal) and made to drink water from the holy Well of St Olaf (Tobair an Naoimh Oluaidh) [*recte* Tobar an Naoimh Moluaidh] and was then copiously sprinkled with the same water, but unless the patient slept within the Temple after this preparatory treatment there could be no cure' (Murray: n.p.; cf. Mould 1953, 176).

Murray's description is supplemented by the earlier account of Arthur Mitchell:

> 'The patient walks seven times round the temple, is sprinkled with water from St Ronan's Well, which is close at hand, is then bound and deposited for the night on the site of the altar. If he sleeps, it is believed that a cure will follow, if not, the powers are unpropitious, and his friends take him home, believing it to be the will of Heaven that he shall remain as he is. The water was formerly brought from the well in an old stone cup, which was left in the keeping of the family, regarded as the descendants of the *clerk of the temple.*' (Mitchell 1862, 268; cf. also - although erroneously ascribing the temple to 'St. Clement' - Daniell 1820, v, 62).

Mitchell goes on to recount that patients have even been brought to the temple from the mainland, though the cure only worked for two islanders, one of whom later had a relapse.

Mitchell's elaborate and apparently trustworthy account, checked by 'a native of Lewis' (probably the Rev. Malcolm Macphail), implies that the ceremony was still being observed. Macphail himself records that the last visits for such a purpose 'as far as I can guess from memory, occurred in the latter end of the forties' (Macphail 1898) - a time of great distress in the island during the Potato Famine. This is substantiated by Second Corporal Hayes of the Ordnance Survey, who recorded in 1852, on the authority of his informant John Morrison of Cnoc Àrd, that the temple:

> 'remains under the protection of some Saint or Angel by whose power or through whose Intercession insane People who sleep in it one night

are Restored to their senses. The Experiment they say was successfully made a few years ago by An Uig man'.[36]

Tradition in Ness, however, apparently suggests that the practice was last carried out as late as 1874, when 'a woman from the West Side [was] taken in a cart by her husband to the Temple, in an attempt to find a cure for her insanity.' A young girl at the time remembered her terror at the sight: 'but her mother, who was with her, explained the situation to her. The woman was shouting. She had to sleep all night in the Temple with her head on the stone' (MacLeod 2008, 98). Lewis was certainly not alone in these practices: for similar rites in the nineteenth-century Gàidhealtachd (see Campbell 2003, 226-7, 490).

Memory of some of the curative practices connected with the church has of course survived in *Sgìre Nis* down to the present day, with small but telling details, such as the stone pillow (now lost) mentioned above, demonstrating the durability of tradition. The *Teampall Mór* itself remained a shell until it was restored under the auspices of the episcopalian church at the beginning of the twentieth century (see Barber 1981; Meaden 1921).

Conclusion

During the late medieval era two major kindreds, the Morisons and the MacLeods, possessed power bases in *Sgìre Nis*, the former in Tàbost, the latter in Eòropaidh. This implies a degree of close mutual cooperation and coexistence that is corroborated in the extant contemporary documentary evidence (see MacCoinnich, above). Traditional accounts, however, suggest quite otherwise, asserting that *Clann a' Bhritheimh* and *Sìol Torcail* were always at loggerheads (for example Thomas 1878, 517; Matheson 1979). Although some degree of long-term mutual suspicion can scarcely be discounted, we might suspect that open and protracted hostility only broke out late in the sixteenth century, when the dominance exerted by the MacLeods over Lewis began seriously to be eroded with the outbreak of internecine strife between the sons of the aged chief Ruairidh. Later heroic clan traditions appear to have projected the factional antagonisms of this convulsive era backwards; local toponymic evidence, however, offers alternative perspectives.

The sanctuary of *Sgìre Nis* serves as a reminder that whatever the ambit might have been of more extensive clan jurisdictions in the late medieval Gàidhealtachd, a patchwork of local customary judicatures lay underneath. The demise of this relatively flexible and less adversarial justice system may have had substantial repercussions well beyond their particular localities. The violent mayhem of the internecine civil war, incited by outside interests, which convulsed the MacLeods of Lewis in the late sixteenth century has of course its parallels elsewhere in the Gàidhealtachd and beyond. Nevertheless, the inability of Ruairidh MacLeod's sons to come to any form of mutual arrangement among themselves, even to the point of the annihilation of the entire kindred, may have been exacerbated in the aftermath of the Reformation by the collapse of the local ecclesiastical structure, the concomitant breakdown of the sanctuary system, and by the internal dissension which split the Morison kindred whose leader the brieve had previously enjoyed 'ane absolut Judicatorie, unto whose authoritie and censure the people willinglye submitt themselves and newer appeal from his sentence qn he determineth any debatable question in controwersie betwixt partie and partie.' (Macphail 1916, 266; see also Gordon 1813, 268). The Morisons' loss of status as acknowledged brokers in island society may have contributed to the incapacity of the various factions among the MacLeods and their followers to achieve a lasting peace. The resulting mistrust and acrimony affecting all levels of island society - and indeed all surviving branches of the kindred in the North Minch basin, mainland as well as island - may have been all the more lethal given the heavy militarisation of members of the *fine* as a result of mercenary participation in the wars in Ireland (MacCoinnich 2007; MacCoinnich, above).

Where does this leave Dùn Èistean? Firstly, it should be noted that the fort was situated in territory that formed part of a major sanctuary during the late medieval period. Indeed, its apparent besieging and slighting in 1597/8 underscores the final destruction of the sanctuary system in Lewis. Dùn Èistean's position on a coastal stack was, however, peripheral to the main complex of power in the area, focused upon the *Teampall Mór*, the 'mansion house' of the MacLeods nearby, and the brieves' residence of *An Taigh Mòr Thàboist*. Aonghas MacCoinnich makes the astute and persuasive suggestion that, during the later medieval era at least, the dùn's principal importance, commanding as it did a wide expanse of strategic sea routes, was as a lookout in the front line of potential retaliatory raids from Orkney (see MacCoinnich, above). For her part, Mary MacLeod has made the stimulating observation that Dùn Èistean may be considered together with Dùn Eòradail as two gateposts guarding the landing place of Tràigh Chealagbhal (pers comm). Local tradition claims that the beach was once the entrance to a channel extending between the Minch and the Atlantic, of which only Loch Stiapabhat remains: the ballast from Viking galleys was, supposedly, deposited on the bottom. Recent survey and pollen analysis, however, suggests that the loch has been silted up since at least the Iron Age (see Ramsay in Barrowman, C S 2015, 154-7).[37] It is possible that there may have been a portage for smaller and lighter skin boats during the early medieval era, but the route is more likely to have been used as a thoroughfare to avoid transporting local cargoes through the treacherous waters around Butt of Lewis/*Rubha Robhainis*.[38] Twin sites of secular and ecclesiastical authority connected with the two major kindreds in late medieval Lewis thus straddled a 'choke point' on what may have been a locally important trade route linking east and west coasts.

A synthesis of disparate categories of historical evidence, derived from archaeological excavations and fieldwork, place-names, and oral and orally-derived traditions, allows for the construction of a speculative framework for the interpretation of the history of *Sgìre Nis* during the late medieval era before documentary sources commence in the sixteenth century. It is hoped that this paper might stimulate further research into the traditional historical perspectives of the people themselves, combining them with insights of modern archaeologists, historians, and onomasticians. It is hoped that this report might, in some small manner, encourage the preservation and passing on of such traditions to future generations of Nisich: what they, and Gaels elsewhere in the Gàidhealtachd, have to say about their own history matters.

Edinburgh University Library (EUL)
Carmichael Watson MSS
MS 3097 (Rev. Colin Campbell collection)

Museum nan Eilean, Stornoway
Donald Murray, "Remin[isc]ences of Hebridean history", (unpublished article), Box 21.

National Library of Scotland (NLS)
MS Adv. 29.4.2 (Hutton correspondence)
Acc. 9711 (William Matheson Collection)

National Museums of Scotland (NMS)
Society of Antiquaries of Scotland MS 28 (Capt FWL Thomas papers)

National Records of Scotland (NRS)
CH2/473 (Presbytery of Lewis)
RH4/23/148 (Ordnance Survey Place-Name Books: Ness)

School of Scottish Studies Archives (SSS)
PN (Place-Name Survey)
SA (Sound Archive)

Scottish Catholic Archives (SCA)
SM (Scottish Mission papers)

References to manuscripts and recordings

Endnotes

[1] The interviews, place-name evidence and stories that were collected by the History Project, directed by Stiùbhart, form the background to this paper, although the totality of the material remains unpublished. However, many of the place-names collected by the fieldworkers, Cairstiona Smith, Mairi MacIver and Anne MacLeod, has been combined with the Ness Archaeological Landscape Survey (NALS) database (Barrowman, C S 2015).

[2] I am grateful to Dr Thomas Brochard, Dr Alison Cathcart, Professor Allan Macinnes, Dr Alasdair Ross and Mr W. David H. Sellar all of whom kindly read drafts and made many helpful suggestions. My thanks in like manner to the editor. They are, of course, not responsible for any errors in this essay. An earlier and much shorter version of this discussion appeared in 'Criomagan' (the newsletter of *Comann Eachdraidh Nis*) no. 38, December 2006, 8-10.

[3] The MacLeod of Lewis papers were placed in Mackenzie 'safe-keeping' by Torcaill Conanach sometime in the 1570s or 1580s. They were still in the possession of the Mackenzies of Kintail and Seaforth in the 1620s and some of the MacLeod charters, dating 1432-1596, are listed in an inventory made of the Mackenzie charter chest in *c* 1627 (Macphail 1916, 267. MacCoinnich 2004, 421-2).

[4] Dòmhnall Càm Macaulay of Lewis, fl. 1609, for example, is variously shown by Donald Morison, the seanchaidh of the early 1800s, as being active in the reign of James IV (d. 1513) and Henry VIII (d. 1547), and fighting for the crown in wars in Ulster. In reality the Macaulays would have accompanied their MacLeod masters over to Ireland probably during the 1590s and are more likely to have fought with Ó Neill or Ó Domhnaill against the [English] crown, an uncomfortable fact best altered to fit the circumstances of the late eighteenth/early nineteenth century. The same source, Donald Morison, the seanchaidh, drew on the tales of the MacLeods featured in Robert Gordon's 'History of the Earldom of Sutherland' (1813). Gordon's manuscript of 1630, but not published until 1813, may thus have given a significant stimulus to local history and oral tradition in early nineteenth century Lewis (Macdonald (ed) 1975, 24-6, 121; MacCoinnich forthcoming).

[5]See, for example, the account given by Roderick Campbell, born in North Dell around 1842, of his mother's ancestry from the Morrison and 'Britheamh' family (Campbell 1901: xi-xii, 9-12). See also the genealogical detective work of William Matheson in his appendices to *An Clàrsair Dall* (Matheson 1970, 186-203), Captain Thomas' account (1878, 517-26, 527-36) and Stiùbhart (2006a; 2006b).

[6]The surname 'Brown' associated with Tiree and Islay may mask an early Gaelic form 'Mac a' Bhriuthainn,' a form of the word '*britheamh*.' Tradition claims a link between the Morisons of Ness and the Morison families associated with Harris and Pabaigh. This tradition may be correct although it seems impossible to prove one way or the other. However, it is worth noting that the form 'Ó Muirgheasan,' of Irish origin, appears in the bounds of the MacLeods of Harris in and around 1614, and this may lie behind the adoption of the form 'Morrison/ Morison' by some families in these areas. The Ó Muirgheasáins probably came back with Ruairidh Mòr MacLeòid from Ireland in the 1590s. Similarly in Mull, 'Clann na h-oidhche' or Ó Muirgheasáin use the form 'Morison' in English, but are clearly not related to the Lewis 'Morisons' (Bannerman 1980, 21, 23; Black, 1994). Neither the Mull nor Harris families used the appellation '*britheamh*' at this time to my knowledge.

[7]Forsyth, Broun and Clancy 2008, 134, 138-9. See also entries under the headings 'Judex/ *britheamh*', in the *PoMS* database.

[8]This text and the translation RPS, A1504/3/124. http://www.rps.ac.uk/mss/A1504/3/124. Date accessed: 9 July 2011. I am grateful to Mr W.D.H. Sellar for bringing this to my attention.

[9]My thanks to Mr Andy Morrison for drawing this last reference to my attention.

[10]My thanks to Dr Thomas Brochard for bringing this manuscript to my attention. For the identification of Mr John Ross as minister to the Fife Adventurers in both 1598 and again in 1605, see MacCoinnich (forthcoming).

[11]According to this manuscript of 1734, the second son of Uillleam Munro of Meikle Allan in Easter Ross (fl. 1540 x 1565) married the daughter of 'Mr Allan Morishon brive of the Lewis' (Munro 1978, 8). For Ailean the Brieve (fl. 1572-1600) see Table 3.1 on CD in back of book. Adam 1991, 244. Alexander Mackenzie was unsure about Uilleam Munro's wife, but gave Uilleam's dates as 1535-1580 (Mackenzie 1898, 292-3).

[12]I am grateful to Rachel Barrowman and Mr Sellar for discussion on this point.

[13]In 1568 Barbara Stewart, Lady Lewis, and her daughter from her previous marriage to James Sinclair of Sanday, Margaret Sinclair, had the feu lands of Barrie in Orkney. *TA xii*, 129. Margaret Sinclair was a half sister of Torcaill 'Oighre' MacLeod of Lewis who died without issue in 1566. A further possible marital link between Lewis and Orkney may have arisen in the shape of 'Jonet McLud' (MacLeod ? possibly a daughter of Torcaill Conanach ?) who died in 1622. Jonet was married to James Stewart in Burray in Orkney. *(NAS CC 17/2/1, reg. 22 April 1625)*. Jonet was possibly the mother of 'Barbara Stewart spous to 'Williame Stewart of Mainss and oy and air of Umqle Torquel Mc Claud of the Lewis hir guid[fathe]r' who tried to make a claim on the Lewis estate in 1630. NAS SC 11/5/1630/5.

[14]http://www.historic-scotland.gov.uk/kinlochberviedescription.pdf [accessed 19 February 2011]; http://canmore.rcahms.gov.uk/en/site/194560/details/ kinlochbervie+wreck+bagh+poll+a+bhacain+north+minch/ [accessed 19 February 2011].

[15]My thanks to Mr Sellar for this reference.

[16]My thanks to Professor Allan Macinnes for this last reference.

[17]They witnessed the same deed or had business together on the following dates 11 June 1607, *NAS GD 46/21/2* fol. 18; 30 May 1609 *NAS GD 1/1149/4*; 19 January 1608, *NAS RS 36/1* fol. 329r, 329v-331r; 14 May 1616, *BL Add Ch. 61928;* 17 February 1620, *NAS RS 37/1* fol. 195; 31 May 1623, *NAS GD 1/1149/6.* 14 April 1627, RPCS (2nd ser.), i, 688.

[18]This article was begun under the auspices of the Dùn Èistean Archaeological Project, managed by Glasgow University Archaeological Research Division (GUARD) and funded by the Heritage Lottery Fund, Historic Scotland, the Clan Morrison Society, Comunn Eachdraidh Nis, Western Isles Enterprise, and Comhairle nan Eilean Siar. It was brought to completion as part of the Carmichael Watson Project at Edinburgh University Library, generously funded by the Leverhulme Trust.

[19]SSS PN1966/15 [Alan Gillies (1891-1970) 'Candal', from Dail bho Dheas but living at 28 Gabhsann bho Dheas], no.16 and notes.

[20]SSS PN1966/16 [John Smith, 'Ceocaidh', from Cros but living at Druim Fraoich, Dail bho Thuath], no.26 and notes.

[21]SSS PN1966/17 [Angus Campbell, 'Am Puilean', Suaineabost], no.51 and notes.

[22]SSS PN1966/9 [Lewis Murray (1906-89) ('Louis Noraidh'), Tàbost, with Norman MacLeod (1904–68) ('Contair', 'Am Bàrd Bochd'), Lionail], no.9.

[23]SSS SA1949/9/A6.

[24]SSS PN1966/14 [Norman MacRitchie (1906-78), 'Ceogaidh', Na Còig Peighinnean], no.77.

[25]SSS SA1949/9/A6 [Aonghas Caimbeul, 'Am Puilean', Suaineabost].

[26]For Crùisle nam Ban Torrach, 'where the frail [i.e. expectant] women were put', cf. EUL Carmichael Watson MS 115, fos.2ᵛ, 5. For Candlemas, cf. Hutton 1996, 138-45; also Martin 1703, 29; Daniell 1820, v: 63.

[27]My thanks to Aonghas MacCoinnich for his comments on the importance of driftwood to Hebridean communities.

[28]It is unfortunate that we do not have an account of Teampall Mholuaidh from William Watson, who gathered lore in Ness in 1867: cf. EUL Carmichael Watson MS 95, fo.31ᵛ; NLS Acc. 9711, Box 1/4, 285.

[29]For possible additional Morison connections with Trotternish in Skye, see MacCoinnich, this volume.

[30]NMS SAS MS 28/'(d) Lews', 1; /'2(f)', fo.7; SSS PN1966/10 [Louis Murray, Tàbost], no.44; cf. EUL Carmichael Watson MSS 95, fo.35ᵛ; 115, fo.4ᵛ.

[31]SCA SM3/14, '75'.

[32]NLS Adv. MS 29.4.2 (xi), fos.192ᵛ-193; cf. ibid. (xiii), fo.50ᵛ.

[33]NRS CH2/473/1, 297-8; also 324; Matheson 1970, 199.

[34]NRS CH2/473/1: 211-12; also 215, 224.

[35]NAS CH2/473/2, 50, 57, 69-70, 74, 80, 82, 84, 115-18, 134-5, 138, 154-6, 163-4, 165-8; NLS Acc. 9711, Box 7/2, 28-9.

[36]NRS RH4/23/148; cf. NMS SAS MS 28/'3', fo.10: 'the daft lad of Aird Bheag'.

[37]My thanks to Rachel Barrowman for this reference.

[38]My thanks to Aonghas MacCoinnich for this observation. The local Yachtsman's Pilot recommends that 'unless the wind is both fair and moderate, and the tide is going in the same direction, [the Butt of Lewis] should be given a berth of at least 5 miles, which must be added to the length of the passage' Lawrence 1990, 172.

groun

dwork

Illus 4.1 Work in Trench A.

four

Structure A consists of two rectangular stone and turf buildings in a triangular-shaped enclosure on the west side of the island. Excavations in Area A investigated in and around two buildings, A1 and A2, an area north of A1 and cuttings through the enclosure walls to the north and south of the buildings. The excavations identified seven phases of activity, from the earliest to the latest: (1) the natural subsoil, (2 and 3) the construction and occupation of the buildings and the enclosure walls, (4 and 5) their abandonment and collapse, (6) a turf and rubble shelter built into the ruins at the north end of A1, and (7) the development of topsoil. Ash and midden material found in the earthen core of the Phase 2 building walls suggests that the turf used in the walls of A1 and A2 was cut from an area of the island where there was already occupation and A1 and A2 cannot therefore be the earliest buildings on the site. A sample of ash from the base of the north wall of building A2 has been radiocarbon dated to AD1450-1635.[1]

The excavations have shown that the buildings were set end to end with a narrow gap between them, and aligned south-west to north-east with the prevailing wind. Whilst A1 was built from low walls of stone, earth and turf, only the north end wall of A2 was built with stone, the rest being solely turf. Each building had a turf roof, an entrance on the east side and a central hearth on the floor in the interior. Modelling of the radiocarbon dates suggests that the buildings were near contemporary (see Chapter 13).

The hearth in A1 was large and contained several layers of ash and burnt material, but the A2 hearth was smaller with only one layer of ash. This would suggest that A1 was the main building for gathering

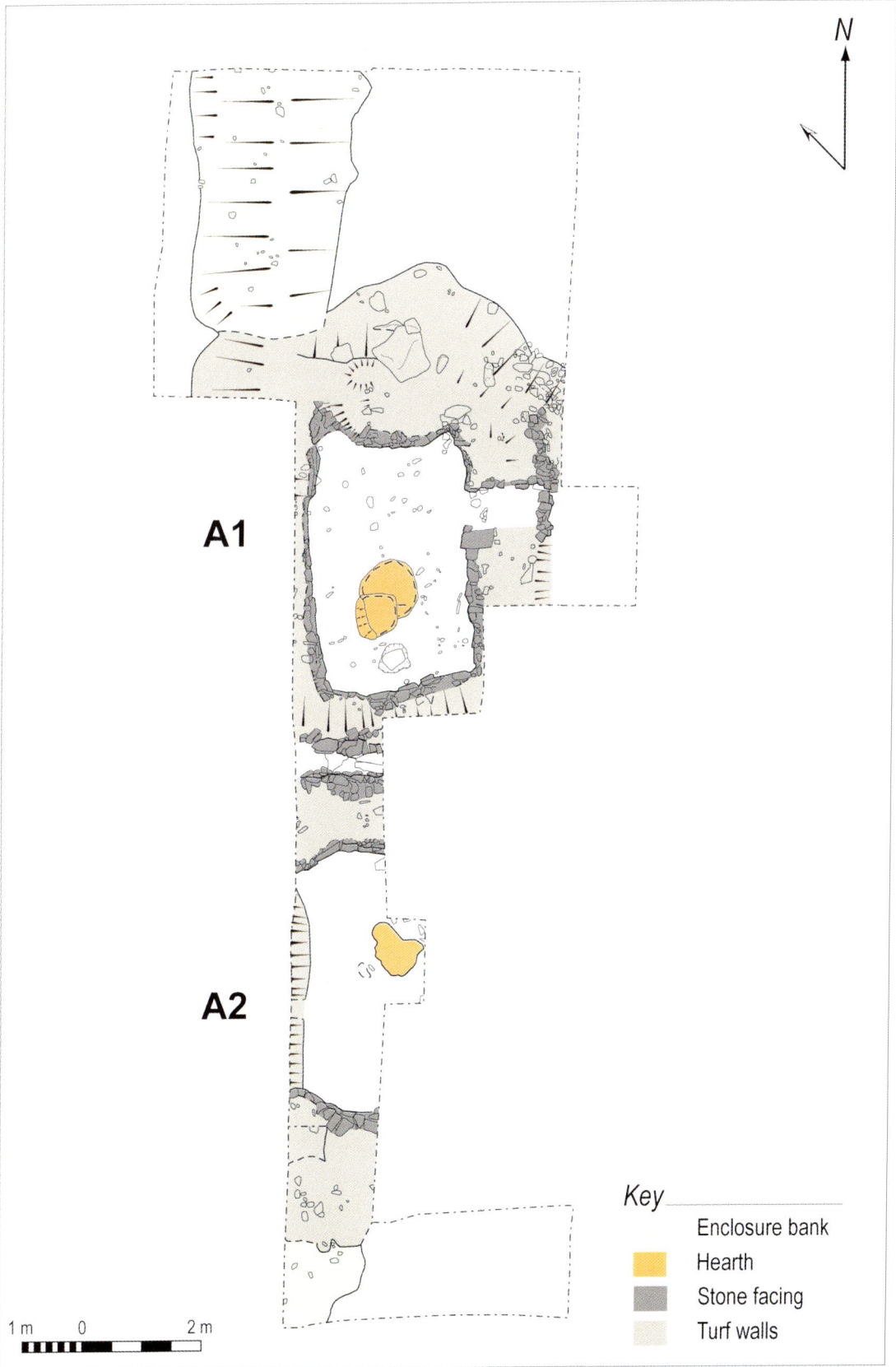

N

A1

A2

Key

Enclosure bank
Hearth
Stone facing
Turf walls

1 m   0   2 m

and sleeping, whereas A2 may only have been used for human occupation for a short period of time. The island was accessed from the mainland opposite at this corner. The enclosure around A1 and A2 functioned as a forecourt or entrance corral to gather personnel and supplies and control admission onto the stronghold.

The artefactual assemblage recovered from the excavations in this area comprises mainly sherds of local, hand-made pottery from storage and cooking vessels (see Chapter 10). The burnt material found in the hearth in A1 contained material evidence of the activities that took place in the building. Chips of flint and a droplet of lead and piece of lead scrap suggest that gunflints were manufactured or modified at the fireside, and that small-scale lead casting also took place, probably to make musket balls or pistol shot. Environmental finds of carbonised oat and barley grains indicate that grain was dried at the hearth, and although peat was the main fuel, charcoal from locally-growing tree and shrub species such as birch, hazel and heather demonstrate that these were also burnt, together with driftwood, as indicated by finds of conifer charcoal and fragmentary iron nails (see Chapter 11). Carbonised haddock and saithe bones and small fragments of mammal bone reveal that meat and fish were cooked and eaten around the fire, with the bones being discarded into the hearth afterwards. Plant remains such as buttercup, sedge and dock provide a glimpse of the surrounding environment. Radiocarbon dating of hearth samples demonstrates that buildings A1 and A2 were occupied some time between AD1445-1640.

When the buildings and enclosure banks went out of use, the collapse of the turf roofs and upper walls was fairly rapid as suggested by the slump and collapse layers found directly above floor and wall deposits. Pottery and other artefacts such as a musket ball and sherd from a glass bottle were found in slumped turf and stone from the ruined building (Phases 4 and 5). Some time later in the eighteenth century a small, rough shelter was built into the north end of the ruined building A1 (Phase 6). This was probably used as an occasional shelter by those fishing, or moving sheep on and off the island for grazing.

Results

with Chris Dalglish, Chris Barrowman, and Mary MacLeod

Trench locations

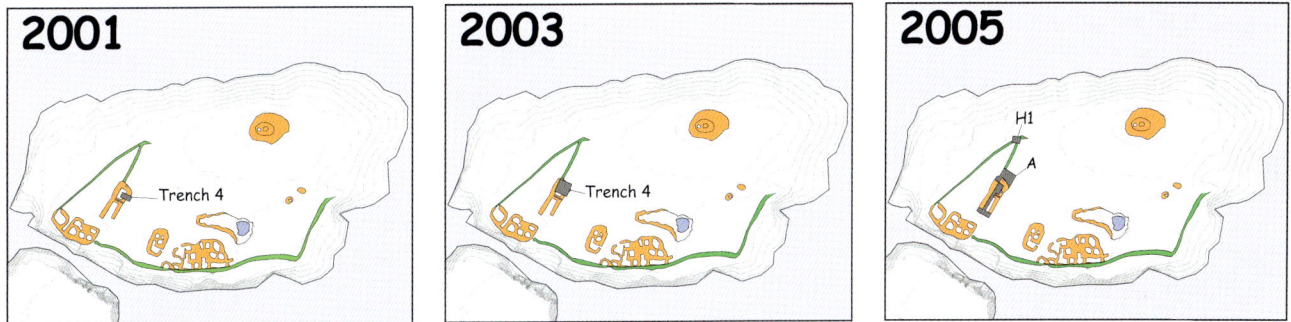

2001

Trench 4

2003

Trench 4

2005

H1

A

2001 Trench 4: 4 x 2m

Aims: The survey described Structure A as the best preserved of the archaeological structures on Dùn Èistean and suggested that this may be the most recent building on the site. This trial excavation was positioned over the entrance in the E wall of A1 and investigated this by looking at the nature and depth of the deposits within and around the building.

Work completed: Turf and topsoil removed, initial surfaces cleaned and recorded, but no other contexts excavated.

2003 Area 4: 5 x 5m

Aims: To excavate part of the interior and part of N and E walls of A1 during filming for BBC 'Time Fliers' programme about Dùn Èistean.

Work completed: Rubble and turf shelter found set into the ruins of A1, recorded and excavated.

2005 Trench A (and H1): N of A1 (7m x 6m), interior of A1 (5m x 3.2m) plus sections through walls, W half and SE exterior of A2 (L-shaped, 10.2m x 1.6m, extending 4.9m to E). Trench H1 5m x 2m to N of Trench A.

Aims:

• Understand how A1, A2 and the enclosure wall were built, whether the identification of A1 and A2 as a dwelling and outbuilding was correct, investigate how they related to the triangular enclosure.

• Investigate the anomaly indicated in the geophysical survey to NE of A1.

• Investigate S end of A2.

• Date the use of the building.

Work completed: Excavation and sampling of all deposits down to natural subsoil and bedrock over entire Trench A and in wall cuttings. Trench H1 stripped of topsoil and turf to investigate the enclosure wall, but no archaeological deposits excavated.

Phase 1: Bedrock and natural subsoils

The gneiss bedrock on this part of the island forms a roughly flat surface, sloping gradually N from the S end of the structure to the N. It was covered by yellow very compact sandy subsoil with black/purple manganese-stained patches, A025=A026, from which a small volume of intrusive charcoal was recovered. Buildings A1 and A2 were built onto the natural subsoil.

Phase 2: Construction of buildings A1 and A2 and enclosure banks

Building A1

A1 was a roughly rectangular building, 4.5m x 2.7m internally. Excavation uncovered the inner faces and core of all four walls of the building, and an entrance in the E wall. Three cuttings were made through the walls to investigate the outer face and core construction. All four walls were faced internally and externally with undressed stone and had an earth core.

The S and W walls of A1 survived to a height of between 0.17m and 0.45m, and were up to 1.1m wide. The inner faces of the walls, A005=15 and A007, were built partly from orthostats and partly coursed stone, of which one to three courses survived. Only one course survived of the outer faces of the S wall. Between the two stone faces was a core of grey brown sandy silt A061=A051 and A050.

The E long wall was of similar construction to the W, having a stone face A006=407=17 and an earth core A047=17=401. Face A006 included no orthostats and instead was built from two to four courses (with an overall height of 0.2m to 0.4m) of stones. The earth core A047 was a mid brown sand silt.

An entrance, 0.7m wide, was found towards the S end of the E wall, on the sheltered side of the building. It was defined on its S side by a return in the wall face A006, which formed a door-jamb. No evidence was found for a similar return face/door-jamb on the N side of the gap, but the N side was more ragged, having been modified later when a small shelter was built into the ruins of A1 after it had gone out of use. When the entrance was first excavated it was thought that a large block of stone set into the entrance was part of the original structure, so making the entrance in to A1 only 0.35m wide. However, further excavation demonstrated that the stone block was placed there later during the building of the shelter in Phase 6, when the shelter wall was keyed in to the gap in the wall where the old entrance had been.

The N wall of A1 was also built from a stone inner face A004=3 and an earth core A039/A040 with three to six courses of stones surviving, standing to a height of up to 0.5m. At its E end, face A004 abutted stone face A006 of the E wall, but at its W end, there was a gap 0.9m wide filled with degraded turf between the end of the stone face of the N wall, and the stone face A005 of the W wall. A slot was excavated to investigate this gap, to test in particular whether it was an entrance, and this showed that the gap was due to the robbing of the stone inner face when the Phase 6 shelter was built into the ruins of A1 (see below).

The exploratory cutting excavated through the N wall did show that the basal layers of the earth core were built first, and the retaining stone faces added subsequently. In the slot through the N wall it was also found through the excavation of the basal layer of earth core, a mid brown silt sand A040, that the S wall (that closest to Structure A2) and both of the long walls on the E and W sides of the building were all built at the same time as each other, with the N wall then built last. This said, it is likely that all three walls, together with the S end wall A007/A061/A064, were part of the same construction event. The cutting through the N wall also showed that the wall cores of the N and W walls (A040 and A050) shared a common capping

Illus 4.6-4.8 Blocked entrance in A1 and Illus 4.9 N, S and W walls of A1 from E

Table 4.1 Phase 2 A1 context descriptions, finds and environmental on CD at back of book

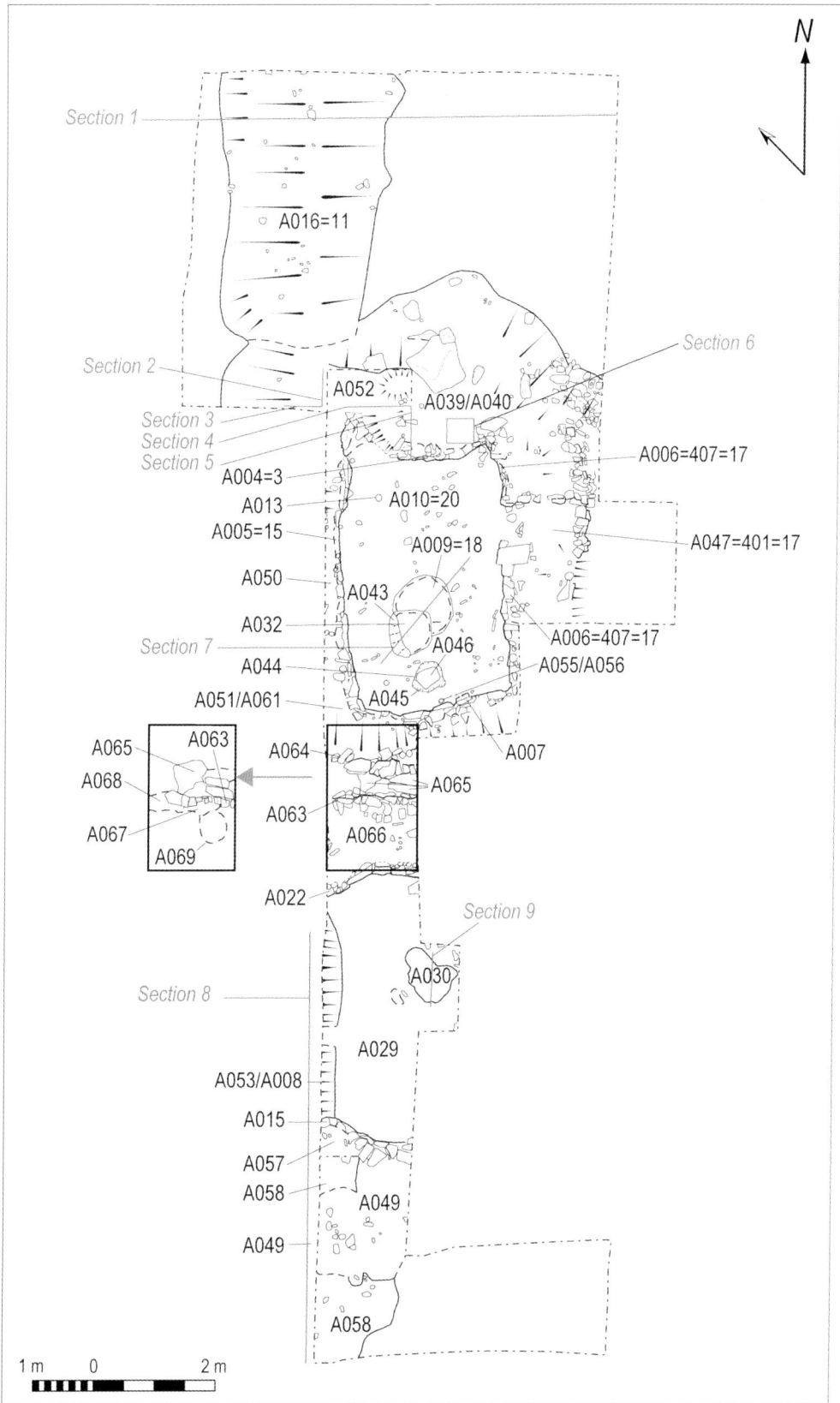

N

Section 1

A016=11

Section 2

Section 6

A052

A039/A040

Section 3
Section 4
Section 5

A006=407=17

A004=3

A013

A010=20

A005=15

A047=401=17

A050

A009=18

A043

A032

A046

A006=407=17

Section 7

A044

A055/A056

A051/A061

A045

A007

A065   A063

A064

A068

A065

A067

A063

A069

A066

A022

Section 9

A030

Section 8

A029

A053/A008

A015

A057

A058

A049

A049

A058

1 m   0   2 m

Illus 4.10 Phase 2 and 3 plan

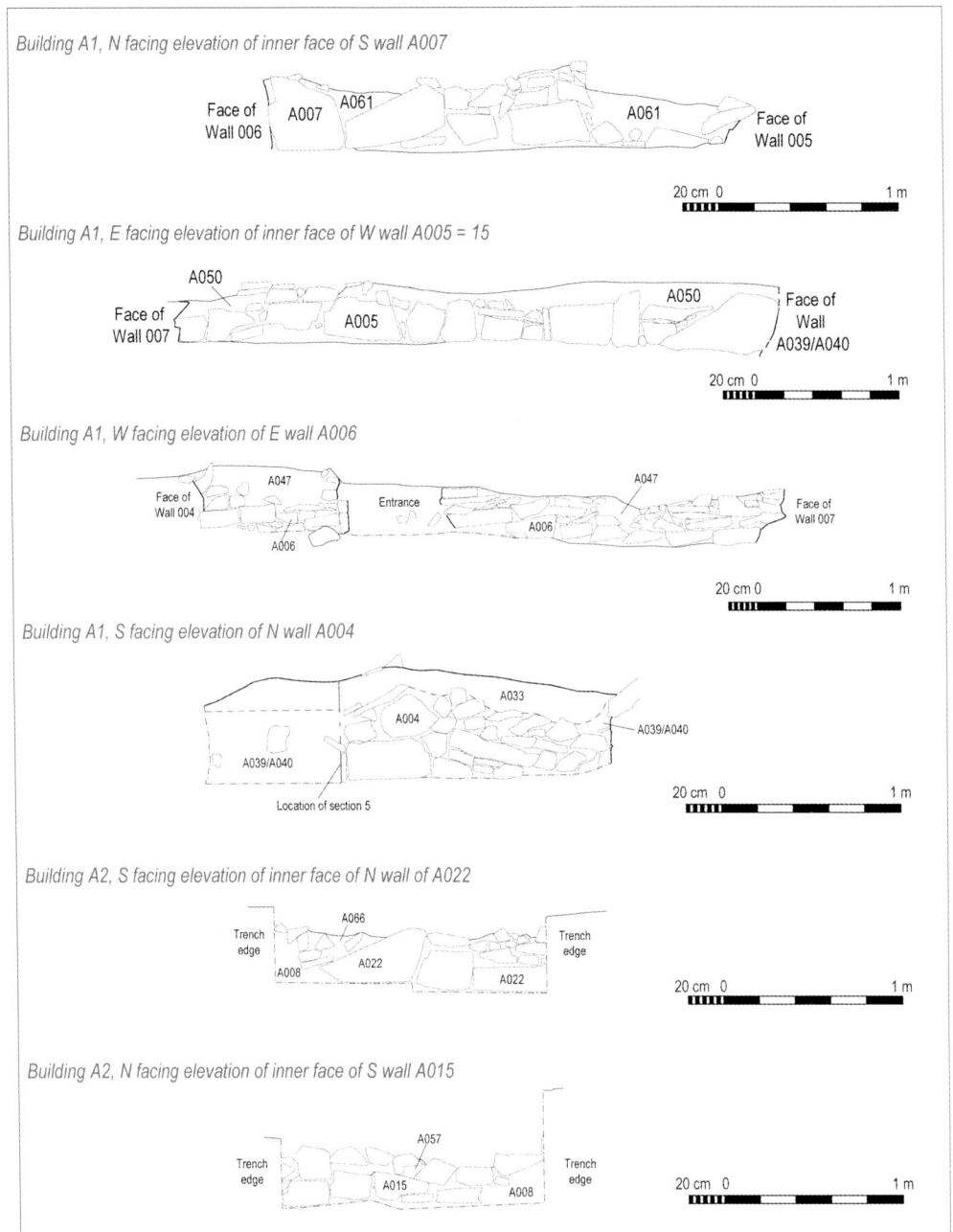

Building A1, N facing elevation of inner face of S wall A007

Face of
Wall 006

A007 A061

A061

Face of
Wall 005

20 cm 0   1 m

Building A1, E facing elevation of inner face of W wall A005 = 15

A050

Face of
Wall 007

A005

A050

Face of
Wall
A039/A040

20 cm 0   1 m

Building A1, W facing elevation of E wall A006

Face of
Wall 004

A047

Entrance

A047

Face of
Wall 007

A006

A006

20 cm 0   1 m

Building A1, S facing elevation of N wall A004

A033

A004

A039/A040

A039/A040

Location of section 5

20 cm 0   1 m

Building A2, S facing elevation of inner face of N wall of A022

Trench
edge

A066

A008 A022

Trench
edge

A022

20 cm 0   1 m

Building A2, N facing elevation of inner face of S wall A015

A057

Trench
edge

A015

Trench
edge

A008

20 cm 0   1 m

Illus 4.11 Structure A
elevations

layer of dark brown sand clay A052. So, while the base layer of the N wall is later than the base layers of the two adjacent long walls, the clay capping indicates that the walls were all built together above base level.

The walls of A1 were built directly on to the natural subsoil in most parts, but in some places, the inner stone faces of the walls appeared to lie on earth core material. This suggests that the basal earth cores, and possibly the outer faces, of the walls were put in place first, and the interior of the structure was then faced once it had been delimited by the earth banks.

All four earth wall cores contained artefactual and carbonised botanical material, and suggest that the turf, ash or midden material used to build the walls derived from areas of older occupation, not necessarily many years (or even months) older however as the material recovered is of the same general late medieval date. Sherds of local pottery were found in all four cores, and quartz flakes, chunks and chips were found in the E and W wall cores. Carbonised barley grains were found in A039, the N wall core, and Scots pine type charcoal was found in the S wall core A051=A061.

Building A2

Half of building A2 was uncovered in the excavations – the W wall and half of the N and S walls. Like building A1, A2 was rectangular with rounded corners, orientated N to S, and 4.4m long. The earliest of the three walls to be built was the W long wall, which was constructed entirely from turf, in two distinct deposits, A008 and A053, up to 0.5m high, onto the natural subsoil.

The S and N walls of A2 were both built after the W wall. The S end wall had an inner stone face A015 comprising up to three courses of stones, and an earth core up to 0.25m thick, and 0.6m wide. There was no outer stone face to the wall, which sloped to the S to form a banked profile and for this reason it had not been picked up by the topographic survey, surviving as only a low bank of turf. The S wall was built after the W wall as A015/A057 overlay the upper deposit of the W wall A008. At the SW corner of the building a dump of midden/hearth sweepings of charcoal flecks and occasional lumps of charcoal, clay, ceramic sherds (some burnt), and corroded iron objects in grey brown sand silt A049 had been deposited on top of the wall. It was unclear if this dump A049 had been placed within the earth core of the SW wall of A2 during the construction of that wall, or if it had been dumped over or against the wall when building A2 was in use, but it was overlain by the earth enclosure bank A058 to the S of and tacked on to building A2. This deposit contained sherds of local pottery, including a rim sherd and a shoulder sherd, four indeterminate iron objects, and fir, alder, birch, spruce, spruce/fir and Scots pine type charcoal, and carbonised oat, six-row barley and indeterminate cereal grains.

The N end of A2, unlike the W wall, was faced in coursed stone on both the inner and outer faces A022 and A063, with an earth core A066. The overall width of the wall was up to 1.4m, and the stone wall faces survived up to three courses to a maximum height of 0.27m. Patches of ash A067 and A068 were found below the earth core of the N wall and were interpreted at an interim stage as a hearth and hence the fugitive remains of an earlier structure (Barrowman R C 2006a, 27-8). However, a closer look at the ashy 'hearth' deposit A067/A068 in the excavation records showed that there was no evidence for in situ burning, and that the stones below the ash were not burnt but were stained by the peat ash. A067/A068 lay partially within a shallow depression A069 in the bedrock, and a more likely interpretation is that they were deliberately laid with ashy material as a levelling foundation deposit for the building of the N wall of building A2.

No evidence for an entrance was found in the W wall or the parts of the N and S walls that were excavated. It is most likely that the entrance into A2 was, like A1, in the E wall and therefore sheltered from the prevailing wind.

As with A1, all the wall core deposits in A2 contained carbonised botanical material and artefacts, including sherds of local pottery and quartz flakes, chips and chunks. In addition to this a gunflint with worn edges, and birch, conifer, spruce/fir and Scots pine type charcoal, and carbonised barley grains, were found in A008, the W wall core, and birch, heather type and Scots pine type charcoal in A057, the S wall core. Flint chips, a flake and a microblade were found in ash deposit A067 at the base of the N wall, and a flint flake in A063, the other face of the N wall. A067 and A068 were also rich in carbonised plant remains, including birch, hazel, heather type and spruce/fir type charcoals, as well as carbonised oats, barley and indeterminate cereals, and unidentified small fragments of mammal bone.

A charcoal sample from ash deposit A067 was radiocarbon dated and produced a range of AD1450-1635. This date was combined with dates from Phase 3 in modelling to test whether the two buildings, A1 and A2 were contemporary (see Chapter 13 below).

The gap between buildings A1 and A2

Buildings A1 and A2 were separated by a narrow gap between the N wall of A2 and the S wall of A1. In this gap, below turf slump from the two walls, three flat stone slabs A065 were uncovered

Table 4.2 Phase 2 A2 and enclosure banks context descriptions, finds and environmental on CD at back of book

Illus 4.12 Close-up of inner face of N wall of A2 and Illus 4.13 Gap between A1 and A2

Illus 4.14 Enclosure bank to N of A1 and Illus 4.15 Enclosure banks to N of A1 from W

in an area 0.4 x 1m. In the centre of the SW side of this paved surface, a gap in the paving formed an incomplete circle and it was considered that this might indicate the former presence of a post, although no accompanying posthole was revealed in removing the slabs of A065. The slabs were situated directly onto the subsoil with no cut or drain below, and against the stone facing A063 on the N side of the N wall of A2, but partially below and therefore pre-dating the stone facing A064 of the S wall of A1, if only by a short time. Five sherds of local handmade pottery were found amongst the paving.

The enclosure banks to the N of A1 and S of A2

Excavation demonstrated that the two enclosure banks, A016=11 and A058, had been tacked on to the N and S ends of Structure A after buildings A1 and A2 had been built. These banks were identified during the topographic survey, and together, the W walls of A1 and A2 and banks A016=11 and A058 formed a continuous N-S line defining and enclosing an triangular-shaped open space, perhaps an entrance courtyard, at the SW corner of the island.

No indication of burning, metal-working or other activity was found in the trench outside the N end of A1 to explain the anomalous readings that had been identified by the geophysical survey in this area, and it seems most likely that the readings originated from the bedrock, and not from an archaeological feature.

Bank A016, at the N end of building A1, stood up to 0.5m in height, with steep edges on the E and W sides breaking sharply to a shallow slope at 0.2m above the base of the bank where it had slumped to a width of up to 2m wide. When a cutting was excavated through the bank it uncovered a narrow steep-sided core, no more than 0.6m wide, probably reflecting the original profile of the bank before the turf slumped outwards. Only 4.5m of the bank was uncovered in Trench A in 2005, from its S end to the point where it disappeared into the trench edge at the N, but the survey indicated that the bank extended for another 10m to the N, where it joined with H, the perimeter wall around the island.

The N end of the bank was uncovered, but not excavated, in Trench H1 H101=A016 where it joined a second turf enclosure wall H102/H103/H104 at the W edge of the island (see Illus 4.22, and Phase 5, below). A short gap between the SW end of bank A058 and Structure B to the S may suggest there was an entranceway here into the enclosure at its SW corner.

Bank A058, at the S end of building A2, was 3.30m long and sloped down to the S from the S end wall of building A2 A015/A057 where it formed a small bank. It had eroded more extensively than A16, and remained standing to a height of only 0.28m. Only half of the width of the bank was excavated as the rest lay outside the edge of Trench A, but the entire length of the wall was uncovered. No finds were recovered from bank A016, but 23 sherds of local pottery and three indeterminate iron objects were recovered from bank A058.

Phase 3: Occupation of buildings A1 and A2

A1

The interior of A1 appeared to have an earthen floor A010=20, on which was set a central hearth slightly towards the S end of the building. The interface between the floor layers and the first layers of turf collapse that had slumped/collapsed onto it when the building went out of use (see Phase 4 below) was hard to distinguish during the excavation, having become intermingled during the decay and leaching of silt from the collapsed turf. As a result, occupation material from the interior of A1 was removed with the post-abandonment layers above the floor during the excavation.

When the central hearth was excavated, a complex sequence of burning and cleaning layers were identified, showing that it had been used several times in succession. The hearth was set in the floor in a shallow oval depression A038, 1.3m by 0.5m and 0.12m deep, which had clearly been burnt at the base A042. The hearth spot was partially enclosed by a small turf or earth kerb A043, 0.8m by 0.2m, situated on the opposite side from the entrance, presumably to stop ash from the hearth blowing into the building if the wind was in the N or E and blowing in the entrance. A small patch, 0.1m in diameter, of pale orange sand clay peat ash A013, found at the N end of the floor A010 may have blown or dropped from the hearth.

Within the hearth itself there was a sequence of distinct in situ burning layers A032, A034, A035, A036, A037 and A009, a layer of ash that had formed in sweeping out the hearth spot. Within the overall area of the hearth, individual layers of burning were small and often overlapping, showing that each burning event took place in a slightly different part of the overall hearth spot each time. The earliest burning event was A037, covered by A036, A034 and A035, and finally the uppermost layer, A032, represented the final use of the hearth.

A large piece of bedrock A046 was found protruding through the floor near the hearth, on its S side. A roughly circular cut, 0.5m in diameter and up to 0.1m deep around the stone (A044; filled with mid grey brown sandy silt A045) may have resulted from an attempt to remove it either during the construction or use of A1. A small stake hole A055 was found to the W of the stone and may suggest that the stone served as a pivot for a pole embedded in the stake hole in the floor– the purpose of this pole being to suspend items over the hearth (eg cooking pots).

104 sherds of local pottery, including rim and shoulder sherds, and a possible hammerstone, as well as 10 pieces of unidentified burnt mammal bone were found in floor layer A010=20. Sampling of all hearth deposits recovered a wide range of material including alder, broom, conifer, hazel, birch, heather-type and oak charcoal, as well as carbonised oats, barley, including hulled barley, and indeterminate cereal, and small unidentified fragments of mammal bone. In addition to these species, sedge and dock were recovered from hearth deposit A009, haddock and saithe bones from intermediate hearth layer A034, and buttercup and a hazel nutshell from A036. Small numbers of local pottery sherds and chips and chunks of quartz were found in all the hearth deposits. Chips or flakes of flint were also found in deposits A032, A034, A035 and A036, and a possible gunflint in A032. Lead residue or droplets were found in A009 and A036, and indeterminate iron objects and nails, in A009, A035 and A036 probably originate from burning driftwood, as also demonstrated by the recovery of conifer charcoal from A032, A034 and A036.

Charcoal samples from hearth deposits A032, A034, A036 and A037 were also radiocarbon dated and produced a range of AD1445-1640 (A032 AD1445-1635, A034 AD1465-1640, A036 AD1445-1630 and A037 AD1450-1635). This date range can be slightly modified by modelling (see Chapter 13 below).

Illus 4.16 Interior of A1 from N and Illus 4.17 Section through hearth in A1

Table 4.3 Phase 3 A1 and A2 context descriptions, finds and environmental on CD at back of book

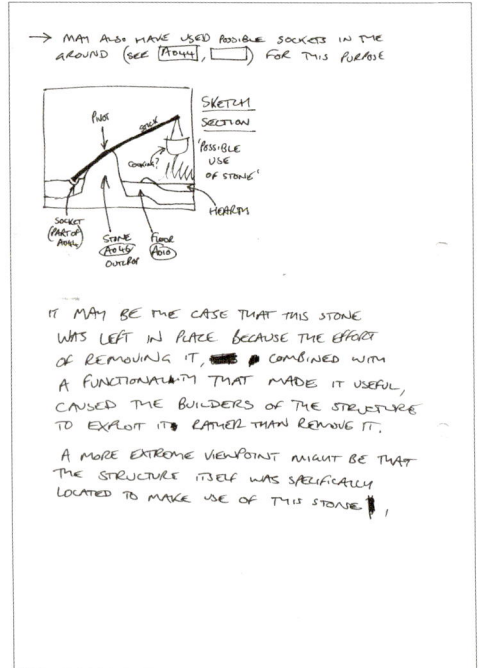

A2

A2 also had an earth floor A029 and a central hearth A030. The floor and hearth deposits were less substantial than those in A1 however, and the hearth covered a smaller area of 0.90m by 0.80m and contained only one layer of burning A030 up to 0.06m deep.

The smaller finds assemblage from A2 also suggests less intensive occupation here. One body sherd of local pottery and a quartz chip and flake, was all that was recovered from floor A029. A small assemblage of birch, oats, barley and indeterminate cereal grains were identified from hearth A030, together with five body sherds of local pottery and a rim with nail indentations.

A charcoal sample from hearth A030 was radiocarbon dated and produced a date range of AD1425–1620. This date was combined in modelling with dates from A1 to investigate whether the two buildings were contemporary (see Chapter 13 below).

Illus 4.19 Floor in A2 from S

Phase 4: Initial abandonment and collapse of buildings A1 and A2 and the enclosure banks

The lower deposits in this series represent the initial collapse of the stone facings of some of the walls and slump from the earth cores of the building walls and enclosure banks.

The enclosure banks

To the N of building A1, clay silts A019 and A059 had slumped and washed from the turf of bank A016 to form a slope of degraded material at the foot of the bank. On the W side of bank A016, a similar slump deposit of silt clay A060 had collected. These layers, A019, A059 and A060 were the first deposits to slump and collapse from bank A016 after the site was abandoned. A019 was the same as A033, a deposit of slump/wash from the N end wall of building A1.

No finds were recovered from deposits A059 and A060, but 22 sherds of local pottery, including a rim and two shoulder sherds, were found with two flint pebbles and two iron objects in A019. Birch, conifer and willow were identified from the environmental sample from A019.

A1

The collapse of building A1 can be seen in a series of deposits excavated from around the lower stone walls of the building, representing the collapse of the stone facings and turf of the upper walls and presumably roof.

Outside the E wall of A1 in Trench 4 in 2001, silt clay 403 and loose sandy clay and large stones 404 were uncovered but not excavated. 403 and 404 contained 70 sherds of local pottery, including three decorated body sherds, two decorated rim sherds and a decorated neck sherd. As most of the sherds were large and had fresh edges, it was suggested that the rubble collapse was mixed with midden that had accumulated against the outside the building while it was still occupied, to the side of the E doorway into building A1. Birch, heather-type, conifer and oak charcoal was identified from these two deposits, together with indeterminate carbonised cereal grains.

On the other side of this wall, a layer of stone rubble A020=16 covered the interior of the building, abutting the interior faces of the S, E and W walls (wall faces A005, A006, A007). A020 comprised only a single layer of rubble, and probably represents the collapse of the stone wall facings of the interior of the building. Three body sherds of local pottery were found in this deposit.

Above these layers of rubble several deposits very similar in character were excavated, which had resulted from the slump and degradation of the cores, upper turf walls and possibly roof of building A1. Over rubble A020 was a layer of silt sand A021=10=14, which abutted the building walls, forming a bank running around and sloping down from the inner wall faces and extending 0.3 - 0.60m into the interior. In common with the in situ wall core deposits excavated from Phase 2, these slumped turf wall deposits contained a considerable assemblage of pot sherds, 99 sherds of local pottery in total, including neck, rim and shoulder sherds, but also three pieces of burnt mammal bone, eight quartz flakes, indeterminate iron objects and a nail shank, a smoothing stone, a hammer/anvil stone and a possible pot lid.

Above A021, linear bands of mid brown silt sand, A011=21=22 and A012=19, were found along the inner faces of the E and W building walls. A011 lay adjacent to the interior face of the W wall, and A012, which was an L-shaped band, lay adjacent to the interior faces of the E wall and, part of the N wall before terminating near the centre of that wall face. These had been interpreted in 2003 as evidence of turf benches running along the inside of the walls of A1, but excavation in 2005 demonstrated that they were slump deposits from the upper turf building walls.

Directly below deposit A012, a cluster of small, amorphous patches of sand silt A062 were found in undulations in the earth floor of A1, and a silt sand A028 was found infilling a gap in the E wall. Three body sherds of local pottery were found in A062 and A028. Above layers A011 and A012 reddish brown clay patches 13, excavated in 2003, were interpreted as the remains of slumped turfs.

Table 4.4 Phase 4 context descriptions, finds and environmental on CD in back of book

Illus 4.20 Slump and collapsed turf in A2

Illus 4.21 Phase 5 slump in trench

Table 4.5 Phase 5 context descriptions, finds and environmental on CD in back of book

Along the N wall, degraded turf A033, containing patches of black, highly organic clay, had slumped over an area over the N wall of A1, and the enclosure bank A016. A033 is probably the same as deposit A019, a turf slump from the enclosure wall A016 (see above).

Along the S wall, and between the S end wall of Structure A1 and the N end wall of Structure A2, turf walling material had slumped and degraded to form a grey sand silt A054=A048, which had accumulated up to 0.23m deep in the gap between the walls. Seven body sherds and four rim sherds of local pottery, and three flint flakes were found here, and conifer, oat and six-row barley grains were identified in the sample from A054.

A2

Outside building A2, to the S, a shallow grey brown silt clay layer A014/A024, had washed from the earth core A057 of the S wall of A2 and the earth bank A058 abutting that wall. Two body sherds and a rim sherd were found in this deposit and a small volume of unidentified charcoal.

In the interior of A2 four abandonment layers were excavated representing the collapse of the stone wall faces and turf walls and cores of building A2. Silt clay A031 covered an area in a linear band around the edge of the interior faces of the walls of A2, up to 0.8m wide, and in patches on the floor A029. A layer of rubble in grey mottled orange and yellow silt A041 was also found in an area 1.5m wide, abutting the inner face A022 of the N wall of A2. As with other collapsed wall core layers in the trench, these deposits contained a large assemblage of pottery sherds – 68 body sherds, two neck sherds, four shoulder sherds and four rim sherds, one with nail indentations, and a chip of flint. Many of these finds are likely to derive from the occupation of the building, but have become incorporated with the turf collapse that accumulated onto the floor of the building after it was abandoned. The exception to this may be the find of a clear glass vessel shoulder sherd that is probably 18th century (see Murdoch below in Chapter 10).

Above these collapse layers collapsed and degraded turf, grey black silt clay A027, and above that, dark, almost black, clay with a high organic content and peaty consistency A023 were found, within the interior of A2. Deposit A023 extended from the W wall of A2 (A008) to the limits of the excavation in the S and had accumulated within a depression in the centre of the collapsed building. Both deposits contained sherds of local pottery, including 70 body sherds, one with decoration, two shoulder and two rim sherds.

Phase 5: *Further slump and wash of abandonment and collapse layers*

The upper post-abandonment deposits represent subsequent wash into the depressions created after the initial collapse and slump from buildings A1 and A2, and the enclosure banks A016 and A058. Silt clay, A002 (=12=7=406), which had been washed from the turf walls of A1 through

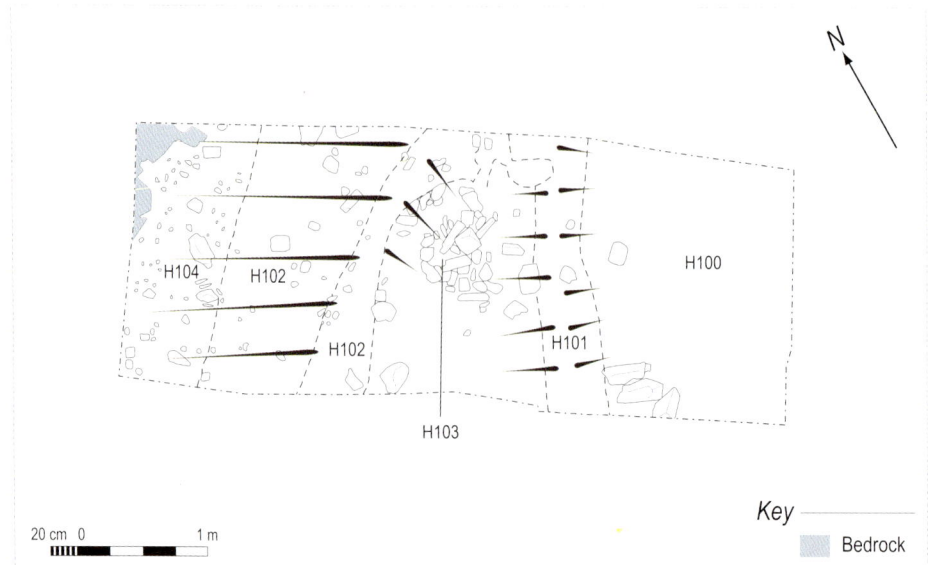

Illus 4.22 Plan of Trench H

N

H104 H102

H100

H102

H101

H103

20 cm 0   1 m

Key

Bedrock

Trench H

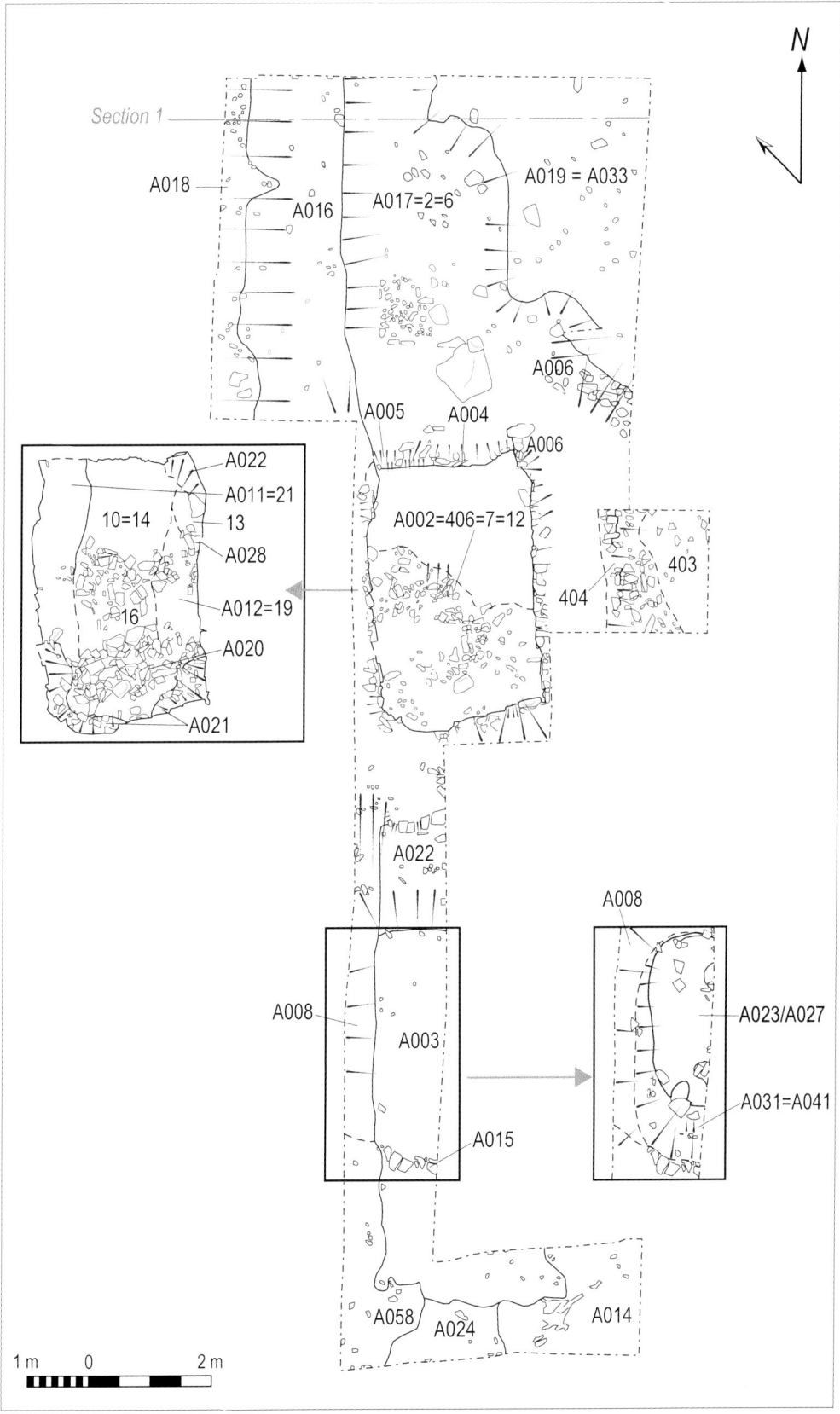

Section 1

A018

A016

A017=2=6

A019 = A033

A006

A005   A004

A006

N

A022
A011=21
10=14   13
A028
16   A012=19
A020
A021

A002=406=7=12

404   403

A022

A008

A008   A003

A015

A008

A023/A027

A031=A041

A058   A024   A014

1 m   0   2 m

Illus 4.23 Phases 4 and 5 plan

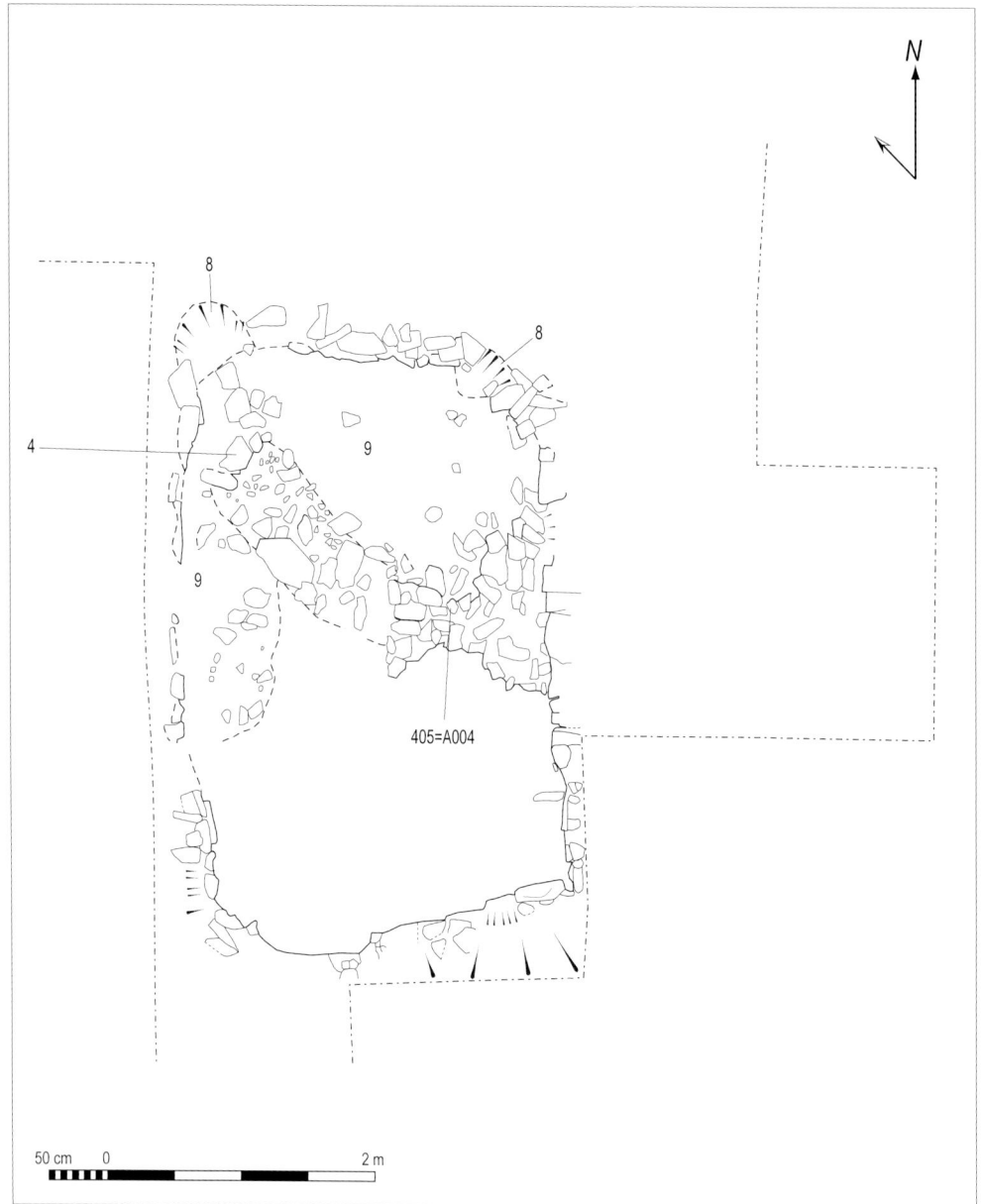

Illus 4.24 Phase 6 plan

50 cm   0   2 m

weathering, was found in a hollow depression in the interior of A1. An assemblage of 11 body sherds of local pottery, a quartz flake, a quartz chunk and two flint flakes, with birch conifer, heather type and spruce/fir charcoal and carbonised oat grains, was found in A002. A similar deposit, A003, was found in the interior of A2, and contained 31 body sherds of local pottery, and a rim sherd with nail indentations.

Clay silt A017 (=2=6=11), had washed up to 2m E down from the E of the enclosure bank A016 along its length and a sand silt A018 similar in character to A017 was found along the W side of the length of bank A016. A017 and A018 appear as two spatially distinct but similar deposits, separated by the intervening bank A016, and they can be interpreted as post-abandonment wash layers from that bank. A small trench (H) opened up over the N end of the enclosure bank N of Structure A uncovered similar upper post-abandonment layers H102-4, but no further excavation took place.

Relatively few finds were recovered from these wash deposits, but included four body and three rim sherds of local pottery, and 72 conjoining body and rim sherds from one vessel, and a chunk, flake and microblade of quartz. Notable finds were a small sherd, probably from a cold-colour painted vessel or bottle, of a type common in Germany, Austria and Bohemia in the second half of the 18th century/early 19th century (although possibly of earlier Venetian date; see Murdoch in Chapter 10 below), and a musket ball from context 6 which has teeth marks on it (=2=11=A017). It is possible that this musket ball was in the enclosure wall, and then collapsed with it.

Phase 6: Temporary shelter

After A1 was abandoned and had collapsed, a small turf and stone shelter was built inside the N end of the ruined building. The shelter comprised a rough, semi-circular wall (4=405) built from rubble collapse and blocks of turf (degraded to grey/brown sandy clay) cleared from inside the building. The wall was up to 0.65m wide and curved round from the old entrance in the E wall of A1 to the NW corner. When the rubble wall was built the original entrance into the E side of A1 was blocked by turf and a large block of stone was placed in to key the shelter wall into the old entrance. The entrance to the shelter was instead on the opposite side of the building, in a gap in the W wall, and accessed from the NW corner of the slumped walls of A1.

A floor surface of gravel sand and silt 009 was found inside the shelter and trodden out through the entrance and along the inner face of the ruined W wall of A1, suggesting that this route was the access in to the shelter through the ruins. Above the floor lay the collapsed turf roof, 5=402, which had degraded to a layer of dark brown clay silt loam with sand and roots and contained three sherds of local pottery (one a decorated rim sherd) and a chunk of quartz, birch heather and spruce charcoal and a carbonised barley grain. This material presumably derived from the older occupation of the buildings, and was contained in the turf stripped from them to build the shelter. When the shelter itself went out of use, slumps of greyish brown sandy silt 008 washed from the NW and NE corners of the shelter walls.

Phase 7: Topsoil

Topsoil A001=400=1 of dark brown silt clay covered the area to a uniform depth of 0.15m to 0.2m. 10 body sherds of local pottery, and three rim sherds and three flint flakes were found in the topsoil.

Endnotes

[1] All radiocarbon dates are calibrated and quoted at 95.4% confidence: see Chapter 13

Table 4.6 Phases 6 and 7 context descriptions, finds and environmental on CD in back of book

Section 1: S facing section of N edge of Trench A

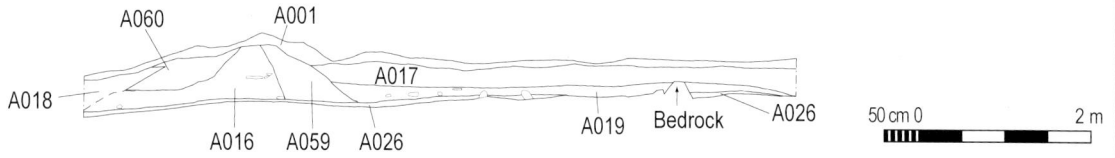

A060 A001 A017 A018 A016 A059 A026 A019 Bedrock A026

50 cm 0 2 m

Section 2: W facing section of slot through W wall of A1, A050 and enclosure bank A016

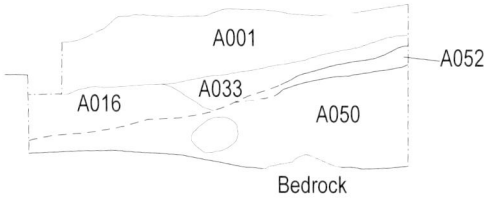

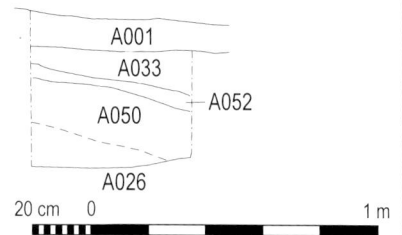

A001 A052 A016 A033 A050 Bedrock

Section 3: N facing section of slot through W wall of A1, A050, and enclosure bank A016

A001 A033 A052 A050 A026

20 cm 0 1 m

Section 4: S facing section of slot through W part of N wall of A1

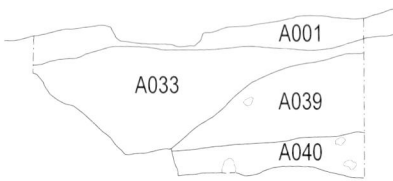

A001 A033 A039 A040

Section 5: W facing section of slot through W part of N wall of A1

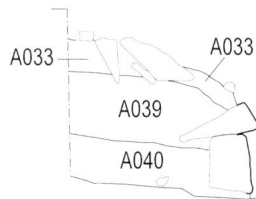

A033 A033 A039 A040

Section 6: S facing section of slot through E part of N wall of A1

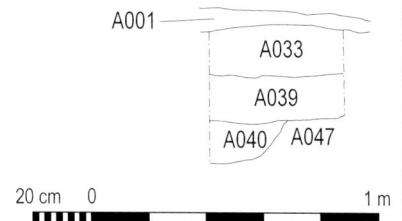

A001 A033 A039 A040 A047

20 cm 0 1 m

Section 7: SE facing section through hearth in A1

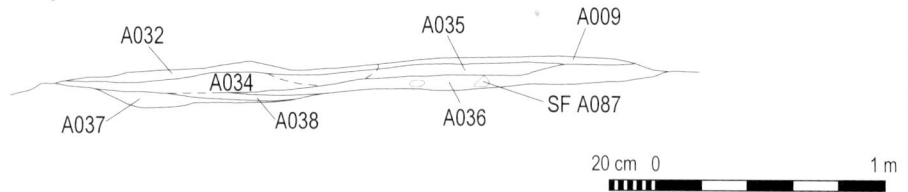

A032 A035 A009 A034 A037 A038 A036 SF A087

20 cm 0 1 m

Section 8: E facing section at S end of Trench A

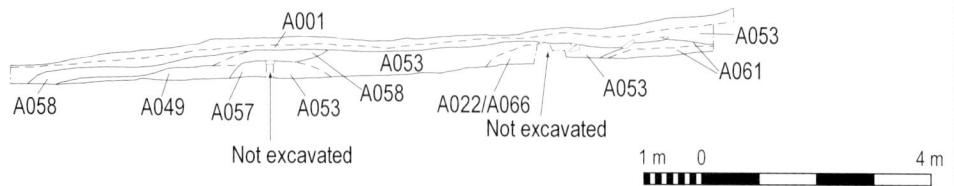

A001 A053 A053 A061 A058 A049 A057 A053 A058 A022/A066 A053 Not excavated Not excavated

1 m 0 4 m

Section 9: W facing section through hearth in A2

A030

20 cm 0 1 m

Illus 4.25 Trench A sections

Illus 5.1 Working in Trench B

Structure B is a group of six stone and turf buildings set against the perimeter wall H at the south-west corner of the island. Excavations in Area B investigated four of the six buildings (B1 and B4-6), a cutting through the perimeter wall Structure H and an area between Structures A and B. Six phases of activity were identified, from earliest to latest: (1) the natural subsoil, (2) original ground surfaces, (3) structures and occupation pre-dating Structure B, (4) construction and use of Structure B, (5) its abandonment and collapse, and (6) the development of topsoil.

Artefacts and carbonised botanical material from Phases 2 and 3 demonstrate that there was already occupation on the island when Structure B was built. Old ground surfaces (Phase 2) contained evidence for the burning of peat and driftwood (conifer species and larch), and the drying of oats and barley in the vicinity. Above these surfaces, in an area that had shown up as blank in the geophysical and topographical surveys, excavations revealed the robbed-out footings of a stone and earth wall and a spread of artefactual material such as a gunflint and flint flakes, and sherds of local pottery (Phase 3). A rich assemblage of carbonised grain, peat ash and hearth material was also found below the walls of building B1, with flint flakes, local pottery, an iron object and lumps of slag. One particular deposit (B102) contained clear evidence of cultivation (off-site, see Chapter 11, below) and processing of grain. Radiocarbon dating of samples from layers predating building B1 returned an overall date range of AD1430-1630.[1]

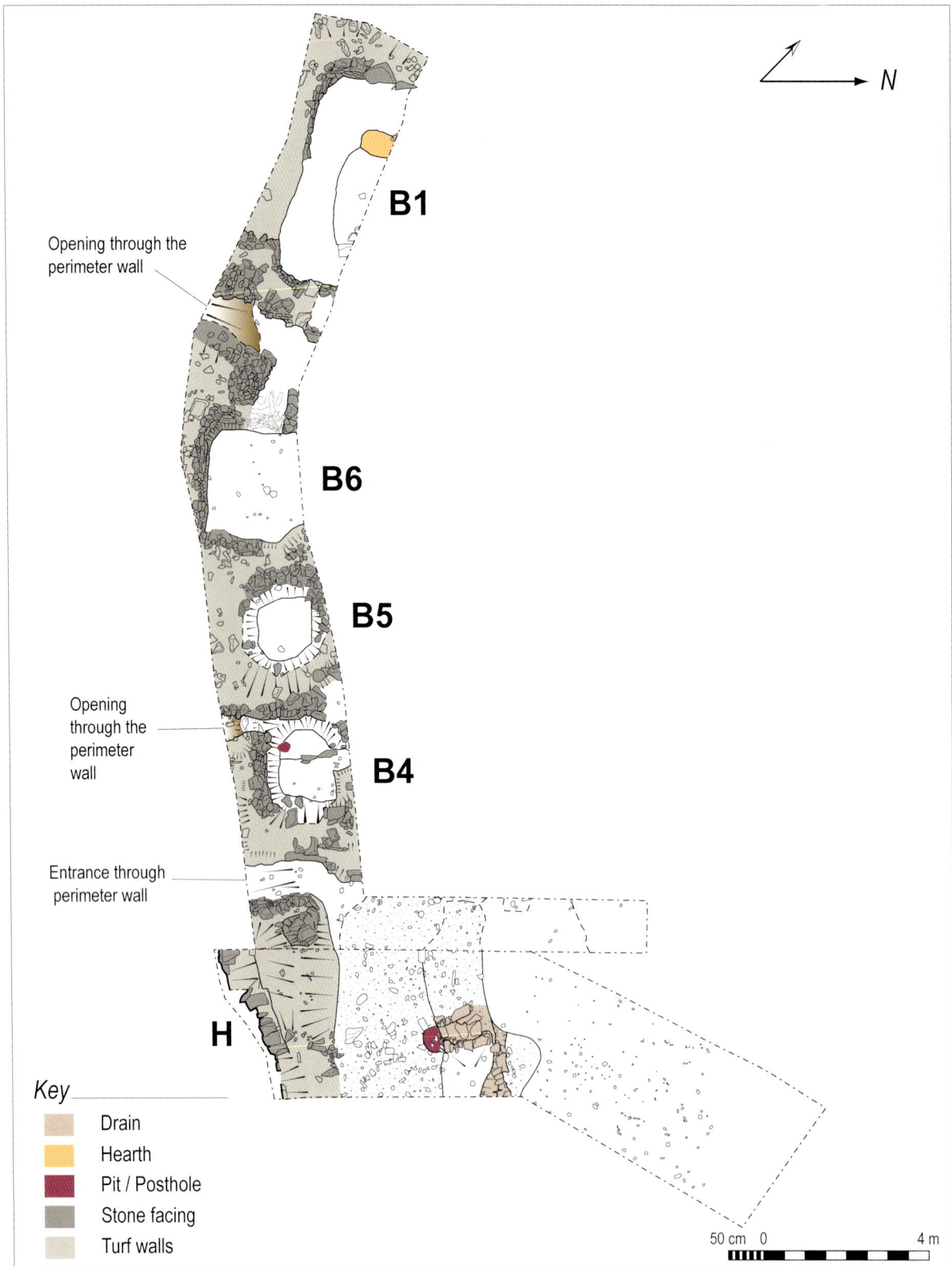

Illus 5.2 Interpretation plan

Key
Drain
Hearth
Pit / Posthole
Stone facing
Turf walls

B1

Opening through the
perimeter wall

B6

B5

Opening
through the
perimeter
wall

B4

Entrance through
perimeter wall

H

50 cm 0   4 m

N

Buildings B1 and B4-6 (Phase 4) were then built together as one unit onto these old ground surfaces. B1, the largest building at the west end of the complex, was separated from the rest by a metre-wide gap. It had a sunken floor and a central peat hearth, which contained burnt material evidence for the drying and cooking of barley, oats, mammal and fish bone, suggesting that B1 would have been the gathering and eating place for the rest of the complex. Ashy material (probably from the hearth) was found dumped in the gap between B1 and B6, and this also contained slag, as well as local pottery and carbonised cereal grains, birch, heather, oak and Scots pine type charcoal. Adjacent to this, the remaining buildings, B4-6, were smaller and built side to side, with conjoining earth and stone lower walls, and upper turf walls and roofs. Like B1, B4-6 also had sunken floors, and some evidence of occupation layers, but they had no hearths. The occupation and hearth deposits in buildings B1 and B4-6 contained local pottery, including rim and decorated sherds, two lumps of slag, quartz and flint flakes, and further evidence for the burning of peat, shrubby species, and driftwood. Radiocarbon dating of occupation deposits B092 in B4 and B079 in B5 returned date ranges of AD1445-1635 and AD1470-1645 respectively.

Excavation through the perimeter wall H to the east of Structure B showed that it had also been constructed from stone facings with a turf and earth core. The external face rested on the bedrock terrace at the cliff-edge, and the interior face was built on an old ground surface of small stones and gravel set into the subsoil. There was also evidence that the wall had subsequently been repaired after it was built. The turf walls and earthen wall cores of Structures B and H contained sherds of local pottery, lithics, charcoal and carbonised cereal and plant remains, suggesting that the material used to build them derived from existing areas of occupation.

Phase 5, representing the abandonment and collapse of Structures B and H, contained the most varied range of material and the largest assemblage of local pottery sherds (over 260 sherds), but, as with Structure A to the north, it is likely that this material originally derived from the Phase 4 floor layers below. It includes sherds of medieval and post-medieval glazed ceramics, gunflints, a pistol ball and a musket ball, flint and quartz flakes, iron objects, lumps of slag and a shard of late seventeenth/early eighteenth century glass. The recovery of two coins adds an extra dimension to the dating of the site - an Elizabeth I silver sixpence dating to 15[8?]0 was found in slump in the interior of B6, and a James VI billon plack (eightpenny Scots) issue of 1583-90 was recovered from a sample of turf slump lying between buildings B1 and B6. Many, if not the majority, of these finds no doubt originate from the use of Structure B, and the late sixteenth/early seventeenth century date provided by the coins is corroborated by radiocarbon dating of deposits from Phases 3 and 4 (see above).

Excavations within Structure B itself suggest that buildings B1 and B4-6 were probably built together as one contemporaneous unit. Modifications were made during the use of the building however, such as the blocking of an entrance in the west wall of B6 that once gave access to a passageway to the perimeter wall around the site. The position of Structure B at the top of the two main access routes on to the site, with a view across to the mainland only 15m away, suggest that it was probably used as a lookout to defend the site from the landward side. An entrance onto the site was found in the perimeter wall H at the top of an access route up the cliff to the site at the east edge of B6 where the gap between the island and the mainland is at its narrowest. The entrance had been paved and lined with stone uprights and could also have been used to haul supplies up onto the site. Gaps in the south walls of B1, B4 and B6 were also found filled with turf slump, and could originally have provided access to lookouts through the defensive wall. These features all support the interpretation that Structure B was a gatehouse, which worked together with the triangular enclosure and Structure A to defend and organize access on to the site.

Results

with Chris Dalglish and Chris Barrowman

Trench locations

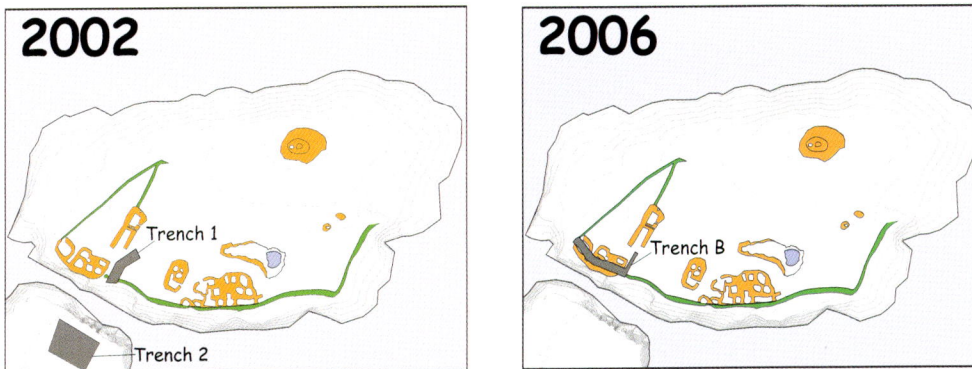

2002 Trench 1: 3.5m x 5m with a 6m extension parallel and E of Structure B from the cliff edge to SE corner of Structure A, Trench 2: 25m x 11m on mainland opposite.
Aims: To excavate and record any archaeology found in the areas of the footings for a steel footbridge that was to be built across to the island.
Work completed: Excavation down to natural subsoil in both trenches. Trench 1: Cutting excavated through the perimeter wall H and its construction investigated. Trench 2: No further deposits or features identified other than topsoil and subsoil.

2006 Trench B: 22m x 3m with narrow extension 1m x 5m N-S, at the E end. Trench aligned E-W across Buildings B1, B4, B4 and B6. Trench extension at E end of and perpendicular to the main trench met up with W edge of Trench 1 from 2002.
Aims:
•Understand how B1 and B4-6 were built, determine their function and date, to investigate how they related to perimeter wall H and to explore their interpretation as a gatehouse controlling access on to the site was correct.
•Investigate the 'blank' area to the N of B4, between Structures A and B.
•Investigate the area to the E of Structure B and link deposits with those excavated adjacent in Trench 1 in 2002 at the bridge footing.
Work completed: Excavation and sampling of all deposits down to natural subsoil over most of the trench and in wall cuttings.

Phase 1: Bedrock and natural subsoils

The gneiss bedrock was covered by the natural subsoil B064=003=025=018.

Phase 2: Original ground surfaces

The earliest deposits encountered above the natural subsoil were a series of old ground surfaces and topsoils found preserved under the E wall of B4 (B099), the W wall of B4/E wall of B5 (B105) and the area between the E wall of B1/W wall of B6 (B070/B108).

Adjacent and to the E of Structure B, a compact silty sand B059=1/B056 was found in the gap between B4 and the perimeter wall Structure H. The upper surface of the deposit was eroded from the passage of traffic through the gap, but otherwise it was the same as 2, the old ground surface excavated to the N of Structure B in Trench 1 2002, and B099 excavated from below the wall of B4 to the W. These deposits overlay B082=023=024, silty sand with gravel and stones overlying the natural subsoil, from which nine body sherds of local pottery and a quartz blade were recovered.

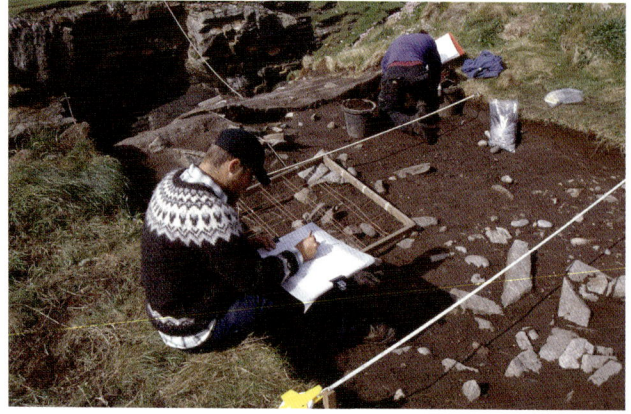

Illus 5.5 and 5.6 Bridge trenches 2002

Illus 5.7 Photo record sheet for B056 and Illus 5.8 Cutting through perimeter wall in 2002

Table 5.2 Phase 3 context descriptions, finds and environmental on CD at back of book

A scattering of finds was recovered from these old ground surfaces. Three chips of quartz and a limpet shell, and six row barley (including hulled), birch and burnt peat were found in B059, and carbonised birch in 024. A rim and a body sherd of local pottery were found in B070, and birch, conifer, larch, burnt peat, oat, hulled and six row barley and indeterminate carbonised remains were recovered from deposit B108, both below buildings B1 and B6.

Phase 3: Construction of perimeter wall H and structures and occupation pre-dating Structure B

5m of the perimeter wall, Structure H, were excavated. The wall stood to up to 1m high and was built from an outer face of three or four courses of stonework 009, a turf core (012, 013, 016, 017 and 028) and an inner face of stonework 008. The wall extended E-W along the S edge of the island, stopping just short of the E edge of Structure B, where there was an entrance gap. The terminal of the wall at the W end had a stone face B010 of unbonded, coursed stones, which survived to a height of up to six courses or 0.6m.

The N side of the bank was made up of three deposits: 13=B006, a loose sandy silt mixed with loose and tumbled stones and an area of burning within it, overlay the edge of layer 012=B007, a mixed layer of silty clay that had the consistency of degraded turf, with a high degree of peat-like fibrous material. This in turn overlay and completely sealed layer 016, one of the best preserved layers, exhibiting a patchwork of yellow and grey, presumably where individual turfs had decomposed. Below these layers was a further degraded turf layer of grey sandy clay 017, spreading across the entire width of the wall, from behind the external stone facing 009, over a sequence of gravels and across approximately 1m.

A quartz blade, mammal bone fragments and carbonised conifer, barley and indeterminate cereal remains were found in 013=B006. A burnt flint chunk, and birch, conifer, oak and barley carbonised remains were found in 012=B007. Only small quantities of unidentified charcoal were found in 016 and 017, although they contained the largest assemblage of local pottery sherds in H, including 24 body sherds, four shoulder sherds, six rim sherds and a neck sherd. The earliest turf layer (028) recorded in Structure H lay in a hollow in the bedrock. It appeared similar to the previously described layers, with a high sand content and no stone or artefactual inclusions. To the S of this, and forming the bedding for the external masonry 009, was a sandy loam 027.

Parallel to, 2m away from, the perimeter wall, the compact gravel footings of a wall 006=B065 were excavated, extending under a mass of stones and earth to the E. This rubble feature, on further excavation, proved to be the footings of a wall consisting of stone facing 010 with a turf or earth core 004 composed of silty clay. The wall had a distinct edge to the N, consisting of no more than two courses of dry stone, the turf or earth core appeared as

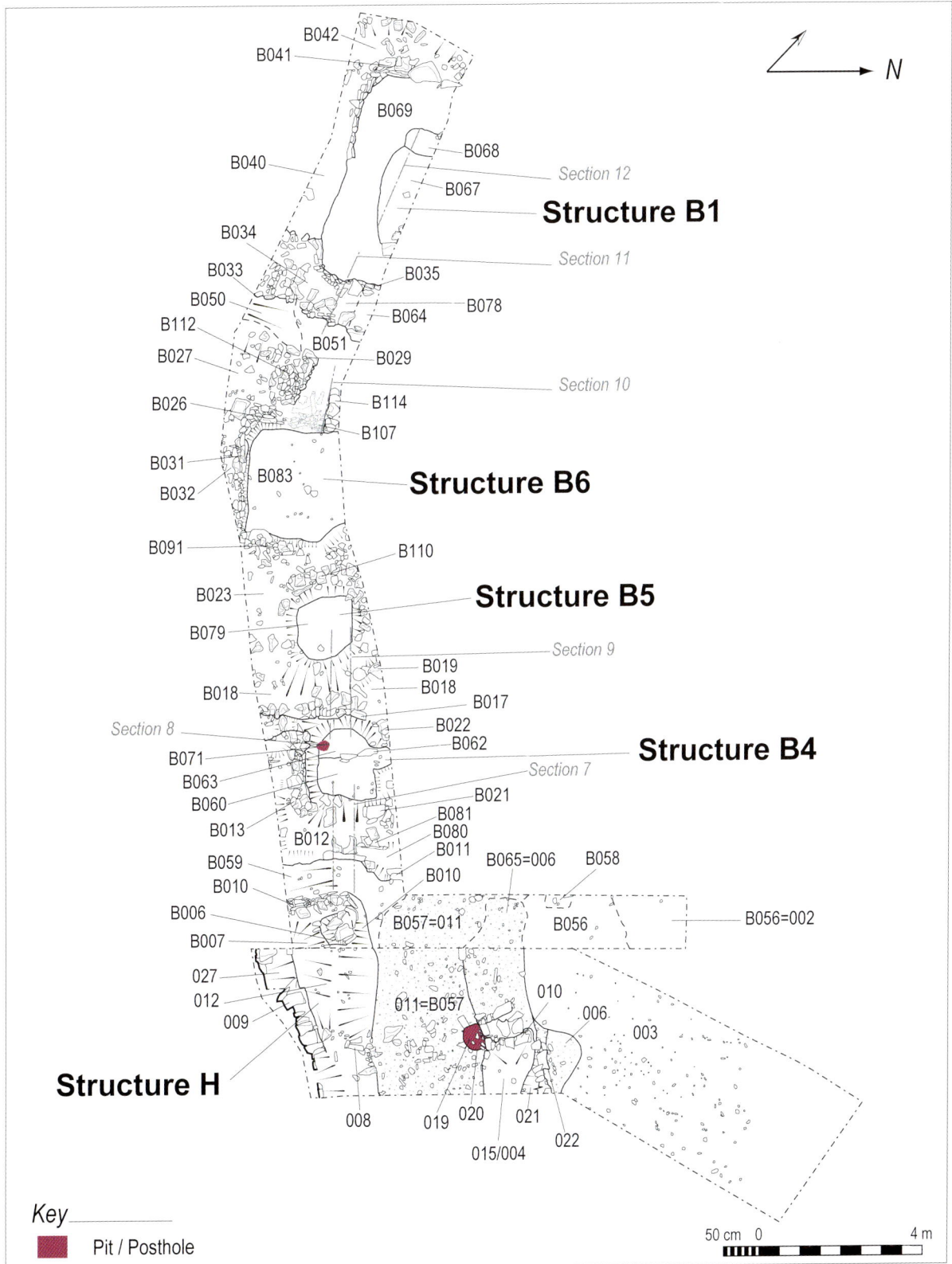

N

B042
B041
B069
B068
B040
Section 12

Structure B1

B067
Section 11
B034
B033
B035
B050
B064   B078
B112
B051
B027   B029
Section 10
B026   B114
B107

Structure B6

B031
B083
B032

B091   B110

Structure B5

B023
B079
Section 9
B019
B018
B018
B017
Section 8   B022
B071   B062

Structure B4

B063
Section 7
B060   B021
B013   B081
B012   B080
B059   B011
B010   B010
B006   B065=006   B058
B007   B056=002
B057=011   B056
027
012   011=B057   010
009   006   003

Structure H

008   019   020   021   022
015/004

Key

Pit / Posthole

50 cm 0   4 m

Trench B,

a slight bank, and the S edge was formed by a slight channel suggesting evidence of robbed stonework. The wall was 1.6m wide. A gap between two finished wall ends in the wall, 0.5m wide, was possibly an entrance. On the W side of the entrance the wall was entirely robbed out. On removal of the wall structure on the E side a similar gravel to 006 was present (014/015) underneath, along the same line and of the same composition, confirming the hypothesis that the W side had been robbed. The two gravel deposits were separated by the entrance paving stones, which had been set into the natural subsoil. Finds recovered from the wall and entrance gap 010 included local pottery, a flint flake and core, an iron object and unidentified charcoal fragments. A similar range of material was found in the turf core of the wall, and included local pottery, flint flakes and a gunflint.

Between this wall and the perimeter wall an occupation layer or floor surface, 011=B057, of loose sandy clay with frequent stone inclusions was excavated, and contained 26 sherds of local pottery, a chip of flint, and carbonised birch, oats, barley and hazelnut fragments. It is possible that this structure was robbed to construct the perimeter wall H, as evidenced by the pot sherds and other debris found in the basal turf layers 016 and 017 of Structure H. However, it is also possible that the early, robbed building is of the same date as H and was robbed to build Structures A or B nearby. Unfortunately no deposits linking this structure and Structures A and B were found, other than subsoil and topsoil, despite the whole area between the three structures being excavated, and so it is not possible to determine which of these scenarios is most likely.

On the S side of the entrance, in the building interior, a circular pit 019/020 was also excavated, 0.7m wide and 0.23m deep with a flat base, filled with 019, sandy loam with frequent stones. A body sherd of local pottery and fragments of wood were found preserved in the pit. On the N side of the wall a shallow drain or gutter 021/022 was excavated, measuring up to 0.3m wide, with a maximum depth of 0.07m. The building was situated in a low lying, flat area of the island, and it is clear that a drain would have been necessary to keep water away from the building in this part of the site. A deposit of silt (B058) excavated on the W side of the building, may possibly be the remains of a feature.

A series of three deposits in a small slot trench excavated through the E wall of B1 are also evidence of occupation that pre-dated Structure B. The earliest of these was a thick layer of peat ash, B078, thought to be a dump of hearth material. This was covered by B103, a sandy clay layer, and then B102, a deposit of charcoal with lenses of peat ash. Above B102, and directly under the earth core of the E wall of B1, was a light grey silt/clay B096. Significant assemblages of finds and environmental material were collected from these deposits considering such a small proportion of the deposits were excavated. Sherds of local pottery were found in layers B078, B096 and B102, a lump of slag, an indeterminate iron object and a flake and chunk of quartz were found in B102, and four pieces of flint in B096. Carbonised plant remains in B078 included birch, Scots pine type, oak, oat and six-row barley, and fragments of calcined mammal bone were also found. The environmental assemblage recovered from B102 was completely different in character from B096, B103 and B078, as it contained considerably larger amounts of cereal grains, chaff, and arable weeds, such as corn marigold, corn spurrey and stichwort. This significant assemblage is discussed further by Ramsay below in Chapter 11.

Charcoal samples from hearth and ash deposits B078, B102 and B103 were radiocarbon dated and produced ranges of AD1440-1630, AD1430-1620 and AD1445-1630 respectively. These dates were combined with dates from Phase 4 in modelling (see Chapter 13, below).

Phase 4: Construction and use of Structure B

This phase includes the construction and use of the four buildings, B1, B4, B5 and B6 in Structure B.

B4

At the E end of the complex, the E, W and S walls, and interior, of B4 were excavated. The walls comprised earth cores and stone faces of un-mortared stone. The E wall of the building

Section 1: Trench 1 2002 E facing section

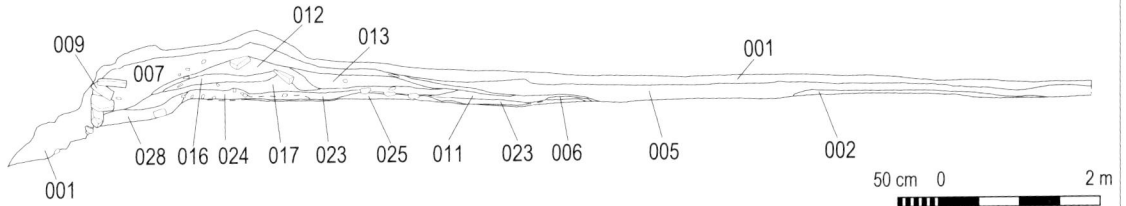

009
012
013
007
001
028 016 024 017 023 025 011 023 006 005 002
001

50 cm 0 2 m

Section 2: N facing section through interior slump deposits in B4

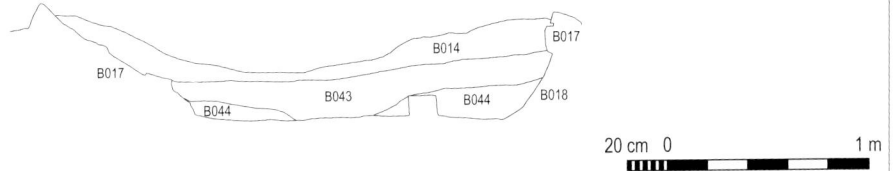

B014
B017
B017
B043
B044
B018
B044

20 cm 0 1 m

Section 3: N facing section through interior slump deposits in B5

B020
B046
B045

20 cm 0 1 m

Section 4: S facing section through interior slump deposits in B6

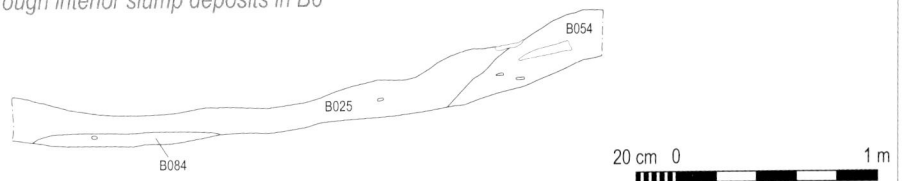

B054
B025
B084

20 cm 0 1 m

Section 5: N facing section through deposits between B1 and B6

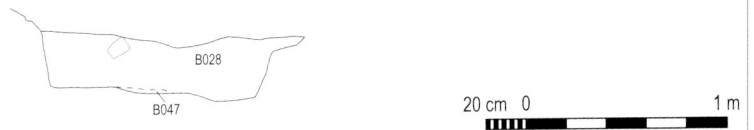

B028
B047

20 cm 0 1 m

Section 6: W facing section through B1

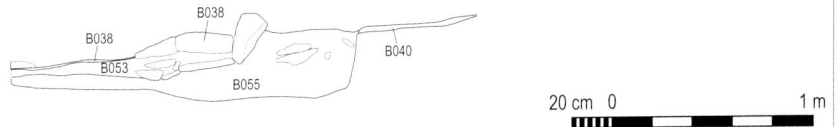

B038
B038
B040
B053
B055

20 cm 0 1 m

Illus 5.13 Trench B sections (1)

Section 7: N facing section through E wall of B4

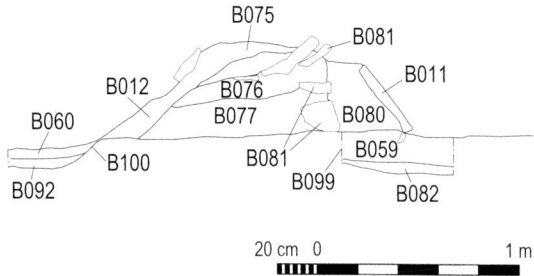

B075
B081
B012
B076
B011
B060
B077
B080
B100
B081
B059
B092
B099
B082

20 cm 0   1 m

Section 8: E facing section of posthole B071 in B4

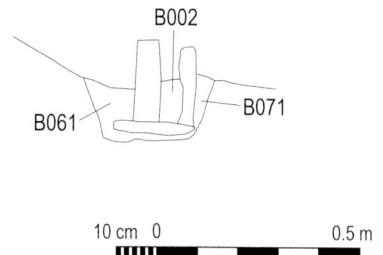

B002
B061
B071

10 cm 0   0.5 m

Section 9: S facing section through W wall of B4

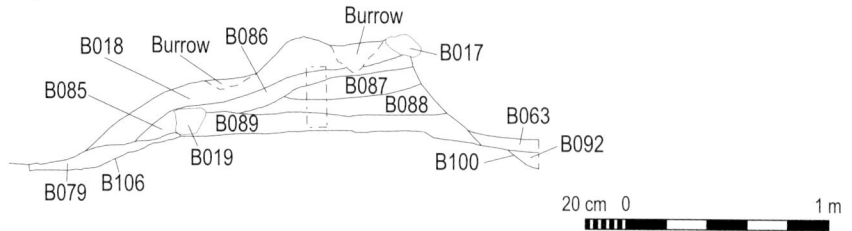

B018   Burrow   B086   Burrow   B017
B085
B087
B088
B063
B089
B100
B092
B019
B079   B106

20 cm 0   1 m

Section 10: S facing section of W wall of B6

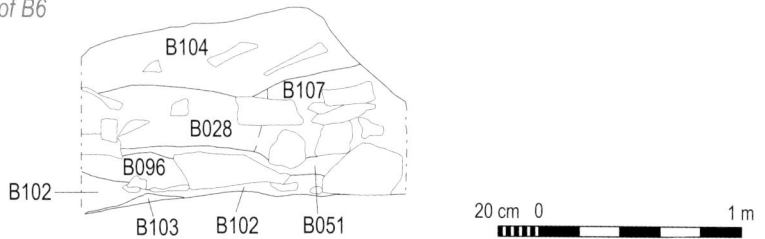

B104
B107
B028
B096
B102
B103   B102   B051

20 cm 0   1 m

Section 11: N facing section of E wall of B1

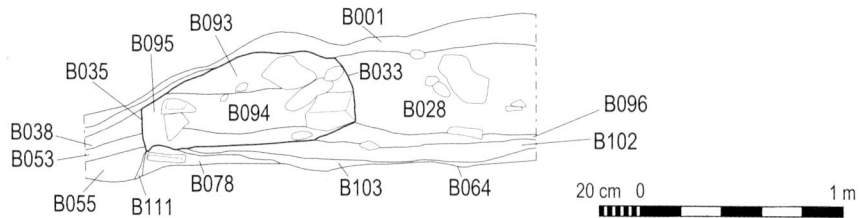

B093   B001
B095
B035
B033
B038
B094
B028
B096
B053
B102
B055   B078   B103   B064
B111

20 cm 0   1 m

Section 12: N facing section of hearth in B1

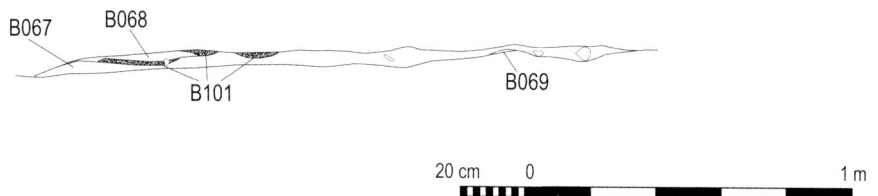

B067   B068
B101
B069

Key

▪ Charcoal

20 cm 0   1 m

Illus 5.14 Trench B sections (2)

had been built directly on to the old ground surface B099 and had a partially-preserved interior stone face B021 and an exterior stone face B081. Lying between these faces was a series of earth core deposits (contexts B012, B075, B076 and B077). The internal face B021 survived in a fragmentary condition, perhaps having been partly demolished and robbed. In places it survived to three courses high. The external face B081 survived in a much better condition, comprised unbonded, coursed stones, and was 1.5m long (disappearing into context B012 at each end) and 0.35m wide, surviving to a height of up to five courses. Both wall faces B021 and B081 had been set directly on the old ground surface B099 (see Phase 3 above).

At some point, the E external side of this E wall was re-faced with four large orthostats and some coursed stone walling (B011), and the gap between the original wall face (B081) and this new face (B011) was filled with an earth core deposit B080. Secondary wall face B011 also formed the W face to an entrance gap or passageway to the E of B4. The E side of the 0.8m wide gap was defined by the terminal of Structure H (see Phase 3 above).

The W wall of B4 was common to B5, and was also set directly on to an old ground surface (B105). This wall also had two stone faces – B017 internal to B4, and B019 internal to B5. In between these faces lay a series of earth core deposits (contexts B018, B086-89). Stone face B017 was abutted by the upper wall core layer B018 and by wall core layer B086 (see B5 below). However, wall face (B017) did not extend to the base of the wall and was apparently set into intermediate wall core layer B087 – the lower course of face B017 sat at approximately 0.5m above the floor level of B4 and comprised unbonded, coursed stones. The wall was 1.8m long, and it appeared to run for a further 0.8m to the S into the fabric of the S wall of B4 (although this was not established through excavation). It survived to a height of two courses.

The interior stone face (B013) of the S wall of B4, as the interior stone face (B017) of the E wall, was set at knee height – the absence of stone below this level remains to be explained. Wall face B013 also backed on to an earth core (B012), shared with the E wall of the building. B013 consisted of unbonded, coursed stones surviving to a height of four courses, up to 2.1m long and with a maximum visible width of 0.5m. No stone facing was found in the SW corner of the interior, where a hollow in the turf walls was filled with turf slump. This was probably once a gap in the wall that enabled access from the interior of B4 to the perimeter wall H and a view across to the Ness mainland.

The N wall of B4 only partly intruded into the trench. A gap in the N wall formed an entrance up to 0.6m wide, although originally it may well have been wider. The W part of the N wall had a stone face (B022), which was a continuation of the interior W face B017, and the E part of the N wall was a continuation of the E wall earth core (B012). Face B022 comprised only four angular stones, protruding from the N trench edge and this section of walling survived to a height of two courses, was 0.5m long, and had a visible width of 0.3m. The E part of the N wall was, similarly, formed of a return to the E wall. This E part of the N wall was formed of context (B012) (described above). In the E wall of B4, core layer (B012) lay on top a series of layers of earth core, B075, then B076, mixed deposits of sand and silt, then the initial earth core deposit (B077) a slightly compact dark brown silty clay.

The interior of building B4 had a sunken floor cut B100 1.3m x 0.9m, and 0.15m deep with a sharp break of slope at the top, sides at an angle of 45° and rounding to a flat base. The floor was cut through an old ground surface/topsoil B099, and contained an initial occupation deposit B092 of compact mid grey/brown clay with charcoal flecks, charcoal concentrations, and small lumps of peat ash.

Above this occupation deposit, on the W side of the entrance a small stone kerb B062 divided the interior of the structure into two halves. The kerb comprised two large, angular stones laid end-to-end on a N-S alignment on the W side of the entrance to the structure and lying either side of this kerb were two further occupation-phase deposits, B060 and B063. The difference in the character of these deposits reflects the division of space within the building and, presumably, a difference in use of the two halves. In the E half, dark brown silty clay B060 was greasy to the touch and contained charcoal flecks and trampled fragments of pottery – all indicating that this was an occupation deposit created through the trampling of the floor of the structure in this area. B063 was a light brown cleaner silty sand and contained no such charcoal

Illus 5.15 Structure B4, from the NW excavated, Illus 5.16 Area S of B011 after removal of B049 at entrance onto site and gap in perimeter wall and Illus 5.17 Slump and hollow in SW corner of B4 filling access to perimeter wall

flecks and pottery fragments. It may be that deposit B063 lay under a piece of furniture, defined to the E by kerb B062. Further evidence for this was found in the form of a small posthole at the S end of the kerbed area. The cut B071 for this posthole was oval in plan, measuring 0.33m by 0.28m, and had a depth of 0.15m. The lower fill B061 of the posthole was a compact sandy clay, into which had been set a flat-laid stone (a post-pad) and three upright packing stones. The latter, which protruded above the surface of silty sand B063 were arranged so as to form a triangular post setting. The space in the middle of these packing stones had been filled by a deposit of sandy silt B072.

Finds and environmental material were recovered from the occupation deposits and wall cores of B4. Two sherds of local pottery, three quartz flakes, five quartz chips, a flint flake and an iron object were found in the E wall core layers, together with an environmental assemblage of birch, hazel, heather, larch, Scots pine type, burnt peat, hawthorn, dog rose, oat and barley grains and saithe and unidentified fish bones. Two body sherds of local pottery, a chunk of quartz, mammal bone fragments and barley grains were found in occupation deposit B060 E of the kerbed feature, and worked quartz, birch, heather type charcoal, burnt peat and saithe bone were found in occupation deposit B092.

Radiocarbon dating of occupation deposit B092 returned a date range of AD1445-1635.

B5

B5 lay directly to the W of B4, and the two buildings shared a common wall. The S wall of B5 had no apparent stone face, and comprised a continuation of earth wall cores B023 and B018, ie the earth cores of the E and W walls of the building. The E wall of B5 also formed the W wall of B4. The uppermost context forming this common wall was earth core layer B018, which abutted the interior face of B5 to the W and the interior face of B4 to the E. The deposit had also slumped somewhat beyond face B019 to the W.

The W wall of B5 was shared in common with the E wall of adjacent building B6, with an internal stone face B110 surviving to two courses in height set into the wall core B023. Parts of the wall comprised orthostats with a maximum height of 0.3m. The overall length of the wall face was 2m, and it was aligned N-S, but curved towards the E at both its S and N ends, also forming a partial face to the N and S walls of the building. A slot was excavated through the W wall of B4/E wall of B5, and the upper wall core layer B018 was found to overlie a series of layers of earth core, silty clays B086 then B087, B088, a mixed layer of silty sand and clay and clay B089 at the base, which appeared to abut B019, the stone face of coursed, unbonded stones forming the wall interior to B5, surviving to a height of up to three courses.

B5 had a sunken floor cut B106, sub-rectangular in plan. The base of the cut measured 1m by 1.1m and had been made through the old ground surface. The cut was filled by an occupation deposit B079, of dark brown clayey silt with frequent flecks of charcoal, occasional crushed sherds of pottery, and occasional, small, angular and sub-angular stones.

As with B4, no hearth was found, but unlike B4, there was no division of space and there were no features within the interior of B5. A piece of worked quartz and a sherd of local pottery were found in the wall core layers in the W wall, with an environmental assemblage of alder, birch, hazel, Scots pine type, oak, oat, barley, indeterminate cereal and burnt peat. A sherd of local pottery and birch charcoal, carbonised barley and mammal bone fragments were found in occupation deposit B079. Radiocarbon dating of occupation deposit B079 returned a date range of AD1470-1645.

B6

B6, a larger, sub-rectangular building, lay to the W of B5, with the E wall of B6=W wall of B5. In the interior of B6, this wall had a stone face B091 of unbonded, coursed stones, and some orthostats, and behind this lay an earth core B023. The wall as a whole survived to four courses high. The earth core B023 was exposed in plan but not excavated. The S wall of B6, which was slightly bowed, also had an interior stone face B031 of unbonded, coursed angular stones

Illus 5.18 Stone kerb and posthole in B4 and Illus 5.19 Structure B5 from N

Illus 5.20 Structure B6 from the N and Illus 5.21 Gap between B1 and B6 (on LH side of photograph) showing access to H

surviving to up to four courses high. To the S of the wall face B031 lay earth core B032, a silt with occasional stones exposed in plan but not excavated. The W wall of B6 had an interior stone face B026 of unbonded, coursed stones, surviving to a height of 0.55m, an exterior stone face B029 of unbonded, coursed stones 0.55m high, and an earth core B027 which was exposed in plan but not excavated.

Removal of slump layer (B028), which partly lay over the W wall of B6, revealed a blocked entrance from a passageway W of B6, into the building. This entrance had a N jamb B114 and a S jamb B112 of coursed stonework up to 0.9m high, and the gap between the two jambs had been filled by context B107 – a blocking deposit of silty clay faced with coursed unbonded stone on its E side built so as to continue the interior stone face B026 of the W wall of B6 to the N. The removal of B107 revealed an underlying deposit B102 that also ran under the W wall of B6 (see Phase 3 above).

In the gap between B1 and B6, a silt sand deposit B050 of the partially-collapsed remains of blocks of turf were found which had been used to block the gap between the S walls of buildings B1 and B6 so that there was a continuous turf bank along the cliff edge. Access to this bank from B6 was afforded by the gap between B1 and B6, and may suggest that there was a second loophole or opening in the turf bank here, similar to that suggested in the S wall of B4, through which the Ness mainland, only 30m across from the building, could be viewed. Adjacent and below B050 a deposit of greasy black clay B051, perhaps an occupation deposit, was found in the gap between buildings B1 and B6, and in the blocked entrance through the W wall of B6 (underlying the blocking deposit B107 in that entrance).

Like the other buildings, B6 had a sunken floor cut B113, 0.15m deep and 2.85m x 2.5m, through old topsoil, down to the upper surface of the natural which formed an earth floor B083 exposed in plan but not excavated. No features were evident in the interior of B6, and apart from three sherds of local pottery found in wall core layer B032, the only deposit to contain artefactual and environmental material was B107, which contained five body sherds and one neck sherd of local pottery, a piece of flint, and carbonised remains of birch, hazel, heather type, beech, larch, spruce/fir, Scots pine type, grass/sedge, oat, barley, burnt peat and mammal bone fragments, suggesting that midden was used as blocking material.

B1

B1 was the largest building in Structure B, measuring up to 5m x 4m internally (only around half of the building was uncovered in Trench B). B1 lay to the W of B6, and was separated from it by a gap of around 1m. The W wall of B1 and the W part of the S wall had a common interior stone face B041, comprising unmortared, orthostats and coursed stones standing to a maximum height of one orthostat or four courses. Behind stone face B041 lay earth wall core layers B040 for the S wall and B042 for the W wall. Up to 4.1m by 1m of B040 was uncovered and had slumped into the interior of the structure at a point where the stone face of the S wall had collapsed. B042 was virtually indistinguishable from B040.

The E wall of B1 had an interior stone face B035 up to 0.6m high, of unbonded, coursed stones of which up to seven courses survived and a similar exterior stone face B033

which survived to a maximum height of six courses (0.7m). Lying between these was an earth wall core made up of layers of silty clay B034, B093, B094 and B095, which were investigated in a slot through the N part of the wall. The basal turf layer B095 was set onto B096, a layer of ash that pre-dated the building (see Phase 3 above).

The interior of B1 also had a sunken floor, comprising a sub-rectangular cut B111, 5m x 1.6m. The cut was 0.15m deep, and made through an old topsoil deposit B070 down to the upper surface of the natural subsoil, which had been utilised as an earthen floor. This compact, charcoal-flecked floor deposit B069 extended over a maximum area of 5.8m x 2m N-S (disappearing into the N trench edge). Lying on top of this floor was a hearth, located towards the W end of the interior of B1 and only partially exposed in the trench. The hearth comprised three distinct layers of peat ash and charcoal B068, B101 and B067. The presence of the hearth in B1, the largest building in Structure B, suggests that it was the main area of occupation in Structure B.

Building B1 contained by the far the richest artefactual and environmental assemblage of all the buildings excavated in Structure B, due partly to the presence of thicker occupation deposits and hearth deposits. The wall core layers also contained finds and carbonised plant remains. The upper earth core deposits of the S and W walls of B1 contained a lump of slag, five body sherds and a neck sherd of local pottery and birch, Scots pine type, burnt peat and oat remains. A large assemblage derives from the slot trench excavated through the E wall of the building. Here three rim sherds, one with fingernail decoration, 21 body sherds and one neck sherd were found in deposits B093-B095, and the carbonised remains included birch, spruce, Scots pine type, willow, alder, heather type, ash, oat and barley, as well as carbonised fish and mammal bone fragments. The occupation deposits excavated in the gap between B1 and B6,

Illus 5.22 Structure B1, from the N and Illus 5.23 Hearth B067 after removal of peat ash B068 and charcoal B101 in Structure B1, from the S

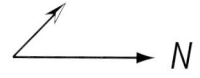

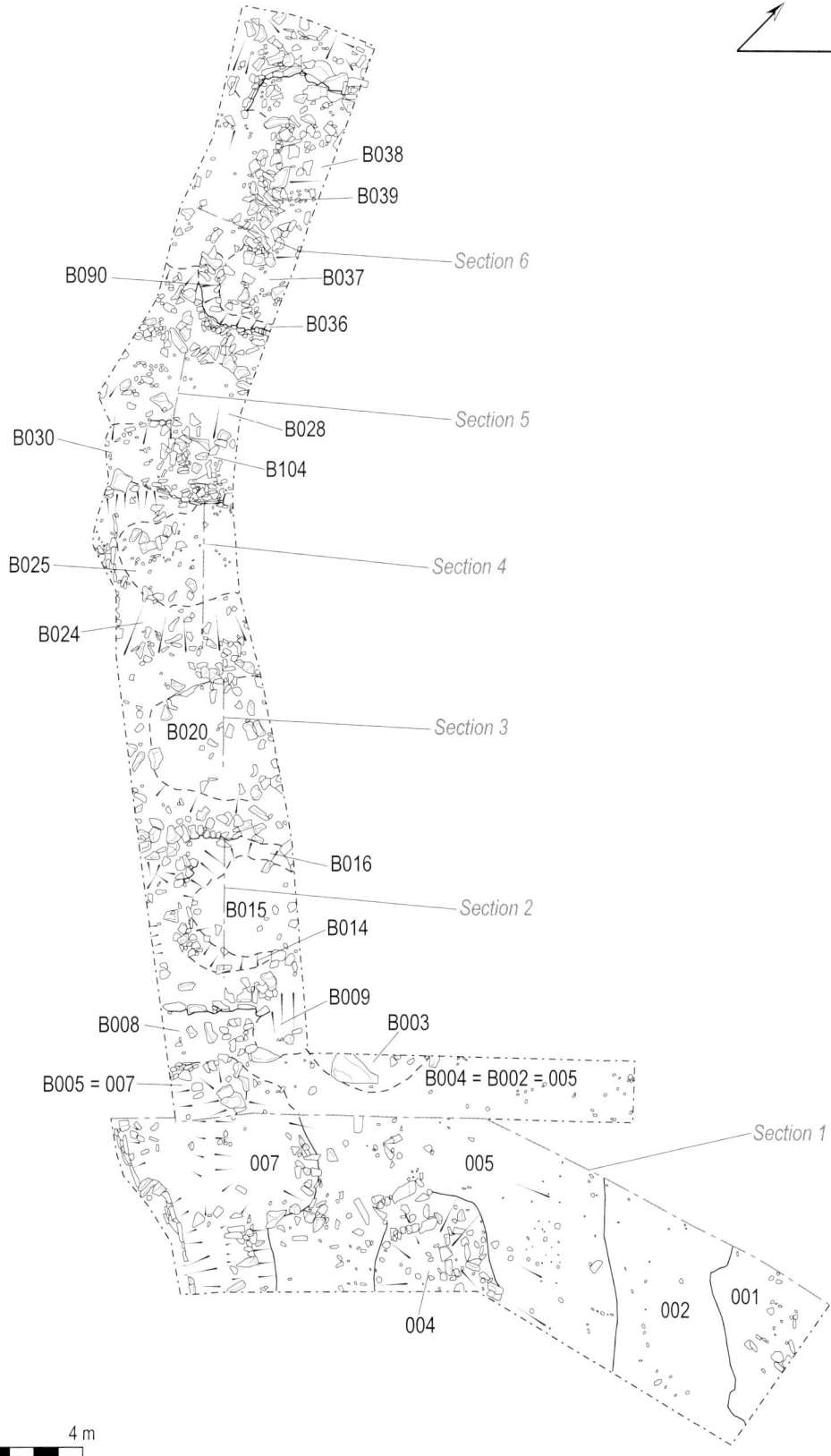

N

B038

B039

Section 6

B090   B037

B036

Section 5

B028

B030

B104

Section 4

B025

B024

Section 3

B020

B016

Section 2

B015

B014

B009

B008   B003

B005 = 007   B004 = B002 = 005

Section 1

007   005

001

002

004

50 cm 0   4 m

Illus 5.24 Phase 5 plan

and within B1 itself contained larger artefactual/environmental assemblages. 32 sherds of local pottery, two iron objects and two lumps of glassy black slag were found in occupation deposits lying between buildings B1 and B6, together with an environmental assemblage of birch, heather type, Scots pine type, oak, oat, barley and mammal bone fragments. In addition to this 18 sherds of local pottery, four of which were decorated, and mammal bone fragments were found in the earth floor of B1. The hearth deposits contained 11 sherds of local pottery, and four flakes and a chip of flint. Plant remains included alder, birch and heather type, burnt peat, oat and barley fragments, and carbonised mammal bone and fish fragments were also recovered.

Charcoal samples from hearth deposits B068 and B101 were radiocarbon dated and produced ranges of AD1520-1955 and AD1480-1645 respectively. These dates were combined with other dates from Phase 3 and modelled to produce a range of AD1500-1670 and AD1485-1645 respectively at 95.4% confidence (see Chapter 13, below).

Phase 5: Post-abandonment
Area E of Structure B

Table 5.4 Phase 5 context descriptions, finds and environmental on CD at back of book

To the E of B4, and in between that structure and Structure H, a series of post-abandonment deposits were excavated which included initial wash/collapse from buildings B3, B4, and Structure H (contexts B049 and B056), further structural collapse (B048 and B009) and final silting/washing of material (B002-B0044=005 and B008).

Context B002/3/4=005 covered the N part the trench, and at its S side, 005 overlay B005=007, the uppermost slumped turf layer of Structure H, indicating that B002/3/4=005 was final slump and wash from the perimeter wall collapse. Silty clay B008 was found in the gap between building B4 and Structure H, also extending beyond that gap for a distance to the N, to B009, which was found to be the same as B003-5, and again represented final wash from those collapsed structures. Below B009, in the gap between Structure H and the E wall of B4, silty clays B048 and B049 were both a result of post-abandonment wash/collapse from B4 and H.

27 body sherds, four rim sherds and two neck sherds of local pottery were found in the post-abandonment layers in this area. Two late medieval brown glazed pottery sherds were also found, with a gunflint, two flint flakes and a flint chunk. The environmental assemblage included the familiar range of birch, conifer, heather type, Scots pine type, hazel, oat and barley grains, burnt peat and mammal bone fragments seen in earlier contexts on the site.

B4

Illus 5.25 N facing section through slump in B4

In the interior of B4 a sequence of post-abandonment deposits were excavated, from the latest, B015, through B014, and B043, to the earliest, B044. Deposit B015, was roughly circular in plan, as a final wash of material filling the hollow created by the preceding post-abandonment contexts. The stratigraphically intermediate contexts B014 and B043 represent collapsed earth wall core/turf walling spread across the entire interior of the structure, each up to 0.15m thick. B043 contained occasional, small, abraded fragments of pottery, small, angular stones, and flecks and small lumps of charcoal and filled the whole interior of the structure and sloped down from the walls of the building towards the centre. The earliest post-abandonment context B044 represents the initial collapse of the wall core/turf walling and/or roofing and contained frequent charcoal flecks and lumps and very small fragments of highly abraded pottery, and lay in a ring around the fringes of the interior of B4, extending into that interior from the inner wall faces by up to 0.5m. B044 had a banked profile, being deepest where it abutted the interior wall faces and thinning towards the centre of the building before petering out. It lay directly on the occupation-phase contexts associated with B4.

Eight body sherds, two shoulder sherds, three lumps of slag a quartz flake, a flint flake, an iron nail shaft and a gunflint were recovered from the slump deposits in B4. The environmental deposits included the same range of species seen in the area to the E of Structure B, but also included sheep/goat bones, saithe, herring and sand eel bones, bird bone, limpet and crab shell fragments.

B5

The latest post-abandonment deposits in B5 were B020 and B045 both up to 0.17m thick. B020 contained occasional flecks of charcoal, abraded pieces of pottery, and small stones and extended over the larger part of the interior of B5. B045 contained occasional lumps of charcoal and small, sub-angular stones, lay in the E half of a bowl-like hollow in the interior of B5. This hollow had been created by the walls of the structure and by two banks of earlier post-abandonment silty clays, B046 with a banked profile which abutted the interior edge of the W wall of the building, and earlier deposit B085, banked up against the interior edge of the E wall of B5. All the post-abandonment deposits represents material which had collapsed or washed into the interior of B5 from the walls and roof of the building - B020 and B045 may represent collapsed turf walling which spread and washed to cover a large part of the interior, B046 and B085 may derive from discrete collapse events when individual sections of wall core fell into the interior of the structure from its W and E walls, respectively.

18 body sherds and three rim sherds of local pottery, and a body sherd of brown glaze late medieval pottery were found in the slump deposits in B5. A lump of slag, four quartz chips, two quartz flakes, fragments of iron and a gunflint were also found. The environmental assemblage included Scots pine type, birch, heather type, spruce/fir, burnt peat, oat and barley grains and calcined mammal and fish bone fragments.

B6

Another distinct series of silty clay deposits, representing discrete collapses of wall material, filled the interior of B6 – deposits B030, found in the SW corner and extending into the interior of the building, B073, in the NW corner, and B074 in the SE of the interior.

Silty clay B074 overlay B024, an earlier and more extensive collapse of earth wall core material into the E part of the interior. Below B024, B030 and B073, B025 extended across the entire excavated portion of the interior of B6 to a depth of up to 0.25m and represents another, earlier and yet more extensive, collapse of the walls into the interior. This deposit was preceded by what appears to be an initial slump from the E wall B054 located on the E edge of the interior abutting the interior edge of the E wall, and an initial post-abandonment accumulation on the floor of the building B084, possibly from a turf roof.

A rich and varied artefactual assemblage was recovered from the post-abandonment deposits from this building, and from the gap between buildings B1 and B6. 174 sherds of local pottery were found, including nine rim sherds, one of which was decorated, one neck sherd and one decorated body sherd were recovered. In addition to local pottery, several other finds of late medieval/post-medieval date were recovered from the interior of B1. These included a modern earthenware brown glazed sherd, and an unglazed undecorated Scottish Medieval Reduced ware medieval sherd. Also ten pieces of worked quartz, a fire flint, two square-headed nails and fragments of iron nails, a green neck/rim sherd of late 17th/early 18th century glass, four lumps of slag, a gunflint, a lead pistol ball, a lead musket ball and a silver sixpence of Elizabeth I dating to 1580. The environmental assemblage included the range of species seen in other buildings in the phase.

B1

The gap between B1 and B6 was filled by another series of post-abandonment deposits B104, B028, B047 and B052, representing collapsed/slumped turf deriving from the N wall of Structure B6, the S wall of B1 and the N wall of B6, early post-abandonment accumulation of material in the gap between B1 and B6, and initial silting up of the area between B1 and B6 respectively.

The interior of building B1 was filled with a series of deposits, B036, B037, B038, B039, B053, B055 and B090 from the initial silting up of the interior of the structure, the collapse of its S wall, the collapse of turf walling and roofing, and the final filling up of the interior of the collapsed structure by wash/wind-blown soils.

The upper post-abandonment context B036 abutted the E interior wall face B035 of B1, sloping from E to W into the interior, and covered B037=B038, an earlier post-abandonment

Illus 5.26 N facing section through slump deposit in B5 and Illus 5.27 N facing section through slump deposit in B6

Illus 5.28 Excavation in Trench B, Illus 5.29 Trench B after topsoil clean-off from the E, and Illus 5.30 Slump between buildings B1 and B6

deposit with a relatively level surface and only 0.02m thick in the bottom of the bowl-like feature that had been created by the collapse of B1. Below this a deposit of rubble of stones B039 up to 0.25m thick and in a linear band aligned approximately E-W and coinciding with a similarly-sized gap in the interior face of the S wall of B1 was the result of the inward collapse of the interior face of that wall. Behind rubble (B039), to the S, the earth core had slumped S.

B039 lay on top of a series of earlier post-abandonment contexts, B053 0.2m thick, with charcoal flecks and stones lying in the N part of the exposed section of the interior of B1,

B055 0.31m thick extended across most of the interior of B1, and B090, a small, initial post-abandonment deposit at the E end of the interior, overlying the floor of the building. Silt B053 and silt/sand B055 may represent collapsed turf walling deriving from the various walls of the building.

A series of post-abandonment deposits were also found in the gap between buildings B1 and B6. Uppermost of these was B104, collapsed/slumped turf walling in a break in the W wall of B6. Below this, extending into this break in the wall but also found throughout the whole of the gap between B1 and B6, was B028, collapsed turf walling from the upper E wall of B1 and the W wall of B6, then B047 which was found in a small area in the centre of the gap between B1 and B6, and a thin layer of light grey silt B052 which abutted the E wall of B1 and W wall of B6. In the area between the two buildings a rich assemblage was recovered, including a pinkish fabric/ orange/brown glaze post-medieval pottery sherd, a green body shard of 19th century glass, two lumps of porous slag, three fragments of furnace lining, three iron objects, a complete iron rove, an unusual copper alloy/iron object, a flint flake and a billon plack (8d Scots) coin of James VI, of issue 1583-90, type 3.

A much smaller assemblage in comparison to the assemblage from neighbouring building B6 was recovered from the slump deposits in B1. These included 14 body sherds and a neck sherd of local pottery, two quartz chips and a quartz flake. The environmental assemblage was also smaller and included birch, heather, Scots pine type, oat, barley and burnt peat, as well as burnt mammal bone fragments.

Phase 6: Topsoil

Topsoil B001=1=050-053 covered Trench B and the bridge footings trenches to a depth of up to 0.3m. Finds recovered from the topsoil included 93 body sherds, six shoulder sherds, nine rim sherds and one decorated neck sherd of local pottery, three flakes and a chip of quartz, two flint flakes, an iron nail and a lead pistol ball. Unidentified charcoal, and sheep/goat, mammal and fish bone was also recovered. Finds from the mainland footings Trench 2 included a possible gunflint flake and two body sherds of local pottery and are a hint at activity off the site, despite the lack of structures identified.

Endnotes

[1] All radiocarbon dates are calibrated at 95% confidence: see Chapter 13

Table 5.5 Phase 6 context descriptions, finds and environmental on CD at back of book

Illus 6.1 Excavating in Trench C

S tructure C is a sub-rectangular building situated between Structures A and D on the S side of the island. Excavations in Area C investigated the northern two thirds of the building, and an area immediately surrounding it, and identified it as a large barn, with a corn-drying kiln in the north end. Six phases of activity were identified, from earliest to latest: (1) bedrock and natural subsoil, (2) original ground surfaces, (3) the construction and use of the kiln barn, (4) robbing and collapse of the kiln and construction of later small shelters, (5) final collapse, and (6) topsoil.

The remains of the Phase 2 old ground surface were found in and around Structure C, and contained carbonised oat grains that had probably been dropped whilst the kiln barn was in use. The kiln barn (Phase 3) was built onto this old ground surface. Slot trenches excavated through the walls of the building showed they were constructed from outer skins of stonework and inner earthen cores. Although charcoal, local pottery, a flint flake, an iron object and a globule of lead were found in the earth cores of the walls, compared with the number of artefacts found in the walls of other buildings on the site this was a small number. This suggests that Structure C was built on a relatively 'clean' and previously unoccupied part of the site. This was confirmed by the analysis of soil samples taken from the walls of the building (see Chapter 12, below).

Most of the other Phase 3 finds from the layers associated with the use of the kiln barn, flue and kiln bowl comprised mainly sherds of local pottery. A flat stone slab found at the end of the flue in the entrance to the kiln bowl may have been a 'spark stone' to prevent sparks from setting fire to the grain and straw over the kiln bowl when in use. Conifer and spruce charcoal, burnt peat and iron nails found in these deposits demonstrate that peat and driftwood fired the kiln. In all, only small quantities of cereal grain were found in the kiln, suggesting it was cleaned out after its final use. No evidence for carbonised grain or burnt wood was found in the kiln bowl itself, but small amounts of carbonised oat and barley grains, and willow, birch, ash and oak charcoal were found in peat ash at the south end of the flue. No chaff was found amongst the grain, suggesting that it was thoroughly cleaned before being dried. Radiocarbon dating of the kiln deposits suggests that it was used

Illus 6.2 Interpretation plan (opposite)

N

KILN PLATFORM

FLUE

KILN

KILN BARN

Key

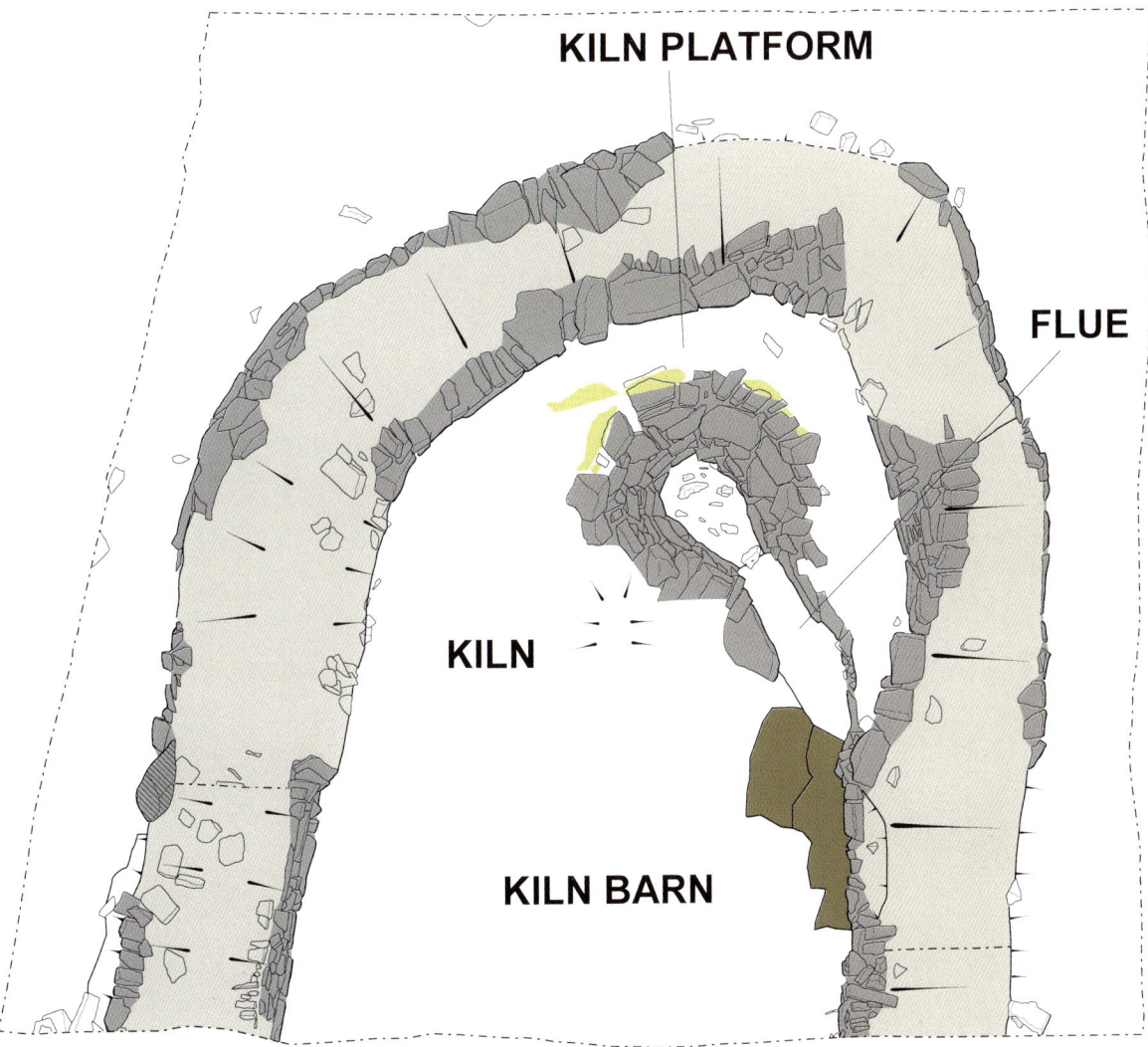

Clay
Orthostat
Peat ash
Stone facing
Turf walls

50 cm   0   2 m

between AD1460-1640.[1]

After the kiln had gone out of use it collapsed and was abandoned. The next phase of activity, Phase 4, then followed, with three small turf and rubble shelters (C1, 2 and 3) built into the ruins at the north end of the barn. These shelters were built from the collapsed turf roofing and turf and stone walls from the abandoned kiln below, and subsequently most of the artefacts found in them actually derive from the kiln barn below. They include small assemblages of local pottery, a shard of seventeenth century glass and environmental material. These small shelters then themselves collapsed (Phase 5). Again, the artefacts from the collapsed shelters derive from the turf material of the original kiln barn. They include a shard of bottle glass from no later than the seventeenth century and a pistol ball found in the collapsed east kiln barn wall. As with other buildings on the site, the lack of any later finds, such as mass-produced ceramic, in Phase 5, and an almost total lack of artefactual material in the topsoil confirm that the site does not seem to have been occupied or in use after the seventeenth century on anything but a small, local scale for example as shelter overnight when fishing.

Overall the assemblages of material from Structure C were small in comparison to nearby Structures A, B and D and may indicate that the kiln had a short life. The lack of occupation material in the wall cores of the kiln barn indicate that it was built towards the beginning of the occupation on the island, but unfortunately due to the lack of surviving deposits associated with the use of the kiln, there are limited possibilities for modelling and therefore refining the radiocarbon dates further than the general mid-fifteenth to mid-seventeenth time scale (see Chapter 13 below). The discovery of the kiln barn is particularly significant as it adds a new dimension to the interpretation of the occupation on Dùn Èistean. Other buildings on the site have revealed evidence for drying and processing small quantities of grain at the hearth, but the kiln barn is evidence for the drying of larger quantities of grain, and suggests the presence of a larger and more permanent community on the island.

Results

with Tessa Poller

Trench locations

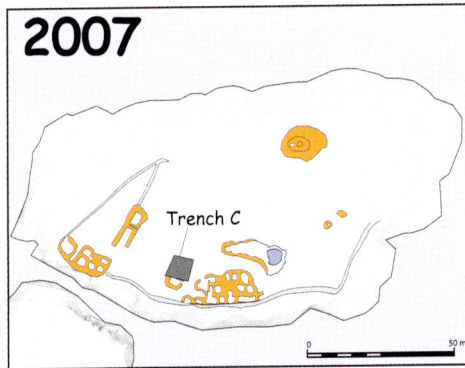

2007 Trench C: 6.8m long when first opened, then extended by 1.5m to the S to cover final area of 8.3m N-S, and 8.3m wide at the S end, narrowing to 7m at the N end and covering two thirds of Structure C, including C1, C2 and C3 and the N part of C4 and outside the building to the N, E and W.

Aims:
• To test the topographic survey conclusions that Structure C was divided into four separate parts (C1 to C4) and that it may have been a dwelling house of the Norse architectural tradition.
• To investigate that whether, due to the degree of preservation of the walls, Site C was occupied later than B or D, or perhaps at the same time as A.

Work completed: Excavation and sampling of all deposits down to natural subsoil and bedrock over entire trench. Although structure left upstanding, cuttings taken through walls.

Phase 1: Bedrock and natural subsoils

The gneiss bedrock C044 formed a level plateau covered by degraded bedrock layers C034 found outside the structure on the N side, mottled sandy silt C037, and sand C083 in the NE corner of the trench.

Phase 2: Original ground surfaces

Above the bedrock a sandier deposit of natural subsoil C083 and the remnants of a relict turf layer C071 was identified. A chip of quartz and carbonised oat grains were found in this context.

Table 6.1 Phase 2 context descriptions, finds and environmental on CD at back of book

Phase 3: Construction and use of the kiln barn

A stone-faced wall with an earth core C004 defined the exterior of the structure. In the S part of the trench the E and W walls were up to 1.3m wide at the base, had an earth core with an outer and inner skin of stones and varied in height between 0.5m and 0.8m. The outer skin (contexts C061 and C064) consisted of upright orthostats with stones placed lengthwise in between earth layers, pinning together the core and thus adding stability to the construction. The inner skin (contexts C062 and C065) differed on either side of the structure, being regular on the W side, utilising small stones in the upper courses, while on the E side the stone face was more irregular. This may reflect that the stonework of the lower walls on the E side would have been covered by the flue and therefore would not have been visible. On the outer face the stone was visible at the same height of *c* 0.7m all around the building.

     A slot 1m wide was excavated through the wall on the W side. The wall core (contexts C076, C075, C074, C059, C056) consisted of alternating layers of grey sandy silt with mottled dark purplish grey and yellow sandy silt deposits which were interpreted as cut turfs (this was

Table 6.2 Phase 3 context descriptions, finds and environmental on CD at back of book

Illus 6.4 Structure C excavated
from S

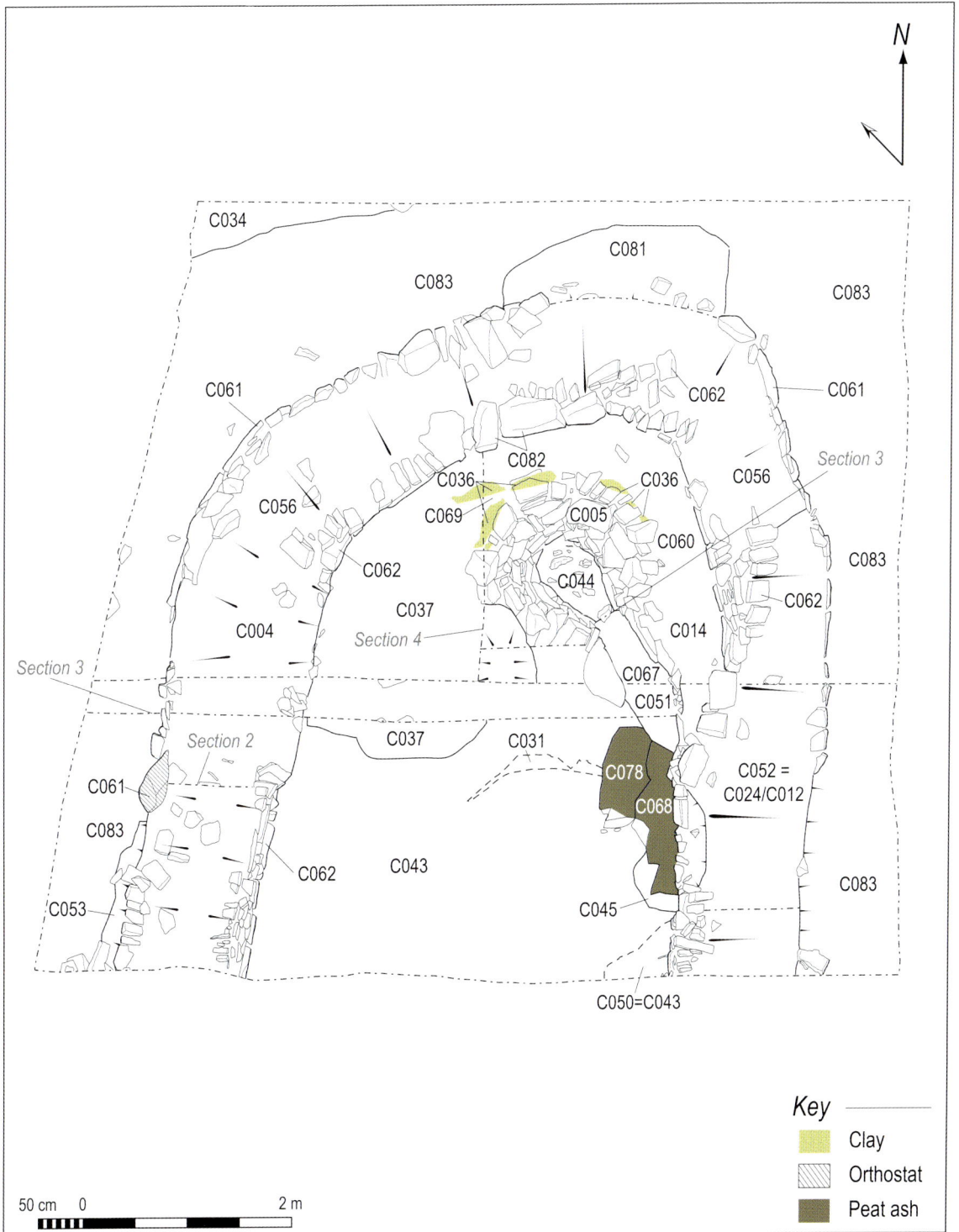

Illus 6.5 Phases 2 and 3 plan

N

C034
C081
C083
C083
C061
C062
C061
C082
C056
Section 3
C036
C036
C056
C069
C005
C060
C044
C083
C037
C062
Section 4
C004
C014
C037
Section 3
C067
C051
Section 2
C037
C031
C061
C078
C052 =
C068
C024/C012
C083
C062
C043
C053
C045
C083

C050=C043

Key
Clay
Orthostat
Peat ash

50 cm   0   2 m

later confirmed by soils analysis, see Chapter 12, below). A turf pocket C084 was noted in section behind a large orthostat and this was interpreted as extra packing material for the outer stone skin. To the S of the wall slot, at the S end of the barn wall, a further layer of silt C053 was identified in the wall core and on the E side further layers were noted in the core of the wall but were not excavated (C052, C012, C024, C020). The turf from the wall core of the outer wall may have come from the area on which the kiln barn was built, as supported by the poor and uneven survival of the relict turf layer in Phase 2 (see above). This was also investigated in the soil micromorphological analysis undertaken (see Chapter 12, below). A small assemblage of carbonised oat, heather type charcoal, eight body sherds of local pottery, a flint flake, an iron object and a lead globule were found in these wall core deposits.

At the N end of the structure, the outer skin of the wall C004 was continuous with the S part, but the inner skin C082 was constructed over a platform. This platform consisted of three layers. The basal layer C077 was sandy silt with inclusions of peaty lumps. Above this was a deposit C069 silt with sand and lumps of peat up to 0.5m deep. This deposit was not seen in the main section as it had been truncated by the construction of a later turf-banked shelter C1. On top of layer C069 was a capping of sandy silt C060 interpreted as the surface of the platform. From this height, the inner skin of the wall C004 continued and consisted of a single course of large sub-angular flat stones C082. In this N area some of the core of the wall C056 has slumped to the N (discussed further below). No finds were recovered from the platform, other than a

Illus 6.6 S facing section cut through W wall of Structure C, Illus 6.7 Outer face of N wall of Structure C and Illus 6.8 Looking from the kiln bowl southwards along the flue

Section 1: S facing section of mid baulk

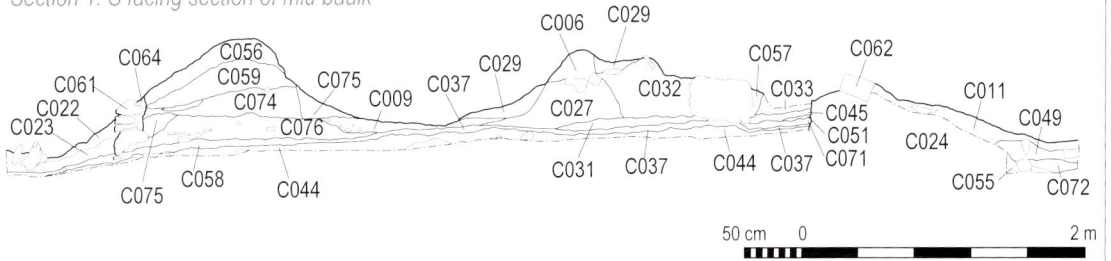

C061
C064
C056
C059
C075
C009
C037
C029
C006
C029
C057
C062
C011
C022
C074
C027
C032
C033
C049
C023
C076
C045
C024
C051
C071
C058
C031
C037
C044 C037
C055
C075
C044
C072

50 cm   0   2 m

Section 2: N facing section of outer wall 004

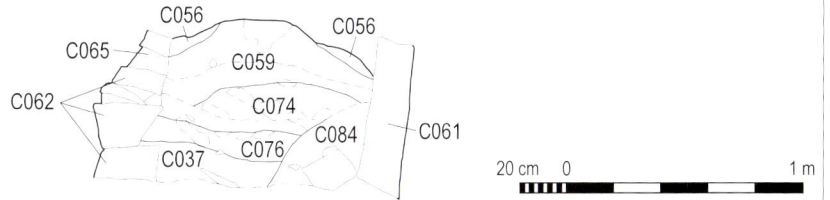

C056
C056
C065
C059
C062
C074
C037
C076
C084
C061

20 cm   0   1 m

Section 3: SE facing section through entrance to kiln bowl

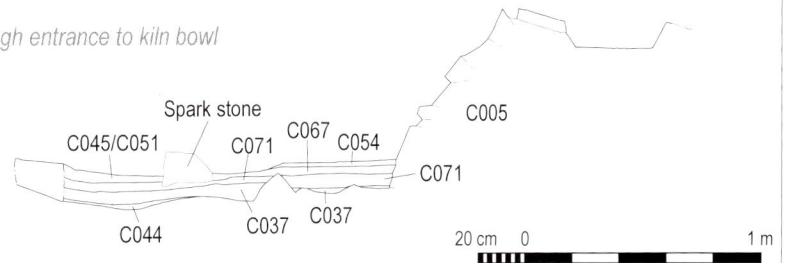

Spark stone
C045/C051
C071
C067
C054
C005
C071
C044
C037
C037

20 cm   0   1 m

Section 4: W facing section through kiln platform

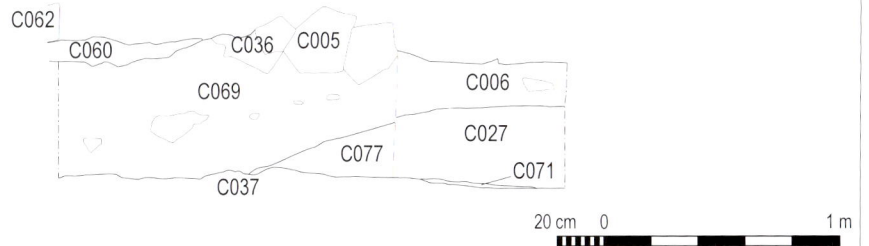

C062
C060
C036
C005
C069
C006
C027
C077
C071
C037

20 cm   0   1 m

Section 5: SE facing elevation of kiln bowl

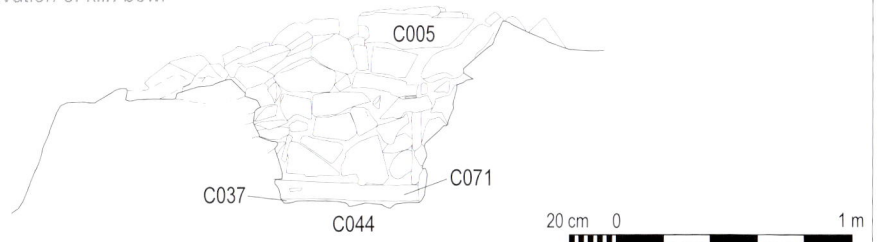

C005
C037
C071
C044

20 cm   0   1 m

Illus 6.9 Trench C sections and kiln bowl elevations

fragment of conifer charcoal in amongst stone C082.

Within the platform a stone-lined kiln bowl had been constructed. A clay deposit (C036) was uncovered around the edge of the kiln bowl, as bonding or backing for a stone lining C005 of stones. The kiln bowl was pear-shaped in plan, and cone-shaped in profile, measuring 1m at the top, and narrowing to 0.54m at the bottom, which was flat. The kiln flue extended to the SE for a distance of at least 0.9m. The stones forming the NE wall of the flue (C014) were interwoven with the lower courses of stones of the inner skin C062 of the kiln barn wall, as if built contemporaneously, whilst the upper coursing of C062 accommodated the shape of the platform around the kiln, curving slightly outwards on the E side, and comprising simply a line of stones on top of the fill of the platform, which was likely built into the core of the outer wall. In plan this construction gave Structure C a slightly skewed appearance on its NE side.

At the junction of the flue and the bowl there were two large flanking stones and a small upright stone SF 128 still in situ in the base of the flue. This feature was interpreted as a spark stone preventing sparks from the fire at the end of the flue entering the bowl. A layer of charcoal C078 and peat ash C068 was also identified to the S of the flue, lying on top of the remains of the relict turf layer C071. This ash extended for 1.6m by up to 0.4m and it abutted the inner skin C062 where it was up to 0.15m deep. The ash was swept up against the wall C062 filling the gaps in between the stones. No other finds were recovered from C068 and C078, although the environmental assemblage included birch, conifer, hazel, ash, oak, heather, Scots pine type, oat, hulled and six row barley, indeterminate cereal, burnt peat and mammal bone fragments.

Within the bowl itself there were three layers that may have accumulated during the use of the kiln. The basal layer C067 was very compact sandy silt with occasional inclusions of clay and burnt peat. Above this was a compact layer of sandy silt with lenses of clay and burnt peat C054, and above this a layer of grey loam with fragments of burnt grain C048. Sealing the ash C068 there were patches of clay C051, which were interpreted as collapsed insulation of the flue sides. Above this was a greasy organic layer C045 within the area of the flue. Birch, conifer, Scots pine type, Douglas fir, grass/sedge, burnt peat, oat and hulled and six row barley were recovered from C045, C048 and C051. A shoulder sherd of local pottery was found in C048.

Contemporary floor surfaces were difficult to distinguish in the S part of the kiln barn as most of it lay beyond the S edge of the trench, but patches of dark sandy silt with an organic content (C043/C050 and C031) under the later shelters, were excavated, and may have been traces of an occupation surface. The entrance to the barn also lay outside the trench and could be clearly seen on the ground as a hollow in the E wall just S of the S edge of the trench. Eight body sherds, a base and a rim sherd of local pottery were found in these contexts, and two iron nails, fragments of burnt mammal bone and oat, six row barley and burnt peat.

Outside the structure in the NE corner and sealing the natural subsoil there were thin layers of sand alternating with organic layers. The basal layer C081 contained a piece of wood SF119 and was sealed by a dark brown organic layer C080 and then a small pocket of sandy silt with turf inclusions C079. Above these layers were thin lenses of brown organic greasy deposits with sand C070. The NE corner was the deepest part of the trench and was wet and peaty. A similar layer, C055, was seen outside the structure further S, to the E. C055 and C070 contained seven body sherds, a rim and a shoulder sherd of local pottery, seven quartz flakes, two quartz microblades and seven chips of quartz, and burnt peat, conifer, indeterminate cereal, oat, birch, spruce and willow charcoal. Radiocarbon dating of the peat ash C068 and charcoal C078 S of the flue returned ranges of AD1470-1640 and AD1460-1635, confirming that the kiln was in use between the last half of the 15th and first half of the 17th centuries AD.

Phase 4: Robbing/collapse of barn and construction of shelters

After the kiln had gone out of use, the bowl was filled with two layers of sandy silt C047 and C046 and large stones C025. The bowl walls had survived fully intact and therefore the rubble within the bowl must have been acquired from elsewhere and deliberately thrown into the kiln bowl. It is possible that the infill was used to make a makeshift surface for the interior of a turf shelter, although this would have been very uneven. This possible shelter was labelled C2

Illus 6.10 Excavating the stone infill from the kiln bowl, Illus 6.11 Stone infill in kiln bowl and Illus 6.12 Shelter C3 from E

Table 6.3 Phase 4 context descriptions, finds and environmental on CD at back of book

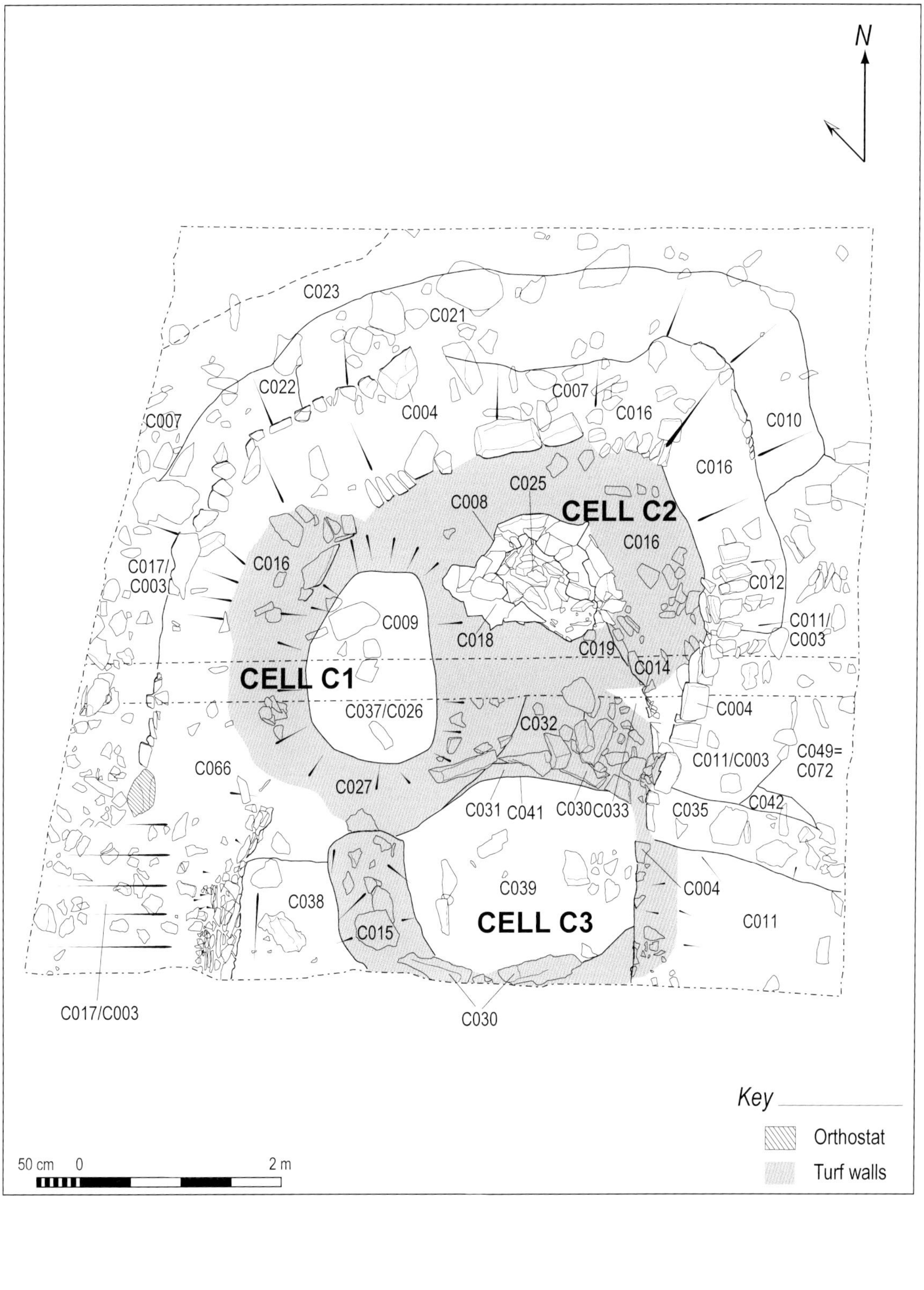

N

CELL C2

CELL C1

CELL C3

C023
C021
C022
C004
C007
C007
C016
C010
C016
C025
C008
C016
C016
C017/
C003
C016
C012
C009
C011/
C003
C018
C019
C014
C037/C026
C004
C032
C066
C011/C003
C049=
C072
C027
C031 C041 C030 C033
C035
C042
C038
C039
C004
C015
C011
C017/C003
C030

Key

Orthostat

Turf walls

50 cm   0   2 m

Illus 6.13 Phases 4 and 5 plan

when it was identified during the survey and lies adjacent to C1, which cut through the turf and stone platform in the N end of the barn, into which the kiln bowl was set. This platform would probably originally have been revetted at its S edge by large stones, as seen in later 19th and 20th century examples recorded from elsewhere in Ness (see the NALS survey; eg Barrowman, C 2007a, 35). It is possible that these stones were pulled out and partly re-used, partly dumped into the disused kiln bowl, when C1 was cut into the W side of the platform. One body sherd, and birch, conifer, oat and indeterminate cereal remains were found in these contexts.

Two further small shelters were also built adjacent to the kiln bowl – C3 to the S in the barn area and C1 to the W. C1 was oval in plan, and built into the NW corner of the kiln barn. It was constructed from two phases of turf walling; the first wall C027 was up to 0.4m high and was sealed by a second phase of turf C006. The shelter measured 1.8m by 1.4m and was cut into the platform C069/C077. Where the shelter abutted the face of the outer wall C004 of the barn, the stone skin had been removed and the inner wall core had slumped slightly before being sealed by the turf wall C027. The shelter had also cut through the W side of the platform, and it is probable that the large stones used in the construction of this building originated from the platform. The turf wall layers contained seven body and one rim sherd of local pottery, Scots pine type charcoal, burnt peat, and carbonised six row and hulled barley, oats, indeterminate cereal and mammal bone fragments. Two limpet shell fragments and a dogwhelk shell were also found.

C3 was also oval-shaped, and had been built before C1. It measured 2.5m by 2m and was defined by seven large recumbent stones C030. Along the N side of the shelter, between it and the kiln bowl, were two rubble layers in medium to light grey and yellowish brown silt, C032 and C033. The material in these layers was probably robbed from the kiln walls and platform, and was the collapsed remains of the turf and stone wall associated with the recumbent stones C030 of C3. The shelter probably utilised the E wall C062 although the stones C030 did not abut it. There may have been an entrance on the NW side where there was a gap in the stones 0.7m wide, which was subsequently blocked with the building of C1, or there was an entrance on the E side of the shelter where the inner wall face stones and the turf core of the E kiln barn wall was eroded. C032 and C033 contained oat, six row barley and indeterminate carbonised cereal grains, as well as birch, conifer, heather type charcoal and mammal bone fragments.

The W side of the flue was destroyed by the construction of this shelter and the

Illus 6.14 Slump across shelters C3 and C1 and Illus 6.15 Excavating slump from the outer face of the W walls

recumbent stones used in its construction were probably robbed from it. This may account also for sparse remains of burnt deposits at the S end of the flue. Abutting the only large stone of the inner face of the flue was a pocket of very dark grey sandy silt C057 and brown sandy silt C063 turf slump. Oat, six row barley, indeterminate cereal, birch, heather type, burnt peat and two haddock bones were recovered from these deposits.

Phase 5: Final collapse

Within each of the two larger shelters, C1 and C3, layers of grey sandy silt were excavated - C039 within C3, and C038 to the W, and C026 and C009 in C1. Most of the finds from Trench C come from these layers, which were interpreted as mixed occupation debris with wall and roof collapse, and many of then will derive from the kiln barn itself. Fourteen body, two shoulder, four rim and a rim and handle sherd of local pottery, and birch, heather type and spruce charcoal, oat, hulled and six row barley and indeterminate cereal grains, and burnt mammal and fish bone fragments were found in C038 and C039. A shard of bottle glass dated to no later than the 17th century was also found in C038, and a flint blade and three quartz flakes in C039. A similar, if smaller, assemblage was recovered from layers C026 and C009. A lump of vitrified material was found in C009.

A rough alignment of rubble in silt C035 was also noted to the E of the E wall C004 of the kiln barn, where the wall had become eroded. It is possible that this may have been an entrance in to C3, although it may be part of the collapse of the E kiln barn wall. The kiln area itself was finally sealed with mixed sandy silts C018 and C019, possibly originating from the turf C2. Conifer charcoal, hulled and six row barley grains and a quartz flake were found in C035. Birch, conifer, heather type, six row barley and indeterminate cereal were found in C018, and oat, burnt peat and a body sherd of local pottery in C019.

Collapse of the kiln barn included slumped material C007 excavated from the barn wall C004, C016 excavated at the platform at the N end of the structure and C008 within the kiln bowl. These contexts contained larger assemblages of material than seen in other contexts, including mammal and domestic fowl bones, heather type charcoal, two haddock and a cod bone, 41 limpets, a dog whelk and a periwinkle, birch, burnt peat, oat, hulled six row barley, corn spurrey and grass/sedge.

In the NE corner peat C002 sealed sandy silt C010. In C1, stone rubble C003 with a sandy silt matrix C041, C042, C013 and C011 on the E side and C023, C022, C021 and C017 on the W side sealed slump from the upper turf wall C006 on either side of the wall (contexts C029, C023, C073). These contexts contained the same general mix of plant remains and marine shells seen in the collapse deposits discussed above. Below this the wall C004 had slumped outwards, the initial slump mixed with the occupation layer below, C058 to the W and C049=C072 to the E. Both of these layers contained more pottery than other collapse layers – 16 body sherds of local pottery in C058, and seven body, four rim, one with finger decoration, and three shoulder sherds of local pottery in C049. A pistol ball was also recovered from C049.

Animal burrows C040 had cut through the upper layers of the platform, the wall C004 and in between the rubble of the kiln C025. Mammal bone fragments and crab and limpet shell were recovered from these burrows.

Phase 6: Topsoil

Turf and silty topsoil C001 and C015 covered the site. A body sherd of local pottery, mammal, including sheep/goat, bone and limpet shells, and a periwinkle shell were found in the topsoil.

Endnotes

[1] All radiocarbon dates are calibrated and quoted at 95.4% confidence: see Chapter 13

Tables 6.4 and 6.5 Phases 5 and 6 context descriptions, finds and environmental on CD at back of book

Illus 7.1 Trench D 2006

seven

Structure D is a group of interconnecting stone and turf buildings set against the perimeter wall, adjacent to Structure C on the south side of the island. Excavations across Area D of seven out of the fifteen buildings identified by the topographic survey found evidence for five phases of occupation within this complicated structure. The latest buildings were a series of small, rough shelters, D4, D7, D8, D10, D13 and D14 built from still partially upstanding conjoining turf and stone walls. Below these were the ruins of earlier settlement. A large hearth or bonfire set into a circular pit was found below turf shelter D7 and has been interpreted as a clamp kiln for firing pots. Below shelters D13 and D10 in the centre of Structure D lay the ruins of a rectangular courtyard D16, with access to the perimeter wall H on the south. To the south-west the traces of one contemporary building, D12, were excavated (see Illus 7.8). Cuttings through the east wall of the courtyard discovered the remains of an even earlier building below it, with an old ground surface and dumps of ash and burnt material (Phases 2 and 3). The finding of so many phases of occupation in the one small part of the structure that was excavated demonstrate that Area D was the most intensively used part of the settlement. An overall date range of AD1440-1640[1] was obtained from radiocarbon dating of Phases 2 to 4. Finds of seventeenth/eighteenth century glass in the later turf shelters D7 and D10 confirm a later date for

Phase 2 to 4

Phase 5

N

D4

D16

D13

D10

D14

D7

D8

Key

	Charcoal
	Clay
	Hearth
	Orthostat
	Pit / Posthole
	Stone facing
	Turf walls

1 m　0　　　　　5 m

Illus 7.2 Interpretative plan

the phase of turf shelters (Phase 5), and eighteenth/nineteenth century glass and glazed ceramics found in shelter D13 suggest a final late use of this small building. Overall seven phases of activity were identified, from earliest to latest: (1) natural subsoil and bedrock, (2) traces of early structures and original ground surfaces, (3) middens below the walls of D16, (4) construction and use of the perimeter wall H, Structures D12, D16 and associated features, (5) abandonment and collapse of earlier buildings and construction and occupation of turf shelters, (6) post-abandonment and final collapse and (7) topsoil.

The finds and environmental material from Phases 2 to 4 included carbonised cereal grains, charcoal from species such as rowan, oak, birch, fir, alder and hazel, iron objects and larch and Scots pine from driftwood burning, local pottery and evidence for gunflints, flint-working, and small-scale metal-working. Particularly rich assemblages of material were found in the thick spreads of ash and burnt grain dumped in Phase 3 as footings for the Phase 4 building walls. Around 2700 oat and barley grains were recovered, as well as flax seeds, burnt peat/turf and possibly the remains of a straw mat or similar on which the grain had been burnt. This large assemblage of grain would seem to be the throw out from more than just drying and processing grain in a small domestic hearth, and may be connected to the corn-drying kiln adjacent at Structure C. A radiocarbon date from this phase produced a date of AD1455-1635.

The rectangular courtyard D16 in the centre of Structure D was buried beneath the later phase of turf and stone shelters (Phase 5) and was not picked up on the topographic survey, although a large central hearth in the courtyard had shown up on the geophysical survey in 2001. D16 was defined by stone-faced earthen walls of the buildings around it on the north and east sides, although these were not excavated. There was a doorway from building D6 into the central courtyard, and also access on the south side of the courtyard to the perimeter wall, Structure H. The large hearth in the courtyard, and the large and varied collection of material recovered from the floor, suggest that this was an area where the occupants on the island gathered and cooked. The width of the courtyard and the results of detailed sampling of sections through the hearth and floor layers for soils micromorphological analysis (see Chapter 12) suggest that it was unroofed and open to the elements. A small building, D12, to the south-west of it was in use at this time, and is dated to the late sixteenth century by a sherd of Cologne stoneware found in peat ash on the floor of the building. Seven radiocarbon dates from hearths and a floor layer in D16 produced an overall range of AD1440-1640.

Also belonging to this phase was another large hearth found below later turf shelter D7, and interpreted as the remains of a clamp kiln used to fire pottery made on the site. The ash deposits in the hearth contained a large assemblage of burnt, mainly animal, bone, of 730 cow, pig, sheep/goat and indeterminate mammal and fish bone fragments and it is possible that bones left over from meat preparation and/or consumption were deliberately collected and burnt as fuel, here, together with driftwood and peat (the main fuel used). Soils analysis identified remains of a collapsed turf layer in the fire, and small quantities of alder, ash and oak identified from the ash may be the remains of a mat or woven layer placed over the fire on which to place the pots before being clamped with turfs. Pot sherds found around the feature, included an almost complete pot found smashed on the original ground surface adjacent (discussed further in Chapters 10, 12 and 14 below). A radiocarbon date taken from this feature produced a range of AD1445-1625.

Overall, the large assemblages of material recovered from Phases 2- 4 suggests a busy occupation area, with activities of the same character as seen in other structures on the island. Like Structure B, this would have been a strategically important part of the site with a view across to the mainland opposite, as well as east along the Minch. The size of the courtyard area, the hearths, the multiple phases of activity and the evidence for the production and processing of significant amounts of resources, such as pots and grain, suggest that this was a gathering place to shelter and feed more than just a few individuals. Although only half of the buildings of Structure D were excavated, the depth of deposits and features identified supports the interpretation that it was the main residential area on the island. The different phases of buildings identified in Phases 2 to 4 demonstrate that Structure D was clearly used, re-used and modified several times. As well as domestic material such as local hand-made pottery sherds, carbonised grain, wood and driftwood charcoal, peat ash, burnt mammal and fish bone found in the buildings, finds of medieval glazed pottery, gunflints and flint-working debris and pistol and musket balls also link to the other buildings on the site, particularly structures A and B, from which finds of the same general date and character were recovered.

After Structure D was abandoned, decayed and collapsed, some time in the early seventeenth century, the area was re-occupied on an ad hoc basis, with the building of small, mainly turf, shelters (Phase 5) that were probably used locally in connexion with agricultural practices such as grazing sheep on the island in the summer, or fishing. The occupation material from these later turf shelters D10 and D13 became mixed with older artefacts due to the re-use and digging up of stone and turf from the ruined buildings, and finds of eighteenth-nineteenth century lamp glass, window glass (from roof lights) and bottle glass were found mixed up with older pistol balls, musket balls and gunflints. Structure D was the only structure to produce finds of eighteenth and nineteenth century glazed pottery and lamp glass, suggesting that this part of the island was used for temporary shelter long after others.

Results

with Alastair Becket and Chris Barrowman

Trench locations

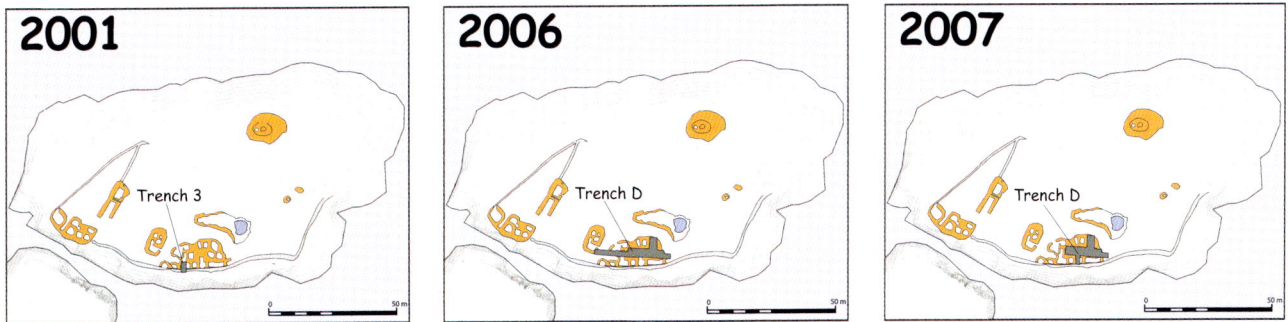

2001 Trench 3: 4m x 2m within D12 of Structure D, and cutting through perimeter wall H on its S side.
Aims: To test the geophysical survey results. D12 chosen to investigate any floor deposits and walling, plus perimeter wall construction.
Work completed: Excavation and recording down to natural subsoil over entire trench.

2006 Trench D: 30m x 2m, widening to 3m towards the E end, with an extension 5m x 3m, perpendicular to the N side of the main trench aligned E-W across D4, D8, D10, D13 and D14, with the trench extension towards the E end over D7.
Aims:
• To partially strip Structure D and take sections through the walls so as to understand the way they were built.
• To investigate the relationship of all the buildings to each other, their construction, phasing, function and date.
• To investigate the 'blank' area outside the buildings between Structures C and D.
• To investigate the relationship between Structure D and the perimeter wall Structure H.
Work completed: Latest layers of post-abandonment excavated across entire trench. Cuttings through buildings and walls completed in D4, D8 and D7. Floor and occupation deposits and old ground surfaces and dumps of ash below the building walls, all sampled and partially examined.

2007 Trench D: E half 15m x 3m of the 2006 trench opened plus extension to the N, 5m x 3m and new extension to the S of D10, 1.5m x 3.3m.
Aims:
• To complete outstanding work, specifically the excavation of D7, newly-identified large rectangular 'courtyard' D16, and traces of earlier occupation in trench.
• To take soil micromorphology samples of floor and hearth deposits.
• Excavation of sondages and sections through the hearth and floor deposits to enable closer study. All hearths excavated 50% at a time, or 25% then 75% and 100% sampling was applied throughout.
Work completed: Interiors of buildings, and all wall cuttings, excavated down to natural subsoil. Post-abandonment deposits, floor and occupation deposits contemporary with the use and construction of the buildings, and old ground surfaces and dumps of ash below the building walls, all excavated and sampled.

Phase 1: Bedrock and natural subsoils

The gneiss bedrock below Structure D formed a small flat-topped hillock, sloping down on the N, E and W sides. It was covered by a compact sandy subsoil D084.

Phase 2: Traces of early structures and original ground surfaces

The earliest archaeological deposit identified was an old ground surface, D064, of compact silty clay with peat, which uniformly covered the slopes on the N and E sides of the trench. This layer was only partially excavated, but was demonstrated to be in excess of 0.15m at its thickest extent, levelling out to 0.03m thick at the base of the slope, and had a high organic content. The occasional lumps of hard peat that were recovered from this layer may indicate that peats were once stacked in this area on the NE sides of the slope. A group of pottery sherds from a single vessel were found in D064 on the E side of the slope. These included three conjoining decorated rim sherds, two shoulder sherds and 28 body sherds from a large coarse pottery vessel which had probably been smashed on the original ground surface during later Phase 4 use of D050 (see below).

The earliest evidence for occupation identified within Trench D was found cut into this surface and comprised the robbed wall footings of the S end of a rectangular building. The building was situated on the N side of the trench, below structures D7, D14, D16 and D6 (the latter just beyond the trench to the N) and the wall footings had clearly been robbed to build these later structures. A corner of the robbed-out building was uncovered, truncated by the trench edge; D048, a row of angular bocks of stone set in sand D062, perpendicular to wall footings D040 and core material D065, a possible return wall D108 parallel to D048 and an occupation deposit, D041, which remained only partially excavated.

Patches of greasy clay were noted above D062, deriving from the walls of later shelter D14 above it (see Phase 5 below). Five stones of D048 survived in situ, although defined patches of D062 indicated that the remaining stones had been robbed at the S end of the alignment in a gap between D048 and return wall D040. D062 extended to the W of D048 in a parallel alignment, suggesting that D048 was the remaining outer face of what was once a double wall.

The return wall at the S end of D048/D062 comprised collapsed inner and outer stone footings D040 and degraded turfy core deposit, D065, which was fully defined by the end of the excavation but only partially excavated. Part of the return wall was covered by later turfy infill D042 from shelter D14 above it (see Phase 5 below). A small assemblage of 13 fragments of burnt mammal bone, two flint flakes, a chunk and a chip of flint, burnt peat, birch, rowan type and oak charcoal, and carbonised oat, six row barley, and indeterminate cereals was found in this context.

The insertion of later wall D010 during later Phase 4 had obliterated the W end of D040, although a second row of possible wall footings D108 of six angular stones aligned SE to NW was identified parallel 2m W of robbed wall footings D048/D062. The remains of an occupation deposit D041 of clayey sand containing moderate inclusions of charcoal flecks, was identified covering a small area truncated by the N trench edge.

Phase 3: Middens below walls

After the early building had gone out of use, its walls were dismantled and robbed and thick layers of ashy midden and burnt material, D105 and D036=D058 were piled on the robbed wall footings to provide a foundation for the next phase of buildings on the site, as represented by a N-S aligned wall, D010 (see Phase 4 below). These layers of ashy midden were identified in a cutting made through the N end of wall D010. The latest midden layer D036 was a mixed layer of silty clay up to 0.14m deep with a high burnt organic content, frequent large patches of peat ash, large chunks of carbonised wood and charcoal, sand and occasional large stones could be seen continuing to the S where it was recorded in section in 2006 as D058 below wall D010.

Below D036 a different layer was identified, D105, a dark grey to black silty clay with sand, patches of ash, small stones and burnt bone, wood, grains, charcoal and ash. This context was more consistent throughout, unlike the D036 above, which was mixed and included unburnt

Illus 7.6 Remains of early robbed-out wall footings below thick layers of later collapsed turf and stone buildings and Illus 7.7 Close-up of robbed wall footings

Table 7.1 Phase 2 context descriptions, finds and environmental on CD at back of book

Table 7.2 Phase 3 context descriptions, finds and environmental on CD at back of book

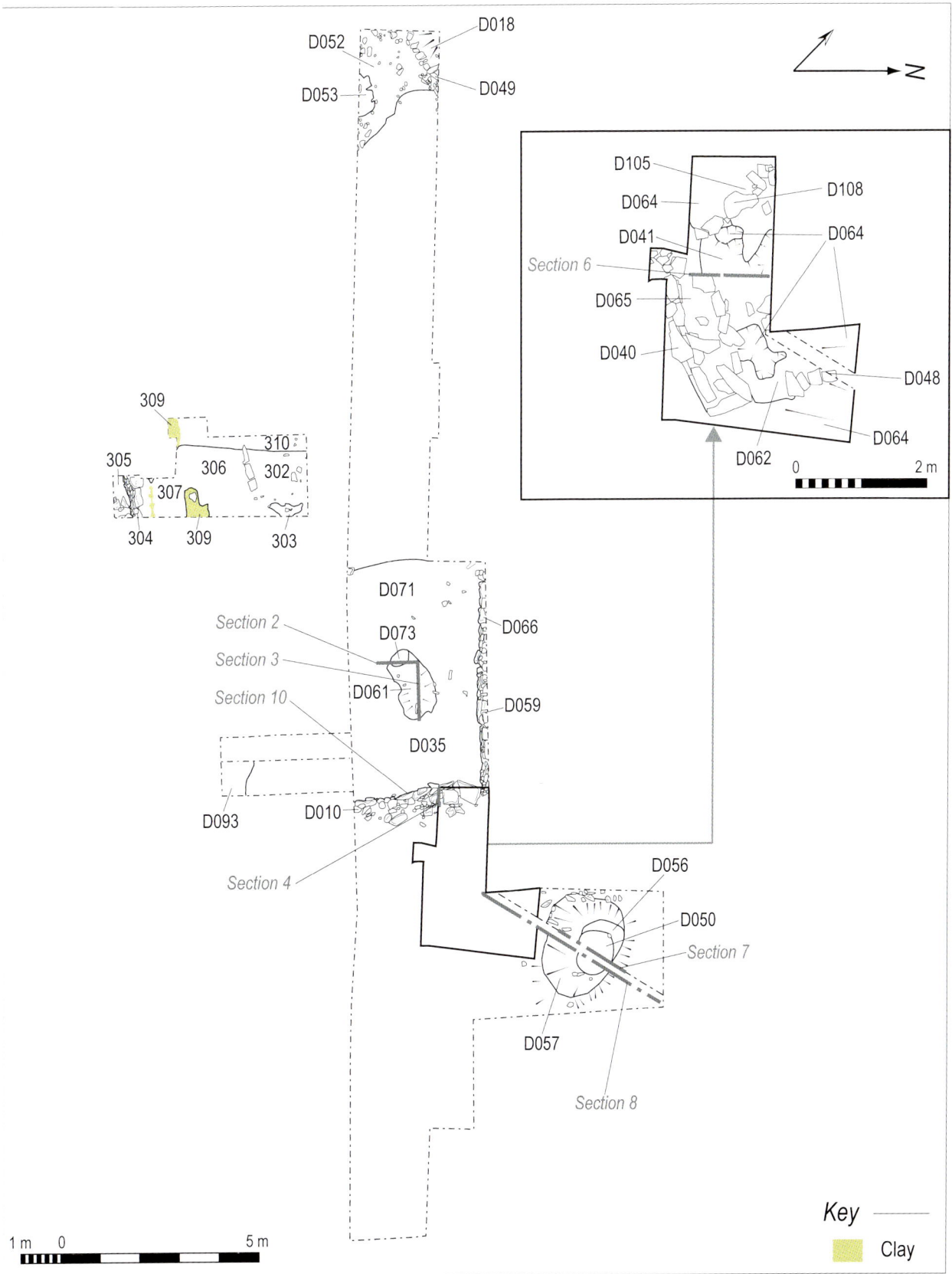

D052
D018
D053
D049

D105
D064
D108
D041
D064
Section 6
D065
D040
D048
D064
D062
0   2 m

309
310
305   306   302
307
304   309   303

D071
Section 2
D073   D066
Section 3
D061
Section 10   D059
D035
D093   D010
Section 4

D056
D050
Section 7
D057
Section 8

Key

Clay

Illus 7.8 D Phases 2-4 plan

1 m   0   5 m

Illus 7.9 Excavation of the midden D036 below wall D010, Illus 7.10 Close-up of carbonised wood and organic material in midden D105 and Illus 7.11 Pottery find SF 390 in midden D058 below wall D010

156 / groundwork

stones for instance. No scorching of the layers below D105 was evidenced, and a spread of stones, D108, directly below D105, was not heat-affected demonstrating that D105 was not the result of in situ burning. A spread of patterned charcoal and grains suggesting that a woven textile or straw-like fabric containing grain was included in this deposit. Total sampling was employed so as to retrieve as much information as possible and it is discussed in Chapter 11, below.

Over 290 fragments and pieces of burnt mammal and fish bone were found in D036, together with fir, alder, birch, conifer hazel, heather type, larch, Scots pine type and oak charcoal, carbonised cultivated flax, docks, club rush and stitchwort, and carbonised oat, hulled, six row barley and indeterminate cereal. The artefacts recovered included 52 body, four shoulder and three rim sherds of local pottery, a gunflint rejuvenation flake, a flint flake and a flint chip, a quartz flake and two chips and an iron ring, an iron nail and two indeterminate iron objects. D058 also contained a large assemblage of pot sherds (three neck sherds, a shoulder sherd and 71 body sherds of local pottery) as well as a lump of slag and a gunflint. It was also rich in mammal bone (102 indeterminate burnt fragments) and contained birch charcoal, and carbonised cultivated flax, oat, hulled and six row barley grains.

The assemblage from D105 was similarly rich, despite only a small area being excavated, and contained 76 body sherds of local pottery, two of which were decorated, two shoulder sherds and seven rim sherds, six lumps of vitrified industrial waste, a quartz flake, two flint chips, an indeterminate iron object and fragments of iron, as well as a varied ecofactual assemblage of 208 sheep/goat, bird, cow and indeterminate mammal bone fragments, burnt peat, fir, alder, birch, Scots pine type and oak charcoal and carbonised sedge, corn marigold, cultivated flax, stitchwort, oat, hulled and six row barley and indeterminate cereal.

A radiocarbon date was produced from material sampled from midden deposit D036, with the resulting date range of AD1455-1635.

Phase 4: Construction and use of the perimeter wall H, Structures D12, D16 and associated features

Large hearth below D7

At the NE edge of Structure D was the site of a large hearth or bonfire, excavated from below the turf walls and floor level of later shelter D7 (see Phase 5 below). It seemed unusual during excavation that the exact spot of an earlier hearth should be used on which to situate a later turf shelter. However, when the walls of the shelter were excavated, it was revealed that the hearth was set into a hollow, and that once it had gone out of use, the hollow had been used as a small, circular shelter, with earthen walls mounded up around it. The hearth was large, appeared more like a bonfire than a domestic hearth, and was clearly related to some sort of industrial process, or cooking on a large scale (frequent fragments of burnt animal bone were found in the ash). No

evidence for metal-working was recorded and the amounts of grain recovered were too small to indicate grain drying or processing. Also, the construction of later turf shelters over the area (Structures D6, D7 and D14, only the latter two of which were excavated) had obliterated much of the earlier stratigraphical evidence. However, later post-excavation analysis showed that given the size of the fire and other factors such as the finding of an almost complete smashed pot on the old ground surface D064 adjacent to D7 (see Phase 2 above) and the evidence for a layer of turf capping within the hearth seen in the soil micromorphological evidence, that this bonfire was used as a clamp to fire pottery (see below).

Careful excavation of the hearth revealed several layers of burning D050A-D, D056-7, and D080-3. The upper part of the hearth comprised two deposits – D050, a thick red peat ash sandy silt, with charcoal lenses, ash, burnt bone fragments and fire-cracked stones, was excavated as one layer in a sondage cut through the hearth for soils analysis NE to SW (25% of the deposit). In excavation in plan of the remaining 75%, four different layers, A to D, within the hearth were noted, probably representing different burning events, or the varying temperatures within the hearth deposit. To the side of D050, D056, a silty peat ash with charcoal and burnt bone, was identified as sweepings from hearth D050. Below hearth D050/D056, a lower hearth comprising four deposits was identified: the latest D080=D055, comprised yellow peat ash with bone, charcoal and fire cracked stones; then D081, a thin spread of grey sand, D082 a concreted layer of charcoal, burnt peat, and burnt bones and stones in the base of the hearth, and finally the basal layer in the hearth, D083, a grey silty sand. An ashy deposit of silty clay with sand, D057, lay around the hearth and it is probable that the majority of the artefactual material incorporated into the turf walls of Structure D7 originated from this layer.

The artefactual assemblage from the hearth layers comprised mainly burnt animal bone, wood and heather charcoal, and burnt peat. 730 cow, pig, sheep/goat and indeterminate mammal and fish bone fragments in total were identified from the environmental samples, together with the carbonised remains of alder, birch, conifer, heather type, Scots pine type, ash, oak, grass/sedge, peat, oat, hulled and six row barley and indeterminate cereal. Seven body sherds and one shoulder sherd of local pottery, three flint chips, a flint core, a burnt flint flake, a quartz chip and an iron object were also recovered. Two body sherds of local pottery, and birch, heather type and spruce charcoal, burnt peat and carbonised oat were found in the ashy deposit D057. One radiocarbon date was produced from this feature, from D056, with a range of AD1445-1625.

D12 and the perimeter wall H

In the small trial trench excavated through D12 in 2001, the edge of the W wall of D12 was excavated, set against the perimeter wall H on its S side. D12 and H had been built onto the original ground surface 306=305. Above 305, within the earthen core of H, a thin layer of clay 307 was excavated from below the main turf of the bank, 301. Conifer and heather type charcoal was recovered from 306.

The perimeter wall H comprised an outer stone face 304 on the S (landward facing) side, and an inner turf face 309 and an earth core 301, 0.46m thick at its apex. Banding occurred at intervals throughout the bank and appeared to be junctions between individual turfs, although this has not been verified by soils analysis. The external stone face 304 on its S side consisted of a single skin of dry-stone masonry built into the earthen bank, standing to a maximum of eight courses in height, or 0.35m. The inner, probably turf, face was seen as a linear band of very dark brown greasy material with a high organic content. A body sherd of local pottery, a small calcined fragment of mammal bone and an indeterminate fragment of carbonised plant material was found in bank 301.

The edge of the W wall of D12 was identified perpendicular to and built against the perimeter wall. Only the foundation of the wall survived, with the core 310 consisting of compact silty clay, with sand and interpreted as degraded turf. The wall 310 appeared to overlie the occupation layer 302 within D12 (see below), although this may be the result of slumping as only the W edge of the wall was uncovered in the trench. Underlying 310 clay 311 was excavated, and also interpreted as degraded turf. Examination of the trench section through the building and perimeter wall revealed cut marks showing that when the building was constructed, turf was cut away from the inner face of the perimeter wall, perhaps to be used elsewhere in the building.

Within D12 silty clay 302 with occasional flecks of charcoal and small stones throughout was excavated. The majority of the finds from the trench came from this context and included 48 body sherds, one of which was decorated, eight rim sherds, three with decoration and five shoulder sherds of local pottery. A sherd of post-medieval glazed pottery was also found, and a lump of unfired clay, a lump of possible furnace lining, two flint flakes, a quartz flake and chunk, eight iron objects including nails and a rove. The environmental assemblage included 18 fragments of burnt mammal bone, birch, conifer and oak charcoal, and carbonised oat and barley grains.

In the NE corner of the trench a spread of peat ash 303 was excavated, cut by the trench edge. As well as local pottery (39 body sherds, three shoulder sherds and two rim sherds, one of which was decorated) a neck sherd of post-medieval Cologne stoneware was also found in this small dump of material. The ash also contained birch, conifer, heather and spruce charcoal, carbonised oat and barley grains, and indeterminate mammal bone fragments.

D16

Structure D16 was identified from excavation only in an area shown as blank on the topographic survey in the centre of Structure D, below later turf shelters D13, D14 and D10. D16 was defined by the outer walls of surrounding buildings, rather than being a discrete building in itself,

Illus 7.15 Perimeter wall H section showing outer stone face and Illus 7.16 Excavation of wall remains in Trench 3 2001

Table 7.3 Phase 4 (i) context descriptions, finds and environmental on CD at back of book

and should be viewed more as a communal courtyard, than a building. Several floor (D035/ D071, D079/D088) and hearth (D061/D073, D074/D075, D076-8, D089-90) deposits were excavated from within it, suggesting that the area was extensively used, as also evidenced by the extensive and mixed artefactual assemblage recovered from it. The hearths within it had been picked up by the gradiometer survey in 2001 (see Chapter 2 above, anomaly A2). Soils analysis has since confirmed that the area was unroofed and open to the elements (see Chapter 12 below). Only the N and E walls of D16 were identified during the excavations. The S side of the structure lay mainly outside the trench, and had been replaced by the edge of turf shelters D10A and D10B above. The W side had been completely removed by the building of later shelters, and the extent of D16 on this side was indicated only the by the W limit of the floor deposit inside it.

The dry-stone wall face delineating the N edge of D16 divided into two distinct builds: D059 on the E side included a doorway with a sill stone, and was built from up to seven courses of neat blocks of stonework, D066 on the W side was of a rougher build, utilising upright stones and rubble rather than a dry-stone facing: The outer faces of the S walls of conjoining unexcavated Structures D5 and D6 to the N of Trench D. A doorway enabled access between Structures D6 and D16 and from this it can be suggested that although D5 and D6 weren't excavated, they were contemporary with D16. The E side of D16 was defined by a N-S aligned wall D010 of earth (probably turf) and stone with a rough stone facing on its interior face, the remains of a contemporary structure only partially excavated in Trench D. At least three courses of stonework survived, and the wall extended beyond the trench edges to the N and S. The stones were set into an earthen core of silty clay, with greasy clay patches (probably individual turfs). The W face of the wall had collapsed slightly and slumped down onto the deposits in the interior of the structure. Excavation of a small section through the N end of wall D010 revealed that wall D059 abutted D010. The S and W extents of D16 were less clear due the insertion of later turf shelters D10A and D10B (see Phase 5, below). No W wall to the area was uncovered either and seems to have been obliterated by the insertion of a later turf building, D13. It is possible that the 'courtyard' area of D16 was accessed from the W, but this must remain conjecture without further excavation.

When a section was cut through wall D010 a varied assemblage of material was recovered from the earth core including 16 body and three rim sherds, two with decoration, of local pottery, in addition to a flint flake, an iron object, a piece of iron strapping, possibly from a bucket, two fragments of broken quern, 10 fragments of burnt mammal bone, birch, heather type and Scots pine type charcoal, carbonised oat, six row barley and indeterminate cereal grains and burnt peat.

The latest floor layer to be uncovered in the interior of D16 was D071=D035, a compact clayey silt with sand and charcoal flecks. There were four different hearths contemporary with the use of this floor: the latest were D061, compact peat ash and charcoal, and D073, a small patch of hearth sweepings, then D073, peat ash and charcoal, then two basal

Illus 7.17 General overhead view of area of D16 after removal of central hearth (burnt area of rock in centre), Illus 7.18 Dry-stone wall face D059 on N side of area D16, and rubble wall D010 to the E and Illus 7.19 Lower hearth D077 D078 and floor layer after removal of upper hearth and floor layer D074-6 from SE

Illus 7.20 Close-up of section through layers in central hearth in area D16

layers, D074, a very thin layer of silty sand with frequent charcoal and carbonised peat, and D075, peat ash and charcoal flecks with burnt bone. Below these deposits was an earlier group of floor and hearth layers. Below D035/D071 was an earlier floor, D079=D088 first identified in a sondage 2m x 1.6m cut for soils analysis through the hearth deposits, but on wider excavation revealed to the S and E of the hearths covering an area 3.24 x 1.2m.

Three hearth deposits were identified that were associated with this floor deposit, layers D076, the latest of these, was a silty sand and peat ash with carbonised peat and charcoal flecks covering an elongated oval area. At the base of D076 was a thin peat ash deposit, D077, with burnt flint and quartz flakes, covering a circular area and below this a thin spread of peat ash and silty sand, D078, situated in a hollow in the bedrock in the centre of the hearth area.

The earliest deposit excavated from this phase of occupation deposits was a small burnt deposit, D090, concreted pinkish red ash situated below the earliest floor layer D079, and above the bedrock.

As would be expected, the floor and hearth deposits produced a rich and varied assemblage of artefactual and ecofactual material. Latest floor layer D035=D071 contained around 250 sherds of local pottery, including 18 rim sherds, three of which were decorated, seven neck sherds and eight shoulder sherds. Two gunflints were also recovered and a blade, two microblades, 18 flakes and 15 chips of flint are evidence of flint working. Two musket balls, a pistol shot, three iron nail and two iron objects and a piece of iron strap or binding were also found. A late 17th/early 18th century glass bottle shard, two sherds of modern glazed pottery, a shard of a probably 19th century glass bottle, a shard of probably 19th century lamp glass and a shard of 17th/18th century window glass are all evidence of a degree of mixing of this latest floor layer of Phase 4 into the occupation of the turf shelters built into the ruins of D16 during Phase 5 above. Finds of later 18th/19th century glass and ceramics were only found in this latest floor deposit below the area of later turf shelter D13 (although the earlier date suggested for one of the shards of window glass is intriguing), and this is as much due to animal burrowing in this area seen in the topsoil during excavation, as to the mixing due to the digging of turf from the area to build the later shelters. The environmental assemblage from this floor layer includes 159 mammal bone and teeth and fish bone fragments, fir, birch, Scots pine type and oak charcoal, carbonised oat, hulled, six row barley and indeterminate cereal grain, a hazel nut shell and cultivated flax, and burnt peat. 17 body and three rim sherds of local pottery, eight flint flakes, 37 flint chips, four chunks, two microblades and a core of flint, two indeterminate iron objects, and a domical spindle whorl fragment were found in hearths D061/D073 and D074/D075 associated with floor layer D035=D071. The environmental assemblage of burnt material included 169 indeterminate mammal and fish bone fragments, alder, ash, birch heather type, Scots pine type, fir, juniper, oak, hazel nutshell, cultivated flax and redshank charcoal, oat, hulled and six row barley and indeterminate cereal grains, and burnt peat.

Lower floor layer D079/D088 contained 62 body sherds, a base and a rim sherd of local pottery, three very small shards of possible vessel glass, a microblade, a flake and a core of flint, a quartz flake, 67 mammal and fish bone fragments, alder, birch, heather type, Scots pine type, fir and oak charcoal, and carbonised oat, six row barley, indeterminate cereal and peat. The hearths associated with these floor layers, D076-D078, contained over 50 body sherds, six rim and two shoulder sherds of local pottery, a quartz flake, a flake, 2 blades and 12 chips of flint, a fire flint, a copper alloy and wood fragment and an iron object. The carbonised assemblage

Table 7.4 Phase 4 (ii) context descriptions, finds and environmental on CD at back of book

Section 1: Structure D4 SE facing section

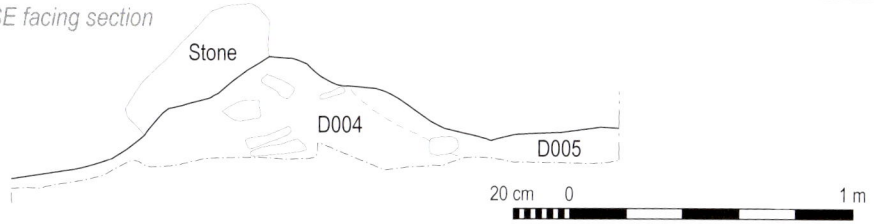

Stone

D004

D005

20 cm   0   1 m

Section 2: E facing section through hearths in Structure D16

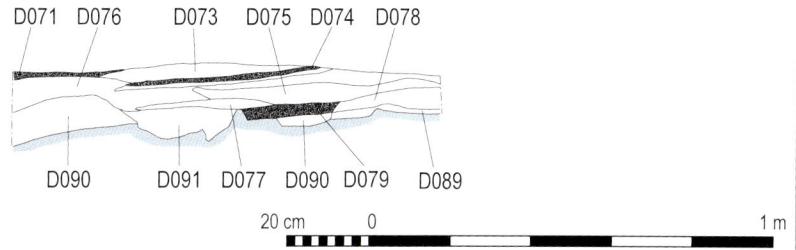

D071   D076   D073   D075   D074   D078

D090   D091   D077   D090   D079   D089

20 cm   0   1 m

Section 3: S facing section through hearths in Structure D16.

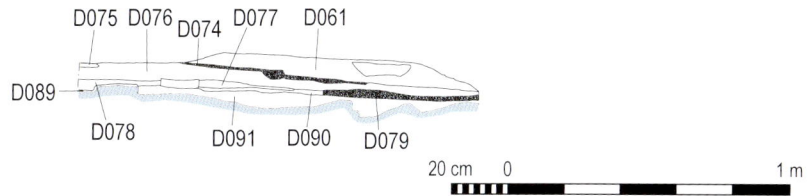

D075   D076 D074   D077   D061

D089

D078   D091   D090   D079

20 cm   0   1 m

Section 4: N facing section through wall D010.

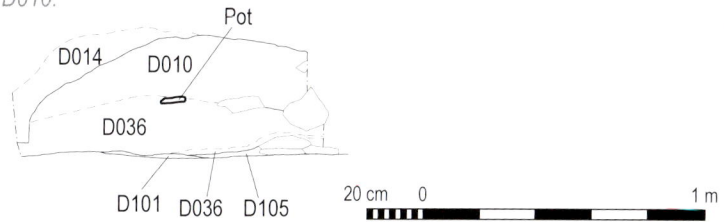

Pot

D014   D010

D036

D101   D036   D105

20 cm   0   1 m

Section 5: W facing section of S extension of Trench D.

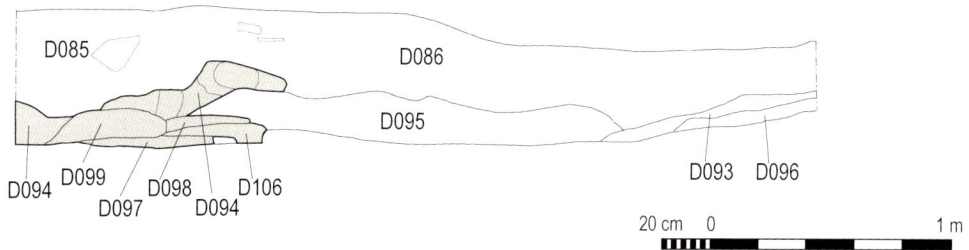

D085   D086

                           D095

D094   D099   D098   D106   D093   D096

D097   D094

20 cm   0   1 m

Section 6: Sondage 3 W facing

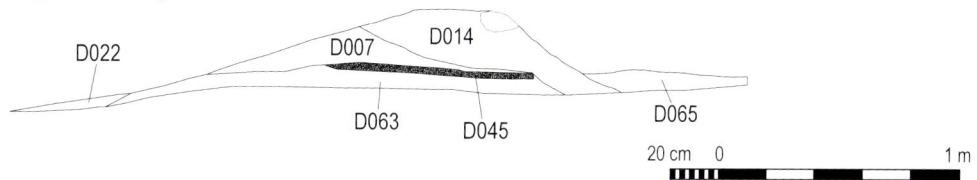

D022   D007   D014

                                        D065

D063   D045

20 cm   0   1 m

Key

Bedrock   Charcoal   Turf walls

Illus 7.21 Trench D sections
(continued over page)

Section 7: W facing section through hearth D050 below Structure D7

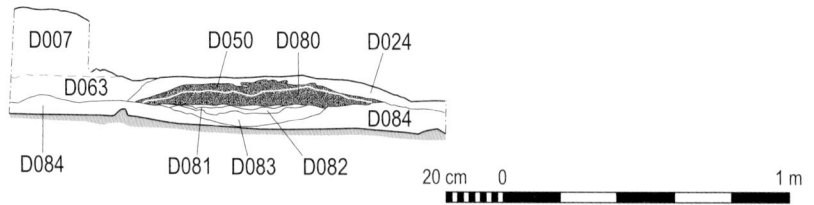

D007
D050   D080   D024
D063
D084
D084   D081   D083   D082

20 cm   0   1 m

Section 8: Structure D7 NW facing section

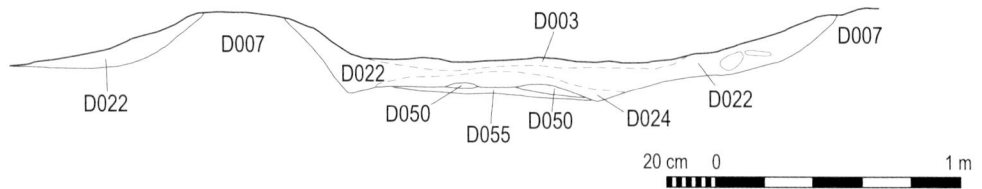

D003
D007   D007
D022
D050   D050   D024   D022
D055
D022

20 cm   0   1 m

Section 9: Structure D8 N facing section

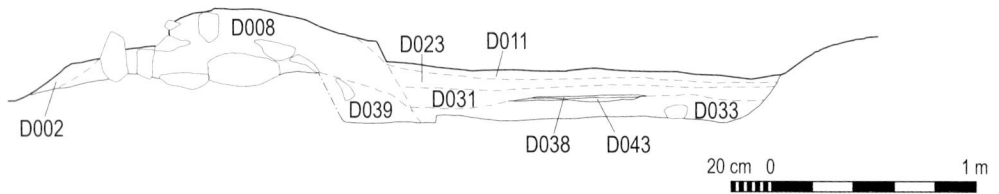

D008
D023   D011
D031   D033
D002   D039
D038   D043

20 cm   0   1 m

Section 10: W facing elevation and section below wall D010.

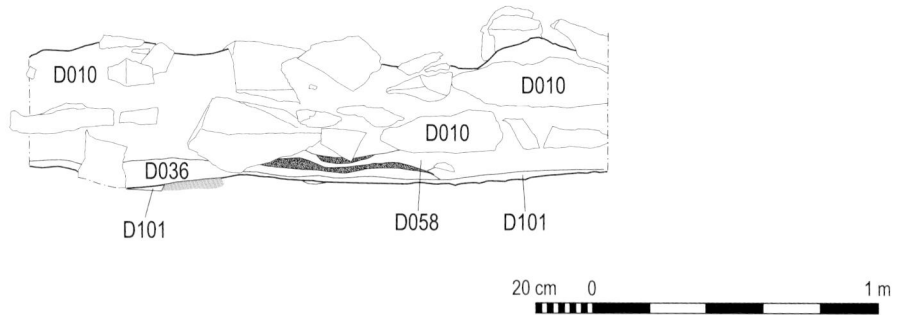

D010   D010
D010
D036
D101   D058   D101

20 cm   0   1 m

Section 11: W facing section, Trench 3.

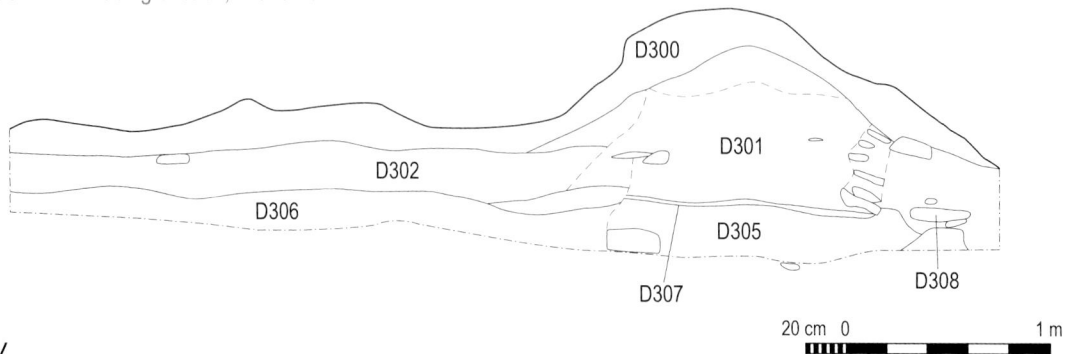

D300
D301
D302
D306   D305
D307   D308

20 cm   0   1 m

Key

Bedrock   Charcoal

included 75 mammal and fish bone fragments, birch, heather type, Scots pine type, larch, oak and cultivated flax, oat, hulled and six row barley, indeterminate cereal grains and peat. The lowest hearth deposit D090 contained a flint chip and a carbonised assemblage of 60 mammal and fish bone fragments, heather type, Scots pine type, oak, cultivated flax, oat, six row barley and burnt peat. Radiocarbon dating of material sampled from five different deposits from D16, including hearth deposits D061 and D074-6 and floor deposit D079, produced an overall date range of AD1440-1640. These dates were investigated further with mathematical modelling and are discussed below in Chapter 13.

Structure C

A small section of the SE corner of Structure C lay at the W end of Trench D and comprised a dark brown turf bank (D018) kerbed with a single course of stone (D049). At the S edge of the trench and sealed by the trample (D052) was a deposit of peat ash (D053) that appeared to have been dumped directly upon the natural subsoil (D051) outside the building, and may be associated with the use of Structure C. The finds and environmental assemblage from this corner included an example of six-row barley from the wall core D049, 19 body and a neck sherd of local pottery, two flakes and a chip of flint, 171 mammal, fish, and bird bone fragments, birch, conifer, heather type, oat, hulled and six row barley and indeterminate cereal from trample D052, and mammal bone fragments, birch, heather type, oat and six row barley from peat ash D053.

Phase 5: Abandonment and collapse of earlier buildings and construction and occupation of turf shelters D4, D7, D8, D10A, D10B, D13 and D14

Uppermost of the occupation phases excavated in Trench D were a series of seven small, sub-circular turf and stone built shelters built into the ruins of the older buildings below them. D7, D8 and D14 were the best preserved of these buildings, D13 and D10A were less well preserved, whilst D4 and D10B lay mostly outside the excavated area. Finds of pottery, peat-ash, stone, charcoal and other material were recovered from the shelter walls, suggesting incorporation of material from earlier structures. The shelters had the overall appearance of temporary buildings, with little or no indication of occupation deposits, and no, or only short-lived, hearths. The walls were built from mixed stone rubble and turf with no evidence for neat courses stone and turf walling as seen in earlier buildings. Animal burrows in the area of shelters D13 and D10 have resulted in mixed assemblages from these structures.

D4

The topographic survey identified D4 as an amorphous building, forming a large cell on the NW corner of Structure D. The SE corner (D069) of the outer wall of D4 was uncovered in Trench D, and comprised an outer face of three rough courses of stonework. From the investigations in Trench D it is likely that D4 as shown on the topographic survey is more complicated structurally than being one contemporaneous building, and is probably made up of later turf walling on an earlier stone-built structure (Phase 4). D069 is included in Phase 5 here as it was built against and used as the NW wall of later shelter D13 (see below).

Further W at the W end of Trench D the SW corner of D4 (D004) was excavated, and a small cutting aligned NE to SW revealed that it was built directly onto the natural subsoil, and comprised a rough core of stones and dark brown clay silt which survived to a height of 0.4m. The wall was hard to define due to the slump on both sides and because the majority of the structure appears to have lain outside the excavated area. The wall core contained artefactual and environmental material such as 20 sherds of local pottery, a pebble, a chip and a flake of flint, a fire flint, a cow tooth and carbonised birch, conifer, oat, hulled six row barley, six row barley, indeterminate cereal and peat, suggesting that the wall core contained material or turf derived from buildings elsewhere on the site.

Illus 7.22 D4 excavated, from above

Table 7.5 Phase 5 (i) context descriptions, finds and environmental on CD at back of book

D7

D7 was a circular, turf and stone shelter built straight over a large hearth, D050 (see Phase 4 above). The hearth was not reused, but became trampled when D7 was in use. Once the turf and topsoil was removed, the walls of D7 proved difficult to define during excavation due to the similarity of the simple earthen bank (D007) and the subsequent slump and collapse deposits around it. Cuttings were made through the walls and discovered that the walls of D7 had not only slumped over the hearth during post-abandonment, they actually post-dated the abandonment of the hearth, thus confirming that the shelter was built over the hearth. The walls were made up of two different layers, D007, the slumped upper layer, and D063, the basal layer. The trampled surface of the hearth D024 was also excavated from the baulk across the centre of the building.

Stones scattered along the turf wall on the W side of the structure were shown to originate from Structure D6 to the W outside Trench D. It appeared that D7 was built against D6, although it was not possible to verify this with excavation. Below D007 deposit D063=D070, silt with sand, clay patches, charcoal flecks, iron pan, burnt peat, burnt bone fragments and small stones, curved around from the S to the E, W and N sides of the structure, and formed the basal layer of the walls. A spread of greyish brown sand D072 along the bottom of the slope at the N edge of the trench was noted in a semi-circular arc at the bottom of the turf walls of D7. This deposit was probably the result of rain wash action, filtering the sand from the later turf walls to the bottom of the slope where it had collected.

A sizeable assemblage of pottery, charcoal and other finds and occupational material contained in the turf wall deposits D007 and D063 of shelter D7 originated from the primary use of the structure and hearth below it, and was mixed with material contemporary with the use of D7 itself, probably due to the cutting of turfs to make the later shelter D7. D007 contained 109 body, 13 rim and four shoulder sherds of local pottery, a sherd of 19th century lamp glass, three shards of 18th century window glass, 18 flakes, six chips, two blades, a core and a microblade of flint, a fire flint, three gunflints, five iron objects, six iron nails and two pistol balls. The carbonised material included 76 mammal bone fragments, a bird bone fragment, birch, conifer and heather type charcoal, oat, hulled and six row barley, and indeterminate cereal grains, and burnt peat. D063 below it contained a similar range of material such as local pottery, 17th/18th century window glass, flint waste, a gunflint, a hammerstone, burnt mammal bone fragments and burnt cereal grains.

In the centre of the shelter D024 was excavated. This had accumulated as a result of the surface of the hearth and surrounding deposits being trampled during the use of the sub-rectangular turf shelter, D7, above it. This mixed deposit contained three body and a rim/shoulder sherd of local pottery, two chips and a flake of flint, a sheet fragment, a rove and an iron object, and a carbonised assemblage of 63 mammal and fish bone fragments, conifer, heather type, oat, hulled and six row barley grains. A radiocarbon date was produced from D024 with a range of AD1445-1630.

Illus 7.23 D7 excavated from NE and Illus 7.24 Excavation working shot

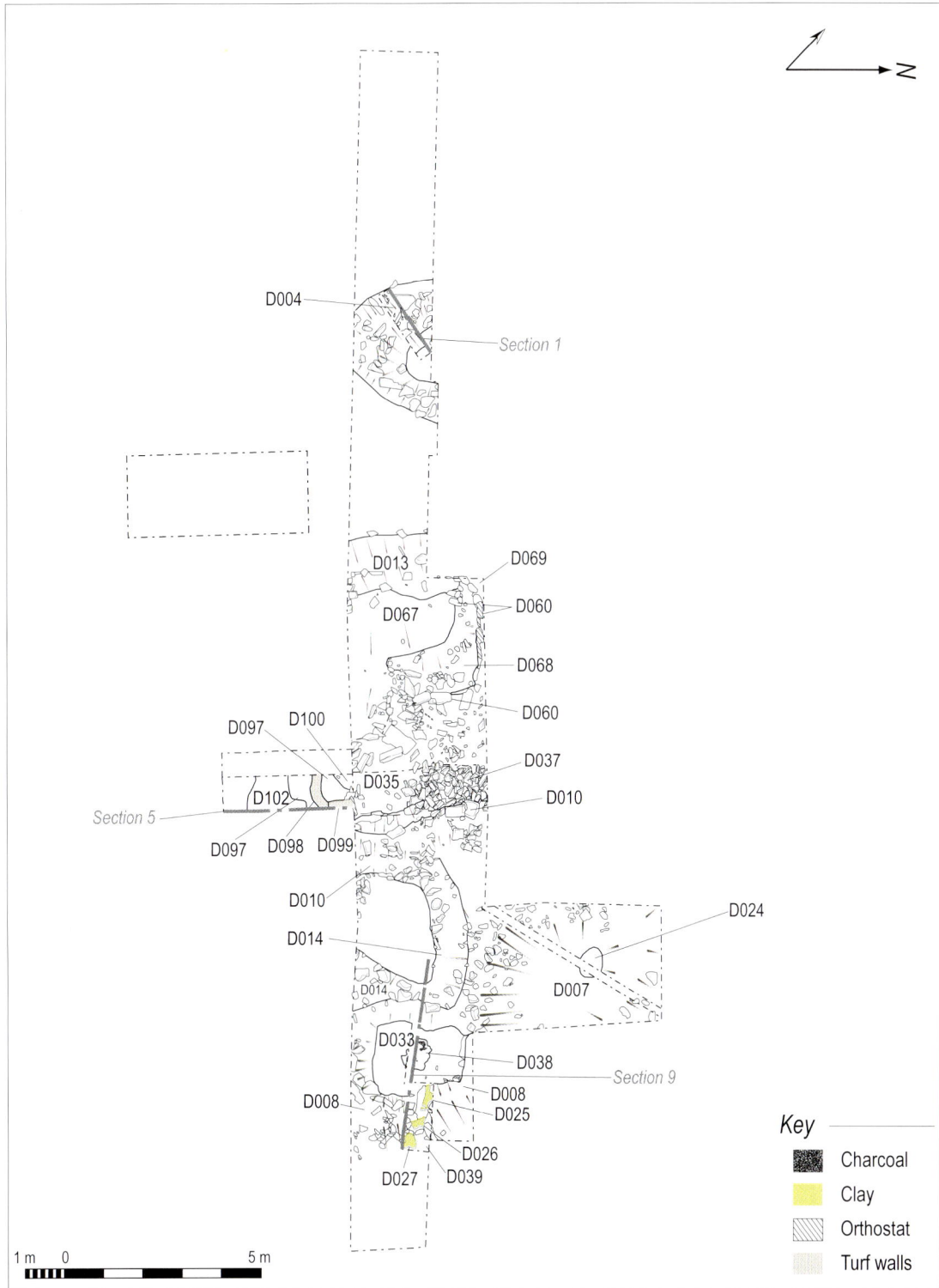

Illus 7.25 Phase 5 plan

Key

- ▪ Charcoal
- ▪ Clay
- ▨ Orthostat
- ▤ Turf walls

D8

D8 was a simply-built shelter constructed from a basic earth and stone bank D008 forming a sub-circular cell with an internal diameter of approximately 2.2m. An orthostatic stone on the S edge of the trench marked a possible doorway into the shelter on the S side. A small, rectangular hearth D047 was found near the centre of the structure dug into a mottled silt clay deposit D033 that formed the floor. The hearth contained three fills: peat ash D038 over a compacted charcoal deposit D043 and a thin layer of mixed ash and charcoal D046. 10 body sherds of local pottery, two quartz chips, 90 mammal and bird bone fragments, birch, conifer, heather type, larch and oak charcoal, and carbonised oat, hulled and six row barley and indeterminate cereal grains were found in floor deposit D033, whilst the hearth deposits contained a familiar range of carbonised mammal bone fragments, cereal grains and plant remains, although cultivated flax and wild radish were also recovered and are more unusual.

Three small cuttings were excavated through the walls of D8 and a baulk was maintained that ran on an E-W alignment through the structure. A cutting through the E wall of D8 revealed several deposits in the base of the wall including three patches of charcoal D025-7 that sat directly upon mixed peat ash and stones D039 that included one large slab measuring 1m x 0.45m. It was suggested at first during excavation that these ashy deposits were earlier than the wall, but further examination in post-excavation revealed that they were a basal wall deposit. The E wall of D8 contained mixed material, including that from earlier occupation, such as local pottery sherds, flint waste, a tiny shard of 18th century window glass, mammal bone fragments and burnt peat, heather and conifer charcoal, and carbonised cereal grains. The ashy deposits in the base of the wall contained three body sherds of local pottery, burnt mammal bone fragments, and a familiar range of carbonised plant remains, that reflect the incorporation of hearth material from elsewhere, such as birch, conifer, oak, ash, willow and heather type charcoal. Unusually however, carbonised weed seeds such as sedge, ribwort plantain, buttercup and docks, and oats, hulled and six row barley, and indeterminate cereal grains, burnt straw and peat, were also recovered, and this is discussed further in Chapter 11 below.

D10

The collapsed and slumped traces of the lower part of the turf walls of shelter D10, and ephemeral traces of associated floor deposits, were excavated. D10 was mainly turf-built, and divided into a N part 10A, and a S part 10B. D10A and B had been set into and re-used the lower dry-stone walls of earlier buildings below them. The two parts, A and B, were separated by an earth, probably turf, wall (D097/D098/D099) and (D103/D106) which was investigated in a small trench extension to the S of Trench D. Small patches of occupation layers associated with this structure, D102, D104 and D100 were also identified.

D10A was considerably more degraded and collapsed than other turf shelters on the site and all that remained of the N and E walls was a considerable depth of degraded turf and stone, which comprised re-used tumble D037 from earlier walls D059 and D010. The W wall of D10A comprised two deposits – stones D060, and D068, a bedding of compact clayey silt, and divided D10 from D13 to the W. Wall D060/D068 survived to a height of 0.25m. D068, the footings of the wall, was situated directly over the latest hearth and floor layer of D16 and occupation material from this layer had become incorporated into the later wall. A large oblong stone at the S end of D060 appeared to be the butt end, and no evidence was found of D068 or D060 to the S of this or curving E or W to join with the S walls of either structure, D13 or D10A. It is likely therefore that there was a doorway here between the two conjoining structures. The opposite side to the possible doorway lay outwith Trench D, although part of the S wall of Structures 10A was partially excavated within the small S extension to Trench D. No occupation deposit associated with the use of D10A was identified, although it is possible that deposits D032/34, seen only in section in 2006, may have been the floor deposits that were covered by rubble collapse.

In the S extension of Trench D, part of the turf wall separating Structures D10A and D10B was excavated and comprised D097, a grey sandy clay, D099, a grey band of sand, and D098, a compact clay lump. It is likely, although unconfirmed by soils analysis, that D098 and D099 were the remains of individual turfs, and D099 had been set behind a large upright stone, D107 which abutted earlier wall D010 to the E. Below D097 further probable degraded turf deposits were identified – D103, very similar to D097, and within that, D106 a lump of silty clay. No finds were recovered from these wall deposits. To the W of the large stone upright D107, and the N of turf D097, a small patch of D100 was identified, a mottled sandy clay deposit containing occasional charcoal and bone flecks. This was probably a small corner of floor layer associated with the use of D10A that had survived, equivalent to layers D032/34.

Shelter D10B occupied the space between the wall described above, and the perimeter wall, Structure H, along the S edge of the site. Only a very small part of this building was uncovered in the trench extension, and perimeter wall H also lay out with it. D10B may not have been roofed, or used for occupation, as no evidence of a turf roof or occupation deposit was found within it. D104, a gravely silt was excavated in a small area respecting the edge of the wall between D10A and B, and D102, a sandy silt covering a small area identified adjacent to this, may have been surfaces associated with the use of D10B.

The finds and environmental assemblage from D10A included nine body and a neck sherd of local pottery, a shard of 18th century bottle glass, a flint pebble, a gunflint, a stone weight and a familiar range of mammal bone fragments and plant remains from stone tumble D037 on the E side of the shelter, and a similar assemblage from the W wall D060/D068, with the addition of a shard of 18th century window glass. The assemblages from the possible floor layer D032/D034 and D100 include a similar range, with additional finds of local pottery, flint waste and gunflints, and late 17th/early 18th century window glass. The assemblage from 10B is smaller as less of the structure was excavated and there is little evidence for occupation as only finds of burnt peat were recovered.

D13

D13 was built into the W half of D16, and the dividing wall between it and D10 (D060/D068) is discussed above. Clay bedding layer D068, found beneath the stones of dividing wall D060 forming the E wall of D13, was found to curve around from the N end of D060 and along the N edge of the trench, against earlier dry-stone wall D066, and D069, the SW corner of the unexcavated building D4 to the W. The W wall of D13 was identified as a single N-S aligned earth and stone bank D013. The S wall lay outwith the confines of the trench to the S. An occupation layer D067 was identified in an oval area defined by D068 and the S trench edge.

Material from this building includes a flint chip, mussel and limpet shell fragments and the familiar range of mammal bone fragments, birch, conifer, heather type and oak charcoal, and carbonised cereal grains from wall D013. A varied assemblage of 50 body and two rim sherds of local pottery, two sherds of modern glazed ceramic, two conjoining rim/neck sherds of post-medieval glazed Cologne stoneware and one sherd of post-medieval unglazed pottery, a crucible fragment, a shard of late 18th/early 19th century window glass, flint waste, a fire flint, a gunflint and a musket ball were recovered from the floor layer of D13, together with an environmental

Illus 7.28 D10A wall D060/D068 from N and Illus 7.29 Section through turf and rubble wall D010, showing ashy midden and earlier deposits below

assemblage of 37 mammal, cow and fish bone fragments, birch, heather type, Scots pine type charcoal, and carbonised corn marigold, cultivated flax, oat, hulled and six row barley, indeterminate cereal and burnt peat. The sherds of Cologne stoneware were found to conjoin with a rim/neck sherd found in adjacent D12 from Phase 4 and are an indication that many of the finds from shelter D13 originate from earlier phases of occupation and have become incorporated with the re-built turf and stone walls. The finding of two sherds of later, mass-produced modern ceramics in D067 also demonstrates that the stoneware sherds were not found in context in the floor of D13.

D14

D14 was located between D7, D8 and D10 and as a result was very hard to define as its walls D014 were almost indistinguishable from the walls of the surrounding buildings. The W wall of D14 was partially investigated in a section cut through earlier wall D010 adjacent to it, and this confirmed that D14 post-dated D16. Wall D014 comprised degraded turf-like material of sandy clay with silt, stones and flecks of charcoal throughout, which was built up against the earlier wall D010. D014 also overlay earlier wall footings D040 along the E side of D010. Although occasional stones were found scattered in D014, they were not structural. The basal layers of the wall were identified as D045 and D042=D044. D045, a compact silty clay with frequent roots and a high peat and clay content was also related to the conjoining shelter D7 and indicated that D7 and D14 were contemporary. D042=D044 was the basal fill of D014 only, and comprised a clayey silt with peat and charcoal flecks. Both of these layers overlay earlier wall D010 below.

D014 contained the familiar range of material seen in other contexts from this phase, but also included a shard of 18th century window glass and five pieces of slag. Lower contexts D042=D044 and D045 contained a body and two shoulder sherds of local pottery, a mammal bone fragment, birch, conifer, heather type and oak charcoal, and carbonised oat, hulled and six row barley grains. One radiocarbon date was produced for this phase, from turf wall footing deposit D068 in Structure D10A/D13, and gave a date of AD1480-1640, although this material derives from occupation deposits elsewhere that were then utilised in the wall and cannot be used to date the occupation of D10A/D13 itself.

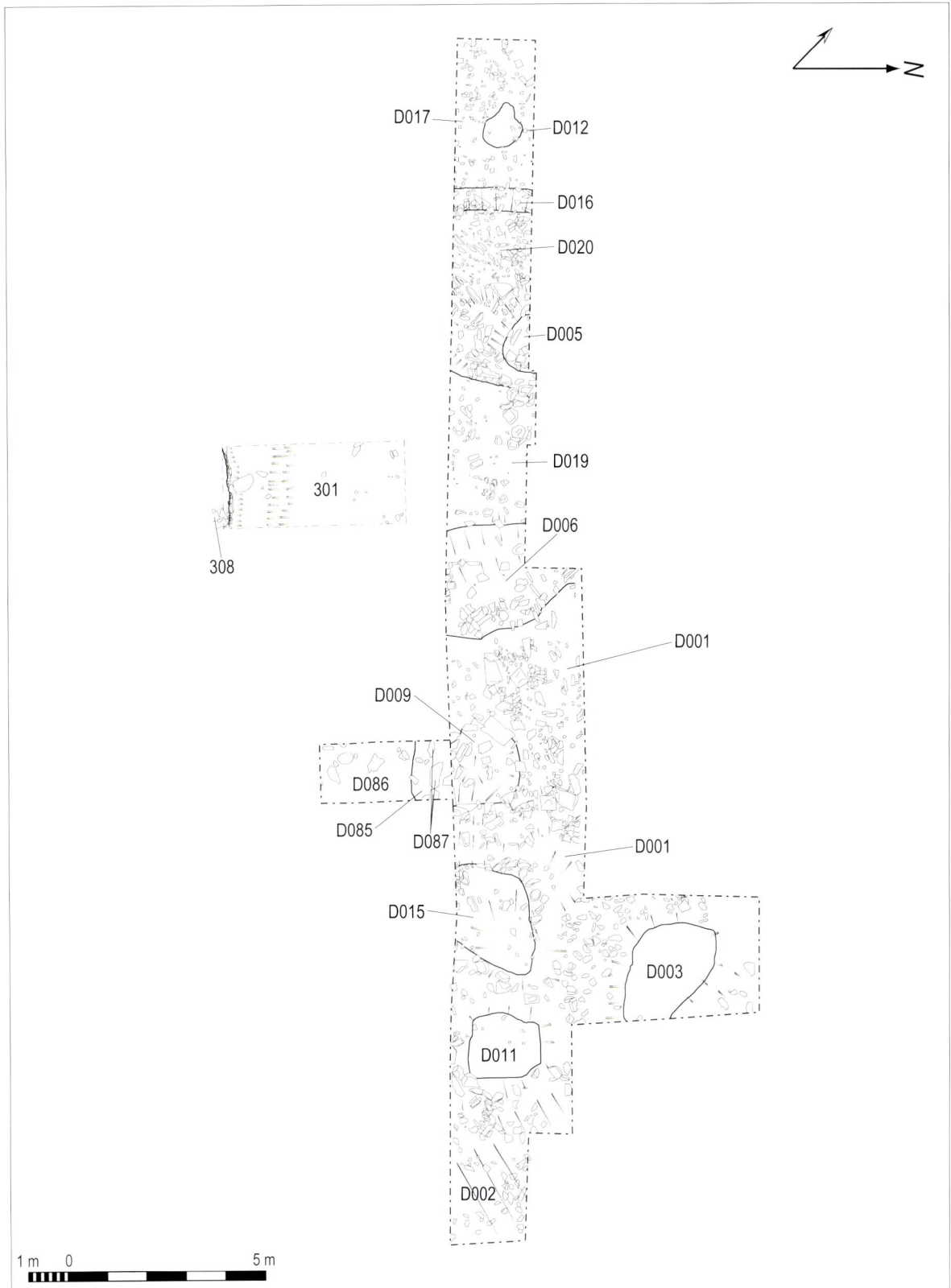

D017

D012

D016

D020

D005

D019

301

D006

308

D001

D009

D086

D085

D087

D001

D015

D003

D011

D002

1 m   0   5 m

Illus 7.31 Phase 6 plan

Phase 6: Post-abandonment and final collapse

After the turf shelters had gone out of use Structure D was covered in thick layers of abandonment and collapse deposits of slumped and rain-washed turf and collapsed walling.

At the W end of the trench D4 was covered by silty clay D005 in the interior of the building from slump from the walls and also possibly the roof. Slump deposits of sandy clay and stones, D016, D019, D020 and D021, were also recorded to the W and E of the structure. Also at the W end of the trench a silty clay deposit D012 and a collapse of stones in soil D017 had slumped from Structure C. Local pottery sherds, a shard from a glass vessel, flint waste and an example of vitrified fuel ash were recovered from slump deposits in and around shelter D4, together with a carbonised assemblage of mammal bone fragments, birch, conifer, Scots pine

type charcoal, corn marigold, burnt peat and carbonised oat, hulled and six row barley grains. A larger assemblage of local pottery sherds, including decorated sherds and rim and neck sherds was recovered from slump deposits from Structure C.

To the E, a roughly linear deposit of stones D006 was found collapsed from the E wall of D13, and overlying a slumped turfy deposit of greyish brown sandy clay D054, possibly the turf roof of the shelter. Finds from these slump deposits included both local and glazed modern pottery, a shard of 19th century glass vessel, flint waste, and a carbonised assemblage of mammal bone fragments, birch, conifer, larch, Scots pine type, oak, cultivated flax, stitchwort and oat and barley grains.

Adjacent shelter D10A was covered by turfy sandy clay deposits D029 and D028/ D030, and stone tumble D009. D085, a sandy clay, and contemporary layer D087, a spread of large stones, excavated in shelter D10B to the S were probably equivalent to these collapse layers. To the S of these layers and covering the remainder of D10B D086 was excavated, a slightly bowl-shaped deposit of clayey sand with small stones and iron pan that had accumulated from slump and wash of material N from the perimeter wall, Structure H, on the edge of the trench, and S, from the wall of D10B. Below this an earlier post-abandonment deposit D095, a sandy

Illus 7.32 D4 pre-excavation from the NE, Illus 7.33 General view of working in D on slump deposits from the SW and Illus 7.34 Structure D10, from the W, showing later collapse over structure

clay layer had washed in to the hollow in the centre of the trench, and D094, sandy clay collapse from the wall between 10A and 10B was identified.

Finds from the slump layers in D10A included 11 sherds of local pottery, including decorated sherds, an iron nail head and evidence for flint working, as well as the burnt assemblage of mammal bone fragments, birch, conifer, heather type and oak charcoal, burnt peat and carbonised oat, hulled and six row barley. A similar assemblage was recovered from slump layers in D10B, with the addition of two sherds of modern glazed ceramic, a sherd of glazed post-medieval pottery, a fire flint and carbonised remains of hazel and corn marigold.

In shelter D7 on the N side of the trench two silty clay slump deposits, D003 over D022, covered the interior of the structure. 61 sherds of local pottery, including rim, neck and decorated sherds, were recovered from these layers, with evidence for flint working, an iron nail, and burnt mammal bone fragments, birch, conifer and heather type charcoal, cultivated flax and oat, hulled and six row barley grains.

At the E end of the trench, a collapse deposit of clayey sand and stones D015 and lower slump of silty clay D021 were found over and around the turf walls of shelter D14, and a thick slump D002 covered silty clays D011, D023 and D031, that had collapsed from the walls and possibly the turf roof of shelter D8. 200 sherds of local pottery, including rim, neck sherds and decorated sherds, were found in slump layers from shelter D8, together with flint waste, iron objects and nails, and finds of carbonised mammal bone, birch, conifer, Scots pine type, ash, oak and heather type charcoal, burnt peat and cereal grains common to many contexts from this phase. Slump from shelter D14 contained a similar assemblage, with the addition of a shard of 18th/19th century bottle glass and a lump of vitrified fuel ash.

Along the S side of the trench, a small collapse of stones 308 was found on the S (exterior) face of wall H, from which a body and a rim sherd of local pottery were recovered.

The finds from the slump layers over all the shelters on the site demonstrate that the turf and stone material used to build these shelters derived from older buildings on the site, although finds contemporary with the use of the shelters, such as 18th/19th century bottle glass were also found.

Phase 7: Topsoil

Trench D was covered by topsoil, from which, as is to be expected, a mixed assemblage of finds was recovered. Amongst the more interesting these included 42 body, five rim and two decorated neck sherds of local pottery, two sherds of modern glazed ceramic, three shards of 18th century bottle glass, an iron flesh hook, a sub-angular copper object and a copper candle holder.

Endnotes

[1] All radiocarbon dates are calibrated and quoted at 95.4% confidence: see Chapter 13

Table 7.7 Phase 6 context description, finds and environmental on CD at back of book

Illus 7.35 Slump and collapse over Structure D14

Table 7.8 Phase 7 context descriptions, finds and environmental on CD at back of book

Illus 8.1 Trench F working shot

eight

area F

Structure F comprises two hollows, F1 and F2, set into the slope down from Structure G on the east side of the island, adjacent to the top of the natural gully, *Palla na Birlinn* (Ledge of the galley). In Area F, half of Structure F1 was excavated, and this revealed that it was a D-shaped turf and stone building built into the hillside. The interior of the building walls were lined with stonework, and a wall across the front of the building was built from double faces of neat stonework with an earthen core and an entrance looking out to the sea across the Minch. Two phases of occupation in the form of floor layers and hearth sweepings were identified, overlying a carefully built drain to channel water out from the slope behind. These two phases of occupation followed each other in quick succession with no build-up of abandonment deposits between them and the artefact assemblages from them are very similar. There was also evidence that midden material was scattered in the building and used in the construction of the walls, and possibly to build up the floor layer. Above these deposits, layers of collapse accumulated after the building had gone out of use. Two samples from each phase of occupation were radiocarbon dated and suggest that the building was in use some time between AD1440-1640.[1] The excavations identified six phases of activity, from earliest to latest: (1) bedrock and natural subsoil, (2) construction of the building, (3) first phase of occupation, (4) second phase of occupation, (5) post-abandonment and collapse, and (6) topsoil.

Finds from occupation Phase 3 included evidence for the

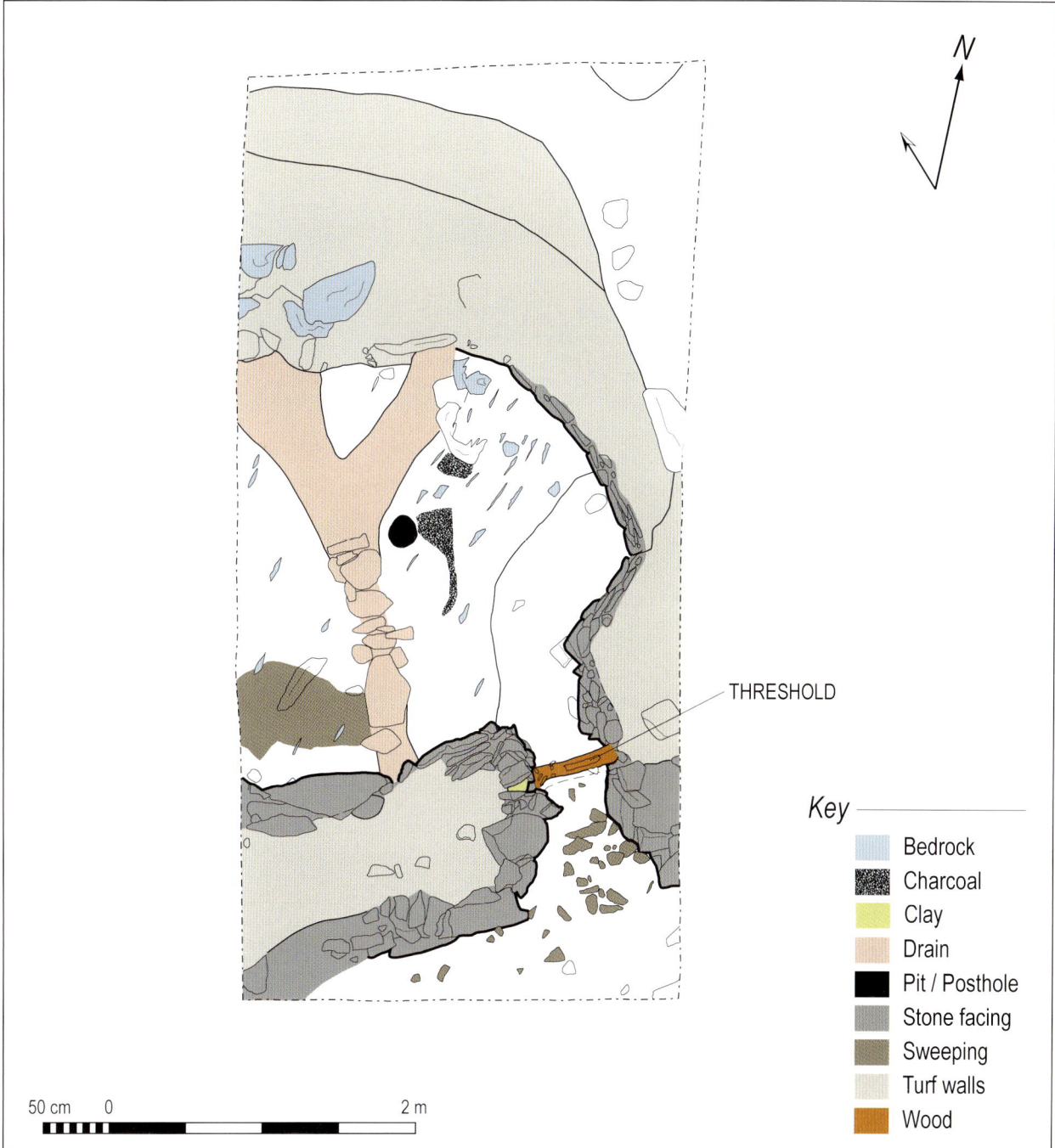

THRESHOLD

Key

	Bedrock
	Charcoal
	Clay
	Drain
	Pit / Posthole
	Stone facing
	Sweeping
	Turf walls
	Wood

50 cm   0   2 m

Illus 8.2 Interpretation plan

burning of driftwood, oak and peat, and the drying and processing of cereals on a domestic scale, oats being more common than barley. Body, shoulder and rim sherds of local pottery, mammal bone fragments and burnt cereal grains suggest domestic food cooking and processing. However, against this general background of material, notable finds of a misshapen musket ball, discarded in the fire after being poorly cast in a two-part mould, and a piece of lead scrap, are evidence for the casting of lead projectiles in Structure F1. A small shard of green glass, probably from a pre-eighteenth century bottle, was also found.

The deposits from the second phase of occupation, Phase 4, were less substantial and may suggest that this was short-lived. An oak wood threshold was inserted in the entrance to the building during this phase, and the interior was swept out, with the sweepings being found as trample just outside the entrance. These sweepings included a group of local pottery sherds, nine of which were decorated, and a gunflint. Flakes and chips of quartz and an iron nail were also recovered, and carbonised remains reflective of hearth material, such as burnt mammal bone fragments, burnt peat, heather, Scots pine, broom, crowberry and cereal grains. The Phase 4 floor deposits contained the usual range of mixed occupation material, including flint and quartz flakes, sherds of local pottery, burnt saithe and cod bones, and carbonised plant species, heather, spruce/fir, and cereal grains.

Despite the same general range of materials and species represented in the assemblages as from other areas of the site, Structure F is different in two key respects. Namely that there is a lack of earlier deposits under the building, and therefore, unlike Structures A, B or D, it was built on a 'clean' previously unoccupied site, and also unlike all the other structures on the site, it was not re-used for shelter after it had been abandoned and collapsed. Furthermore, work on soil samples from the building suggests that it collapsed rapidly (see Chapter 12), and there is therefore the possibility that it was deliberately demolished. It is probable that due to the position of Structure F at the top of the natural gully, Palla na Birlinn, it was a lookout building watching the seaward approach on the east side, and as such was, like Structures B and D, at a strategic point on the island.

Results

with Alastair Becket and Donna Maguire

Trench locations

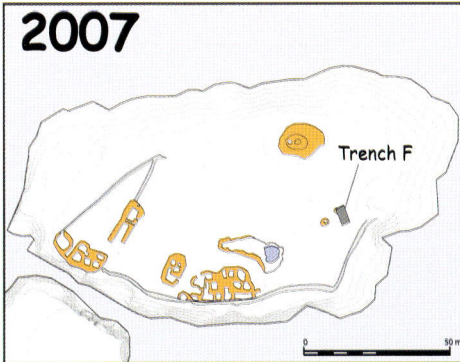

2007 Trench F: 3m x 5m aligned NE-SW across 50% of Room 2 of Structure F.
Aims:
• To investigate whether the hollow was a built structure or a natural scoop in the rock, and to investigate whether it was related to the use of Palla na Birlinn.
• To determine the function and extent of the structure.
• To excavate cuttings through the walls of F where appropriate, so as to understand the construction of the building.
• To take soil micromorphology samples of floor and hearth deposits.
• To sample all undisturbed deposits for environmental and dating material to ascertain whether Structure F was contemporary with other structures on the site.
Work completed: Interior of building excavated down to natural subsoil. A baulk excavated through the wall and hearth/floor deposits.

Phase 2: Construction of building

The building was set into a hollow in the Phase 1 bedrock F018 and natural subsoils F002 and F072. The N and E walls of the building were built from an earthen bank, probably turf, set onto

Illus 8.4 Structure F excavated

the natural slope at the NW (top) and NE sides. The bank comprised an upper deposit F004 of grey brown silty sand and lower deposits of dark brown and yellowish orange silty sand F005 and F020 that may represent lower turf layers or perhaps topsoil that the wall was built directly upon. The bank had been constructed on the hill slope above the structure and a shallow drainage channel F016 had been cut on the N side of the bank which silted up over time with silty sand F013. Within the structure on the E side the bank F004 had been lined with stones F032 laid up to five courses high and continued through the entrance of the structure. No evidence for a stone lining was found on the N exterior face of bank F004, although there may have been a stone lining at the base of the slope that had later collapsed inwards, as suggested by the post-abandonment tumble deposit F028 in Phase 5. A small assemblage of material was recovered from samples of the wall cores and included two quartz chips, and examples of hulled six row barley, oat, heather type, spruce/fir and burnt peat.

The S wall comprised an earthen wall core F007 of mixed sandy silt with a lining of stones F017 at the base of the slope across the front of the hollow, with an entrance gap. The stone lining in this case was slightly more varied in construction with a mix of coursed stones such as those used in F032 and much larger stones that had been set flat against the core as orthostats. In places lumps of firmly compacted orange brown clay F008 were found around the stones and may have been used as a bonding material although the majority of stones appear to have been laid with no bonding. A small lens of sandy silt F041 was found within the earth core F007. This deposit contained three sherds of local pottery and may have represented material that had been transferred from the floor of the structure up into the wall during the

Illus 8.5 Front (S) wall of structure, from N

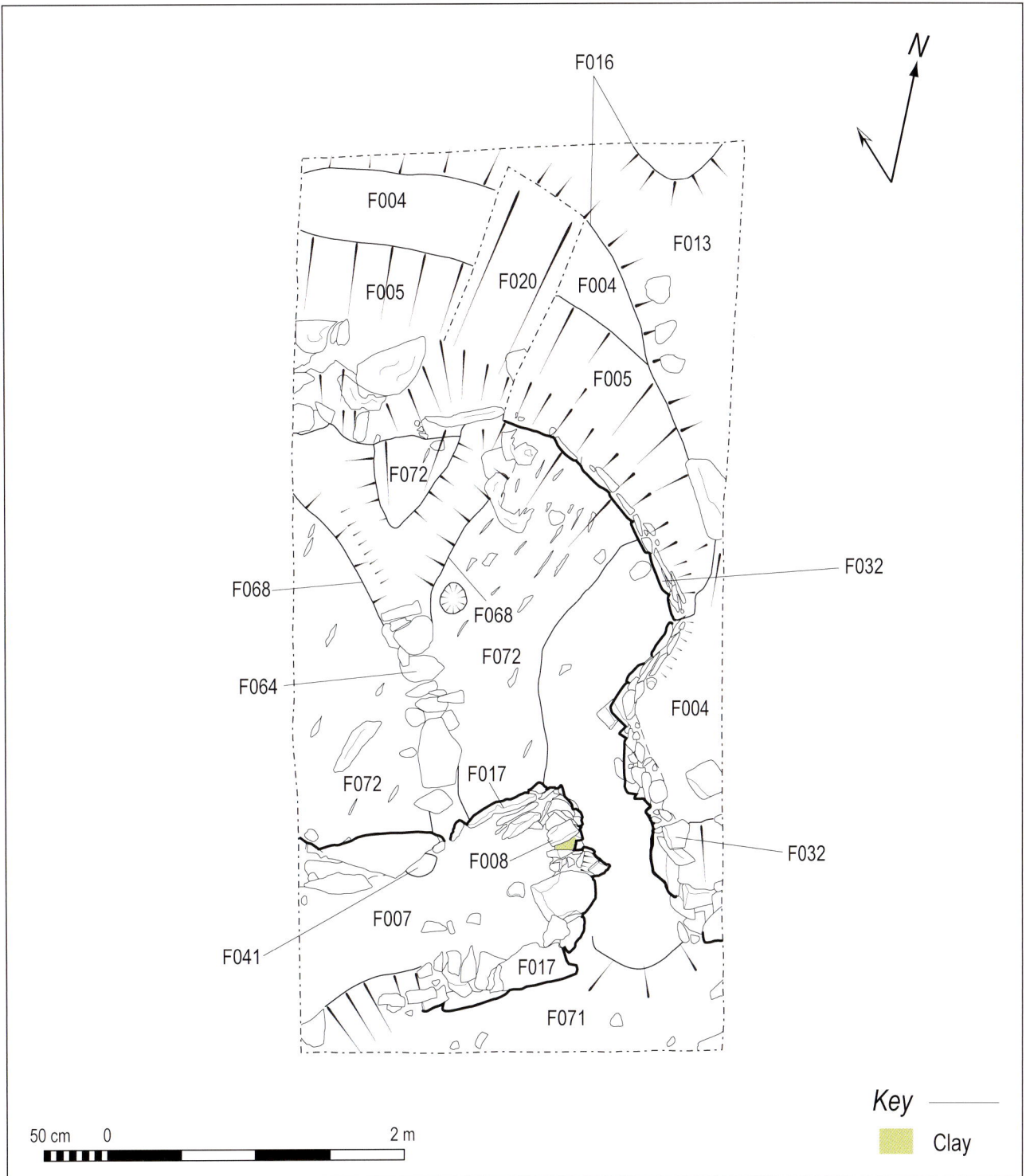

F016

N

F004

F013

F005

F020 F004

F072

F005

F068

F032

F068

F072

F064

F072

F004

F017

F072

F008

F032

F007

F041

F017

F071

50 cm   0   2 m

Key

Clay

course of repair. That the wall may have been repaired at some stage may also explain the mixed construction of the stone lining F017. A small assemblage of two body sherds of local pottery, and heather type, Scots pine type, oat, cf oat, cf and six-row barley, indeterminate cereal and burnt peat was recovered from samples of the wall core F007.

Running under the S wall was a drain F062 that had been cut as a channel to take water away from the N wall of the structure, through the building, and outwards down the slope. This

Illus 8.6 Phase 2 plan

cut was Y-shaped in plan with two open channels to the N feeding into a single channel with a capping of stones F064 and sandy clay F048. This drain had been cut directly into the natural subsoil and may have been cut out when the site was first dug into the hillside although where the limits of the main construction cut begins and the natural slope ends was somewhat unclear. The S half of the drain had been capped with stones and clay forming a fairly flat surface over which floor deposits had been laid. A body sherd of local pottery, a quartz chip, an indeterminate iron object, fragments of mammal bone and burnt peat were recovered from the clay capping F048.

To the E of the drain, in the centre of the building, was a small circular posthole F066 filled with grey sand and upright packing stones F065. This posthole had been dug into the natural subsoil at the time of the construction of the drain and may have held a post to support the roof. The posthole had gone out of use by the time of the second phase of occupation however, as it was sealed by grey sand F037 of Phase 4. A flint chip, conifer charcoal, burnt peat, mammal bone fragments and cereal grains were found in posthole fill F065.

Phase 3: First occupation phase

Once the building had been constructed, a floor of sand was laid in the interior, heavily trampled and compacted, onto which a large number of thin layers of peat ash and other hearth sweepings were dumped and at various stages trampled. The presence of the drain F062 created a linear division in the floor deposits between mixed grey sandy silt F033 on the W side of the drain and mixed darker grey brown sandy silt F046 on the E. A lead musket-ball was found within the floor F046 to the E of the drain. A scattering of environmental material was recovered from these deposits and included the familiar range of fragments of mammal bone, burnt peat, carbonised cereal grains, and burnt conifer, birch and heather. A dark blackish brown lens of sandy silt F058 was seen within the floor layer F033. Two thin layers of black, charcoal-rich material, F042 and F043, had been trampled onto the natural subsoil to the NE of the drain and also formed part of the floor horizon. Two further deposits that formed part of the floor were located in the entrance of the building; a firm, heavily trampled mixed sandy silt F059, over a less compacted mixed sandy silt F071. A thin layer of darker floor material F054, a sandy silt, overlaid the capping stones of the drain F064 in the centre of the structure. A scattering of carbonised cereals, mammal bone fragments, heather, conifer and peat was found in these deposits, together with a flint chip and an indeterminate iron object.

A further deposit of yellow grey sand (F024) in the buildings interior was heavily compacted but very clean, not mixed like the overlying floor (F046). This deposit was seen in the E corner of the building, possibly remaining clean and untrampled due to its location. The other floor layers may have been the same as this deposit when they were originally laid down. A small assemblage of two shoulder, three body and a rim sherd of local pottery, and carbonised birch, six row barley and cereal grains was recovered from this deposit.

A series of peat ash deposits, F034, F035 and F056, F049, F052, F057, F050, F051 and F060 were located in the SW of the excavated interior of the building, spread thinly on top of one another. This series of deposits were the sweepings from a hearth, and suggest that the building did have a hearth but that it probably lay in the unexcavated W side of the interior. Iron nail shank fragments, indeterminate objects and two pieces of porous slag were recovered from these deposits, and the peat ash contained a mixed carbonized assemblage of mammal bone and tooth fragments, birch, conifer, hazel, heather type, oak, burnt peat, sun spurge, oat, six row barley and cf six row barley, and indeterminate cereal grains. A blackish brown deposit of sandy silt with peat ash F053 overlaid the hearth sweeping deposits and was notable for appearing slightly trampled and for containing two indeterminate iron objects, two iron nails, two possible lumps of slag, and a sherd of local pottery.

A discrete dump of sand with clay F038, interpreted as probably degraded turf, was located to the N of the peat ash deposits and may represent a repair to the floor surface over the drain F062. This material also partially overlaid a sub-circular area of scorching F070 that may represent the location of a hearth, albeit a small, possibly temporary, one, or possibly a dump

Illus 8.7 Sandy floor F033/F046 either side of drain and Illus 8.8 Section through hearth sweepings/peat ash from Phase 3

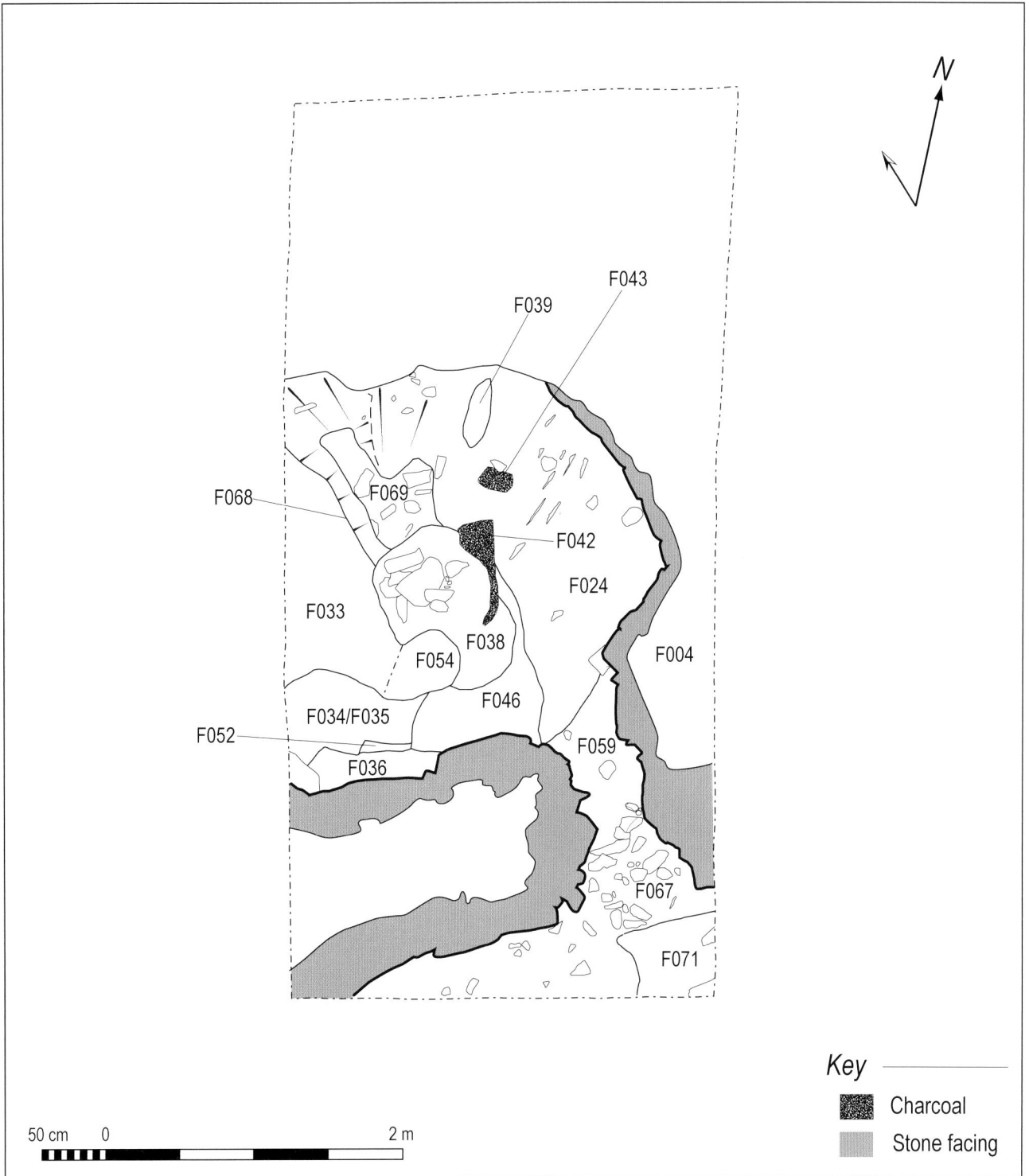

N

F043

F039

F068

F069

F042

F033

F024

F038

F054

F004

F034/F035

F046

F052

F059

F036

F067

F071

Key

▓ Charcoal

▓ Stone facing

50 cm   0   2 m

of burnt material. Similarly, within the peat ash dump deposits, a thin layer of ash F049 had the texture and appearance of being scorched suggesting that a small fire had been burnt on top of the layers of earlier hearth sweepings. The peat ash hearth sweepings were located tight against the stones of the S wall F017 and sealed a thin, dark layer of dark black brown sandy silt F036 that had formed through trampling of a lower peat ash deposit F061. A small piece of glass, probably from a bottle, was found within the dark layer F036, as was a piece of flattened and

Table 8.2 Phase 3 context descriptions, finds and environmental on CD at back of book

folded lead. Otherwise these deposits contained the same general assemblage of carbonised material. Two radiocarbon dates were produced from this phase - AD1440-1630 from trampled charcoal deposit F042, and AD1450-1635 from floor layer F033.

Phase 4: Second occupation phase

The second phase of occupation was made distinct from the first by the insertion of a new floor layer. The reasons for the insertion of the new floor are unclear although the old floor may have become too saturated with ash and other dirt to make it easily cleanable. The deposit of firm grey sand F037 covered the entire interior of the building and was contemporary with similar deposits, F010 that was spread out of the doorway to the exterior, and F031 located against the N wall. These deposits had been spread out to form the base for the floor and all of the deposits relating to the second phase of occupation were built up upon this base. Two further deposits, silty sand F055 and a stony deposit in sand F067, were seen at the entranceway to the structure and appear to have been inserted to create a gentle slope down into the building, something that may have helped to keep draughts out. A rim and a shoulder sherd of local pottery were found in F037, with an iron nail shank. The environmental remains from this sandy deposit contained the usual range of mammal bone fragments, birch, conifer, oak, burnt peat, cereals and grass family. A flint flake and quartz flakes and chips were recovered from F010. A similar range of material was recovered from the deposits at the doorway.

In the doorway of the building was a piece of oak wood set into a linear cut feature, forming a threshold to the building. The wood itself was very fragile and had partly decomposed into the surrounding material F030. The wooden sill protruded slightly above the upper edges of the shallow cut F040 into which it was set, forming a low sill under the doorway. The threshold had been set into the walls on either side of the entrance.

The threshold was sealed by a floor layer F023, a peaty sand, and hearth sweepings F026, silty peat ash. However, there was not the complexity or number of deposits seen in the earlier phase suggesting that the period of occupation may have been shorter or that perhaps the function of the structure had changed. The thin floor layer of dirty, trampled sand F023 covered most of the interior of the structure and contained many pottery sherds. This sealed a further deposit of hearth sweepings F047, orange peat ash and sandy silt, and the threshold in the

Illus 8.10 Sandy floor deposits in interior of building and Illus 8.11 Oak threshold and pottery sweepings in doorway

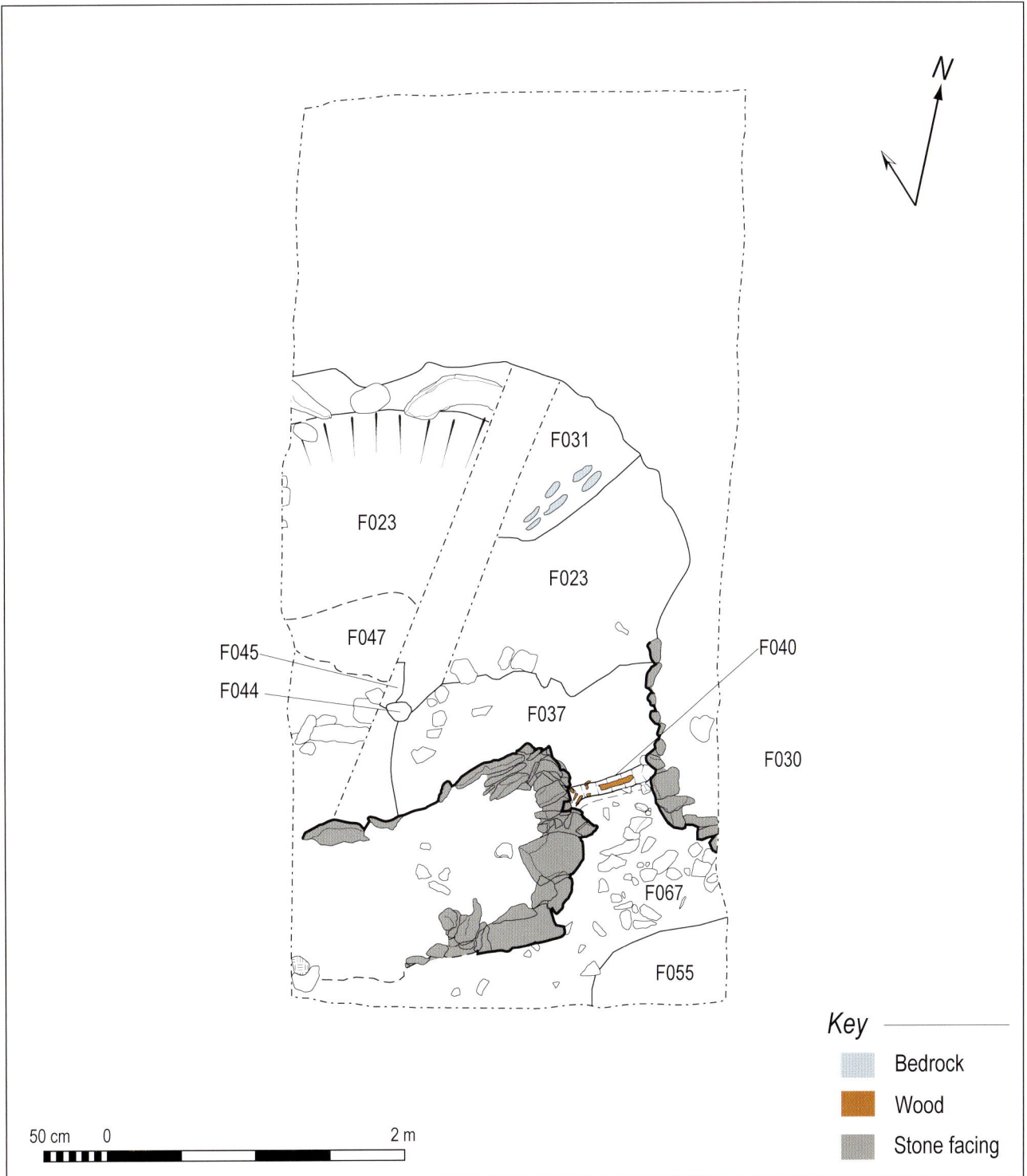

Key

Bedrock	
Wood	
Stone facing	

doorway of the structure. A trampled deposit F009, a silty sand containing many pottery sherds and lenses of ash and clay had formed just outside the entrance to the structure, part of the same horizon as the floor layer F023, perhaps the result of sweepings from the interior of the structure being trampled in the entranceway. A thin layer of hearth sweepings F026 formed the uppermost layer sealed by the collapse and slump deposits and represents the final occupation of Structure F. This material contained peat ash and burnt bone but there was no evidence that the

Illus 8.12 Phase 4 plan

Table 8.3 Phase 4 context
descriptions, finds and
environmental on CD at back
of book

material had been burnt in situ.

Not surprisingly the floor layers and hearth sweepings contained the largest assemblages of material in this phase. 43 body and a rim sherd of local pottery, a flake of quartz and a possible hammerstone were recovered from F023, with a varied environmental assemblage of saithe and cod bones, birch, conifer, heather type, spruce/fir, Scots pine type, grass/sedge, oat, cf oat, six row barley and burnt peat. Lower floor deposit F047 also contained many sherds of local pottery, including four decorated sherds, five rim sherds, a neck/handle sherd and five shoulder sherds, including two decorated. The carbonised plant remains were similar to F023, with the addition of examples of broom and crowberry. A body sherd of local pottery, a flint flake, iron objects, a nail and a rove, and a gunflint were recovered from hearth sweepings F026, with the environmental assemblage including examples of cultivated flax, as well as birch, conifer, heather, and mammal bone fragments.

Two radiocarbon dates were produced from this phase – AD1455-1635 from hearth sweepings F026 and AD1480-1640 from trampled floor layer F023.

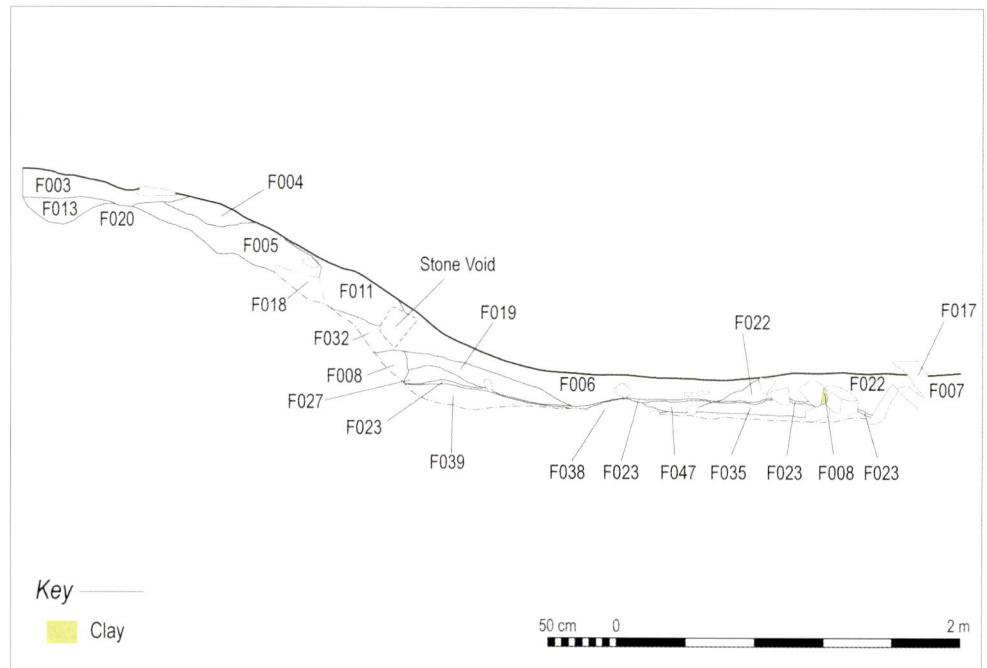

Phase 5: Post-abandonment and collapse

When the building was abandoned its collapse can be seen in the slump deposits that were excavated. A large number of pottery finds were made from these collapse deposits suggesting that the turf and midden used in the building construction had come from an area of previous occupation. Two deposits of tumbled stone were found in the interior of the building, F022 and F028, and may represent stone lining of interior walls that had collapsed as the structure had gone out of use.

To the N of the building were slump deposits F003 and F021 resulting from gradual erosion and slump of the turf walls. These deposits were less substantial than slump deposits found within the structure, and contained sherds of local pottery, a quartz flake, fish and mammal bone fragments, and an environmental assemblage of birch, spruce, oats, barley and burnt peat, consistent with material contained within the turf used to build the walls, as seen elsewhere on the site. There were also slump and collapse deposits located on the S exterior of the structure. These silty clay and silty sand deposits, F029, F025 and F014, were all located around the entrance to the structure, in the SE corner of the trench. Two body sherds and a rim sherd of local pottery, three flakes of flint and corroded iron nail fragments were recovered

from these deposits, together with a similar environmental assemblage to the other slumped wall deposits, but with the addition of carbonised grass/sedge.

Further deposits relating to the slump and collapse of the structures walls were found in the interior of the structure. These included grey silty sand slump deposits from the back wall of the structure, F019 and F027, as well as a deposit containing angular stones that may represent the collapse of a stone lining F028. A similar stone tumble deposit F022 was seen abutting the S interior wall of the structure. This tumble sat directly on top of deposits relating to the final phase of occupation of the building. Three body sherds, one of which was decorated, two quartz chips and two flint flakes were recovered from these deposits, and an environmental assemblage of burnt peat, cereal grains and conifer charcoal, as well as examples of birch and dock.

Uppermost of the collapse deposits in the interior of the structure were grey silty sand deposits F006 and F011. A lens of darker, more richly organic, material F015 was found within the main roof collapse deposit F006 as well as a large number of craggan-ware pottery sherds. It is not clear why so much pottery should be contained within the collapsed walls and roof, other than as an indication that the turfs used to build Structure F were cut from an area of pre-existing settlement or midden. A similar range of carbonised plant and animal bone fragments were found in these deposits as elsewhere, although F006 was particularly rich in pottery, containing 17 body and one rim sherd of local pottery, and F011, one shoulder sherd of local pottery. Flint waste and an iron nail were also recovered.

Phase 6: Topsoil

Trench F was covered by topsoil F001, and an animal burrow was also excavated from the NE side of the slope F012. Indeterminate mammal and sheep/goat bones, and limpet and dog whelk shells were recovered from the topsoil.

Endnotes

[1] All radiocarbon dates are calibrated at 95.4% confidence: see Chapter 13

Table 8.4 Phase 5 context descriptions, finds and environmental on CD at back of book

Table 8.5 Phase 6 context descriptions, finds and environmental on CD at back of book

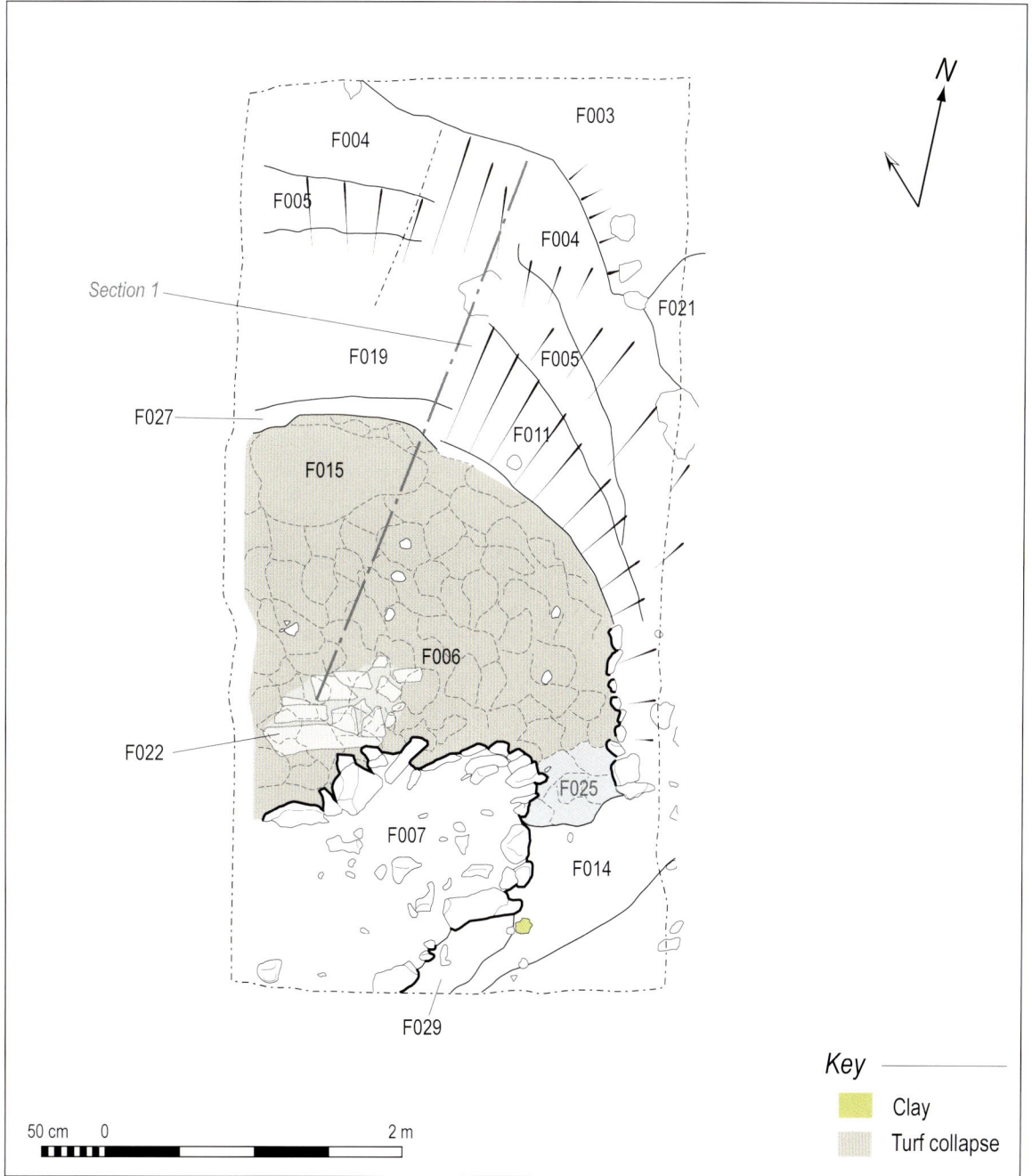

N

Section 1

F004
F003
F005
F004
F021
F019
F005
F027
F011
F015
F006
F022
F025
F007
F014
F029

Key

Clay
Turf collapse

50 cm   0   2 m

Illus 8.16 Phase 5 plan

nine

Structure G is situated on the highest point of Dùn Èistean, on the north side of the island where there are commanding views across the Minch to the Scottish mainland and northwards to the North Atlantic. Excavations took place in Area G in and around the ruined building on the rocky plateau on which it was built, with narrow trenches extended to the south and east down the slope, and a small area beyond the plateau to the south-west. Excavation of the main structure showed that only the lower part of the building survived, the upper storey having completely collapsed in antiquity, covering the ruins in a thick mound of stone rubble and clay. Below this rubble, excavations of half the mound revealed the lower story of a rectangular tower built from thick, 2m wide double-skinned walls with an outer face of neat clay-bonded stonework, and an inner core of compressed peat ash, midden and turf. The upper storey of clay-bonded stonework had been built onto the heads of the thick lower walls and fallen lintel stones found around the base of the building suggest that there was a door and/or window at the upper level. The building had functioned as a small lookout tower or keep for the stronghold, with only room for two or three people inside. Excavation of a section of the tower wall revealed that it had partially collapsed whilst being built, before the upper storey had been added, and the collapsed lower storey walls were simply repaired and incorporated into a second, successful, attempt. This may suggest that the tower was built hurriedly, perhaps in response to a specific threat.

By the nineteenth century all that remained of the tower was a large mound of rubble, and it had became known as *'Tigh nan Arm'* (House of the Armoury, or Arms) in oral tradition. In 1866-7 local antiquarian Malcolm MacPhail dug a hole into the top of the mound, and the hollow left by his excavation was used occasionally for shelter in the late nineteenth/early twentieth centuries, when a memorial cairn was built adjacent to it on top of the mound. Eight phases of activity are in evidence in Area G: (1) bedrock and natural subsoil, (2), original ground surfaces, (3) construction and collapse of the first tower, (4), rebuild and repair of the tower, (5) final collapse, (6) MacPhail's excavations, (7) temporary shelter, and (8), topsoil and marker cairn.

Compared with other buildings on the site, the assemblages of finds and environmental material from Structure G are small. Pottery sherds and two gunflints, burnt cereal grains, mammal bone fragments, peat and charcoal were recovered from the ground surfaces surrounding the tower and probably derive from ash and midden material trampled around the tower whilst it was being built. Burnt peat and charcoal, iron nails and roves from the burning of driftwood, sherds of local pottery, a fragment from a broken whetstone, and burnt mammal bone fragments and cereal grains found in the wall core and clay bonding deposits in Phases 3 and 4 are evidence for the incorporation of domestic and hearth waste into the earthen cores of the tower walls. Two notable finds of a complete schist whetstone and a sherd from a late medieval/post-medieval glazed pot were recovered from a patch of material found on the old ground surface at the base of the tower wall and this deposit, and also a wall core layer, have been radiocarbon dated and produced and overall range of AD1435 -1635[1] for the construction of the tower. The finding of the late/post-medieval glazed ceramic in this context would seem to suggest a date towards the latter half of this range, confirming that the tower was an integral part of the defended settlement, and contemporary with the other buildings on the island.

Corroded iron nails found in the collapsed rubble from Phase 5 when the tower was abandoned suggest that driftwood timbers may have been used to support the tower roof. Three notched flat stones that were also found could be roofing slates, although these are far

Illus 9.2 Interpretation plan (opposite)

REBUILT TOWER

ORIGINAL TOWER

Section 1

ORIGINAL TOWER

1 m   0   5 m

Section 1

Collapse

Collapse

Collapse

Foundation

1 m   0   5 m

Key

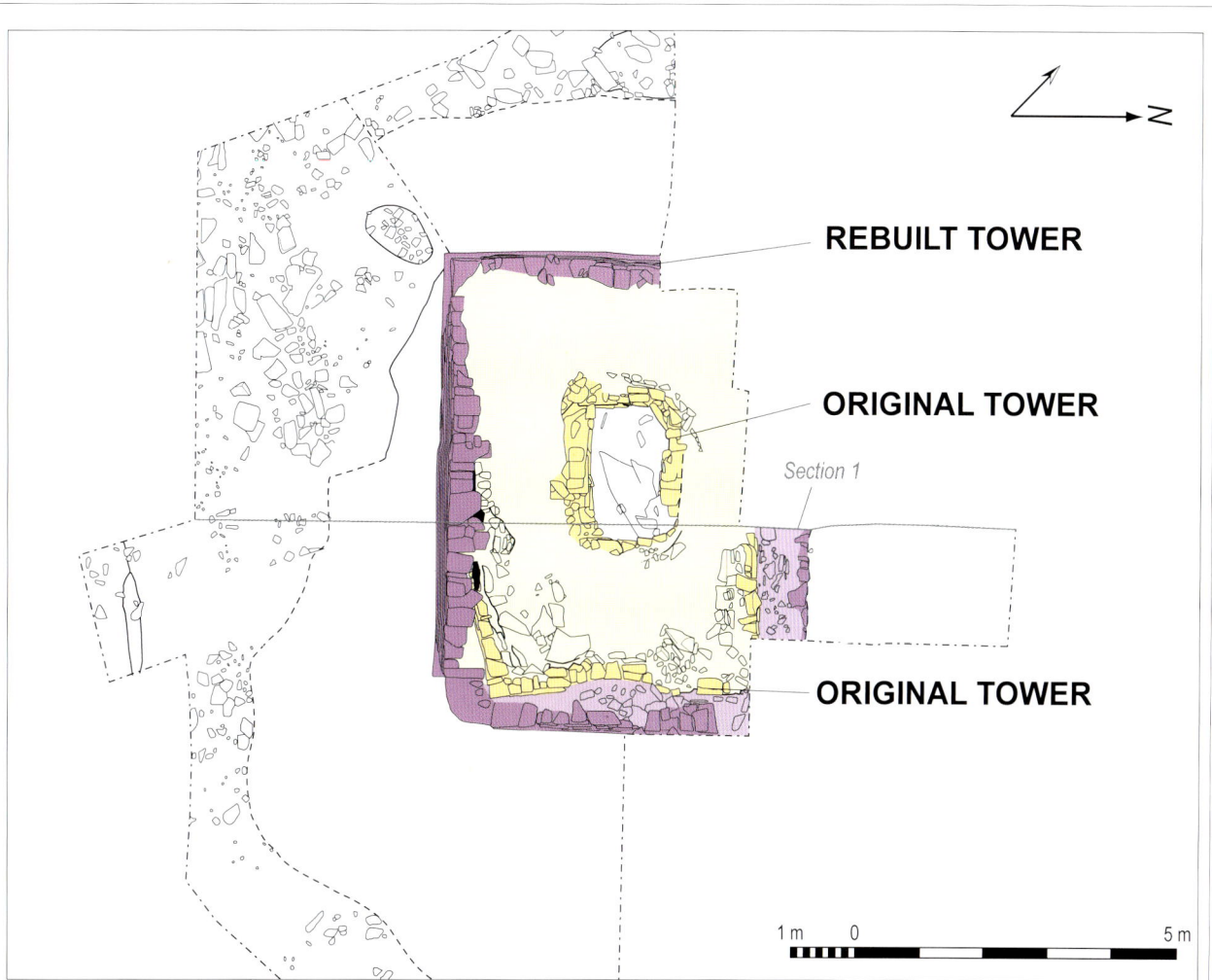

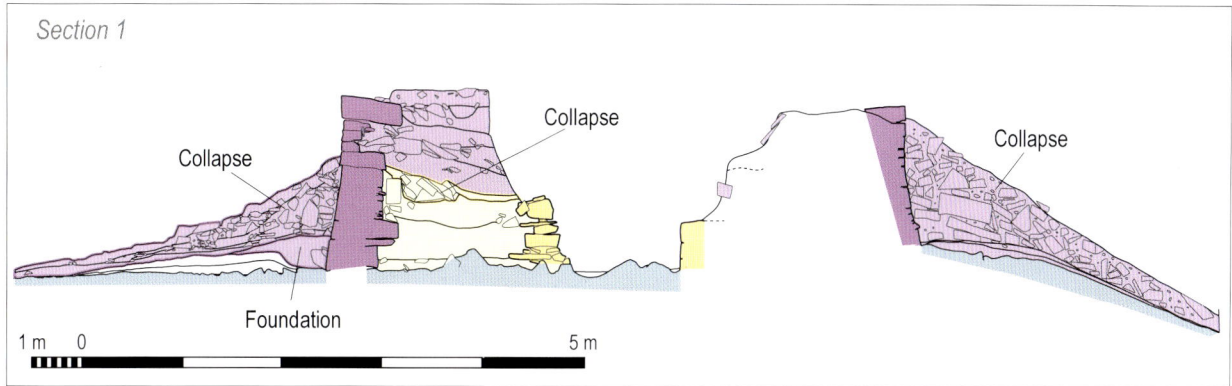

Bedrock	Stone facing of rebuilt tower	Turf walls of original tower
Void	Stone facing of original tower	Turf wall of rebuilt tower

from definite and it is perhaps more likely that the tower had a turf and heather/straw roof like the other buildings on the site. A musket ball, a gunflint and flint-working debris, also found in the rubble, suggest that artillery was being used in or near the tower. Excavation of the rubble from around the tower identified that the upper tower collapsed in two short catastrophic events, suggesting that either the gunflint, musket ball and other items were contained within these walls before they collapsed, or they accumulated during the collapse of the tower eg during deliberate demolition. Three gunflints and a stone gaming piece found in the backfill left by MacPhail's excavations (Phase 6) may have derived from the central chamber of the tower that was cleared out by MacPhail in 1867. Modern Phases 7 and 8 produced as expected pieces of metal, a whisky bottle top, shells and modern sheep and small mammal bones. A 1936 George V bronze penny provides the earliest dating for the memorial cairn.

Large areas outside the tower were also excavated as well as the structure itself, but no evidence was found for any surviving archaeological features. Excavations on the edge of the rocky plateau failed to find any evidence for earlier buildings or occupation, and although the geophysical survey had indicated the possibilities of a rock-cut ditch around the tower, these were revealed to be natural faults in the bedrock. No residual earlier Iron Age material was found in any deposits, confirming that the tower was not a re-used Iron Age structure but, like all the other buildings excavated on Dùn Èistean, was built and used between the 1500s and early 1600s AD.

Results
with Ian McHardy

Trench locations

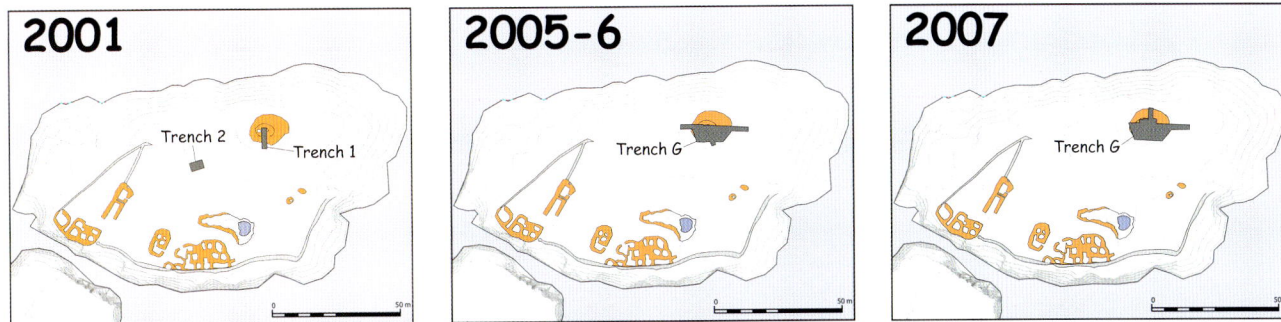

2001

Trench 2
Trench 1

2005-6

Trench G

2007

Trench G

2001 Trenches 1 and 2: Trench 1 8m x 2m N-S across Structure G, Trench 2 3m x 5m E-W over a geophysical anomaly on plateau 20m SW of Structure G.

Aims: Trial Trench 1 to investigate Structure G and whether earlier structures or ditches were present. Trial Trench 2 to assess geophysical anomalies outside Structure G, such as a possible rock-cut ditch and other structures.

Work completed: Trenches excavated to natural subsoil. Walling of Structure G left in tact to protect structure. No archaeological deposits identified in Trial Trench 2. Geophysical anomalies proved to be natural features and not structural remains.

2005 Trench G: 30m across S half of Structure G extending S to 9m, with 2m-wide extensions to the E and W.

Aims:
• To remove stone collapse from 50% of exterior of G and examine edges of rock plateau.
• To uncover top of 50% of Structure G walls to assess erosion and record the remains of rectangular tower identified.
• To record and dismantle marker cairn on the summit of Structure G.

Work completed: Marker cairn recorded, removed and stone stacked for reconstruction. Part of collapse around tower excavated to bedrock. A modern shelter and 19th century excavation trench identified in collapsed interior of the tower.

2006 Trench G: As in 2005

Aims:
• To remove collapse from exterior of G and investigate how and why tower collapsed.
• To examine condition of tower wall to assess its potential for conservation in the future.
• To excavate interior of G as far as possible and assess the condition of any in situ deposits.
• To complete excavation of outlying areas of rock plateau.

Work completed: Central part of trench excavated down to subsoil. Total removal of rubble and collapse from W half of the trench. Modern shelter, 19th century excavations and remnants of interior of tower excavated. Outer arms of trench excavated to bedrock.

2007 Trench G: E half of Trench G and E extension 7m x 2m re-opened, plus 5m x 2m extension to the N, and 1.8m extension on N side of the trench

Aims:
• To complete outstanding work from previous years, specifically the process and nature of the collapsed layers and N side of the wall heads of Structure G.
• To take soil micromorphology samples of the wall core material in tower wall.

Work completed: Interior of building, cutting through wall core, and exterior of SW corner of tower excavated down to natural subsoil. Collapse, wall core deposits and possible floor deposits all excavated but N half of mound and walls left in tact to protect structure.

Phase 2: Original ground surfaces

The tower was built on bedrock and natural subsoil G064=G067=G076. Geophysical survey in 2001 had indicated the possible presence of a rock-cut ditch on the S and W sides of the tower (see Chapter 2 above, anomalies A5 and A6), but no evidence for this was found in the excavations. Excavations in Trench 2 in 2001 to the SW of G found no archaeological remains and revealed that the geophysical anomaly B9 (and by implication B6 and B10) was a bedrock outcrop and the circular raised area upon which the tower was built was a natural platform in the bedrock and had not been artificially raised or enhanced.

Above the natural subsoil the earliest archaeological deposits identified were the original ground surfaces (silty sands) G056=G078=G065, G027=G028=G055=G072=108, 109, 110 and G026 over the areas S and E of the tower. These layers were overlaid by G054, thin lenses of red iron pan spread patchily over the area. Similar layers G081 and G080 were excavated in the trench on the N side of the tower. A group of slates G082 infilling a natural hollow were excavated outside the SW corner of the tower.

Finds from these original ground surfaces include a body sherd of local pottery and carbonised larch, Scots pine type and oat from layer G078, and a base and seven body sherds of local pottery, a burnt chunk of flint and indeterminate iron object and a gunflint from G055=G072=108-110. Alder, oak and Scots pine type charcoal, and carbonised oats and six-row barley were also recovered from G072. Nine body sherds of local pottery and a gunflint were found in G080 and G081 on the N side of the tower, together with unidentified small calcined fragments of mammal bone, alder, birch, spruce, oak and Scots pine type charcoal, burnt peat, and carbonised oats and hulled and six row barley grains.

A flint chip and fragments of birch and Scots pine type charcoal, and indeterminate carbonised cereal grains found in the Phase 1 natural subsoils are intrusive, having been washed down by water action and settled on to the natural subsoil from the layers of collapse and wall core above.

Table 9.1 Phase 2 context descriptions, finds and environmental on CD at back of book

Phase 3: Construction and collapse of first tower

A slumped and buckled outer wall face G005 and clay bonding G041 of an earlier wall within the later tower wall was identified, backed by wall core layers 66, and 73=61, and an inner face G032=G057 defining an oval-shaped hollow in the centre of the tower. The face of the earlier wall G005 had twisted and collapsed, but was found still in situ within the outer wall face of the second and more substantial and well-built wall G004 (of Phase 4), which represented the repair of the tower simply re-built around the earlier collapsed wall. When the rebuilt tower itself later collapsed, the remains of the buckled earlier wall G005 had survived within it at the E side and stood to a higher level than the later re-built face G004 around it. This presented a very confusing picture during excavation, with the earlier collapsed phase of tower actually standing proud of the in tact courses of later masonry around it, so that during the topographic survey, and subsequent excavations in 2001 and 2005, G005 was thought to be a later addition sitting on top of G004, even perhaps the remains of the upper walls of the tower, rather than the remains of an earlier structure surviving within the later wall core.

Under normal circumstances the later wall would be dismantled so as to investigate the earlier wall below/within it. However in this case the tower walls had to be left intact to protect them and to leave open possibilities for conservation of the structure in the future presentation of the site. As a result only the upper 0.6m of G005 could be uncovered and investigated. It could still be seen from this shallow investigation however that the stonework of G005 was ragged and irregular compared with the neatly-coursed work of later wall G004 around it.

The wall core layers that were contemporary with G005 were also still partly in situ and comprised G066, a silty clay with grey silty sand lenses, overlaid by G073=G061, mixed lenses of peat, sandy clay and silty sand. They slumped downwards with a defined kink, suggesting a slump in the wall core during its construction, outwards to the S and W. The survival of only the E half of the stonework of the first tower wall G005 supports this. A remnant of stonework G074 that had tumbled from wall G005, some with clay bonding attached, was also excavated, and included a large cornerstone.

Illus 9.6 Phases 2 and 3 plan (opposite)

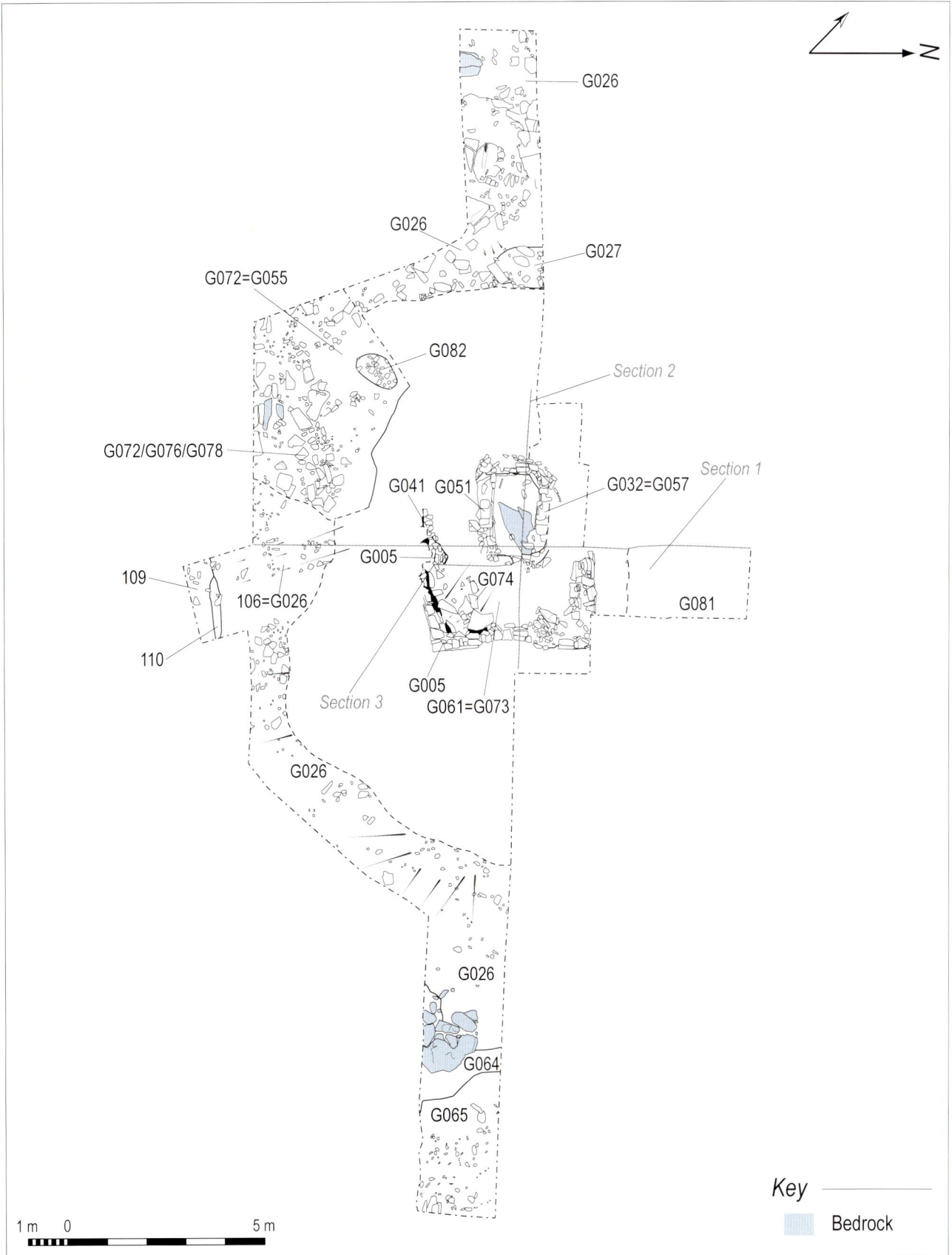

G026

G026

G027

G072=G055

G082

G072/G076/G078

Section 2

Section 1

G041 G051

G032=G057

G005

109

106=G026

G074

G081

110

G005

Section 3

G061=G073

G026

G026

G064

G065

1 m   0   5 m

Key

Bedrock

Illus 9.7 Full extent of collapsed tower wall G005, Illus 9.8 Close-up of first tower wall G005, slumped, with collapse G074, Illus 9.9 W facing section through lower wall core on S side of tower, showing collapsed stones G074 and slump in wall core material and Illus 9.10 Interior 'chamber' in base of tower, from above E

Table 9.2 Phase 3 context descriptions, finds and environmental on CD at back of book

The finds and environmental assemblages from the wall layers are suggestive of the use of midden material in the wall core mix. Finds included nine body sherds of local pottery, two of which were decorated, a chunk of flint and flakes of flint and quartz, and a possible whetstone fragment. A thin piece of iron wire and an iron nail head probably originated from driftwood ash. The environmental assemblage included larch and Scots pine type charcoal, as well as alder, birch, oak and burnt peat, carbonised oat, six-row barley and hulled six row barley grains. A mink skull fragment however, suggests that there was some later disturbance in upper layer G061 from mink burrowing (as seen in the layers of topsoil and collapse above).

Within the interior chamber in the centre of the tower a compact sand G049 was excavated, which was overlaid by a mixed silty G050 and which may be the remains of a surface that accumulated during the building of the tower. No finds were recovered from these layers, although an environmental assemblage of spruce and Scots pine type charcoal, burnt peat and oat, six row barley and indeterminate carbonised cereal grains was recovered from the upper layer G050.

Samples from floor layer G050 from the tower interior, and wall core contexts G061 and G073 were radiocarbon dated to AD1440-1630, AD1440-1630 and AD1450-1635.

Phase 4: Rebuild and repair of the tower

This phase of rebuilding and repair of the tower was investigated in the excavation of the southern half of the surviving lower storey of the tower, a small trench on the N face and in the section cut through the wall cores of the S wall.

On the S side of the tower G004 was set into a foundation cut G058 with a small amount of silty fill, G077, from which a quartz flake, burnt peat and alder, Scots pine type and oat carbonised remains were recovered. A small deposit of trampled silty clay with peaty clay and orange/yellow clay patches, G029, similar to wall core material, was also found in the foundation cut at the base of the wall face G004. A complete schist whetstone, a sherd of post-medieval glazed ceramic and two sherds of local pottery were found in context G029, together with an environmental assemblage of the usual range of material associated with other wall core contexts on the site. One body sherd of local pottery was found in layer G031=106. Wall G004 comprised a substantial wall of neatly coursed large slabs and blocks with small pinning stones and larger tie stones reaching into the core and clay bonding G068=G062=118 between the stonework. This stonework face had a deliberate inward batter of c 0.3m over a 1.5m height, with the wall widest at the base and narrowing towards the top, and was backed by further thick layers of mixed turf, clay, peat and midden wall core layers. The walls survived to a height of 2m, at which the tower

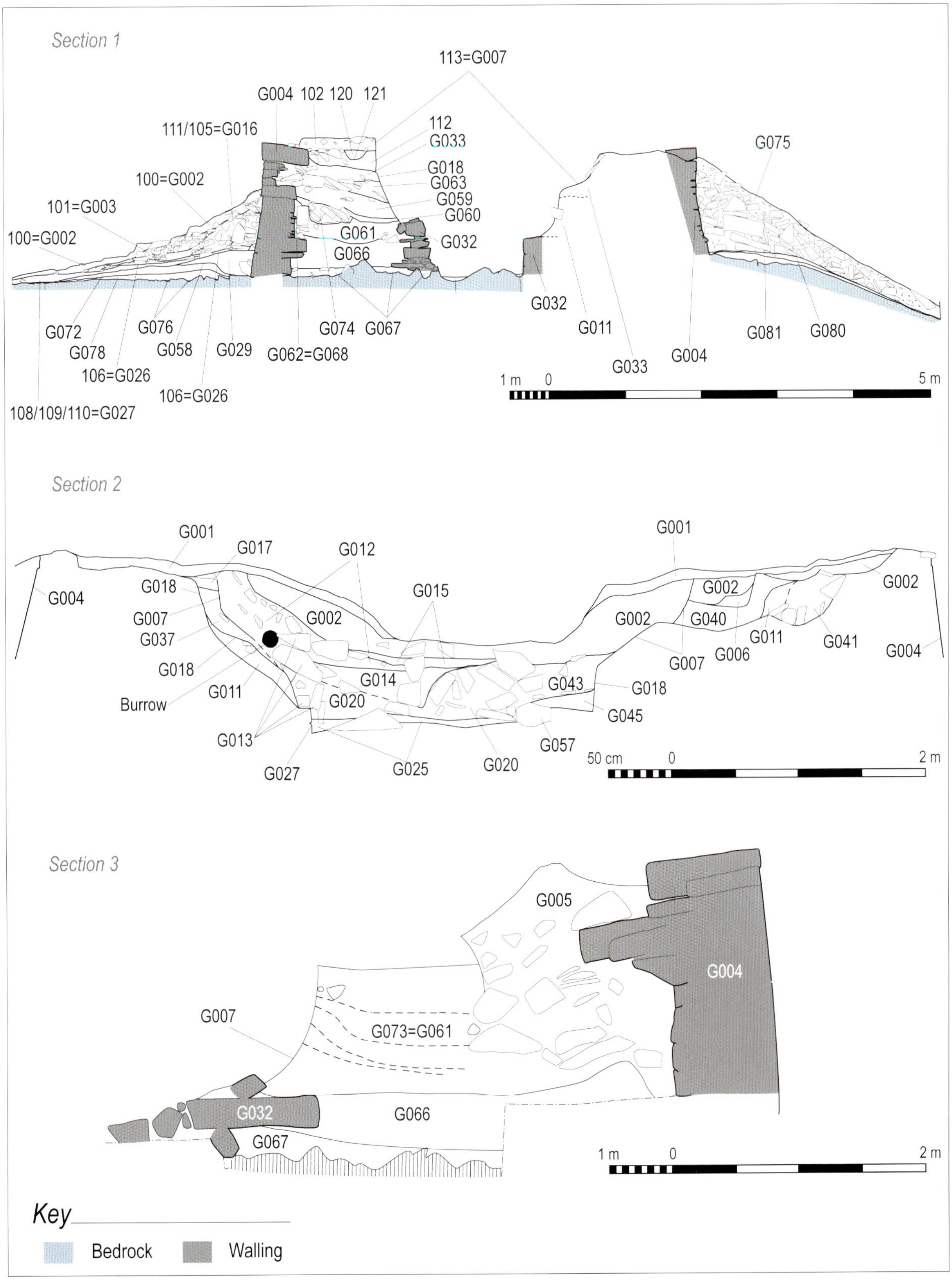

Section 1

113=G007

G004 102 120 121

112
G033

111/105=G016

G018
G063
G059
G060
G032

100=G002

101=G003

G061
G066

100=G002

G075

G072
G078
G076
G058
106=G026
G029
G074 G067
G062=G068
106=G026

108/109/110=G027

G032

G011

G033

G004

G081 G080

1 m   0   5 m

Section 2

G001

G017

G012

G001

G018

G015

G002

G004

G007
G037

G002

G040

G002

G018

G002

G006
G011

G041

G004

Burrow

G011

G014

G043

G007

G018

G020

G045

G013

G027

G025

G020

G057

50 cm   0   2 m

Section 3

G005

G004

G007

G073=G061

G032

G066

G067

1 m   0   2 m

Key

Bedrock   Walling

Illus 9.11 Trench G sections

area G / 199

Illus 9.12 Foundation cut at base of tower wall from above N and Illus 9.13 W side of tower from W, working shot (opposite)

Illus 9.14 E facing section of wall core on W side of tower showing upper wall core layers tipping, lower layers level

Table 9.3 Phase 4 context descriptions, finds and environmental on CD at back of book

had external measurements of *c* 7m x 4.5m, with the long axis aligned E-W. The thick layers of collapsed stonework around the exterior of the tower were all that remained of the upper storey, although it was estimated that this once stood to 2m to 3m, judging by the amount of fallen masonry excavated. No evidence for a door was found in the parts of the lower storey wall face uncovered. Wall G004 incorporated the remains of the earlier wall G005 with the two walls were knitted together half way along the S face. The W side of the tower therefore had only one exterior wall face, whereas on the E side where part of the first phase of tower wall was still standing, the new wall G004 was built around the outside of the collapsed and buckled remains of earlier wall G005.

Behind the stone face G004 new layers of wall core material were built up. Initially when the tower walls were uncovered the wall core was given one context number, G011, but further investigation revealed the complexity of the layers. In the SE corner of the tower only one wall core layer was added, G071, but to the W, where the earlier tower wall had completely collapsed, three layers were needed - G060, G059 and G063. These wall core layers contained a mixture of turf, peat, peat ash and midden material, and this was confirmed in the analysis of soil micromorphology samples taken of the section of wall core layers excavated on the S side of the tower (see Chapter 12, below). Finds from these wall core layers were limited, but included three body sherds of local pottery, a flint chip and an iron rove with a nail shank. Environmental material recovered includes calcined mammal bone fragments, larch, pine, fir, Scots pine type, spruce, alder and oak charcoal, and burnt peat, all indicative of the inclusion of domestic hearth waste. Carbonised oat, hulled and six-row barley, indeterminate cereal grains and a single example of wheat in layer G063, probably a contaminant, were also present.

In the SE corner on the wall heads of the lower storey a concreted layer G069=G040 above a trampled deposit G070 was excavated. The very hard, concrete nature of G069 suggests that the wall heads of the lower storey acted as a platform around the inner edge of the upper tower, similar to the earthen platform utilised around the kiln bowl in the interior of the N end of Structure C. Certainly when the collapsed stonework from the upper storey was excavated from around the tower no evidence for collapsed wall-core material was found (see Phase 5 below), suggesting that the upper storey comprised clay-bonded stonework only. Context G070 below G069 was very similar to wall core material, being made up of peat and yellow/yellow-brown clays. No artefacts were recovered from these contexts, and the small calcined fragments of mammal bone, alder, birch, Scots pine type and heather charcoal, and carbonised cereal grains were all that was recovered from the environmental assemblage. Radiocarbon dating was undertaken of samples from wall core context G059 and deposit G029 at the base of the tower wall, with a resulting range of AD1435-1635 and AD1450-1635, respectively.

Wall G004 South facing elevation

25 cm   0   1 m

Wall G004 West facing elevation

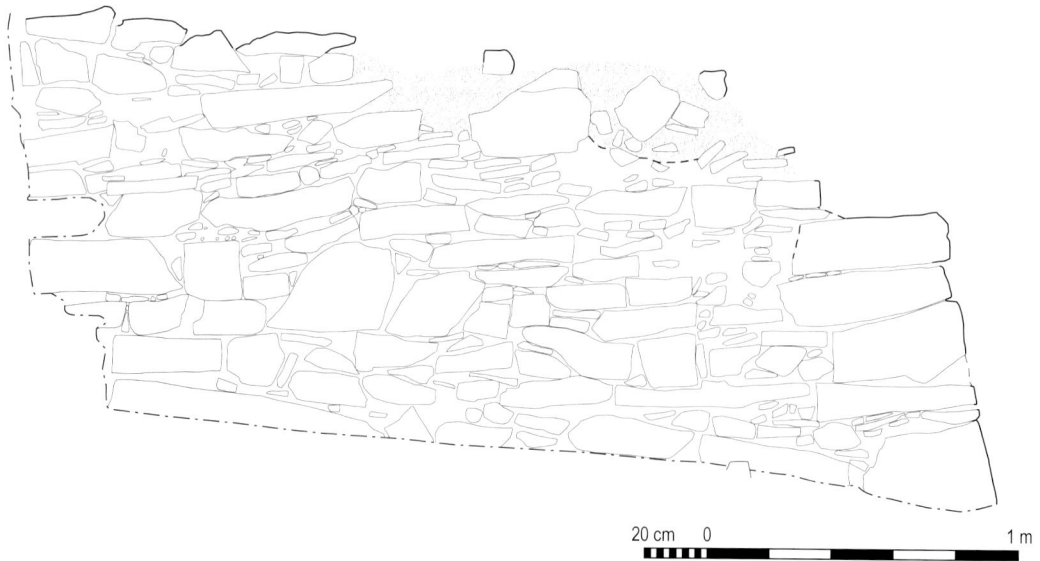

20 cm   0   1 m

Key

Recess in stonework   ■ Void in stonework

Illus 9.15 Tower wall elevations

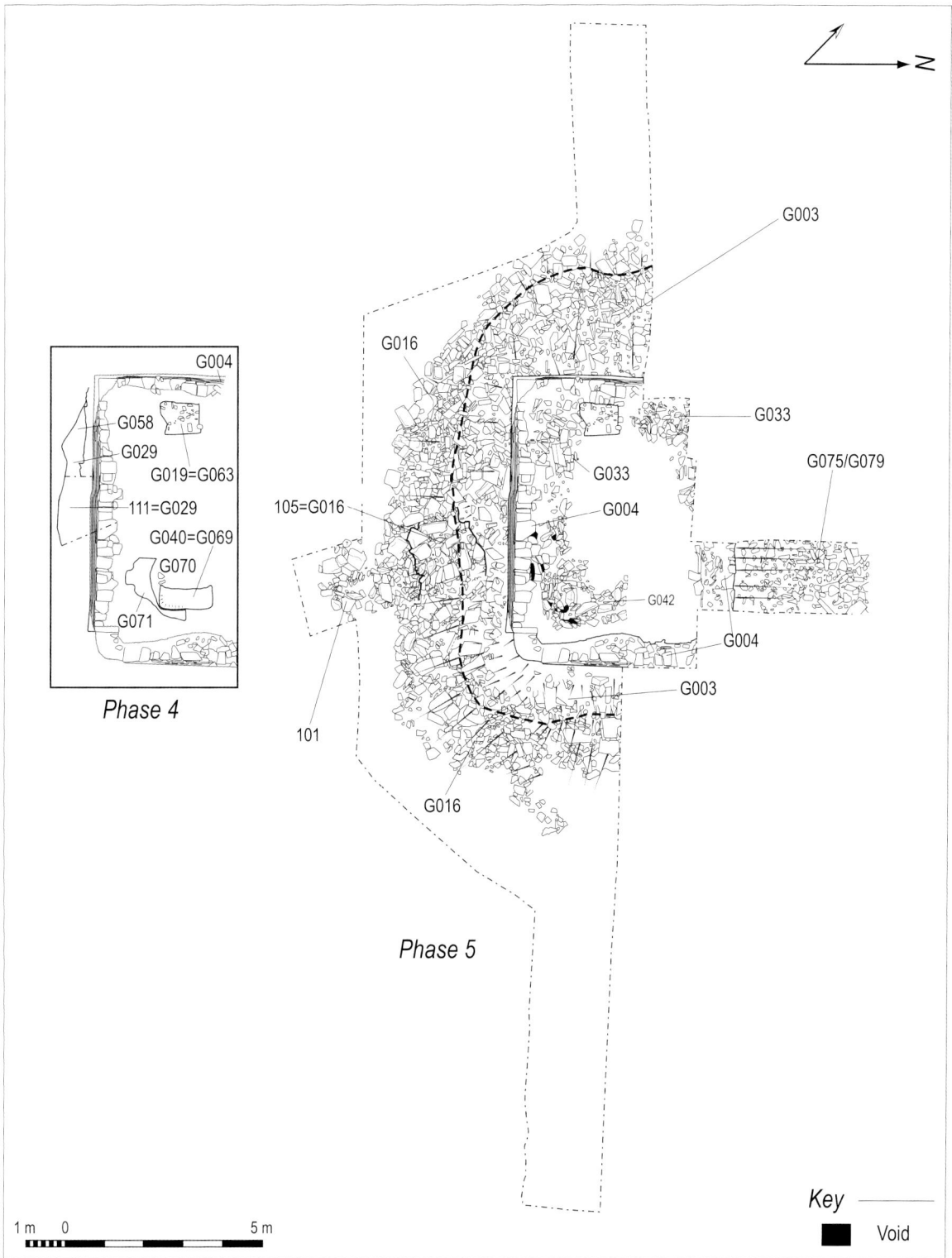

Phase 4

Phase 5

G003

G016

G033

G075/G079

105=G016

G033

G004

G042

G004

G003

101

G016

G004

G058

G029

G019=G063

111=G029

G040=G069

G070

G071

N

Key

Void

1 m   0   5 m

Illus 9.16 Phases 4 and 5a plan

Phase 5: Collapse of the second tower

Two distinct layers of collapsed stonework were identified during the excavation on the S and W sides of the tower, and suggest that rather than a gradual collapse of two or three stones at a time, the upper tower suffered two major collapses, which left only the lower walls intact. This raises the question as to whether the upper storey of the tower was deliberately slighted. Unfortunately this cannot be proven either way from the collapse deposits. As discussed above, no wall core material was excavated from amongst these collapse layers, but a thick layer of leached clay bonding material was identified amongst the stones, suggesting that the upper part of the tower wall was stone-built and bonded with clay, with no earthen core.

Collapsed stonework (5a)

The primary collapse layer G016=105=111 was a very compact clay containing approximately 60% gneiss blocks, which had accumulated up to 0.7m deep where they abutted the tower wall. The clay matrix of this context no doubt derives from clay bonding from the collapsed wall. Above this layer a second, clearly different, layer of collapse, G003=101, a moderately compact yellow silt containing around 40% gneiss blocks was excavated. The layer had accumulated to up to 0.8m deep where it abutted the tower wall and spread increasingly thinner outwards to the S and W. It is probable that much of the compact grey clay found in G016 may have leached from G003 above. Large corner stones were found down the slope from the corners of the tower building within rubble G003. G003 also contained mink burrows and modern contamination as it lay directly below the topsoil.

In the trench extension on the N side of the tower only one context of collapse could be discerned, G075, a sandy clay with 60% gneiss blocks, 1.3m deep against the tower wall G004, thinning as it fell away towards the cliff. Patches of clay bonding G079 were found adhered to many of the stones in this deposit. The lack of two separate tumble deposits, as found to the S, could possibly be due to the proximity of the cliff, shedding the latest deposit into the sea. Large stones, possibly lintels, were found in the base of this context.

Three body sherds of local pottery, a flint flake, four corroded iron nails and an iron fragment and a hammerstone were found in G016, together with a musket ball, and a possible roofing slate. As would be expected, the environmental assemblage was limited, containing a narrower range of material than seen in the wall core contexts. Other than mammal bone

Illus 9.17 Stone collapse around outside of tower on E, W and S sides and Illus 9.18 Outer face of N wall of tower showing stone collapse on N side of tower in section

fragments, only a limpet shell, conifer charcoal, and examples of carbonised oat, six row barley and sedge remains were recovered. The later layer G003 contained only two sherds of local pottery, an unidentified mammal long bone fragment, and conifer and oat remains. Two rim sherds, a shoulder sherd and a body sherd of local pottery were found in the collapse deposit on the N side of the tower.

In the interior of the tower two layers of collapsed stones and clay were identified – G042 in the SE corner of the tower, and G033=120/121 on the SW side. There was no significant difference between G033 and G042, both layers comprising sandy clay and tumbled gneiss blocks. A second possible schist roof tile, an indeterminate iron object and a flint flake were found in G042.

Illus 9.19 Lower collapse deposit G016 at SW corner of tower showing collapsed cornerstones

Leached clay bonding (5b)

These layers of collapse inside the tower were sealed by a compacted layer of sandy clay G006=102, which had become compact and trampled during later phases when the top of the mound was used as a shelter (see Phase 7 below). G006 spread over the entire top of the mound of collapse (apart from the area of MacPhail's trench, which contained patches of G006 in its backfill). Excavation discovered that the stone collapse from the tower wall G004 was surrounded and sealed by G006, and that G006 was probably the leached and collapsed clay bonding. Three body sherds of local pottery, a rectangular whetstone and a chip and flake of flint, unidentified mammal bone fragments, burnt peat and carbonised oat, hulled and six row barley and indeterminate cereal grains were found in G006.

Table 9.4 Phase 5 context descriptions, finds and environmental on CD at back of book

Phase 6: Macphail's excavation 1867

Macphail's trench cut G018=G030=G047 was sub rectangular, c 3.5m by 2.5m, and had been dug downwards into the centre of the mound to expose the base of the original interior wall, G057=G032. It had been backfilled with re-deposited material G017=G025=G034=G037=G046=G048=G035. Macphail appears to have started small and deep, and worked outwards once he had discovered the internal room. At the NW corner, he excavated down to the floor level and then worked outwards, perhaps in an attempt to find an entrance. A section of the SE corner of the wall-face of the small interior chamber is totally missing, and it seems likely that Macphail took this section of wall away to investigate behind it.

The finds in MacPhail's backfill presumably derived from the occupation deposits

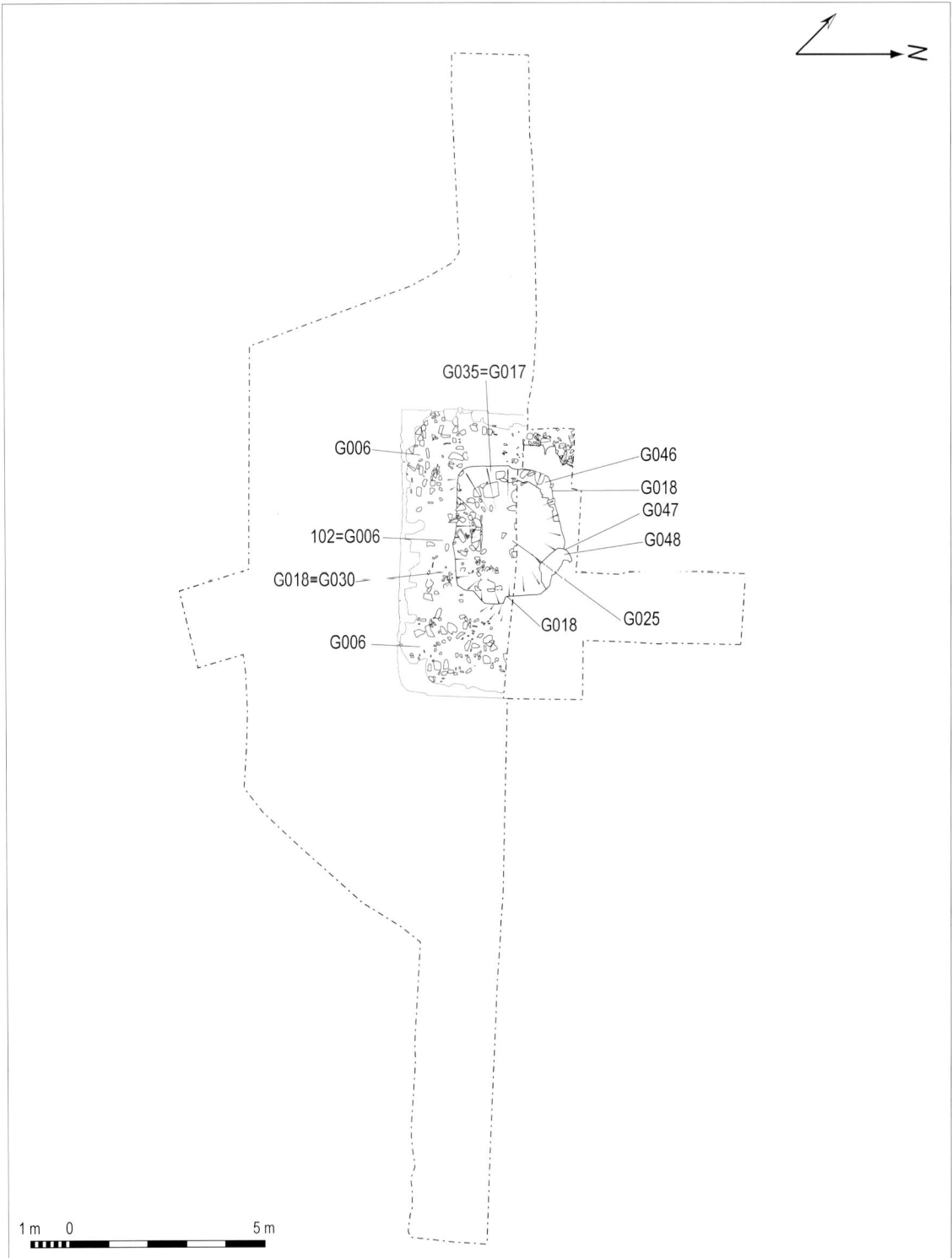

G035=G017

G006

102=G006

G018=G030

G006

G046

G018

G047

G048

G018

G025

Illus 9.20 Phases 5b and 6
plan

Illus 9.21 S half of MacPhail's excavation trench

which he dug out from the central room, and it is worth noting that as well as the usual range of environmental material, and finds such as lumps of cinder, two sherds of local pottery, a flint flake and a flint chip and fragments of iron nails, a gaming piece and three gunflints were recovered.

Table 9.5 Phase 6 context descriptions, finds and environmental on CD at back of book

Phase 7: Modern shelter

The hollow left by MacPhail's trench cut was subsequently re-used as a temporary shelter G007=G036=117, 4m by 2.5m, cut into the backfill in MacPhail's trench and lined with up to three courses of poorly-built dry-stone walling G013=G044=115 around the sides of the hollow, a possible seat G022 which rested upon the remains of the central chamber wall head, and a paved entrance area G052. The shelter wall had slumped in places and completely collapsed on the E side. A revetment deposit of loamy clay with sand G023, possibly originally of turf, was excavated from behind the wall of the shelter, and a sandy loam with silt and clay G010=117 was found in the bottom of the shelter cut.

Outside the shelter wall G013, to the S, a sandy loam with stones G009=114 was deposited during the occupation of the shelter. On the N side two similar contexts, G043 and

Area detailed

G020

G009

G009=114

G012=119

G014

G043/G045

G009

G053

1 m   0   5 m

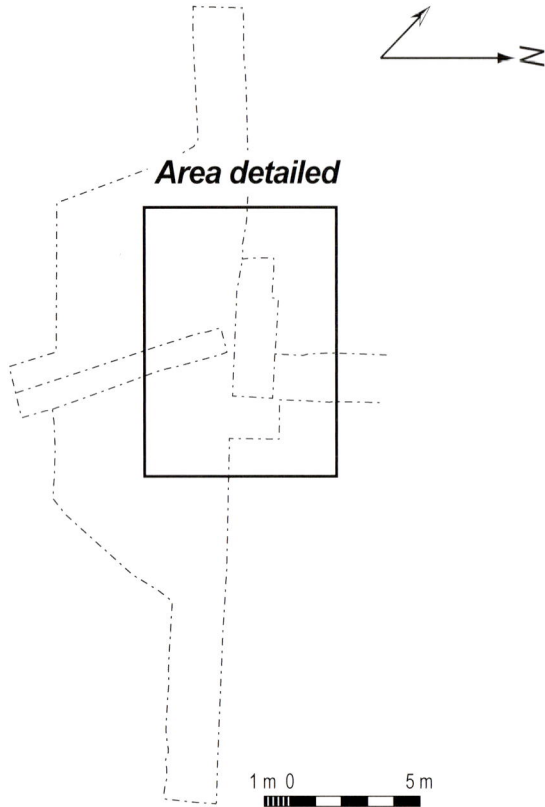

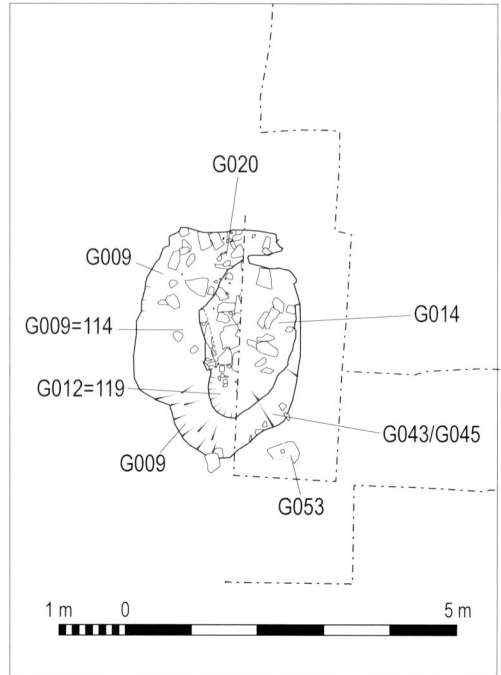

Trench G,
Phase 7c

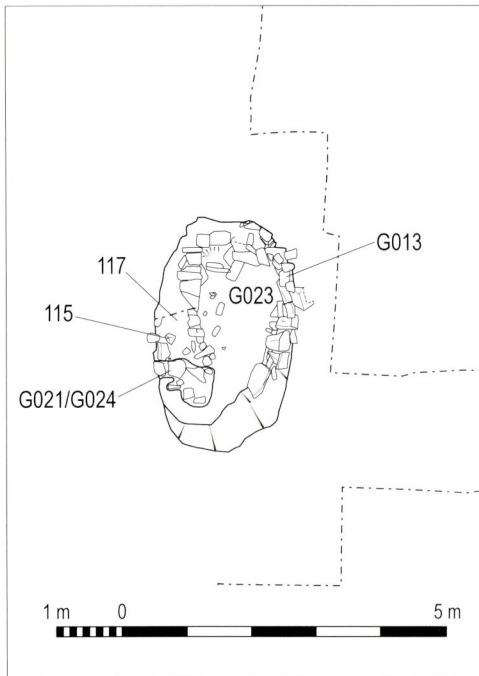

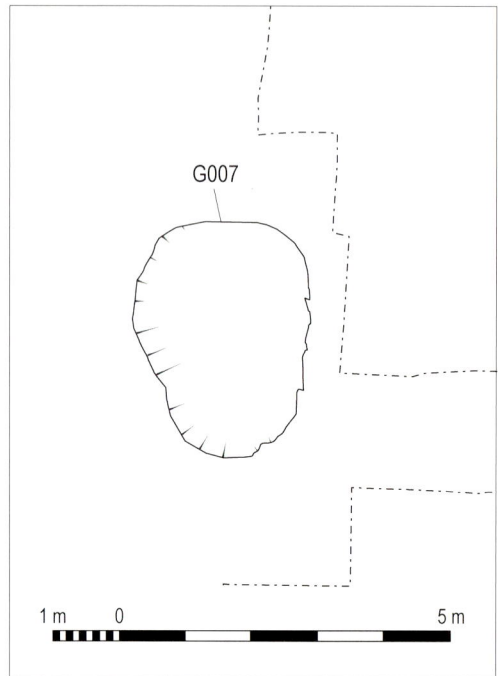

1 m   0   5 m

117

G013

115

G023

G021/G024

1 m   0   5 m

G007

1 m   0   5 m

Illus 9.22 Phase 7 plan

G045 were found deposited behind the shelter walls. G053, a rounded slab of gneiss with a small pivot depression was also found at the edge of the shelter, and whilst this may have been used in the shelter, it may originally have been used in the tower itself. Contexts G021, a loamy clay with silt and stones, and G024, a sandy clay with stones were also deposited during the occupation of the shelter. As G009, G021, G024, G043 and G045 built up in the space between the cut G007 and the newly built shelter walls the walls were pushed inwards and had clearly begun to slip from their foundations on the old interior tower walls, and the large pivot stone G053 had been used to prop them up.

Layers of collapse then built up over the shelter when it went out of use. These included gneiss blocks G012=119, and stony loams G014 and G020. A layer of partially-degraded buried turf G015=116 was excavated above this collapse and represents a later re-use of the hollow for shelter. Modern bottle tops from "Vat 69" whisky were recovered from this context, confirming its modern date.

The finds and environmental assemblages from this phase contain mainly modern material, or material disturbed from earlier contexts, such as fragmentary iron objects, a sherd of local pottery and a flint flake, shells and small mammal bones, and a scattering of conifer, birch and willow charcoal, burnt peat and cereal grains.

Table 9.6 Phase 7 context descriptions, finds and environmental on CD at back of book

Phase 8: Topsoil and marker cairn

The rubble mound was covered in topsoil G002=100=103=107. On the W side of the mound a cone-shaped cairn G001, 2.05m tall was built as a marker cairn and memorial. It was set in a shallow circular scoop G008 cut through the topsoil. A 1936 penny and a 1999 penny were found pushed into the stones of the cairn, and a scattering of material, including a possible gunflint, a strip of copper alloy, corroded iron objects, four coarse stone tools and a stone pot lid, shell and fish and mammal bone fragments, alder, conifer, willow and birch charcoal and carbonised cereal grains were found in the topsoil.

Endnotes

[1] All radiocarbon dates are calibrated at 95.4% confidence: see Chapter 13

Illus 9.23 Marker cairn

Table 9.7 Phase 8 context descriptions, finds and environmental on CD at back of book

anal

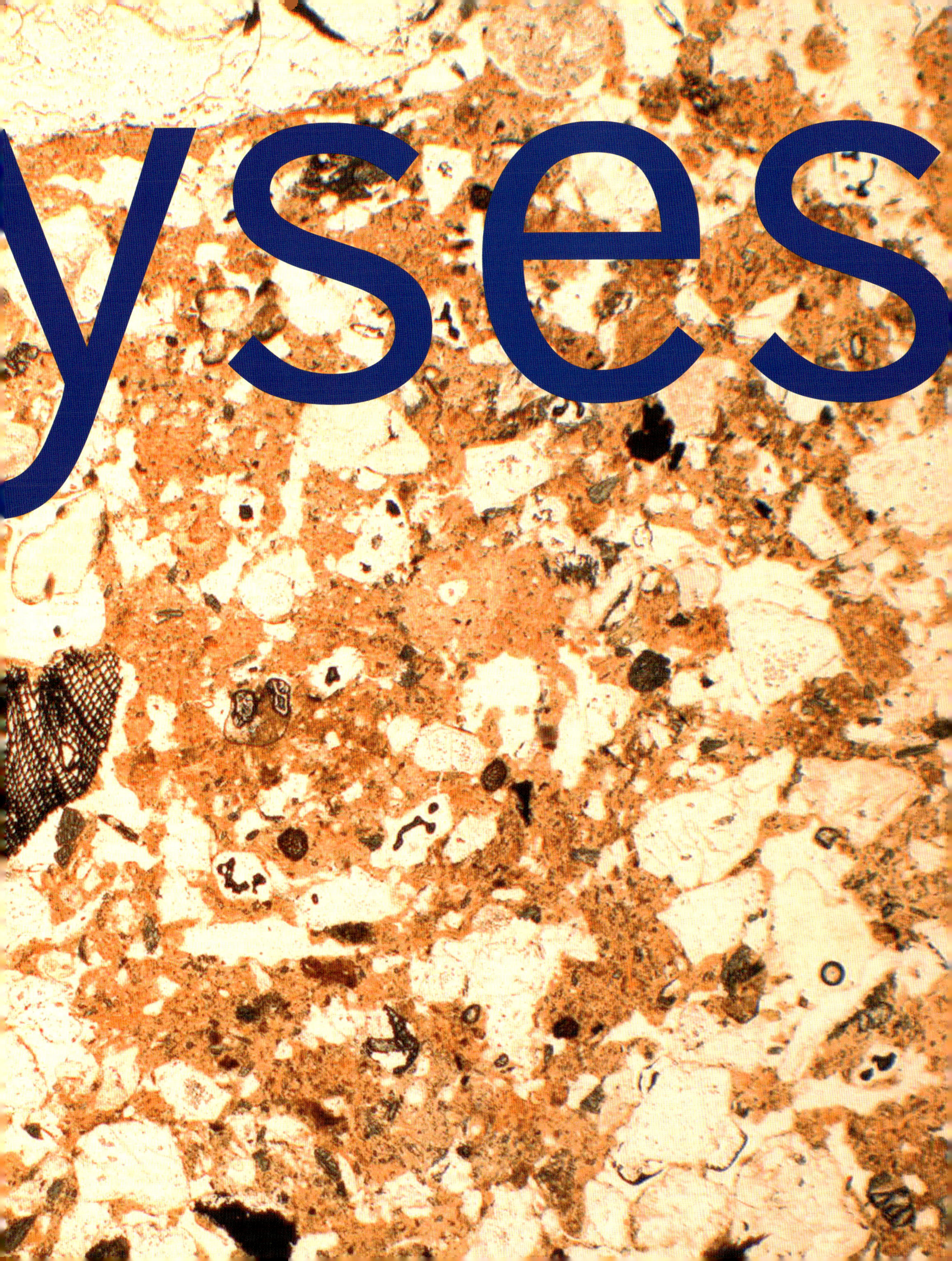
yses

Illus 10.1 Pistol shot found in Trench B

ten

In this chapter specialists study over 4,250 artefacts that were found from the excavations on Dùn Èistean. These discarded fragments of material culture are evidence of the everyday activities and other events that took place on the site over 400 years ago.

The chapter begins with Campbell's report on the largest group of artefacts from the excavations, the 3,500 sherds (broken pieces) of local, coarse pottery called 'craggan' (from the Gaelic 'cragain', for pots). This unique tradition of hand-made pottery vessel is found in the Highlands and Islands and west coast of Scotland, and the sherds from Dùn Èistean comprise by far the largest excavated assemblage of craggan to have been studied and dated to the late medieval period. Campbell identifies that the pots were made and fired on or close to the site, and included vessels for a variety of cooking and storage functions, as well as decorated cups for drinking.

Further signs of domestic life on the island are found in the stone and metal objects, both reported on by Batey. These include stone weights for fishing nets or lines, spinning whorls, whetstones for sharpening, a fragment of a quern, hammerstones for pounding or grinding grain and pot lids for sealing pottery jars. The small fragmentary group of metal objects includes a piece of metal binding strip from a bucket or barrel, and this hints at the wood and leather storage and food-processing vessels and tools that must have been used on the site but do not survive in the archaeological record. In addition to these small traces of domestic tools, Ballin identifies amongst the lithics assemblage fire-flints for firelighting and flint flakes used as cutting tools, and Sneddon reports on lumps of slag that are evidence of small-scale metal-working on the site, probably at the hearth.

Some of the finds from the excavations give us clues as to the materials that were used to construct the buildings on the island, especially the roofs. A small collection of iron nails and roves from all structures on the site are identified by Batey as originating from driftwood timber that was collected and used for roofing supports. In Structure D, Murdoch identifies ten shards of glass as probably deriving from roofing lights, and in Structure G Batey reports on two possible stone roof tiles but concludes that their identification is tenuous.

The remaining finds from the excavations are evidence for the unusual nature of the late medieval occupation on Dùn Èistean, and the reason that this tiny island was sporadically occupied. Ferguson reports on the small group of lead projectiles found across the site, which includes eight musket balls, five pistol balls and a piece of buckshot. She concludes that whilst these are not evidence for a battle on the site, they do suggest that there were small scale skirmishes or sieges, as suggested by the example of a projectile with impact damage recovered from one of the turf walls of Structure D. Ferguson is of the opinion that these projectiles were made on the island itself, and three pieces of scrap lead reported by Batey and most probably collected to be melted down at the hearth for this reason, support this. These projectiles are not the only evidence for skirmishes on the island. An assemblage of used gunflints has been found from the excavations, and these are reported on by Ballin. As well as the gunflints themselves, he also identifies waste from their manufacture, demonstrating that the gunflints, like the lead projectiles, were made on site. A gunflint assemblage of this date is unique in the UK, as is the evidence for the production of flints on the island. Most of the gunflints were found in sizes associated with smaller firearms and Ballin suggests that it is likely that the flints are linked to one or more specific conflict events, with the guns being discharged on the site in the sixteenth and early seventeenth centuries AD.

A small group of imported objects not made in the local area are also testament to contact with the wider world. A number of sherds from glazed, wheel thrown pottery vessels are reported on by Will and include three decorated rim and neck sherds from a small Cologne stoneware wine bottle or flask, six sherds from earthenware bowls and a sherd of medieval redware from the Scottish mainland. Also, Bateson reports on five coins, including one Scottish issue billon plack of James VI, struck between 1583 until 1590, and an English Elizabethan sixpence of 1580, that were found in slumped deposits in Structure B. These small collections of imported material demonstrate that the inhabitants on Dùn Èistean were in touch, even if indirectly, with the wider political scene, specifically with the mainland and continental seaborne traffic that passed north Lewis on the busy trade routes between mainland Scotland and the Isles, and between Britain and northern Europe. Further evidence of this may be seen in shard from a painted, possibly Venetian, glass bottle identified by Murdoch from Structure A.

Across the finds reported in this chapter a small group were recovered from the temporary shelters that were built on the site in the eighteenth and early nineteenth centuries. Lamp glass and wine bottle shards, a copper alloy candle holder, a fragment from a possible fleshing fork and a piece of metal sheet, probably from a cooking cauldron have all been identified. The general lack of later, modern material (apart form a small group of modern glazed ceramic from Area D and modern coins from the marker cairn in Area G) is a reflection of the position of the island away from modern settlement at this time.

Local pottery

by Ewan Campbell

Local pottery catalogue, Summary of local pottery by context, and a note on organic residue analysis by B Derham on CD at back of book

Introduction

The assemblage of over 3500 sherds, comprising around 24 kilos of pottery, is one of the largest excavated from a late/post-medieval site in the Hebrides. Despite the large number of sherds, only around 75 individual vessels can be identified, showing that the assemblage largely consists of material that has not been much disturbed since its breakage (see Table 10.1). The vast majority of the pottery falls into the category of Hebridean handmade pottery known to archaeologists as craggan wares (from Gaelic crogan, pl. crogain; Cheape 1993, 109), but which can be better defined as a tradition rather than a ware. As most of the pottery is undecorated, and all the vessels are globular or bowl-shaped with no flat bases, vessels can only be differentiated on the basis of their rim and neck forms. It has proved possible to reconstruct the profiles of a few vessels, but finding joining sherds in assemblages of craggans is very difficult and time-consuming due to the uniformity of body shape, variability of fabric within vessels, and the general lack of decoration. However, as this is the first large stratified and radiocarbon dated assemblage of this date to be published, it is important because of the light it can throw on a little-studied ceramic tradition.

Background

Previous research on craggans has consisted mainly of ethnographic accounts of late nineteenth and early twentieth century survivals of the tradition (Mitchell 1880, 43-56; Beveridge 1903, 70; Mann 1908; Cheape 1988, 1993; Holleyman 1947), which provides valuable details of construction methods and folklore associated with the wares. Accounts of excavated material have tended to be

Illus 10.2 Fingernail decorated sherd

from poorly-dated contexts: a complete vessel from Ensay (Lane in Miles 1989, 18-19, fig 13); another from Dun Cueir, Skye with a few decorated sherds (Young 1956, fig 5); a small assemblage from Northton, Harris (Johnston 2006) including stabbed and rim-decorated vessels; and a small sixteenth/seventeenth-century assemblage from Druim na Dearcag, North Uist (Campbell 1997). The only well-stratified assemblages are the unpublished excavations at the Udal, North Uist; Guinnerso, Lewis; Gunna, Coll; and the published small assemblage from Breachacha Castle, Coll (Turner and Dunbar 1970), which has some decorated material in fifteenth/sixteenth-century contexts. There is also one vessel from Stornoway associated with a late seventeenth-century coin hoard (Dean 2007, 451-2, illus 6). From these accounts it has so far been impossible to propose any chronological changes in craggan wares from the late medieval to twentieth-century periods. Decoration may be one feature that can be given chronological significance. Stabbing around the rim and shoulder seems to be a medieval feature, at least at the Udal and Eilean Olabhat, North Uist (Campbell in Armit et al 2008, 68), and the Breachacha Castle assemblage suggests its continuation in craggan wares into at least the sixteenth century. However, there may be wide variations even within the Hebrides as there is no decoration in the assemblages at Bornais, South Uist, from the tenth to fourteenth centuries (Lane 2005, 194). The use of fingernail impressions as the main means of decorating the Dùn Èistean pots may be a local characteristic, as it has not apparently been recorded elsewhere.

Fabric

The fabric is generally coarse, and typical of Hebridean pottery from the Iron Age to twentieth century. The clay is derived from glacial tills, in turn derived from the underlying Lewisian gneisses, and is full of coarse rock fragments and minerals derived from the breakdown of these rocks. Detailed petrographic work by Phillips (2006) has confirmed the opinion of the author (Campbell 1991; 2002) that the variability in fabric is not significant and merely reflects a very variable source of raw material. It is therefore not worthwhile to subdivide the fabric as it is all of immediate local origin.

A small proportion of the material has variable amounts of organic temper added. This is always in the form of chopped grass stems, or possibly dung (Lane 1983, 140). Occasionally, this seems to have been applied preferentially to the exterior surfaces (cf Cheape 1993, figs 8, 9), looking very similar to grass-marked pottery characteristic of Norse Hebridean assemblages (Lane 2007, 10), but is not confined to bases. This would appear to be a case of independent development of a useful technique for constructing pottery in two different periods.

The vessels have been fired in clamps or bonfires, resulting in very variable degrees of oxidation/reduction, even within one vessel. While most vessels are various shades of brown to black, a few are oxidised red or orange. The fabric is usually fairly well fired, similar to Iron Age vessels from the region, but occasional vessels are crumbly due to poor firing.

Illus 10.3 Close-up of coarse fabric and Illus 10.4 Differential burning on exterior of pot CAT 28a

Area A (* = illustrated sherds)

1* Rim of small cup, simple upright rim. Buff fabric. Rim diam c 120mm. Context A021, SF026.
2* Rim of small cup, simple in-turned. Fabric buff. Rim diam c 100mm. Context A035, SF100.
3* Rim of medium cup, simple upright. Fabric grey. Rim diam 160-180mm. Context A031, SF 066
4* Rim of cup or bowl. Rim flattened with slight lip on exterior and interior. Fabric orange/grey. Context A014, SF025
5* Rim of large jar. Flaring rim, thinning at top edge. Fabric poor, crumbling, buff/grey. Rim diam 220-240mm. Context A019, SF045
6* Rim of large jar. Flaring rim, smoothed on interior. Fabric grey. Context A019, SF033
7 Rim of medium jar, simple. Fabric buff. Context A021, SF030
8 Rim of jar, out-turned. Fabric grey. Context A021, SF012
9 Rim of jar, out-turned. Fabric buff. Context A031, SF069
10 Rim of small cup/jar. Fabric grey. Context A030, SF037

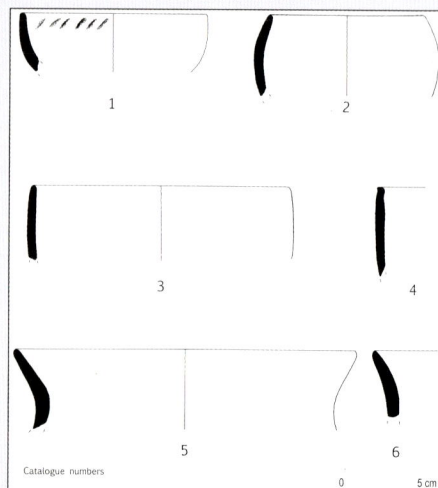

Illus 10.5 Area A sherds

Area C

25* Rim and shoulder of large jar. Rim upright, shoulder sharply angled. Fabric buff/grey. Rim Diam c 130mm. Context C049, SF096, SF69, Sf61, SF122
26* Rim and shoulder of medium jar. Rim upright. Fabric grey, exterior sooting, interior carbonized deposit. Rim diam c 120mm. Context C039, SF038
27 Rim of jar. Fabric orange. Context C031, SF055

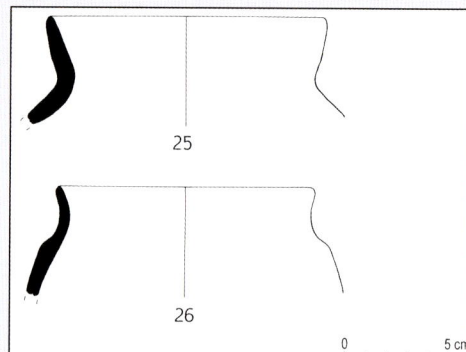

Illus 10.7 Area C sherds

Area D

28* Complete profile of large jar with upright, slightly out-turned neck. Sharp shoulder, body globular. Decoration of closely-spaced fingernail impressions on interior of rim. Fabric buff with grey core, grass-tempered, with grass-marking on basal area. Exterior surface lumpy, with some irregular wipe marks. Interior smoother. Exterior sooted on one side, no interior deposits. Rim Diam 180mm, maximum body diam 230mm, Height 200mm, T 6-10mm. Many sherds from D064, D022, D007: SF382, SF372, SF375, SF383, SF839, SF837, SF831, SF1230, SF449, SF375, SF382, SF372
29* Complete profile of small globular jar, rim slightly flaring. Sharp shoulder, body globular. Fabric buff to grey, grass-marked on base. Exterior lumpy, some scoring marks, interior more smoothed especially around shoulder. Some exterior sooting, interior with patch of carbonized residue on one side. Rim diam 12cm cm, maximum body diam 160m, Height 140m, T 6-8mm. Many sherds from D058, SF390
30* Rim and neck of small decorated cup. Neck upright, with fingermarked carination on exterior where rim coil has been added. Decoration of slanting fingernail impressions on exterior of rim. Fabric buff, hard, fine. Rim Diam 90mm, T 3-5mm. D035, SF283; D034, SF196; D007, SF479
31* Rim of large jar. Decorated with strong slanting fingernail impressions on inside of rim. Rim flattened on top. Context D036, SF1069; D015, SF171, SF169; D007, SF474
32* Rim of small jar, slightly flaring rim. Decorated with strong slanting closely-spaced fingernail impressions on interior and exterior of rim. Slight carination on neck. Fabric pale buff. Context D010, SF230
33* Rim of jar with slightly flaring rim. Decorated with strong fingernail impressions on exterior and interior. Interior has vertical and horizontal row, exterior horizontal. Fabric buff/grey. Context D035, SF338
34* Rim and neck of jar. Neck upright, decorated with single row of widely-spaced stab-marks. Rim Diam 120mm,. Context D010, SF925; D104, SF275
35 Rim of small cup similar to 30 but thicker, decorated with one row of internal fingernail impressions on rim. Context D063, SF903
36* Profile of small cup with vertical sides and rim. Fabric grey, hard, fine. Interior and exterior smoothed. Basal angle rounded, with flat or sagging base. Height 80mm, Rim diam c 100mm, T 4-5mm. Context D031, SF268
37* Rim of small cup, slightly in-turned. Fabric buff. Rim diam c 100mm. Context D032, SF180
38* Rim and shoulder of large jar. Neck upright, flaring rim, large globular body. Fabric pale buff, fine, smoothed interior. Some exterior sooting. Rim diam c 160mm, max body diam c 380mm, T 8-10mm. Context D015, SF189; D061, Sf704; D001, SF431

Area B

11* Rim of medium jar, upright. Neck decorated with three lines of fingernail impressions: the upper and lower simple, the middle crossed. There is a carination on the exterior of the neck. Fabric buff. Context B025, SF242; B104, SF260

12* Rim, decorated with fingernail impressions. Fabric buff. Context B069, SF219

13* Rim and shoulder of small jar. Rim simple, neck upright. Rim diam c 10cm. Body diam c 180mm. Fabric grey, hard. Context B054, SF245; B055, SF226, B070, SF195

14* Rim and shoulder of small jar. Rim simple, out-turned. Fabric buff/grey, hard. Rim Diam 80-100mm. Context B009, SF143

15* Rim and neck of large jar. Rim simple, neck upright, shoulder very sharply angled. Fabric buff. Rim Diam c. 120mm. Context B025, SF159

16   Rim of large jar, flaring, slight exterior lip. Fabric buff. Context B093, SF234

17   Rim of large jar, flaring. Fabric buff/grey. Context B095, SF237

18   Rim of large jar, flaring. Fabric buff. Rim diam c 12cm. Context B095, SF238

19   Rim of large jar, flaring. Fabric pale buff. Context B001

20   Rim of small jar, flaring. Fabric buff. Context B024, SF109

21   Rim of medium jar, flaring. Fabric grey. Context B009, SF172

22   Rim of medium jar. Fabric orange. Context B128, SF131

23   Rim of medium jar. Fabric orange. Context B024, SF118

24   Rim of small jar with lip. Context B028, SF071

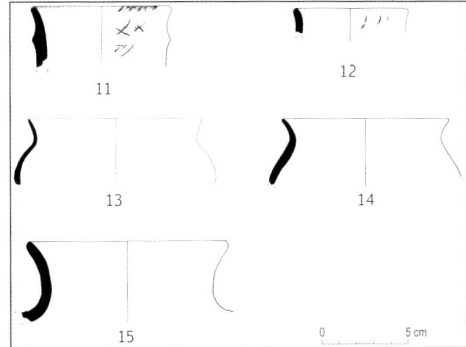

Illus 10.6 Area B sherds

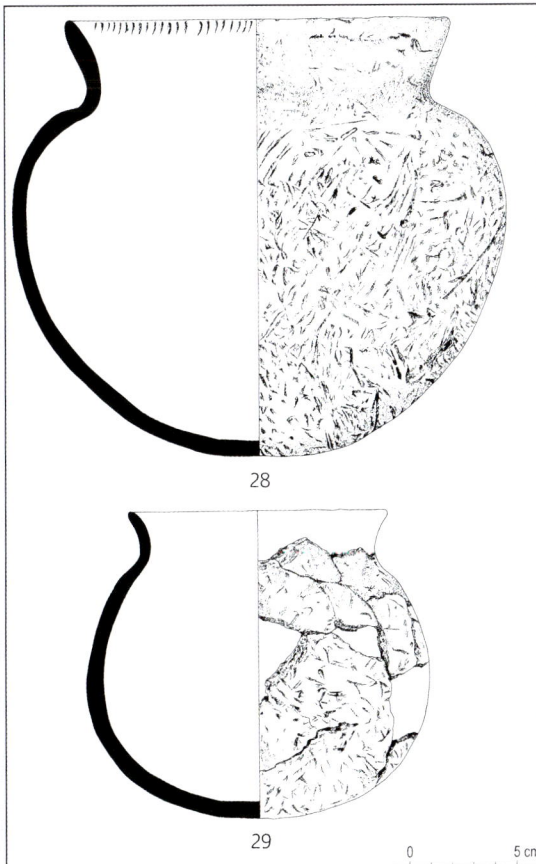

Illus 10.8 Area D sherds

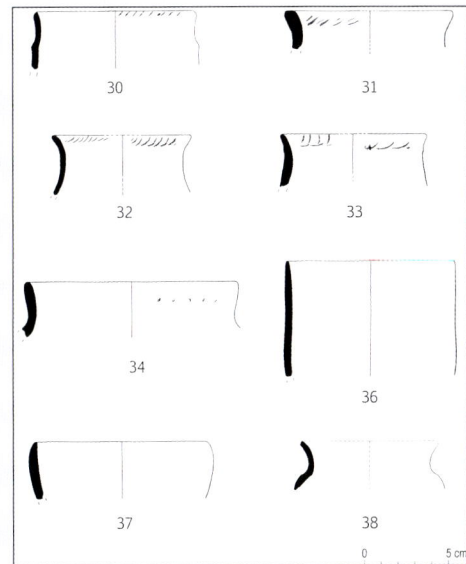

Table 10.1 continued

Area D continued

39* Rim of large jar, flaring. Neck height 45mm. T 10mm. Sooted exterior. Fabric orange/grey. Context D035, SF346

40 Rim of large jar, upright. Exterior sooted. Rim Diam c 220mm, Neck height 40mm. T 8-11mm. Context D035, SF735, SF348, SF734

41* Rim of large jar, upright. Thick and crudely formed with fingermarks still visible. Heavy sooting on exterior. Rim Diam 180mm, T 10mm. Context D077, SF1165; D076, SF1110, SF892; D035, SF339

42* Rim of large jar, tall and flaring, shoulder angle sharp. Neck height 35mm. Exterior sooted. Context D015, SF76

43* Rim and shoulder of medium jar. Rim upright, shoulder angle sharp. Interior with smooth turning marks. No sooting. Rim Diam c 140mm, T 7-8mm. Context D012, SF270

44 Rim of large jar. Rim flat-topped, heavy sooting on exterior. Context D007, SF547

45 Rim of medium jar, flaring. Context D032, SF214

46 Rim of large jar. Context D012, SF227

47* Rim and shoulder of small jar. Rim upright slight flare. Rim Diam 90mm, Body diam c 140mm, T 4-5mm. Grass-tempered. Context D086

48* Rim and shoulder of small jar. Rim flaring. Rim Diam 90mm, body diam 140mm. Sooting on exterior. Context D035, SF995, SF394

49 Rim and shoulder of small jar, flaring. Context D035, SF956

50 Rim of small jar, flaring. Context D007, SF083

51 Rim od small jar. Context D017, SF292

52 Rim of very small jar. Context D035, SF350

53 Rim of medium jar, flaring. Context D063, SF797

54 Rim of medium jat. Context D071, SF759

55 Rim of medium jar. Context D071, SF773

56 Rim of medium jar. Context D105, SF1208

57 Rim of small jar. Context D002, SF204

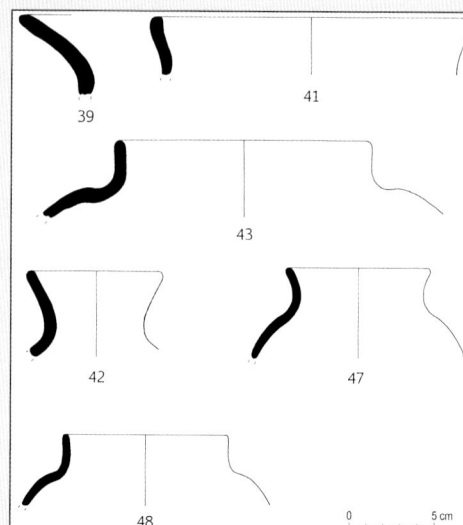

Trial trenches 02 (Trench 1, Area B, Bridge footings)

60* Rim and profile of cup, vertical sides. Rim diam c 140mm. Fabric fine, smoothed, orange to black. Context 02/17, SF199

61* Rim of small jar, flaring. Fabric fine, buff. Context 02/007, SF114; 004, SF137, 001, SF029

62 Rim of tiny cup. Diam c 6 cm. Context 02/007, SF201

63 Rim of large jar. Light buff fabric. Context 02/001, SF042

64 Rim of large jar. Smoothed buff fabric. Context 02/004, SF132

65 Rim of small jar. Context 02/005, SF090

Trial trenches 03 (Structure A, Trench 4)

66* Rim and shoulder of large jar. Rim flaring. Fabric grey, smoothed interior. Rim diam c 220mm. Context 03/020, SF055

67* Rim and body of cup with in-turned sides. Diam c 160mm. Sooted exterior. Context 03/010, SF57, SF45; 03/022, SF101; 03/020, SF74

68* Rim and body of small cup with in-turned sides. Diam c 100mm. Context 03/020, SF61

69* Rim and body of small bowl. Rim slightly out-turned, slight carination at shoulder. External sooting. Fabric grey/buff, grass-tempered, interior smoothed. Body diam 120mm. Context 03/001, SF1, SF33

70* Rim and shoulder of medium jar. Rim flaring. Fabric buff. Context 03/006, SF16

71* Profile of small jar. Rim flaring. Fabric hard, buff/grey. Body diam c 100mm. Context 03/010, SF42

72 Rim of large jar. Context 03/020, SF85, SF73

73 Rim of small cup. Context 03/020, SF100

74 Rim of medium jar. Context 03/020, SF88

Illus 10.9 Area D, Area F and small trenches sherds

Area F

58* Rim and shoulder of large jar. Rim flaring, crudely made
     with finger marks. Carination at shoulder. Interior smoothed.
     Fabric grey. Sooting on exterior below shoulder. Rim Diam
     c 240mm, body diam c 300mm, T 5-11mm. Context F023,
     SF077
59   Rim of medium jar, flaring. Context F009, SF032

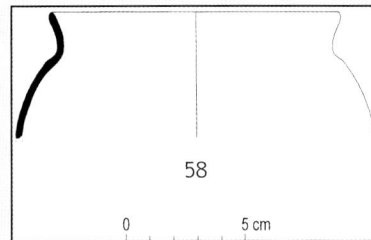

58

0   5 cm

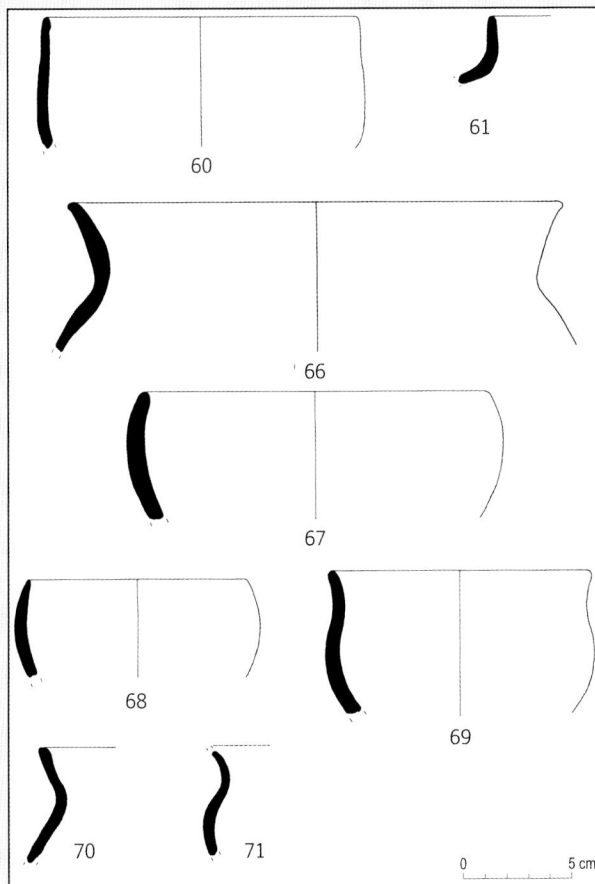

61

60

66

67

68

69

70   71

0   5 cm

Construction

The characteristic that distinguishes most craggans from other, earlier, handmade Hebridean wares is the construction and surface treatment. The exterior surface is usually uneven and 'lumpy', due to the method of pressing the clay between the fingers while forming the pot, which creates a pot wall of variable thickness. In earlier handmade wares, the exterior surface is smoothed to a greater or lesser extent after the initial forming as a coil or slab, often with a scraping tool or by wiping with a pad of grass or cloth. Surprisingly, this feature of craggans does not appear to have previously been discussed in print, though the pinching construction of small vessels has been described (Holleyman 1947, 208). The date of this change in practice cannot be accurately determined, but presumably lies after the date of the thirteenth/fourteenth-century Bornish wares (Lane 2005), which do not have this feature, and before the Dùn Èistean material of the sixteenth century. In the Dùn Èistean examples there is occasional scraping of the shoulder area to smooth out major unevenness, which can look superficially similar to decoration. Surprisingly, given the exterior treatment, the interior surfaces are often smoothed, or smoother than the exterior. This may indicate that the vessels were partly made on a former such as a round boulder.

There are occasional signs of slab construction, with overlapping joins, a continuation of Norse period construction method (Lane 2007, 11). The join between the neck and shoulder, which is often at quite an abrupt angle, is clearly a weak point and is often thickened. Rims were always simple, with the neck vertical or out-turned, except in the case of straight-sided cups where the rim was sometimes in-turned. Firing was done in a clamp, so the colour and hardness is very variable both between and within pots.

Illus 10.10 Examples of out-turned rim sherds

Vessel form

The large majority of the vessels are of the typical craggan form - a globular jar with a high, upright neck, often slightly out-turned at the rim or even flaring. The shoulder is often very marked, sometimes being at right angles to the neck (cat no 42). The rim diameter is often small in relation to the maximum body diameter, making a very closed form. The base is completely rounded, with no differentiation of the base, producing a truly globular body (eg cat no 28). The size can range from large, at up to 400mm diameter, down to very small, around 100mm. This type of vessel is well known from ethnographic studies in the Hebrides, having being made up until the beginning of the twentieth century (Cheape 1993). One small well-dated example from Stornoway contained a late seventeenth-century coin hoard (Dean 2007, 451-2, illus 6) is very similar to one of the reconstructed vessels (cat no 28). Mann illustrates a group of eleven nineteenth-century examples from Tiree, showing a range of sizes and neck forms very similar to those at Dùn Èistean. There do not seem to have been any standard sizes of vessels, and it is clear from the Dùn Èistean material that forms have not changed in any significant way over the whole of the post-medieval period.

Other vessels (13 out of 75) are mainly simple but well-finished small cups with slightly inturned profiles. No complete profiles could be reconstructed, but the indications are that they have sagging bases (cat no 36). This basic shape was originally used in the Norse period (Lane 2007, 10, fig 8), but seems to have continued throughout the medieval period (Campbell in Armit et al 2008, 76, illus 28, 29). Four decorated cups were found in stratified contexts in Structure D alongside normal craggan vessels dated to the sixteenth century, and there is no sign of other characteristic Norse wares such as platters at Dùn Èistean, so Norse occupation can be ruled out. Finally, there is a single example of an open bowl-shaped vessel, unfortunately from an unstratified context (cat no 69).

The only obvious chronological variation in the assemblage is that Area A has proportionally more cups than jars, in both the sixteenth-century occupation levels, and in the later post-abandonment layers. It is possible of course that this difference could be due to the different function of the drinking cups.

The craggans were used for a variety of cooking and storage functions. A

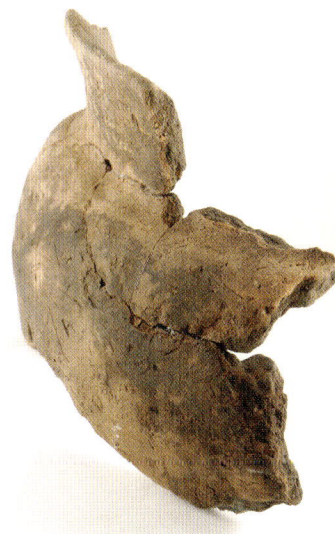

Illus 10.11 Reconstructed vessel, CAT 28, showing rim, Illus 10.12 CAT 28, different view and Illus 10.13 Sherd from small decorated cup, CAT 30

proportion of the vessels is sooted on the exterior, or have carbonised residues on the interior (detailed in the spreadsheet; see CD catalogue), showing they were used as cooking pots. Others are known from ethnographic accounts to have been used for ale, milk and fish oil storage. There seems to be no correlation between vessel form or size and the presence of sooting or residues. In contrast, the small cups, and the bowl, were probably used as drinking vessels. Hollyman (1947, 208) reports that on Tiree the cups were associated with medicinal use, particularly for heated milk for consumptives, known as *bainne gun ghaoth* (Gaelic 'milk without wind'), and were used well into the twentieth century. There is no oral evidence for this type of use in Lewis (Hugh Cheape pers comm), but the preservation of these cups in households in Tiree long after craggans had gone out of use illustrates how some types of vessel could have highly charged symbolic properties.

Decoration

Decoration is rare in the assemblage, being found on less than 2% of the sherds. In terms of vessels however, 12 out of 75 were decorated (16%). Almost all the decoration is formed using fingernail impressions around the rim and neck. These fingernail impressions usually consist of a single row, on the inside (four examples) or outside (four examples), or both (cat nos 32, 33). One vessel (cat no 11) has a more complex pattern on the neck, with three rows of impressions, the middle one consisting uniquely of crosses. The impressions on the interior of the rim are usually on those vessels where the rim is out-turned, so the decoration would have been visible from above when the vessel was in use. Most of the vessels with decoration are small cups, though one is a globular jar (cat no 28). The use of fingernail decoration has not been reported in other craggans, and may be a feature of the Ness area. There are however, vessels with superficially similar decoration from Gunna, Coll, though most of the decoration is stabbed (Heather James pers comm).

There is also a single example with a row of stab marks on the neck (cat no 34). This type of decoration is typically found on Hebridean handmade medieval vessels (though often on the rim), for example at Eilean Olabhat (Campbell in Armit et al 2008, illus 28, 122) and derives from Late Norse forms (Lane 1990, 123). These are difficult to date but have been suggested to lie between the thirteenth and sixteenth centuries. Mann (1908, fig 2) illustrates

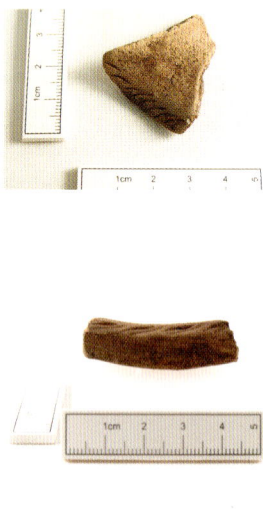

Illus 10.14 Decorated sherd, CAT 32 and Illus 10.15 Rim decoration, CAT 11

Phase	A	B	C	D	F	G
Pre-occupation	0	0	0	1.2	0	0
1st occupation	0	0	0	3.7	0	0
2nd occupation	0	4	0	3.3	0	0
Post-occupation	0	1.1	0	1.9	0	0

Table 10.2 Local pottery percentage decorated sherds

a complete vessel from a midden at Kilkenneth, Tiree, with rows of stabbing on the top of the rim and at the shoulder, and there is a similar vessel from Dun Vulan, South Uist (Parker-Pearson and Sharples 1999, fig 8.5). The Dùn Èistean example differs in that a point, rather than a bird bone, has been used for stabbing. At Breachacha Castle stabbing occurs in fifteenth/sixteenth-century deposits (Turner and Dunbar 1970, fig 13). The Dùn Èistean example may be a late example of this decorative tradition, as it appears in stratified deposits with standard undecorated craggan forms, possibly suggesting a sixteenth-century date. This date is re-enforced by the radiocarbon dates and later sixteenth-century Rhenish stoneware from the same phase.

The stratigraphic distribution of decoration can be illustrated by dividing the occupation into two broad phases of building, which from the radiocarbon dates both date to the sixteenth-century, with no more than a generation between them (Table 10.2). Decoration starts to appear along with the first buildings in Area D (Phase 4), and the secondary buildings in Area B (Phase 4). There are three decorated sherds in the pre-building phases in Area D, from two vessels (cat nos 28 and 31), found in Phases 5 and 6 in post-occupation layers where they are presumably residual. The main period of decoration thus can be dated with confidence to centre on the sixteenth century. This is comparable to evidence from Breachacha Castle and Gunna (Coll) for a sixteenth-century date for similar types of decoration. The horizontal distribution of decorated material is discussed below.

Distribution

Table 10.3 shows the statistical distribution of sherds across the site. Area D has by far the greatest amount of pottery, both in terms of sherds, sherd weight and numbers of vessels.

Trench	No. of sherds	Wt (g)	No. of vessels	Sherds: vessels
A	620	3247	10	62:1
B	450	2740	14	32:1
C	124	1791	3	41:1
D	1589	10625	30	53:1
F	137	1377	2	69:1
G	47	256	1	47:1
Trial trenches	592	3854	15	40:1
TOTAL	3559	23890	75	48:1

Table 10.3 Pottery sherd distribution

Illus 10.16 shows the percentage of rim and decorated sherds, and this reveals a different pattern. Area C has a much higher percentage of rim sherds than normal for the rest of the site. This might suggest that the vessels in use

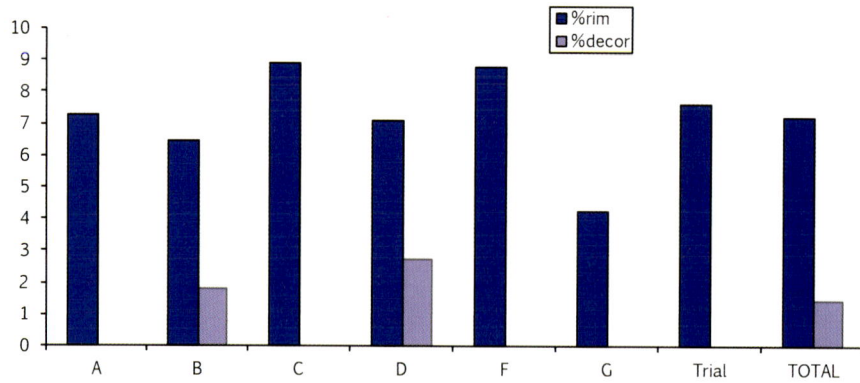

there were smaller (so the rims form a greater part of the assemblage), or there may be some unexplained taphonomic process at work. Looking at the decorated sherds, only Areas B and D produced these. This difference could be attributed to several factors, but as we have seen, chronological differences cannot be the explanation. One possible explanation would be that the decorated vessels had a specialist function that was carried out in the buildings on Areas B and D. Alternatively, they could represent the idiosyncratic style of one individual potter (probably a woman), and the spread to Structure B in the later phases could be seen as springing from a familial relationship (a daughter?). Ethnographic evidence shows that household-scale pottery production is almost always undertaken by women, and there is direct evidence of this in the Hebrides, 'Each township had its potter who was always a woman, and she... passed on the art to one of her daughters' (Holleyman 1947, 208).

Taphonomy

Table 10.3 shows the sherd to vessel ratios across the trenches. All the figures are high, indicating that most of the pottery is primary refuse which has been broken more or less in situ, rather being redeposited in middens or being residual. Illus 10.17 shows the average sherd weights across the site.

It can be readily seen that Area F stands out as having a much higher average sherd weight than normal. This should mean that the pottery on Area F is

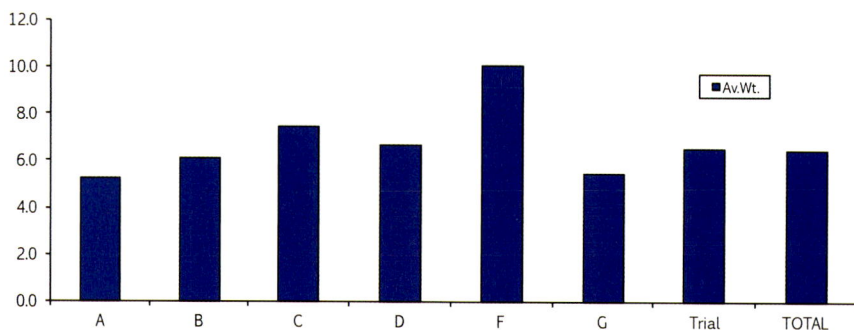

Illus 10.17 Average sherd weights by area

less broken than on other sites. However, there is strong variability between contexts within each site, and rather than look at general patterns, it may be more instructive to see how individual contexts vary. The spreadsheet shows which contexts have abnormally high or low average sherd weights, and this may aid interpretation of the taphonomic conditions of deposition at work. Low average weight suggests a heavily trampled assemblage, while a high average weight suggests little disturbance after breakage. For example, context C49 has a high average weight and high sherd to vessel ratio, suggesting that the pottery represents in situ breakage. However, this context is a post-occupation deposit formed from collapse of a structure. It may well be that the smashed vessels found in this context belonged to the underlying deposits, or that the vessels had been suspended from the roofs or walls of these buildings when they collapsed. The same high values apply to contexts D22 and D64, which are associated with the possible clamp kiln for firing the craggans, which would explain the breakages of apparently complete pots here (eg reconstructed vessel C28).

The taphonomic study shows that certain contexts contain assemblages that are probably in situ, being smashed and abandoned on structure floors. Whether these represent abandonment contexts or a lack of cleaning of floors is debateable. Midden material was a valuable resource in the Hebrides, and one would expect floors in use to be kept clean, but Dùn Èistean is unusual in that midden material is unlikely to have been used on site, or taken off the stack.

Discussion

The Dùn Èistean assemblage has enabled us to make more definitive statements about the craggan tradition. Firstly, we can see that craggans are not just a late devolved form of earlier pottery traditions. On the contrary, they have their own unique form of vessel (the globular jar with narrow neck) and construction technique. It is not clear where the inspiration for the globular form came from - it may be a skeuomorph of leather bags, or be derived from late medieval imported round-bellied sagging-based cooking pots. Whatever the case, it is a unique local development that seems to have fulfilled a functional niche, which allowed it to continue to be made over at least four centuries. It has not been properly appreciated what an innovation this form was, given the flat-based wares of the preceding Norse period. The jar form must have appeared sometime between around the fifteenth century and remained unchanged till the end of craggan production. The technique of production, with the characteristic thumbing producing a lumpy outer surface, seems to have been widespread in the Hebrides, with other examples from the mainland as far south as Loch Glashan in Argyll.

The small cups or bowls, which form a significant element of the assemblage, have a longer history, being similar to those from Late Norse period contexts at the Udal, but at Dùn Èistean they dominate the assemblage in the latest levels of Structure A in the sixteenth century occupation levels, re-deposited in the post-abandonment layers which may date to the eighteenth/ nineteenth century. The lack of more than a scattering (14 fragments of the same ceramic in Area D, see Will, below) of mass-produced factory wares of the later nineteenth century from all the excavated areas, suggests that all occupation on the site had ended by that time, as most sites of this period have produced quantities of these wares (Barker 2005). The fingernail decoration, which occurs mainly on the cups in the sixteenth-century levels, is so far unique to Dùn Èistean. However, similar types of decoration, of stab marks, occurs more widely, and appears to be the only chronologically sensitive part of the craggan tradition, being mainly confined to the sixteenth century and earlier. This opens up the potential for dating other sites in the Hebrides.

The taphonomy of the pottery suggests that most of it represents in situ breakage, giving an indication of living conditions in the buildings, and possible abandonment processes. Study of the decoration shows that it is confined to certain buildings and it was suggested that we may be seeing the actions of an individual family of potters at work. Overall, the assemblage is important in giving a glimpse of the pre-modern living conditions on this isolated settlement, and allowing a fixed point in the chronological development of post-medieval handmade pottery in the Hebrides.

Medieval and later wheel thrown pottery
by Robert Will

Introduction
A small assemblage of 27 sherds of wheel thrown medieval and later ceramics was recovered from the excavations, and included three decorated rim and neck sherds from a small Cologne stoneware bottle or flask, six sherds from earthenware bowls and a sherd of Scottish medieval redware. There are very few published comparable sites of the late medieval to post-medieval period in north-west Scotland, making the small assemblage from Dùn Èistean of some importance

Fabric	Total	Rims	Bases	Handles	Body-sherds	Weight (g)
Modern white earthenware	14	1			13	13.4
Modern red earthenware	2				2	7.8
Cologne stoneware (all join)	3	2			1	20.4
Post/late medieval redware	6		1		5	29.9
Post/late medieval whiteware	1				1	1
Scottish medieval redware	1				1	6.5
Total sherds	**27**	**3**	**1**		**23**	**79**

Table 10.4 Medieval and later wheel thrown pottery: Breakdown of fabrics and sherds

Methodology

All the sherds retrieved from the three seasons of excavation and pilot seasons were individually examined and weighed with diagnostic features such as rims, handles and bases, and differences in fabric and decoration recorded. The breakdown of sherd numbers and fabrics present are summarised in Table 10.4. The pottery was catalogued according to guidelines and standards produced by the Medieval Pottery Research Group (MPRG 1998; 2001).

Medieval pottery catalogue on CD at back of book

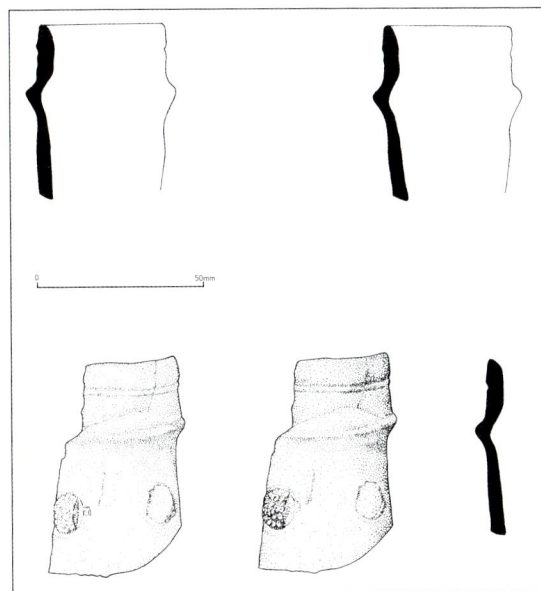

Cologne stoneware

Three conjoining sherds forming the rim and neck of a Cologne stoneware bottle or flask were recovered from Area D: two from Area D Phase 5, context 067, SF 525 and 1225, and the third from Trench 3 Phase 4, context 303, SF 3/89, with a combined weight 20.4g. The sherds are thin-walled and quite fine with a pale pink to buff fabric that may have been burnt in places once broken. The exterior has a speckled dark brown and grey appearance with an incised double band or groove just below the rim and a pronounced cordon on the neck. Unusually there are two applied decorative prunts on the outside although one has been damaged. The rim has a diameter of 34mm and is glazed on the inside. The sherds represent the rim and neck from a small bottle or bellarmine (Bartmanmkruig).

These distinctive stoneware bottles, usually with an incised face mask on the neck and shoulders, date from the late sixteenth century through to the eighteenth century. A similar vessel with the distinctive prunts more commonly seen on glass has been dated to 1525-1575 (Haggarty pers com) and this may be the first example of this type of decoration recovered from Scotland. Although relatively common on urban and east coast urban excavations few sherds have been recovered from the north or west of Scotland. Several sherds of stoneware

Illus 10.18 Cologne stoneware sherd 3/89 and Illus 10.19 Cologne stoneware sherd SF D525 have been recovered from excavations at Inverness (Wordsworth 1982) and Urquhart castle on Loch Ness (Banks unpublished) but this was probably connected to east coast or North Sea trade. Another point to note is that due to different soil conditions during deposition there are differences in the surface colour of the sherds and the fabric colour as SF 1225 is darker than the other two and may have been burnt.

Post-medieval/Late medieval earthenwares

Six body sherds (29.9g) were recovered that represent three different vessels of possible late medieval or post-medieval date. Four sherds from Area B (Phase 5, contexts B009, SF 174, two sherds; B020 SF 49 and B028 SF 8) and one each from Areas D (Phase 6, context D086 general) and G (Phase 4, context G029 SF 85). The sherds from Area B are in a pink/orange fabric with a light-brown glaze and appear to be from the base of the same vessel - a bowl - as the glaze is on the inside.

The sherd from Area D may also be from a bowl. The fabric is orange/red in colour and thicker than the sherds from Area B. The glaze is a yellow/brown colour and there is a hint of white slip underneath it to mask the red colour of the fabric. The sherd from Area G is in a smooth red fabric that is thicker than the others and has throwing marks on the exterior. The interior glaze has been burned or heated and has bubbled and ran down two of the edges, presumably once the pot was broken or discarded. The heating process has obscured the true colour of the glaze but it appears to be a dark-green or brown colour and as the glaze is on the interior, the pot is probably a bowl.

Scottish medieval redwares

One body sherd (Phase 5, B025 SF 155) in a Scottish medieval redware fabric was recovered from Area B. The sherd has a red/orange fabric and is reduced to a grey colour on the interior. The sherd is unglazed with no decoration. Similar fabrics have been recovered from excavations throughout Scotland and tend to date from the thirteenth to the fifteenth century.

Modern ceramics

The assemblage includes fourteen sherds of modern industrial nineteenth or twentieth century white earthenware sherds (weight 13.4g). Most of the sherds were small fragmentary body sherds from plates that had often split, possibly as a result of frost damage or weathering. Only one sherd, a rim sherd from a plate, had any decoration, in this case moulded feather edge pattern. In addition, there were two sherds of red earthenware with brown glaze.

Discussion

There are very few published comparable sites of the late medieval to post-medieval period in the north-west of Scotland never mind the Isles, therefore the assemblage from Dùn Èistean although small, is important. The key sherd,

Illus 10.20 Example of a similar Cologne stoneware bottle decorated with sprigged flower heads. The neck and handle are missing. Museum of London collection.

although from a mixed context, is that of the neck from a stoneware bottle or flask. These are relatively common on particularly urban sites on the east coast of Scotland but rare on the west, so to recover one from Lewis is important. The decoration is unusual and may be the first example of this from Scotland. The remaining medieval and post-medieval sherds while few and fragmentary confirm that wheel thrown and glazed pottery if not being made on the island was certainly getting there by trade or more likely had been brought in on a more casual and personal level but not in great quantities. Medieval pottery has been recovered from Rodel on Harris from trial trenching (Hunter 2005) but no details are given. Although there were large scale excavations at Finlaggan on Islay (Caldwell) where medieval pottery including imported wares were recovered the results are presently unpublished although they suggest that again wheel thrown imported wares from mainland Scotland and abroad were a minority of the overall assemblage which was dominated by local hand made wares.

Glass
by Robin Murdoch

Discussion
This small assemblage of glass from Dùn Èistean is difficult to assess because of the small shard sizes and their relatively good condition, ie lack of denaturing. The presence of denaturing on glass after prolonged burial can give a very approximate idea of date. However, denaturing normally occurs in the presence of alkali, ie lime mortars, whereas typical acidic Scottish clay soils have little effect. Only three shards retained any significant manufacturing detail to assist in identification/dating.

Glass catalogue on CD at back of book

Ten of the shards were of window glass (all from trench D) and again the lack of denaturing on these left few clues as to date except perhaps the fact that most had a distinct greenish tinge. This tinge, due to the presence of iron in the raw materials or in the clay of the crucibles in which the glass was made, tends to be stronger in earlier window glass, ie seventeenth/eighteenth rather than nineteenth century. However, individual batches of nineteenth century glass may have ended up more strongly tinged and would have been sold off cheaply. Fortunately it was possible to have two shards, SF D716 from context D068 and SF D1229 from context D071, analysed. These shards turned out to be HLLA (high lime low alkali) glass that means they almost certainly date to before 1700 AD.

Recent research by English Heritage has indicated that HLLA glass was superseded by mixed alkali (derived from kelp) glass around that date, at least in England. However, James Ord, one of the early seventeenth century pioneers of the indigenous Scottish glass industry, was known to have sought a monopoly of kelp making in 1621 (Turnbull 2001, 9). This may be an indication that kelp alkali was being used in the Scottish industry considerably earlier than in England. Research on glass composition just beginning in Scotland may help to clarify this. It may be that one or more of the remaining window shards may also date to the seventeenth century or earlier, but only analysis could resolve this.

It is also highly probable that some of the window glass is eighteenth century and none looked likely to be later than early nineteenth. This is supported by the fact all of the shards are thin blown and a few have variable thickness indicative of crown, or spun disc, glass. Crown glass was rapidly replaced by improved sheet glass around the middle of the nineteenth century, Pilkingtons closing their last crown furnace in the 1870s. Regarding a possible source for the window glass, late eighteenth and early nineteenth century material would almost certainly have come from Dumbarton. The great Crown glassworks there was set up *c* 1777 and operated through to *c* 1850 (Logan 1972, 177). In simple logistical terms for transportation to Lewis, Dumbarton would be the obvious choice for that period. Glasgow produced crown window glass from 1752 and limited earlier production had occurred at Loch Maree and Wemyss, Fife in the early seventeenth century. Leith in the later seventeenth century and Port Seton in the early eighteenth also produced window glass (Turnbull 2001). We do not know as yet what composition the early Scottish made window glass comprised and as such provenance for the HLLA glass would be purely speculative. It could as easily have been imported as made here.

The other items of particular interest were as follows: SF7 (context 006), a small shard of cold-colour painted vessel or bottle. This technique involves the painting of scenes or designs in what is either oil paint or lacquer and is not fired into the parent surface as with enamel. This means that the decoration can be easily removed. Often described as peasant-painted, this technique was common in Germany, Austria and Bohemia in the second half of the eighteenth century and the early nineteenth. Not enough survives here to look for specific parallels but the bottles in Van den Bossche 2001, 276-279 give a good idea of the typical product. It is, however, just possible that the cold colour shard could be sixteenth century but impossible to verify. Coincidentally, two shards of cold colour decorated glass were recovered from excavations at Fast Castle, Berwickshire, from a sixteenth century context (Mitchell et al 2001, 84), Fast Castle being a promontory fortification similar to Dùn Èistean in location and topography.

The very small shard of wine bottle neck and lip SF B037 (context B025) is of a form of the late seventeenth century. The surviving string ring is neatly finished and at a considerable distance below the lip which is flared out. The string ring is also nipping in the neck slightly (Dumbrell 1992, 57). Later wine bottles tended to be cruder in execution and the string ring much nearer the lip, suggesting that this is an earlier example.

Finally the possible wine bottle body shard SF C023 (context C038) is also reminiscent of the body curvature of a mid to late seventeenth century item. The puzzling thing here is its condition, very poor with heavy denaturing 1mm thick. The rest of the assemblage exhibits very little denaturing and it remains a mystery why this item should be so bad unless its local buried environment was alkaline for some reason. Again, because of its small size and lack of detail, the interpretation of it as a wine bottle may not be correct and

Illus 10.21 Glass shard SF7

it could date to possibly much earlier than seventeenth century, although the location of the site might militate against that.

Metalwork
by Colleen E Batey

Iron

The iron finds from this site are numerous, but unfortunately the exceptionally poor condition of the iron fragments recovered, often lacking any metallic core (see Clydesdale 2007) provides for very little identifiable or diagnostic material. Apart from the quantity of finds which are completely indeterminate in form or function, nails form the dominant element of the assemblage, supplemented by a small number of well-preserved roves and a small collection of miscellaneous items including metal sheet and possible vessel bindings.

The indeterminate iron assemblage comprises 69 finds out of a total of 140 finds (approx 49.3%). The combination of a dense layer of corrosion products with the ravages of maritime, salt laden atmosphere deprives us of any chance to work further with this material. The spread of this material across the site is detailed in Table 10.5.

Metalwork catalogue and metalwork catalogue with phasing on CD at back of book

Trench	Quantity	Percentage of total (approx)
A	6	8.70%
B	11	15.94%
C	2	2.90%
D	27	39.13%
F	5	7.24%
G	12	17.39%
T1 (2002)	6	8.70%

Table 10.5 Indeterminate iron assemblage

From these figures it is clear that Area D, a complex structure of several cells has the largest percentage of indeterminate iron pieces (as indeed it does of nails and nail fragments). The indeterminate fragments are scattered through several phases, eg eight finds in Phase 5 a period of collapse of earlier structures and the construction/occupation of turf structures and from earlier Phases 3 and 4 on that part of the site, underlying middens and the construction of earlier buildings there are slightly fewer examples. This does not necessarily assist in identifying the functional activities in Area D. The corroded rather than fragmented condition of the pieces does not suggest an area of trample, but perhaps localised drainage issues or heavily salt-laden soils in this part of the site.

Miscellaneous

12 iron finds have been allocated to this category, of which four are metal sheet, from Areas D, B and G. Of these, SF G018 (Phase 7 in Area G) is rather thin and of indeterminate function from the surviving fragments. They could have

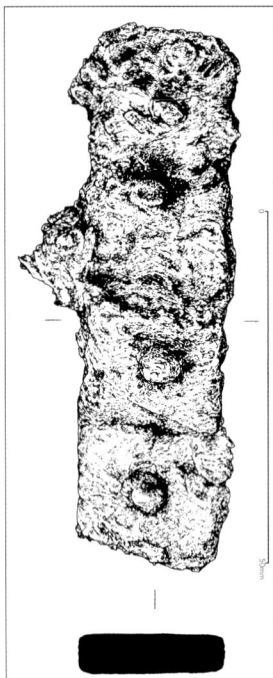

Illus 10.22 Iron binding strip
SF D997/D1118

been part of larger objects, which would include a thin metal segment, such as a box or padlock. However, SF D434 from Area D (Phase 7) is a thicker fragment, with a slight curvature and identified as being part of a vessel. There are a number of similar examples of metal vessels which have been distinguished, although as Egan in the seminal work on The Medieval Household (1998) has indicated, vessels in iron are seldom recorded, either in the written documents or in the archaeological record (Egan 1998, 152 and 177). Copper alloy vessels are more commonly identified. Nevertheless this find from Area D meets the criteria for a kitchen vessel with curving base/wall, probably resembling a cauldron for use over an open fire. In addition to these a fragment of a possible mould for shot found in Area F (from sample F028, context F009, Phase 4) adds further to the assemblage of lead projectiles and gunflints from the site.

The finds D997 and D1118 (see Illus 10.22), although from different contexts within the area (D035 and D010 of Phase 4) are probably part of the same object that is interpreted as a metal binding strip for a bucket or barrel. Examples of such fittings have been noted by Ottaway in Viking age contexts (1992, 623, not illustrated). This is presumed to be a storage vessel, and could have held water if luted or any bulky product such as oatmeal.

The much corroded ring (SF D1135 from context D036, Phase 3) may have been part of a suspension chain, and there are many similar items which have been identified in assemblages of several periods, ranging from the Viking age for example (Ottaway 1992, 649, fig 274), although its narrow diameter of only 30mm would suggest it is unlikely to have held any significant weight itself. Egan illustrates an example that was used to support a possible candleholder (Egan 1998, 146 fig 114), and such a light attachment would be more likely than a link in a chain to support a metal vessel.

Elsewhere in the miscellaneous category are a small number of clearly modern items, such as G056 a length of thin wire, and G017 which is the cap of a VAT 69 whisky bottle and B004 a piece of aluminium foil.

Roves

These small pierced plates were used with clench bolts, where overlapping timbers were affixed by a nail and the point was secured by being hammered (or clenched) over the rove on the inner face. Ottaway has noted two forms of simple rove (or rivet, clench plate), one of which is essentially rectangular (cf SF Area G US) and the other diamond-shaped (cf SFs B053 (Phase 5), D126

Illus 10.23 Iron roves D126 and D122

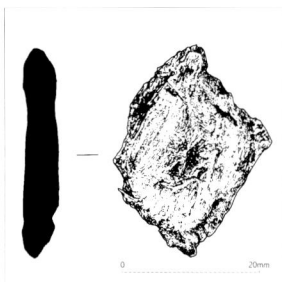

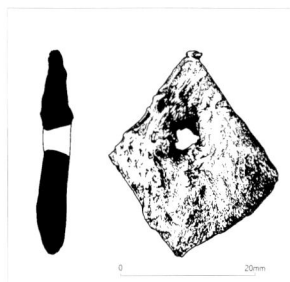

(see Illus 10.23; Phase 5) and Trench 3, 122 (see Illus 10.23; Phase 4)) (Ottaway 1992, 615). The rectangular example from the site retains a section of its square-sectioned nail shank. The four examples are of very similar size, less than 30mm at the broadest point and 3-5mm thick. These are clearly for securing two pieces of wood together and in rare cases where both broad flat head and rove survive intact, the thickness of that wood can be assessed. The fragmentary nature of these pieces does not allow this assessment. In the nail collection, discussed below, SF F019 from Phase 4 Area F has both shank and rove surviving, but no head.

Nails

This overall find group comprises 59 finds, which is over 42% of the total assemblage. They are distributed over much of the site as noted below, and are a ubiquitous find on archaeological sites of most periods. They can be sub-divided into groups which are larger and clearly structural as distinct to smaller ones which may have been ancillary to larger structural or boat timbers, this has been extensively discussed by Ottaway in relation to the finds from Coppergate in

Trench	Shank only	Head/shank	Flat head	Structural
A	8		1	
B	2	1 square; 1 round	1	1 square
C	1	1		
D	14 (incl 1 round)	3	3	
F	9			1
G	8	1 square; 1 round		1 flat head
Topsoil	1 (round)			
TOTALS	43	8	5	3

Table 10.6 Iron nails assemblage and Table 10.7 iron nails assemblage, with phasing

Trench	Number	Phase
A	2	2
A	5	3
A	2	4
B	5	5
B	1	6
C	2	3
D	1	3
D	7	4
D	5	5
D	7	6
F	5	3
F	3	4
F	2	5
G	2	3
G	4	5
G	2	6
G	1	7
G	2	8

York (Ottaway 1992, 616-618).

Most of the nail finds are simply shanks (43), all highly corroded and in most cases indeterminate in section, although there seems to be a marked predominance of square sectioned shanks. Where head and shank survive, in seven cases only, there is a split between round and squared shanks. The six finds with flat heads are all round in form. There are three nails that are distinguished specifically as structural, and this is based on the sole criteria of size; in each case these are larger and more substantial. Single examples of structural ironwork, one from each of Areas B, F and G do not particularly suggest the presence of timber structures on the site, and it is just as likely that ship's timbers were being brought up to the site for fuel and the larger quantities of unidentified nail shanks from Areas D, F and G (20, 10 and 11 respectively) may represent areas of greatest activity.

The flat circular head to those nails which have that evidence surviving are predominantly to be found on shanks of squared section, although this is possibly fortuitous as there are very few round sectioned shanks recovered in this assemblage. It is unclear if there is likely to be a functional difference, or indeed chronological difference between these two forms of shank section, although Ottaway also noted in relation to the earlier assemblage from Coppergate, that the predominant form of shank section is squared (1992, 615). This is as likely to be a reflection of production skill as function, in that it is easier to hammer out a squared shank than create a rounded one.

In Area A, the few finds of nails are spread across the three main phases of the site that cover the abandonment. Area B phases are related to post abandonment, and although there is a suggested structural nail from Phase 5 the small group from Phase 5 (five in total) is likely to be indicative only of decaying timbers after the building abandonment. In Area C, two finds only were noted in this category of material and these relate to the construction /use of the kiln barn. Area D has a greater number of nails, and also the predominance of the indeterminate fragments. Phases 4 and 6 have the largest number of nails from activity related to the construction/occupation, and then abandonment collapse of the buildings and construction/occupation of turf shelters onsite. The most likely association here is with the demise of the collapsed buildings. With Area F, the numbers are also very small, with 10 pieces spread across Phases 3, 4 and 5 which are respectively the first and second occupation phases (with an overall date range of AD1440-1645) and the abandonment and collapse of the onsite structure.

The numbers are very small for this part of the iron assemblage, even though it represents some 42% of the total. It would seem likely that the metal was actually being removed to be reworked elsewhere; despite the fact that almost 50% of the overall iron assemblage is of indeterminate function the quantities are very small for this period. This would be in agreement with the conclusions in regard to the industrial debris from the site.

Lead

There are just three lead finds in this assemblage. SF C115 from Area C (Phase 3) is an amorphous fragment, that from Area A (SF A086, Phase 3) is a perforated flat piece which may have been affixed to something, and Area F (SF F045 unseen, Phase 3) is a folded piece which is also likely to have been flattened. It is difficult with this small (and scattered) quantity to identify its source. Identification as residue from the melting of small item(s) is the most likely, as such a commodity was mined further south in the British Isles (Homer 1991). The possibility of a melted down roofing nail or indeed vessel fragment are possibilities for its origin, and there is a suggestion that the find A086, may well have served the function as an applied mount, although it is clearly incomplete and of amorphous form. It is a rare and presumably prized commodity, so the possibility of recycling or reworking has to be considered.

Although these three finds are from Phase 3 in each case, the phases represent different activities at different parts of the site. Area F is the first occupation phase, Area A is the occupation of Buildings A1 and A2 and Area C is the construction and use of the kiln barn.

Copper alloy

Seven finds fall within this category; one from Area B (SF 060 Phase 5, the abandonment and collapse of the buildings), the identification of which remains elusive, two from Area G and four from Area D (three Phase 7, topsoil and one Phase 4, construction and use of earlier buildings and hearths). Within this small group, two are too small, surviving only as tiny fragments (SFs G200 and D888). A small copper strip (Area G, unstratified) could have derived from an applied band or a fixing to secure a binding, as a knife handle or similar. The fragmentary find D002, a sub angular section of metal sheeting with a cylindrical edge and a large perforation is of unclear function, as indeed is what appears to be a complete object B060 (composite with iron; see Illus 10.24) that is impossible to

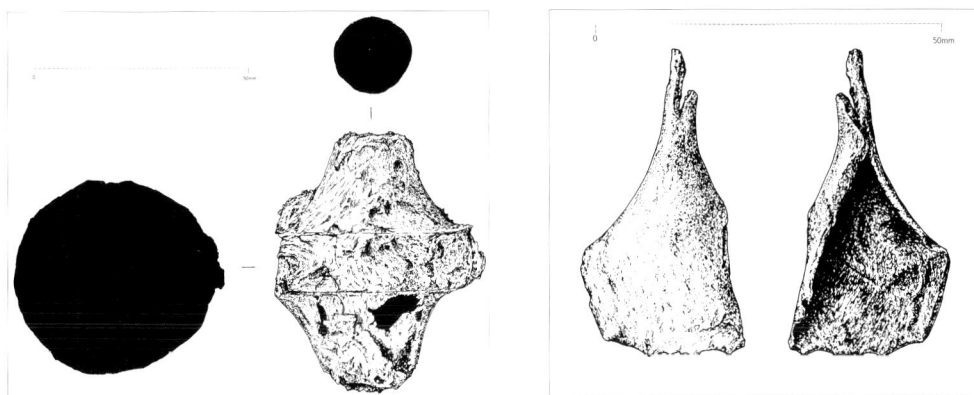

Illus 10.24 Copper alloy object SF B060 and Illus 10.25 Copper alloy part of candle holder SF D422

parallel at this stage.

There are two finds in this group however, which are identifiable and diagnostic. SF D422 is a flattened shallow shovel with a rough tapering handle (see Illus 10.25). This is very similar, although incomplete, to a find discussed by Ottaway in relation to the material from Coppergate (Ottaway 1992, 679, fig 293 find 3676). This is identified as a candle holder, where the tapering handle could be stuck into the wall and a rush or wick placed in the tray. Its simplicity of form suggests expedient workmanship, and it cannot really be seen as being chronologically distinctive, but it is appropriate in this identification. SF D001 is a hook-shaped item that was initially identified as a bracket, secured by the extended flat length. However, it is very similar to a fragment of a fleshing fork, of the type discussed by Egan (1998, 155-156, fig 124, no 436), which would have been used to select pieces of meat being cooked in a large cauldron like vessel. It is appropriate that it was recovered in Area D, where the putative remains of an iron cauldron were noted, and the presence of such finds could support the suggestion of a kitchen area. The predominance of indeterminate metal fragments and small numbers of nails may indicate either in situ rotting of wooden walls/flooring or even the dumping of scrap material in a suitable hollow.

Coins
by J Donal Bateson

The billon plack of James VI

A small, but interesting, group of five coins was recovered from the excavations on Dùn Èistean. Among these there is one Scottish issue, a billon plack of James VI. Such eightpenny (and fourpenny) groats or placks (and half placks) were struck from 1583 until 1590.

The early ones have fuller inscriptions (type 1) which are subsequently

shortened (type 2) and then have inner circles added (type 3), as here. The mint was ordered to stop production in 1587 but on 30th July 1588 the Privy Council authorised a further striking to fund a proposed expedition to the Northern Isles or Outer Hebrides in order to restore order there. The king had entrusted this to Francis Stewart, first Earl of Bothwell, and the coin issue was to provide an advance to buy powder, bullets, victuals, provisions, and to make other preparations necessary for the undertaking. This is the background in which the coin was produced and it is unlikely to have been long in circulation (the expedition never, to our knowledge, took place; A MacCoinnich pers comm).

A smaller, much baser, twopenny plack or hardhead was introduced in July 1588 and an altered type struck from November of that year is very common. The eightpenny groat or plack was demonetised and ordered to be brought into the mint for re-coining in August 1591. A final and small issue of 'saltire' placks (tarriffed at fourpence) commenced in 1594 but in 1597 billon was replaced by copper in Scotland as the medium for small change.

Finds of the eightpenny groat, and more so the hardhead, are relatively common, around twenty sites having yielded examples of the former and double that number the hardhead. It is difficult to be precise about the date of deposition of single finds but few billon coins are likely to have circulated much beyond 1600. The latest hoard containing a number of such coins is one recovered on Skye, at Kyleakin, Castle Maol, concealed shortly after 1601. The find consisted of 72 coins of which 13 were silver and 59 billon including 35 eightpenny groats and 18 hardheads. Thereafter only the occasional straggler is found such as the half plack in a hoard of 42 silver and one billon coins found at Cromarty but surprisingly one eightpenny groat survived into the 1670s when it was included in the Inverary find of 261 coins along with an even earlier billon bawbee of Mary.

The specimen from Dùn Èistean was therefore most probably lost before 1600 and possibly about 1590.

The Elizabeth I sixpence

The second coin found is one of the common English sixpences struck in large numbers by Elizabeth I from 1561 until 1602. These bear the date on the reverse above the shield and though the third numeral is unclear here, the initial mark is a long cross indicating it was struck in 1580. Hoards suggest large quantities of Elizabeth's silver coinage consisting of shillings, especially sixpences, but also groats, threepences, half groats and pennies, reached Scotland after the accession of James VI to the English throne in 1603. While a few finds may represent more contemporary losses the majority belong to the seventeenth century. Elizabethan silver still made up a large part of the Civil War hoards deposited in Scotland. The Kelso hoard, probably, concealed in 1643, is dominated by worn silver of Elizabeth and James I. The find consists of 1,375 coins, of which 1,163 are English issues including 519 Elizabethan sixpences. A hoard from Ardnave on Islay, concealed in the early 1640s contained 23 shillings of Elizabeth though

Illus 10.28 Elizabeth I, silver sixpence, obverse and Illus 10.29 Elizabeth I silver sixpence, reverse

no sixpences. So plentiful were these issues that they continued to play a part in the currency of Scotland well into the second half of the seventeenth century. The Inverary find, deposited about 1675 still had nine Elizabethan sixpences among its silver element of 41 coins while most of the remainder of the total of 261 coins were copper tuners or twopences.

The sixpence of 1580 from Dùn Èistean was thus probably lost sometime during the seventeenth century but since it not heavily worn this seems likely to have occurred early in the century rather than later.

George V bronze penny, and modern decimal penny

Also recovered from the site were a bronze penny of George V dated 1936. The bronze penny had been introduced in Britain by Queen Victoria in 1860 and continued to be issued until 1967 when production ceased in advance of the official change-over to the decimal currency in 1971. Such pennies are frequently found in a variety of sites throughout the country. Since this specimen displays only slight wear it is probable it was inserted into the marker cairn about 1940 or in the early 1940s.

The final coin recovered is a modern decimal penny of 1999, again slightly worn, and found in the marker cairn.

1. Sample B053, context B109, Trench B, Phase 5: Post-abandonment slump between buildings B1 and B6.
    Scotland, James VI, billon plack (8d Scots), issue of 1583-90, type 3
    obverse: crowned shield with lion rampant left, beaded inner circle
        [IACO]B' 6 ·D ·G ·[R ·SCO' ·]
    reverse: crowned thistle, beaded inner circle
        OPPID' ·EDINB ·
    wt.1.30gm (20.1g); axis 135°; corroded, fairly worn
    Burns 1887, fig. 962, no.6

2. SF no. B241, context B025, Trench B, Phase 5: Post-abandonment slump in interior of building B6
    England, Elizabeth I, silver sixpence, 15(8?)0
    obverse: crowned bust left, rose behind
        +[ELIZABE]TH ·D ·G ·ANG FRA Z HIB REGINA
    reverse: arms upon floriate cross, date above 15[8]0, initial mark long cross
        POSVI / DEV ·AD / IVTORE / M ·MEVM
    wt.1.91gm (29.5g); axis 310°; corroded, fairly worn
    North 1991-6

3. SF no. G002, context G002, Trench G, Phase 8: Marker cairn
    United Kingdom, George V, bronze penny, 1936, slightly worn

4. SF no. G001, context G002, Trench G, Phase 8: Marker cairn
    United Kingdom, Elizabeth II, bronze penny, 1999, slightly worn

Lead projectiles
by Natasha Ferguson

Introduction

Lead projectiles catalogue on CD at back of book

An assemblage of sixteen artefacts had been identified as either a lead projectile or as lead residue of the casting process. Out of this assemblage eight were

Illus 10.30 Composite photo of all 15 lead projectiles, all same scale

identified as musket balls; five as pistol balls; one piece of buckshot and one fragment of lead residue. Two artefacts were not made of lead, including one of the possible musket balls, which was identified as a stone ball (SF G063), and what appears to be a fragment of a tooth (SF no F045).

Illus 10.31 An early 17th century Scottish snaphaunce lock pistol © Granite Productions. Licensor www.scran.ac.uk and Illus 10.32 An early 17th century Scottish snaphaunce lock musket © National Museums Scotland. Licensor www.scran.ac.uk

Diameters and weight

The musket balls ranged in size and weight with the smallest measuring 12.74mm in diameter and weighing 10g (SF no D487), and the largest measuring 17.18mm in diameter and weighing 26g (SF no G010). The range size and weight of pistol balls was much closer with the smallest measuring 11.83mm in diameter and weighing 8g (SF no B116), and the largest measuring 14.25mm in diameter and weighing 6g (SF no D4860. The piece of buckshot was a fraction of this size measuring only 9.52mm in diameter and weighing 6g (SF no 1032). The stone ball measured 17.58mm in diameter and weighs 6g (SF no G063), the size of this ball would certainly suggest that it has the potential to have been used as a projectile if sources of lead were low or non-existent, although it could equally have been used in nineteenth century bottles as a stopper which is a common misinterpretation.

Lead condition

The condition of the lead in this assemblage was poor which is not unexpected if the soils are acidic in nature as this accelerates the corrosion of the patina ie surface. Only two appeared to be in good condition with only minor flaking of the patina SF no 10 and SF no B154. Lead projectiles will oxidise relatively quickly in the soil forming a white patina that appears pitted and flaky. Many of the projectiles, particularly the pistol balls, have a fragmentary and unstable patina resulting in layers disintegrating in large areas across the surface of the ball. A resulting factor is that many diagnostic features such as firing marks, often preserved in the patina, could not be identified. The corrosion also affected the shape of some of the projectiles, and in one example a musket ball SF no D487 appears to have lost mass because of severe corrosion.

Casting features

Quality of casting across the assemblage is generally poor with a number of projectiles either poorly cast or with casting errors. SF no F098 and SF no G010

Illus 10.33 SF F098 and Illus 10.34 SF G010

both contain casting errors. The first has been miscast in a faulty two part mould as both halves are slightly offset. The latter showing signs of an air bubble formed during casting creating a small hole and depression on the surface, which is a result of the lead becoming too hot to pour effectively into the mould. Four projectiles, SF nos A071, C071, D613 and D758, are slightly oval or egg shaped, which is often a result of poor casting. This shape may occur if the mould is of poor quality or the crisp spherical form required for the mould has not been achieved. This is usually a product of hand carved moulds, often of stone or some kind of organic material. Further evidence of small scale casting on site is supported by (A071), a small droplet of lead residue.

Interesting diagnostics

SF no 10 has been covered extensively in teeth marks and may have been chewed deliberately to alter its size and shape if it was too big to fit down a particular muzzle. Alteration of shape may also have the effect of destabilising the projectile when fired, with the result of increasing damage to a potential target ie a dum-dum.

Illus 10.35 SF 10

SF no B154 has evidence of banding, which occurs when the ball expands in the barrel particularly if it is a tight fit. This is indicated by the presence of a regular band running around the equator of the ball, which contains a series of regularly spaced indentations. Banding is a feature that has been noted on a number of projectiles from mid to late seventeenth century assemblages and may be due to a lack of standardisation of firearm calibres.

Illus 10.36 SF B154

SF no D486 is an impacted pistol ball that has been flattened on one side and with rounded edges and has impacted into a hard surface solidly and directly. This compacted residue of soil is still present on the flat area of the ball and appears to have adhered itself to the surface. It is possible that this was the result of impacting into a turf wall and may represent the most significant evidence of conflict within Dùn Èistean.

Illus 10.37 SF D486

Discussion

Those projectiles found in exterior deposits do have signs of impact damage and are mostly associated with Structure D. SF 486 is interesting as it appears to have been fired into a turf wall. This pistol balls shows signs of deformation and the turf seems to have seared itself onto the surface of impact.

The majority of the assemblage was also recovered from interior deposits, which may suggest either taphonomy processes, or that musket balls were cast within structures. Those found within interior contexts show little to no impact damage, except a ball from Structure B found in a slump deposit, suggesting that musket balls may have been fired, but not necessarily within the buildings.

There are some interesting casting features amongst the assemblage. Many of the balls appear to have been poorly cast using a misshapen cast, possibly one that is hand made. F098 has two offset sides, made in a two-part mould, and as it was found in hearth sweepings, it may have been discarded after casting or dropped. It is unlikely to have been fired. SF 010 has an air bubble, resulting from a mistake made during casting. It was found in the collapse of the tower wall and does appear to have been fired.

It is difficult to ascertain for sure what the presence of these lead projectiles indicates. There could be a variety of reasons why they have ended up in the contexts they are in. The primary function may indeed have been as a means of defence. However the distribution of the lead projectiles across various contexts cannot in itself be interpreted as an event of conflict. They may represent the debris of multiple events of conflict, snippets of information making there way into other contexts. It is important to consider other possibilities and the fact that they may not have been fired, some may only represent the process of their manufacture. Muskets may also have been used for hunting purposes, although other methods in this area were probably more effective such as netting for birds or the bow. If the aim is to look for signatures of conflict then what is required is a survey in the areas between the structures in the topsoil, as demonstrated with other battlefield sites.

Conclusion

Both muskets and pistols were readily available from the sixteenth to nineteenth centuries, with pistols retained by the social elite as a symbol of status. Muskets could have been used for hunting however it is likely that the more accurate rifled fowling pieces, or even bow, would have been preferred for this activity. Lead projectiles were relatively easy to manufacture and did not require any specialist knowledge except for some basic skills in smelting and a hand held mould, therefore it is likely all projectiles were manufactured on site.

Due to the assemblage being derived from a variety of contexts it is not possible to link it to any singular event, or events, as the projectiles appear in individual contexts. Events such as skirmishing are more likely to be represented as artefact scatters within the topsoil representing the debris of battle, which may still exist if a topsoil survey was carried out. Rare examples of projectiles recovered from structures such as (SF no D486), potentially the result of hitting a turf wall, offers a rare glimpse of what may have been a small skirmish or attack on the fort.

Lithics
by Torben B Ballin

Introduction

The purpose of the present report is to characterize the lithic finds in detail, with special reference to raw materials, typological composition, technology, and on-site distribution. From this characterization, it is sought to date and interpret the various groups of finds. The evaluation of the lithic material is based upon a detailed catalogue of all the lithic finds from Dùn Èistean (see catalogue on CD in back), and in the present report the artefacts are referred to by their number (CAT no.) in this catalogue.

Lithics catalogue on CD at back of book

As the characterization and cataloguing of the lithics indicated that the lithics sub-assemblages represent different prehistoric and historic events, it was decided to subdivide the present report into the quartz assemblage (most probably dating to the prehistoric period) and the flint assemblage (thought to represent a local gunflint industry). The assemblages are summarized in Table 10.8. Natural flint pebbles were retained, as they are thought to represent stored raw material for the gunflint industry. A large number of natural quartz pebbles and granules were discarded. The quartz group (173 pieces) includes no strictly diagnostic material, and with its low research potential, it was decided to make the presentations and discussions of this material brief. The flints from the site, on the other hand, are quite unique, as this relatively large assemblage (429 pieces) allows the detailed characterization and discussion of a probably early, and very distinct, gunflint industry. In general, it is difficult to find references to other gunflint industries than those at Brandon in Suffolk (eg Skertchley 1879; de Lotbiniere 1977), and most references to gunflint production concern industries from the latest part of the eighteenth century and, mostly, the first half of the nineteenth century (Napoleonic times). This report focuses on the characterization and discussion of the lithic waste and implements associated with the Dùn Èistean gunflint production.

Table 10.8 General list of flint and quartz artefacts

	Flint	Quartz	Total
Debitage			
Chips	171	63	234
Flakes	157	75	232
Blades	13	3	16
Microblades	13	6	19
Indeterminate pieces	12	23	35
Total debitage	366	170	536
Cores			
Pebbles	6		6
Split pebbles	4	1	5
Bipolar cores	11		11
Single-platform cores		1	1
Total cores	21	2	23
Tools			
Gunflints	25		25
Gunflints(?)	5		5
Gunflint chips	3		3
Fire-flints	6		6
Retouched pieces	3		3
Hammerstones		1	1
Total tools	46	1	47
TOTAL	429	173	602

The quartz assemblage

The 173 quartz artefacts from the DEAP excavations include 98% debitage, supplemented by two cores and one tool. The quartz is mostly fine-grained material, with some milky quartz, and the fact that the assemblage consists almost entirely of inner (ie cortex-free) pieces suggests procurement from one or more vein sources, rather than from shore deposits. Almost one-quarter of the quartz is burnt.

The debitage is composed of 63 chips, 75 flakes, three blades, six microblades, and 23 indeterminate pieces. Approximately 14% of the technologically definable blanks were produced in hard percussion, and the remainder in hammer-and-anvil technique. One blade is a hard-hammer specimen, whereas all other blades and microblades are bipolar pieces. In comparison, hard percussion was used approximately two and a half times less at Dùn Èistean than at the NALS sites (see Barrowman, C S 2015), indicating the application of a simpler, single-step operational schema at Dùn Èistean (the reduction of quartz by the exclusive application of hammer-and-anvil technique).

The assemblage includes two cores, namely one split pebble (CAT 557) and one single-platform core (CAT 483). The split pebble is an exceedingly small piece (18 x 19 x 15mm), which was placed on an anvil and probably struck once. The knapper's intention may have been to split the pebble into two halves (for example for thumbnail-scrapers) or four orange-segment flakes, but the action only detached two thin primary flakes, and the piece was abandoned. CAT 483 is a small, crude single-platform core (32 x 29 x 19mm), with a plain, untrimmed platform. It was knapped along most of its circumference. The collection only includes one tool (CAT 554), namely a large hammerstone (66 x 54 x 34mm). CAT 554 has one rounded end with some surviving cortex (the handle-end), whereas its other end is defined by a crushed, convex ridge (the working-end).

The assemblage is devoid of any datable typo-technological elements but, in Scotland, quartz would not be expected to have been used in domestic contexts after the prehistoric period (Ballin 2009, 75). The dating of the DEAP

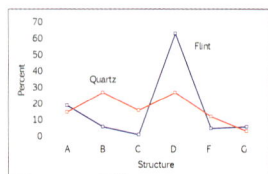

Illus 10.38 General distribution of flint and quartz across the site graph

Trench	Quantity			Percent		
	Flint	Quartz	Total	Flint	Quartz	Total
A	77	22	99	19	15	18
B	26	41	67	6	27	12
C	2	24	26	1	16	4
D	259	41	300	63	27	54
F	19	19	38	5	12	7
G	24	4	28	6	3	5
TOTAL	407	151	558	100	100	100

Table 10.9 Distribution of flint and quartz across the site

quartz to a part of prehistory (that is, suggesting that it is not contemporary with the post-medieval flint assemblage) is supported by the distribution of flint and quartz across the Dùn Èistean site (Table 10.9; Illus 10.38). The distribution of the flint indicates two activity 'hotspots' (Structures A and D), and three areas of less intense activity (Structures B, F, and G), whereas flint was not – as expected – worked in the area around the kiln (Structure C). In contrast, the quartz seems to have been distributed relatively evenly across the site, including Structure C, defining the quartz as most likely residual in relation to the site's post-medieval activities.

The Dùn Èistean flint assemblage – the gunflint industry

Although it cannot be ruled out that a minor proportion of the flints from Dùn Èistean are prehistoric pieces, the site's flint assemblage constitutes a logical coherent whole, including waste from several stages of gunflint manufacturing, as well as finished and damaged gunflints. The total DEAP flint assemblage is listed in Table 10.8 (429 pieces), and it includes 366 pieces of debitage (85%), 21 cores (5%), and 46 tools (10%). In general, actual gunflint workshops are only known from Brandon in south-east England, and they are mostly late (see dating, distribution and discussion sections, below), making a thorough presentation and discussion of the relatively early Dùn Èistean material important. As the present assemblage is clearly linked to the production of gunflints, and to a lesser extent fire-flints, this presentation is introduced by a brief terminological section, which explains the most important terms relevant to the understanding of those two types.

Terminology (Ballin 2005)

Gunflints: The description of the Dùn Èistean gunflints follows a terminology adapted from Nelson (2004) (Illus 10.39). A gunflint generally has two faces and four sides. The flat face is referred to as the lower face and the bevelled face as the upper face. The functionally defining elements of a gunflint are its back and leading edge. The back, which is usually relatively steep, has been modified from the lower face to allow the piece to be fitted into the jaws of the cock, where it would be held in place by a leather pad. The leading edge, which is supposed to create the spark and discharge the gun, is more acutely angled in relation to the lower face, and in many cases a slight bevel has been formed on its underside by retouch from the upper face. The two lateral sides of a gunflint are usually modified by either fine retouch, or by a relatively coarse retouch corresponding to the stout retouch of the back.

Gunflints were produced in the form of two general varieties, the so-called English and French types. The English type was produced on large conical single-platform cores, from which regular broad blades were detached (Knapp 1996). These blades were then subdivided by a number of opposed notches and subsequently broken into small wedge-shaped pieces, the gunflints. By retouch of the four sides, the English gunflint then acquired its regular rectangular shape (as in Illus 10.39). French gunflints, on the other hand, were made by detaching thick, bi-convex flakes ('Janus-flakes') from the ventral face of a larger flake (Chandler 1917; McNabb and Ashton 1990). These blanks, which were frequently characterized by a quite prominent bulb of percussion, were then transformed into gunflints by producing a steep convex back, which did not form corners with the lateral

Lithic terminology on CD at back of book

Illus 10.39 Descriptive terminology of gunflints

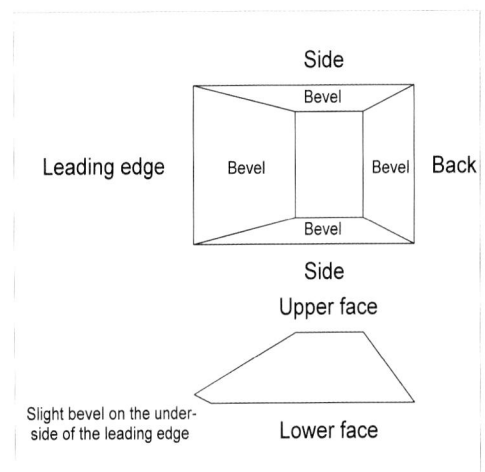

sides. The finished product is, in popular terms, D-shaped, rather than rectangular. Generally, English gunflints are dark-brown to black, whereas French gunflints are honey-brown. Due to the different forms of manufacture, the former are also referred to as blade gunflints, and the latter as spall gunflints (Stone 1974).

However, rectangular and D-shaped gunflints were produced in France as well as in Britain, and the D-shaped gunflints were occasionally based on blades as well as on spalls (though Hume [1982, 220-1] describes French gunflints as D-shaped, his illustrated piece is clearly based on a blade). The gunflint industry of East Anglia was dominated by the manufacture of D-shaped gunflints (spall gunflints) from the 17th to the end of the 18th century, but from approximately 1800 the rectangular blade gunflints became standard (Barnes 2004). This is, for example, demonstrated by finds from British shipwrecks, where the gunflints from the Invincible (sunk 1758) are D-shaped spall gunflints (Bingeman 2004), whereas the gunflints from the Earl of Abergavenny (sunk in 1805) are rectangular blade gunflints (Reis 2004). Consequently, the author recommends avoiding the terms 'French' and 'English', and he suggests their replacement with the more descriptive terms 'spall gunflint' and 'blade gunflint'. Skertchley (1879, 4) noted that 'a good flint will last a gunner about half a day', explaining the huge production of gunflints at places like Brandon, Suffolk (Barber et al 1999, 18; Martingell 2003) and the equally huge number of gunflints found at some battle sites (eg Le Vieux Fort, Placentia, Canada; Crompton 2004).

Fire-flints: The most basic part of the fire-flint terminology is the name of the category, the purpose of which is to allow distinction between flints involved in prehistoric (eg Stapert and Johansen 1999) and historic fire-making (eg Koch 1990). Two different techniques were applied to produce fire, with prehistoric fire-making involving a flint and a piece of pyrite, whereas historic fire-making involved a flint and a mostly bullhorn-shaped steel implement. It is proposed

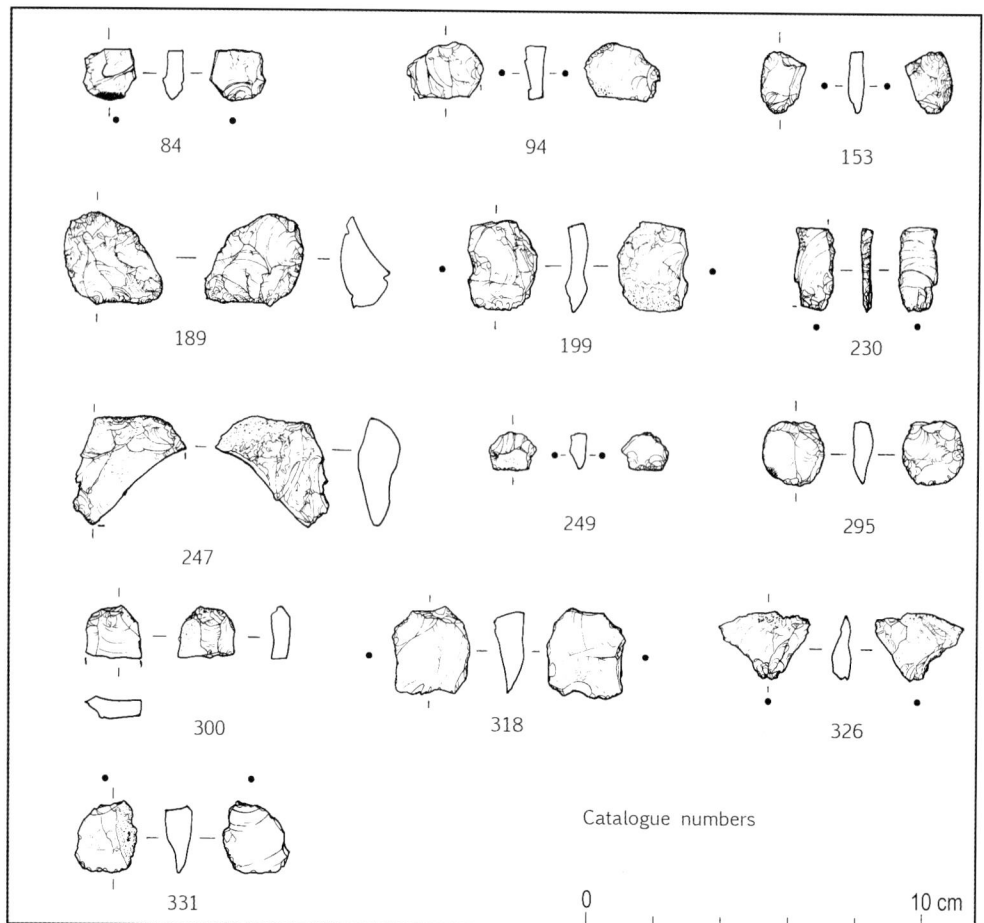

Illus 10.40 The gunflint assemblage

to limit the use of the term 'strike-a-light' to the implement doing the actual striking (subject), and not the material that is being struck (object). This means that, in prehistoric fire-making, the flint is the strike-a-light (as it strikes the pyrite), whereas, in historic fire-making, it is not (as it is being struck by the steel strike-a-light). The author suggests referring to the struck historic lithics as 'fire-flints'. The fact that the prehistoric and historic fire-making flints are subjects and objects, respectively, results in notably different wear-patterns, with the former developing smooth abraded points, whereas the latter develop chipped and crushed, mostly concave edges. Gunflints vs fire-flints: As noticed by many analysts of gunflints and fire-flints, gunflints were frequently used as ad hoc fire-flints (Carovillano 2002, Barnes 2004). This creates a problem with attempts at classifying such artefacts unequivocally and, in this description, a pragmatic approach has been followed. Pieces with a specific size (average diameter: 18 x 17 x 7 mm) and shape (square, rectangular or trapezoidal), and/or gunflint-specific use-wear (particular forms of chipping, polish, 'powder-burn') were defined as gunflints as a matter of course, although some were probably also used as fire-flints.

As noticed by gunflint specialists, fire-flints were produced in the Brandon area in a number of standard shapes and sizes, such as 'ordinary (like large French or old English gunflints), horseshoe, straight-sided round-edged, half-round, and circular' (Whittaker 2001). Particularly some of the gunflints referred to the groups 'minimally shaped pieces' and 'thin quadrilaterals' (below) appear to be particularly thin, or thin-edged and, despite their general shapes and sizes, they may be fire-flints. Some pieces were defined as gunflints on the basis of gunflint-specific wear, introducing so far unknown gunflint forms, such as pieces based on bipolar cores.

Specimens listed in Table 10.8 as fire-flints are pieces which – due to their sizes and shapes – are unlikely to be gunflints, and which have fire-flint specific edge-wear. They are generally larger than typical gunflints, and several are relatively thin. Usually, pieces struck repeatedly by a steel strike-a-light have edges characterized by shallow concavities, and pieces that were only struck once or twice may have relatively deep cuts in their lateral edges. Where some forms of lithic edge-wear may, on occasion, look very much like regular retouch, the worn edges of fire-flints tend to appear more splintered or bruised.

Raw materials – types, sources and condition
It is difficult to distinguish macroscopically between flint types, particularly when the pieces are relatively small and many are patinated. However, an attempt was made to characterize the raw material of the gunflints, and the following flint types were defined: 1) Dark-brown (five pieces); 2) grey (18 pieces); 3) dark black and grey (four pieces); and 4) spotted black (one piece).

Although the dark-browns and the greys could have been procured from sources in Yorkshire (cf Ballin 2011), the cortex of the greys is generally abraded and battered, and they may have been obtained in the form of ballast flint from shores in SE or E England. The find of a very large, perfectly formed, 'standard' D-shaped gunflint in dark-brown flint suggests that this flint variety may have been procured from the workshops in Brandon in SE England, possibly even in the form of finished pieces (Skertchley 1879; de Lotbiniere 1977). The dark black and grey flint is generally slightly cruder/grainier than the grey and dark-brown types, and it is more impure than the site's other flint forms. It corresponds to much of the post-medieval flint discovered in connection with excavations in, for example, Scottish ports (Ballin forthcoming a), and this raw material was almost certainly procured in the form of ballast flint. The solitary gunflint in spotted black flint may have been manufactured on local beach flint, although procurement as ballast flint cannot be ruled out.

A total of 35 pieces of flint are burnt, corresponding to a ratio of 8%. This total includes one bipolar core (CAT 391) and one possible gunflint (CAT 12).

Debitage
The 366 pieces of debitage consist of 171 chips, 157 flakes, 13 blades, 13 microblades, and 12 indeterminate pieces. This material is generally thought to represent waste from the site's gunflint workshops, and it is possible to subdivide it into two technological groups, namely

Illus 10.41 Four re-fitted oange-segment flakes from the Norwegian site Lundevaagen 21, SW Norway and Illus 10.42 Ditto with flakes separated

micro-waste and macro-waste. The former includes the chips, whereas the latter includes the flakes, blades, and microblades. The general characterization of the site's larger pieces showed that approximately 85% are bipolar flakes and blades, whereas examination of the chips by the application of a magnifying glass showed that those are almost exclusively small hard-hammer flakes. This fact is crucial to the interpretation of the operational schema responsible for the production of the site's gunflints (below).

Eighteen of the flakes and blades are so-called orange-segment flakes, formed when a pebble was struck on an anvil, thus splitting it into usually four or five flakes with a triangular cross-section. Orange-segment flakes are highly diagnostic of the bipolar technique (Illus 10.41-10.42) (Ballin 1999).

Although the assemblage includes 26 blanks defined as blades or microblades, it is important to emphasize that those pieces are 'metric blades' and not 'qualitative blades'. Metric blades are defined simply as flakes that are more than twice as long as they are broad, whereas qualitative blades are defined partly in metrical terms, but they also have parallel lateral sides and arrises. The latter is a characteristic of blades detached by the application of soft or hard percussion (ie platform techniques), whereas the blades from the present site are all bipolar (with one exception – microblade CAT 226). Consequently, the Dùn Èistean blades have curved or irregular lateral sides (not straight, parallel sides), and they mostly have a solitary proximal-distal arris or no complete arrises at all. The indeterminate pieces are predominantly pieces that have been burnt beyond recognition (54% of this category is burnt), or they may be pot-lid flakes or cubic waste.

Cores

The 21 cores include six pebbles, four split pebbles, and 11 bipolar cores. The six pebbles were included in this category, as they must represent stored raw material, whether it was procured from local beaches or in the form of ballast flint. They measure on average 30 x 22 x 16 mm, with their greatest dimensions (GD) varying between 20 mm and 40 mm.

The four split pebbles (CAT 162, 163, 266, 279) are basically early-stage bipolar cores, from which less than three flakes were struck. They measure on average 38 x 28 x 28mm (GD 28-55mm). The 11 bipolar cores proper (CAT 85, 189, 214, 227, 231, 234, 247, 248, 254, 300, 330, 391) vary greatly in size and shape. Two are broken-off terminals (CAT 248, 300), and the intact pieces have the following measurements: length 16-50mm; width 10-39 mm; and thickness 8-20mm. The smallest bipolar core measures 16 x 10 x 10mm, whereas the largest measures 50 x 39 x 13mm.

Approximately half of the bipolar cores are unifacial pieces (CAT 85, 214, 227, 235, 330, 391), with the remainder having been reduced bifacially (CAT 189, 247, 248, 254, 300). Most of the pieces only have one reduction axis (ie one set of terminals), while two (CAT 85, 189) have two axes. Pieces with one axis were not re-orientated during the reduction process, whereas pieces with two axes were.

CAT 227 is heavily water-rolled, and may be a prehistoric artefact. CAT 391 is a small trapezoidal piece (25 x 26 x 8mm) based on the medial fragment of a primary flake. It has 'crush-marks' at either end, but although this makes it look very much like an early stage bipolar core, one 'terminal' is very regularly shaped and the modification at this end may be actual retouch, whereas the modification of the other 'terminal' may be use-wear. Or in other words: this piece may be an expedient gunflint, where the former end is the back and the latter the leading edge.

Tools

The tools include 42 pieces, 33 of which are associated with the production of gunflints (80%), with six being fire-flints, and three artefacts are retouched pieces. The gunflint-related tools include the following specimens: 25 gunflints (as explained above, some of these may be combined gunflint/fire-flints or fire-flints), five likely gunflints, and three gunflint chips detached either during use or implement rejuvenation. Although the expedient character of some gunflints, in conjunction with the general gunflint wear, prevents the 25 suggested gunflints from being classed unequivocally, it was possible to subdivide these pieces into a number of subjective formal categories: 1) minimally shaped pieces; 2) D-shaped pieces; 3) straight-backed pieces; 4) thin quadrilaterals; 5) heavily worn ('amorphous') pieces; and 6) larger fragments. Whether these categories have any validity in relation to a larger statistical body of contemporary gunflints from less 'stressed' circumstances (raw material scarcity, possible conflict event(s)) needs to be tested.

As the morphology of most of the Dùn Èistean gunflints differ considerably from the well-known later Brandon gunflints, the identification of typical gunflint use-wear was crucial to the classification of these implements. In general, chipped leading edges is a certain determinant in the identification of 'normal' late gunflints, but as this chipping may give an edge an appearance very much like the terminal of a bipolar core, the situation is less straight forward in assemblages based on bipolar reduction. However, it has been possible to identify one type of wear, which is unique to this group, namely the so-called 'powder-burn'. This form of wear is usually associated with the leading edge, or the faces near the leading edge (this form of wear was identified in Ballin 2005, Fig. 4). Although it is presently uncertain whether this wear type represents discrete areas of micro-crazing from the exposure to fire, or whether it represents a chemical reaction, a deposit, polish, or a combination of the above, it seems to be an unequivocal attribute of some used gunflints. At Dùn Èistean, six gunflints had this type of wear (CAT 84, 295, 79, 101, 161, 308), as well as one gunflint chip (CAT 115).

Gunflints

The 25 gunflints are mostly based on bipolar flakes, although some hard-hammer flakes were also used as gunflint blanks, as well as two bipolar cores (CAT 75, 295). The average dimensions of the site's intact gunflints are 18 x 17 x 7mm (Illus 10.43), with the smallest gunflint measuring 11 x 14 x 5mm (CAT 249) and the largest 25 x 23 x 10mm (CAT 318). CAT 249 and CAT 318 are both D-shaped gunflints.

A trendline has been inserted into Illus 10.43 and the line's correlation coefficient calculated ($R^2 = 0.0961$). An R^2 of only 0.0961 indicates that the Dùn Èistean gunflints do not form a morphologically homogeneous category

The gunflints include five minimally shaped pieces (CAT 96, 149, 245, 255, 190). One rectangular hard-hammer flake is entirely unmodified (CAT 149), and it was only possible to identify it as an expedient gunflint by the use-wear defining its leading edge. The other pieces are generally simple flakes with sporadic retouch or rubbing along their lateral sides and back and use-wear along the leading edge. Two pieces have a retouched leading edge (CAT 190, 255).

Three flake-based pieces have a D-shaped outline, with the curvature of the D forming the lateral sides and back, and the straight line of the D forming the leading edge. Two of the D-shaped specimens (CAT 249, 318) are highly regular, well-executed gunflints, with retouched leading edges, whereas one is more irregular (CAT 331). The latter piece forms a misshapen D, and one lateral side and the back have been formed by sporadic retouch and rubbing.

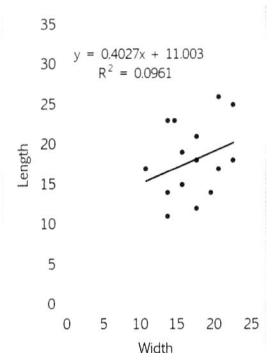

$y = 0.4027x + 11.003$
$R^2 = 0.0961$

Illus 10.43 The lengths and widths of all intact gunflints

The gunflints also include three <u>straight-backed pieces</u> (CAT 84, 199, 295). CAT 295 is based on a thin bipolar core, and the lateral sides appear to be defined by the cores two opposed crushed ridges (terminals). Its back was shaped by regular retouch. The category's two flake-based specimens were formed mainly by a combination of sporadic retouch and rubbing.

Two pieces were defined as <u>thin quadrilateral specimens</u> (CAT 150, 158). They are both based on 3mm thick rectangular flakes, and they have three or four sides characterized by fine retouch/rubbing. CAT 150 is intact, and it has regular modification along all four sides, whereas CAT 158 broke diagonally, detaching the leading edge. Most likely, CAT 158 also had four modified edges.

Five <u>'amorphous' pieces</u> (CAT 4, 79, 101, 161, 308) are sufficiently intact to be defined as gunflints, but they are so heavily worn that safe determination of their original sizes and shapes is impossible. CAT 161, for example, is missing most edges. The other four pieces were generally formed by initial crude shaping, followed by a combination of retouch and rubbing of lateral sides and back. CAT 101 has a retouched leading edge.

A group of <u>larger gunflint fragments</u> consists of three lateral halves split from back to leading edge (CAT 75, 103, 153), two broken-off convex backs, possibly from D-shaped pieces (CAT 94, 232), and one piece (CAT 132) is either a lateral fragment or a detached back (whether one thing or the other, it appears to have been a D-shaped piece). These pieces were in the main shaped by a combination of retouch and rubbing.

Gunflints(?)

Five pieces were defined as likely, albeit it misshapen, gunflints (CAT 12, 87, 88, 148, 197) on the basis of their sizes, shapes and wear patterns. Apart from CAT 197, which is a small sub-triangular/rectangular flake (13 x 10 x 4 mm) with one retouched lateral side and one side blunted by cortex, all pieces are characterized by having been retouched along the entire circumference and by having an uneven outline. Of the latter, the larger specimen (CAT 87) is large enough (18 x 18 x 10mm) to have functioned as a fire-flint, but the three smaller specimens (CAT 12, 88, 148) are only slightly larger than CAT 197, and they do not have enough mass to have functioned in connection with a steel strike-a-light. It is therefore most likely, that these pieces are totally exhausted gunflints.

Gunflint chips

Three small pieces (CAT 115, 287, 337) are either small waste flakes (average diameter: 11 x 7 x 2mm) from the production or rejuvenation of gunflints or - more likely - they were detached from gunflints in battle. CAT 287 is a piece with a straight lateral retouch and a corticated platform remnant, and CAT 337 is the distal fragment of a thin flake with an angled lateral retouch. Both may be so-called 'Janus flakes', ie flakes with two ventral faces (detached from the ventral faces of implements), and they both display flat spin-offs from what is assumed to be the

Illus 10.46 Gunflints (1): Top SF B019 and SF G075, bottom SF D305 and SF D1014 and Illus 10.47 gunflints (2): Top SF D569 and SF D1123, bottom SF D791 and SF D417

Illus 10.48 Production chips from Sample D088 Context D073

specimens' oldest faces. The latter indicates that the pieces may be chips detached from gunflints during use. CAT 115 is a small elongated chip detached from the corner of a gunflint, along one of its lateral sides. Its dorsal face is defined by one modified edge and one with 'powder-burn'. The examination of gunflints has shown that the detachment of gunflint corners is a common occurrence during use, and this piece was probably detached in connection with the discharge of a gun.

Fire-flints

Six pieces (CAT 95, 185, 191, 268, 326, 670) form a small heterogeneous group of flakes or flake fragments with concave wear along various edges. The concavities were clearly formed by violent, poorly aimed strikes by another tool (a steel strike-a-light?), and the lateral modifications are not regular enough to warrant the use of the term 'retouch'. The blanks are in all cases bipolar or indeterminate flakes, and four specimens are intact (CAT 95, 191, 268, 670). The greatest dimension of the intact pieces varies between 17mm and 29mm. Three pieces (CAT 185, 191, 326) are relatively thin pieces (Th = 5-6mm), whereas the other three (CAT 95, 268, 670) are somewhat thicker (Th = 10-13mm). Flint strike-a-lights and fire-flints have been discussed on a number of occasions (Koch 1990; Stapert and Johansen 1999; Ballin 2005; Mikkelsen 1991; 1994).

Retouched pieces

Three implements (CAT 130, 173, 230) are characterized by relatively regular edge-retouch. CAT 230 (24 x 12 x 4mm) is the proximal fragment of a flake in obviously exotic, homogeneous dark-brown flint. It has regular backing along one lateral side, but unfortunately the opposite lateral side has been snapped off. Most likely, this is the fragment of a backed knife that has lost its cutting-edge. CAT 173 (31 x 16 x 7mm) is a broad flake with a shallow retouched concavity along one of its long edges. This is probably a spoke-shave, plane or concave scraper. CAT 130 (7 x 17 x 2mm) is a small fragment of a thin flake tool. One lateral edge is characterized by crude rubbing, whereas the other edge is notched (chord = 6mm). The function of this specimen is uncertain. The raw material and applied technique of CAT 230 suggests that this piece may be contemporary with the gunflint assemblage, whereas the character of the retouch of CAT 173 indicates a possible prehistoric date. CAT 130 is too small and uncharacteristic to be placed in any form of context.

Utilized blanks

Nine flakes and blades display no intentional retouch, but instead they are defined as tools by their lateral use-wear. Two of these pieces are blades (CAT 83, 321) and seven are flakes (CAT 9, 76, 118, 146, 152, 179, 240). CAT 179 may have acquired its 'use-wear' in connection with general battering to break up the parent piece further, whereas the 'use-wear' of CAT 152 may be modern damage (rust traces). The wear of three specimens (CAT 9, 240, 321) is relatively flat, and it may have been formed in connection with cutting.

The operational schema of the gunflint industry

Only one of the NALS and DEAP assemblages appears to be chronologically well-defined (see dating section), namely that of the post-medieval flints. The finished implements and the waste suggest that the finds may represent a gunflint industry. In the present section it is attempted to reproduce the operational schema applied in connection with the manufacture of the site's gunflints.

At Brandon in Sussex, the production of gunflints was divided into three stages, namely quartering, flaking, and knapping (Davis 1997, 9; Whittaker 2001). During quartering, nodules were made into cores; during flaking, either flake ('spall') or blade blanks were produced; and during knapping, the blanks were transformed into finished gunflints. The first stage of the Brandon operational schema, quartering, was not needed at Dùn Èistean, as the small beach pebbles available (most of which may have been ballast flint) were too small for the production of traditional gunflint cores: the pebbles at hand simply did not have enough mass to be thoroughly prepared (ie decorticated, crested and trimmed), for which reason gunflint blanks were produced by the application of bipolar technique.

Where, at Brandon, the flaking stage was concerned with the production of large hard-hammer flakes or blades, at Dùn Èistean flaking produced blanks in the form of, mainly, bipolar flakes and blades (a small number of hard-hammer gunflint blanks have also been identified), as well as bipolar cores. As a consequence, the Dùn Èistean gunflints differ considerably from their more southerly, and probably mostly later, 'cousins' (see dating section, below). In some cases, bipolar flakes were modified into the same standard types as those known from Brandon (for example, large and small versions of D-shaped gunflints), but in several cases, Dùn Èistean gunflints have lateral sides defined by the two terminals of bipolar flakes, blades, and cores (eg CAT 94, 153, 295). An obvious visible difference between these two types of gunflints is that the former have four-sided cross-sections and the latter pointed-oval cross-sections. In connection with the identification and orientation of gunflints based on bipolar blanks, pieces with pointed-oval sections pose a problem, as it may on occasion be difficult to distinguish between their lateral sides (defined by terminals splintered during the primary production) and used leading edges (characterized by detached flat spin-offs, and/or splintering).

Where the pointed-oval pieces (for example based on bipolar cores) were almost fully formed in connection with the flaking process (creating an overlap between the flaking and knapping stages), pieces with four-sided cross-sections were formed into final gunflints when blanks had their lateral sides and back modified by mostly coarse retouch. This process is evidenced by two sets of attributes, namely series of circular impact scars along the sides and back of the gunflints, and the site's chips, which are mostly small cubic and/or hinge-terminated hard-hammer chips. The small D-shaped specimen (CAT 249) is a good example of this approach, and it is almost certain that a small pointed steel hammer and an anvil would have been needed to carry out this work (cf Whittaker 2001) in a fashion which could best be described as a modern 'sur enclume' technique.

One consequence of this approach is the formation of a dichotomous operational schema: it includes a flaking stage, characterized by the manufacture of flake, blade and core blanks almost exclusively in bipolar technique, and a knapping stage characterized by the detachment of small hard-hammer chips from the various edges of the gunflint blanks. Four-sided as well as pointed-oval specimens would occasionally have had their leading edges modified by fine retouch.

It is thought that gunflint types, such as 'minimally shaped pieces' and 'thin quadrilaterals', may represent a unique historic situation, which required the site's gunflint stock to be urgently replenished (possibly a conflict event, such as a siege; see distribution and discussion sections, below), and they are not necessarily typical early gunflints or typical NW Scottish pieces. Their general attributes may be the results of 1) the use of blanks which would normally have been deemed unsuitable and 2) expedient (ie fast) modification.

As mentioned above, the Dùn Èistean flints also include a small number of fire-flints, pieces with edge-retouch, and pieces with lateral use-wear. Although one retouched piece may be prehistoric, the remaining finds (and not least their use-wear), suggest that the post-medieval settlers at the site occasionally used flint for other purposes, such as fire-making and cutting (cf Ballin forthcoming a).

Dating

A total of 33 radiocarbon dates were produced, and they all fall within the period AD1465-1670 (see Chapter 13). These dates are supported by the collection's gunflints, their raw material, shapes and use-wear, which clearly identify them as mostly early gunflints. A number of factors suggest a general pre-Napoleonic date, such as the complete absence of blade-based rectangular gunflints, in conjunction with the common occurrence of D-shaped pieces (CAT 249, 318, 331; probably also fragments CAT 94, 132, 232). It is in the main accepted that assemblages produced prior to *c* 1800 are flake-based and commonly D-shaped, whereas post 1800 assemblages are heavily dominated by blade-based specimens (Barnes 2004). However, D-shaped pieces were manufactured relatively early, and they are for example known from the 17th century Le Vieux

Fort, Placentia, Newfoundland (Crompton 2004).

A number of gunflints and gunflint fragments in dark-brown raw material may be relatively late pieces, with this superb flint indicating procurement from early (pre-1800) workshops at Brandon, Suffolk. This 'black' Brandon flint was quarried from shafts sunk into the local chalk (Whittaker 2001). The collection's largest piece is in Brandon flint (CAT 318), and it is thought that specimens in this raw material may date to the second half of the 18th century. Most of the gunflints are clearly somewhat smaller than CAT 318, and they are generally in grey, less homogeneous flint. These specimens are probably mainly based on ballast flint from SE England, and their small sizes and varying shapes may indicate an earlier date (as mentioned, literature on early gunflints is exceedingly rare).

However, it is uncertain to what extent local raw material availability and heavy use may have influenced the shape and size of the Dùn Èistean gunflints, and at present it is not possible to determine whether the distinct appearance of the assemblage (raw material, artefact morphology, artefact size) is chronologically or geographically diagnostic, or both. It is obvious that the shape of some gunflints is due to the use of bipolar flakes and cores as blanks (eg CAT 75, 295), but does this technological choice simply represent an adaptation to a local procurement situation dominated by the use of ballast flint (relatively small pebbles, albeit larger than the more scarce local beach pebbles)? The wear of many pieces (chipping, polish, 'powder-burn') indicate prolonged use, but how much did heavy use and possibly rejuvenation affect artefact shape and size?

Unfortunately, neither vertical nor horizontal distribution patterns add much to the understanding of the site's chronology, although the incorporation of gunflints and gunflint waste into various site contexts clearly define the assemblage as post-medieval.

Distribution and activities

The vertical, as well as the horizontal, distribution of artefacts across the location demonstrates how complex the Dùn Èistean site is, with the remains representing an immensely intricate sequence of construction, use, abandonment, and repair/re-use/replacement of buildings. Moreover, the interpretation of the artefact distribution is complicated by the fact that recovery policies varied across the site, and that, for example, the spoil from the individual structures were not consistently sieved. Instead, sieving was carried out as part of a sampling procedure defined by other concerns than lithic distribution. With reference to Binford's toss-drop model (1983, 153), chips are likely to be the best indicators of the location of the site's gunflint workshops, as larger blanks, cores and finished pieces may have been removed, either as still usable raw material/blanks or in connection with preventive or post hoc site maintenance (ibid, 189) (also see Ballin forthcoming b).

Vertical distribution

Attempts were made to test the vertical distribution by examining the stratigraphy of a number of certain gunflints, gunflint fragments, and pieces with typical gunflint wear (eg 'powder-burn') (CAT 79, 94, 101,115, 153, 161, 190, 249, 295, 318, 331). Basically, no vertical distribution pattern could be discerned, with the various artefact forms being scattered through early as well as later contexts.

The two typical D-shaped pieces (CAT 249, 318) were found relative to each other as one would have expected, namely with the smaller grey one recovered from midden layers below wall D010 of Structure D16, whereas the much larger D-shaped piece in dark Brandon flint was found in the later context D071, a Structure D16 floor layer. However, if simpler gunflints precede pieces of more complex shape, and if pieces manufactured in simpler ways precede pieces based on more complex operational schemas, then a piece like CAT 295 (gunflint produced in bipolar technique; minimal modification) ought to be older than CAT 318 (gunflint produced in platform technique; extended modification). Yet, CAT 295 was retrieved from context D068, incorporated into a later wall above the Structure D16 hearth and floor layers. An asymmetrical D-shaped specimen (CAT 331) was recovered from context D100, a floor layer in Structure D10, and a minimally shaped piece (CAT 190) was found in context D007, a Structure

Quantity

Trench	A	B	C	D	F	G	?	Total
Debitage	73	20	2	226	17	27	1	366
Pebbles	3			3				6
Cores				14		1		15
Gunflint-related objects	3	5		14	1	10		33
Fire-flints		1		5				6
Retouched pieces				2	1			3
TOTAL	79	26	2	264	19	38	1	429

Percent

Trench	A	B	C	D	F	G	?	Total
Debitage	92	77	100	86	90	71	100	85
Pebbles	4			1				1
Cores				5		3		4
Gunflint-related objects	4	19		5	5	26		8
Fire-flints		4		2				1
Retouched pieces				1	5			1
TOTAL	100	100	100	100	100	100	100	100

Production of gunflints

Trench	A	B	C	D	F	G	Total
Pebbles (stored raw material)	3			3			6
Chips	55	6		98	6	6	171
Orange-segment flakes	1			17		1	19
Cores				14		1	15
TOTAL	59	6	0	132	6	8	211

Use of gunflints

Trench	A	B	C	D	F	G	Total
Gunflints etc.	3	5		14	1	10	33
Powder-burn/polish (heavy wear)		2		2		3	7
TOTAL	3	7	0	16	1	13	40

Table 10.10 Distribution of main lithic artefact categories across the site and Table 10.11 Distribution of the most obvious gunflint production and gunflint use indicators across the site

D7 wall layer (thus pre-dating that building).

Several gunflints and gunflint fragments were retrieved from various forms of abandonment tumble associated with Structures B and G (CAT 79, 94, 153, 161), and they pose a particular problem. CAT 94, for example (the broken-off back of a D-shaped piece), was found in upper Structure B5 deposits, which may represent collapsed turf walling that spread over a part of that structure's interior. However, did CAT 94 originally form part of the floor deposits of that structure; was it part of the collapsed wall, thus pre-dating Structure B5; or was it deposited in the tumble after the destruction of the affected walling? Basically, it is not possible to be absolutely certain as to whether this specimen pre- or post-dated Structure B5, or whether it was contemporary with it. The 'powder-burned' chip CAT 115 pre-dates Structure B1, whereas CAT 101 must have been deposited in the later phases of Structure B6.

Horizontal distribution

As shown in Table 10.10, post-medieval flint was recovered from all areas of the Dùn Èistean site, albeit with the most notable concentrations being associated with Structures A and D. There are smaller concentrations in Trenches B, F and G but, as expected, practically no flint was recovered from Structure C, the kiln barn. Table 10.11 shows the distribution of elements thought to be indicative of gunflint production ('workshops') (stored flint pebbles, chips, larger flakes, and cores), as well as elements indicative of gunflint use or conflict (the gunflints themselves, most of which are used, and pieces with 'powder-burn').

Although varying recovery policies (sieving) may have influenced the recovery of chips (which would represent Binford's drop-zones or the actual foci for primary production; Binford 1983, 153), the areas with few chips also generally have no stored raw material, and almost no larger flakes or exhausted cores. This fact (Table 10.11), in conjunction with the general flint distribution (Table 10.10), suggests that most gunflint production took place in Structures A and D. As the analysis of the site as a whole has not yet been completed (including the many non-lithic finds), the specific functions of the various structures are still uncertain. However, whether the structures were domestic or not, or whether their main functions were industrial or defensive, there is little doubt that specialized gunflint workshops were associated with Structures A and D.

The indicators of gunflint use, on the other hand suggests that gunflints were used throughout the stack-site, but with the heaviest use occurring around Structures B, D and G. These structures were located at the most strategically important points on the stack, namely immediately across the narrowest point of the abyss between the stack and the mainland (Structure B), at the centre of the defensive wall towards the S (Structure H), and at the highest point of the stack (Structure G, the tower).

Conclusion and discussion

The composition of the flint assemblage shows quite clearly that the flints from Dùn Èistean represent mainly used and exhausted gunflints as well as waste from the manufacture of gunflints. In addition, six fire-flints, three retouched pieces, and nine pieces with macroscopic use-wear were recovered, representing fire-striking as well as (mainly) cutting work. It is not always easy to distinguish between gunflints and fire-flints, as some use-wear patterns are related, but the combination of small sizes, particular shapes, and certain use-wear patterns has allowed the characterization of 25 gunflints, five likely gunflints, and three pieces detached from gunflints during use, whereas five slightly larger pieces with concave used edges were defined as fire-flints. Also, at Brandon, some designated fire-flints are known to have been produced in the shape of gunflints (Whittaker 2001), and the analysis of Colonial American gunflints has shown that some gunflints were used ad hoc as fire-flints (Carovillano 2002; Barnes 2004).

Technologically, the manufacture of the gunflints was organized in two stages, namely the primary production (the production of blanks by bipolar technique) and the secondary production (the shaping of blanks into gunflints by hard percussion sur enclume). This resulted in two sets of distinct waste, namely bipolar, frequently orange-segment flakes, and hard-hammer chips. Most likely, steel-hammers were used during the entire procedure, with a robust hammer for the first part of the reduction process and, most likely, a smaller and pointed hammer for the final work (Davis 1997, 9). Both processes involved the use of an anvil. In spatial terms, the gunflint production is likely to have been organized in workshops associated with Structures A and D.

As mentioned above, it is presently unknown whether the various structures were mainly domestic, industrial or defensive, but most likely most of the buildings represent a combination of functions. Although actual specialized workshops have only been suggested for Structures A and D, limited (probably expedient) knapping also took place in other areas.

The worn gunflints, mostly in sizes associated with smaller fire-arms, were recovered from the entire site, although the densest concentrations were found in Structures B, D and G. The complex stratigraphy of the site makes it almost impossible to refer the gunflints to one or more specific conflict events, but a number of factors suggest that the gunflints were generally discharged at the site, possibly in connection with one or more sieges: 1) the presence of minimally shaped pieces, exceedingly small specimens, and expedient modification, suggest speedy production of gunflints as well as limited raw material supplies; and 2) most likely the small gunflint chips (three pieces from Structures B and D) were found where they broke off the gunflints (ie where the gunflints were discharged), as these pieces are too small to have been picked up (Binford 1983, 153).

Due to the almost complete lack of literature on early (seventeenth and early eighteenth century) gunflints, it is impossible to precisely date the assemblage or its individual pieces by typo-technological analogy. This means that it is also presently impossible to determine whether the distinct character of the Dùn Èistean assemblage is due to age (ie it is older than other known gunflint-bearing assemblages), or whether the assemblage attributes are the results of local adaptation to generally scarce raw materials (for which reason relatively impure ballast flint dominates dark-brown flint from primary sources ['Brandon flint']), or whether gunflint morphology and technology may represent ad hoc adaptation to a specific stress scenario, such as for example a siege. Typo-technologically, the only certain dating evidence suggests that all gunflints may be pre-1800 (the complete lack of blade-based pieces indicates that they may be datable to a period substantially earlier than 1800; Barnes 2004).

Thirty-three radiocarbon dates were produced, and they all fall within the period AD1465-1670 (see Chapter 13). It is presently possible to define three gunflint operational schemas, namely 1) the production of D-shaped gunflints on bi-convex 'Janus-flakes' struck from the ventral faces of thick flakes (a form of 'flaked flake' or Kombewa approach; Inizan et al 1992, 57; Ashton et al 1991); 2) the production of rectangular gunflints on segments of large blades from large conical cores (Whittaker 1991); and 3) the production of D-shaped and straight-back gunflints from the segmentation of elongated bipolar flakes and relatively thin, flat bipolar cores (the Dùn Èistean approach).

The important Dùn Èistean gunflint industry and its various components have been included in a discussion of gunflint production in general (Ballin 2012). In this paper, the finds from Dùn Èistean are used as a point of departure for a discussion of early (ie pre-Napoleonic) gunflint production, and how gunflints, bi-products from gunflint production, and operational schemas applied to manufacture gunflints may have varied prior to the industrialization of gunflint production experienced during and after the Napoleonic Wars.

Industrial waste
by David Sneddon

Industrial waste catalogue on CD at back of book

A full description of each piece of industrial waste from the Dùn Èistean excavations is given in the accompanying catalogue (see CD in back). The assemblage of industrial waste retrieved from the excavations at Dùn Èistean was very small scale and does not provide any clear indication that large scale metal-working/production was being undertaken on the site, although it is feasible that evidence of larger scale metal-working is still present in unexcavated areas.

Most of the material came from within Trench B, and from slumped deposits between and within the structures, suggesting that the material was residual in nature. However, a small amount of material was also found in Structures D and F, from earlier occupation and ash deposits, either contemporary with, or earlier than, the buildings, and is worthy of further note. In particular a lump of slag from the base of a hearth/furnace found in Structure B in a Phase 3 peat ash deposit, is evidence of small-scale in situ metal-working.

Illus 10.49 Slag, possible hearth base fragment, SF B257, scale:20cm

SF B009: (from Phase 5: Post-abandonment, context B028: Deposit of slump lying between Structure B6 and Structure B1). Consisted of one very small fragment and two slightly larger fragments of vitrified ceramic. Contained glassy porous inner face where heat has been highest and an orange fired clay outer area (no clear face visible). Likely originates from a clay lined furnace/smithing hearth although clearly not in situ

SF B257: (from Phase 3: Structures and occupation pre-dating Structure B, context B102: Charcoal and peat ash deposit. Midden deposit or spread/sweepings from possible hearth B078). A relatively large piece of dense but porous slag with a lightly glassy surface. Earth concretions on base. Drip like extension attached to the top. Likely to have formed by dripping/running down and gathering at the base of hearth/furnace. Given its context it may have originated from within the hearth and, therefore, represent small scale smithing/bloom working.

SF B136: (from Phase 5: Post-abandonment, context B025: Slump deposit in interior of Structure B6). A small piece of extremely porous and light material. Very small patch of slightly glassy outer surface. Possible vitrified material/pumice stone?

SF C002: (from Phase 5: Final collapse, context C009: Turf slump from outer wall 004 or possible collapse of turf roof of Cell 1). Extremely porous and light material, slightly discoloured on one outer face. Contains a few attachments of stone. May be unidentified vitrified material rather than slag.

The remainder of the pieces were very small and fragmentary pieces of slag and cinder that do not lend themselves to further interpretation.

Worked stone
by Colleen E Batey

Introduction

Stone catalogue on CD at back of book

Although a substantial quantity of stone finds were recovered from the excavations at Dùn Èistean, some 83 finds units in total, only 26 (approximately 31%) are in fact worked or utilised. These range across several different find categories, including fire-cracked stones, simple hammerstones, pot lids, a quern and weights amongst others. In turn, the finds are scattered through many different contexts and consequently in small numbers per context which makes the potential for wider observations more limited.

Fire-cracked stones

Three finds in this category have been recovered from contexts D007 (wall of D7), D075 (hearth deposit in D16) and G006 (collapse deposit). D7 was notable for having a very substantial hearth within the limits of the turf built structure. Such finds are ubiquitous on settlement sites of most periods and are not period specific. They are formed by the heating in a fire of locally available stones, often pebbles (as in SF G036) and then commonly by the transfer of those heated stones to heat water for cooking.

Several excavations have commented on the presence of fire cracked stones in the assemblages, such as Freswick Links in Caithness, where extensive examination of the middens revealed different concentrations of fire cracked beach pebbles. Area 5 for example had a quantifiably higher proportion of fire cracked stones, generally in association with middens containing high shell and fish content (Morris et al 1995, 265). In terms of function, they could have

Excavation code (year)	SF no.	Context	Trench	No. pieces	Notes
Fire-cracked stones					
2217 (06)	D097	D007	D	1	Possibly fire cracked
2378 (07)	D884	D075	D	1	
2378 (07)	G036	G006	G	1	Fractured beach pebble
Hammerstones					
(03)	50	10	Tr 4/A	1	Hammer or anvil stone. Flat edge of beach pebble has strike marks. 140 x 90 x 60mm
2000 (05)	A166	A010	A	1	Possible. Hammer. Barely beaten at either end
2378 (07)	D822	D063	D	1	Hammer stone? Half fractured beach pebble with small chip at apical end.83 x 51 x20mm
2378 (07)	D1239	D001	D	3	2 natural; one coarse pebble with possible hammer use. 82 x 70 x 65mm
2378 (07)	F021	F023	F	1	Slight evidence of hammering at one end of cobble, smoothed flat face. 140 x 90 x 45mm
2378 (07)	G072	G016	G	1	Beach cobble possibly with slight hammering damage at each short end. 150x105x70mm
Pot lids					
2378 (07)	G057	G025	G	1	Possibly trimmed to disc shape, ?gaming piece. D 27mm
2378 (07)	G101	Topsoil	G	1	Roughly trimmed thick disc. ?Pot lid. D 150mm, Thickness 29mm
(03)	83	10	Tr 4/A	1	Possible half of pot lid. 72 x 100 x 13mm
Querns					
2217 (06)	D231	D010	D	1	Three small circular depressions within a larger depression. ? cup marks. Possible quern, broken. Minor depressions could be solution holes or result of handle position for grinding? c420 x 260 x 45-80 mm
Roofing slates					
716.3 (01)	3	105	G	1	Conserved
2378 (07)	G093	G042	G	1	Rounded edge, flat indeterminate piece
Smoothing stone					
(03)	39	16	A	1	Very flat and smooth stone on one face, rough on other. 132 x 75 x 24 mm
Whetstones					
2378 (07)	G080	G029	G	1	Probably complete fine grained whetstone, quadrilateral section. Good example. 71 x 13 x 13mm
2378 (07)	G108	G073	G	1	Small fragment of fine grained schist whetstone.28 x 11 x 7mm
Weights and whorls					
2217 (06)		D037	D	1	Coarse beach pebble weight with slight mid point waisted groove for suspension. 85 x 72 x 65 mm
2378 (07)	D315	Topsoil	G	4	1 with pecked hole
2378 (07)	sample D087	D061	D	-	Small fragment of slightly domical stone whorl. D c 25-28mm

Table 10.12 Stone finds assemblage by type

been hearth debris (used for the flooring of the hearth), or to heat water on a domestic scale or on a quasi-industrial scale for the processing of marine products. Large quantities of fire-cracked stones are still visible on the surface at Jarlshof (personal observation), but could have derived from any of the many periods represented on the site. The isolated examples at Dùn Èistean are probably indicative of larger numbers across the site in areas remaining to be excavated.

Hammerstones

Six probable hammerstones have been identified, from Areas A, D, F and G. They are distinguished as simple beach pebbles or cobbles that show signs of percussion damage at one or both narrow ends. Clarke has categorised this type of artefact as being either a pounder or grinding stone '...distinguished by broad areas of faceted wear on one or both ends of the cobble...' (Clarke 2006, 45). The stones used tend to be longer than they are broad and obviously the degree and form of wear depends on longevity of the find, its biography as well as the stone type. Clarke cites examples of varying degrees of "sophistication" from sites such as Kebister and Scalloway in Shetland and large examples from Pool in Orkney (Clarke op cit, 45), and clearly there is a potentially long time period for the utilisation of such items. In terms of use of this artefact type, crushing and grinding activities as the most commonly suggested. SF 050 from context 10, Area A, has indications of striking along the flat edge of the pebble and is thus distinguishable from the rest of the group, and may fall into Clarke's category of faceted and facially pecked cobbles (Clarke op cit, 46). This find was identified on site as a possible anvil stone, but it is not matched by hammerscale finds in the industrial waste report from this area.

These finds are scattered across a number of areas and phases on the sites. Two are from Area D Phases 5 and 7, one from Area G Phase 5a, Area F Phase 4 and Area A Phase 3. It seems clear from this distribution that they are unlikely to be period-sensitive and probably served a number of different percussive functions.

Pot lids

Two of the finds are from Area G, SF 057 is from Macphail's backfill deposit and therefore essentially unstratified, likewise SF G101 is from the topsoil. The two larger finds have diameters of 100-150mm, whereas one is considerably smaller at 27mm and is more likely to be a gaming piece than a very small pot lid. They are all fabricated in the same fashion, having been crudely chipped into a disc of thin or laminated stone. In all three examples there are no signs of the chipped edge having been further refined, by grinding or smoothing for example. Clarke has distinguished this type of additional treatment as being generally of earlier date (prehistoric) than those which are more crudely shaped and has made the further distinction of suggesting that the larger diameter stone discs are more commonly earlier as well (at least in the large Pool assemblage) (Clarke 2006, 37). However, size differential is also likely to be at least partially a result of the function of such items and commonly these discs are identified as pot lids. Clarke interestingly differentiates in the assemblages she examines between those lids that have signs of burning at their periphery and those that do not. The larger ones with burning could have been used as covering vessels that were being heated and those without perhaps covered storage vessels (Clarke op cit 37). Neither of the two larger examples from Dùn Èistean shows signs of burning.

Of relevance to this discussion is the material excavated at Tintagel Castle in Cornwall. The site is known for the large quantities of imported amphora storage jars from Spain and the Mediterranean in the fifth to seventh centuries AD, which presumably arrived with a ceramic disc seal intact. When opened, and the contents partially discharged, a replacement cover was made of a local stone disc, crudely chipped around the edges, and in some cases, these showed signs of subsequent reopening by a pick or similar which had created a pecked notch at one edge (Batey 1997, 202 and fig 107 and 114).

The smallest disc, with a diameter of only 27mm could have served as a gaming counter. Similar finds have been noted from Birsay Brough Road,

Orkney (Batey 1989, SF 203, illus 155) and also by Hamilton at Jarlshof in Shetland (1956, fig 77, 10-13) all from Norse contexts. It should be noted however that this is an expedient use of a locally available resource that is not necessarily period specific.

Querns

A single quern (SF D231; Illus 10.50) was recovered from context D010, that is, the stone facing of the east side turf wall of Structure 10. This is from Phase 4, representing the construction and use of earlier buildings and hearths and with a radiocarbon determination of AD1445-1625. It was described on excavation as having cup marks. The stone has an area of considerable smoothing, although it is irregular in form and clearly incomplete.

Roofing slates

Two finds fall within this group, SFs 3 and G093, and both are from Area G, from Phase 5a collapse deposits from the rebuilt tower (see Table 10.12; Illus 10.51 and 10.52). Stone roofing slates have been noted from work at Tintagel Castle in Cornwall, particularly in relation to Site F that is considered to date to the era of the thirteenth century castle (see Barrowman et al 1997, 21 and foot note 29). Throughout that assemblage there are several perforated slates that fall into earlier activities on the site, some of which are considered to be roofing cover (op cit, eg illus 115 and illus 119). The examples from Dùn Èistean could be an indication of how Structure G may have been roofed, although due to their simple nature and manufacture from local stone, they are difficult to date and are far from definite.

Illus 10.50 SF D231 quern fragment, Illus 10.51 SF G003 possible roof tile and Illus 10.52 SF G093 possible roof tile

Smoothing stone

This find has a single flat and smoothed face and could have been used for burnishing a softer material such as leather or bone. No obvious striations are visible on the smoothed surface. This class of tool is dealt with very briefly by Clarke (2006, 50) and it clear that these are a ubiquitous find, maximising suitable locally available material and without any kind of standardisation.

Whetstones

There are two good quality whetstones in this assemblage; SF G080 (Illus 10.53) from context G029 (from wall core material making up the construction of the rebuilt tower wall in Phase 4 with a C14 determination of AD1450-1635); this is a complete four-sided piece of sandstone that is most likely to be an import to Lewis. SF G108 from context G073 (the wall core from the first tower, Phase 3, which shares the Phase 4 dating horizon) is a smaller fragment of a fine-grained schistose stone, also potentially an import to the island. The excavators noted that the rebuilding of the tower was a hasty event, utilising locally available materials. It is unlikely that such useful items as good quality whetstones, albeit one that is fragmentary, would have been deliberately incorporated into the wall core material, it is more likely that they had been gathered together amongst other materials and deposits to be used as filler for the wall. It is presumed the original context for these items may have been the immediate vicinity, and potentially they were part of a working context, perhaps the minor industrial activity noted elsewhere by Sneddon (see above).

Weights/whorls

There are three finds in this category; a grooved beach pebble (SF D315; Illus 10.54, context D037 from Phase 5 the collapse of earlier buildings and construction/occupation of turf structures), a stone piece with pecked hole (U/S, G001) and a small fragment of a domical stone whorl (find from sample D087, context D061, from Phase 4 construction and use of earlier buildings and hearths) which is similar to examples from Jarlshof (Hamilton 1956, fig 56, 120 and fig 66, 144). Phase 4 has been dated to the period AD1475-1640 and Phase 5 AD1455-1630.

The crudely waisted beach pebble/cobble has similarities with more proficiently made examples from Jarlshof in Shetland (Hamilton 1956, fig 77, 166 no 2). The simple grooved pebble could have served as a line sinker or weight for counterbalance of a door for example, or a weight for holding down thatch. Similarly the stone piece with pecked hole recovered from the topsoil in Area G has common parallels at Jarlshof for example (Jarlshof, Hamilton 1956 Plate XXXV, 1-3), although it is a ubiquitous find. Clarke distinguishes pecked and faceted cobbles in the Pool assemblage from Orkney, and find PL4030 is a crudely modified beach pebble which has pronounced grooving on four sides as well as at its waist (Clarke 2007, illus 8.2.4, 363) unfortunately it was an unstratified find.

The whorl fragment was found in a sample taken from the upper hearth deposit in Structure D10 and its fragmentary nature clearly supports a discard. The simple domical form indicated has a number of parallels, such as PL1802 from Pool in Orkney (Smith and Forster 2007, illus 8.5.12, 429) and several examples discussed by Walton Rogers from York who sees a decline of the type there into the eleventh century (eg 1997, fig 806 6541and 6542).

Illus 10.53 SF G080 whetstone and Illus 10.54 SF D315 stone weight

Miscellaneous stone
SF G033 has been described as a trimmed stone, and the find from Sample F024, context F035 is a worked but indeterminate fragment.

Overall comments
This small assemblage includes some items whose function is clear, weights and whorls, whetstones, hammerstones and pot lids for example. There is however a number of items that are more obscure and identification is not assisted much by the contexts in which they were recovered. Few of the stone finds are chronologically diagnostic and it would seem that in most cases the finds represent the expedient use of a locally available resource, potentially supplemented by specific stones, such as for whetstones. The inclusion of the quern in the wall lining of Structure D10 could have been associated with the kiln barn from Area C, but this would assume a small scale activity which would seem to be at variance with the scale of activity suggested by the building of a kiln barn. Earlier, domestic grain processing is therefore a more likely interpretation for this evidence. The very small assemblage of roofing slates from Structure G give us an indication of how this building may once have been roofed, although the slates are far from definite and difficult to tie down chronologically.

Illus 11.1 Taking soil samples on site

eleven

A significant assemblage of environmental remains was recovered from the excavations on Dùn Èistean. Due to the acidity of the soil on the site only burnt organic material survived. This included carbonised plant remains, animal, bird and fish bone, and marine shells. In this chapter specialists report on their analysis of this important assemblage. Over 400 bulk samples of up to 28 litres of soil each were taken from every archaeological deposit excavated on Dùn Èistean and processed through an environmental flotation tank so as to recover the carbonised remains of plants and seeds. Significant quantities of charcoal, burnt peat/turf and cereal grain were recovered, and these are analysed by Ramsay below, who discusses the evidence for the building materials used on the site, the fuel burnt in the fires, and the foods, especially cereal grain, that was dried and consumed by those living on the island. She also identifies sixteen different types of wood amongst the assemblage, some from local woodlands, but the majority non-local species collected as driftwood. Some of the driftwood originated from mainland Scotland but exotic conifer types such as spruce, larch and fir probably came across the Atlantic from North America. The wood identified was used mainly for fuel, with the exception of an oak threshold identified in the doorway of Structure F.

The environmental assemblage contained abundant cereal grain with over 17,000 carbonised grains being recorded from the site. Oats and barley were the most common. Ramsay identifies that only trace amounts of chaff or weed seeds were present in the grain, suggesting that it had been processed before it was taken onto the island, where the final stages of drying and grinding would have taken place. Her report on the preliminary pollen analysis and AMS radiocarbon dating of a core sample from the silt deposits in the man-made pond, Structure E, demonstrate that the basal deposits of the pond can be radiocarbon dated to AD1440-1640.[1] The pollen contained within the pond was local and provided information on the vegetation that grew on the island in the late fifteenth to early seventeenth centuries. Plantains were common, showing evidence of trampling. No evidence was found of heather growing locally, and only one cereal pollen grain was identified, demonstrating that cereals were not grown on the island but in the vicinity. Seeds of flax were also recorded from the site, suggesting that this was grown locally for fibre and/or oil production.

The animal bone recovered from the excavations was almost all burnt and so fragmentary that Masson-MacLean is able to identify only a small number of fragments to species and element. However, he is able to report that cattle and sheep bones were the most numerous, and were a source of meat and probably dairy products. He also notes cut marks on some of the bone fragments, made as a result of meat removal using metal bladed knives and which demonstrates that butchery activities did occur on the site. Small numbers of domestic fowl and wild bird bones are also identified, suggesting that these were also used as food. The small group of burnt fish bones recovered are studied by Cerón-Carrasco, who identifies mainly cod, saithe and haddock caught from the rocks or from boats in shallow water. A small number of unburnt marine shells were also recovered, including limpets, periwinkles, mussels and pieces of crab shell. Cerón-Carrasco suggests that this was an easily accessible food source from the coast, but may also have been used as bait.

Carbonised plant remains

by Susan Ramsay

Methodology

Sample processing

A programme of bulk sampling was undertaken during the excavations in order to examine the carbonised archaeobotanical remains from the site. 28 litres of all excavated deposits, apart from topsoil and backfill, were bagged, and taken off site to be processed by flotation for the recovery of carbonised remains. More than 28 litres were sampled if a deposit was particularly rich or suitable for dating. In total, 413 bulk samples, representing 349 contexts, were analysed. The majority of the samples were processed by flotation using standard methods and sieves of mesh diameter 1mm and 500µm for flots and 2mm for retents. There was no indication that any of the samples had the potential for the preservation of uncarbonised plant remains through waterlogging.

Macrofossil analysis

Dried flots and sorted retents were examined using a binocular microscope at variable magnifications of x4-x45. For each sample, estimation of the total volume of carbonised material >4mm was made and modern contaminants were scored using a scale of 1-3 'plus' marks. For each sample, all carbonised seeds and a representative volume of the total charcoal >4mm was identified. When this volume was less than 100%, the percentage of the total volume of charcoal >4mm that was identified is given in the results tables.

The testa characteristics of small seeds and the internal anatomical features of all

Illus 11.2 Taking soil samples on site

charcoal fragments were further identified at x200 magnification using the reflected light of a metallurgical microscope. Reference was made to Beijerinck (1947), Schweingruber (1990), Jacomet (1987), Cappers et al (2006), and the extensive botanical reference collection held at the University of Glasgow. Vascular plant nomenclature follows Stace (1997) except for cereals, which conform to the genetic classification of Zohary and Hopf (2000).

Uncarbonised wood was sectioned, mounted on a glass slide and then identified under high magnification of x100 to x400. Identification was made with reference to Schweingruber (1990).

Results

Results will be discussed initially by trench and then by phase and feature grouping within each trench. Numbers in brackets indicate individual context numbers; round brackets relate to deposits or fills and square brackets indicate cuts or features.

The results are shown in Tables 11.1 –11.6, which are too extensive to include here and are instead published on the CD in back in the back of this volume. Multiple samples from the same context were added together in these tables for ease of interpretation. Contexts in which no carbonised remains were recorded have been omitted from the tables. The results from each table are summarised in the account below.

Trench A
Phase 2: Construction of A1 and A2 and enclosure banks
The stone walls of A1 and A2 all contained earth cores, but within Structure A1 contexts A061 and context A039 were the only wall core contexts to contain any carbonised remains, albeit only at trace levels. This is in contrast to many of the walls from other structures on the site, which show obvious use of midden material within the wall cores. The earth cores A008 and A057 of the N and S walls of Structure A2 both produced small quantities of a mixed charcoal assemblage but no cereal grains. A discrete deposit of midden or hearth waste A049 within the earth core A057 contained fir/spruce, alder, birch and oak charcoal together with a few cereal grains and is consistent with hearth remains, with cereals insufficient to suggest processing. Ash deposits A067 and A068 found below the base of the N and S walls of A2 and A1 respectively produced charcoal assemblages of birch, spruce/fir and heather type together with cereal assemblage of oats and barley.

Of the two earth enclosure banks A016 and A058 joined on to the ends of Structure A, samples from context A016 produced only a few fragments of coniferous charcoal and a single grain that was possibly an oat and are much less rich in carbonised remains than many of the other wall/bank deposits recorded elsewhere on this site. There is no evidence that midden or hearth material was used within the structure of this bank.

Phase 3: Occupation of A1 and A2
The hearth in the centre of the floor, towards the S end of Structure A1 contained a sequence of five separate hearth deposits. The primary deposit A037, radiocarbon dated to AD1450-1635, contained mainly heather charcoal and cereal grains, primarily barley, suggestive of a domestic hearth with heather, rather than peat/turf, being used as fuel. Directly above this deposit, A036, radiocarbon dated to AD1445-1630, contained a diverse range of charcoal types, including alder, birch, hazel and conifers but was dominated by heather type charcoal. A large number of cereal grains (> 1800 grains) were recorded from this context, with approximately equal numbers of oats and barley, suggesting that cereal processing, in the form of parching, was being undertaken over this hearth, rather than simply cooking of pre-processed grain. Overlying A036 was context A034, radiocarbon dated to AD1465-1640, which contained a similar carbonised assemblage to that recorded in A036 but with significantly fewer cereal grains. A034 also contained a greater proportion of oats (c 80%) than barley (c 20%), suggesting that this context is the result of a separate cereal processing event to that recorded by A036. Above A034 was the penultimate hearth layer A009, containing a different charcoal assemblage of birch, alder, heather and oak, but a cereal assemblage similar to that from (A034) with oats by far the largest component. The

Table 11.1 Results from Trench A on CD at back of book

Illus 11.3 Sieving samples in a Siraf flotation tank and Illus 11.4 Oat crop, Eorodale, Ness

uppermost layer of hearth deposit A032 radiocarbon dated to AD1445-1635, contained a charcoal assemblage of ash, with heather type and conifer also present, together with a cereal assemblage dominated by oats. The significant amount of ash charcoal within this context is unusual on this site but may simply record random collection of wood from the shoreline rather than being of real significance.

The central hearth in Structure A2 contained only a single deposit A030, radiocarbon dated to AD1425-1620. The hearth had been fuelled solely with birch but it also contained >300 cereal grains, with oats making up c 85% of the identifiable grain. This would appear to represent a single episode of cereal parching.

Phase 4: Initial abandonment and collapse of A1 and A2 and the enclosure banks

Contexts A021 and A054, slumped wall deposits in the centre of Trench A, contained negligible amounts of carbonised material and so provide little further evidence to add to the interpretation of this part of Trench A. In the N of the trench the initial abandonment deposits were also largely devoid of carbonised remains. Only A033, slump from the end of the N wall of Structure A1, produced any carbonised material with charcoal of birch, conifer and willow together with a substantial quantity of carbonised cereal grain. The cereal assemblage was dominated by oats with approximately 80% of the assemblage being oats and only 20% barley, and was also very well preserved with none being unidentifiable to type. This suggests a single episode of burning

Illus 11.5 Birch scrub and Illus 11.6 Heather growing on the moor in Ness

and a limited period before redeposition and burial. Assuming this is wall core material, it is possible that the material was incorporated into the wall core directly from a hearth rather than via a midden deposit. Further slump material 404 and tumble 403 from the main E wall of Structure A, contained small amounts of charcoal and cereal grains, together with burnt peat. As before, this seems to represent the remains of domestic hearth waste.

Of the initial abandonment deposits within Structure A2, the uppermost deposit A023 contained only a single carbonised barley grain, whilst lower deposit A027 contained small quantities of a mixed charcoal assemblage together with a few cereal grains, consistent with redeposited midden material, and the latest deposit, rubble A041, which again produced only limited carbonised remains that are not considered to be of significance.

Phase 5: Further slump and wash of abandonment and collapse layers
Two slump/wash deposits A002 and 406, from the further collapse of Structure A1 produced additional evidence for the use of hearth waste within the walls of this structure, with birch, heather type and spruce/fir charcoal identified.

Phase 6: Temporary shelter
The floor deposit 406 in later shelter in the N end of Trench A contained only traces of birch, heather type and spruce/fir charcoal together with a single cereal grain, and it is possible that it is the remains of redeposited hearth waste from earlier phases rather than from a Phase 6 fire.

Trench B
Phase 2: Original ground surfaces
Only a small amount of birch charcoal, burnt peat/turf and a single barley grain were recovered from decayed turf layer B059 between Structures B4 and H. Directly below B059 was a layer of gravel 024, which only produced trace amounts of charcoal, and a possible earlier occupation layer 011, which produced birch charcoal, burnt peat, a few cereal grains and a fragment of hazel nutshell. This is consistent with domestic occupation waste and is one of only a few finds of hazel nutshell from this site. Another old ground surface B108 located beneath the S wall of Structure B1 produced birch and larch charcoal, together with burnt peat/turf and a few cereals. This was a comparable assemblage to many of the wall core deposits and suggests a similar origin.

Phase 3: Structures and occupation pre-dating Structure B
Overlying the old ground surface were a sequence of deposits, which were thought to represent a hearth or dumps of hearth waste. However, although all these deposits contained large amounts of carbonised material, there were significant differences between the assemblages. The lowermost deposit B078 produced only small amounts of charcoal, two cereal grains and some burnt animal bone. This was overlain by B103, which also contained only traces of charcoal with a small numbers of cereal grains (barley and oats in almost equal numbers) and a few culm nodes and a cereal glume, suggesting some cereal processing waste. Context B103 however was sealed by a layer of charcoal and ash B102, which contained large amounts of birch and Scots pine charcoal and extremely large numbers of carbonised cereal grains and fragments of chaff. In total, over 2000 cereal grains were recovered from this context, with approximately 50% barley, 40% oats and 10% indeterminate. The most interesting finds were the large numbers of chaff fragments, with over 500 culm nodes recorded and large quantities of culm (cereal stem) fragments also present. In addition, there were blocks of carbonised organic material that contained a large proportion of straw-like material. This context also produced a few carbonised weed seeds that are associated with arable crops, including corn marigold and corn spurrey, together with other weeds with a wider habitat requirement such as cabbage family, common hemp nettle, bristle club rush, dead nettle family, cinquefoil and stitchwort/mouse-ear. The assemblage from B102 appears to include a significant proportion of cereal processing waste, together with accidentally burnt cereal grain, probably as a result of overheating during parching prior to grinding. The processing waste may simply have been used as additional fuel on the fire.

Illus 11.7 Hazelnuts and Illus 11.8 Ears of modern barley

Table 11.2 Results from Trench B on CD at back of book

Illus 11.9 Corn spurrey and Illus 11.10 Tormentil

Phase 4: Construction and use of Structure B

Within Structure B1, the core B042 of the W wall and the stony basal deposit B093 of the E wall contained only small amounts of carbonised material, consistent with the re-use of midden material, and clay deposit B094 only traces of carbonised material. The earliest wall core deposit B095 contained a significant amount of carbonised remains, dominated by birch and Scots pine charcoal but with alder, heather and ash also present. Cereal grains were common, with barley and oats almost equally represented. Of particular note was the presence of burnt animal bone within this context. This is further evidence for midden material being incorporated into the walls of these buildings. The hearth in the interior of Structure B1 contained uppermost deposit B068, radiocarbon dated to AD1520-1955, over a thin carbonised layer B101, radiocarbon dated to AD1480-1645, then a spread of charcoal B067. The carbonised assemblage from these hearth deposits was dominated by birch and heather charcoal, together with significant quantities of burnt turf/peat. The cereal assemblage contained both oats and barley but included a significant proportion of indeterminate grains that had probably been subjected to repeated episodes of burning. It is not possible to say if hearth deposit B067 represents the remains of an earlier hearth as it has a carbonised assemblage that is consistent with the upper hearth deposit B068.

Within Structure B1, overlying B102 from Phase 3, was a further layer B096 that was rich in carbonised remains, significantly different to those from B102. Although birch and Scots pine dominate the charcoal assemblage in both contexts, B096 also contained a significant amount of oak, together with hazel, larch and willow. Cereal grains were present, but in much reduced numbers and although a few culm nodes were recorded, culm fragments and weed seeds were absent. It is clear that B096 represents a completely different episode of burning from B102 and should be placed into this later phase of occupation. A thin layer of greasy black clay B051 sealed B096 and contained very similar carbonised assemblage, suggesting that some mixing had occurred between these contexts.

The E and S walls of Structure B4 shared an earth core layer B012, which contained a carbonised assemblage similar to that seen in context B087 ie within the core of the shared wall between Structures B4 and B5, with a diverse range of charcoal types (but lacking oak) and cereals grains with culm nodes present. Layer B012 sealed a further three layers of core material B075, B076, B077, which all contained oak charcoal and cereal grains. Contexts B075 and B077 also contained birch charcoal and heather type but these were absent from B076. Between the original E wall of Structure B4 faced with stone B081 and a secondary facing B011 that was added later was a silty deposit B080, which contained a small amount of carbonised midden material. The primary occupation deposit B092, filling the area of sunken floor within B4 radiocarbon dated to AD1445-1635, contained only traces of birch and heather type charcoal and cereal grains were absent. Above it were two further occupation layers B060 and B063 but these also contained little in the way of carbonised remains and certainly no evidence for hearth waste. A small posthole [B071], with fill (B061), within the interior of Structure B4 produced only a small amount of carbonised peat/turf but no further carbonised material.

The E wall core B018 of Structure B5 was also the W wall of Structure B4 and sealed another layer of wall core material B086. These contexts contained mainly birch and Scots pine charcoal, although both also contained fragments of oak, together with a small cereal assemblage dominated by barley. They sealed a further three earth layers, and although B088 and B089 contained only traces of carbonised remains, B087 contained a significant carbonised assemblage. Charcoal was mainly Scots pine, with birch, heather type and hazel also present and the cereal assemblage was dominated by barley but with lesser quantities of oats. However, there was a significant number of cereal culm nodes present, together with single glume and rachis fragments suggesting that cereal processing waste made up part of this assemblage. It is clear that this midden/hearth material is from a different source to that used as packing within the upper wall core contexts B018 and B086. The occupation layer B079 that filled a hollow in the centre of Structure B5 contained only a trace of carbonised material was recovered from this deposit.

Only a single context was examined from the construction/occupation phase of Structure B6 to the E of Structure B1. Context B107 was a deposit that blocked an entrance in the W wall of Structure B6 and contained an extremely rich carbonised assemblage. As with many of the contexts from Trench B, the charcoal assemblage was dominated by birch and Scots pine type but with the addition of hazel, heather type, beech, ash and spruce/fir as well as burnt peat/turf. The cereal assemblage contained both oats and barley, but with oats predominating. This carbonised assemblage is much more diverse than the midden assemblages present within the wall cores of Structure B6 and so, presumably, had a different origin ie it came from a different but contemporaneous midden or was from a later episode of midden deposition.

To the E of Structure B, a trench was excavated through the perimeter wall Structure H, the perimeter bank with a stone outer facing 009 and a turf core, which included contexts 012 and 013. These wall core deposits produced birch, conifer and oak charcoal, together with a few cereal grains. Broken pottery was also common within the wall core and it is likely that midden waste was used as packing and filling material within the wall. The remains of a robbed structure represented by a section of wall 010 produced some evidence for possible midden material packing within the wall core 004. A posthole fill 019 also produced indeterminate conifer charcoal and wood, together with Scots pine type charcoal. This may be evidence for the post having been made of Scots pine and that it was burnt in situ. To the N of the wall was a shallow drain 021, which produced only slight traces of charcoal but nothing of significance.

Phase 5: Post-abandonment

The abandonment deposits B036 and B038 within Structure B1 contained little in the way of carbonised remains, with only a few cereal grains present with burnt turf/peat. A further series of post-abandonment deposits below collapsed wall B040 included B053, which contained only traces of birch, heather and pine charcoal with a few cereals, and B055, probably collapsed turf walling, which contained a single large fragment of Scots pine charcoal and a few cereals. Whether the Scots pine was structural or hearth waste is impossible to determine. Between Structures B1 and B6 was a further slumped layer B109 that also contained charcoal of birch and Scots pine, together with cereals grains. This is consistent with the midden deposit packing that seemed to be present within many of the wall cores from this site.

The upper post-abandonment layer B015 in Structure B4 contained birch and Scots pine charcoal, with a few cereals, and sealed clay deposits B014 and B043. These clay deposits contained very similar carbonised assemblages dominated by birch, Scots pine, larch and oak, with significant amounts of burnt peat/turf and the cereal assemblages were mainly barley, with smaller quantities of oats also present. As before, this assemblage is consistent with midden material that has been reused as packing material within the walls of the structure. Structure B5, to the E of Structure B6, also contained post-abandonment deposits, thought to represent wall collapse. Contexts B020 and B045, within a hollow in the interior of the structure, contained mainly Scots pine charcoal with a few cereal grains. A slump layer B085 and an upper layer of wall core B018 contained a more diverse charcoal spectrum of birch, heather, spruce/fir as well as Scots pine and cereals but all these contexts are consistent with wall core deposits, containing midden material.

The uppermost post-abandonment deposits B030, B073 and B074 in Structure B6 contained similar carbonised assemblages of birch and heather charcoal with a few cereal grain and burnt peat/turf. In addition, small quantities of hazel, oak and Scots pine charcoal were also present. The assemblages from these contexts are consistent with wall core collapse. Below these deposits, were two further wall collapse contexts, B024 and B025, which also contained mixed charcoal and burnt peat/turf deposits with a greater concentration of cereal grains than was seen in the upper deposits. Again, these are consistent with wall core material, with a significant midden component. The greater concentration of cereals may suggest that the midden material was in the lower, middle of the wall cores and when the walls collapsed this material was buried beneath less midden-rich deposits from the outer sections of the wall.

In the gap between the E wall of Structure B4 and the perimeter wall H there were a further series of collapse deposits, from uppermost to lowest, B008, B009, B048 and B049. These contexts contained very similar carbonised assemblages, dominated by birch and Scots pine type charcoal, with burnt peat/turf and a cereal assemblage of barley and oats and may have been deposited over only a short period of time. Again, they are consistent with collapsed

Illus 11.11 Peat burning in a modern hearth, Illus 11.12 Alder tree scrub and Illus 11.13 Common mouse ear

wall material, with a midden component that was incorporated during construction. Another layer of possibly collapsed wall material (005), associated with Structure H, contained a variety of charcoal types, degraded wood and a few cereal grains. This is again consistent with midden material that has been used to infill the wall.

Trench C

Phase 2: Original ground surfaces

Only one context C071 was examined from this phase and contained a few carbonised oat grains, adding little to the interpretation of this area.

Table 11.3 Results from Trench C on CD at back of book

Phase 3: Construction and use of kilnbarn

The charcoal assemblages from the majority of contexts associated with the construction and use of the kilnbarn were varied and showed little sign of selection for specific types. Only context C078, which was ash from the kiln fire within the flue, had a notably different charcoal assemblage with ash dominating and oak and Scots pine also common. These charcoal types may have been used for fuel, or they may represent a structural component from the kiln, such as the remains of a platform that was accidentally destroyed. If these types had been the favoured fuel for the kiln it would seem likely that charcoal fragments of these types would have been common in the general background scatter. However, ash charcoal, in particular, was found exclusively in context C078 and oak was only found in trace amounts elsewhere in Trench C. Several fragments of burnt animal bone were also recovered from this context. It is not clear why these should be present within the kiln, although they may have been used as an additional fuel supply either intentionally or perhaps as part of midden material. An alternative explanation may be deliberate burning of animal bones to flavour the grain as suggested by Fenton (1997, 387).

Although this area was identified as a corn drying kiln, the quantities of cereal grain recovered were generally limited. Only context C068, a deposit of ash from the kiln fire, contained more than a small quantity of cereal grain. Oats were the dominant type recovered from C068, although six-row barley (including the hulled variety) was also present. There was no evidence for chaff of any description, suggesting that the grain was fully cleaned prior to drying.

Radiocarbon dating of a sample from C068 produced a range of AD1470-1640, and from C078, AD1455-1635.

Phase 4: Robbing/Collapse of barn and construction of shelters

The charcoal assemblage from this phase of Trench C was very similar to that from the final collapse, described above. Charcoal was not abundant, with only small quantities of birch, conifers, heather and oak present. A small amount of hazel charcoal was recorded from the lower turf C027 of the C1 wall but this is unlikely to represent deliberate structural use of hazel rods. A background scatter of cereal grain was also recorded, with similar amounts of barley and oats present. Again the quantities involved are not sufficient to indicate waste from a corn-drying kiln.

Phase 5: Final collapse

Only small quantities of charcoal were recovered from this phase of Trench C. Birch was the commonest type recorded, with lesser amounts of various conifers, heather stems and occasional oak. Burnt peat/turf was also present in many of the contexts, although never in large quantities. Carbonised cereal grain (equal quantities of barley and oats) was found in the majority of the contexts but only in small amounts, as a general background scatter. There is little evidence from this material for the previous use of this area as a corn-drying kiln. The quantities of cereal recovered are small and fuel waste is also minimal. The material from this phase is mainly structural debris from the turf collapse associated with the core of the outer wall of Structure C with only small quantities of hearth waste or kiln waste mixed into it.

Illus 11.14 Ash tree in winter

Trench D

Phase 1: Natural subsoil and bedrock

Only one context D084 under the earliest hearth deposit was examined from this phase, and yielded only a few fragments of carbonised peat/turf.

Table 11.4 Results from Trench D on CD at back of book

Phase 2: Traces of early structures and original ground surfaces

The remains of an early turf wall or bank, a degraded turf deposit, D065, contained small quantities of charcoal and cereal grains, which are in keeping with assemblages recorded from many of the other turf walls on the site. An old ground surface D064 contained only a small quantity of carbonised peat/turf but no other carbonised remains.

Phase 3: Middens below wall footings

Deposit D036, a thick, ashy deposit below wall footings D010 in Structure D16, contained an extremely charcoal-rich assemblage, with a high diversity of charcoal taxa present. Birch was by far the most abundant type but fir was also very common. In addition, alder, hazel, heather type, larch, Scots pine and oak charcoal were all represented. This suggests general collection of wood for fuel, probably with a high component of driftwood, with little evidence for selection. Of particular note were the very large numbers of cereal grains present within this context. Over 1700 cereal grains were identified, with approximately 15% oats, 70% barley and the rest indeterminate. There were also more than 50 cereal culm nodes recovered, indicating that cereal processing waste was part of this deposit, rather than simply cleaned grain. Seeds of cultivated flax were also recorded, confirming a domestic, rather than industrial, origin for this material. Midden deposit D058 also contained cereal grain and flax seeds, although at a much lower concentration to that seen in D036. However, there was almost no charcoal recorded from D058 suggesting that the cereal grain may have percolated down into this deposit from above but that larger fragments of charcoal remained in situ. Also of note are the large numbers of burnt animal bone fragments present in this context (in addition to those larger pieces removed as small finds – see Masson-MacLean, below).

Below D036/D058 the basal deposit D105 contained a much higher proportion of burnt peat/turf than the upper deposits but charcoal was also frequent, as was burnt animal bone. Alder was the commonest type identified, with oak, fir, birch and Scots pine also present. A significant quantity of cereal grain (almost 1000 grains) was identified from this context with approximately 30% oats, 55% barley and the rest indeterminate. Oats are twice as common in context D105 as compared to D036 suggesting that more than one phase of activity is represented. However, as with the upper midden contexts, flax seeds were also present. Of particular note in D105 were large quantities of carbonised straw fused into lumps of burnt organic and mineral material. It was noted during excavation that the spread of charcoal and grain within D105 suggested a woven textile, perhaps containing grain, had been burnt in situ. This cannot be confirmed from the above analysis but it does appear that cereal processing was being undertaken and that possibly a mat or layer of straw had been laid beneath the grain, possibly with textile between the straw and the grain, although no fragments of textile were noted in the flots or retents analysed from this context.

Phase 4: Construction and use of earlier buildings and hearths

Below Structure D7, hearth D050 and associated contexts D055, D056, D057, D080, D081 and D082 were interpreted as the fire site from a clamp kiln. These deposits produced charcoal assemblages dominated by conifers (Scots pine and spruce) and heather type charcoal, with smaller quantities of alder, birch and oak, and burnt animal bone, also present. There were also substantial quantities of burnt peat/turf within these contexts. The heather charcoal may have been a component of the peat or collected specifically for fuel. Finds of carbonised sedge/grass rhizomes provides further evidence for the burning of turves in this hearth. Although carbonised cereal grains were recorded from the hearth contexts, these were not abundant, and generally at a lower concentration than elsewhere within Trench D. It seems unlikely that any cereal processing was being carried out using this hearth and that the majority of food preparation may also have

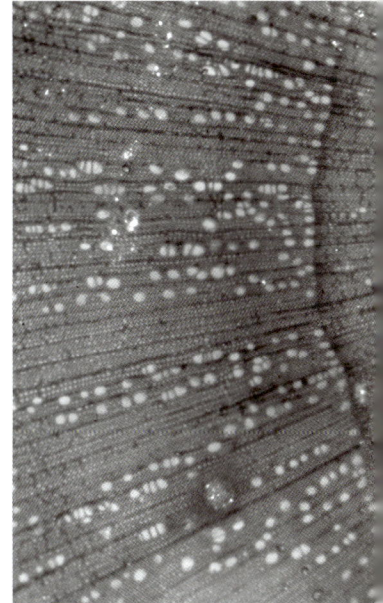

Illus 11.15 Hazel charcoal and
Illus 11.16 Flax in flower

been undertaken elsewhere. Context D056 was radiocarbon dated to AD1445-1625.

Elsewhere in Trench D the turf bank 301 of Structure D12 produced no carbonised remains but a possible occupation layer 302 abutting the turf bank produced birch, conifer and oak charcoal, together with cereal grain. In the NE of the trench was a deposit of burnt material 303, which contained a very similar assemblage to that recorded from 302 and they may have a common origin ie midden waste. Beneath 302 was a silty clay layer with small stones 306 that contained only slight charcoal traces.

Large rectangular courtyard area Structure D16 contained a series of floor layers and hearths. The uppermost floor layer D071 contained a mixed charcoal assemblage dominated by birch but with fir, Scots pine and oak also present, along with burnt peat and there were also a significant number of cereal grains, mainly barley with lesser amounts of oats. Other evidence for food plant remains included three fragments of carbonised hazel nutshell and three flax seeds. There were four different hearths in the area D061, D073, D074 and D075, which are considered to be contemporaneous with floor layer D071, and these contained a mixed charcoal assemblage with carbonised cereals and occasional fragments of hazel nutshell, flax seeds and burnt animal bone. This suggests that the hearths were used for domestic cooking and that the carbonised assemblage from floor layer D071 is the result of rake-out from these hearths. A number of these hearth contexts were radiocarbon dated with context D061 dating to AD1475-1640, D074 dating to AD1450-1635 and D075 dating to AD1440-1630 ie the dates are contemporaneous. Below this, an earlier floor layer D079/D088 contained only small quantities of charcoal and cereal grain but substantial amounts of burnt peat. Context D079 was radiocarbon dated to AD1450-1635. Three hearths D076, D077, D078 were associated with this floor and produced mixed charcoal assemblages with cereal grain and were similar in composition to the later hearths. Context D076 was dated to AD1445-1635. The earliest occupation deposit excavated in Structure D16 was a burnt deposit D090 located below the earliest floor layer D079 and above the bedrock. This produced only small quantities of heather, Scots pine and oak charcoal, together with a few cereals and two seeds of flax and is consistent with domestic hearth detritus and the other hearth contexts from Structure D16. A section through context D10, the E wall of Structure D16, contained a mixed charcoal assemblage of birch, heather type, Scots pine and oak, together with a significant number of cereal grains, and is yet another instance of midden material being incorporated into the structure of a wall.

A small section of the SE corner of Structure C lay within Trench D at the W end of the trench and comprised a turf and stone bank D018/D049, which produced traces of cereal grain. At the S edge of the trench, a deposit of peat ash D053 and trample D052 associated with the use of Structure C contained similar carbonised assemblages of birch, conifer and heather type charcoal, with some cereal grains.

Phase 5: Collapse of earlier buildings and construction and occupation of turf shelters

Structure D4: One context D004 was analysed from the collapsed wall but produced only a small quantity of birch and Scots pine charcoal, with a few cereal grains of barley and oats. Context D016, another possible wall, contained a similar assemblage to that from D004.

Structure D7: Turf wall contexts D007, D045 and D063 produced evidence for the reuse of midden material within the wall structure and a trampled layer D024, radiocarbon dated to AD1455-1630, over earlier hearth (D050) showed a similar carbonised assemblage to that seen in these earlier hearth deposits, indicating mixing of material had occurred.

Structure D8: Charcoal from the main wall D008 was a mixture of birch, conifer, heather type and oak, with a small amount of cereal grain and appeared to be hearth material that had become incorporated into the wall during construction. Three patches of charcoal, D025, D026, D027, were located under wall D008 and were considerably different from other contexts within this structure in that they contained significant quantities of burnt straw, together with cereal grains and weeds seeds of ribwort plantain, buttercup and dock. This might suggest that cereal processing had occurred in this area prior to the construction of Structure D8 or that the material may have come from a byre floor and had been burnt as fuel. Context D027 also contained an unusual charcoal assemblage of ash and willow, and a small amount of animal bone. These charcoal types were only found in this context within Structure D8 and could be the remains of a wicker container or basket. The hearth contexts, D038, D043, D046, from Structure D8 contained similar carbonised assemblages, with heather type stems dominating the charcoal, along with lesser quantities of birch, confer and oak. Burnt peat/turf remains were also common, suggesting the heather type stems may have been brought in within cut peats/turves. Although cereal grain was only present in trace amount, a total of 18 seeds of cultivated flax were identified from the hearth contexts. A possible floor layer D033 contained a very similar carbonised assemblage to that seen in the hearth deposits and it is likely that these remains originated from hearth scatter.

Structures D10A and D10B: Turf contexts D098 and D099 associated with the walls of the structures contained only the remains of carbonised peat/turf. Possible floor layers D032, D034 and D100 contained small quantities of charcoal, including birch, conifer and oak, together with cereals (mainly barley with some oats) but did not provide much additional information regarding the occupation of these structures. The carbonised assemblage from D068, bedding for the stones of the W wall of Structure 10A, radiocarbon dated to AD1480-1640, contained a variety of charcoal types dominated by birch and Scots pine but with lesser amounts of alder, heather, larch and oak, together with a significant number of cereal grains. Again, this assemblage is characteristic of midden material, which appears to have been re-used to form the bedding for the later wall. Context 037, wall collapse, also contained a carbonised assemblage that was consistent with reuse of midden material.

Structure D13: The remains of the N-S turf wall D013 yielded a carbonised assemblage similar to those seen elsewhere. Birch was by far the commonest component, with oak, conifers and heather type also present. Carbonised grain was also frequent, with barley (including the hulled six-row variety) the dominant type present with lesser amounts of oats. This again suggests midden material had been used in the construction of the wall. An occupation layer D067 produced a typical charcoal assemblage but also included a significant number of cereal grains, with barley the commonest type present. Seeds of cultivated flax and corn marigold were also present in trace amounts suggesting midden material was present.

Structure D14: The W turf wall D014 and its basal fill D042 had very similar carbonised assemblages dominated by birch charcoal, with conifer, hazel, oak and heather type also present. A few cereal grains were also present, with barley the commonest type found along with smaller quantities of oats. This assemblage is very similar to other wall contexts from the site and appears to represent midden material used in the construction of the wall.

Illus 11.20 Birch growing in heather moorland

Phase 6: Post-abandonment and final collapse

The post-abandonment layers, mainly slump and collapse from walls, showed very consistent charcoal assemblages across the trench. Birch was generally the commonest charcoal type recorded, with lesser quantities of conifers (including Scots pine and larch) and oak also present. Heather type charcoal was also frequently found although it is difficult to determine whether these heather type stems had originally come from cut peats rather than from collected stems. Burnt peat/turf was common in this trench and so the heather stems may be contemporaneous with the formation of the peat rather than the occupation of the cells within Trench D.

Cereal grain was present in most of the contexts examined, in moderate concentrations. Barley, including the hulled six-row variety, was the commonest cereal type, although significant quantities of oats were also present. Only a single context (D069) contained traces of chaff, suggesting that the grain that was recovered from the abandonment deposits was from cleaned crops. Two seeds of corn marigold and six seeds of cultivated flax were recorded from the post-abandonment layers, suggesting that arable agriculture had been practiced nearby as corn marigold is a weed of cultivated machair (Dickson and Dickson 2000) in the Outer Hebrides, whilst cultivated flax may have been grown as a crop in its own right or may have occurred as a weed within the cereal crop.

The cereals and charcoal from this phase of Trench D probably represent general domestic scatter from the previously occupied structures, possibly mixed with midden material. There is no definite evidence for the use of wood as a structural component of the buildings, with the charcoal probably all originating from fuel.

Trench F
Phase 2: Construction of building

The N and E wall F004 of Structure F produced only a single carbonised cereal grain, rather than the midden-like material that was recorded from many of the other turf walls on this site, and the silty sand F005 below it, which also produced little in the way of carbonised remains. The core of the S wall F007 contained only a trace of charcoal but significant quantities of burnt peat/turf and a few cereal grains. Although this may be midden material used to fill the wall core, it is not as clear cut as the midden fill recorded from many of the other wall cores on this site. Drainage channel F016 contained a silty fill F013 with a similar limited carbonised assemblage to F005 and F007, suggesting that a scatter of carbonised material had been present across most of this area. Drain F062, that ran through Structure F was capped with clay F048 but this context produced no significant carbonised remains. A posthole F066 in the centre of Structure F, filled with F065, contained only traces of charcoal and cereals but substantial amounts of burnt peat/turf, which may have been deliberately used as additional packing material. There was no evidence for a post having been burnt in situ.

Phase 3: First occupation phase

The uppermost of these first occupation deposits F034 and F035, contained charcoal assemblages dominated by birch and Scots pine, together with a few cereal grains and seeds of sun spurge. This assemblage is similar to that in the second occupation phase floor F037 above it and may contain some of the same material. The lower deposits F051, F052, F053, F054, F056, F057 and F060 contained only traces of charcoal and cereal grain but more significant amounts of burnt peat/turf. If these lower deposits are also hearth sweepings, the hearth was being used for a different purpose to that from the second phase of occupation.

To the N of the peat ash deposits was a dump of turf-like material F038 that may be a repair to the drain F062. This context contained only coniferous charcoal together with significant numbers of cereal grains (mainly oats) and is consistent with midden material or midden used in wall construction. The drain F062 contained a silty fill F069 that contained birch, heather type and oak charcoal together with large amounts of burnt peat. This may be the remains of hearth waste or burnt turves, rather than midden material, as cereal grains are scarce in this deposit. A small area of scorching F070 was thought to represent a hearth but produced only a few carbonised barley grains and so it is unlikely to have been a hearth. Below the peat ash

Illus 11.21 Peat moorland in Ness

Table 11.5 Results from Trench F on CD at back of book

Illus 11.22 Modern peat banks in Ness

sweepings was a trampled deposit F036 that formed over another peat ash deposit F061. These contexts contained very little charcoal, but substantial quantities of burnt peat/turf together with a few cereal grains, and are more likely to represent burnt structural material rather than hearth sweepings. The above deposits had all formed over a sandy floor within Structure F.

The floor in this phase was denoted F033 to the W of the drain and radiocarbon dated to AD1450-1635, and F046 to the E. A trampled deposit F042, radiocarbon dated to AD1440-1630, was located on the floor to the NE of the drain and contexts F033 and F042 contained similar assemblages, with a mixture of charcoal types and significant numbers of cereal grains, dominated by oats. This suggests occupation detritus from a midden.

In contrast, floor context F046, to the E of the drain, context F054 overlying the drain and a further sandy floor deposit F024, contained only a trace of charcoal and cereals and cannot be attributed as midden material but may simply be background scatter. Another floor deposit F059 was located in the entranceway to Structure F and contained a similar carbonised assemblage to the midden-rich floor deposits inside the structure.

Phase 4: Second occupation phase

The uppermost layer was a thin layer of hearth sweeping F026 that itself overlay a thin floor layer F023. These contexts contained very similar assemblages, with charcoal dominated by birch, conifer, heather type and oak and significant numbers of cereals grains, with oats being more common than barley. These are consistent with remains from a domestic hearth, with F023 radiocarbon dated to AD1480-1640, and F026 radiocarbon dated to AD1455-1630. A further layer of hearth sweepings F047 directly below floor F023 but produced little in the way of identifiable carbonised remains. Outside the entrance ash layer F009 produced a similar carbonised assemblage to that from F026 within the structure, although with a higher proportion of burnt peat/turf and it is likely that it is the remains of hearth sweepings from the interior of the structure that have been trampled out into the doorway. A piece of oak wood F030 set into a linear cut, forming a threshold to the structure was cut into a grey sand deposit F037 that contained similar carbonised material to that identified as hearth sweepings. Deposits of similar mineral composition outside the structure F010 and against the N wall F037 produced little in the way of carbonised material. At the entrance to the structure material had been dumped to form a slope down into the entranceway of Structure F. A stony deposit F067 contained only scarce carbonised material, but a mixed deposit F055 was rich in charcoal and contained cereal grain. It is likely that either hearth waste or midden material had been used to build up this slope.

Illus 11.23 Oak wood threshold during excavation in Structure F at the doorway of the building

Phase 5: Post-abandonment and collapse

Contexts F011 and F015 related to the collapse of the turf walls and roof of the structure and contained only fragments of heather type twigs and burnt peat respectively, in keeping with turfs from the roof of a structure. However, context F006, which was also although thought to be the main roof collapse, contained a diversity of charcoal types, including birch, conifer, heather and Scots pine, together with a small amount of carbonised cereal grain, and this is not consistent with roofing turfs, being more akin to the material that was recovered from the turf walls within Trench D.

To the N of Structure F, slump deposits F003 and F021, and F014, F025 and F029, on the S exterior of the structure contained a mixed charcoal assemblage and cereal grain, with oats dominating, although F003 contained little carbonised material. Again, this is consistent with midden material being used during the construction of turf walls on this site.

Further turf slumps F019, F027 from the interior of the structure contained only limited carbonised material. Stone tumbles F022 and F028 produced carbonised assemblages similar to those from the turf walls, with mixed charcoal of birch, conifer and heather, together with small numbers of cereal grains.

Trench G

Phase 1: Bedrock and natural subsoil

The bedrock layer G076 contained only traces of carbonised remains and added little to the interpretation of the area.

Table 11.6 Results from Trench G on CD at back of book

Phase 2: Original ground surfaces

Three examples of the original ground surface were excavated outside the S of the tower. Contexts 108 and G072 contained carbonised assemblages of mixed charcoal and a scatter of cereal grains, similar to overlying wall core material G029, suggesting some mixing of these deposits, whilst G078 contained little in the way of carbonised remains.

On the N side of the tower, two original ground surfaces G080 and G081 contained significant quantities of Scots pine charcoal, burnt peat and cereal grains, suggesting that occupation had occurred on this ground prior to the construction of the tower.

Phase 3: Construction and collapse of first tower

Wall core deposits G061, G066 and G073 contained mixed charcoal and cereal assemblages, with a small amount of burnt animal bone, consistent with the use of midden material within the

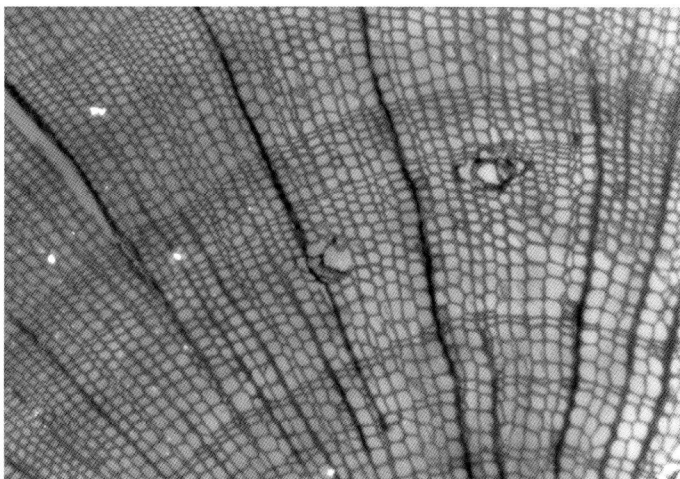

Illus 11.24 Scots Pine charcoal

structure of the walls, as commonly seen elsewhere on the site.

The only context identified as a possible occupation layer was G050 within the interior room of the tower. This context contained a limited carbonised assemblage of spruce and Scots pine charcoal together with a few carbonised cereal grains and fragments of burnt animal bone and provide little evidence for the living conditions within the tower.

Phase 4: Rebuild and repair of tower

During excavation it was determined that there was a single phase of interior wall construction and two phases of exterior wall construction, but only on the E side of the tower. The main wall G004 was constructed using blocks of gneiss bonded together with clay. Clay bonding material was recorded in context G062 and G041/G068 and the carbonised assemblages from these contexts suggest that a small amount of midden material had become incorporated into the clay, although it is not clear whether this occurred by accident or by design. An area of trample G029 outside the tower was thought to be contemporaneous with the construction of the walls and was radiocarbon dated to AD1450-1635. This context contained a scatter of oat and barley grains, and a single fragment of cf larch.

The wall core deposits 112, G011, G059, G060 and G063, contained very similar carbonised assemblages, generally dominated by Scots pine charcoal, with occasional other conifer types, birch, oak and burnt peat present. Cereal grains were common with the identified grains comprised of approximately 70% oats and 30% barley. The uniformity of these assemblages indicates that the wall cores were filled with midden material from a single midden deposit. The abundance of Scots pine was particularly notable in Trench G and may suggest that there was some degree of selection involved in the fuel that eventually ended up in the midden deposits that filled these walls. A possible floor surface G069 within the tower contained little in the way of carbonised material. Layer G070, directly beneath G069, was interpreted on site as a layer of construction trample and contained significant amounts of carbonised material, dominated by Scots pine charcoal but with significant amounts of alder also present. Cereal grain was also common, with oats being slightly more abundant than barley. Below this trample was a sandy layer G071 that was thought to have built up after the first tower collapsed. It contained a very similar assemblage to that recorded for trample layer G071, with Scots pine and alder the commonest charcoal types, together with frequent cereal grains. This suggests that G070 and G071 are more or less contemporaneous, but that the carbonised material within them was from a different source to the midden material used within the wall cores.

Phase 5a: Collapse of the second tower

Three separate layers of collapse 111, G003 and G016 outside the tower, produced only limited carbonised remains consistent with the midden scatter found over much of the site.

Phase 5b: Collapse and leaching of clay bonding

Only a single context G006 was attributable to this phase and was thought to represent leached clay bonding from the collapsed walls. The carbonised assemblage was consistent with the midden material that was utilised within many of the wall cores, and contained cereal grains (oats and barley) and a weed seed.

Phase 6: MacPhail's excavation

Three contexts G017, G025 and G037 represented the main backfill of Macphail's trench. These contexts contained mixed charcoal and cereal assemblages consistent with the incorporation of scattered midden material. A pit G047 had been cut into the backfill of Macphail's trench and the fill G048 of this pit contained similar redeposited midden material to that seen elsewhere within this trench.

Phase 7: Modern shelter

The modern shelter was constructed within cut G007 and comprised a wall G013 and G022 and contained fills G010, G021, G023 and G043. These fills contained only traces of charcoal and a

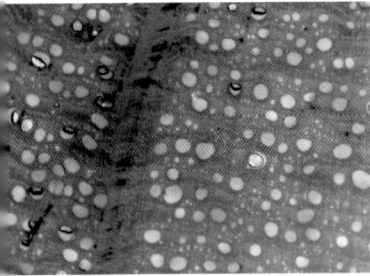

Illus 11.25 Oak charcoal

few cereal grains, suggesting that the carbonised remains are probably redeposited material from midden/hearth scatter that was apparent across much of the site. Contexts 114, G009, G014 and G024 relate to the collapse of the modern structure. These contexts contained similar carbonised assemblages to those from the fill of the structure and again are probably simply redeposited midden material from the earlier phases of the site.

Phase 8: Topsoil and marker cairn

The modern cairn G001 produced a mixed charcoal assemblage with carbonised oat grains, suggesting that the cairn material contained midden deposits from elsewhere on the site. The topsoil deposit G002 produced only limited carbonised remains consistent with the midden scatter found over much of the site.

Discussion

Materials used in the construction of the buildings on Dùn Èistean

The structures identified on the stack were constructed using stone and turf for the walls, with midden material used extensively as packing and infilling material within the wall cores. The peat/turf remains often contain a minerogenic component suggesting that peat/turf used for construction purposes was not generally cut from areas of deep peat but more usually from shallow mire/grassland areas.

There was no evidence for the use of wood within the main fabric of the buildings. The only fragment of wood that clearly formed a structural component was within the doorway of Structure F, where there was a piece of oak wood set into a slot to form a threshold to the building. There is little evidence for oak growing on the Isle of Lewis at this time (Bennett et al 1997) and it is more likely that this wood was imported onto the island, collected as driftwood or recovered from a shipwreck. The fact that it was a piece of oak, a hard wearing and durable timber, that was utilised as the threshold indicates deliberate selection of this type of wood rather than random collection.

It is impossible to determine, for certain, from the evidence obtained during this study what materials were used for the roofs of these structures. Turfs were certainly available in abundance and may be the most obvious option. However, heather type stems were also commonly found as carbonised and uncarbonised remains in the samples, as were a few concentrations of carbonised cereal straw eg in Trench B and Trench D. A combination of heathy turfs and straw may have formed the roofs of the structures at Dùn Èistean, as can be seen in the reconstructed blackhouse at Arnol on the Isle of Lewis. Turfs were used as the under layer of the roof and straw as the upper, weatherproofing layer. The straw was not laid in bundles but randomly across the roof and then held down by netting laid over the top. There is also evidence from other thatched buildings in the Hebrides that heather could be used as the outer covering, over the turf, instead of straw (Scott 2007).

An unusual charcoal assemblage of ash and willow was recorded in Structure D8 in a layer of ash and midden material found in the base of the turf wall of the building; the only occurrence of this particular combination of charcoal types recorded on the site. This could be evidence for a woven/wicker object such as a basket or other container having been burnt. Ash wood can be

Illus 11.26 Shallow mire/grassland and Illus 11.27 Roof at Arnol blackhouse

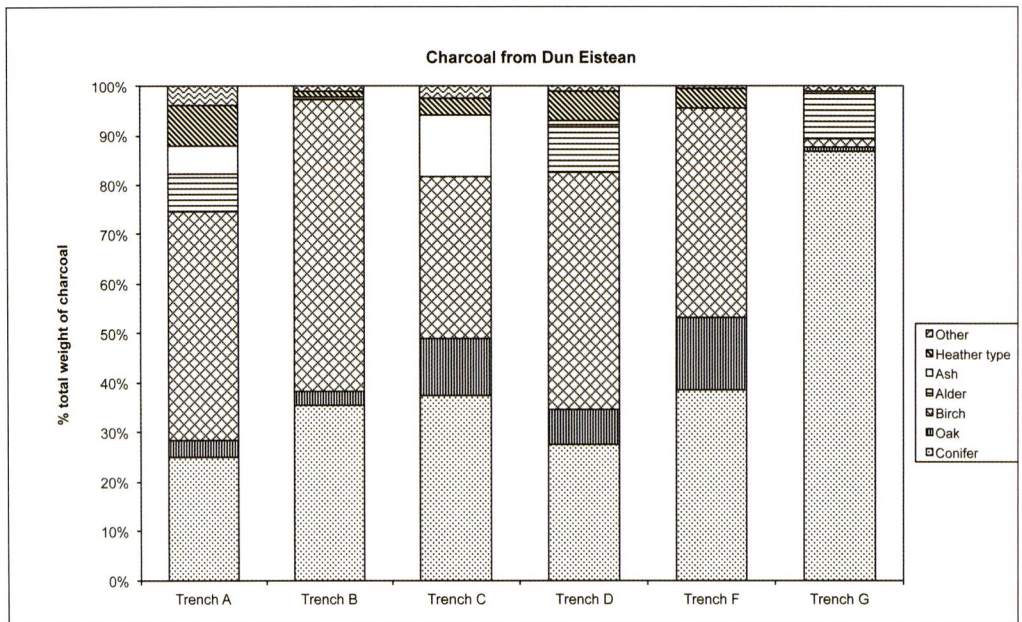

Charcoal from Dun Eistean

Legend:
- Other
- Heather type
- Ash
- Alder
- Birch
- Oak
- Conifer

Y-axis: % total weight of charcoal (0% to 100%)

X-axis: Trench A, Trench B, Trench C, Trench D, Trench F, Trench G

used as the uprights for a woven basket or processed to make binding strips, whilst willow withies are the commonest wood used in basketry manufacture.

Fuel

The charcoal assemblage from Dùn Èistean was extremely diverse, considering the exposed and treeless nature of the site and its surroundings today. In total, sixteen tree genera were recorded from the site, but it is extremely unlikely that more than a few of them were growing locally. Most of the wood recorded from the site would have had to have been imported or collected as driftwood. Illus 11.28 shows the proportions of different charcoal types from each of the main trenches excavated at Dùn Èistean. It is clear that birch and conifer were the commonest types of wood used for fuel. Birch burns quickly but with a hot flame and makes good charcoal (Gale and Cutler 2000), but there is also the possibility that some of the charcoal recorded from Dùn Èistean could have been contained within peat that was subsequently burned as fuel. Types such as birch, Scots pine, heather type and willow could have grown on areas of bog and been enveloped within the growing peat. However, a significant number of the samples analysed from Dùn Èistean contained only charcoal remains and no evidence for burnt peat and it is considered more likely that the charcoal is largely derived from contemporaneous wood rather than more ancient buried wood in peat.

The charcoal from the broadleaved taxa is all representative of species that are native to Scotland. However, it is likely that only small numbers of stunted birch, hazel and willow trees could have been growing on the Isle of Lewis at this time as, by 2600 years ago, the Isle of Lewis was more or less treeless (Fossitt 1996; Bennett et al 1997). The remaining broadleaved tree types may have been deliberately imported onto the island or perhaps, more likely, been collected as driftwood from the surrounding shores. The position of Dùn

Illus 11.29 Birch and heather twigs preserved in peat cut for fuel

Èistean, at the north tip of the Isle of Lewis, would have allowed driftwood to be washed ashore not just from mainland Scotland, but from across the Atlantic and perhaps from the Baltic region. There is also significant potential for the collection of wood from vessels shipwrecked on this area of coast.

More definitive evidence for the utilisation of driftwood is the presence of several non-native coniferous types within the charcoal assemblage. Fir, spruce, larch and cf Douglas fir were all recorded from the site. None of these types would have grown in Scotland prior to the planting of these species within the last 200 years or so, initially as specimen trees on large estates and only more recently as commercial forestry plantations. It is highly unlikely that the coniferous driftwood burned on Dùn Èistean was the product of commercial forestry on mainland Scotland. Dickson (1992) considered that most, if not all, coniferous driftwood identified from archaeological sites on the west coast of Scotland and its islands was of North Atlantic origin, carried north-west by the Gulf Stream and the North Atlantic Current. The practice of utilising driftwood

Illus 11.30 Peat stack

for fuel and even construction purposes seems to have been widespread in the Western and Northern Isles throughout recorded human occupation of these areas (Dickson 1992). The most definitive evidence for driftwood use on an archaeological site is the presence of Teredo (shipworm) holes within charcoal/wood recovered from a site. Unfortunately, these shipworm holes were not noted in any of the charcoal samples from Dùn Èistean.

Heather type charcoal was common in many of the samples analysed. Heather may have grown on the stack itself or, more likely, have been collected from the mainland, most probably to be used as fuel, although it can have a multitude of uses including packing, bedding, thatching etc although there was no definite evidence for any of these other uses here. Some of the heather may have come from heathy turfs, either used for fuel or in the construction of walls. When wood was in short supply, minerogenic heather turf was often the fuel of necessity in the Highlands and Islands of Scotland, and frequently formed the main component of walls or wall cores in many marginal environment dwellings (Dickson and Dickson 2000). Fragments of burnt animal bone were also found in hearths and in midden material in wall core deposits in all the structures on the site and may be a reflection of the use of animal bone domestic waste as fuel.

Cereal grain and arable agriculture

Cereal grains were commonly found in the samples from Dùn Èistean, with over 17,000 grains recorded from the site as a whole. Oats and barley were the commonest cereal types present, with wheat only recorded in trace amounts, probably as a contaminant within the main cereal crop. Histograms of the proportions of each cereal type in each trench are shown in Illus 11.31.

Barley was commonest within Trench B and, particularly, Trench D. Hulled barley was definitively identified from the site, with no examples of naked barley

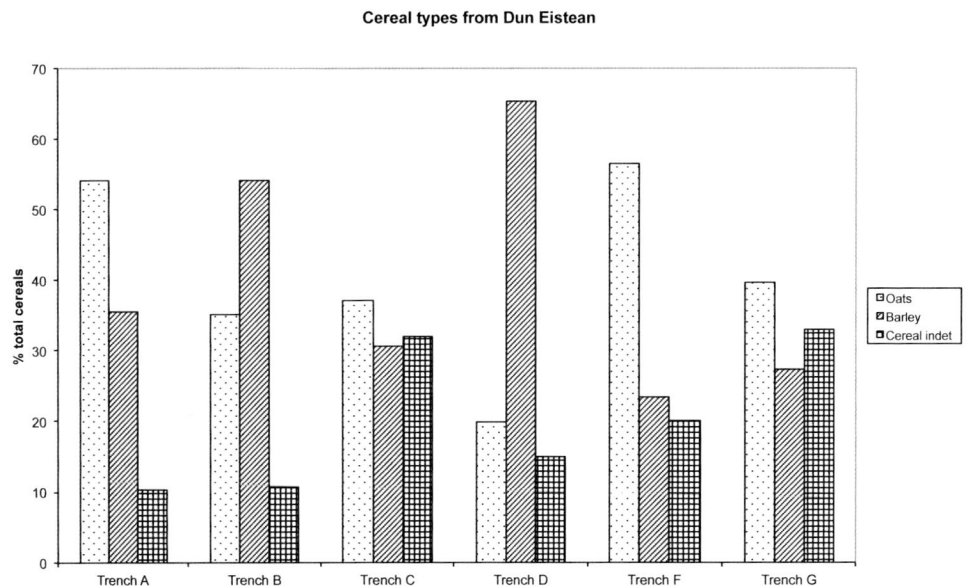

Illus 11.31 Cereal types from Dùn Èistean

present. In addition, at least some of the hulled barley was of the six-row type as a significant percentage of the grains had an asymmetric morphology. Barley has been the commonest cereal type grown in Scotland from the Neolithic to the medieval period, when oats began to become more dominant. Naked barley was generally grown in the Neolithic period, but was superseded by the hulled variety in the Bronze Age and Early Iron Age (Dickson and Dickson 2000), probably as a result of climatic downturn and a trend towards cooler, wetter summer weather (van der Veen 1992), that frequently resulted in naked grain either sprouting or rotting in storage. Hulled grain is generally better protected from damp and fungal attack as a result of the grain being enclosed in papery fused glumes whereas the naked, free threshing variety was prone to fungal infestations.

Oats dominated the cereal assemblages in Trench A and Trench F and were on a par with barley in Trench C and Trench G. Oats are only usually recorded from Scottish archaeological sites that date to within the last 1500 years and are particularly common from the medieval period onwards (Dickson and Dickson 2000). Oats are well suited to the damp, cool climate that prevails in much of Scotland, especially in the Western and Northern Isles. The identification to species of oats is problematic, and is based on the grain size and shape of the abscission scar. In this study the grains were not confidently identifiable to species, although many were sufficiently large to be of cultivated origins, implying that common oat (*A. sativa*) or bristle oat (*A. strigosa*) were present rather than simply wild oats (*A. fatua*).

It is difficult to determine whether the cereal grain that was being utilised on Dùn Èistean came from barley and oats that were grown as separate crops or together as a maslin crop. Much of the cereal grain was from deposits that were identified as having originally been dumped in middens but had then been used as packing material within the walls of structures. It is therefore unlikely that many of the cereal assemblages represent single processing accidents and so it would be expected that a significant amount of mixing of grain would have occurred.

Most of the grain assemblages discussed above contained no more than trace quantities of chaff or weed seeds and so are considered to have been from grain that had been almost fully processed. Crop processing is the name given to the series of events that result in the removal of chaff and arable weed seeds from the grain. The successive stages progressively remove more and more contaminants; thereby leaving a 'fully cleaned' crop that has few, if any, weed seeds remaining (Hillman 1981). Chaff was only found in significant quantities in Trench B and Trench D, where there was evidence for burnt straw, with a few rachis fragments and glumes. However, these remains may have been evidence for the use of straw as thatching or as woven mats, rather than cereal processing waste. Very few arable weed seeds were recorded from the site, with only rare occurrences of fathen, corn marigold, and corn spurrey together with occasional weed seeds of more varied habitats such as stitchwort/mouse-ear, docks, buttercups, ribwort plantain, cinquefoil, sun spurge, wild radish and common hemp-nettle. All these weed species could have grown on the Isle of Lewis and there is no evidence that grain was imported from further afield. The lack of processing waste on this site suggests that the majority of grain processing may have taken place elsewhere with only the final drying of oats, prior to grinding taking place on the stack itself, or in the case of hulled barley the process of gradaning which requires drying before gentle grinding to remove the hulls from the grain (Fenton 1982).

The corn-drying kiln that was excavated within Trench C actually produced very few cereal grains, which suggests that it was thoroughly cleaned after each period of cereal drying. Burnt animal bones recovered from this trench may have been deliberately burnt in the kiln to add flavour to the grain (Fenton 1997), although the burning of animal bones is also seen as a general occurrence in hearths and ash dumps on the site (eg contexts D050, D058/D105 and D080, see Masson-MacLean, below).

Flax

Flax seeds were recorded from contexts within Trenches D and F, although large numbers were never present. Flax grows best on well-drained soil and does not compete well as a casual weed within cereal crops (Clapham et al 1987, Bond and Hunter 1987). It is unlikely to have grown naturally in this locality and is more likely to be the remnants of a crop, either grown for fibre (linen) or for oil from the seeds (linseed). The low numbers of flax seeds recorded from the site may be because flax does not usually require drying as part of its processing and so there is a much lower chance of it being preserved through carbonization than there is for cereal grain.

When grown for fibre flax plants are best harvested before they are allowed to fully ripen the seed, although it is possible to collect both products from one crop. Flax may be a Norse introduction, with many sites in the Northern Isles containing significant quantities of flax seed from the Norse period onwards (Dickson and Dickson 2000). However, in other parts of Scotland, flax is more likely to be medieval or post-medieval in date.

Other food plants

Very little evidence for food plant remains, other than cereals, was found on Dùn Èistean. Only a few fragments of hazel nutshell, a seed from a rose hip and a seed from a hawthorn berry were the only other potential food plant remains recovered from the site. It is not possible to say that these food plants were actually being eaten as the remains were scarce and could easily have arrived on the site accidentally with wood that was collected for fuel.

Pollen analysis and AMS dating of Structure E

by Susan Ramsay

Methodology

Sampling procedures

Structure E is a circular, artificial pond up to 7m in diameter in the centre of the island. At the time of sampling it was holding up to 0.3m of fresh water. The sediment build up was relatively shallow and so was sampled using an auger, rather than the Russian corer. Two cores of sediment, each 20cm in length, were taken through the basal sediments towards the middle of the small pond.

Illus 11.32 Taking a pollen core in the pond Structure E

Sample preparation and analysis

The pollen preparation procedure followed the standard methods outlined in Moore et al (1991) using 1cm^3 of sediment from each sample to be analysed. The concentrated pollen samples were stained with safranin, dehydrated with tertiary butyl alcohol and mounted in silicone oil prior to preparation of microscope slides.

The pollen slides were scanned using high power microscopy at magnifications of x400 and x1000 for critical determinations. Identification of pollen types was by reference to Moore et al (1991) and to the Northwest European Pollen Flora Vols 1-6 (Punt 1976-1991). Any critical determinations were checked against the University of Glasgow pollen reference collection. Pollen nomenclature follows Moore et al (1991). Vascular plant nomenclature follows Stace (1997). Broken, crumpled, corroded and obscured pollen grains were recorded during the counts to give information on the general state of pollen preservation. Pollen counts of at least 500 identifiable land pollen grains were made for each level.

Microscopic charcoal particles >10μm were counted on the pollen slides and assigned to the size categories suggested by Tipping (1995), ie with a longest axis length of 10-25μm, 26-50μm, 51-75μm and >75μm.

The pollen washings from each sample were also analysed in order to provide an indication of the sediment type and local vegetation growing on each site throughout the depth of the core/column. Two AMS radiocarbon dates were obtained from each site, with a basal date obtained for each site.

Pollen diagram
A 'total land pollen' (TLP) sum was used to produce the pollen diagrams. Other types were expressed using a sum of TLP plus the non-land pollen grouping involved. The pollen diagram was produced using the TILIA and TGVIEW computer programs (Grimm 1991). Where the percentage of a pollen taxon is <1%, this is represented by a '+' on the pollen diagram to increase the visibility of rarer taxa.

Pollen washings
All pollen washings were examined under a low magnification binocular microscope to determine the main organic and inorganic components present.

Results

In total four samples were analysed from the 20cm deep core that was recovered from the pond Structure E. The results of the pollen and micro-charcoal analyses are shown in Illus 11.33. All pollen washings were scanned for organic and inorganic components and the results of this analysis are presented in Table 11.7.

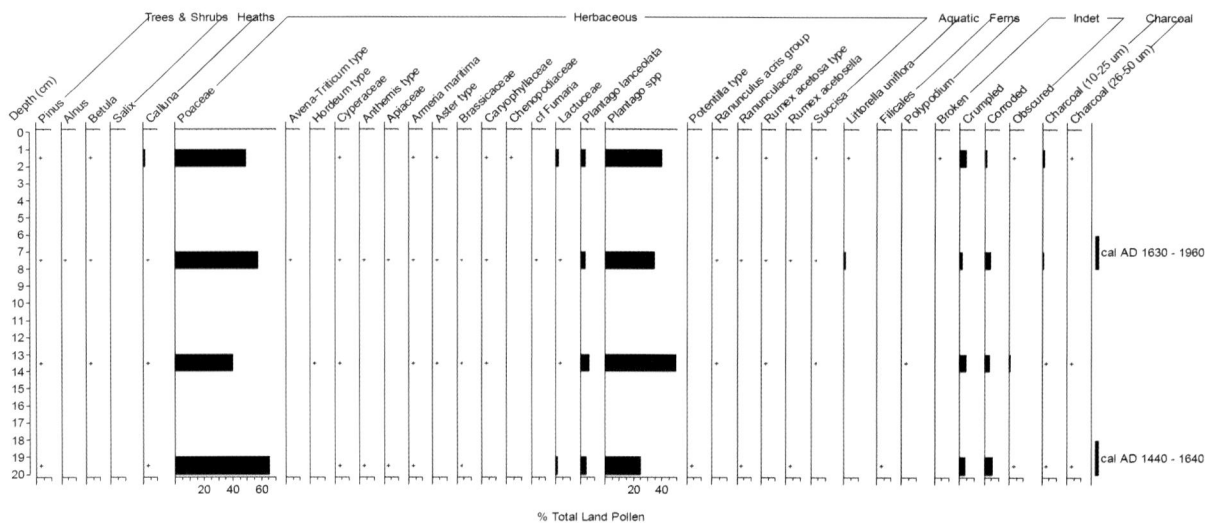

Illus 11.33 Pollen diagram

Very few identifiable plant macrofossils were recovered fro the pollen washings from the pond. Mineral, in the form of fine sand, was present in all samples along with very humified organic matter. Only the sample at 12-13cm contained any identifiable plant remains in the form of moss (bryophyte) leaves and stems although even these were badly degraded. Insect remains were present in two levels. The extensive humification of the organic material and the presence of insect remains indicate that the silts in the pond were very biologically active and so the possibility of bioturbation will have to be considered when interpreting the pollen results.

Two AMS radiocarbon dates were obtained for this core: a basal date at 18-20cm and one at 6–8cm to date the only occurrence of cereal pollen within the core. The results of the AMS dating for this site are shown in Table 11.8.

The pollen preservation and concentration within the samples from the Structure E pond was generally good, although there were a significant number of crumpled and corroded grains present. This may be a result of biological activity within the sediment. Radiocarbon dating of the sediments showed that the basal deposits date to AD1440-1640 and are contemporaneous with the main occupation of Dùn Èistean. This provides evidence for the

Sample depth	Description of pollen washings
1 - 2 cm	Mineral – fine sand
	Very humified organic material occasional
	Insects abundant
7 - 8 cm	Mineral – fine sand
	Very humified organic material occasional
12 - 13 cm	Mineral – fine sand
	Very humified organic material occasional
	Bryophyte stems and leaves occasional
	Insects abundant
19 - 20 cm	Mineral – fine sand
	Very humified organic material occasional

Sample depth	Uncalibrated AMS date	Calibrated AMS date (1σ)	Calibrated AMS date (2σ)
6 - 8 cm	220 ± 35 BP	cal AD 1640 - 1960	cal AD 1630 - 1960
18 - 20 cm	385 ± 35 BP	cal AD 1440 - 1620	cal AD 1440 - 1640

Table 11.7 Pollen washings and Table 11.8 Structure E AMS dates

pond having been dug, or thoroughly cleaned out, during the main occupation period of the stack.

The pollen diagram shows a more or less unchanging environment throughout the period during which the sediment was deposited. The local environment was grassland, with significant numbers of plantains (*Plantago spp*) growing through the sward. The high abundance of plantains would indicate either grazing pressure or, more likely, trampling pressure on the grassland habitat. There is a diverse range of other weedy herbaceous types within the pollen diagram but none, apart from dandelion type (Lactuceae), occurs at more than trace levels. Heather (*Calluna vulgaris*) pollen is very low, suggesting that no significant areas of heathland were present in the local area. A single pollen grain of oat/wheat type (*Avena/Triticum*) was identified at 6-7cm depth but this is insufficient to determine whether cereal growing was taking place nearby. From the carbonised plant macrofossil work also undertaken on excavated material from Dùn Èistean, large quantities of cereal grain, both oats and barley, was being brought onto the stack and this single pollen grain may have originated from this imported grain.

The only evidence for aquatic plants from the pond was pollen grains of shoreweed (*Littorella uniflora*) within the upper half of the core. Shoreweed can survive under fully immersed conditions but will only flower when above water. This suggests that the water level within the pond may have fallen during the period when the upper sediments were deposited.

Considering the quantities of charcoal and carbonised grain that have been identified from the structures excavated on Dùn Èistean, only negligible quantities of micro-charcoal were identified from the pollen slides. This may simply be because of the topography of the stack. The pond is situated within a small hollow, possibly leading to micro-charcoal within smoke being blown up and over the pond, with little charcoal actually being deposited onto the pond surface.

Discussion

The pollen analysis results from Structure E are similar to other sites studied on the Isle of Lewis. Fossit (1996) looked at a lake sediment core from Loch Buailaval Beag (on the west coast of the island) that covered the entire postglacial period. The pollen diagram shows the main vegetation changes to have occurred around 6500 - 6800 cal BC when much of the woodland was cleared. Since that point the vegetation became dominated by grass, heather and sedge, with only slight representations of "weedy" herbs in the diagram and only scarce cereal grains present. Pollen analysis of the area around Callanish by Bohncke (1988) also showed a very similar spectrum to that shown by Fossitt (1996). Birks and Madsen (1979) undertook pollen analysis on a peat core from a valley mire at Little Loch Roag, which also covered much of the postglacial period. Tree pollen was shown to be very low throughout the last 5000 years or so. The last 2000 years showed very little change in tree pollen representation, with the only potential fluctuation being a slight decline in hazel/bog myrtle pollen in the last *c* 600 years. As before, the vegetation appears to be dominated by grass, heather and sedge, with cereal-type pollen even rarer than at Loch Buailaval Beag and Birks and Madsen suggesting that there 'are no unambiguous pollen indicators of human influence on the vegetation over the last 5000 years' (1979, 840).

These previously analysed sites show a very similar environmental picture to that obtained during the study for the Ness area as a whole (see Barrowman, C S 2015, 101-12). Tree pollen is very low, with the dominant vegetation types being heathland and grassland, with sedges being important in particular localities. The effects of agriculture are more clearly visible with the pond Structure E on Dùn Èistean in particular, showing high levels of agricultural indicators, although these effects are most notable for sediments deposited within the last few hundred years. This emphasises the need to analyse sites associated with archaeological finds in order to investigate small-scale agriculture, rather than just expanses of raised bog that will only give a more regional picture of the environment through time.

Animal bone
by Edouard Masson-MacLean

Methodology
Field recovery methods

Animal bone catalogue on CD at back of book

The excavations at Dùn Èistean were undertaken by hand with approximately 28l of soil collected from all undisturbed deposits for environmental flotation, with additional samples taken from particularly rich deposits, or those particularly rich for dating. The majority of the samples where processed through a Siraf tank located at the Comunn Eachdraidh Nis in Habost (Barrowman, R C 2007, 12).

Archaeozoological methods
Identification

All specimens were identified to species or taxonomic group where possible. Ribs and vertebrae (excluding the axis and atlas) and unidentifiable specimens were assigned to size class (large/medium). Large mammal bones were most likely to have come from cattle, but could also have come from horse or red deer. Similarly, medium mammal bones were most likely to have come from sheep, but could possibly have originated from goat, pig or roe deer. All other mammalian fragments for which neither species nor bone could be ascertained were described as indeterminate mammal.

Boessneck's (1969) and Prummel and Frisch's (1986) criteria for differentiating between sheep (*Ovis aries*) and goat (*Capra hircus*) bones, which are morphologically very similar, were applied where feasible. The Hunterian Museum and University of Glasgow vertebrate skeleton reference collections were used for identification purposes.

No measurements could be made as there were no complete bones in the assemblage and the majority of the specimens are small calcined fragments. As bones that have been in a fire and subjected to high temperatures (ie calcined or carbonised) become smaller, they should not be measured (von den Driesch 1976, 4-5).

Taphonomy

The recovery method, state of surface preservation, presence/absence of root etching, angularity of breaks, gnawing, burning and completeness were all recorded. The type of burning was recorded because it provides a crude measure of temperature and may indicate cooking or a disposal method. Burnt specimens were recorded as "burnt" (carbonised) or "calcined". The type and location of butchery was also recorded.

Ageing

Post-cranial epiphyseal fusion stages were recorded and ages assigned using Silver (1969). The fusion stages for mammalian long bones were recorded as 'unfused', 'fusing' and 'fused'. A bone was recorded as 'fusing' when spicules had formed between the shaft and epiphyses with open spaces still present and 'fused' when the line of fusion was closed (Albarella and Davis 1996, 5).

Results

Condition

The faunal assemblage from Dùn Èistean is nearly entirely composed of burnt bone (93.4%). The fresh bones are in poor condition due to the acidic nature of the soils, with an average pH for the site of 5.68 (G. Petersen pers comm), and also show signs of weathering due to exposure to the severe environmental conditions of the Outer Hebrides. In an acidic burial context, calcined bones usually have a higher survival rate than fresh bones thus explaining their higher percentage survival (77.8%). As a result, the assemblage is characterised by the presence of bone fragments smaller than 10mm (with an average weight per specimen of 0.66g) and shaft fragments that have split longitudinally. These make faunal identification to species difficult and only 5.2% could be identified to family or species (this includes fish that were not identified to species and all bird bones). Small calcined bone fragments (less than 2mm) could not be assigned to any animal class (28.1%) though they are most likely to be mammal bone and in some cases bird bone.

Species present and relative frequency of species (Table 11.9)

Mammalian species present in the hand-excavated material included cattle and sheep/goat as well as two possible pig fragments. The bones identified are more likely to be sheep and at least one specimen (ulna) could be identified as sheep/goat. Among the bird bones recovered were gull species (*Larus sp*) and domestic fowl (*Gallus gallus.*). Shell fragments were also recovered and are likely to be oyster shells. Fish bones are also present in the assemblage including vertebrae, fins and ribs. The sieved samples (retents) revealed a similar range of species with the addition of crustacea (probably crab). In addition, bones identified only as large- or medium-sized mammal, indeterminate mammal, indeterminate bird and fish were noted.

In total 3170 bone fragments were present in the faunal assemblage with a total weight of 2192.6g. In total, 2629 fragments were recovered from the hand-excavated material and 705 fragments from the sieved samples (retents). It should be noted that the fragment size of the bones recovered by sieving was smaller, sometimes of the order of less than 5mm, than that from the hand-excavated contexts.

Mammal bones are most numerous with 2274 fragments (68.2%), followed by fish with 98 fragments (2.94%), bird with 22 (0.66%) and molluscs with three shell fragments. Only 60 fragments (1.78%) were identifiable to family or species. Cattle and sheep/goat were the better represented species with respectively 25 and 24 fragments. At least two individuals for cattle can be attested on site with the presence of two proximal ends of the right metatarsal.

Illus 11.34 Modern Hebridean breed sheep

Table 11.9 List of taxa per trench/area

Taxa	Trenches					
	B	C	D	F	Total	%
Medium-sized Mammal	11	5	83		99	3.0%
Fish	7	2	89		98	2.9%
Large-sized Mammal	1	1	90		92	2.8%
Cattle			25		25	0.7%
Sh/Goat	2	8	12	2	24	0.7%
Bird	1	1	16		18	0.5%
Mollusc			3		3	0.1%
Larus sp. Total		1	2		3	0.1%
Suidae ?			2		2	0.1%
Domestic fowl		1			1	0.0%
Lagomorpha ?			1		1	0.0%
Mammal Ind.	38	18	1961	14	2031	60.9%
Unidentified	14	13	910		937	28.1%
Total	74	57	3194	16	3334	100.0%
%	2.2%	1.5%	95.8%	0.5%	100.0%	

Ages of animals at death

Bones of cattle and sheep/goats were assessed as to the state of fusion of their epiphyses as an indicator of their chronological age. However, the number of specimens permitting this was very limited due to the poor state of preservation of the assemblage, and the less resistant bones of immature, juvenile and neonatal individuals are less likely to have survived.

For cattle only the distal epiphyses of two proximal phalanges (Phalanx I) and two middle phalanges (Phalanx II) could be used. These are all fused indicating that the age at death was at least 1½ years. Even though more numerous, cattle metatarsals and phalanges I & II, for which proximal fusion was recorded were present, they are not a good indicator of age as epiphyseal fusion occurs before birth (Silver 1969, 285-286). However, one cattle metapodial had an unfused distal epiphysis suggesting the individual was less than 3 years old.

For sheep/goats, unfused proximal epiphysis of a femur and a tibia indicate ages at death under 3 and 3½ years respectively. The fused proximal epiphysis of an ulna indicates that the individual was at least 2½-3½ years old (Schmid 1972; Silver 1969). Two other bones indicate that the individuals were at least 16 months old (fused distal epiphysis of phalanx I) and 1½ year old (fused distal epiphysis of tibia).

It should be remembered however that because of variations in the age at which particular epiphyses fuse, there is a certain degree of overlap between the age categories and in many cases it is impossible to determine whether an animal is juvenile or immature (or, indeed, immature compared with adult). Mandibular evidence is always considered more reliable than epiphyseal evidence.

The small quantity of material available for age determination did not allow distinction of any animal husbandry patterns.

Site distribution

The general bone distribution over the site is summarised in Table 11.9. Most bone fragments were recovered in trench D (95.8% of total fragment count). In trench D, contexts that contained the most fragments were D047 (12.1%), D036 (10.3%), D056 (9.3%), D105 (6.5%), D052 (5.1%), D050 (3.8%) and D058 (3.1%) that in total counted for 50.3% of the total assemblage. These contexts (from Phases 3, 4 and 5) are mainly related to hearths including sweepings from hearths or ash middens, which could indicate that the faunal material is the result food waste disposal.

Elements	Trench B				Trench C			Trench D				Trench F	Total	
	Burnt	Calcined	Unburnt	Total	Calcined	Unburnt	Total	Burnt	Calcined	Unburnt	Total	Unburnt	NISP	%
Shaft	1	3	3	7	5	2	7	24	215	1	240		254	37.7%
Enamel								113	28	90	231	1	232	34.4%
Rib			3	3				20	20	2	42		45	6.7%
Feet bones					1	2	3	12	26	2	40	1	44	6.5%
Isolated teeth								7		33	40	1	41	6.1%
Vertebrae			3	3		2	2	8	17	3	28		33	4.9%
Cranial fragments	1		1	2		1	1	2	2		4		7	1.0%
Tibia					3	1	4		1	1	2		6	0.9%
Femur			1	1		1	1			1	1		3	0.4%
Ulna									2		2		2	0.3%
Radius						1	1						1	0.1%
Sacrum			1	1									1	0.1%
Humerus									1		1		1	0.1%
Man ?								1			1		1	0.1%
Axis ?									1		1		1	0.1%
Pelvis			1	1									1	0.1%
Scapula									1		1		1	0.1%
Total NISP	2	3	13	18	9	10	19	187	314	133	634	3	674	100.0%
% Total	0.3%	0.4%	1.9%	2.7%	1.3%	1.5%	2.8%	27.7%	46.6%	19.7%	94.1%	0.4%		

Table 11.10 Mammal bone elements per trench/area

Body representation

Mammal bones were recovered from trenches B, C, D, and F, and like the rest of the faunal assemblage were nearly entirely recovered from Trench D. Table 11.10 summarises mammal bone elements present in the assemblage. Bones from all parts of the carcass were represented in the assemblage with elements of the axial skeleton (ribs and vertebrae), feet bone (metapodials, carpals and tarsals, phalanges) and isolated teeth being most numerous. However, these elements are not necessarily over-represented as they are more numerous in the skeleton. Long bones are rare in the assemblage, but the high frequency of shaft fragments (37.7% of all mammal bones) indicates that their under-representation is due to intense fragmentation and consequently difficulties to identify them to a specific element. There is no evidence that high meat-bearing bones were more prevalent than bones that bear little meat, such as those from the feet.

Cattle	Trench D			
Element	Burnt	Calcined	Unburnt	Total NISP
Feet bones	11	7		18
Isolated teeth			3	3
Cranial fragments	1			1
Axis ?		1		1
Feet bones		1		1
Ulna		1		1
Total	12	10	3	25

Table 11.11 Body part representation for cattle

Cattle are represented only by feet bone (phalanges, metapodial, carpal and tarsal bones) and isolated teeth that were the only none-burnt elements. All the bones come from Area D on the site. Three specimens likely to be cattle included also axis and ulna fragments (Table 11.11).

Sheep/goat were slightly better represented than cattle with elements from the hind (pelvis, femur and tibia) and fore (scapula, ulna and radius) limbs, including feet bones, as well as isolated teeth. Sheep/goat bones were present in trenches B, C, D and F though most numerous in trench D.

	Trench									
	B		D			F		C		Total
Element	Unburnt	Burnt	Calcined	Unburnt	Total	Unburnt	Calcined	Unburnt	Total	NISP
Feet bones			6		6	1	1	1	2	9
Tibia				1	1		3	1	4	5
Femur	1			1	1			1	1	3
Isolated teeth		1		1	2	1				3
Radius								1	1	1
Pelvis	1									1
Ulna			1		1					1
Scapula			1		1					1
Grand total	2				12	2			8	24

Table 11.12 Body part representation for sheep

Unlike cattle, only 13 of the 24 sheep/goat bones were either burnt or calcined (Table 11.12).

However, if we include specimens that could not be identified to species but recorded as

Element	Trench B				Trench C	Trench D				Total
	Burnt	Calcined	Unburnt	Total	Unburnt	Burnt	Calcined	Unburnt	Total	NISP
Shaft	1	1	2	4	2		33	1	34	40
Rib			3	3		4	13	1	18	21
Vertebrae			3	3	1	5	7	2	14	18
Isolated teeth						5		4	9	9
Feet bones					1		7		7	8
Cranial fragments					1					1
Sacrum		1		1						1
Humerus							1		1	1
Grand Total				11	5				83	99

large or medium mammal, then all body parts are represented on the site including cranial fragments, axial (vertebrae and ribs), limb and feet bones (Tables 11.13-11.14). Even though these fragments could belong to deer, pig, goat or horse bones it is more likely that they are from sheep or cattle.

Table 11.13 Body part representation for medium-sized mammals

Element	Trench B	Trench C	Trench D			Total	Total
	Calcined	Unburnt	Burnt	Calcined	Unburnt	Total	NISP
Shaft	1		7	36		43	44
Isolated teeth					13	13	13
Enamel				13		13	13
Rib			9	2		11	11
Feet bones			1	2	2	5	5
Vertebrae		1			1	1	2
Man?			1			1	1
Tibia				1		1	1
Grand Total	1	1	18	54	16	88	90

Table 11.14 Ditto for large-sized mammals

Butchery (Table 11.15)

Only four sheep/goat bones showed evidence of butchery activity. A femur from context B002 was sawn and a femur from context D037 was sawn and also had cut marks indicative of attempts to cut meat away from the bone. Chop-marks visible on the proximal end of the sheep ulna from context D057 result from attempts to subdivide the carcass. Only five cattle elements had chop-marks: two metatarsals and a tarsal bone from context D036, a phalanx from context D056 and a metapodial from context D067. These marks could correspond to the removal of the feet.

Chop and cut marks were also observed among 24 fragments that could only be identified to animal size. Four rib fragments showed cut marks indicating attempts to remove meat from the bone as ribs are major meat bearing bones (Dobney et al 1996, 23). Chop and cut marks were visible on 18 shaft fragments indicating attempts of meat removal and the reduction of the carcass in smaller joints. Based on the small amount of evidence for butchery from the assemblage, it is likely that the implements used were cleavers, saws and metal knifes. The high frequency of fractured specimens, mostly longitudinally, can not be associated with butchery alone, burning being more likely to be responsible.

| Taxa | Element | Trench B | | Trench D | | NISP Total |
		Saw	Cut	Chop	Chop + Cut	
Large mammal	Shaft			4		4
	Rib		3			3
	Mpd		1			1
	Total		4	4		8
Medium mammal	Shaft		6	2	5	14
	Phlx		1			1
	Rib		1			1
	Total	1	12	6	5	16
Total		1	16	10	5	24

Table 11.15 Butchery marks on medium and large-sized mammals

Burnt bones (Tables 11.16-11.17)

The faunal assemblage is heavily affected by burning (93.4% of total NISP) most of which is calcined (77.8%). Carbonised bones represent 15.7% of the assemblage, while only 6.6% of the specimens where unburnt. Considering the low proportion of identified bones to taxa and element, and thus identifying burning patterns, it is difficult to assess if the carbonized bones where a result of cooking practises (roasting) or if the bones where burnt after flesh had been removed. Calcination, which requires temperatures of over 450 °C to 500 °C could be a consequence of the disposal of food waste or the use of bones as fuel for fires (Lyman 1994). The high percentage of calcined bones could also be a consequence of better preservation in an acidic burial context.

| Burning | Trench B | | Trench C | | Trench D | | Trench F | | Total | |
	NISP	%	NISP	%	NISP	%	NISP	%	NISP	%
Calcined	51	68.9%	32	64.0%	2508	78.5%	2	12.5%	2593	77.8%
Carbonized	2	2.7%			510	16.0%	10	62.5%	522	15.7%
Unburnt	21	28.4%	18	36.0%	176	5.5%	4	25.0%	219	6.6%
Total	74	100.0%	50	100.0%	3194	100.0%	16	100.0%	3334	100.0%

Table 11.16 Summary of burnt bones

Illus 11.35 Burnt bone fragments in peat hearth deposit

Conclusion

The condition of the faunal assemblage does not permit a clear view of animal-based activities on Dùn Èistean, as recognizing patterns is almost impossible given the very small number of identifiable specimens to species and element. However, butchery activities did occur on the site as cut marks were observed as a result of meat removal using metal blade knifes. Cattle and sheep were a source of meat and probably dairy products. Other sources of food (primary or secondary products) would probably have included domestic fowl, fish, molluscs and crustacean (see shell fish and fish reports), as these species are all present in the assemblage. Birds could also have been consumed. It is not possible to distinguish cooking methods from the assemblage alone but it is likely that the occupants disposed their food waste in hearths after meals and or used the bones as fuel for fires.

For domestic mammals, it is plausible that entire carcasses where

				Trench				
Taxa	Burning	B	C	D	F	Total	%
Mammals	Calcined	32	13	1615	2	1662	74.8%
	Burnt	2		369	10	381	17.1%
	Not burnt	16	11	151	?	180	8.1%
Total		50	24	2135	14	2223	100.0%
Unidentified	Calcined	14	13	812		839	89.5%
	Burnt			96		96	10.2%
	Not burnt			2		2	0.2%
Total		14	13	910		937	100.0%
Fish	Calcined	5	2	48		55	56.1%
	Burnt			31		31	31.6%
	Not burnt	2		10		12	12.2%
Total		7	2	89		98	100.0%
Cattle	Burnt			12		12	48.0%
	Calcined			10		10	40.0%
	Not burnt			3		3	12.0%
Total				25		25	100.0%
Sheep/Goat	Calcined		4	8		12	50.0%
	Not burnt	2	4	3	2	11	45.8%
	Burnt			1		1	4.2%
Total		2	8	12	2	24	100.0%
Bird	Calcined			13		13	59.1%
	Not burnt	1	3	4		8	36.4%
	Burnt			1		1	4.5%
Total		1	3	18		22	100.0%
Mollusc	Not burnt			3		3	
Total				3		3	
Pig ?	Calcined			2		2	
Total				2		2	
Total		74	50	3194	16	3334	

Table 11.17 Burnt bones per taxa and trench/area

transported to Dùn Èistean but it is unclear if these carcasses were disarticulated before accessing the site. Given the difficulty of access to the site today, it is logical to assume that large mammal carcasses, at least, may have been disarticulated.

Fish remains
by Ruby Cerón-Carrasco

Methods
Twenty-six contexts from Dùn Èistean produced fish remains, recovered by sieving. The analysis of the material was done by trench, and phase. Identification of species was made using modern comparative reference collections of fish skeletons and by reference to standard guides (Watt et al 1997). All fish bone elements were identified to the highest taxonomic level possible, usually to species or to the family group, but otherwise classed as unidentifiable when these consisted of mainly broken fragments. Nomenclature follows Wheeler and Jones (1989, 122-123).

Where appropriate, all major paired elements were assigned to the left or right side of the skeleton. All elements were also examined for signs of butchery and burning. Measurements

Fish remains catalogue on CD at back of book

Table 11.18 Summary of fish remains from Dùn Èistean

*Key to Gadidae size categories: VS= Very Small < 15-cm total length, S=Small 15-30 cm total length, M=Medium 30-60 cm total length

Trench	Context	Phase	Sample no	Number	Species	*Size	Comment
A	A035	3	A019	3	Unidentifiable	Unknown	burnt black
	A034	3	A016	1	Haddock	M/L	burnt white
				2	Saithe	VS	burnt white
B	B012	4	B023	1	Saithe	VS	
				1	Saithe	VS	proximal
				4	Unidentifiable	Unknown	
	B014	5	B048	1	Saithe	VS	proximal
				1	Saithe	S	
				2	Saithe	VS	
				1	Herring	adult	
				10	Unidentifiable	Unknown	
	B015	5	B002	1	Sandeel	adult	
	B018	5	B029	3	Unidentified	Unknown	
	B020	5	B008	6	Unidentifiable	Unknown	
	B036	5	B022	1	Saithe	S	
				1	Saithe	S	
				5	Unidentifiable	Unknown	
	B092	4	B037	1	Saithe	VS	burnt white
	B093	4	B038	1	Unidentifiable	Unknown	
	B109	5	B053	1	Thornback ray?	Unknown	
				1	Saithe	S	
C	C018	5	C008		Rodent/bird?		
	C007	5	C002	1	Haddock	S	
				1	Haddock	S	
				1	Cod	S	
	C057	4	C038	2	Haddock	M	burnt white

Table 11.18 Summary of fish remains from Dùn Èistean continued

Trench	Context	Phase	Sample no	Number	Species	*Size	Comment
D	D024	5	D014	1	Thornback ray?	Unknown	burnt white
	D050	4	D013	1	Cod	M	burnt black
				1	Cod	S	burnt black
				1	Saithe	S	burnt black
	D054	6	D048		Bird?		
	D055	4	D054	2	Cod	M	burnt black
				1	Cod	S	burnt black
				1	Saithe	S	burnt black
				1	Cod	M	burnt black
				2	Cod	M	burnt black
				1	Cod	M	Proximal, burnt black
				1	Cod	M	Proximal, burnt black
				10	Unidentifiable	Unknown	
	D061	4	D065	1	Saithe	VS	Proximal, burnt black
				10	Unidentifiable	Unknown	
	D078	4	D075	1	Cod	M	burnt white
				1	Saithe	VS	burnt white
	D080	4	D077	2	Cod	M	burnt white
				1	Cod	S	burnt white
				1	Saithe	S	burnt black
	D080	4	D104	1	Cod	S	burnt white
F	F011	5	F002	1	Cod	M	
	F021	5	F009	1	Unidentifiable	Unknown	
	F023	4	F027	1	Cod	S	burnt white
				1	Saithe	VS	burnt white
G	G002	8	G004	1	Gadidae	S	
				2	Cod	S	
				1	Haddock	S	
				13	Unidentifiable	Unknown	burnt black
	G043	7	G025	1	Cod	S	proximal
	G048	6	G027	1	Cod	S	

were not taken on the identified elements; instead, elements were classified into size categories for total body length. This was done by reference to modern specimens of known size. For specimens belonging to the Gadidae (cod family group), some elements were categorized as 'very small' (150-200mm), 'small' (200-300mm) and 'medium' (300-600mm). For the non-gadoid species a classification of either 'juvenile' or 'adult' was made.

The recording of preservation of the bone was based on two characters: texture on a scale of 1 to 5 (fresh to extremely crumbly) and erosion also on a scale of 1 to 5 (none to extreme). The sum of both was used as an indication of bone condition; fresh bone would score 2 while extremely poorly preserved bone would score 10 (after Nicholson 1991).

All the above information is recorded in the catalogue (see CD in back of book). Quantification was calculated as NISP (the number of identified species) by fragment count.

Summary of the results

Introduction

A summary of the results of the analysis of the fish remains from Dùn Èistean is given in Table 11.18. The full identification of element, erosion, texture, condition and completeness for each bone is recorded in the catalogue (see CD in back of book). The level of preservation of the fish bone was consistent throughout the site, in terms of fragment size and condition. Bones were most frequently 5-70 % complete. Their condition score was generally in the range of 6-9, indicating well-preserved to extremely poorly preserved bone. A total seven taxa were identified consisting of six identified to species and one to family level.

Discussion by trench and phase

Trench A produced very small amounts of fish remains from a Phase 3 hearth deposit. These were mainly from very small saithe although remains of haddock of up to 600mm total length were also present.

Trench B produced mainly remains of immature saithe from a Phase 4 wall core deposit and Phase 5 slump deposits, whilst herring and probable thornback ray were also present in Phase 5.

Trench C produced very few fish remains, from Phase 4 and 5 turf collapse and slump layers. These were mainly from small cod and from small and medium size haddock.

Trench D produced the greatest amount of fish remains from this assemblage, all from Phase 4 hearth layers. The greatest amount of identifiable fish skeletal elements was from medium size cod, whilst small size cod and very small and small size saithe were also recovered though in smaller numbers. Most of the remains recovered in Trench D were burnt white and black.

Trench F produced the smallest amount of fish remains, from a Phase 4 occupation deposit, and Phase 5 slump layers. These were from small and medium cod and from small saithe.

Trench G produced a small amount of fish remains from later contexts (Phases 6 to 8), with mainly small cod as well as small haddock present.

General notes on the species identified

Information on the habitat and size of the species described below derived from Wheeler 1969 and 1978. The assemblage has a representation of three family groups of marine fishes. The main group represented was the cod family group ie the Gadidae of which cod, saithe and haddock were identified in the assemblage.

Saithe (*Pollachius virens*) is a common fish occurring in N inshore waters, some of its most important spawning areas are in the NW of the coast of Scotland. Saithe spawns from January to April and by midsummer the young fish are found close inshore among weed-covered rocks and open bays. This immature phase lasts for at least two years, mature fish are found slightly offshore. Its growth pattern is of an approximate average of 150mm increase in length annually for the first three years followed by a pattern of 100mm annual growth for the next three years. Saithe can reach a total length of 1m in their eleventh year. Saithe represented at Dùn Èistean were immature fish of up to 150mm total length.

Cod (*Gadus morhua*) has been one of the most important food fishes of in North Atlantic Europe. Its value as prime food is enormous its firm flesh allows for preservation as 'stock fish', dried or salted and it keeps well for winter consumption or trade. In the northern North Sea, cod spawns in February and early March. Its growth rate varies with different populations, in the North Sea it can grow to an average of 180mm in their first year, 360mm in their second year, 550mm in their third year and 680mm in their fourth year. A mature cod can reach 1.5m in length and weigh up to 40kg.

The cod is widely distributed in a variety of habitats from the shoreline to well down the continental shelf, in depths of 600m. Young, smaller fish, usually live close inshore. Cod represented at Dùn Èistean were 'small' (300-600mm Total Length category) and 'medium', size (300-600mm Total Length category) specimens.

Haddock (*Melanogramus aeglefinnus*) is another important food fish and in the North Sea, spawning takes place from late February to early June. It may attain up to 1.2m though nowadays it is found at 650mm the best fish coming in the main from deep-water. It is mainly cured by drying and in the recent past also by smoking.

Herring (*Clupea harengus*) (Family Clupeidae) was also present with vertebrae from adult specimens of up to 300mm in length.

The thornback ray (*Raja clavata*) (Family Rajidae) is distinguished by dense prickles over the entire back, and larger thorns in the mid-line from mid-disc to the dorsal fins. In sexually mature specimens these thorns are very large, with button-like bases (known as 'bucklers'). The thornback ray may attain a length of 850mm and a width of 610mm. This is the most common ray in shallow waters and is found in a variety of substrates. It is often caught by inshore fishing vessels and caught by line.

Sandeel (*Ammodytes tobianus*) (Family Ammodytae) is found on sandy substrates in shallow waters, it may grow up to 200mm in length. The specimen recovered at Dùn Èistean may have been the stomach contents of a larger fish as sandeels are an important part of the food chain of fish as well as of seabirds.

General discussion

Fishing at Dùn Èistean appears to have been a mainly inshore activity, which took part throughout the year from the safety of rocky locations, and from small boats close inshore using baited lines. The importance of Gadids, the cod family fish, to the inhabitants of Scotland, particularly in the islands has been quite

Illus 11.36 Trying out the 'taigh thàbhaidh'. Photo: Dan Morrison, 1987; Reproduced by kind permission of Angus Morrison (Morrison 1997)

Illus 11.37 Line basket in Comunn Eachdraidh Nis collection. From exhibition 'Ness Remains', photographed by Angus MacIntosh

notorious: they are common in all periods (Barrett et al 1999). Saithe found in shallow water particularly during their first three to four years when they range from 150mm to 550mm, have been the target of seasonal exploitation from the earliest of times. This fishery has been widely recorded in the Northern and Western Isles (Low 1813; Fenton 1978; Cerón-Carrasco 2005).

In the recent past, immature saithe were caught by net ie the 'poke-net' or 'tabh' as it known in the Western Isles, and used from rocky locations, or by simple rod and line, or from boats in shallow waters. This was essentially a year-round activity beginning in August with the catch of the smaller saithe measuring from 150-250mm through to May when specimens of up to 300-350m were caught. Young saithe particularly caught during the months of June,

July and August were highly appreciated, their livers also removed to extract oil used mainly as fuel for lamps (Cerón-Carrasco 1994, 1998a, 1998b, 2005). Traditionally saithe were hung and left to dry by the wind and sun without the use of salt or by the peat fire in blackhouses. Remains of saithe recovered at Dùn Èistean were present in all phases that produced fish remains and were from specimens of between 150 and 300mm in length. Their size would fit with the ethnographic accounts here described.

Cod of less than 600mm total length can be found from the shore

Illus 11.38 Rock fishing at Stoth. Photo: Dan Morrison, 1955; Reproduced by kind permission of Angus Morrison (Morrison 1997)

line into deeper waters, larger individuals tend to inhabit deeper waters. Larger cod have been caught from boats using baited lines. Haddock would also have been taken from boats as well as thornback ray. Herring were present in small amount, these may have been caught by line rather than using nets which would have produced larger catches thus larger quantities of their remains, however substantial amounts of herring remains have so far only been recovered from sites in the Western Isles dating to the Norse period, presence of herring before this date is constant but in very small quantities (Cerón-Carrasco 2005; Ingrem 2005).

Conclusion

Although small amounts of fish remains were recovered at Dùn Èistean, these have provided information to consider the use of marine resources by the inhabitants of the islands during the late medieval period. Fishing from rocks or from boats in shallow water appears to have been a year round activity and of a subsistence nature. It would have produced young saithe that could have been eaten fresh or preserved for later consumption as well as the use of their livers for oil. The use of boats from the safety of inshore shallow waters would have produced larger gadids, particularly adult cod and haddock.

Marine mollusca, with a note on crustacean remains
by Ruby Cerón-Carrasco

Methodology

Table 11.19 Catalogue of the marine shells from Dùn Èistean Key: * = present (minimal amount) ** = common (relatively large amounts)

The marine shell remains from Dùn Èistean were identified to species using standard guides (Campbell and Nicholls 1989; Moreno-Nuño 1994a). Frequency was estimated by counting shell apices for gastropods and valve umbos for bivalve species (Moreno-Nuño 1994b). Where only

Trench	Context	Phase	Sample	Species	Adult	Juvenile	Broken shell	Broken burnt shell
B	B073	5	B019	Limpet	2	1		
B	B087	4	B032	Crab				claw burnt/ black
B	B107	4	B049	Landsnail				
B	B109	5	B053	Limpet		1		
B	B014	5	B003	Limpet	1		*	
B	B014	5	B003	Crab				claw/ partially burnt
B	B059	2	B028	Limpet			*	
B	B018	5	B029	Landsnail				
B	B014	5	B049	Limpet		2		
B	B014	5	B049	Crab				claw
C	C001	6	C132	Limpet	18	16	*	
C	C001	6	C132	Periwinkle	1			
C	C007	5	C133	Limpet	17	24	**	**
C	C007	5	C133	Dogwhelk		1		
C	C016	5	C131	Limpet	48	32	*	
C	C006	4	C130	Limpet			*	
C	C006	4	C016	Limpet			*	
C	C006	4	C016	Dogwhelk		1		
C	C040	5	C135	Limpet	2	1	*	1 partially burnt
C	C040	5	C135	Crab			*** body shell	
C	C040	5	C135	Crab			** claw	
	C003	5	C008	Limpet	4			
				Rough periwinkle	1			
	C008	5	C018	Periwinkle	1			
	C002	5	C007	Mussel			*	
D	D013	5	D034	Limpet			**	
D	D013	5	D034	Mussel			*	
F	F012	6		Limpet	3	3		
F	F012	6		Dogwhelk	2			
G	G002	8	G001	Limpet	1	1		
G	G002	8	G001	Dogwhelk	1			
G	G015	7	G005	Limpet	1	3		

crushed shell was present for individual species, this was indicated with the symbol * (present, indicating minimal amount) and ** (common, indicating relatively large amounts). The crustacean remains were also recovered, these were classed by part ie mainly as 'claw' and 'carapace' and where possible identified to species.

Results

The marine shell examined derived from twenty-two contexts containing the remains of edible species such as limpets (*Patella vulgata*), periwinkles (*Littorina littorea*), and mussel (*Mytilus edulis*). Remains of non-edible species were also recorded; these included dog whelk (*Nucella lapillus*) and rough periwinkle (*Littorina saxatilis*). Recording of these mollusks is presented in Table 11.19. The presence of crustacean remains was also incorporated in the table. The table illustrates the relative importance of the species represented by trench, and phase.

The main species represented at Dùn Èistean was the limpet (*Patella vulgata*); this is a species of major importance on most littoral shores and in shallow waters (Branch 1985). It is present on all rocky shores from the most sheltered ones to the most exposed.

Limpets on the lower shore are more exposed to wave impact than limpets on the upper shore therefore limpet shells are more conical at the upper shores and flatter at the lower shore (ibid). A flatter shell has a smaller wave impact area than a more conical shell and is less likely to be knocked off the substrate if it has a more streamlined shape. The limpet shell size and shape from Dùn Èistean suggest that these would have been gathered from exposed areas, as their flattened shape would have protected them from strong wave action. The majority of species recovered from archaeological sites throughout the Scottish islands still occur in the local fauna as found at present, thereby facilitating identification and the consideration of habitat. Furthermore, Fenton (1978) indicated that the occupants of the Northern Isles in relatively recent times, collected limpets from low tide locations since they were considered to be tender and more palatable than those collected from higher parts of the shore, these were mainly used as fishing bait. There was a greater amount of adult limpet compared to juvenile limpet specimens in this assemblage and this may imply that these were largely used as component of diet, although they could have equally been used as bait.

The edible periwinkle (*Littorina littorea*) was also present though in very small quantities. Although it has been demonstrated that a variety of environmental factors can influence the shells of molluscs, studies done on edible periwinkles, suggested that there is no significant allometric differences of *Littorina littorea* shell of individuals from different environments (Hylleberg and Christensen 1977). Mature periwinkles are slightly more abundant in the Dùn Èistean assemblage and it is therefore concluded that periwinkles were gathered mainly to be consumed by humans.

Both limpets and periwinkle inhabit rocky locations, which would also explain the presence of the dog-whelk Nucella lapillus though in very small amounts, which may have been caught accidentally whilst, gathering periwinkles. The rough periwinkle specimens may have been gathered along with seaweed with which these species are associated.

Fragments of mussel shell were also identified. These would also have been gathered from rocky locations. Unlike the gastropods however, mussel is a bivalve with a very fragile shell which breaks easily and is recovered generally as fragments in archaeological deposits, it is therefore difficult to assess their relative importance in comparison to limpet and periwinkle consumption as it is probable that only a very small proportion of the original amount of mussel consumed would have survived.

Discussion by trench, and phase

Trench B: Remains of marine shell were recovered from Phases 2, 4 and 5. The remains are of limpet whole specimens and fragments and a significant amount of crustacean remains, some of which were burnt.

Trench C: Contained the largest amount of shell, from Phases 4, 5 and 6, although most of the shells were from collapsed stone and turf, a burrow and topsoil. The main species present were limpet and periwinkle of mainly adult individuals. Mussel fragments were also recovered here

Illus 11.39 Limpets on rocks at Dùn Èistean and Illus 11.40 Periwinkles on rocks at Dùn Èistean

though in small quantities. Only two species of non-edible species were recovered and in very minimal numbers, these were dogwhelk and rough periwinkle. Crab carapace and claw were also recovered, some of which were burnt.

Trench D: A very small amount of mainly crushed shell was recovered from one Phase 5 turf wall deposit in this trench and these were from limpet and mussel.

Trench F: Very small amounts of shell were present in a mink burrow in this trench. These were remains of limpet and dogwhelk. The molluscs may have accidentally been incorporated into the burrow. It must be noted that minks were only introduced in the British Isles in 1929 from America for fur farms (Nixon and Whiteley 1972), many have escaped and been living ferally since then. The mink is acquatic and mainly found close to freshwater sources, it is a hunter praying mainly on geese, ducks, coots and other birds and game. This author is not aware that minks feed on marine molluscs; even if they did, the shells would have been broken, particularly those of periwinkles and those recovered in the burrow were whole. It is more likely that this predator was attracted to the Artic Terns which nest intermittently on the stack.

Trench G: Very small amounts of shell were present in buried turf and topsoil in Phases 7 and 8 in this trench. These were remains of limpet and dogwhelk.

Note on the crustacean remains
Claw and carapace remains of the edible crab Cancer pagurus were recovered in contexts from Trenches B and C, these fragments were burnt implying possible rubbish burning of food residue.

Conclusion

The marine shell remains from Dùn Èistean suggest the use of an easily accessible food source from the coast concentrating on rocky shore species. Limpets were the main species present, their shell shape are consistent with an exposed location. It may be assumed that shellfish were predominantly harvested during summer months when the weather was milder and that although some of the smaller specimens of limpet may have been used as bait, most of the shellfish was gathered and used for human consumption, and the presence of periwinkles and mussel would also support this statement. Crab was also an important source of nutrition and is present in Trenches B and C. Most of the crustacean remains showed signs of burning, indicative of domestic rubbish disposal.

Endnotes

[1] Radiocarbon dates calibrated at 95.4% confidence

Illus 12.1 Close-up of sample K30 in section in Area C

twelve

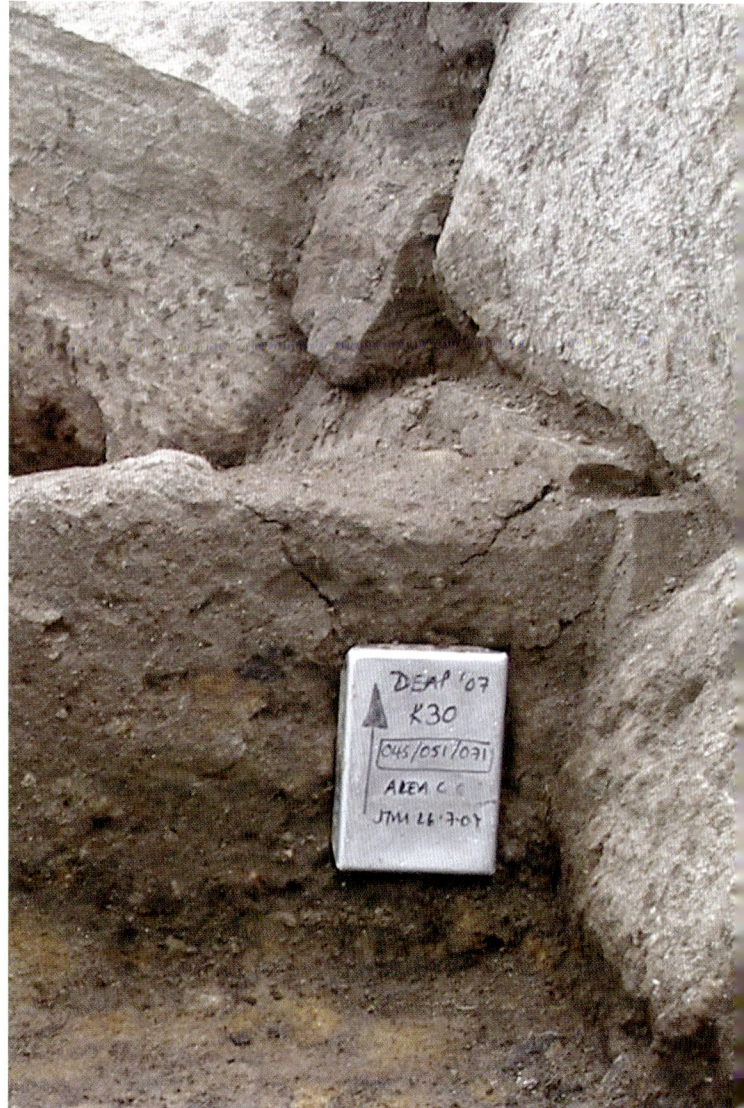

soils and micromorphology

The properties of the soil and sediments found on an archaeological site are an indication of the environment in which they have been formed. Thin section micromorphological analysis of samples taken from these soils and sediments can help understand the ways in which the community living on Dùn Èistean used the resources and materials found in the surrounding environment for the construction of buildings or for fuel. This technique can also identify finer microscopic layers of activity such as burning or surface trampling and occupation, which are not usually visible in the field. Also, chemical analysis of bulk soil samples taken from the same deposits can be used to study the role of human-induced and natural processes in the makeup of the archaeological deposits, and to identify the source of the deposits studied. Samples taken from the wall core of Structure G, and turf wall constructions within Structures C, D and F illustrate that construction at Dùn Èistean took a range of forms and used a range of materials. For instance, dark organic-rich material such as charcoal, peat and degraded plant material was mixed with lighter areas of mineral-dominated material in the Structure G wall cores, whereas the turf wall core sampled in Structure C was more compact and mineral dominated. In addition to these samples, those from the slumped turf walls of Structures D7 and F show that occupation material was mixed into the wall deposits. Particle size analyses confirm that the sandy soils found on Dùn Èistean are the likely source of construction material throughout the structures on the site.

In addition to the study of the building walls on the site, the large central hearth in Structure D16 and the smaller hearth below Structure D7 were intensively sampled in thin section, revealing a huge range of incorporated materials. The D16 hearth included charcoal, burnt and charred mossy peat, peat ash, decomposed plant matter, large peat fragments and bone. Very high levels of phosphate in both hearths in certain bone-rich deposits suggest the deliberate use of bone as a fuel source. Samples from the smaller hearth below D7 indicate a similar range of fuel residues as D16, with evidence of burning episodes at a range of temperatures between 400 and 800°C. The soils analyses also highlight events and features not visible through excavation such as a band of turf-like material within the D7 hearth, which indicates a collapse of roofing material or a turf cover to the hearth. Another example is the presence of fungal spores, only visible under the microscope, in some turf wall and turf roof related deposits such as in Structure C, but not in others, such as Structure F, indicating that different kinds of turf materials were used on the site. Overall, the soils analyses have made a significant contribution to our understanding of life on Dùn Èistean in the fifteenth to seventeenth centuries.

by Jo McKenzie *with* Laura E McKenna and Rachel Barrowman

Soils thin section micromorphology

by Laura E McKenna and Ian A Simpson

Introduction

Soil and sediment properties reflect the environment in which they have been formed, and so the recovery of known anthropic sediments from archaeological contexts has the potential to assist archaeologists to understand the ways in which past communities utilised their available construction and fuel resources. During the Dùn Èistean excavations 25 soil/sediment samples were recovered using 8x5x5cm Kubiena tins from hearths, floor surfaces and turf walling for thin section micromorphological analysis. This microscope-based investigative technique can provide a detailed consideration of finer discrete stratigraphies representing events such as burning or surface trampling and occupation, which are not usually visible in the field. Slides prepared from Dùn Èistean trenches C, D, F and G are investigated to satisfy a range of objectives:

Area C, turf walls: Examine the structure of a turf wall and later turf bank, determine the source of construction materials and investigate for evidence of burning or an occupation layer.

Area D, turf walls, floors and hearth deposits: Identify what fuels were used and the temperature the fires burned at. Examine the construction material of turf walls to identify whether it was sourced from old areas of settlement.

Area F, floor layer, roof collapse and wall slump: Investigate occupational floor layers and turf walls to assist in determining the function of Structure F and whether its use was contemporary with other structures on the site.

Area G, turf wall core: Examine the wall core construction and identify where a second phase of wall construction was deposited upon an earlier, collapsed wall and explore samples for evidence of construction techniques.

The methodology and results from Areas C and D are reproduced below as examples, with the overall conclusions then taking into account the results from all the areas. The full soils analysis results are included on the CD in the back of this volume.

Methodology

Thin sections were manufactured at the Thin Section Micromorphology Laboratory, University of Stirling. All water was removed from the samples by acetone exchange. The samples were then impregnated using polyester 'crystic resin type 17449' and the catalyst Q17447 (methyl ketone peroxide, 50% solution in phthalate). The mixture was thinned with acetone and a standard composition of 180ml resin, 1.8ml catalyst and 25ml acetone used for each Kubiena tin. An accelerator was used and the samples were impregnated under vacuum to ensue complete outgassing of the soil. The impregnated soils were cured, culminating with a period in a 40°C oven. Resin impregnated soils were sliced, bonded to a glass slide and precision lapped to 30µm thickness, and cover slipped to complete the manufacture of the thin section.

By following procedures laid out in the International Handbook for Thin Section Description (Bullock et al 1985) and the most recent methods of Stoops (2003), soil properties are to be recorded semi-quantitatively on a standard table designed to work alongside research objectives, and adapted specifically for each context (hearth, building materials etc). The thin sections were analysed using an Olympus BX-50 petrological microscope at a range of magnifications (x10- x400) and with several different light sources. Plane polarised light (PPL), crossed polarized light (XPL) and oblique incident light (OIL) each allow identification of specific microscopic features, such as, mineral and organic components, pedofeatures and fuel residues. Interpretation of the observed features rests on the accumulated evidence of a number of workers, notably Courty et al (1989) FitzPatrick (1993), and more recent research carried out at the University of Stirling. Research objectives laid out in the 2007 data structure report for Dùn Èistean have been carefully considered throughout the design, description and interpretation process to facilitate a discussion of results which leads to a substantiated site interpretation (Barrowman et al 2007).

Results
Area C
The lowest horizon in Area C, thin section K22 represents the natural bedrock [C044]. In the field this was recorded as 'Yellow and purple dark grey degrading stone"; in thin section it is characterised by dominant coarse minerals (approximately 27-70%). The turf built wall and bank in Area C were sampled using 7 Kubiena tins (turf wall-K22-26 and later turf bank-K29 and K30) to investigate structure and whether the turf used in its construction came from the immediate area and to see if there is any evidence of burning, or of a floor.

Illus 12.2 Area C, turf wall core, Kubiena tins in situ

Turf wall core
There is no evidence for fuel residues or any other domestic waste material within thin sections K22 to K25.
K22
The sample for this thin section was selected to intersect the boundary between context [C037], a natural layer of decaying bedrock and context [C044]. The dominant schist-related mineral content is consistent with the local geology, containing quartz and compound quartz grains (5-20% and 20-40%) with hornblende/biotite (5-20%), feldspar (1-5%) and traces of garnet and muscovite (<1% each). The bedrock within the sample has clearly undergone granulitization and

Legend:

t = trace (<1%) :. = very few (1 -5%) ... = few (5 -20%) .... = frequent (20-40%) ..... = very frequent (40-50%) ...... = dominant/very dominant (50%-70%)

◊ = trace (<1%) ◊ = rare (1-2%) ◊◊ = occasional (2 - 5%) ◊◊◊= Many (5 - 10%)

E= Enaulic CP= Close phorphyric

K22 C037/C044 SINGLE	K23 C076 SINGLE	K24 C074 SINGLE	K25 C059 SINGLE	K26 C056 SINGLE	THIN SECTION REFERENCE / CONTEXT / MICROSTRATIGRAPHIC UNIT	
⋮	⋮	⋮	⋮	·	Compound Quartzite/Schist	COARSE MINERAL MATERIAL (>63µm)
⋮	⋮	⋮	⋮	⋮	Quartz	
t	·	↑	↑	↑	Garnet	
·	·	·	·	·	Feldspar	
t	↑	↑	↑	↑	Muscovite	
·	↑	·	⋮	↑	Hornblende/Biotite	
⋮	↑	↑	⋮	↑	Phytoliths	
					Diatoms	
Brown Organo-Mineral (PPL) · Stipple-Speckled Micro-Crystallitic	Brown Organo Mineral (PPL) :. Stipple-Speckled Micro-Crystallitic	Brown Organo Mineral (PPL) :.. Stipple-Speckled Micro-Crystallitic	Brown-Brown Organo Mineral (PPL) :.. Stipple-Speckled Micro-Crystallitic	Dark-Brown Organo Mineral (PPL) ⋮ Stipple-Speckled Micro-Crystallitic	NATURE OF FINE MINERAL MATERIAL / GROUNDMASS b FABRIC (XPL)	FINE MINERAL MATERIAL (<63µm)
↑	↑	·		⋮	Plant tissues (slight/moderate decomposition)	COARSE ORGANIC COMPONENT (>63µm)
				↑	Plant tissues inc. peat (strong/very strong decomposition)	
					Charcoal	
↑		↑			Fungal Spores	
↑		·	↑	⋮	Organic fine material (black)	FINE ORGANIC COMPONENT (<63µm)
			↑		Amorphous (reddish brown)	
↑					Amorphous (yellow)	
	↑				Rubified Material (OIL)	OTHER INCLUSIONS
↑					Pale yellow ash (OIL)	
					Bone (moderate to high intensity burning)	
					Bone (unburned or low intensity burning)	
Chambers and Channels	CP	CP	Inter-grain micro-aggregates	Inter-grain micro-aggregates	MICROSTRUCTURE	STRUCTURE
Granulitized /Random	Random	Random	Granulitized compound quartzite/ schist	Random	COARSE MINERAL ARRANGEMENT	
CP	CP	CP	E	E	COARSE/FINE RELATED DISTRIBUTION	
	◊◊				Sandy Clay Coatings/Infill	PEDOFEATURES
	◊◊	◊◊◊			Silty Clay Coatings/Infill	
					Limpid Clay Coating/Infill	
◊	◊	◊	↑	◊	Iron Accumulation	
					Iron Depletion	
			◊	◊	Pseudomorphic plant material	
			↑	◊	Excremental	

it is interspersed with birefringent clay fine material containing trace amounts of fungal spores related to weathering processes; the only indication that the close-packed minerals towards the extreme lower portion of the slide are bedrock comes from an iron-pan (Illus 12.3) and other fine material, otherwise the whole sample appears to be decaying bedrock.

K23

Centred on context [C076] identified in the field as a turf layer within the outer-wall, this thin section exhibits a slightly different mineral content when compared with K22. The minerals are related to the local geology, however there are far fewer instances of hornblende and biotite and garnet is more prevalent (see Table 12.1). There are trace amounts of peat and fragmented plant roots/lignified tissue indicating that the turf material was removed from a layer near a land surface.

K24

This sample, collected from context [C074], exhibits a similar mineral content but contains a higher proportion of organo-mineral fine material when compared with K23; this is consistent with its position higher up the profile.

K25

This sample was collected from context [C059] and is strongly related to the granulitization of small pebbles (approx. 11mm diameter) and granules (approx. 2-4mm) composed of compound quartz and schist (20-40%); it is distinguished from samples K22-K24 by Enaulic coarse/fine ratios and an inter-grain micro-aggregate microstructure. The fine organo-mineral material is dark due to high silt and clay sized mineral content (Illus 12.4). The thin section exhibits small amounts of plant material as both fragmented anisotropic pseudomorphs and isotropic decomposed organic tissues (1 5%).

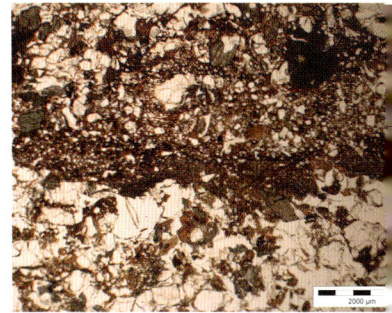

Illus 12.3 K22, iron pan (PPL)

Illus 12.4 K25 groundmass showing sand and silt sized minerals, speckled clay fine material, inter-grain micro-aggregates and plant root pseudomorphs PPL - left and XPL - right

K26

The sample for this thin section was collected from the upper layer within the turf wall core [C056]; in thin section it appears closely related to the micromorphology of sample K25 with fewer compound quartz/schist minerals (1-5%), a greater amount of fragmented plant root

Table 12.1 Thin section description, Area C – Turf wall core (opposite)

pseudomorphs (5-20%) and occasional excremental pedofeatures (2-5%). There is one fragment of charcoal present within this slide.

Later turf bank

Illus 12.5 Area C, later turf bank, Kubiena tins in situ

K29

Within this slide there are two micro-stratigraphic units, A and B related to contexts [C031] and [C037] respectively (Illus 12.5; Table 12.2).

Unit A

This unit is dominantly mineral in composition (up to approx. 65%, all related to underlying bedrock) with grain sizes ranging from silt (4-62μm) to pebbles (4000-64000μm); there is a high ratio of minerals within the organo-mineral fine material (Illus 12.6 (a)). In the field this context was described as decaying bedrock, the micromorphology supports this statement. There is a high amount of iron accumulation within this context (5-10%). Fungal spores (<1%) indicate the

Illus 12.6 K29, groundmass within Unit A - left, and B - right (XPL)

weathering of bedrock was in part biological and the channels, chambers and vughs are evidence of the activity of soil fauna and indicate that the natural weathering process at this horizon continued for an extended period of time through dry periods as well as wet.

Unit B

Unit B contains a more balanced ratio of organo-mineral fine material than Unit A (Illus 12.6 (b)); the coarse minerals are less dominant (frequent only, up to 25% of the unit) and are

Table 12.2 Thin section description, Area C – Later turf bank (opposite)

K29 C031/C037		K30 C045/C051/C071			THIN SECTION REFERENCE CONTEXT MICROSTRATIGRAPHIC UNIT	
B	**A**	**C**	**B**	**A**		
.	:	.	:	:	Compound Quartzite	**COARSE MINERAL MATERIAL (>63µm)**
:	:	:	.	:	Quartz	
t	t	t	t	t	Garnet	
t	.	t	.		Feldspar	
t	t	t	t	t	Muscovite	
t	t	t	t	t	Hornblende/Biotite	
				T	Phytoliths	
					Diatoms	
Brown Organo Mineral :. / Stipple Speckled Micro-Crystallitic	Brown Organo Mineral (PPL) :. / Stipple Speckled Micro-Crystallitic	Grey Brown Organo Mineral :. / Stipple Speckled Micro-Crystallitic	Brown Organo Mineral (PPL) :. / Stipple Speckled Micro-Crystallitic	Brown Organo Mineral (PPL) :. / Stipple Speckled Micro-Crystallitic	NATURE OF FINE MINERAL MATERIAL GROUNDMASS b FABRIC (XPL)	**FINE MINERAL MATERIAL (<63µm)**
.	.	t	t		Plant tissues (slight/moderate decomposition)	**COARSE ORGANIC COMPONENT (>63µm)**
t			:		Plant tissues (strong/very strong decomposition)	
.	t	t	t	t	Charcoal	
					Fungal Spores	
t		.	:		Organic fine material (black)	**FINE ORGANIC COMPONENT (<63µm)**
t					Amorphous (reddish brown)	
t			t	t	Amorphous (yellow)	
					Rubified Material (OIL)	**OTHER INCLUSIONS**
					Orange (OIL)	
					Bone (burned)	
					Bone (unburned)	
Channels, Chambers and Vughs	Channels, Chambers and Vughs	Intergrain-micro-gregate(few vughs)	Channels, Chambers and Vughs	Channels, Chambers and Vughs	MICROSTRUCTURE	**STRUCTURE**
Random	Random	Random	Random	Random	COARSE MINERAL ARRANGEMENT	
CP	CP/E	CP	CP	CP	COARSE/FINE RELATED DISTRIBUTION	
					Amorphous Crypto-crystalline nodules/Coatings/Infill	**PEDOFEATURES**
					Sandy Clay Coatings/Infill	
◊	◊	◊◊◊	◊◊	◊	Silty Clay Coatings/Infill	
				t	Dirty Clay Coating/Infill	
t	◊◊◊	◊		t	Iron Accumulation	
					Iron Depletion	
◊◊		t			Excremental	

t = trace (<1%)   . = very few (1-5%)   ∴ = few (5-20%)   ∴∴ = frequent (20-40%)   ∴∴∴ = very frequent (40-50%)

t = trace (1-2%)   ◊ = rare (1-2%)   ◊◊ = occasional (2-5%)   ◊◊◊= Many (5-10%)   ...... = dominant/very dominant (50%-70%)

(<1%)

E = Enaulic   CP= Close phorphyric

predominantly sand-sized (124-2000µm) with silt-sized minerals incorporated into the fine material. There is evidence for increased biological activity (fungal spores 1-5%, excremental pedofeatures (1-2%), channels, chambers and vughs); this indicates that the layer has accumulated over time and was close to a land-surface. There is no evidence of cultural activity within this layer.

K30

This slide exhibits three micro-stratigraphic units, A, B and C related to contexts [C071], [C051] and [C045] respectively.

Unit A

This unit is micromorphologically very similar to unit B within sample K29 although it exhibits increased instances of coarse minerals (up to approx. 45%) related to underlying geology. Small amounts of herbivore dung evidenced by discrete areas of amorphous yellow material containing phytoliths (<1%), fungal spores, calcium oxalate spherulite under XPL (Guttman et al 2006). Along with channels, chambers and vughs, these features indicate that the context was near to a land surface but there is no evidence for cultural/domestic activity at this level.

Unit B

This unit appears very dark due to the frequent amounts of both charcoal and black amorphous material (5-20% each). Much of the black amorphous material contains phytoliths (Illus 12.7) and exhibits the characteristics of grass charcoal outlined by Umbanhower and McGrath (1998); larger fragments of charcoal correspond to charred plant tissues indicating that this context is composed of burnt turf or heath plants. Silty clay (textual) pedofeatures and bioturbation features indicate that this horizon was exposed as part of the land surface for some time and eventually included in the natural accumulation of the sediment.

Unit C

This unit is dominantly mineral (up to approx. 45% + highly crystallitic organo-mineral material) and contains very few examples of black amorphous fine sand or silt-sized flecks interpreted as charcoal (1-5%) which may have blown or trampled into the profile; the former is more likely as lower horizons are not densely packed. Bioturbation features indicate the context was near-by a land surface and silty clay pedofeatures (5-10%) demonstrate the down-profile movement of material as higher horizons were disturbed. Iron accumulation features reveal that the context was exposed to periods of wetting and drying during formation.

Area D
Structure D7

Samples K17 to K20 (Illus 12.8) were collected from Structure D7 to identify floor layers and investigate fuel residues in order to characterise occupational floor deposits for comparison with turf wall construction materials.

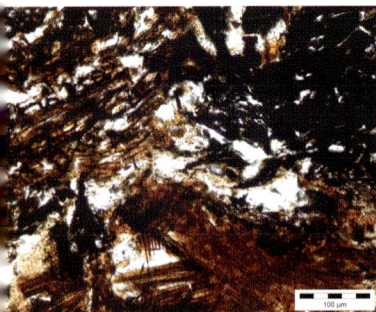

Illus 12.7 K30, phytoliths in amorphous black material, interpreted as grass charcoal (PPL)

Illus 12.8 (a) and (b) Structure D7 showing Kubiena tins in situ

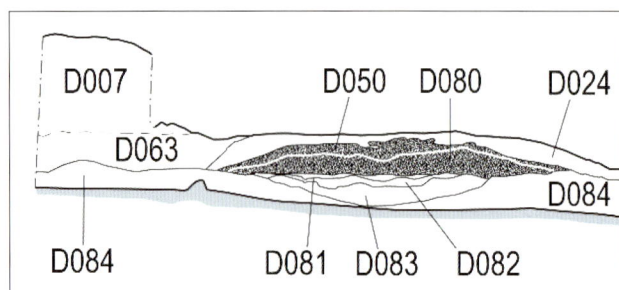

Table 12.3 Thin section description, Area D – Structure D7 (opposite)

K17

This sample was collected from the slumped turf wall [D007] that post-dates the hearth sequence in Structure D7. In thin section there is a single dominantly mineral (approximately 65%), microstratigraphic unit with phytolith rich (5-20%) organo-mineral fine material and well decomposed plant roots (1-5%); consistent with the turf context. The moderate degree of

Legend:

- • = trace (<1%)
- •• = very few (1 – 5%)
- ••• = few (5 – 20%)
- •••• = frequent (20–40%)
- ••••• = very frequent (40–50%)
- •••••• = dominant/very dominant (50%–70%)

- t = trace (<1%)
- ◊ = rare (1–2%)
- ◊◊ = occasional (2 – 5%)
- ◊◊◊ = Many (5 – 10%)
- E = Enaulic CP = Close phorphyric OP = Open phorphyric R = Random

THIN SECTION REFERENCE	K17	K18	K19			K20		
CONTEXT	D007	D056 or D063/D084	D084/D050/D080			D080/D082/D083		
MICROSTRATIGRAPHIC UNIT	SINGLE	A	C	B	A	C	B	A
COARSE MINERAL MATERIAL (>63μm)								
Compound Quartzite/ Rock Fragments	•••	•••	t	t	t	t	•••	t
Quartz	•••	•••	••	••	••	•	•••	•••
Garnet	t	t	t	t		t	t	t
Feldspar	•	t	t		t	t	•	t
Muscovite	t	t	t				t	t
Hornblende/Biotite			t			t	t	•
Phytoliths	•••	t	t			t		
Diatoms						t		
FINE MINERAL MATERIAL (<63μm)								
NATURE OF FINE MINERAL MATERIAL	Pale Brown Organo-mineral (PPL)	Brown Organo-mineral (PPL)	Brown Organo-mineral (PPL)	Brown Organo-mineral (PPL)	Brown Organo-mineral (PPL)	Light Brown to yellow Organo-mineral (PPL)	Very dark Brown Organo-mineral (PPL)	Brown Organo-mineral (PPL)
GROUNDMASS b FABRIC (XPL)	Stipple-Speckled Micro-Crystallitic	Stipple-Speckled Micro-Crystallitic	Stipple-Speckled Micro-Crystallitic	Stipple-Speckled Micro-Crystallitic	Stipple-Speckled Micro-Crystallitic	Stipple-Speckled Micro-Crystallitic	Stipple-Speckled Micro-Crystallitic	Stipple-Speckled Micro-Crystallitic
COARSE ORGANIC COMPONENT (>63μm)								
Plant tissues (slight/moderate decomposition)	•	t	•			t	t	t
Plant tissues inc. peat (strong/very strong decomposition)	•	••	t	••	•	•	••	
Charcoal/Charred Peat/Moss	•	t	•			t		t
Fungal Spores								
FINE ORGANIC COMPONENT (<63μm)								
Organic fine material (black)	•	•	•	•	••	•	••	
Amorphous (reddish brown)			t			t		
Amorphous (yellow)	t	t	t			••		
OTHER INCLUSIONS								
Rubified Material (OIL)						t	t	
Pale yellow ash (OIL)		•	t	•		••	t	
Red/Orange ash (OIL)				••••	•			
Bone (moderate to high intensity burning)								
Bone (unburned or low intensity burning)	t	t	t	t	t	•		
STRUCTURE								
MICROSTRUCTURE	Channel & Chamber	Channels, chambers & vughs	Channels & Vughs	Channels & Vugh	Channel & Vugh	Vughs & Vesicles	CP	CP
COARSE MINERAL ARRANGEMENT	R	R	R	R	R	R	R	R
COARSE/FINE RELATED DISTRIBUTION	CP	CP	CP	OP	CP	CP	CP	CP
PEDOFEATURES								
Microlamination		◊◊		◊◊		◇		
Sandy Clay Coatings/Infill								
Silty Clay Coatings/Infill				◊◊	◇		◊◊◊	◇
Dirty/Limpid Clay Coating/Infill				◊◊	◇		t	◇
Iron Accumulation							◇	◊◊
Iron Depletion	t	t						
Pseudomorphic Manganese / Ferruginous	t	t						◇
Excremental			t	t				

bioturbation (evidenced by channels and chambers within the microstructure) probably occurred post-abandonment, following the slump of the walls. There are two examples of bone burned at moderate and high intensities (Hanson and Cain 2007), several discrete areas of burnt peat (1-5%) and black amorphous material/punctuations; these features occur at random throughout the slide and suggest that the material used in the wall construction was sourced in areas of occupation.

K18

This sample was collected from the basal layer of the turf wall [D063] and the underlying context [D084]. The thin section exhibits a single microstratigraphic unit with frequent minerals (approximately 20-40%) related to the background geology. Charcoal, charred moss and peat fragments contribute 5-20% of the slide and there are a few instances of lightly burned bone (<1%). Pale yellow ash (OIL) is interspersed throughout the slide (1-5%) with a large accumulation to the upper left portion; it contains both melted and articulated phytoliths (<1%). The burning temperature responsible for these features is likely to have been between 600°C and 800°C (Guttmann et al 2006, Parr and Boyd 2002). All material is densely compacted and slight clay banding is present within the lower portion of the slide, this demonstrates that the material was subject to compression. Fragmented bands of homogenised ash and peat could indicate a floor layer towards the lower portion of this slide (context [D084], Illus 12.9); however, this was much disturbed by later anthropogenic re-working (possibly in the construction of turf walls).

K19

This sample intersects three contexts within D7; the lower hearth [D080], the main hearth [D050] and a trample layer over the hearth [D024]. In thin section the boundaries between each context are diffuse but the differences are discernable and these are labelled A, B and C (respective to contexts).

Unit A

Within this unit the coarse mineral component contributes approximately 5-20% of the total groundmass and is related to the background geology; fine organo-mineral material interspersed with yellow and orange ash (<1% each -OIL) indicating different intensities of burning. Other inclusions include charcoal and burnt peat (1-5%), black amorphous material (5-20%) and fragmented bone burned at high intensities. All of these features are thoroughly homogenised with the fine material together with silty/limpid/dirty clay pedofeatures (1-2% each) it is likely they have filtered down profile over time; this cannot however explain the large (2.8cm) bone fragment within this context so perhaps deliberate burial of small amounts of waste material should be considered.

Unit B

This unit is dominantly composed of orange and pale yellow ash (40-50% and 1-5% respectively), charcoal and burned peat (5-20%) and black amorphous material (1-5%). The mineral component (approx. 5-20%) is related to the local geology. There are a few fragments of bone, burned at high intensity (<1%). Channels and excremental pedofeatures (<1%) indicate a degree of bioturbation and silty/dirty/limpid clay and laminated pedofeatures (2-5% each, Illus 12.10) are related to the sequential down profile movement of materials caused by trampling of higher contexts and illuviation of fine material.

Unit C

The fine material in this unit is compacted and contains a greater variation in minerals than Units A and B (Table 12.3), these were likely brought in accidentally on the soles of the feet etc and are related to the background geology. Large channels and excremental pedofeatures (<1%) demonstrate the one-time close proximity of this context to a land surface though the absence of plant roots and phytoliths indicate it was not vegetated.

K20

This sample was taken from the lower hearth sequence; [D083], [D082] and [D080], consequently there are three corresponding microstratigraphic units, A, B and C respectively (Illus 12.11).

Unit A

This unit is closely related to the decaying bedrock visible in Kübiena tin samples K22 and K29

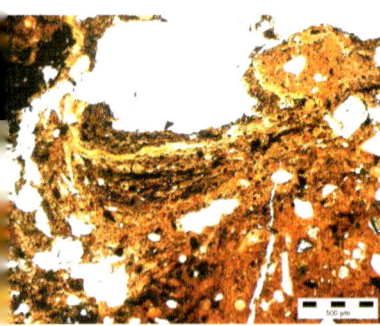

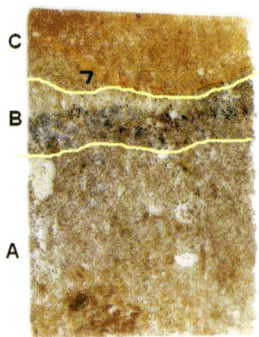

Illus 12.9 K18, possible floor layer (PPL) (opposite), Illus 12.10 K19, laminated silty/limpid clay pedofeature in Unit B (PPL) (top, this page) and Illus 12.11 K20, showing microstratigraphic units and the turf capping of the lower portion of Unit C (bottom, this page)

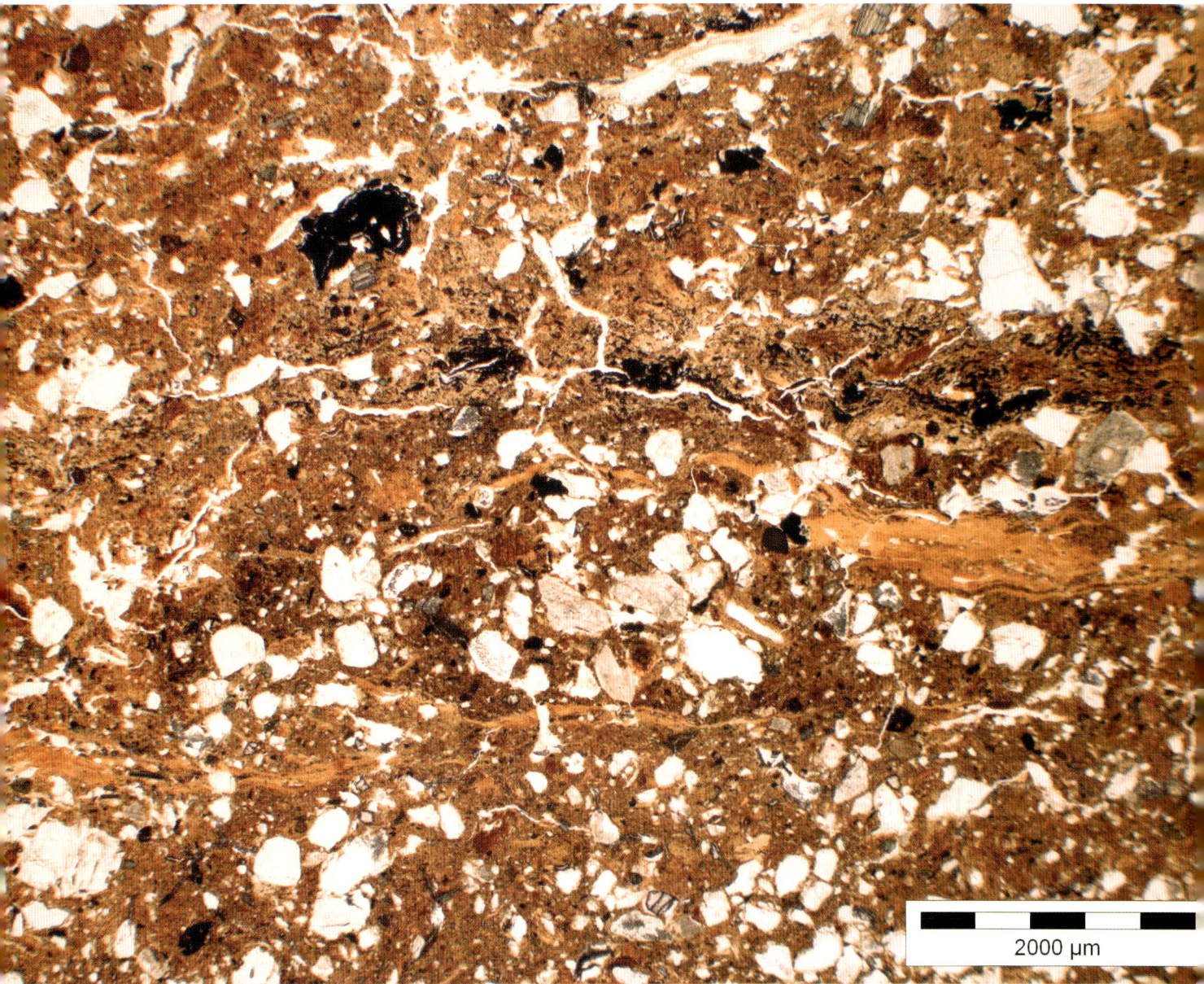

2000 µm

as it contains abundant weathered minerals (approx. 25-60%) related to the underlying geology. The unit also contains iron accumulation and related pedofeatures and silty/clay infill and coatings, which, along with the absence of bioturbation features, indicate a wet environment where chemical and clay illuviation has occurred. There is no evidence of cultural activity within this slide.

Unit B

This unit contains frequent occurrences of fragmented amorphous black fine material interpreted morphologically as burnt peat (20-40%) which are densely packed in between un-heated coarse mineral grains (approx. 11-45%) and cemented with organo-mineral fine material which coats and in-fills pore space. This context contains no ash and peat is highly fragmented which leads to the suggestion that the residues from peat fires were flattened and mixed with coarse minerals, perhaps to create rough flooring.

Unit C

In thin section, Unit B and Unit C are separated by a band of turf material 3200μm thick (Illus 12.12); this could represent a period of abandonment or partial roof collapse as micromorphologically it resembles the turf roof collapse seen in Area F. A distinctive, well decomposed turf capping covers this band of material right across the thin section: the groundmass from this point upwards is compacted with frequent charred/burned peat (21-45%), rubified material and burned bone (<1% each) and represents a period of occupational accumulation.

Structure D16

Kubiena tin samples taken from Structure D16 intersected several hearth layers, with the result that all thin sections from this area exhibit a degree of bedding at the macro-scale and have been scanned (using an Epson SX100 scanner) to aid interpretation/description (eg Illus 12.14). In addition to this, several heterogeneous layers and sequences can be observed at high magnification. Samples K31 - K33 were retrieved from the E facing section of trench D (Illus 12.13; Table 12.4) whilst samples K34 - K36 were retrieved from the S facing section (Illus 12.27; Table 12.5).

E facing section

K31

There are two main stratigraphic units: Unit B, corresponding with context [D076] (mottled dark greyish brown, yellow and black sandy silt peat ash and burnt peat), and lower hearth deposit [D078] and Unit A corresponding with the leached natural deposit [D091]. Within Unit B it was possible to observe a repeating sequence of thin bands (B1 and B2). A third 'homogenisation layer' (A/B) was observed between contexts [D078] and [D091] (Illus 12.14).

Unit A

This unit is highly mineral in composition (approx. 27-70% of the total sample), including

Illus 12.12 K20, band of turf material separating Units B and C. Yellow turf capping to top of micrograph (PPL)

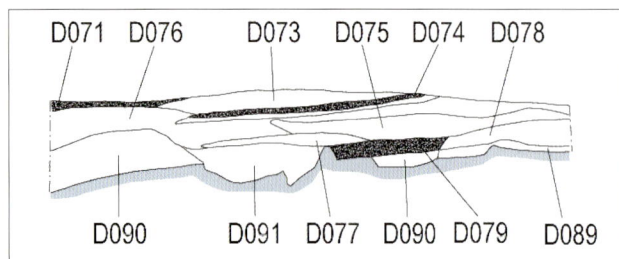

Illus 12.13 E facing Section, Trench D, Structure D16 (showing contexts) and Kubiena tins in situ

quartz, feldspar, compound quartzite, hornblende, garnet and muscovite that are products of the natural decomposition of the gneiss bedrock. The trace (<1%) of yellow amorphous material is derived from plant roots and together with bioturbation vughs and channels indicates Unit A was once near to a land surface. It contains fine material that has filtered down from higher up the soil profile, including a trace (<1%) of the amorphous black punctuations that can be observed in Units B and A/B.

Tables 12.4 Thin section description, Area D – Structure D16

Thin Section Ref.	Context	Microstrat. Unit	Compound Quartzite/Rock	Quartz	Garnet	Feldspar	Muscovite	Hornblende/Biotite	Phytoliths	Diatoms	Nature of Fine Mineral Material	Groundmass b Fabric (XPL)	Plant tissues (slight/mod decomp)	Plant tissues* incl. moss (strong decomp)	Charcoal/Charred Peat/Moss	Fungal Spores	Organic fine material incl. burned peat (black)	Amorphous (reddish brown)	Amorphous (yellow)	Rubified Coarse Material (OIL)	Pale yellow/White ash (OIL)	Orange ash (OIL)	Bone (mod-high burning)	Bone (unburned/low burning)	Microstructure	Coarse Mineral Arrangement	Coarse/Fine Related Distribution	Amorphous Crypto-crystalline nodules/Coatings/Infill	Sandy Clay Coatings/Infill	Silty Clay Coatings/Infill	Limpid Clay Coating/Infill	Iron Accumulation/nodules	Iron Depletion	Pseudomorphic Manganese/Ferruginous
K33	D090	A SINGLE	t	··		·	t				Brown Organo-mineral (PPL)	Stipple-Speckled Micro-Crystallitic				·	.....			t	···					Cracked	Random	OP					◊◊◊		
K33	D078	B SINGLE	·	··		t	·				Brown Organo-mineral (PPL)	Stipple-Speckled Micro-Crystallitic	t		t	t										Fissure & Chambers	Random	CP	◊		◊◊◊				◊
K33	D075	C SINGLE	·	··		·	t	t			Reddish Brown Organo-mineral (PPL)	Stipple-Speckled Micro-Crystallitic		·	··		···	·								Massive, Cracked	Random	OP					◊		t
K33	D073	D SINGLE		···	t	·	t	t			Light Brown Organo-mineral (PPL)	Stipple-Speckled Micro-Crystallitic	t	·	···	·			···							Channel	Random	OP					◊		
K32 D073/D075/D078		A 2	t	·		t	t				Yellowish Brown Organo-mineral (PPL)	Stipple-Speckled Micro-Crystallitic	t	·	·····	t	t		t	···			t	t		Channel & Chamber	Random	OP							
K32 D073/D075/D078	B	1	·	····		·	t	t			Brown Organo-mineral (PPL)	Stipple-Speckled Micro-Crystallitic		t	·		t	t	t	···				t		Channel & Chamber	Random	OP							
K32 D073/D075/D078		2	·		t	t					Brown Organo-mineral (PPL)	Stipple-Speckled Micro-Crystallitic		···	·		·									Massive (very dense)	Random	OP							
K32 D073/D075/D078	C	1	·		t	t					Brown Organo-mineral (PPL)	Stipple-Speckled Micro-Crystallitic		·		t	t	··					t			Cracked	Random	OP	t		◊				
K32 D073/D075/D078		SINGLE	t		t	t					Brown Organo-mineral (PPL)	Stipple-Speckled Micro-Crystallitic	t	·	···	t	·	·	···				t			Cracked	Random	OP							t
K32 D073/D075/D078	D	SINGLE	··	···	t	·	t	·			Brown Organo-mineral (PPL)	Stipple-Speckled Micro-Crystallitic	t	t	t	t										OP	Random	OP					◊◊		
K31 D076/D078/D091	A	SINGLE	t	··	t	t	t	t	·t		Brown Organo-mineral (PPL)	Stipple-Speckled Micro-Crystallitic	··	·	····	·	··		t	···	t					Channels, locally spongy	Random	OP					◊	◊◊◊	
K31 D076/D078/D091	A/B	2	·	·		t					Brown Organo-Mineral (PPL) Undifferentiated		t	·	t	·····	·		t			t			OP	Random	OP	◊◊◊	◊	◊				
K31 D076/D078/D091	B	1	·	···	t	··	t	t			Brown Organo-mineral (PPL)	Stipple-Speckled Micro-Crystallitic	··	t	···	t	·	·	····	··				t		OP- Vesicles, Chamber or Cracked	Random-Locally Banded	OP	◊◊◊ ◊◊						
K31 D076/D078/D091		2	·t	·							Brown Organo-mineral (PPL)	Stipple-Speckled Micro-Crystallitic	t		·····											Cracked	Random	OP					◊◊◊		

t = trace (<1%)   · = very few (1-5%)   ·· = few (5-20%)   ··· = frequent (20-40%)   ···· = very frequent (40-50%)   ····· = dominant/very dominant (50%-70%)

t = trace (<1%)   ◊ = rare (1-2%)   ◊◊ = occasional (2 – 5%)   ◊◊◊ = Many (5 – 10%)

E= Enaulic   CP= Close Phorphyric   OP = Open phorphyric

Table 12.5 Thin section description, Area D – Structure D16

Thin Section Reference	Context	Microstratigraphic Unit	Compound Quartzite/Rock Fragments	Quartz	Garnet	Feldspar	Muscovite	Hornblende/Biotite	Phytoliths	Diatoms	Nature of Fine Mineral Material	Groundmass b Fabric (XPL)	Plant tissues (slight/moderate decomposition)	Plant tissues* including moss (strong decomposition)	Charcoal/Charred Peat/Moss	Fungal Spores	Organic fine material incl. burned peat (black)	Amorphous (reddish brown)	Amorphous (yellow)	Rubified Coarse Material (OIL)	Pale yellow/White ash (OIL)	Orange ash (OIL)	Bone (moderate to high intensity burning)	Bone (unburned or low intensity burning)	Microstructure	Coarse Mineral Arrangement	Coarse/Fine Related Distribution	Amorphous Crypto-crystalline nodules/Coatings/Infill	Sandy Clay Coatings/Infill	Silty Clay Coatings/Infill	Limpid Clay Coating/Infill	Iron Accumulation/nodules	Iron Depletion	Pseudomorphic Manganese/Ferruginous
K36 (D076/D090/D091)	A	SINGLE		·		t	t	t	t		Brown Organo-mineral (PPL)	Stipple-Speckled Micro-Crystallitic	···		·			··						t	Spongy	Random & weak OP bands		◊◊◊		t				
	B	5	t	·		t					Light Brown Organo-mineral (PPL)	Stipple-Speckled Micro-Crystallitic						···							OP	Random OP		◊◊◊						
		4	t	·		t					Brown Organo-mineral (PPL)	Stipple-Speckled Micro-Crystallitic	t		··		·				·	t	t		OP	Random OP		t			◊◊			
		3	t	·		·	t				Dark Brown Organo-mineral (PPL)	Stipple-Speckled Micro-Crystallitic	t	·	·····	t	t		t					t	Crack	Random OP								
		2	·	··		t					Brown Organo-mineral (PPL)	Stipple-Speckled Micro-Crystallitic		t		·			t				t		OP	Random OP								
		1	t	·		·	t				Dark Brown Organo-mineral (PPL)	Stipple-Speckled Micro-Crystallitic		t		··			t				t	t	Crack	Random OP					◊	t		
		SINGLE	··	··	t	··	t	·			Dark Brown Organo-mineral (PPL)	Stipple-Speckled Micro-Crystallitic	t		t		t						t		CP	Random CP					◊			
	C	SINGLE	t	···		t	t	t	t		Brown Organo-mineral (PPL)	Stipple-Speckled Micro-Crystallitic	···	t	t	··		·		t				t	Spongy	Random with local banding OP		◊◊◊		t				t
K35 (D061/D074/D076)	A	SINGLE	t	·		t	t				Brown Organo-Mineral (PPL)	Stipple-Speckled Micro-Crystallitic	t	··	·····				t						Vesicular/ Spongy	Linear, trapped within layers of Charcoal OP		◊◊◊	◊	t				t
	B	SINGLE	·	···		·	t	t	t		Brown Organo-Mineral (PPL)	Stipple-Speckled Micro-Crystallitic	·	t	t	··		t		t					Channel & Vugh	Random OP		◊◊◊		◊◊◊				t
	C	SINGLE	··	·		t	t	t	t		Brown Organo-mineral (PPL)	Stipple-Speckled Micro-Crystallitic	·	t		···		·	t		··			t	Channel	Random OP		◊◊		t				
K34 D078	A	SINGLE	·	·		t	t	t			Brown Organo-mineral (PPL)	Stipple-Speckled Micro-Crystallitic	··			··		·	t		·			t	Channel	Random OP		◊◊		t				
D076	B	SINGLE	t	·	·	t	t	t	t		Dark Brown Organo-mineral (PPL)	Stipple-Speckled Micro-Crystallitic	··			···			t						Channel	Random OP		◊	◊◊◊	◊				

t = trace (<1%)   · = very few (1–5%)   ·· = few (5–20%)   ··· = frequent (20–40%)   ···· = very frequent (40–50%)   ····· = dominant/very dominant (50%–70%)

t = trace (<1%)   ◊ = rare (1–2%)   ◊◊ = occasional (2–5%)   ◊◊◊ = Many (5–10%)

E= Enaulic   CP= Close Phorphyric   OP = Open phorphyric

Unit A/B

This unit displays a similar mineral composition to Unit A though there is a higher incidence of black amorphous material including punctuations (40-50%). The general groundmass is randomly interspersed with peat ash (yellow 1-5% and orange 20-40% in OIL), rubified minerals (<1%) and burned bone fragments (<1%) which have filtered through from higher up in the soil profile. Orange peat ash indicates moderate temperature burning (approx. 400°C) whilst yellow peat ash indicates higher intensity burning at temperatures of approx 800°C (Guttmann et al 2006).

Unit A/B rests upon a discrete band of material (Illus 12.15) which marks a boundary between A/B and A; it is observed in thin section as a linear red-amorphous organic horizon containing large fragments of grass, wood and leaf charcoal, plant fragments very few silt-sized mineral grains, fungal spores and limpid clay textual pedofeatures.

Unit B

B1 begins the repeating sequence (Illus 12.16) in this unit at its lowest extremity; it is characterised by the distinct pale yellow fine material (OIL) containing black amorphous flecks and burned plant material; it is interpreted as peat ash ranging from 8000μm and 118μm in depth and is evidence of fires burned at moderate to high temperatures (approx. 800°C). B2 follows B1, it is highly organic with a mineral component of between 5.1% and 10.9% and contains occasional vesicles and a dominant proportion of black amorphous material (>50%) often broken down into silt-sized (2 μm - 60μm) punctuations or sand-sized (60 μm - 2000μm) particles. These particles exhibit the characteristics of grass and leaf charcoal outlined by Umbanhower and McGrath (1998); together with the very few (1-5%) large fragments of recognisable charcoal it is inferred that B2s are compacted charcoal layers between 9500μm and 462μm in depth. The sandy pedofeatures account for the coarse mineral grains within B2. Two discrete inclusions of plant material interpreted as moss (following Canti 2009) are visible before the second and fourth repetitions of the B1-B2 sequence. A black 'crust' visible under low magnification coats the top of one of these features; under higher magnification is shown to be the same black punctuations present within B2 and B1 which have become 'trapped' as they filter down profile. The moss is an inclusion and has not formed in situ, it contains a trace of vivianite indicating that the moss came from a wet area with low oxygen levels.

Sequence B1 and B2 is capped by a layer of non-rubified organic fine material containing fungal spores which is interpreted as peat (Illus 12.17). The sequence can again be discerned above this, though heavily homogenised through to the top of the slide.

K32

Four stratigraphic units were observed in thin section (Illus 12.18), A, B, C and D. Unit A corresponds with context [D079], identified in the field as dark yellowish brown with black and orange peat ash patches sandy grit with silt and charcoal patches. Unit B corresponds with context [D075], identified in the field as bright yellow silty sandy peat ash, Unit C with contexts [D076], mottled dark greyish brown yellow and black sandy silt peat ash and burnt peat and [D074], black compacted silty clay ashy deposit with frequent charcoal and Unit D corresponds with context [D073], orangey brown to yellowish brown sandy silt peat ash.

Unit A

This unit is very dark in colour due to the high levels of amorphous black fine material (20-40%); it also contains orange peat ash (20-40%) and corresponds with context [D079]. The coarse mineral component throughout the slide corresponds to the local parent material; in Unit A it contributes approx. 21-45% of the total groundmass. There are traces (<1%) of recognisable though decomposed plant tissue and limpid clay coatings (1-2%) that indicate the low-energy downward movement of fine material from the surfaces above.

Unit B

This unit corresponds with context [D075], the lower hearth deposit. Two separate sediments are visible in thin section, differentiated by the colour of the fine material and abundance of coarse minerals. The first of these, B1 is composed of coarse minerals (approx. 42-60%) and orange peat ash (20-40%) that is mixed with the brown-organo mineral fine material, black amorphous punctuations and charcoal (1-5% each) and trace amounts of yellow/white peat ash, and yellow amorphous material (<1% each). It is approx. 15000μm in depth. B2 (Illus 12.19) contains fewer

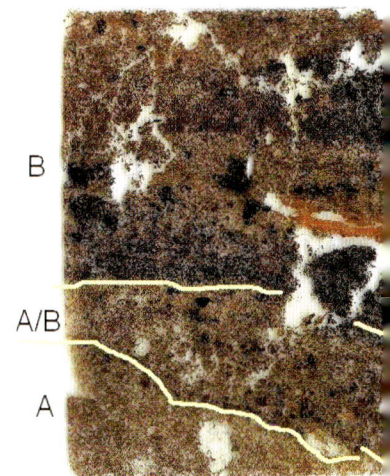

Illus 12.14 K31 scan, annotated showing microstratigraphic Units A, A/B and B. The sequence (B1 and B2) cannot be distinguished at this scale

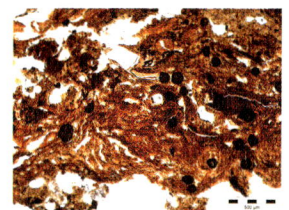

Illus 12.15 K31, discrete layer in Unit A/B (PPL), Illus 12.16 K31, Unit B, sequence B1, B2 (OIL) and Illus 12.17 K31, peat layer in Unit B (PPL)

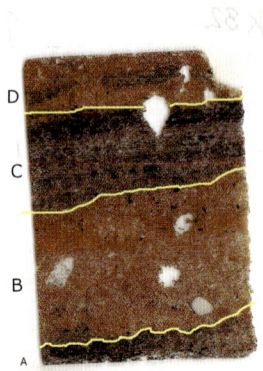

coarse minerals (approx. 5-20%) but more orange peat ash (50-70%) with black amorphous punctuations and charcoal (1-5% each) and traces (<1% each) of both burned and unburned bone fragments. It is approx. 10000μm in depth.

Unit C

This unit comprises several compacted charcoal and ash layers (Illus 12.20) labelled C2 and C1 respectively. The sequence begins with a homogenised C1/C2 layer (300μm -650μm in depth); this is followed by a thin band of C1 (25μm- 150μm in depth) containing few minerals (approx. 1-5%) and orange peat ash (5-20%). The sequence culminates with a thick (up to 7500μm) band of C2 containing an identical mineral component to C1, large amounts of recognisable charcoal material (20-40%) and black amorphous material (20-40%) interpreted as finely broken down wood and grass charcoal. The boundaries between micro-stratigraphic units (C1 and B2), and (C2 and A) are irregular but clearly discernable; therefore Unit C as a whole is likely to correspond with a separate context [D074], another lower hearth deposit.

Unit D

This unit corresponds with context [D073], sweepings from the western hearth. In thin section there are few minerals (approx. 1-5%) as the groundmass is largely composed of both orange (20-40%) and yellow (1-5%) peat ash with black amorphous punctuations interpreted as fine particles of leaf and grass charcoal. There is also a trace (<1%) of unburned bone.

K33

Four micro-stratigraphic units were observed in thin section (Illus 12.21), A, B, C and D corresponding with contexts [D090], [D078], [D075] and [D073] respectively.

Unit A

Within this context (the earliest hearth layer deposit), charcoal (5-20%), black amorphous fine material (5-20%) and orange coloured ash (20-50% in OIL) may be observed in thin section; these demonstrate that wood and grassy materials were burned at temperatures of approximately 400°C. The coarse and fine materials including charcoal fragments, heat altered clay nodules, burned bone, peat ash and black-punctuations are arranged randomly, homogenised with dark brown organo-mineral fine material demonstrating that the unit accumulated over time and did not relate to a single in-situ burning event. Many iron accumulation pedofeatures (up to 10%) evidences a high degree of trampling. The context is capped with convoluted but sequential turf and ash material; the ash exhibits a variety of colours in OIL (Illus 12.22) evidencing burning at varying temperatures. The mineral component relates to the local geology rather than in situ decomposition of bedrock.

Unit B

In this unit the hearth context is confirmed with the presence of dominant black amorphous fine material (>50%) related to both burned grass, wood, charcoal (1-5%), pale yellow peat ash (20-40% OIL) and heat altered clay (Illus 12.23). The coarse mineral fraction of this unit is again related to the local geology but it is more prevalent (approx. 20-40%).

Unit C

This unit contains more coarse minerals than the other units in the thin section (between 23.01% and 55.9%); together with the pale yellow to white (OIL) ashy material this accounts for the light colouration in the macro-scale (Illus 12.21). Ash makes up 20-40% of the unit. Individual constituents are invisible even at high magnification so it appears amorphous with interspersed fine minerals visible under XPL. The unit also contains a trace (<1%) of well-decomposed plant matter which also appears as yellow amorphous material, this is however discernable from the ash component as it is entirely isotropic in XPL and contains occasional pseudomorphs of the original cell structure (Illus 12.24). In some areas the ash is filled with coarse minerals (Illus 12.25), these may have filtered down from higher up in the profile following diagenesis of ash-derived minerals (Schiegel et al 1996) and trampling. Charcoal is not present in this unit but some of the black amorphous fine material exhibits morphological characteristics of wood charcoal; other similar features that do not exhibit these characteristics are iron/manganese nodules.

Unit D

This unit consists of very densely compacted fine organo-mineral matrix interspersed with coarse minerals (7.02%-30.2%) and chemically altered bone. The bone fragments exhibit the

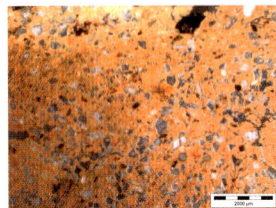

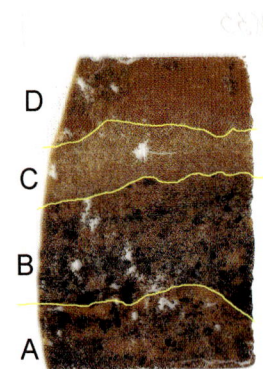

Illus 12.18 K32, scan showing microstratigraphic units, Illus 12.19 K32, red peat ash in microstratigraphic Unit B2 (OIL), Illus 12.20 K32, Sequence C1, C2 in microstratigraphic Unit C (OIL) and Illus 12.21 K33, showing approximate boundaries of the microstratigraphic units

characteristics of low to medium intensity burning (Illus 12.26) described by Hanson and Cain (2007). The planar cracks, fragmentation of bones and high instances of iron accumulation indicate this context was trampled.

K34

There are two weakly formed micro-stratigraphic units; A and B corresponding with contexts [D078] and [D076] respectively (Illus 12.27) with a narrow (50μm) band of light material running horizontally through Unit B. The mineral content of the whole sample is consistent with the local geology.

Unit A

This unit exhibits many signs of burning and it appears that variations in temperature are present evidenced by ashy peds, minerals fused together with ash (Illus 12.28), black amorphous material (5-20%), charred plant remains (1-5%) charcoal (<1%), pale yellow ash (5-20%), orange ash (5-20%)(both OIL) and a bone fragment burned at low intensity (Hanson and Cain 2007). All of these features occur in a random distribution pattern within a densely compacted matrix of fine organo-mineral material.

Unit B

This unit incorporates several phases of accumulation/deposition, evidenced by the weak bedding of the sediment together with a random distribution of coarse minerals, charcoal (1-5%), black amorphous material (5-20%), pale yellow ash (1-5%) and orange ash (5-20%). Below the horizontal band running across this unit there is a higher ratio of black amorphous material, pale yellow ash and charcoal than the upper portion of the unit, and there are several inclusions of peat, moss and bone fragments which have been affected by chemical decomposition. The lighter band is composed of pale yellow ash, coarse mineral grains, rare inclusions of black amorphous fine material and silty pedofeatures from further up the profile. Above this band the nature of the inclusions vary to those below it; they include moss and peat fragments, bone burned at high intensity and black amorphous material which exhibits the same micromorphology as control samples of animal manure burned at 400° (Simpson et al 2003).

K35

There are three micro-stratigraphic units; A, B and C (Illus 12.29) corresponding with contexts [D076], D074] and [D061] respectively. The mineral content of the whole sample is consistent with the local geology.

Unit A

This unit contains a single sinuous band of coarse minerals and white ash (OIL) at its centre; otherwise, white ash (<1%), black amorphous fine material including fine punctuations (5-20%) and charcoal (<1%) are well homogenised with organo-mineral fine material (<1%), silty clay pedofeatures (5-10%) and frequent (20-40%) decomposed root/plant material and peat (with fungal spores <1% of slide, high frequency within peat inclusions). In contrast with the rest of Unit A, the peat fragments do not contain coarse minerals indicating that they have been imported from another area; the diatoms, fungal spores, iron nodules and vesicles present within the peat demonstrate that its source was probably wet or saturated (Simpson et al 1999).

Unit B

This unit appears very dark due to the dominant black amorphous fine material (50-70%) and charred moss/peat (5-20% - Illus 12.30). White ash (<1%, OIL) coats three vughs, and the entire fine organo-mineral component of the unit is comprised of silty pedofeatures containing black punctuations and silt sized minerals. Trampling is evidenced by the dense accumulation of Iron (up to 10%). With the exception of one horizontal band of quartz grains trapped between layers of amorphous black material there is no coarse mineral component.

Unit C

The organo-mineral fine material within this unit is highly compacted, though there are soil fauna channels and occasional large vughs. Included within this matrix are several turf fragments and one pot sherd; the turf fragments are identified by their heterogeneous coloration and the higher ratio of black amorphous material compared with the rest of Unit C. The mineral components of both of these features match the local geology.

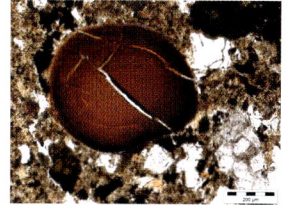

Illus 12.22 K33, disturbed compacted ash and turf layers in Unit A (OIL), Illus 12.23 K33, heat-altered clay in Unit B (PPL) after Goodman-Elgar (2008), Illus 12.24 K33, well-decomposed plant matter PPL, Illus 12.25 K33, ash in Unit C PPL and Illus 12.26 K33, groundmass Unit D showing anorthic iron nodule, iron accumulation and bone fragment (OIL)

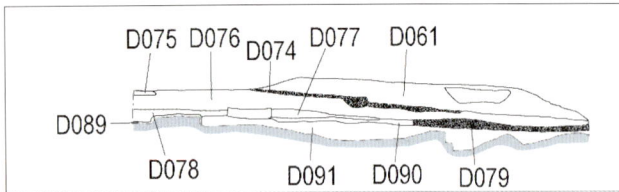

K36

There are three micro-stratigraphic units, A, B and C corresponding with [D091], [D090] and [D076] respectively (Illus 12.31). Within Unit B several layers of ash, charcoal and turf represent different phases of deposition/accumulation. The mineral composition throughout the slide is consistent with the background geology.

Unit A

This unit is highly mineral (approx. 31-85%), reflecting the close proximity of this context [D091] to the underlying bedrock; it is anthropogenically sterile.

Unit B

This unit is composed of five layers of material, B1-B5; layers B2-B4 are well bedded with smooth horizontal boundaries whilst B1 and B5 exhibit irregular boundaries. B1 is a dark deposit incorporating black amorphous material (5-20%), charcoal (<1%) and bone burned at low and moderate intensities (<1% each). It is approximately 2334μm in depth. B2 is a homogenous well decomposed turf layer containing white ash (<1%) and charcoal (<1%), it is approximately 2158μm in depth. B3 is a burnt peat layer (dominant 50-70%) containing charcoal (<1%) and bone burned at moderate intensity (<1%). It is approximately 5839μm in depth. B4 contains ashy peds (white ash, OIL 1-5%), black and yellow amorphous material (5-20% and 1-5%) and bone burned at moderate and low intensities (<1% each) within brown coloured matrix. It is approximately 5745μm in depth. B5 is the final layer within Unit B, it is characterised by a light coloured matrix that is due to the concentration of white ash (20-40%); this layer also contains charcoal (5-20%), burnt peat (1-5%) and a compact layer of turf material (1-5% - Illus 12.32).

Unit C

This unit contains very frequent un-burnt peaty moss (20-40%) containing fungal spores and diatoms (1-5% and <1%); it is responsible for the over-all spongy microstructure (together with channels and vughs). There are many silty and impure clay infill pedofeatures (5-10%) some contain diatoms. The unit also contains amorphous black material (1-5%), unburned bone (<1%) and turf inclusions with smooth borders).

Conclusions

Area C

Turf wall core

In thin section the wall core is noted to be loose soil mixed with turf. The materials used to construct turf walls at Dùn Èistean were of local origin and were likely collected from areas free of human settlement as there are no indications of cultural or domestic activity within the sample set, with the exception of one charcoal fragment within K26. The construction materials in thin section do not exhibit high densities of either phytoliths or organic matter that indicates that topsoils and subsoils were preferred over O horizons.

Later turf bank

The micromorphology suggests the contexts recorded within Kubiena tins K29 and K30 were accumulation layers that built up over time. It is unlikely that bioturbation features and in situ iron accumulation would have occurred at the same time, as soil fauna requires relatively dry conditions whilst iron

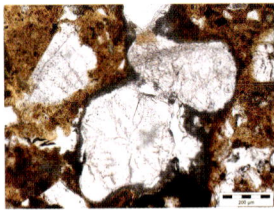

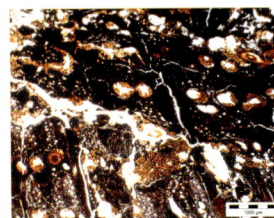

Illus 12.27 S facing section, Trench D, Structure D16 (showing contexts) and Kubiena tins in situ, Illus 12.28 K34, coarse mineral grains fused together with ashy material in microstratigraphic Unit B (PPL), Illus 12.29 K35, scan showing micro-stratigraphic units and Illus 12.30 K35, groundmass, Unit B showing charred mossy peat (PPL)

accumulation occurs in the wet; it is therefore inferred that the contexts became very wet at some point, perhaps due to the deposition of extra material upon the land surface. If this is the case, the earlier occupation phase where grass/peat was burned (perhaps for vegetation clearance), was covered by the later turf bank (this is supported by the presence of textual pedofeatures).

Area D
D7 turf wall
The turf wall slump contains small amounts of cultural material such as burned bone and charcoal though is mainly composed of dry sandy turf; this demonstrates that the materials used in the later turf wall construction were sourced from an occupied area, though not directly from a midden or hearth context. Ashy material incorporated into the basal turf layer originates from an area of high temperature burning (not the hearth within the original structure (D050)).

Earliest deposit below hearth
This context (D084) contains a compacted layer of ash and charred peat. Although this is truncated by the construction of the later turf wall, it could be the only evidence of a floor layer visible within the D7 samples.

Hearth and later deposit
The layer below the hearth (D080) appears to be natural sandy turf mixed with ash, charcoal and bone relating to various burning temperatures. There is not enough ash or burned material to suggest this context was a hearth or that ash has filtered down higher up the profile; another hypothesis is that the section of the context sampled by K19 may be close to an earlier cooking fire which pre-dates the main hearth (D050) (or even the original structure) by enough time to allow wind-blown and alluvial sedimentation (sand and textual pedofeatures).

Above this, the main hearth appears much disturbed by later bioturbation and trampling; it appears to relate to moderate burning temperatures, with a few areas of high intensity.

The trample layer above the hearth reflects the structure falling out of use, and cultural material may have washed, or blown in or been accidentally trampled in around this time. The occurrence of bioturbation features throughout K19 indicates the contexts were reworked by soil fauna; and the high frequency of textual pedofeatures in the lowest two contexts gives rise to the possibility that the structure was neglected or unroofed for a period of time.

The lowest microstratigraphic unit within sample K20 relates to the decomposition of bedrock with no evidence for cultural activity; this was followed by a gradual phase of sediment accumulation evidenced by textual pedofeatures. Carbon and burned peat was then deposited upon this layer before a partial turf roof or wall collapse occurred; immediately after this, a turf capping was placed over the collapsed material and the accumulation of domestic material including bone and charcoal began.

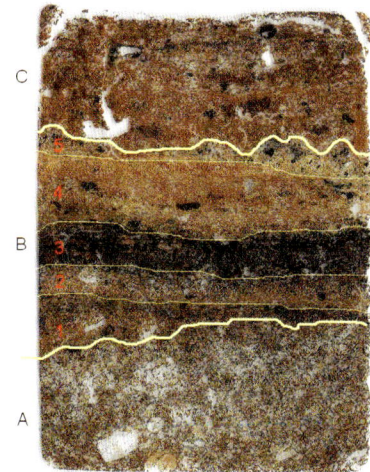

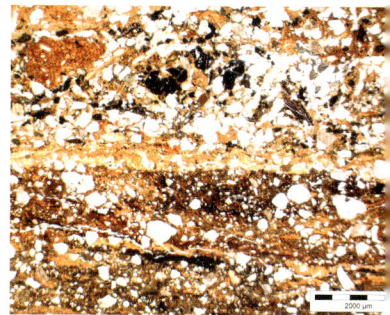

Illus 12.31 K36, scan showing micro-stratigraphic Units A, B (including 6 layers) and C, and Illus 12.32 K36, showing compact turf layer within Unit B5 (PPL)

D16

East and south-facing hearths or floors

All samples typically exhibit horizontal bedding with massive microstructures and very few pore spaces, demonstrating they were subjected to post deposition trampling. Evidence of domestic activity such as bone, grass/peat ash, burnt peat/ animal manure and charcoal indicate that hearth fires were burned at a variety of temperature ranging from low (evidenced by bone fragments) to high (evidenced by white and pale yellow ash). Inclusions of peat or moss, horizontally oriented with spongy microstructures, few minerals and high occurrences of fungal spores appear to have been brought in from another, wetter, area to cap fires or provide a new surface. Very few of the 'ash layers' are wholly composed of ash, most contain textual pedofeatures or unheated minerals and have undergone extra, post-depositional processes. When considered together, these features do not support a simplistic interpretation of the area as either hearth sequences or floor layers alone; instead it appears the area may have been exposed to surface weathering (evidenced by linear bands of minerals, textural pedofeatures, diagenesis of bone material, ferruginous pseudomorphs of plant matter, iron nodules and accumulation, black punctuations of fine material and the moderate amount of soil fauna bioturbation features) and the gradual accumulation of domestic waste material by trampling, washing and blowing in.

Area F

The turf used in construction came from a drier, sandier area than that used in Area C; evidence from sample K20 may suggest that Structure D7 in its early phase was roofed with similar material. In the roof collapse, there is very little evidence of domestic or cultural material visible in thin section but the wall slump contains a moderate concentration of burnt peat and charcoal. The fuel residues suggest high intensity/temperature burning, though not in situ. The steady accumulation of domestic material over time is visible in K2 (Illus 12.34) and in K4/K5 high intensity occupation debris (including fish bone) display features of frequent iron movement; all of this evidence suggests that the structure was occupied for a long period of time. The boundary between the turf roof collapse and the floor layer in K4 and K5 has been shown to be very sharp, leading to the suggestion that the turf roof collapsed whilst the structure was in use. There is no evidence of ashy material incorporated into the floor, but randomly oriented plant stem remains indicate thresh-like material could have been utilised.

Area G

The samples recovered from Area G can be sub-divided into two categories, K7, K8 and K9 exhibiting one construction technique and K11 and K12 a second. The natural and basal layers were detected in K7 (Units A and B), and the hypothesis that turf material was spread over the ground prior to wall construction can be confirmed.; coarse sand was then deposited upon this layer

Area F Results: Illus 12.33-12.38 and Table 12.6 on CD at back of book
Area G Results: Illus 12.39-12.46 and Table 12.7 on CD at back of book

before the main wall core was added. The early phase of building (identified in samples K7, K8 and K9) incorporated a mix of amorphous peat and slightly humic sand forming separate, compacted microstratigraphic and discrete units with sharp boundaries. Such boundaries demonstrate the deliberate stacking of different materials that could have then been trampled and 'puddled' (K9 is the best example of this possibility), however it is also possible that the weight of materials further up the profile could have caused the compaction. Samples K11 and K12 are entirely composed of well-compacted sandy turf and represent a different phase of construction using materials gathered after the site had been occupied for a period of time (eg charcoal). Visually and once semi-quantified, all materials appear to have been sourced from a different area to those in Areas C, D and F.

Soils analyses
by Jo McKenzie

Introduction and objectives
Forty soil samples, each consisting of approximately 100g of soil, were taken from a range of locations within excavation areas C, D, F and G during the DEAP 2007 excavation season. Sampling focused on hearths, floor surfaces, and wall constructions, as detailed below. In addition, two non-archaeological 'background' samples (listed as B1 and B2 in the data charts herein) were taken from two locations elsewhere on the stack, at least 20m from any known archaeological activity, and from a point within the A horizon, approximately 10-15cm below the current ground surface. These were intended to provide a natural baseline for all the soil properties measured in the analysis. All samples were analysed for pH, loss-on-ignition (organic content), magnetic susceptibility, and total phosphate content. Laboratory work was undertaken at the University of Stirling.

The bulk soil sampling strategy was aligned with that of the micromorphological analysis, with each micromorphologically-sampled deposit having its accompanying bulk sample (the exception to this was Area F, for which only one soil sample could be processed: only the most general points may therefore be made here about this part of the excavation). Many of the soil properties listed above are of use in aiding interpretation of micromorphological features, and thus the two analyses exist in tandem. The objectives of each area investigation identified within the accompanying micromorphological analysis can therefore be revisited, alongside further aims relating more directly to the soil analysis:

Structure C: To examine the makeup of the turf walling at C004, examining the source of construction materials and investigating the nature of related occupation/ground surface layer(s). To this can be added investigation of the nature of the deposits identified as relating to the kiln itself (C045, C051).

Structure G: To examine the wall core construction and explore samples for evidence of construction technique.

Structures D7 and D16: To characterise the hearths sampled in both structures, examining burning temperature and fuel materials used.

Structure F: To examine the makeup of material identified as originating from floor layers, hearth deposits and turf walls within this structure. This aim was unfortunately compromised by the successful processing of only one sample from this structure.

Methodology

Prior to analysis, soils were air-dried for two weeks and then sieved to 2mm.

Soil pH

This follows the standard method of Bascomb (1974). 10g of the <2mm fraction of each sample was weighed into a glass beaker, to which 25ml distilled water was added. This was stirred and left to stand for 30 minutes, after which determination of the pH of the solution was made using a glass electrode pH meter calibrated to pH 4, 7 and 10 one hour prior to the commencement of measurement. 2ml of 0.01M calcium chloride was then added by pipette to each soil solution and the pH measured again using the same method as described above. The addition of calcium chloride simulates the salts normally present in soil, thus making the solution more buffered against variability between samples, and it is this second measurement that is quoted in the text. Soils were measured twice to ensure that a stable measurement had been reached.

Loss on ignition

Here, the air-dried, <2mm fraction was further oven-dried at 105°C to ensure complete dryness. Approximately 10g of each sample was then accurately weighed out into a crucible and placed into a muffle furnace and left overnight (16hrs) at 375°C (Ball 1964). After being left to cool in a dessicator, the samples were then re-weighed to determine the percentage loss of mass resulting from the ignition of the organic fraction. The long-cool burn scheme was chosen out of caution and the possibility of shell, carbonates and clay fractions being affected were a higher temperature used.

Magnetic susceptibility

This was measured using a Bartington MS2B desktop meter (Dearing 1994), using standard 10g sample pots. Samples were measured at both low and high frequency, enabling frequency dependant as well as mass specific magnetic susceptibility to be measured.

Particle size

25 g air-dried soil was carefully disaggregated using a pestle and mortar and clay particles dispersed by addition of Calgon. The sand fraction was then separated by sieving, and the clay fraction measured by sedimentation using a 500 ml cylinder and following Stoke's Law. The silt fraction was calculated by difference: Silt (%) = 100% - (sand + clay).

Total phosphate

This was determined through the sodium hydroxide fusion method, following the procedure given in Smith and Bain (1982). Colorimetric determination of a 5ml aliquot of the treated sample was then undertaken using an ammonium molybdate/ascorbic acid reagent, with an allowance of 2 hours for colour development. Standard solutions were made ranging from 0-10 mg P. The absorbance of the standards and samples was measured in a 40 mm cell at 880 mm. The standards were used to plot a graph of absorbance against relative concentration (mg P), from which the total phosphorus (mg/100g) was calculated for each sample and then converted to total phosphate ($P_2O_5/P_2 = 9141.96/61.96 = x\ 2.29$).

Structure C: the kilnbarn

Samples were taken from two locations along the main east-west section through Structure C. To the west, six samples were taken through the four layers of wall core (C056, C059, C074, C076) making up the interior of main barn turf wall C004, degraded bedrock layer C037 and natural bedrock C044. Moving east, five additional samples were taken: one through possible occupation/use layer C031, a second through C037 at this point, and, still further east, three through sequence C045/C051/C071 (organic material in kiln flue, possible collapse of flue clay lining, possible ground surface under kiln bowl).

The turf wall

pH for the turf wall sample set (Illus 12.47-12.48) ranges between 5.37 (at uppermost context C056) and 6.20 (at natural bedrock context C044). Thus the deposits become increasingly more alkaline towards the base of the turf wall and into the natural. Although the varied chemical character of Lewisian Gneiss makes it hard to predict a typical pH for the bedrock, this pattern

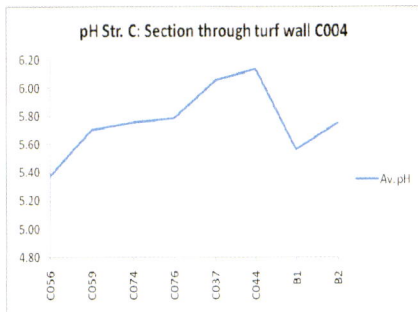

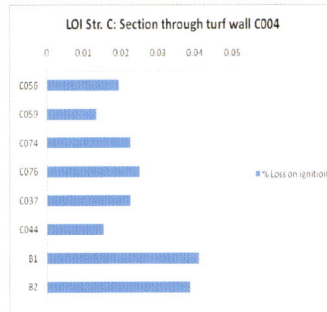

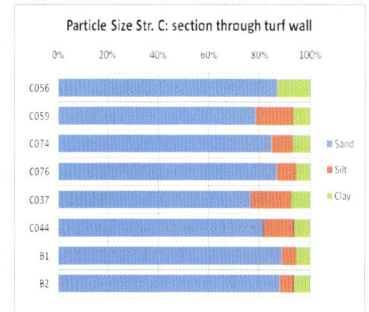

is not surprising: the higher soil organic matter component which would be expected from a turf wall structure is associated with lower pH, due to higher levels of biological action leading to organic decomposition and subsequent production of humic acids (Entwhistle et al 2000, 183). For the same reason, pH is significantly lower in both background samples than in the bedrock. However, it can be seen that the loss-on-ignition plots for the turf wall do not in fact follow the same pattern, with LOI varying throughout the profile, upper context C059 showing a lower organic matter component than bedrock C044, and background samples B1 and B2 having a significantly higher LOI than all of the archaeological samples. Clearly the composition of the turf wall may be more varied than the pH values might suggest. Looking at the micromorphological data, it can be seen that although indicators for organic materials are relatively rare, there are clear variations through the profile: traces of fungal spores can be seen at context C076, but after that, only in bedrock C044. C076 (the highest of the LOI values) also shows more organic fine material than C059 directly above (see McKenna and Simpson, above). It appears that this context may represent a particular concentration of degraded organic matter. Iron accumulations are also seen throughout the profile, indicating a general lack of free drainage and therefore the potential for 'pockets' of material with differing composition to survive.

Finally, LOI values for the profile as a whole are very low. This is perhaps surprising, and again suggests that the composition of the turf wall may be more varied than expected, with a high overall percentage of solid mineral material relative to turfy/peaty matter going into the original construction. Again, this is supported by the micromorphology, with very little extant organic material, such as peat or plant tissues, being seen.

The results of the particle size analysis do not provide any further insight into the precise makeup of the turf wall. There appears to have been an error in the processing of Sample C056, for which a >100% total of clay and sand resulted in a minus figure for silt content. The graph in Illus 12.49 shows no silt content for this sample, and the sample should be discounted. Otherwise, all deposits are sand-dominated, with varying minor percentages of silt and clay present (Illus 12.49). While the sandy nature of the profile overall supports

Illus 12.47 pH through Structure C turf wall samples, Illus 12.48 Loss-on-ignition (organic matter) through Structure C turf wall samples and Illus 12.49 Particle size analysis of the Structure C turf wall samples

the suggestion that the wall core was largely made up of solid mineral material, there is little correlation between those deposits showing higher levels of organic matter (eg C076) and those showing higher levels of silt/clay (eg C037) which could assist with further interpretation of the derivation of the turf wall material. A comparison with the two very similar background samples, however, clearly shows a homogenous, strongly sandy natural for the Dùn Èistean stack which the turf wall deposits deviate from strongly enough to demonstrate their construction from the amalgamation of a variety of materials.

Moving on to the total phosphate values, some similarity to the loss-on-ignition results can be seen, with a gradual increase to the centre of the wall core with a small 'peak' at context C074, then a drop to bedrock C044. As a measure of organic 'additions' to a deposit and therefore the extent of direct anthropogenic activity, the total P patterning supports the picture of the turf wall seen in the micromorphological and LOI studies: as a potentially very variable series of deposits, with perhaps the input characteristics of individual turves being seen thanks to a general lack of drainage through the core. As with the LOI, these values are relatively low, suggesting a high mineral matter content relative to additions with higher phosphate such as surface organic material.

Illus 12.50 Total phosphate through Structure C turf wall samples and Illus 12.51 Magnetic susceptibility through Structure C turf wall samples

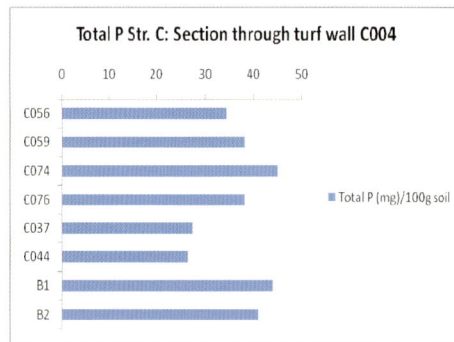

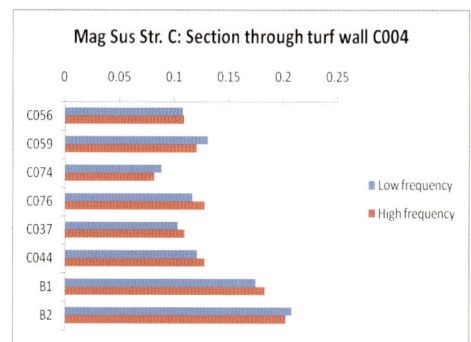

The magnetic susceptibility readings show a slightly different profile and one that provides another angle on the makeup of the wall core deposits. As well as reflecting local geological conditions (the variability of which upon Lewisian Gneiss precludes a 'typical' reading here), the magnetic susceptibility of a sample chiefly indicates heating and disturbance of a deposit. Samples are measured in both 'low' and 'high' frequency magnetic fields. Both readings (Illus 12.50-12.51) give an overall measure of magnetic susceptibility. The difference between these two readings gives the frequency dependant susceptibility, which reflects the amount of ultrafine ferrimagnetic minerals present in the deposit. Such particles are often formed through high intensity burning (Dearing 1994) and thus both a high magnetic and frequency dependant susceptibility can be a good indicator of the presence and intensity of burning activity as well as redeposition of materials or other disturbance. Here, it can be seen that overall magnetic susceptibility is low compared to the background samples, and that frequency dependant susceptibility is fairly low, with high and low frequency readings similar for all contexts. It would seem that the wall core contexts show little sign of disturbance (especially organic-richer context C076 – a reason for the greater survival of its organic materials?) and heated or burned materials are minimal. This concurs with the micromorphology, which identified only one fragment of charcoal and very little identifiable peaty material present in the sequence. The material used in the wall core is therefore likely to have originated from an area some distance from any settlement, and appears not to have seen heating, mixing or other disturbance once in place within the structure.

The kiln and surface deposits

PH values here are far more varied, potentially reflecting the very different character of these latter series of samples (Illus 12.52-12.54). A wider range is seen, from 5.50 in kiln flue residue

Illus 12.52 pH through Structure C kiln/surface samples, Illus 12.53 Loss-on-ignition (organic matter) through Structure C kiln/surface samples and Illus 12.54 Particle size analysis through Structure C kiln/surface samples

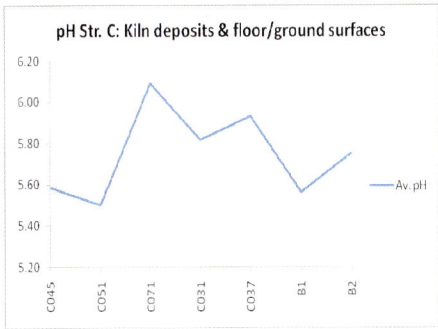

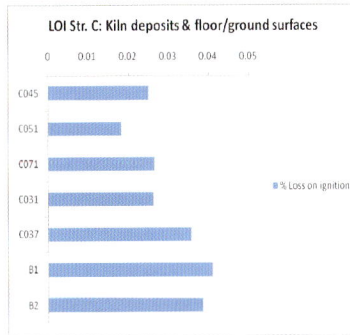

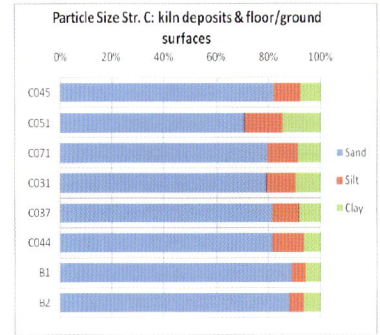

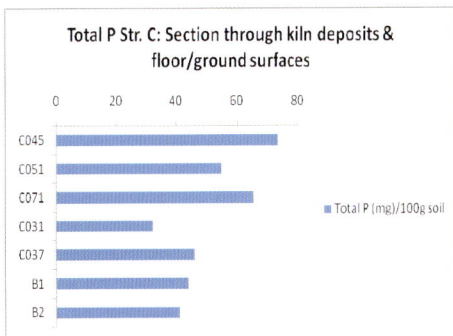

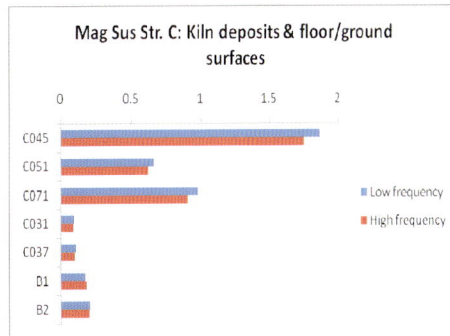

C045 rising to 6.09 immediately below, in kiln flue clay lining C051. The lower pH of C045 would support its interpretation as an organic residue. pH for degrading bedrock context C037 is slightly lower here than seen in the wall core profile, though it is comparable, and rises slightly from possible occupation surface context C031 above – in general, it seems that pH still rises to the base of the profile and the natural bedrock. The higher pH of clay lining C051 may relate to this, indicating its derivation from natural clay source.

Despite the interpretation of C045, however, LOI results show this deposit as lower in organic matter than degrading bedrock context C037, and with similar LOI to possible occupation layer and old ground surface contexts C071 and C031 (again, all values are very low overall, although these values are higher than those for the wall core sequence). This pattern is supported by the particle size analysis, which shows remarkable similarity between all deposits (apart from C051) - again, there is no indication from soil texture that C045 has a markedly different makeup to C037 or C071. Micromorphological analysis supports this, with C045 showing a dominantly mineral profile and little sign of organic inclusions (McKenna and Simpson, above). It would appear that the kiln residue material is not primarily organic in nature.

Particle size analysis once more shows that the Structure C deposits are generally sand dominated, though with markedly larger silt and clay components than seen in the natural background soil. The exception to this is context C051, whose significantly larger clay (14.5%) and silt (14.7%) component confirms the on-site interpretation of this deposit as a clay lining for the kiln.

The total phosphate results turn this on its head however, with C045 showing a markedly higher total P than the rest of this and the wall core sample sequences (Illus 12.55-12.56). Likewise, magnetic susceptibility results for this sequence show a massively higher reading (and greater frequency derived susceptibility) than elsewhere here and in the wall core samples. The nature of the residue deposit at C045 is therefore highly puzzling. In particular, a magnetic susceptibility reading which eclipses the (still high compared to the wall core samples) kiln lining context would not be expected.

Illus 12.55 Total phosphate through Structure C kiln/surface samples and Illus 12.56 Magnetic susceptibility through Structure C kiln/surface samples

One possible interpretation is that the impermeable nature of the kiln lining deposit C051 directly below this context may act to prevent leaching of materials from C045, resulting in a relatively high P content despite there not being significant levels of organic matter present. However, a more plausible explanation (particularly given the magnetic susceptibility readings) may be indicated by the micromorphological analyses through context C045, C051 and C071. These do not fit the expected profile, with clay kiln lining context C051 described as 'very dark due to the frequent amounts of both charcoal and black amorphous material...contains phytoliths...larger fragments of charcoal correspond to charred plant tissues indicating that this context is composed of burnt turf or heath plants' (see McKenna and Simpson, above). This does not sound at all like a clay lining context. By contrast, C045 above is described as largely mineral and lacking organic material. It is possible that, despite the peculiarities of the C051 particle size profile, there is more of a degree of mixing of materials (and thus more varied soil chemistry) than was indicated in the field. Should this be the case, then it is puzzling: the nature of these contexts (clay lining, subsequent residue) should result in their being discrete and clearly defined. This location may therefore repay further study. Overall, however, the significantly higher magnetic susceptibility readings seen in the three contexts adjacent to the kiln confirm their relationship to the structure – all have clearly seen significant heating events.

Structure G: the tower wall-core

Seven samples were taken through a series of deposits making up the core of wall G004 in Structure G, the ruined rectangular tower set at the highest point of the stack. These were: natural (possibly levelling) deposit G067, primary wall core deposit G066 (two samples), subsequent wall core deposits G061 (three samples), G060 and G059.

pH readings for this sequence are the lowest in the whole sample set (ranging from 4.84-5.48), and show very little variation through the sample set (Illus 12.57-12.59). They are very similar to that of the background samples. Organic matter values show similarly little variation, and are uniformly low, notably lower than the background samples. Clear patches of what are interpreted as peat deposits are intermingled with more mineral-dominated material in Illus 12.59. The variability in the Total P values from this sample sequence may be a result of sampling through such a variable profile. Despite the relatively frequent incidence of peaty and 'turfy' organic components identified in the micromorphological analysis (see below), it would appear that the overall chemical 'profile' of the Structure G samples is mineral.

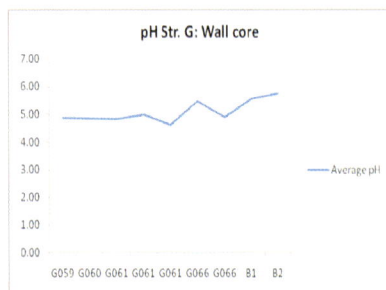

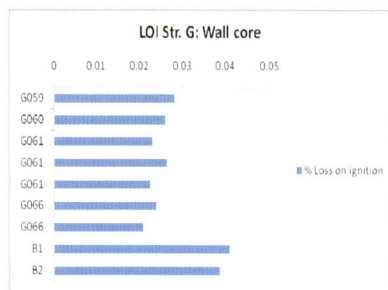

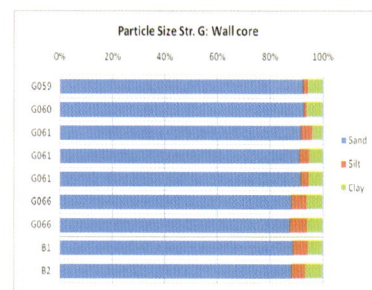

Illus 12.57 pH through Structure G tower wall-core samples, Illus 12.58 Loss-on-ignition (organic matter) through Structure G tower wall-core samples and Illus 12.59 Particle size analysis through Structure G tower wall-core samples

This is very much supported by the particle size analysis. An overwhelmingly sand-dominated series of deposits is seen, with upper deposits G059 and G060 showing minimal amounts of silt and clay. Clay and silt percentages increase slightly through G061 and further into G066, which, as with pH, is exceedingly similar to the background samples. Overall however, the tower wall core is made up of a series of coarse, sandy deposits which appear to have resulted in a heterogeneous, poorly mixed matrix as seen under the microscope.

Following the same pattern, magnetic susceptibility values are similarly uniform, and lower than the background samples (Illus 12.60-12.61). Total phosphate values are more variable. Overall, they show slightly lower P than the Structure C wall core samples, with values of 20-30 mgP/100g soil. There are however notable 'spikes' of P at uppermost context G059 and the lower sample of mid wall core context G061.

Although visible organic components increase towards the top of this sample set in

Total P Str. G: Wall core

Mag Sus Str. G: Wall core

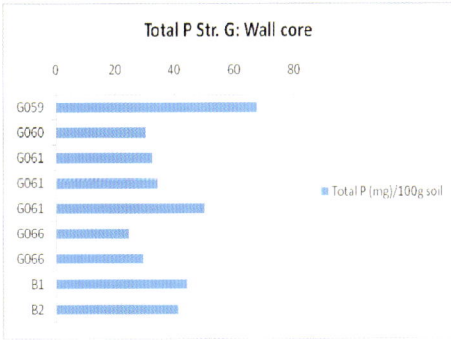

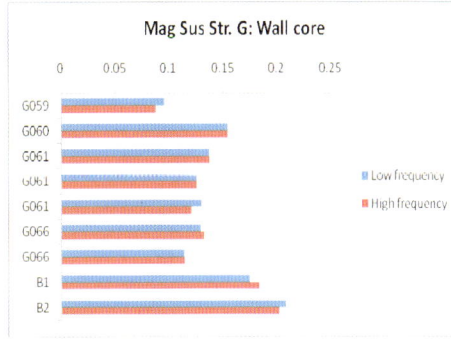

Illus 12.60 Total phosphate through Structure G tower wall-core samples and Illus 12.61 Magnetic susceptibility through Structure G tower wall-core samples

the micromorphological data, there is no clear reason for these spikes apart from as a reflection of the general variability of the wall core material as displayed by the micromorphology (Illus 12.62). Micromorphologically, there is a clear contrast between the structure of the wall core material seen here, and that seen in the Structure C wall core – where the latter is completely mineral dominated, almost all micromorphology samples within the Structure G wall core show clear patches and/or inclusions of peat, turf and amorphous organics, implying either a greater reliance on these materials in this construction, or perhaps a more coarsely mixed, possibly less compressed and less comprehensively degraded structure.

Illus 12.62 Kübiena sample K9 showing context G061

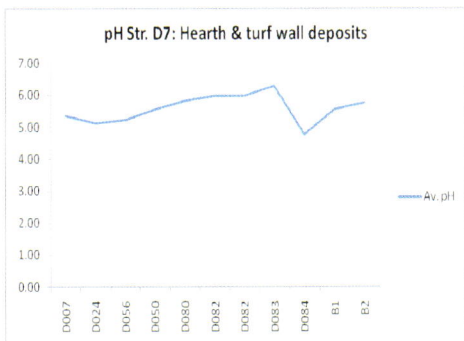

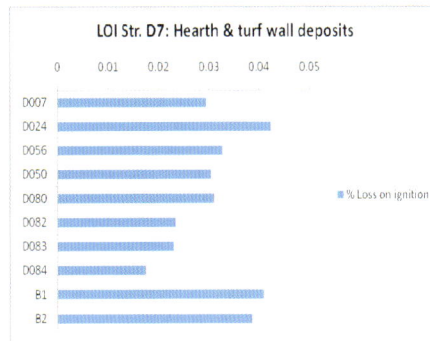

Structure D7: Hearth and turf wall deposits

Eight samples (nine for pH) were taken from the area of the central hearth in Structure D7, a small sub-rectangular to circular turf building on the edge of the Structure D complex. These were as follows: base of hearth deposits D084, D083 and D082, lower hearth deposit D080, main hearth deposit D050, hearth sweepings D056, trample over hearth D024, and slumped turf wall D007.

pH shows relatively little variation down the profile, starting at 5.35 at turf wall deposit D007 and gradually becoming more alkaline to 5.97 at hearth base deposit D083 (Illus 12.63-12.64). There is then a sharp swing to acidity at D084. It is possible that this represents a lowering in the (alkaline) ash content at this point in the sequence, below the main hearth activity, although the micromorphological analysis does identify 'fragmented bands of homogenised ash and peat' within this layer (McKenna and Simpson, above). It would seem that ash content further up the profile is far greater than this still relatively ashy deposit.

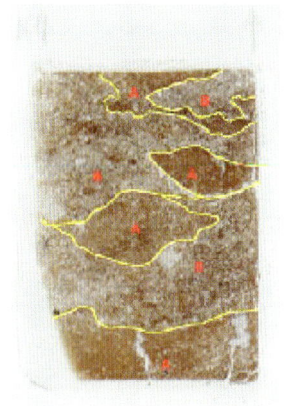

pH Str. D7: Hearth & turf wall deposits

LOI Str. D7: Hearth & turf wall deposits

Illus 12.63 pH through Structure D7 hearth and turf wall deposits and Illus 12.64 Loss-on-ignition (organic matter) through Structure D7 hearth and turf wall deposits

Organic matter content (LOI) appears slightly low for this sample sequence, being only slightly higher than that seen at the two wall core sample sets (Structures. C and G). Although a hearth deposit need *not* show high organic matter content, given that the majority of the material preserved will be (mineral) ash, the micromorphological analysis of the Structure D7 hearth contexts show that charcoal, burnt peat and other organic materials are frequent, with even large fragments of bone present (McKenna and Simpson, above). Within the LOI values, trample over

Illus 12.65 Particle size analysis through Structure D7 hearth and turf wall deposits and Illus 12.66 Magnetic susceptibility through Structure D7 hearth and turf wall deposits

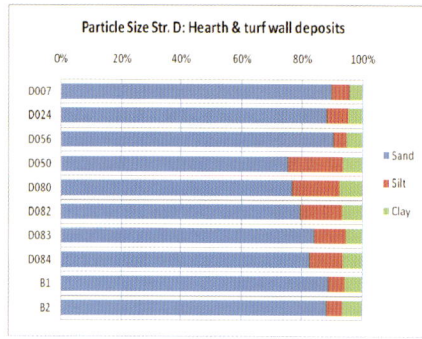

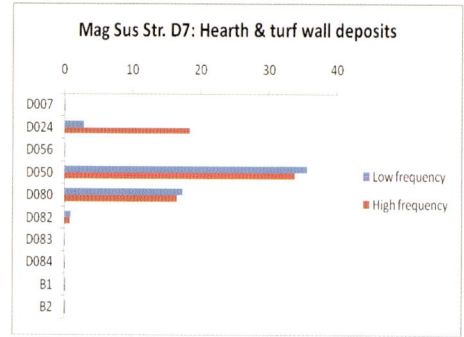

hearth context D024 stands out as an organic matter 'peak'. Micromorphological analysis of this context suggests the opposite: that this context shows an *absence* of organic materials, and is mainly composed of compressed, variable mineral material brought in from a variety of locations as trample underfoot. The organic matter values for this sample set are therefore puzzling.

Particle size analysis is more explicable, showing three very similar and strongly sandy upper deposits (D007, D024 and D056) before a swing to much higher silt and to a certain extent clay percentages within hearth deposits D050, D080 and D082 (Illus 12.65-12.66). This presumably represents the more varied hearth makeup with its higher incidence of organic materials. Only slightly lower silt percentages identify base of hearth deposits D083 and D084 with the hearth itself rather than the sandier upper deposits or with the background samples. Texturally, then, hearth trample D024 fits its micromorphological signature, rather than its unexpectedly high organic matter content, being nearer in textural nature to the slumped turf wall above it.

The total P results are interesting (see Illus 12.67). Values are significantly high, with peaks of 326 and 321mgP/100g soil at main hearth deposits D050 and D080, and even hearth base context D084 producing a P-value of 71 mgP/100g soil, higher than any context previously discussed. This can be related directly to the presence of organic materials, and perhaps especially bone, within the hearth deposits. While the frequent charcoal, peat and turf materials identified under the microscope will have contributed to this very high P-content, very high levels of phosphate have been associated with intensive burning of bone in other Hebridean contexts (McKenzie 2008), and it is suggested from these values that bone inputs account for more of the material processed through the Structure D hearth than would appear from the micromorphological analysis. It would appear that despite lower deposits D082-D084 having a similar texture to the main hearth deposits above, the material inputs into them are entirely different.

An interesting picture is also presented by the magnetic susceptibility results (Illus 12.66). Extreme variability is seen here, with notably high susceptibility seen in main hearth contexts D050 and D080, a less significant enhancement at hearth base context D082, and a higher enhancement with a vastly pronounced frequency dependent susceptibility reading at trample context D024. This is most normally a signifier of high intensity burning, but can also indicate disturbance (Dearing 1994). It is likely that this reading confirms the origin of

Illus 12.67 Total phosphate through Structure D7 hearth and turf wall deposits

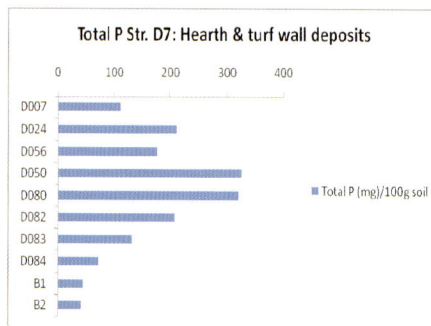

this deposit as trample – having seen repeated disturbance as well as the bringing in to the deposit of a variety of foreign materials and a range of mineral types, as indicated by the micromorphological analysis (McKenna and Simpson, above). The enhancements in main hearth deposits D050 and D080 confirm not only the high intensity burning noted in the micromorphological analysis, but also the lack of real heating in base hearth deposits D082 and D083.

Structure D16: Hearth deposits

The second hearth to be sampled within the Area D buildings complex, large rectangular Structure D16 saw a detailed series of samples taken through the large central E-W and N-S sectioned hearth. This provided a double set of samples for many of the key deposits identified in both sections. The S facing section saw samples taken through main hearth deposit D061 (x2), lower hearth layers D074, D076 and D078, concreted ash deposit D090, and below-hearth deposit D091. The E facing section sampled through D073, representing the sweepings from hearth D061, lower hearth deposits D075, D076 and D078, concreted ash deposit D090 and below-hearth deposit D091.

pH for the two profiles shows a more alkaline signature for the hearth sweepings than the hearth itself – presumably representing a greater quantity of ash rakeout in the sweepings and more organic material in the main hearth area (Illus 12.68-12.70). This is confirmed by the micromorphological analysis, which describes context D073 as mainly orange and yellow peat ash with black amorphous punctuations interpreted as fine particles of leaf and charcoal (McKenna and Simpson, above) while the D061 sample shows turf fragments, plant tissue fragments and even a potsherd. The lower hearth deposits are more variable in pH, which again may be related to differing amounts of organic inclusions. More puzzling are the very different pH values seen for base deposits D090 and D091 in the two profiles. In the E facing section, these show more acidic responses compared to the deposits above them, while in the S facing section, they become more alkaline. Micromorphology sheds some light on this – the two deposits appear to be highly variable in the two sections, with the E facing section deposits showing a higher incidence of organic inclusions, and the S facing section deposits either sterile (appearing as natural bedrock) or ash-rich (McKenna and Simpson, above). These observations highlight the great potential variability in the makeup of apparently discrete, homogenous deposits over a large

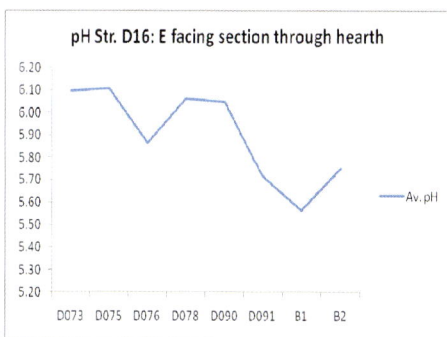

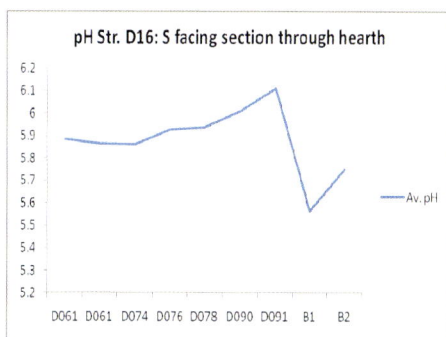

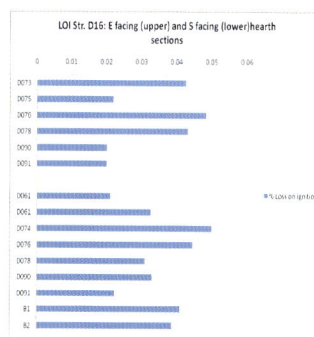

hearth area.

Organic matter values, as is the case with the rest of the DEAP sample set, are generally low. Lower hearth deposits D073, D074, D078 and especially D076 (in both profiles) show the highest organic matter content. Micromorphological analysis of these deposits identify frequent, and large, organic inclusions. The high organic matter for D076 in the E facing section corresponds with the identification of a 'linear red-amorphous organic horizon containing large fragments of grass, wood and leaf charcoal, plant fragments, very few silt-sized mineral grains, fungal spores and limpid clay textual pedofeatures' (ibid). The highest organic matter value, D074 in the S facing section, is seen in thin section as a very dark deposit, composed

Illus 12.68 pH through Structure D16 hearth deposits in E facing section, Illus 12.69 pH through Structure D16 hearth deposits in S facing section and Illus 12.70 Loss-on-ignition (organic matter) through Structure D16 hearth deposits in E and S facing sections

Illus 12.71 Particle size analysis through Structure D16 hearth deposits in E and S facing sections and Illus 12.72 Total phosphate through Structure D16 hearth deposits in E and S facing sections

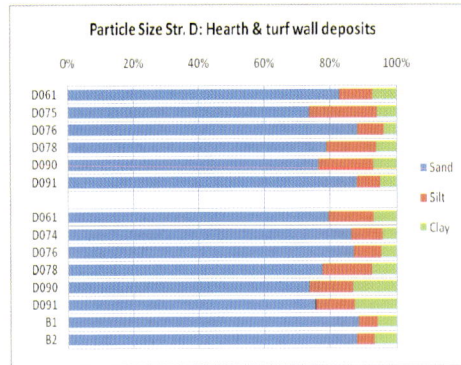

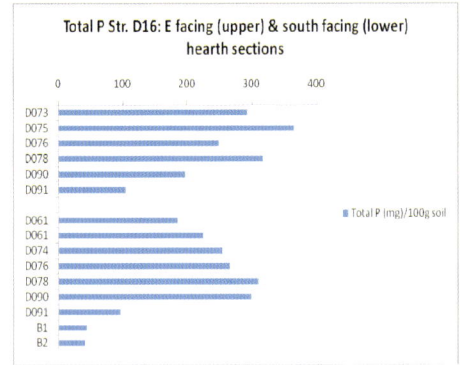

mainly of black amorphous organic material and charred moss/peat (ibid). By contrast, lower hearth deposit D075 in the E facing section is dominated by pale ash and coarse minerals. Both micromorphology and bulk soil analyses build a picture of a series of hearth deposits that vary greatly both spatially and temporally.

This variability is also seen in the results of the particle size analysis (Illus 12.71). Whilst showing the generally very sandy character seen elsewhere on site and within the background samples, the D16 hearth deposits show more within-profile variability than any other sample set. As with the D7 hearth, the deposits are generally siltier than the background samples, presumably reflecting the more variable, organic nature of the hearth inputs. However, unlike D7, the D16 deposits also show significant variation within the clay fraction, which is often significantly higher than that seen in the natural. Again, the great complexity and variability in hearth inputs as seen in the micromorphological analysis is the most probable source of this. Notable contexts here are D075 in the E facing section, with a significantly high silt component most probably derived from its high ash content, a pattern also seen in D078 and D090 (though the micromorphological analysis does not show a high ash content for D078) (McKenna and Simpson, above) and D090 and D091 in the S facing section, whose clay content is almost as high as that seen in the clay kiln lining in Structure C (at 12.9% and 12.5% respectively). A high clay component in these two lower deposits may, through preventing leaching and cycling of nutrients, be at least partly responsible for higher phosphate and organic matter readings throughout this S facing section. Interestingly, deposit D090 in the E facing section shows a completely different texture, and one very similar to the sandier background samples. Once again, the great variability of the deposits through the entire hearth area is highlighted.

Total phosphate values show similar variability, but with some unexpected results (Illus 12.72). Most notable is the fact that the highest phosphate reading comes from lower hearth deposit D075 in the E facing section – the silty, low organic matter deposit described above. Crucially however, micromorphological analysis identifies traces of both burned and unburned bone fragments (McKenna and Simpson, above). These are present in trace amounts through both of the profiles, even within the below-hearth deposit D090 where high phosphate is indicated (S facing section). With phosphate values extremely high overall, it is suggested (as in the Structure D7 hearth sequence) that the burning of bone was likely to have been a highly

Illus 12.73 Magnetic susceptibility through Structure D16 hearth deposits in E and S facing sections

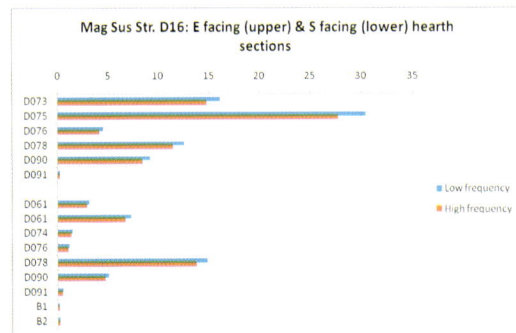

significant part of activity on the hearth.

The magnetic susceptibility readings for the two D16 hearth section sequences show an interesting degree of variability both spatially and temporally (Illus 12.73). Whilst underlining the point made above – that this large hearth feature varies quite substantially in character over time – more specific factors can be noted. The highest readings by far are those for lower hearth context D075 – a context with ash and bone inclusions and a notably silty nature, but certainly not the strongest evidence for heating. The possibility of some disturbance or redeposition of material at this location should therefore be considered. Secondly, unlike hearth D7, here we see that the main hearth deposit itself - D061 - does not show nearly as much enhancement as several of the lower hearth deposits and even 'below hearth' deposit D090. With the micromorphological analysis showing varied amounts of burnt organics, ash, bone and peat/turf material in the majority of these samples, it requires an overall measure such as magnetic susceptibility to identify that the more significant heating episodes may not have been those associated with main hearth D061.

Structure F

The final Dùn Èistean structure to be sampled for bulk soil analyses was Structure F. Unfortunately however, only one of the bulk sample set from this area could be processed. This was F047, a deposit of hearth sweepings relating to the second phase of the occupation of the structure. Although closely related to micromorphologically-sampled contexts F022, F023 and F035 context F047 was unfortunately not sampled in thin section.

The pH for context F047 was 5.83, a reading most comparable to that of degraded bedrock context C037 in Structure C. Although slightly more acidic than the background samples, this is also in the range seen within the majority of the hearth-related deposits in the sample set. The loss-on-ignition value is 0.038% - a reading easily comparable with the rest of the sample set, as it is almost exactly the same as that from the second background sample. As such, it actually represents a relatively high reading in the context of the (very low in organic matter) Dùn Èistean sample set. Looking to the micromorphological evidence available for adjacent hearth sweeping contexts F026 and F035 (McKenna and Simpson, above) organic material appears to be relatively rare within these contexts, with ash predominating. However, with no thin section sample available from F047 it is difficult to draw firm conclusions as to the likely makeup of the deposit. Particle size analysis provides a sand:silt:clay ratio of 84%:8.8%:7.16% - characterising the deposit as dominantly sandy, but with an increased percentage of silt and clay relative to the background samples. Clay is particularly high, comparable with that seen in eg hearth deposit D078. Again, this is within character for the archaeological deposits at Dùn Èistean as a whole.

Magnetic susceptibility readings are 10.15 and 9.28 $10^{-6}m^3kg$ high and low frequency respectively, giving a frequency dependant susceptibility of 8.5%. These are high readings, with a significant frequency dependant susceptibility indicative of disturbance – not surprising for a hearth-related deposit. Total phosphate values are however low, at 14.2 mgP/100g soil – the lowest readings in the sample set, and lower too than the background samples. Again, however, further interpretation of these results is difficult given the lack of supporting data either in the form of related bulk soil data from the trench, or supporting micromorphological evidence from context F047. However, what we can see from thin sections through related deposits F022, F023, F026 and F035 is that those deposits interpreted as hearth - related (F026 and F035) are relatively low in anthropogenic material such as fuel residues, while trampled floor deposit F023 and even wall tumble F022 are richer in burned materials. It appears likely that hearth sweeping deposit F047 follows the pattern seen in these other hearth-related deposits, with a relatively low incidence of fuel residues, although the character of the deposit in general is in keeping with hearth-related deposits seen elsewhere on site.

Overall conclusion
by Jo McKenzie

The micromorphological and bulk soils analyses conducted at Dùn Èistean have made a significant contribution to increasing our understanding of a wide range of occupation activities at the site, and the role of both human-induced and natural processes in the makeup of the archaeological deposits. The inclusion of background samples in the bulk soil analysis has provided a baseline for soil properties against which modification of the natural material on the stack can be assessed. Bulk soil analyses characterise a strongly sandy, slightly acidic soil with low levels of organic matter and a correspondingly relatively low total phosphate values. Micromorphology confirms that the mineralogy of all the deposits relates clearly to the background geology (Lewisian gneiss) of the stack.

A major part of the soil analysis programme was to investigate the nature of construction activity at Dùn Èistean, and to look at variation in this throughout the range of structures extant on the site. Sample sets through the wall core of tower Structure G, and turf wall constructions within Structures C, D and F illustrate that construction at Dùn Èistean took a range of forms and utilised a wide range of materials. Thin sections through the Structure G wall core show a very variable soil matrix, with large patches of dark, organic-rich material showing charcoal, peat and degraded plant material contrasting with more extensive, lighter areas of more mineral-dominated material. Boundaries between contexts appear sharp (eg G067/G066) and the matrix appears relatively loosely packed and the organic components not particularly well degraded. By contrast, the turf wall core sampled in Structure C has hardly any organic inclusions (indicating sourcing a certain distance away from the occupation areas of the site), and shows a far more well compacted soil matrix, again, mineral dominated. Although organic matter and particle size analysis show that both constructions appear to have relied on the sandy stack soils (rather than the organic 'peaty' material which may have been expected to make up the bulk of, for example, the Structure C turf wall), the two constructions are very different in character. Further sampling through the slumped turf wall of Structure D7 shows yet more variation - here, burnt peat and organics indicate that construction material is likely to have been sourced from near to occupation areas, unlike in the adjacent Structure C. Similar inclusions are seen in the Structure F wall collapse deposit. Clearly, construction methods and materials at Dùn Èistean varied from structure to structure.

A second key aspect of the soils analysis was investigation of the makeup of hearth deposits. Two hearths – the large central hearth in Structure D16 and the smaller D7 hearth – were intensively sampled in thin section, revealing a huge range of incorporated materials. The D16 hearth shows a variety of burned and unburned inclusions, including charcoal, burnt and charred mossy peat, peat ash, decomposed plant matter and amorphous organic materials, large peat fragments and burnt and unburnt bone. The presence of diatoms, fungal spores and iron nodules indicates that fuel residues were imported from both wet and dry source areas. Sampling through both the east and south facing sections of this large feature also allowed an insight into the complexity of the hearth stratigraphy at the microscopic scale, with repeating bands of ash and organics in the east-facing section contrasting with the more disturbed, but strongly compacted ash and turf layers of the south-facing section. Bulk analyses highlighted further points of interest, with magnetic susceptibility indicating that in fact, the most intensive episodes of heating may not have been associated with 'main hearth' deposit D061. Very high levels of phosphate in certain bone-rich deposits echo evidence from other Hebridean sites, where high phosphate levels in hearth contexts appear to indicate intensive burning of bone, and possibly the deliberate use of this material as a fuel source. pH, organic matter and particle size analyses for all of these deposits indicate great variation in the makeup of even small areas of the D16 hearth. Although much smaller, the hearth below D7 indicates a similar range of fuel residues in use, and evidence of burning episodes at a range of temperatures-here, variations in ash colour indicate burning through 400-800°C. Once again, high phosphate levels seen in association with bone indicate the possible use of bone as a fuel source.

A look at the results of each of the bulk soil analyses at the site scale helps build a more detailed picture of variation in on-site activity, particularly where soil properties deviate from the 'background norm'. Spikes in pH within the hearth sequences (eg D084) appear to indicate high ash levels, and variation in pH throughout the turf wall of Structure C highlights its potentially poor drainage. Organic matter levels are low throughout the site, making higher readings, such as kiln deposit C045 and hearth deposit D076 particularly interesting. Particle size analyses confirm that the sandy stack soils are the likely source of construction material throughout the structures, but variation in the percentages of silt and clay present help elucidate the nature of certain deposits - confirming for example the interpretation of C051 as a clay lining for the kiln, highlighting the finer texture of many of the key hearth deposits, and confirming the coarse, loose nature of the Structure G tower wall core material. Total phosphate 'spikes' in association with bone in the hearth deposits are discussed, and similarly high readings help to indicate the presence of organic materials in several of the other hearth deposits. Conversely, low phosphate readings, for example in the Structure G tower wall core, help confirm their sterile nature. Patterns of magnetic susceptibility throughout the hearth deposits help build a picture of burning intensity, and high readings in other contexts indicate exposure to heating events (eg C045). Frequency dependant susceptibility, an indicator of disturbance, is low in the Structure C and G wall core sequences, but produces very notable spikes in certain deposits – for example, confirming the interpretation of 'trample' deposit D024.

Both bulk soil and micromorphological analyses also highlight events and features not discoverable through excavation. In D7, thin section slide K20 shows a band of turf-like material separating hearth base deposit D082 from main hearth deposit D080   not visible during excavation, this feature indicates some hiatus in activity here, such as a period of abandonment or perhaps some collapse of roofing material. Adjacent to this in the sequence, organic inclusions, compression features and bands of ash and peat indicate a likely established surface between the basal layer of the turf walls and hearth base deposit D084. Both micromorphological and bulk soil analyses highlight a potential issue with the separation and elucidation of contexts C051 (kiln clay lining) and C071 (the organic debris in the flue), which is discussed in detail in the text. The presence of fungal spores in some turf wall and turf roof related deposits (eg Structure C) but not in others (eg Structure F) indicates different kinds of turf materials – both dry and sandy as well as wet and peaty - being in use on the site.

Illus 13.1 Close-up of carbonised material

thirteen

the dating evidence

Radiocarbon dates were produced for 33 samples from Dùn Èistean of charred barley and oat grains (*Hordeum vulgare* and *Avena sativa*), a charred Hazel nut (*Corylus avellana*) and a fragment of Birch charcoal (*Betula*). The resulting dating evidence produced a coherent chronological sequence ranging from the mid-fifteenth to the mid-seventeenth centuries AD. It was not possible to define which of the features excavated at Dùn Èistean were built first, due to the similarity in the dates. However, the application of a statistical model as well as the input of stratigraphic information identified two broad phases of activity – the earliest grouped between AD1440-1635 and including the construction and use of Structures A1 and A2, early features below B1, the use of the kilnbarn Structure C, the hearth below D7, and midden deposits below D16, the first occupation phase of Structure F and the construction and re-build of the tower in Trench G. The later features returned age ranges spanning AD1465-1670 and included the upper hearth within Structure A1, the use of Structure B1, the later use of the kilnbarn in Trench C, the use of Structure D10, the use of D16 and the second use of the building recorded in Trench F.

by Zoe Outram and Catherine M Batt

Introduction and methodology

The dates have been summarised in Table 13.1, and have been assessed in sequence in order to produce a chronology for the site. The dates have also been assessed within a Bayesian model in an attempt to refine the age ranges using the stratigraphic relationships of the sampled deposits. Note that the phasing information used in Table 13.1, and in the subsequent discussion of the dates relate to trench-specific phases, and not to the site as a whole.

Table 13.1 Summary of the radiocarbon dates produced for Dùn Èistean (continues over)

Trench	Building	Phase	Sample	Material	Context	Description	Depositional context	Uncalibrated (Years BP)	Calibrated 2-sigma	Delta-13C ‰
A	A1	3	GU-20446	Charred barley	A032	Dark red-brown compact clay/charcoal from the upper hearth	Primary	375±30	AD1445-1635	-23.3
		3	GU-20447	Charred barley	A034	Compact orange clay from the intermediate hearth	Primary	345±30	AD1465-1640	-24.9
		3	GU-20448	Charred barley	A036	Dark brown-black compact ash layer from the intermediate hearth	Primary	380±30	AD1445-1630	-25.3
		3	GU-20449	Charred barley	A037	Compact grey-black ash layer in the primary hearth	Primary	365±30	AD1450-1635	-22.5
	A2	3	GU-20450	Charred barley	A030	Black hearth deposit with patches of red and orange compact clay	Primary	420±30	AD1425-1620	-22.3
		3	GU-20451	Charred barley	A067	Orange brown material	Secondary or tertiary	360±30	AD1450-1635	-23.2
B	B1	4	GU-20454	Charred oat	B068	Peat ash hearth deposit	Primary	260±30	AD1520-1955	-24.5
		4	GU-20458	Charred barley	B0101	Brown-black charcoal hearth deposit	Primary	320±30	AD1480-1645	-25.9
	Earlier features below buildings	3	GU-20455	Charred barley	B102	Charcoal and peat ash material interpreted as the possible sweepings from the hearth	Secondary	410±30	AD1430-1620	-23.6
		3	GU-20456	Charred barley	B103	Mid-brown sandy layer overlying the hearth	Secondary or tertiary	380±30	AD1445-1630	-23.8
		3	GU-20457	Charred barley	B078	Orange-yellow silt layer representing a possible hearth	Primary or secondary	390±30	AD1440-1630	-25.1
	B4	4	GU-20452	Charcoal (Betula)	B092	Mid grey-brown clay with charcoal flecks and patches of peat ash interpreted as a possible occupation surface	Secondary	365±30	AD1445-1635	-25.6
	B5	4	GU-20453	Charred barley	B079	Dark brown clay-silt with frequent charcoal flecks and crushed pottery, interpreted as an occupation deposit	Secondary	335±30	AD1470-1645	-24.8
C	Kilnbarn	3	GU-20459	Charred barley	C068	Orange peat ash from within the entrance to the flue and the inner area of the kiln	Primary	340±30	AD1470-1640	-24.6
		3	GU-20460	Charred barley	C078	Black sandy ash from the kiln fire flue	Primary	350±30	AD1455-1635	-24.4

Trench	Building	Phase	Sample	Material	Context	Description	Depositional context	Uncalibrated (Years BP)	Calibrated 2-sigma	Delta-13C ‰
D	D10	5	GU-20462	Charred barley	D068	Dark brown clay bedding	Secondary or tertiary	335±25	AD1480-1640	-25.3
	D16	4	GU-20463	Charred barley	D061	Orange brown-bright orange silt-ash-clay hearth deposits with charcoal	Primary	335±30	AD1475-1640	-24.8
		4	GU-20464	Charred nutshell (Corylus avellana)	D074	Black compacted silty clay ash from the lower hearth	Primary	365±30	AD1450-1635	-22.6
		4	GU-20467	Charred barley	D075	Bright yellow silt-sand peat ash from the lower hearth deposit	Primary	390±30	AD1440-1630	-24.2
		4	GU-20465	Charred barley	D076	Mottled dark grey-brown, yellow and black sandy-silt peat ash	Primary	370±30	AD1445-1635	-24.1
		4	GU-20468	Charred barley	D079	Dark yellow-brown, black and orange peat ash from the lower floor layer	Secondary	365±30	AD1450-1635	-25.3
	Middens below walls of D10 and D14	3	GU-20469	Charred barley	D036	Mixed layer of very dark greasy silt-clay with patches of peat ash	Secondary or tertiary	355±30	AD1455-1635	-25.0
	D7	5	GU-20461	Charred barley	D024	Mottled brown and bright orange/red silty-clay and peat ash – the interface/ trample layer overlying the hearth	Secondary or tertiary	380±30	AD1445-1630	-25.3
		4	GU-20466	Charred barley	D056	Yellow and black ashy-silt with charcoal, interpreted as the sweepings from the hearth	Secondary	385±25	AD1445-1625	-25.2
F		4	GU-20470	Charred barley	F026	Peat ash swept from the hearth	Secondary	350±30	AD1455-1635	-24.3
		4	GU-20471	Charred barley	F023	Trampled floor layer containing peat ash	Secondary or tertiary	320±30	AD1480-1645	-24.9
		3	GU-20472	Charred oat	F042	Trampled floor layer containing charcoal	Secondary or tertiary	385±30	AD1440-1630	-24.2
		3	GU-20473	Charred barley	F033	Mixed floor layer	Secondary or tertiary	360±30	AD1450-1635	-24.3
G	Tower rebuilt	4	GU-20476	Charred barley	G029	Trampled wall core layer deposited on the ground outside the tower	Tertiary	365±30	AD1450-1635	-22.3
		4	GU-20474	Charred barley	G059	Wall core material in tower wall	Secondary	395±40	AD1435-1635	-25.2
	Construction, use and collapse of the first tower	3	GU-20478	Charred barley	G050	Upper surface of floor/basal level of interior 'room' inside the tower	Secondary	395±30	AD1440-1630	-23.8
		3	GU-20475	Charred oat	G061	Wall core layer in the tower	Secondary or tertiary	385±30	AD1440-1630	-28.9
		3	GU-20477	Charred barely	G073	Wall core layer in the tower	Secondary or tertiary	360±30	AD1450-1635	-24.5

Table 13.1 continued Summary of the radiocarbon dates produced for Dùn Èistean

The sampled material

The selection of suitable material for radiocarbon dating is crucial to the production of an objective chronology. The majority of the dates were produced on charred cereal grains (*Hordeum vulgare* or *Avena sativa*), as they represent small, chronologically coherent, seasonal entities that do not require marine correction (Harris 1987). However, the small size of the cereal grains may permit post-depositional movement through interstices in a deposit and so only secure deposits were investigated. In addition, a charred Hazel nut (*Corylus avellana*) and a fragment of Birch charcoal (*Betula*) were also utilised. Care is needed when using charcoal for radiocarbon dating due to the 'old wood' problem (Schiffer 1986), where wood may be reused for several years; this is particularly important for islands such as Lewis, which is largely tree-less in nature, increasing the risk of wood being recycled.

All of the sampled materials related to plant matter, and so it was necessary to investigate if the any of the plants had suffered fractionation, which would result in an overestimation of the age of the material. This was investigated using the delta-^{13}C (δ^{13}C) ratios (Table 13.1), which were compared to the recommended values for terrestrial plants in the area of study, which in this case is -20±1‰ (Richards et al 2006, 123). It was concluded that fractionation had not occurred for any of the plants sampled from Dùn Èistean and so does not need to be discussed further.

Methodology

The archaeological information was used to arrange the dates into stratigraphic order as well as to investigate the formation of the contexts, and the origin of the material sampled. This would affect the chronological significance of the resulting dates, and could also be used to explain the presence of any anomalous dates in the chronology. The methodology used was based on the work of Schiffer (1987), developed by Dockrill at the Old Scatness Broch site, Shetland (Dockrill et al 2007, 46-49). Deposits were defined on the basis of what had happened to them prior to their incorporation into the archaeological record, summarised in Table 13.2.

A primary deposit represents the most chronologically significant information, while the tertiary deposits represented the lowest. In the case of tertiary material, it was not clear how much time elapsed between the initial formation of the deposit and the incorporation of the material into the archaeological record.

The deposits sampled from Dùn Èistean were predominantly primary or secondary in nature, and therefore sampled deposits of the highest chronological significance. The majority of the sampled deposits related to material collected from stratified sequences of hearth deposits

Table 13.2 The definition of the types of archaeological deposits sampled for scientific dating

Deposit type	Description	Example	Reference
Primary	An in situ deposit that was not moved since it was created.	Hearth deposits, dedicatory deposits or microrefuse trodden into a floor.	Schiffer 1987, 58
Secondary	Material moved once from the site of its creation. The boundaries separating deposits would be clear and distinct.	A midden, or the material raked out from a hearth	Schiffer 1987, 58; Dockrill et al 2007, 46
Tertiary	Material moved on more than one occasion before being incorporated into the archaeological record, shown by homogenised deposits with diffuse boundaries.	The use of midden deposits to level an area	Dockrill et al 2007, 46

and occupation surfaces, which therefore directly date to the use of the structures that were sampled. Of the 33 deposits sampled for dating, 13 represented a primary deposition event, eight sampled a secondary deposit, and one sampled a tertiary deposit. A further 10 samples represented material corresponding to either a secondary or a tertiary deposit, with one final sample representing either a primary or a secondary deposit. It can therefore be concluded that chronology was based on the more chronologically significant information, with 66% of the dates being produced from primary and secondary deposition events.

It is clear when the dates in Table 13.1 are assessed that they all returned very similar calibrated age ranges. This is partly due to a plateau within the radiocarbon calibration curve between cal AD1440-1600. This restricts the resolution available for this period, and the conclusions that can be drawn from the dating evidence. In addition to this, the majority of the calibrated age ranges were bimodal in form, giving two possible date ranges at 95% confidence, further complicating the assessment of the chronological information. The dates were therefore statistically assessed in an attempt to reduce the size of the age ranges and increase the resolution of the resulting chronology. A Bayesian model was used, allowing the archaeological information to be combined with the chronological information through the translation of the stratigraphic order of the deposits into a statistical function (Buck et al 1991; Buck et al 1994). The OxCal 4.1.4 programme was selected for the analysis as it allowed chronological models to be built easily and produces clear graphical outputs that display the models imposed on the sequence through the production of probability distributions plots of the selected dates (Bronk Ramsey 1995). OxCal 4.1.4 also utilises the most recent calibration curve, IntCal09 (Reimer et al 2009) to calibrate the radiocarbon dates (Bronk Ramsey 2009).

All dates are presented in this report at 95% confidence (2σ levels). The radiocarbon dates were incorporated into the model as uncalibrated dates (R-Dates), being calibrated during the statistical assessment of the sequence. The dates were arranged into a sequence, representing the stratigraphic order of the sampled deposits. A number of the dates were also placed into a 'phase', defined as an unordered group of events which have no known relationship, but which share stratigraphic relationships outside of the phase (Bronk Ramsey 2010).

The use of the boundary function within an ordered sequence of dates is the most complicated aspect of Bayesian analysis, as the results are very sensitive to the assumptions made about the sequence (Steier and Rom 2000; Steier et al 2001; Bronk Ramsey 2000). A boundary was used at the beginning and end of each sequence produced for the Dùn Èistean dates, with additional boundaries being used to represent breaks in the phases of activity. This may represent an episode where a new floor was re-laid over the previous surface, or where a structure was temporarily abandoned. Two alternative models were utilised to represent a break in a sequence:

1. A contiguous sequence – the sequence of dates before and after the break follow on from each other without a significant hiatus.
2. A sequential sequence – where there is a sequence of dates, a break, and another sequence of dates.

For a number of the sequences, both models were applied in order to determine the impact that they have on the dates. Following the application of the two models if a significant

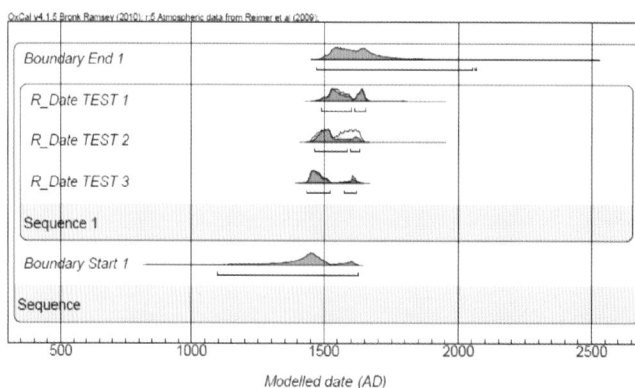

Illus 13.2 An example of the probability distributions produced using OxCal 4.1

difference was not identified the simplest model was used for discussion in the report, which related to a contiguous sequence.

Following the application of the statistical model to a sequence, a second probability distribution was produced that demonstrated how the age ranges were affected by the inclusion of the stratigraphic information, referred to as a posterior density estimate. An example has been shown in Illus 13.2. Two probability distributions are displayed for each radiocarbon date on the same plot. The light grey probability distributions represent the raw calibrated age ranges, while the dark grey probability distributions represent the posterior density estimates produced following the application of the model to the dates.

The 'agreement index' value (A-values) quantifies the degree to which the dates support the proposed model. The critical value defined for the agreement indices is set at 60%: values below this level were indicative of problems within the sequence and may indicate the presence of residual or intrusive material (Bronk Ramsey 2010). Any dates highlighted as being anomalous were reassessed using the site records.

Inclusion of stratigraphic information can refine the resulting age ranges through the production of posterior density estimates, but it is important to note that these age ranges are the result of a statistical model imposed on the data and the interpretation of the stratigraphy within the field. Any new information, such as additional dating evidence or a different model being imposed on the data will produce different posterior density estimates.

The sequences of dates

The site of Dùn Èistean was divided into several trenches, each of which were assigned a letter. Trenches A, B, C, D, F, and G were sampled for radiocarbon dating, and will be discussed in turn in the following sections.

Trench A

A total of six radiocarbon dates were produced from Trench A, summarised in Table 13.3.

Building number	Context	Sample code	Uncalibrated date BP	Calibrated age range 95.4% confidence
A1	A032	GU-20446	375±30	AD1445-1635
	A034	GU-20447	345±30	AD1465-1640
	A036	GU-20448	380±30	AD1445-1630
	A037	GU-20449	365±30	AD1450-1635
A2	A030	GU-20450	420±30	AD1425-1620
	A067	GU-20451	360±30	AD1450-1635

Table 13.3 Summary of the dating evidence from Trench A

Two structures were recorded in this area: Buildings A1 and A2 represented approximately contemporary structures but which could not be related stratigraphically.

The majority of the radiocarbon dates were produced from hearth material, which could be interpreted as primary or secondary deposits. These dates related to the use of the structures and so are highly significant for the chronology of the site. Context A067 was the exception to this, interpreted as an ashy layer dumped at the base of the wall of Structure A2, and associated with its construction. The context may therefore represent a secondary or tertiary deposition event.

As mentioned above, A1 and A2 could not be related stratigraphically. It was therefore necessary to produce two sequences of dates from Trench A: one that assessed the dates from Structure A1, and a second that assessed the dates from Structure A2. Each sequence will be discussed in turn before the chronology of Trench A is discussed as a whole.

Structure A1

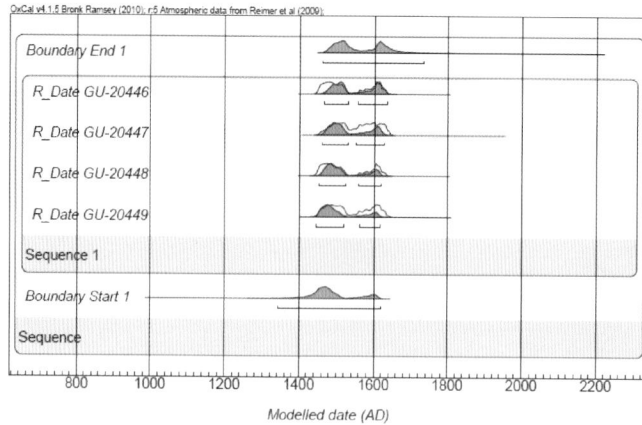

OxCal v4.1.5 Bronk Ramsey (2010); r:5 Atmospheric data from Reimer et al (2009)

Boundary End 1

R_Date GU-20446

R_Date GU-20447

R_Date GU-20448

R_Date GU-20449

Sequence 1

Boundary Start 1

Sequence

800   1000   1200   1400   1600   1800   2000   2200

Modelled date (AD)

Illus 13.3 Probability distributions for the radiocarbon dates from A1

The dates produced from Structure A1 were arranged in sequence, as shown in Illus 13.3. An assessment of the dates in sequence did not highlight any anomalous results, and demonstrated that the dates respected the stratigraphic relationship of the deposits. All the agreement index values returned for the sequence exceeded the critical value of 60%, for the individual dates and for the overall sequence. The application of the model allowed reduced age ranges to be produced following the production of posterior density estimates, summarised in Table 13.4.

Table 13.4 Summary of the posterior density estimates (modelled age ranges) for the dates from Structure A1

Context	Sample code	Unmodelled age range (95% confidence)	Modelled age range (95% confidence)
A032	GU-20446	AD1445-1635	AD1465-1635
A034	GU-20447	AD1465-1640	AD1460-1630
A036	GU-20448	AD1445-1630	AD1455-1620
A037	GU-20449	AD1450-1635	AD1445-1615

The application of the model and the production of posterior density estimates returned age ranges that were reduced by up to 20 years compared to the raw calibrated age ranges. An assessment of the modelled age range could be used to suggest that the phases of activity associated with the use of the primary hearth (context A037) and the use of the upper hearth (context A032) were separated by a minimum of 20 years, or a maximum of 190 years.

Structure A2

Two dates were produced from Structure A2: an ash-based deposit relating to the construction of the structure (context A067), and the material associated with a hearth (context A030) representing the use of the building. The dates were arranged in sequence, as shown in Illus 13.4. A boundary was placed between the two dates to represent the period of time between the construction of Structure A2 and the use of the hearth. The two phases were investigated as a contiguous and then a sequential sequence of events; a significant difference was not noted between the results of the two models, and so a contiguous sequence was applied to the dates (Illus 13.4).

An assessment of the dates in sequence demonstrated that the two dates were not in agreement. Sample GU-20450 returned an agreement index value of only 44.6%, but as there were only two radiocarbon dates produced from this structure, it was not clear which of the samples were anomalous. It is also important to note that the calibrated age ranges produced for the two samples are very similar, with the majority of the age ranges overlapping. A calibrated age range represents the 95% probability of where the true age of the sampled material lies, and

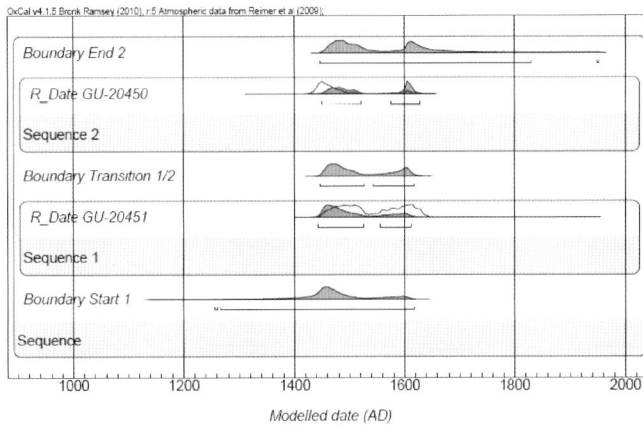

Illus 13.4 Probability distributions for the radiocarbon dates from A2

that the true age may lie at any point within the calibrated age range. Of the 190 years covered by the calibrated age range of GU-20450, 150 of these years completely overlap with sample GU-20451. The model imposed on the sequence can be used to suggest that GU-20450 was anomalous, but this should be regarded as a suggestion only as it is based on the application of a statistical model, and the comparison with one other date. What can be concluded is that the dating evidence from Structure A2 should be investigated further.

Structures A1 and A2

As mentioned above, A1 and A2 were thought to represent approximately contemporary structures. A detailed assessment of the structural remains recorded within Trench A suggested that A2 was built earlier than Structure A1. This hypothesis was investigated by placing the dating evidence from both structures into a single sequence. The sequences were separated by an overlapping boundary that allows approximately contemporary events to be assessed in sequence (Illus 13.5).

The assessment of the dates produced from A1 and A2 together suggested that

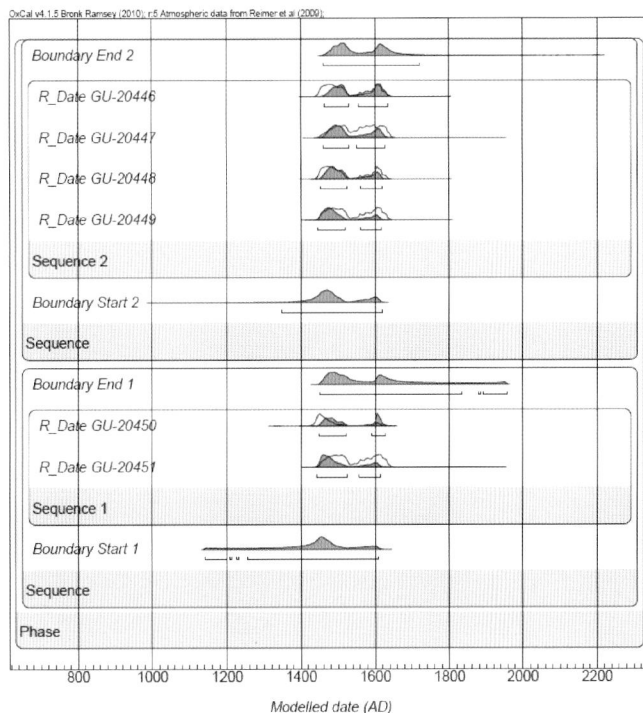

Illus 13.5 Probability distributions for the radiocarbon dates from A1 and A2, investigating the likelihood that A2 was built earlier than A1

sample GU-20450 from context A030, the hearth deposit, potentially sampled residual material and returned a slightly older age range. However, this is based on the assumption that the two structures were approximately contemporary allowing the dating evidence from A1 to be taken into account. It is also important to note that the calibrated age range of GU-20450 was similar to the other dating evidence produced from Trench A: GU-20450 returned an age range of AD1425-1620, compared to the other age ranges grouping between AD1445-1640.

With the exception of sample GU-20450, the assessment of the dates in Illus 13.5 could be used to support the hypothesis that Structure A2 was built slightly earlier than Structure A1; an agreement index value of 78.4% was returned for the overall sequence. In addition, the converse argument was also investigated, assessing the likelihood that Structure A1 was built earlier than A2, summarised in Illus 13.6.

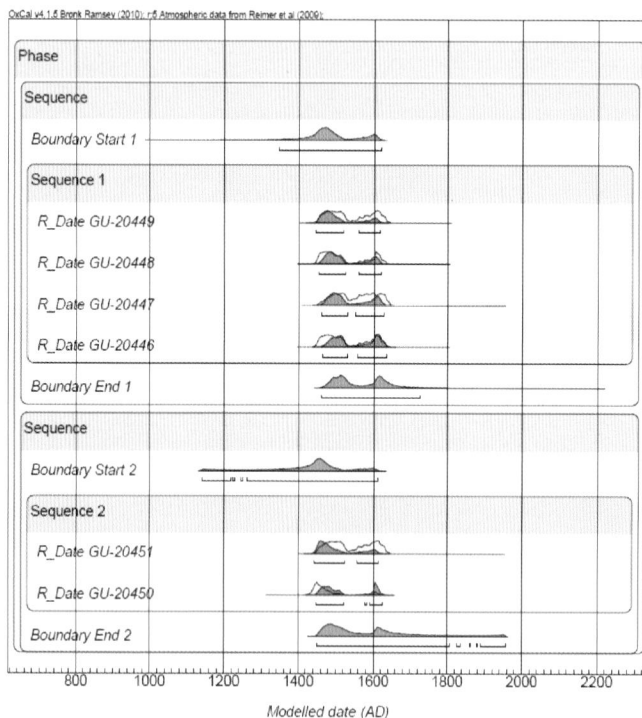

Illus 13.6 Probability distributions for the radiocarbon dates from A1 and A2, investigating the likelihood that A1 was built earlier than A2

The assessment of the model in Illus 13.6 also demonstrated that it was statistically possible that Structure A1 was built earlier than Structure A2. It can therefore be concluded that the strong similarity of the dating evidence from Trench A indicated that the activity recorded was contemporary. The dating evidence supports the archaeological evidence in the hypothesis that Structure A2 was built slightly earlier than Structure A1, but that the converse argument is also possible.

Trench B

A total of seven deposits were sampled for radiocarbon dating from Trench B. The majority of the deposits related to activity within Structure B1 (Phase 4), or from earlier phases of activity that were sealed by Structure B1. A single date each was obtained for Buildings B4 (GU-20452) and B5 (GU-20453), but they could not be stratigraphically related to the other dates from Trench B. The dates will be assessed in terms of how they fit into the chronology of Trench B at the end of this section.

The dates from Structure B1 and the deposits sealed by Structure B1 have been summarised in Table 13.5.

The majority of the dates from Trench B sampled material collected from hearths,

Phase	Context	Sample code	Uncalibrated date BP	Calibrated age range 95.4% confidence
4	B068	GU-20454	260±30	AD1520-1955
	B0101	GU-20458	320±30	AD1480-1645
3	B102	GU-20455	410±30	AD1430-1620
	B103	GU-20456	380±30	AD1445-1630
	B078	GU-20457	390±30	AD1440-1630

Table 13.5 Summary of the dating evidence from Trench B

relating to the use of Structure B1 and the earlier phases. Contexts B068, B101, and B078 sampled material from within hearths and therefore corresponded to a primary deposition event. In contrast, context B102 was interpreted as the sweepings from the hearth across the floor surface, representing a secondary deposition event. Context B103 was described as a sand-clay based deposit overlying the hearth, and may therefore relate to a secondary or tertiary deposition event. The dates were arranged in a sequence, with the two phases of activity separated by a boundary. The boundary represented the period of time between the final use of the hearth in recorded in Phase 3, and the construction and use of Structure B1 in Phase 4. The two phases were investigated as a contiguous and then a sequential sequence of events; a significant difference was not noted between the results of the two models, and so a contiguous sequence was applied to the dates (Illus 13.7).

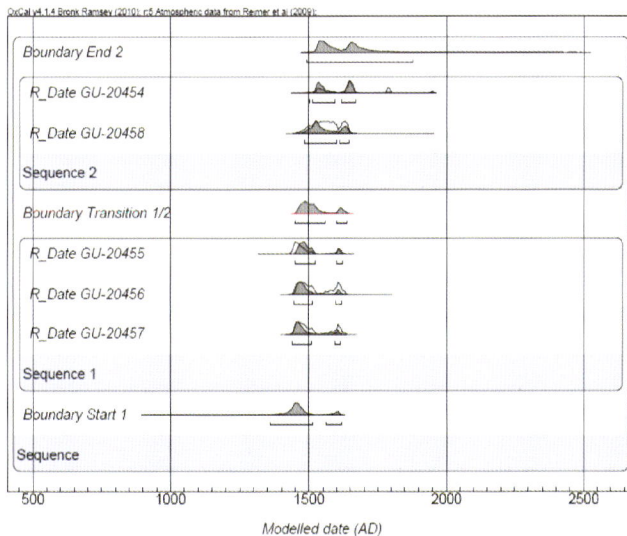

Illus 13.7 Probability distributions and posterior density estimates for the sequence of dates produced from Trench B

The assessment of the dates in sequence did not highlight any anomalous results, with all of the dates respecting the stratigraphic model imposed on them. This was supported by the agreement index values assigned to each individual date, and the overall sequence, which exceeded the critical value of 60%.

The application of the model returned posterior density estimates, which have been summarised in Table 13.6.

The application of the stratigraphic model on the dating evidence has reduced the age ranges of the raw calibrated dates by up to 20 years, with the exception of GU-20454, where the model had a significant impact on the size of the age range assigned to the date. The model used here suggested that the occupation of Structure B1 occurred between AD1485-1670, as indicated by the dates from the upper and lower deposits within the hearth. The application of the model

Context	Sample code	Unmodelled age range (95% confidence)	Modelled age range (95% confidence)
B068	GU-20454	AD1520-1955	AD1500-1670
B101	GU-20458	AD1480-1645	AD1485-1645
BOUNDARY			AD1450-1640
B102	GU-20455	AD1430-1620	AD1450-1620
B103	GU-29456	AD1445-1630	AD1450-1615
B078	GU-20457	AD1440-1630	AD1440-1615

Table 13.6 Summary of the modelled age ranges estimated for the dating evidence from Trench B

suggested that the pre-Structure 1 activity occurred between AD1440 and 1620. It can therefore be concluded that the modelled dates indicated that the two phases of activity dated within Trench B were separated by a minimum of 30-50 years, or a maximum of 230 years.

As mentioned above, the dating evidence from Structures B4 and B5 could not be stratigraphically related to the dates from B1. The dates from the three structures were compared, as shown in Table 13.7.

Structure	Sample code	Date (modelled age ranges in brackets)
B1	GU-20454	AD1520-1955 (AD1500-1670)
	GU-20458	AD1480-1465 (AD1485-1645)
B4	GU-20452	AD1445-1635
B5	GU-20453	AD1470-1645

Table 13.7 A comparison of the dating evidence from Structures B1, B4 and B5

It is clear from a comparison of the dating evidence from the three structures sampled from Trench B were very similar, and may therefore represent contemporary structures. The age range associated from B4 could be used to argue that it represented the earliest structure dated from Trench B. However, this is based on one date, and supporting evidence is required to confirm this suggestion. In addition, the date from B4 was produced on wood charcoal; it is possible that there was a delay between the felling of the tree and the incorporation of the charcoal into the archaeological record, and so further evidence is required to support the evidence from B4.

Trench C

Excavations in Trench C revealed a corn-drying kilnbarn. Two samples were collected from material in the kiln for radiocarbon dating, summarised in Table 13.8.

Context	Sample code	Uncalibrated date BP	Calibrated age range 95.4% confidence
C068	GU-20459	340±30	AD1470-1640
C078	GU-20460	350±30	AD1460-1635

Table 13.8 Summary of the dating evidence from Trench C

The sampled material related to the use of the feature, and could therefore be interpreted as a primary deposit. The two dates were assessed in sequence, as shown in Illus 13.8.

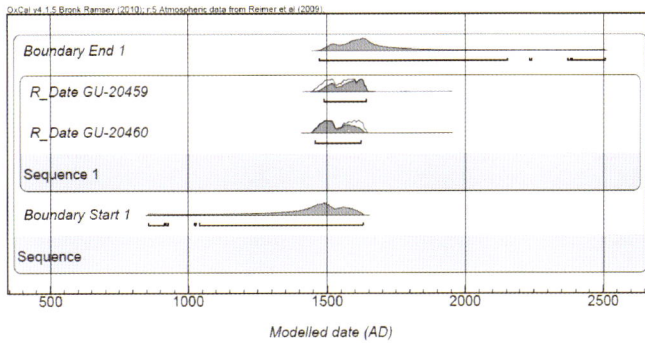

Illus 13.8 The probability distributions and posterior density estimates for the dates from Trench C

The assessment of the two dates in sequence demonstrated that the dates respected the stratigraphic order of the deposits, supported by the agreement index values for the individual dates and for the overall sequence exceeding the critical value of 60%. The model allowed reduced age ranges to be suggested for the dates following the production of posterior density estimates, summarised in Table 13.9.

Context	Sample code	Unmodelled age range (95% confidence)	Modelled age range (95% confidence)
C068	GU-20459	AD1470-1640	AD1490-1640
C078	GU-20460	AD1455-1645	AD1455-1620

Table 13.9 Summary of the modelled age ranges estimated for the dating evidence from Trench C

The application of the model has allowed the age ranges to be reduced by up to 20 years. However, the model has not significantly altered the conclusions that can be drawn about when the feature was in use compared to the raw calibrated dates. This is due to the plateau recorded within the calibration curve at this point in time, and the small number of dates included in the assessment; it has been noted that a statistical model has a greater impact on a series of dates if a greater number of dates are included in the assessment.

Trench D

Trench D represented one of the most complex sequences of events dated at Dùn Èistean. Three separate structures were sampled, Structures D10, D16, and D7, as well as a midden deposit that was directly sealed by the walls of Structures D10 and D14. Structure D16 represented one of the earlier structures within Trench D, with Structure D10 and D7 representing the later structures. With the exception of Structure D7, all of the structures could be related stratigraphically, and so two sequences of dates were therefore assessed: the dates from Structures D10 and D16 were assessed together, as were the dates from Structure D7. The separate sequences will be discussed in turn.

Table 13.10 Summary of the dating evidence from Structures D10 and D16, and context D036

Building and phase	Context	Sample code	Uncalibrated date BP	Calibrated age range 95.4% confidence
D10 Phase 5	D068	GU-20462	335±25	AD1480-1640
D16 Phase 4	D061	GU-20463	335±30	AD1475-1640
	D074	GU-20464	365±30	AD1450-1635
	D075	GU-20467	390±30	AD1440-1630
	D076	GU-20465	370±30	AD1445-1635
	D079	GU-20468	365±30	AD1450-1635
Phase 3	D036	GU-20469	355±30	AD1455-1635

Structures D10, D16

A total of seven dates were produced from material sampled from Buildings D10 and D16. The dates have been summarised in Table 13.10.

The material sampled from Structure D10 related to the bedding for stones of the shelter, sampling a dark brown clay layer that may represent a secondary or tertiary deposition event, and the date will therefore represent a *terminus ante quem* for the event in question: the construction of the wall for Structure D10.

In contrast, contexts D061, D074 and D075 from Structure D16 sampled hearth material that related to a primary deposition event, and therefore corresponded to the use of the structure. The remaining contexts from Structure D16, contexts D076 and D079 were interpreted as possible floor layers that contained mottles of peat ash and charcoal. The well-defined mottles within these contexts suggested that the material had not been disturbed and represented a secondary deposit. The final context dated (D036) related to a midden deposit that was sealed by the wall D010 of Structures D16, D10 and D14, representing a secondary or tertiary deposition event.

It was noted that two dates were produced on material collected from the same hearth: contexts D074 and D075. A comparison of the two dates was interesting as they sampled different materials: GU-20464 from context D074 sampled a charred Hazel nutshell (*Corylus avellana*), while sample GU-20467 from context D075 sampled charred barley grains. The resulting dates were combined using the chi-square test in order to determine if they represented the same deposition event. This hypothesis was upheld following the assessment, with a t-value of only 0.3, compared to the 5% limit of 3.8.

The dates were arranged in stratigraphic order with boundaries placed in between the different phases of activity. The sequences were assessed using both contiguous and sequential sequences; no significant difference was noted and so a contiguous sequence was applied to the

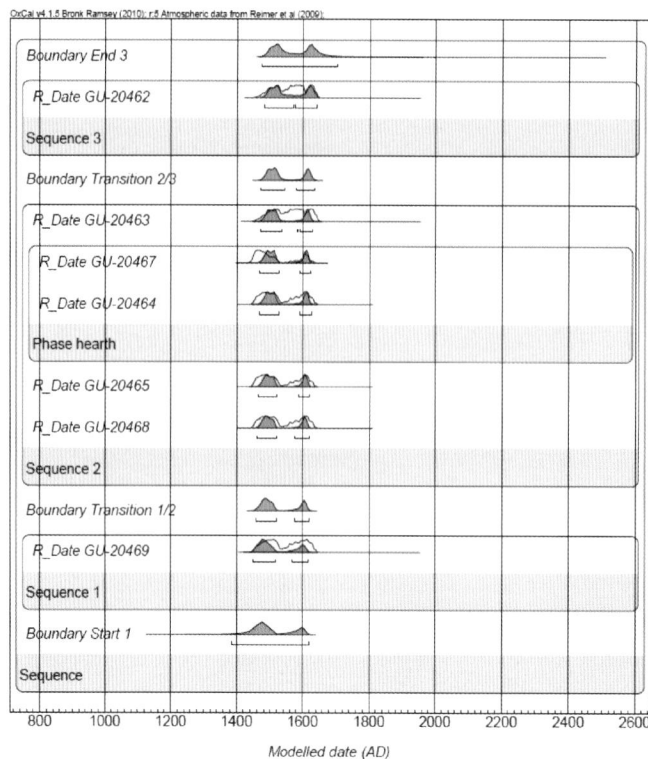

Illus 13.9 The probability distributions and posterior density estimates for the dates produced from Structures D10, D16, and the midden deposit context D079

dates, as shown in Illus 13.9.

The model imposed on the dates returned agreement index values that exceeded the critical value of 60%, demonstrating that the dates respected the stratigraphy. In addition, no

Context	Sample code	Unmodelled age range (95% confidence)	Modelled age range (95% confidence)
D068	GU-20462	AD1480-1640	AD1480-1640
BOUNDARY			AD1470-1635
D061	GU-20463	AD1475-1640	AD1470-1630
D074	GU-20464	AD1450-1625	AD1465-1625
D075	GU-20467	AD1440-1630	AD1465-1625
D076	GU-20465	AD1445-1635	AD1465-1620
D079	GU-20468	AD1450-1635	AD1460-1620
BOUNDARY			AD1455-1620
D036	GU-20469	AD1455-1635	AD1450-1615

Table 13.11 Summary of the modelled age ranges estimated for the dating evidence from Structures D10, D16 and the midden deposit context D079

anomalous dates were identified following the application of the model. The posterior density estimates produced from the applied model have been summarised in Table 13.11, reducing the size of the age ranges by up to 35 years.

The model applied to the dates can be used to suggest that the midden deposit located beneath Structures D10 and D16 was deposited between AD1450-1615. The model also suggested that Structure D16 was in use between AD1460-1630, while the clay bedding for the wall of Structure D10 was laid after AD1480-1640. The modelled age ranges indicate that there was not a significant break between the different phases of occupation in Trench D, with structures being abandoned and built relatively rapidly. It could be argued that the context D036 was deposited less than 10 years before the construction and use of the Structure D16 if the lower limits of the modelled age range are considered. In addition, a minimum of 10 years separated the final hearth sampled from Structure D16 and the building of D10.

Structure D7

The final structure sampled from Trench D was Structure D7, one of the later structures

Phase	Context	Sample code	Uncalibrated date BP	Calibrated age range 95.4% confidence
5	D024	GU-20461	380±30	AD1445-1630
4	D056	GU-20466	385±25	AD1445-1625

Table 13.12 Summary of the dating evidence from Structure D7

recorded in the area. Two dates were produced and are summarised in Table 13.12.

Context D024 sampled a brown and bright orange-red silty clay material that overlay a hearth, and context D056 sampled a yellow and black ashy silt and charcoal layer that was interpreted as the sweepings from the hearth. Both deposits contained mottles of orange and red peat ash that had not been greatly disturbed, suggesting that the contexts both sampled secondary deposition events.

The dates from Structure D7 were arranged in stratigraphic order, with a boundary placed between the phases. A contiguous and sequential sequence was used, but the results produced through the different model were not significantly different. Therefore a contiguous model was applied to the dates, as shown in Illus 13.10.

The assessment of the dates in sequence from Structure D7 did not highlight that any anomalies; all of the agreement index values exceeding 60% for both the individual dates and for the overall sequence. The posterior density estimates for the modelled dates have been summarised in Table 13.13.

The modelled age ranges for the dates from Structure D7 were reduced by up to 10

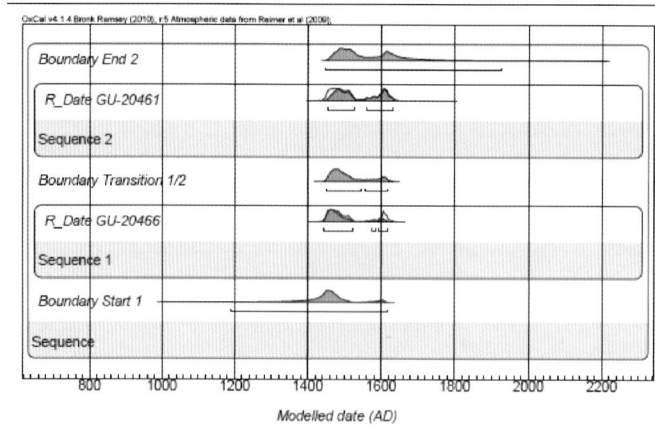

Illus 13.10 Probability distributions and posterior density estimates for the dates from Structure D7

years, and so were not significantly different compared to the raw calibrated ages. It has been noted that a statistical model has a greater impact on a series of dates if a greater number of dates are included in the assessment. In addition, the two sampled deposits were closely related stratigraphically; context D056 represented a hearth, while context D026 was interpreted as an interface/trample layer over the hearth. The close relationship of these deposits suggests that they should also be closely related in time, and so the similarity of the calibrated and modelled age ranges is to be expected. It can therefore be concluded that the hearth was used and then

Table 13.13 Summary of the modelled age ranges produced for the dates from Structure D7

Context	Sample code	Unmodelled age range (95% confidence)	Modelled age range (95% confidence)
D024	GU-20461	AD1445-1630	AD1455-1630
BOUNDARY			AD1450-1620
D056	GU-20466	AD1445-1625	AD1440-1615

abandoned between AD1440-1630 based on the modelled age ranges.

Trench D: conclusions

This section will summarise the chronological relationships of the structures dated from Trench D following the application of the statistical models. The stratigraphic and archaeological

Table 13.14 Summary of the modelled age ranges for the structures from Trench D

Phase of activity	Structure/context	Date (based on the modelled age ranges)
Later phase	D10	AD1480-1640
	D7	AD1440-1630
Earlier phase	D16	AD1460-1630
	Context D036	AD1450-1615

evidence indicates that Structure D16 was part of an earlier phase of activity, while Structures D10 and D7 were part of a later phase (Table 13.14).

The modelled age ranges produced for the sampled areas are very similar for each of the phases of activity, but there is also a considerable overlap in the dates from the earlier and later phases. This could suggest that there was not a significant hiatus between the two phases of activity. The dating evidence could also be used to argue that Structure D7 was constructed slightly earlier than Structure D10.

Trench F

The excavations within Trench F revealed two phases of occupation associated with structural remains. Both phases of occupation contained floor surfaces, with a hearth being recorded in the

Phase	Context	Sample code	Uncalibrated date BP	Calibrated age range 95.4% confidence
Second phase	F026	GU-20470	350±30	AD1455-1635
	F023	GU-20471	320±30	AD1480-1640
First phase	F042	GU-20472	385±30	AD1440-1630
	F033	GU-20473	360±30	AD1450-1635

Table 13.15 Summary of the dating evidence from Trench F

second phase. Four dates were produced from Trench F, two from each phase of occupation, summarised in Table 13.15.

A range of contexts were sampled from Trench F:

F023, F042 and F033 were interpreted as floor surfaces. Contexts F023 and F042 were described as being trampled, which may increase the risk of contamination, as material can easily have been moved on the bottom of the feet of humans and animals. The deposit may therefore represent a secondary or tertiary deposit.

F026 was a charcoal rich layer interpreted as the sweepings from the hearth and represented a secondary deposition event.

No primary deposits were sampled from the structure in Trench F, but the floor surfaces would provide dates that were contemporary with the use of the structure, containing micro-refuse incorporated by the different activities carried out.

The dates were assessed in sequence, arranged with a boundary positioned between the two phases of occupation. A contiguous and sequential sequence was used to assess the dates,

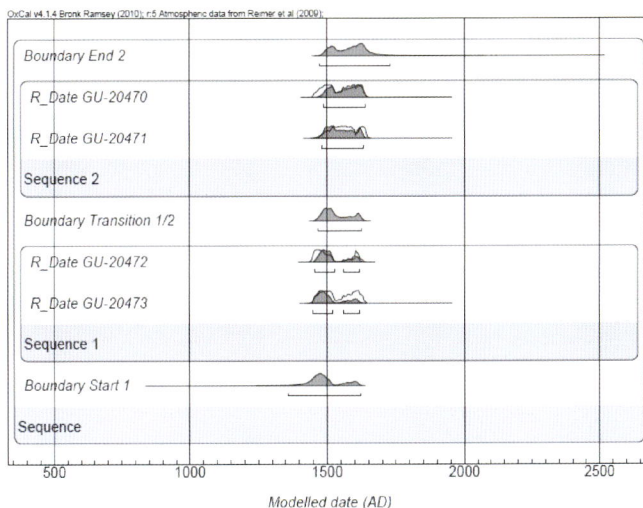

Illus 13.11 The probability distributions and posterior density estimates for the dates produced from Trench F

Context	Sample code	Unmodelled age range (95% confidence)	Modelled age range (95% confidence)
F026	GU-20470	AD1455-1635	AD1485-1640
F023	GU-20471	AD1480-1645	AD1480-1630
BOUNDARY			AD1470-1625
F042	GU-20472	AD1440-1630	AD1455-1620
F033	GU-20473	AD1450-1635	AD1445-1615

Table 13.16 Summary of the modelled age ranges produced for the dates from Trench F

but as no significant difference was noted between the posterior density estimates produced by the different models, a contiguous sequence was applied to the data (Illus 13.11).

The assessment of the dates in sequence demonstrated that the chronological information respected the stratigraphic order of the deposits. Agreement index values exceeding 60% were produced for the individual dates and for the overall sequence. The posterior density estimates produced have been summarised in Table 13.16.

The application of the model has allowed the age ranges to be reduced by up to 30 years. The floor surfaces in the first and second phases were estimated to have accumulated between AD1445-1615 and AD1480-1630 respectively, being separated by a minimum of 15-35 years, or a maximum of 185 years.

Trench G

The excavations within Trench G revealed a sequence spanning the construction and occupation of the tower structure (Phase 3), and then its later reuse (Phase 4). A total of five dates were produced, which have been summarised in Table 13.17. All of the dates were produced on charred cereal grains collected from contexts assigned to either secondary or secondary/

Phase	Context	Sample code	Uncalibrated date BP	Calibrated age range 95.4% confidence
4	G029	GU-20476	365±30	AD1450-1635
	G059	GU-20474	395±40	AD1435-1635
3	G050	GU-20478	395±30	AD1440-1630
	G061	GU-20475	385±30	AD1440-1630
	G073	GU-20477	360±30	AD1450-1635

Table 13.17 Summary of the dating evidence from Trench G

tertiary deposition events. The dates will therefore represent a *terminus ante quem* for the events in question: the construction, use and reuse of the tower.

Two of the dated contexts were thought to represent the same event: contexts G061 and G073. The resulting dates were combined in order to determine if they represented the same population, which was achieved using the chi-square test. This hypothesis was upheld following the assessment, with a t-value of only 0.3, compared to the 5% limit of 3.8. This indicated that the dates could be statistically combined, resulting in a combined uncalibrated range of 373±22BP and a calibrated range of AD1450-1630 at 95% confidence. The combined age range was very similar to the uncalibrated age ranges, which further demonstrates the excellent agreement between the dates produced from the wall core within the tower. This is encouraging considering the deposits were the result of secondary or tertiary deposition events. The combined date for this feature was used for the assessment of the dates in Trench G.

The dates were assessed in sequence, with a boundary being used to separate the

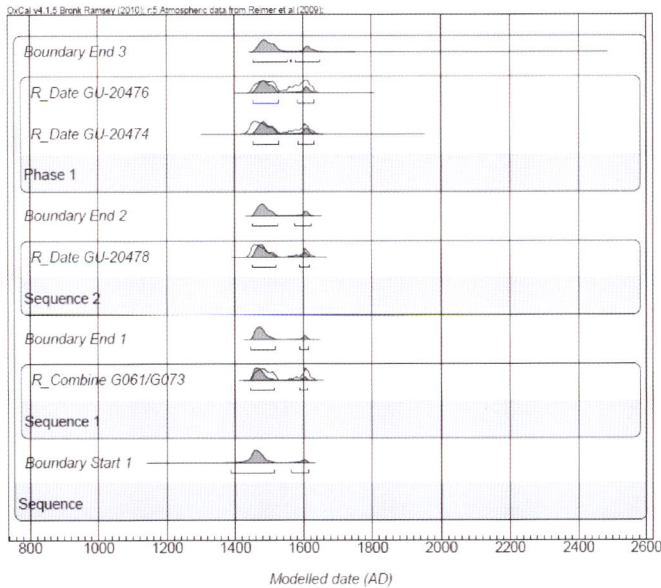

Illus 13.12 The probability distributions and posterior density estimates for the dates produced from Trench G

phases of activity recorded between Phases 3 and 4. An additional boundary was placed between the two dates from Phase 3 as it was assumed that a period of time elapsed between the dated events: the construction and use of the building. A number of models were assessed for the dates from Trench G, using contiguous and sequential sequences. A significant difference was not recorded for the different models, and so the simplest model was applied, as shown in Illus 13.12.

The assessment of the dates in sequence demonstrated that the chronological information respected the stratigraphic order of the deposits. The sequence returned excellent

Context	Sample code	Unmodelled age range (95% confidence)	Modelled age range (95% confidence)
G029	GU-20476	AD1450-1635	AD1455-1630
G059	GU-20474	AD1435-1635	AD1455-1630
BOUNDARY			AD1450-1625
G050	GU-20478	AD1440-1630	AD1450-1620
BOUNDARY			AD1445-1615
G061/G073	GU-20475/ GU-20477	AD1450-1630	AD1445-1615

Table 13.18 Summary of the modelled age ranges produced for the dates from Trench G

agreement index values that exceeded 100% for the individual dates, and for the overall sequence. The resulting posterior density estimates have been summarised in Table 13.18.

The application of the model could be used to reduce the raw calibrated age ranges by up to 20 years. It could be argued that initial construction and reuse of the structure (as dated by contexts G061/G073 and G059 respectively) was separated by a minimum of 10-15 years, up to a maximum of 185 years. The dating evidence could be used to suggest that there was not a considerable hiatus between the initial use and subsequent reuse of the tower. However, the lack of resolution available between the chronological information limits the conclusions that can be drawn.

Conclusions: The chronology of Dùn Èistean

The dating evidence from Dùn Èistean produced a coherent chronological sequence with only one sample being identified that potentially sampled residual material (GU-20450, Trench A, Structure A2). The similarity in the dating evidence was mainly due to the presence of a plateau in the radiocarbon calibration curve between AD1440-1660. The stratigraphic information was used in conjunction with a Bayesian model in order to refine the age ranges and increase the resolution between the dated events.

The application of the model to the sequences of dates resulted in age ranges that were reduced by up to 30 years, which has allowed some subtle patterns to be identified in the chronological information. It was not possible to argue which of the features excavated at Dùn Èistean were constructed first, due to the similarity in the dates. However, the application of the statistical model as well as the stratigraphic information demonstrated that a number of features could be grouped together as the earliest remains on site. This included:

- the construction and use of buildings A1 and A2
- the earlier features sealed by the construction of building B1
- the use of the kilnbarn structure in Trench C
- the hearth below D7
- the midden deposits sealed by structures D16 and D10 wall footings
- the first use of the structure recorded in Trench F
- the construction and rebuild of the tower in Trench G

The dates produced from these structures/features were grouped between AD1440-1635. All of the dates related to the use of the structures, dating hearth deposits, floor surfaces, or the fired material within the kilnbarn in Trench C. The dating evidence therefore represents a *terminus ante quem* for the construction of the buildings. Samples GU-20475 and GU-20477 were the exception to this, sampling material within the wall core of the tower in Trench G and representing the construction of the building; the sampled contexts were interpreted as resulting from secondary or tertiary deposition events and so they provide a *terminus post quem* for the construction of the tower.

The remaining features dated at Dùn Èistean form a group of features/structures that returned later dates. These features include:

- the upper hearth within A1
- the use of B1
- the later use of the kilnbarn in Trench C
- the construction of D10
- the use of D16
- the second use of the building recorded in Trench F

The dating evidence produced from these structures/features returned age ranges spanning AD1465-1670. All of the dates apart from that from Structure D10 relate to the use of the structures, sampling hearth deposits, floor surfaces, and the later use of the kilnbarn in Trench C.

Sample GU-20462 sampled material from the basal wall deposit of Structure D10 and represents the construction of the building; the sampled context was interpreted as resulting from secondary or tertiary deposition events and so it provides a *terminus ante quem* for the construction of Structure D10.

It can therefore be concluded that the remains recorded at Dùn Èistean present an image of a site in continuous use, with no major phases of abandonment. The dating evidence allows several spatially distinct features recorded in the different trenches to be linked, identifying contemporary phases of activity across the site. It is possible to argue that the features/structures representing the earlier phases of activity were constructed as early as AD1440, potentially being in use for up to 230 years.

conclu

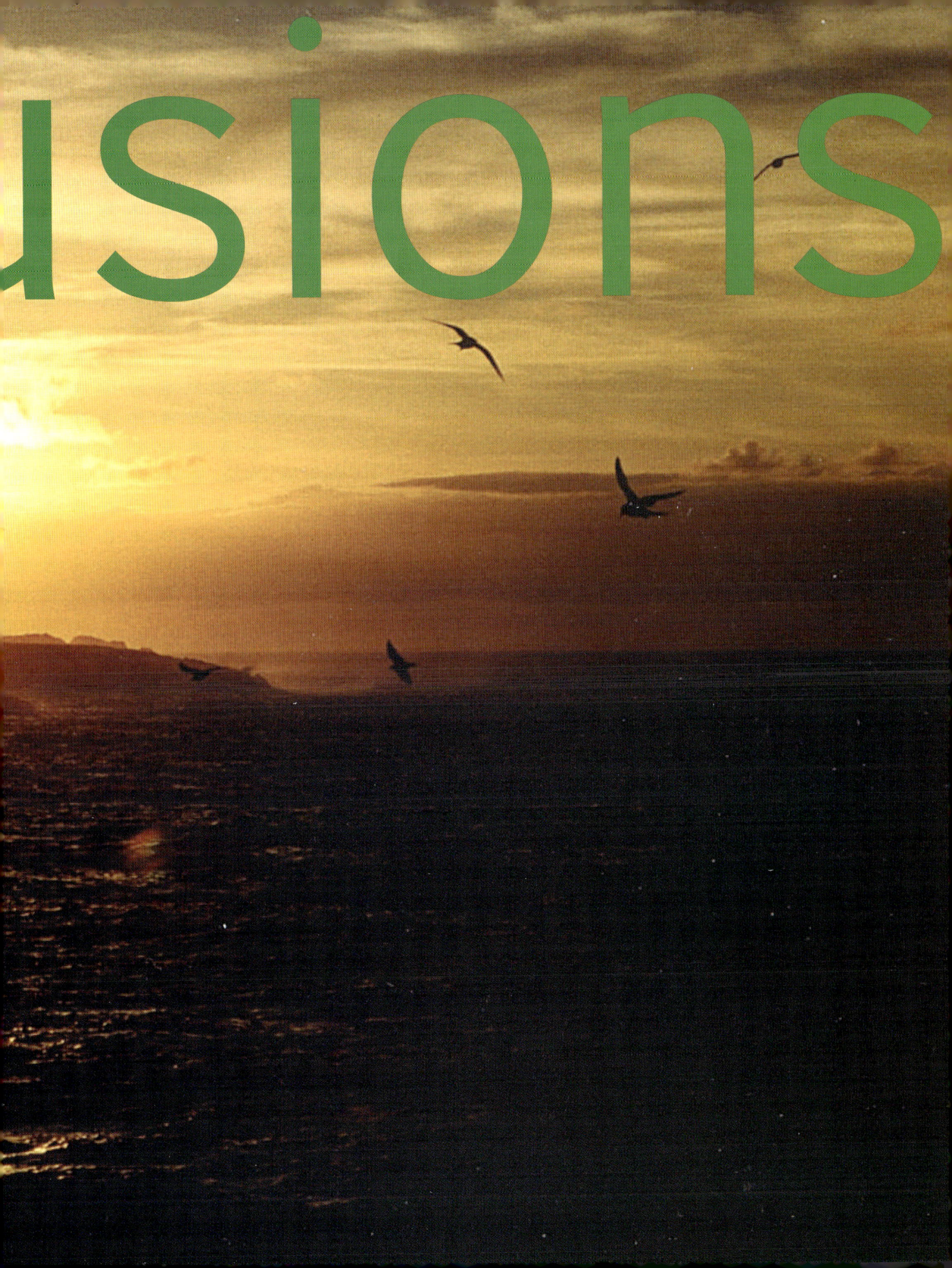

usions

Illus 14.1 General view of Dùn Èistean from the south-east

fourteen

discussion

In this concluding discussion all the detailed results reported in Chapters 2-13 are tied together and the site is looked at as a whole. Apart from a small collection of potentially prehistoric quartz found scattered across the site (see Ballin in Chapter 10) all the material and buildings excavated from Dùn Èistean have been dated to the fifteenth century onwards and can be grouped into three episodes; the first two taking place some time between the late 1400s and early 1600s AD, and the third in the late 1600s to early 1800s (see Table 14.1). There is evidence that the stronghold was occupied several times within each of these episodes, but it is impossible to define all of these uses more specifically than to group them into the three general Episodes, I, II and III.

During Episodes I and II Dùn Èistean was used as a place of refuge in times of trouble, and as a collection point and symbol of power in the Ness district. In Episode I the stronghold had a lookout tower or keep, a defensive wall around the landward perimeter of the island, buildings for shelter and storage, and kilns to fire pottery and dry oats and barley. Episode II followed swiftly, with the corn-drying kiln barn, tower and perimeter wall remaining in use, Structures A and F1 re-occupied, and two new groups of buildings constructed against the perimeter wall –Structure B on the west side of the site, and three small houses (D5, D6 and D12) around a courtyard (D16) on the east. The building of this extra accommodation suggests that the population on the island increased during the second episode.

After this the stronghold was abandoned, and the roofs and walls of the buildings decayed, slumped and collapsed. Dùn Èistean was then re-occupied only on a sporadic basis (Episode III) when rough turf shelters were built into the ruins on the site for short-term shelter whilst the island was being used for grazing or fishing. One of these shelters was found in the north end of the remains of house A1, three in the ruins of the corn-drying kiln C, and six across the collapsed Structure D complex. They were used intermittently between the end of the 1600s and into the early 1800s, with the exception of a small hollow and a marker cairn that was built on the top of the ruined tower in the twentieth century.

Table 14.1 Combined summary of the archaeological sequence on Dùn Èistean (opposite)

EPISODES	Area A	Area B	Area C	Area D	Area F	Area G
EPISODE I ORIGINAL GROUND SURFACES, HOUSES A1 AND A2 AND ENCLOSURE, TRACES OF BUILDINGS, OLDER SETTLEMENT AND CLAMP, KILN BARN (C), SMALL HUTS (F), TOWER (G) AND PERIMETER WALL (H). BETWEEN AD1440 AND 1635	Phase 2: Construction, Phase 3: Occupation, of houses A1, A2 and enclosure banks	Phase 2: Original ground surfaces Phase 3: Construction of perimeter wall H, and structures and occupation pre-dating Structure B	Phase 2: Original ground surfaces Phase 3: Construction and use of kiln barn	Phase 2: Original ground surfaces and traces of structures Phase 3: Middens below wall footings Phase 4: Construction of perimeter wall, construction and use of clamp or fire below structure D7	Phase 2: Construction of building. Phase 3: First occupation phase	Phase 2: Original ground surfaces Phase 3: Construction and collapse of first tower Phase 4: Rebuild and repair of tower
EPISODE II CONTINUED USE OF C, G, H, 2ND OCCUPATION OF A1 AND F, BUILDINGS B1 AND B4-6, D12 AND COURTYARD D16. BETWEEN AD1465 AND 1670	Phase 3: Upper hearth A032 in Building A1	Phase 4: Construction and use of Structure B		Phase 4: Construction and use of structure D16 and D12	Phase 4: Second occupation phase	
EPISODE III ABANDONMENT AND COLLAPSE OF BUILDINGS, TURF SHELTERS BUILT INTO RUINS OF A, C AND D. END OF 1600s TO EARLY 1800s AD	Phases 4 and 5: Abandonment, collapse and slump of buildings, Phase 6: Temporary shelter	Phase 5: Post-abandonment	Phase 4: Robbing/collapse of kiln barn and construction of shelters C1, C2 and C3	Phase 5: Collapse of earlier buildings and construction and occupation of turf shelters D7, D8, D10, D13 and D14	Phase 5: Post-abandonment and collapse	Phase 5: Collapse of second tower and leaching of clay bonding

Episode I: Establishment of the late medieval stronghold
The perimeter wall (Structure H) and the earliest traces of buildings and older settlement

The sparse remains of the wall footings of two buildings (see Area B, Phase 3 and Area D, Phase 2) were found adjacent to the stone and turf perimeter wall (Structure H) which stood to around 1.5m high at the cliff edge on the landward sides of the stronghold. Material found in the buildings, such as a gun flint, a flint blade, sherds of local pottery, peat ash, rowan, oak and birch charcoal and burnt oats, barley and a hazelnut, suggest that they were used for shelter and cooking (see Ballin, Campbell and Ramsay in Chapters 10 and 11). They were then dismantled and re-cycled into new buildings during Episode II (probably Structures B and D). Thick deposits of ash and other hearth debris found below the walls of B and D (see Phase 3 in Areas B and D) contained evidence for small-scale metal-working, and also thousands of burnt oat and barley grains and burnt straw. This leads Ramsay in Chapter 11 to suggest that drying and processing of grain in more than just a small domestic hearth also took place on the island during Episode I.

A large fire or clamp found on the old ground surface on the east side of the island (Area D, Phase 4) also dates to this episode. When in use this clamp would have comprised a large fire lit in a shallow pit, banked up with fuel, then covered with the unfired pots, possibly on a framework of sticks (driftwood). More fuel (peat and wood) would then be piled over the pots and the whole then 'clamped' with earth and turf and left to burn out until the clamp collapsed. Once the kiln had cooled, the fired pots would be taken out from the ashes. Campbell in his study of the local pottery from this area in Chapter 10 identified an almost complete smashed pot found on the old ground surface adjacent to the fire site. Soils analysis by McKenzie et al in Chapter 12 identified a layer of turf within the hearth, a capping of collapsed material, and an accumulation of ash and domestic material above it. They also detect evidence of an earlier hearth, suggesting that there was re-use of this feature. Occasional small hard lumps of peat found on the original ground surface near to the clamp kiln indicate that peats were once stacked in this area on the north-east side of the slope downwards towards the east side of the island.

Houses A1 and A2, Structure A

These two houses were built from low stone and earth walls and roofed with turf and were set in an enclosure on the west side of the island. Each house had an entrance on the east side and a hearth in the centre of the floor. A large stone set upright next to the hearth in A1 may have been used as a seat (a feature also seen in the mid-nineteenth century blackhouses; Mackie 2006b, 76)[1]. Material found in the hearth is evidence for the activities that took place around the fireside: grain was parched or dried (see burnt grain identified by Ramsay in Chapter 11), gunflints were made and refined (see Ballin, Chapter 10) and lead smelting took place on a small scale, probably for the casting of musket balls or

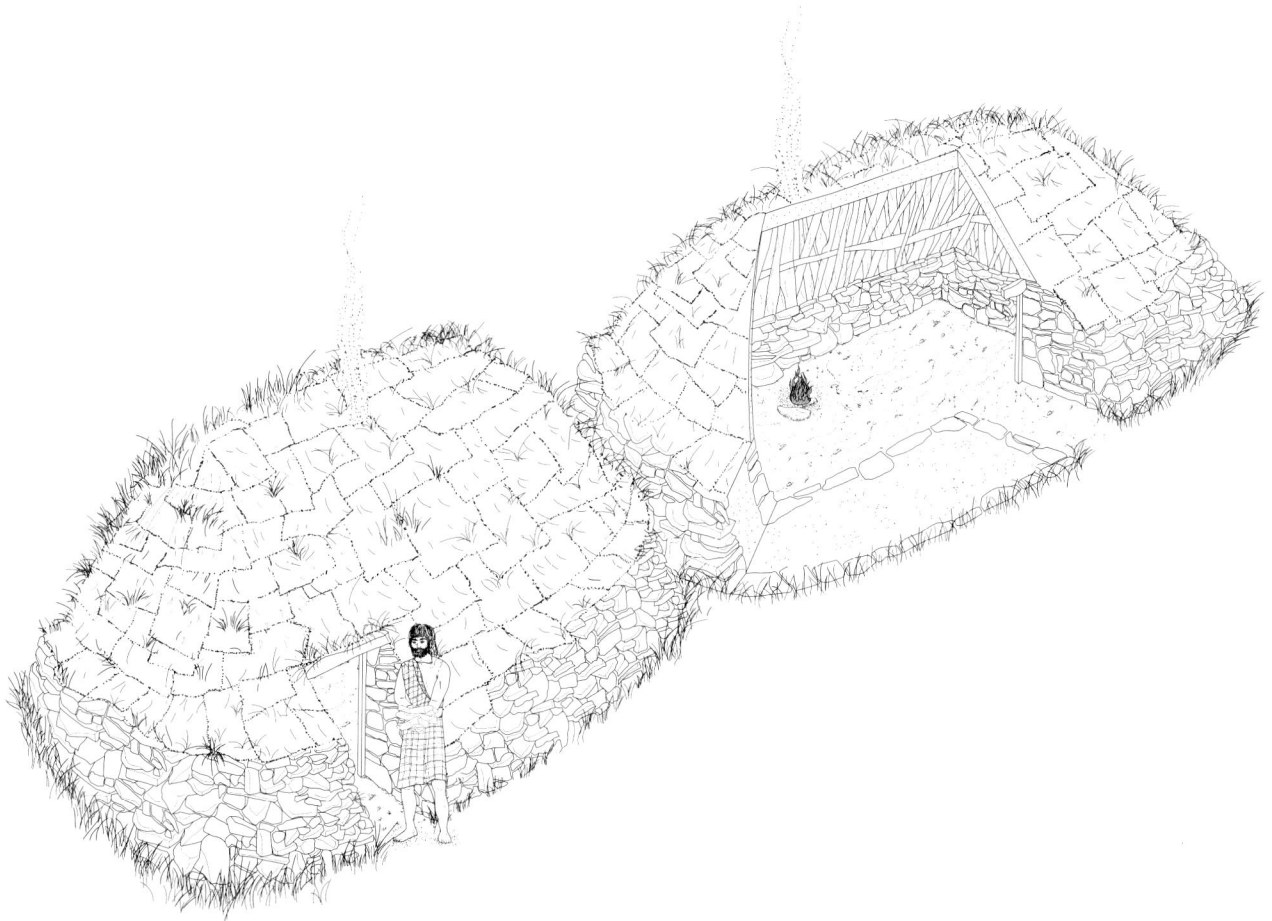

Illus 14.2 Reconstruction
drawing of A1 and A2

pistol shot (see Ferguson and Batey, Chapter 10). Pottery sherds from storage jars, cooking pots and small drinking cups as well as fragments of burnt mammal and fish bones demonstrate that food and drink were also consumed in the building (see Campbell in Chapter 10, and Masson-MacLean and Cerón-Carrasco in Chapter 11).

The hearth in neighbouring house A2 was smaller and shallower. Only birch wood charcoal, probably deriving from birch twigs found in the peat, is identified from this hearth and it contained just a small collection of oat and barley grains and a small number of pottery sherds. This implies that A2 was not occupied for as long as A1, or that it had a different use. The walls of A2 were also less substantial, being built mainly from turf with only the inner face lined with stone. It is possible that this structure was used at times to house animals.

Building F1, Structure F

This structure was one of two little buildings, F1 and F2, which were set into the hillside at the top of a natural gully, *Palla na Birlinn*. With access down to the sea, these buildings may have been lookout posts to guard a landing stage and watch southwards along the coast and across the Minch. F1 was built with turf and stone walls, had an entrance on the seaward side and a drain to take water away from the back of the building and out under the front wall.

Ramsay suggests in Chapter 11 that finds of peat ash and driftwood charcoal on the floor of F1 indicate that there was a hearth in the unexcavated half of the building. Fish and animal bone and a small shard of green glass from a bottle (see Cerón-Carrasco and Masson-MacLean in Chapter 11; Murdoch in Chapter 10) demonstrate that food and drink were consumed in the building, and a piece of scrap lead, a misshapen and discarded musket ball, and a chip of flint (see Batey, Ferguson and Ballin in Chapter 10) are evidence that gunflints and lead projectiles were made there too. A small group of iron objects and a lump of slag suggest driftwood was burnt in the hearth and that small-scale metal-working may have taken place nearby (see Batey and Sneddon in Chapter 10). McKenzie et al in their analyses of the soils in Chapter 12 suggest that randomly oriented plant stem remains found in soil samples could indicate that threshed material was spread on the floor of the building. They also suggest from the build-up of occupation material that F1 was used for a relatively long time, and that because the turf used to build the walls contained very little midden material, it was built on a 'clean' previously unoccupied part of the site, as would be expected in this initial phase of settlement.

The corn-drying kiln and barn, Structure C

This large rectangular building with rounded corners, built from double stone and earth walls and with a corn-drying kiln at one end, was used for storing and drying grain. A flue on the east side of the interior led to a stone-lined kiln bowl set in a revetted, solid clay platform at the north end of the building. No evidence survived for the superstructure that would have been placed over the kiln bowl on which to lay the grain to be dried. Traditionally wooden struts

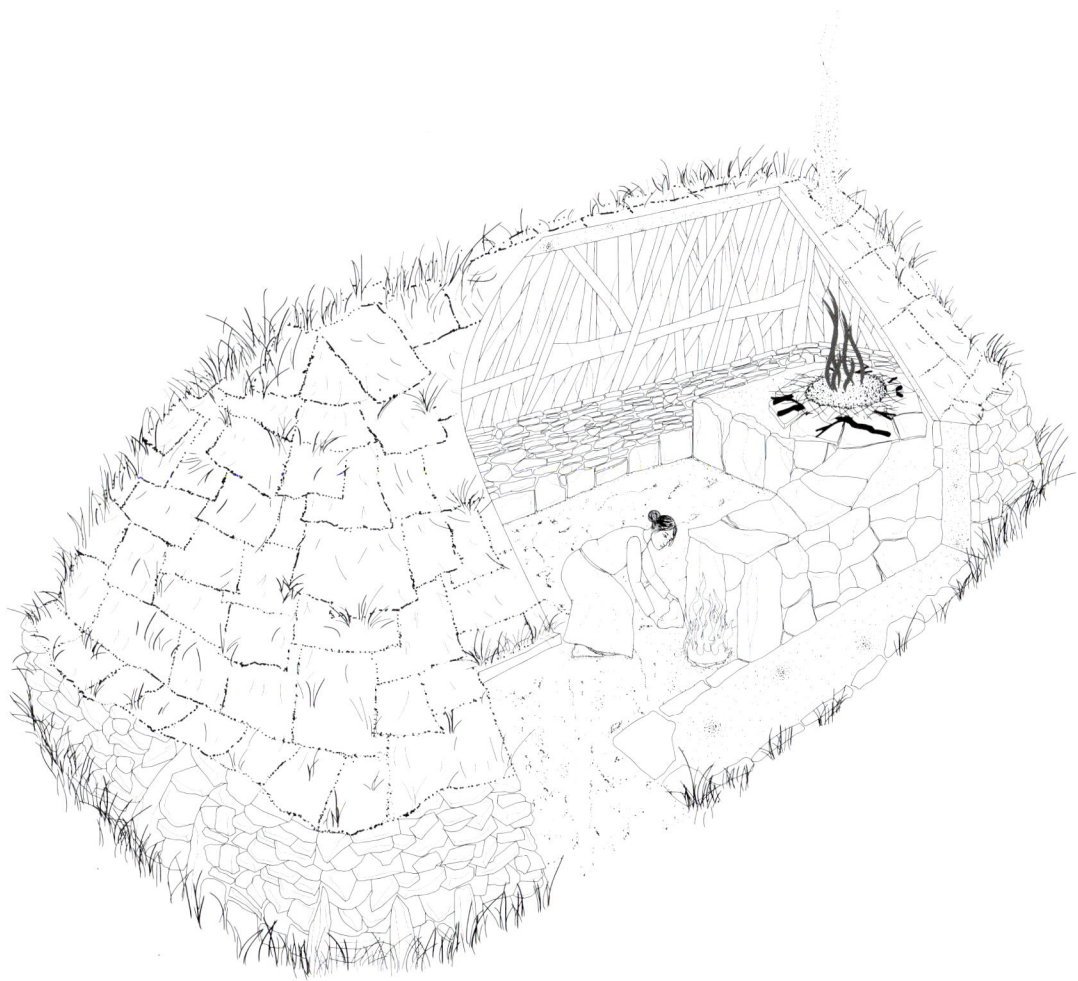

Illus 14.3 Reconstruction drawing of Structure C

were laid across the top of the bowl on which a bedding of hay, straw or cloth of animal hair was placed (Macleod 2009, 35-6; see below). Miller (Chapter 11) draws attention to finds of ash, oak and Scot's pine charcoal in kiln flue deposit C068 as possible evidence for this. Soils analysis by McKenzie et al in Chapter 12 indicates that the area below the kiln barn was stripped of turf before the barn was built, and this turf was used in the wall cores of the building. Very little midden material was found in the walls, suggesting that the kiln barn was, like hut F1, built on a previously unoccupied area of the site. There were also few artefacts and no evidence for a hearth, confirming that the barn was used for storage (of grain and potentially dried peat and other supplies) rather than accommodation.

Ramsay in Chapter 11 has identified small amounts of carbonised oat and barley grains, and ash and oak charcoal, in peat ash at the south end of the flue, and magnetic susceptibility measurements by McKenzie (see Chapter 12) revealed high readings that indicate that this deposit was exposed to heat. Overall though, the small amount of ash from the flue and grain in the kiln may suggest that it was not in use for a very long time, even taking into consideration that the grain would have been taken out after each use.

The tower, Structure G

The rectangular tower, in local tradition called '*Tigh nan Arm*' (House of the Arms, or the Armoury), originally stood to around 5m and was built on the highest point of the island on a natural rock platform. It had two storeys: the lower built from double stone walls up to 2m thick enclosing a small sub-rectangular chamber in the centre, and the upper from clay-bonded stonework set onto the wall heads of the base. Excavation found evidence that there had been a defect in the way the tower was constructed so that whilst it was being built the walls of the base had slumped and collapsed before they were finished. They were then rebuilt and repaired using the same wall construction but with a slight inwards batter to the neat coursed stonework of the outer face of the wall, which was keyed into the earthen core.

The upper storey had completely collapsed by the time of the excavation. Lintel stones hint at a window or a door on the south side of the tower, and iron nails indicate that driftwood timbers were used to support the roof. It is not known what was used to cover the roof. Two flat stones, one with a partial perforation, were identified as possible examples of stone tiles during the excavation, but Batey in Chapter 10 above is cautious as to their identification describing them as 'far from definite'. It is more likely that the tower would have had a turf, or turf and heather, roof, as seen on all other buildings on the site.

Two or three individuals could only have occupied the tower as there was no evidence for a hearth and given the internal dimensions, barely enough room for sleeping. It seems instead to have functioned both as a watchtower out to sea, and as a visible symbol of power from the sea. Gunflints and sherds of local pottery, a whetstone, a glazed post-medieval pottery sherd, and corroded iron and flint waste were found scattered on the original ground surfaces around the

Illus 14.4 Reconstruction drawing of Structure G with turf roof

edge of the tower, and Ballin identifies above, in Chapter 10, that the heaviest use of gunflints is evidenced here and at Structures B and D, the most strategic points on the island. A musket ball found in the stone collapse may have originated from the tower wall. There is the possibility that prisoners or hostages could have been held in the tiny central chamber in the tower's lower storey, which would only have had access from the floor above. This cannot be verified from the archaeology alone however as the excavation by MacPhail in the 1860s removed most of the interior deposits from the tower.

Episode II: Expansion and re-occupation of the stronghold
The re-occupation of buildings A1 and F1

A second floor layer and ash deposits in F1 suggest that it was re-occupied in Episode II, although the second phase of occupation was short-lived compared with the first. An oak wood threshold was inserted in the doorway to the building, the front wall was repaired, and pottery sherds and hearth material found trampled just outside the entrance suggest that the interior was swept out. Soils analysis by McKenzie et al in Chapter 12 reveals that this second occupation in F1 followed the first in quick succession as no build-up or abandonment deposits were detected between them. Re-use of the hearth in A1 suggests that this building was also re-occupied, although again for a shorter time than the previous event. Although it is possible that A2 was also re-used, there is no evidence for the hearth being lit.

Structures B1, B4-6 and H, small house and huts and the perimeter wall

A new group of six stone and turf buildings (Structure B) were built at this time against the perimeter wall in an area of older settlement at the south-west corner of the island. They were used as lookout points to the mainland opposite and guarded the two main access points up the steep cliffs and onto the island. Gaps found in the south walls of the buildings where they abutted the perimeter wall may originally have been 'squints' or 'loopholes' as recorded in local tradition (Thomas 1878, 516). A paved and stone-lined entrance onto the island was found in a gap between the east side of building B6 and the continuation of the perimeter wall. This gap lies at the top of one of the access routes up the cliff to the site where the breach between the island and the mainland is at its narrowest. Supplies may also have been hauled up here on to the site.

A small house (B1) at the west end of the complex, with a sunken floor and a central peat hearth, was the main gathering and cooking area. Charred mammal and fish bones, and barley and oat grains were found in the hearth deposits (see Masson-MacLean, Cerón Carrasco and Ramsay in Chapter 11), and it had been used more than once, with dumps of ash from clearing the hearth found outside the building. Three smaller conjoined buildings B4-B6 adjacent to B1 also had sunken floors but no hearths, and were probably used for storage and lookout shelters. A low earthen platform defined by stones against the west wall of B4 may have been for sleeping on.

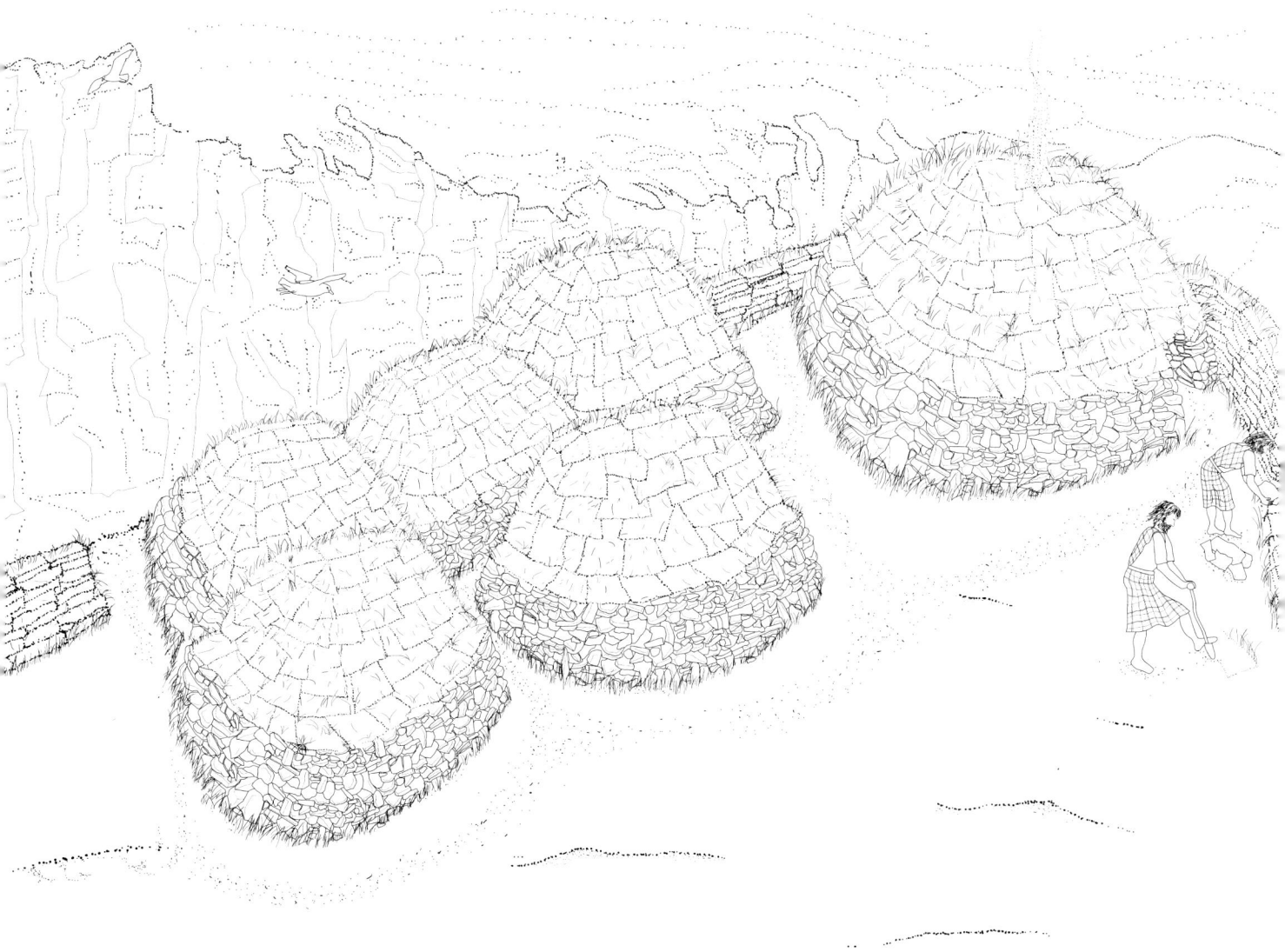

Illus 14.5 Reconstruction
drawing of Structure B

The excavations and modelling of the radiocarbon dates by Outram and Batt in Chapter 13 suggest that buildings B1 and B4-6 were probably built and used together as one contemporaneous unit, although modifications were made whilst the buildings were in use, such as the blocking of an entrance in the west wall of B6. Will, Ballin, Ferguson and Bateson identify medieval glazed pottery, gunflints, a pistol ball, a musket ball, an Elizabeth I silver sixpence dating to 1580 and a James VI billon plack (eightpenny Scots) issue of 1583-90 in slumped wall deposits in buildings B1 and B6, and these no doubt derive originally from the occupation of the buildings. Ballin identifies that this structure, and others at the most strategic points on the island (D and G), contained evidence for the heaviest use (rather than manufacture) of gunflints.

Structures D16, and D5, D6 and D12, courtyard and surrounding buildings

A second new group of at least three buildings; D5, D6 and D12 were built at this time on the east side of the site centred on an open rectangular courtyard, D16, with access to the perimeter wall. It is not possible to reconstruct what the whole of this complex would have looked like as the ruins of most of the structures were subsequently dismantled to build later turf shelters (see General Event III below) and only 50% of the complex was excavated.

However, it is clear that there was access from D5 and D6, two buildings on the north side of the complex, into courtyard D16. Given its large span, it seems unlikely that the courtyard itself was roofed. Several floor and hearth deposits found in the courtyard suggest that it was extensively used, and was perhaps a main gathering place for the inhabitants of the island. Soils analysis by McKenzie et al in Chapter 12 of the hearths and floor layers in D16 show that it had been exposed to surface weathering and the gradual accumulation of domestic waste material by trampling, washing and blowing in, as would be expected in an open courtyard and communal area. The environmental assemblages studied by Ramsay and Masson-MacLean in Chapter 11 from the peat and driftwood hearths in D16 also suggest that they were used for domestic cooking, with finds of burnt mammal and fish bone and small amounts of carbonised grain, weed seeds and flax. Two pieces of an iron object are identified by Batey in Chapter 10 as a metal binding strip for a bucket or barrel and Campbell identifies sherds from four decorated cups found in the floor deposits in the courtyard area, and in the later shelters built into it (and therefore probably originally deriving from it) alongside normal craggan jars dated to the sixteenth century. Like those found in houses A1 and A2, the cups confirm that eating and drinking took place in the courtyard area. A small number of glazed medieval pottery sherds, gunflints and flint-working debris, and pistol and musket balls were also found (see Will, Ballin and Ferguson in Chapter 10). Ballin suggests that most gunflints were both manufactured and used in Structure D. The recovery of a domical spindle whorl fragment identified by Batey may be evidence that women as well as men took refuge here.

One of the buildings (D12) on the west side of the area was partially excavated, but only traces of the foundations of its turf wall and part of an

Illus 14.6 Excavating floor layers in Structure D

occupation surface survived. It appears to have provided access to the perimeter wall and into the courtyard area. Material found in the occupation layer in the building includes a sherd from a glazed Cologne stoneware wine bottle identified by Will in Chapter 10 as dating to the end of the sixteenth century.

Episode III: Abandonment and occasional use for shelter from the late seventeenth to early twentieth centuries

By the mid-seventeenth century the stronghold had been abandoned and the buildings there left to collapse and decay. After this the island was used intermittently for shelter, with small, makeshift turf huts or bothies built mainly from re-used turf with minimal use of stone (usually just the basal course lining the interior of the shelter). None of the shelters that were excavated had a hearth, and the majority of the artefactual material found in them was the debris from the older ruined buildings below them. Finds of glass and pottery date the Episode III turf huts in areas A, C and D to some time between the end of the 1600s, and the beginning of the 1800s AD. Shards of window glass identified by Murdoch from D7, D8, D10A and D14 suggest that the shelters had small door or roof lights, and were built and occupied in the seventeenth/eighteenth centuries. A shard from a cold-colour painted glass bottle/vessel, probably dating from the late eighteenth/early nineteenth century, but possibly Venetian and dating to the sixteenth century (see Murdoch in Chapter 10) was found outside the shelter in the north end of the ruins of A1 in slump from the turf enclosure. A musket ball with teeth marks on it was also found which Ferguson identifies had possibly been chewed deliberately to alter its size and shape so as to be fitted down a particular muzzle. Murdoch also identifies a shard from an eighteenth century clear glass vessel or bottle found in slump inside the adjacent house A2, and a shard of seventeenth century glass in the huts C1-C3, which he suggests, due to its poor condition, may be from an older context.

Many of these artefacts originated from earlier turf walls or floors that were dug up with the turf used to build the later shelters. All of the little shelters contained a mixture of older, late medieval material from the ruined stronghold. Ramsay in Chapter 11 identifies that the lowest layers of the east wall of shelter D8 contained significant quantities of burnt straw, cereal grains and weed seeds, and ash and willow charcoal. These no doubt derive from older ash deposits, and possibly a woven basket or similar from cereal processing (see Episode I, above). Similarly, shelter D7 was built into the sunken circular hollow left by the large fire or clamp from Episode I. Ferguson identifies in Chapter 10 that a lead projectile found in the wall of D7 displayed evidence that it had been fired into a turf wall, but not the wall of D7 itself as the turf used to build D7 was cut from elsewhere (probably the area of the ruined courtyard D16 nearby). This is confirmed by McKenzie et al's soils analysis in Chapter 12, which identifies that the ash and hearth material found in the turf walls of D7 does not derive from the fire site of the clamp kiln which it was built over, but from the adjoining area, again probably courtyard D16. A mixture of sixteenth/seventeenth, eighteenth,

Illus 14.7 Structure D8, from the west

and even nineteenth century ceramic and glass sherds between General Events II and III demonstrates that more re-building and adaptation, and subsequent mixing up of soil layers, happened in Structure D than anywhere else on the site, suggesting that the little shelters were re-used and repaired several times.

These huts were probably used by the inhabitants of nearby Garenin, two clusters of houses situated on the north side of Loch Stiapabhat, and then the later settlement of Knockaird, founded in 1766 (see Barrowman, C S 2015, 267-8; Robson 2008, 14-15; 18). Dùn Èistean was part of the agricultural landscape at this time and was used as a place to keep and tend the cattle and sheep away from the arable crops during the growing season (as seen on other uninhabited off-shore islands in the Hebrides at this time; eg Shaw 1980, 91). Analysis of agricultural soils undertaken in the Loch Stiapabhat area in the late 1990s (see Entwhistle et al 2000, cited in Barrowman, C S 2015, 268) has shown that prior to the nineteenth-century crofting township, the early settlement of Knockaird was more spread out. The system of run-rig agriculture was practised at this time, utilising sets of *feannagan* (lazybeds) laid out within turf enclosures. These preserved field-systems are still clearly visible on the ground today on the mainland opposite Dùn Èistean, covering the coastal area from the Butt of Lewis to Port of Ness, and along with the Episode III buildings on the site are a reflection of the intensification of agriculture in Ness at this time due to population increase and improvements initiated by the Seaforth MacKenzies in the 1700s.

Towards the end of the eighteenth century Knockaird became more of a nucleated settlement, with the first lotting taking place in the 1820s when the crofting settlement was established. Murdoch and Will in Chapter 10 identify a small number of pieces of later eighteenth/nineteenth century glass and glazed ceramics in wall slump layers on Dùn Èistean, including sherds of modern white ceramic found in the shelters D10 and D13. A flattened copper alloy shallow shovel-shaped object with a rough tapering handle interpreted by Batey in Chapter 10 as a candleholder, and a hook-shaped item that she suggests may be part of a fleshing fork were also found in the topsoil in these shelters and probably date to the later eighteenth/nineteenth centuries. By 1852 the buildings on Dùn Èistean are described as ruins in the Ordnance Survey Name Books (see Chapter 2, above), so it seems unlikely that they were used beyond the early nineteenth century. The exception to this is a small hollow in the top of the ruined tower mound in which was found modern metal and glass, and a cairn built next to it on the mound in the 1930s/40s as a memorial.

Local context and everyday life on Dùn Èistean in the sixteenth and early seventeenth centuries

Building techniques

All the Episode I and II (late fifteenth to early seventeenth century) buildings on Dùn Èistean, apart from the tower, were sub-rectangular or roughly circular in shape. The kiln barn C, and small buildings at F, were single units, but those

Illus 14.8 View of lazybeds on coast at Dùn Èistean and Illus 14.9 Marker cairn on Dùn Èistean

at A, B and D comprised two or more conjoining units. Houses A1 and A2 comprised two rectangular buildings joined end to end, but those at B and D were smaller, sub-rectangular and roughly circular conjoining buildings used for a variety of storage and gathering purposes, as well as habitation (sleeping and eating), and as such may be evidence for conglomerated units in the early post-medieval period (see Mackie 2013, 14-15; forthcoming). The Episode I and II buildings at A, B, C, D and F were built from low stone and earth or turf walls, either with inner and outer stone faces and a wall core of earthen turf material, or with only the inner faces lined with stone and the outer faces built with turf to roof level. The soils analysis work by McKenzie et al on samples taken from C, D and F (see Chapter 12) showed that a range of materials were used to build the walls, but that the sandy soils from the island were the main component in the wall cores. Samples taken in Structures B and D showed that different mixes of material were used between buildings and phases, suggesting that re-building and repairing of walls and buildings was an ongoing activity. The exception to this general picture is the tower, Structure G, where soils analysis of sections taken through the walls of the tower base identified that different materials had been stacked in the wall core, then trampled and 'puddled', a method seen in late nineteenth/early twentieth century blackhouse buildings. At Arnol, for instance, the tempered earth core of the blackhouse walls was made up from top soil excavated from the site, mixed with peat dust, blue clay and the ash from the fire, which were then compacted between the masonry faces as they were built (Walker and MacGregor 1996, 4). On Dùn Èistean, above the basal layers soils analysis showed that only well-compacted sandy turf was used, which had been gathered from a different part of the site where there had already been occupation, but from a different area to those in Structures C, D and F.

From the thick layers of degraded turf excavated from within the collapsed buildings on Dùn Èistean it would seem that the roofs of all the buildings on the site would have been turf or turf and heather, resting on wooden supports on the wall heads of the building. As Geddes points out, by modern standards of engineering this roofing technique may seem less than adequate, but experienced use of these local materials produced roofing that could last for generations (Geddes 2006, 22). Ramsay's analysis of the botanical remains reveals that heather type stems were commonly found as burnt and unburnt remains in the samples from Dùn Èistean, as were concentrations of carbonised cereal straw. She suggests that a combination of heathy turfs and/or straw may have formed the roofs of the structures, with turfs used as the underlayer of the roof and straw or heather as the upper, weatherproofing layer, held down by netting or rope laid over the top (see Walker and McGregor 1996, 10-16; also NicAoidh 2000). This is possible as turf and heather roofing was not just used in vernacular buildings in the past. According to the Statistical Account of Scotland 1791-99, Parish of Barvas (Rev Donald MacDonald) the post-medieval Ness parish church, *Teampall Pheadair* (St Peter's) in Suainebost "was … thatched with heath" as late as the eighteenth century (see Barrowman, R C 2006b, 11-15).

Illus 14.10 Cutting through earthen wall core in Structure G and Illus 14.11 North facing section through wall C004 in Structure C

The roof supports in the buildings on Dùn Èistean would have been made from whatever was available, probably mostly driftwood from old ship timbers and other jetsam. Traditionally these timbers would not have been cut, but used in their entirety as wood was so rare, and then re-used as/when necessary, in other buildings. Batey in Chapter 10 highlights that the majority of the metalwork assemblage comprises iron nails, and she suggests that many of the nails most likely derived from ship's timbers brought up to the site, whether for fuel or to be used as roofing timbers, or both. Traditions cited in Stiùbhart's paper in Chapter 3, above, demonstrate the scarcity and therefore importance of roofing timbers in Ness in the past. For instance, there is a tradition that when timber was needed to roof *Teampall Mholuaidh* (St Moluag's) in Eoropie, the saint prayed for a roof and one was found washed up on the beach at *Traigh Shanndaigh* (Eoropie sands) that fitted exactly. This tradition illustrates the scarcity of large roofing timbers, the use and re-use of wood and driftwood, and the value put on it.

In all the buildings tried and tested local building methods were followed that responded to the surrounding environment, and made use of locally-available materials, many of them from the island itself. Soils analysis reported in Chapter 12 above demonstrates that the turf used for buildings was stripped from the island. There was also an ample supply of stone from the island's rocky ledges, as well as the surrounding cliff line and rocky shore.[2] McKenzie et al identify that the clay used to bond the tower walls and cap the top of the walls of the tower base was also of local origin. Some may have come from the island, perhaps from the digging of the freshwater pond, or the hollows for the huts at F, but may also have come from the Ness mainland, where thick deposits of clay subsoil are found below the peat and grassland.[3] In addition to these resources, abandoned buildings were dismantled and the materials re-cycled into new structures, as seen in the evidence for robbed-out wall remains in Episode I.

Many of the construction techniques used in the buildings excavated on Dùn Èistean are seen elsewhere in Ness, in late eighteenth and nineteenth century vernacular buildings. The rich Gàidhlig vocabulary associated with these buildings has been recorded by Catriona Mackie (NicAoidh), during her research on Lewis houses in the nineteenth and twentieth centuries, with particular focus on the Bragar township (NicAoidh 2000; Mackie 2006a; 2006b). Her research demonstrates that there were certain ways of doing things, with every small detail having its own special gaelic term. Interestingly, some of the features she records from the nineteenth/twentieth century buildings are also seen in the excavated Episode I and II (sixteenth to early seventeenth century) buildings on Dùn Èistean, such as '*glutadh*', '*glutaran*', or '*talamh balla*', the inner sand or earth cavity in a wall (used in all the buildings on the site), or '*spalla*' a small, wedge-shaped stone used in stonework (used in the outer face of stonework in the tower) (NicAoidh 2000b, 46; Mackie 2006a, 126-9), and *fàd-bhuinn* (literally, 'sole-sod'), a name originating from when a grassy turf was used as a door step, but also used for a wooden step or stick laid across a door-way to keep out draughts (NicAoidh 2000a, 89) and seen in the oak wood placed across

the threshold of the doorway of hut F1. The relevance of these later Gaelic terms to features seen in the sixteenth/seventeenth century buildings on Dùn Èistean suggests that the building methods used in the nineteenth and early twentieth centuries were local techniques and traditions that may have originated two or three centuries earlier. Unfortunately with so little excavated examples of low status (vernacular) houses and dwellings from the period between the fifteenth and early nineteenth century there is little more that can be said on this possible evidence of continuity of building technique, and there is clearly more archaeological excavation needed to research the development of the form of the Lewis house in the late medieval/early post-medieval periods.[4]

Very little evidence for doors or windows survives. It is possible that rather than doors, the buildings had screens made from scrubby wood such as willow, which would be slotted into the doorway in a notch such as that found to the side of the doorway of F1. Murdoch's identification of small shards of window glass from Structure D Episode II (as well as later Episode III) suggests that the buildings here may have had small door or roof lights (as seen in the turf shielings built out on the moor in Ness in the nineteenth and twentieth centuries; see Illus 14.13). Evidence for interior fittings was also rare. House A1 had a low turf bank at one side of the hearth, possibly to shelter it from any draughts blowing in from the door. In B4 on the east side of the Structure B complex, a low platform defined by stones was found against the west wall and may have been for sitting or sleeping. If this feature is indeed a bed, it is a rare

Illus 14.13 A shieling at Cuidhsiadar, Ness. Photo: Dan Morrison, 1985; Reproduced by kind permission of Angus Morrison (Morrison 1997)

pre-eighteenth century turf and stone example (see Mackie 2013, 11-13, 17. 24-5). Otherwise, fittings were probably made from perishable materials, such as wooden hinges or heather rope, and have not survived in the archaeological record.

One of the debated topics on the site whilst excavations were ongoing inside the Episode I and II buildings was 'Is this the floor of the building?' This may seem like a strange question but on Dùn Èistean it was far from obvious in some buildings which soil layer was the floor. This was partly due to the difficulty of identifying what exactly a floor was. On other sites that had been excavated (eg Tintagel, Cornwall; Barrowman et al 1997) floors had seemed obvious – layers of sandy soil overlying the interior of the building, with a hearth laid on them, and containing debris such as broken pot sherds, bits of bone, flecks of charcoal and so on. However, recent discussions concerning floor layers have brought into question the interpretation of a layer such as this being a floor. Why, it is asked, would the occupants of a building want to walk around on a layer of broken bits of pot and other domestic rubbish, when surely they would sweep the floors clean? (Armit 2006, 240).

The difficulties in identifying and interpreting floor layers on Dùn Èistean were exacerbated by the nature of the deposits resulting from the building materials used. All the buildings were constructed, as we have seen above, using stone and turf walls and turf roofs. When a building was abandoned, the turf would eventually slump onto the interior floor and begin to decay, especially as roof timbers were removed to be re-used. Rubble and stones and further turf and wall core material would then collapse and sink into this turf slump, which became compressed into the floor below as the building walls continued to deteriorate due to exposure to the elements. In addition to this soils would become mixed through bioturbation (worms and weather mixing and churning up the soil on a microscopic scale), and leached due to the heavy rainfall in Ness. As a result of these collapse and decaying processes it could be difficult during excavation to differentiate between the floor layer of a building and the decayed layer of compressed and degraded turf and collapse above it. In many buildings this situation was exacerbated by the disturbance and mixing of layers which occurred as a result of the re-digging and re-use of collapsed turf to build Episode III shelters.

In the unroofed courtyard area D16 in Structure D however, floor layers were easier to identify. The latest floor layer to be uncovered for instance was a compact dark blackish-brown to mid-dark brown clayey silt with sand and charcoal flecks, quite different from the pale greyish-brown sandy degraded turf above it, and it contained four different hearths contemporary with it. Soils analysis of this, and the floor layers below it by McKenzie et al in Chapter 12, confirmed that these were occupation levels containing evidence for trampling, with organic debris such as flecks of charcoal and peat ash blown from the fire. A similar situation was seen in the excavations in hut F1 where two clearly defined phases of occupation/floor deposits were identified, including a compact sandy material that may have been brought in deliberately to level the

Illus 14.14 Floor and hearth in Structure B1 and Illus 14.15 Floor and hearth area in Structure D16 under excavation. The white tags mark the position of finds

floor or provide a clean surface, and evidence that the interior of the hut was swept out and straw used to cover the floor.

In Structures A and B however the floor layers were not so clear. Sunken floors set into the natural subsoil were identified in the buildings excavated in Structure B but there was a general lack of material found on them. However, the abandonment and collapse layers found immediately above the subsoil contained over 260 sherds of local pottery, as well as glazed ceramics, gunflints, lead projectiles, flint, iron objects, lumps of slag, glass and two coins - an Elizabeth I silver sixpence and a James VI billon plack. There is no doubt that many, if not most, of these finds actually derived from the use and occupation of the building, and indeed Bateson's late sixteenth/early seventeenth century date for the deposition of the coins (see Chapter 10) is contemporary with the use of the site (rather than its collapse and abandonment). This same scenario was seen in the interiors of houses A1 and A2, which appeared to have clean floors on the natural subsoil on which were set central hearths, but then large artefactual assemblages in the earliest collapse/turf slump deposits immediately above the subsoil. It cannot be ruled out therefore that the occupation material that accumulated during the use of Structures A and B became incorporated into the lowest layers of turf slump when the buildings were abandoned and collapsed, and the occupation material was then removed with the collapse deposits during the excavation. Campbell in his analysis of the assemblage of pottery sherds in Chapter 10 supports this observation. He identifies that the high average weight and high sherd to vessel ratios for much of the pottery found in these post-occupation collapse deposits indicate that most of the pottery had been broken more or less in situ, rather than being brought in from elsewhere or left over from an earlier phase of use (eg included in turf used to roof the building). He concludes that the smashed vessels may in fact have belonged in the underlying (ie floor) deposits but were removed with the post-occupation collapse as the two layers became fused together during decay.

It would seem therefore that on Dùn Èistean the floor layers of most, if not all, of the buildings contained fragments of discarded occupation material, such as broken pottery sherds, lumps of charcoal and burnt peat, and fragments of burnt bone. This may not be as unacceptable as it seems. It goes without saying that our modern perception of floors and 'cleanliness' will be quite different to the perception of those living on Dùn Èistean 400 years ago. Certainly a floor was to be reasonably level and dry, and therefore presumably warm and comfortable to walk, sit or lie on. However, the numbers of finds of pot sherds and other domestic 'rubbish' found in the floor layers on Dùn Èistean are small and akin to a layer of dust, muddy footprints and a few cobwebs in a busy farmhouse, rather than a knee-deep layer of domestic filth. The occasional pot sherd left behind in the low light of the building interior when a breakage occurred, or a small flake of flint trodden into the floor, was probably not important, or indeed, even noticed especially in the buildings on Dùn Èistean which were only occupied for a short time and on an ad hoc basis. The floors were also not that hard or concreted, another result perhaps of the

Illus 14.16 Collapsed stonework in the north end of Structure A and Illus 14.17 Pottery sherds being excavated in Trench D

successive short-lived occupations of the site, and this would have allowed for the incorporation of small bits of debris. It must be concluded that on this site, scatters of occupation material on an interior surface do not preclude it from being the floor surface of a building *per se*.

Population size and access onto Dùn Èistean

One of the most frequently asked questions by visitors to the site during the excavations was one of the hardest to answer: 'How many people would have lived on Dùn Èistean?' At any one time on the Dùn during Episodes I and II there was clearly more than one area of occupation, and therefore accommodation for more than just one or two people. For instance, around 15 men, women and children could probably have been sheltered and slept in each of the houses at Structure A if necessary for a few days or weeks. With the proviso that not all of the site was excavated, and many of the buildings do not now survive well enough to give an indication of their original size and form, it could be estimated that taken together the buildings on the Dun had the facilities to accommodate upwards of 100 people for a short length of time, provided supplies of peat, grain and other foodstuffs were brought to the site. There were at least two groups of buildings available for warmth and shelter in each episode, in addition to the corn-drying kiln barn for drying grain and storing supplies, and the man-made pond providing fresh water. As will be discussed below, there was also no shortage of local resources in the environment around the Dùn.

Ramsay's analysis of the pollen core taken from the pond in Chapter 11, suggests that on the island at this time (AD1440-1640) there was a significant number of plantains (*plantago* species) growing, which is suggestive of trampling pressure on the grassland habitat. The numbers of pottery sherds recovered from the site also indicates a significant-sized population, especially if we consider that only 50% of most of the buildings was excavated. Logically it would seem most likely that in a time of attack, or during an unsettled time when the local population needed to show their strength, women and children would be brought to the site for protection. Campbell suggests that ethnographic evidence shows that household-scale pottery production was almost always undertaken by women, and the spindle whorl fragment and quern stone fragment identified by Batey amongst the assemblage of stone finds may also support the presence of women on the site, and therefore also probably children.

The second most frequently asked question by visitors who had just walked over the 2002 Morrison footbridge to the site concerned whether Dùn Èistean was joined to the Ness mainland in the past. No evidence for any bridge footings or similar was found during the excavations, although the identification of the entrance gap in the perimeter wall east of building B6 suggests that the route up the steep cliffs here was also used in antiquity, and it is probable that there would have been some kind of stance or rope here to haul up supplies on to the site. Richard Cox in his study of the Ness place-names suggests that perhaps Èistean derives from the Norse for 'the stein of the isthmus' (ie 'rock/ stone of the promontory'; see Chapter 1 above; Cox 2006). Whilst it is most

Illus 14.18 A site tour in progress Illus 14.19 Ness cub scouts visit Dùn Èistean

likely that the promontory referred to would be the peninsula of Ness itself, it could be argued that Dùn Èistean was once linked by land with the adjacent coastline in the sixteenth/seventeenth centuries AD, and that this land has since eroded away and collapsed. By way of comparison, *Luchruban*, a small island similar to Dùn Èistean and situated less than a mile away from it on the opposite north-west coast of Ness, was joined to the Ness mainland when Captain Dymes visited it in the 1630s (see discussion in Barrowman, C S 2015, 158-9). However, whereas the gap between the mainland cliffs and *Luchruban* today is still filled with the rock falls from the erosion and collapse of the land connecting it, the gap at Dùn Èistean is relatively clear with smaller quantities of fallen rock. Also, perhaps the most convincing argument for Dùn Èistean having been an island 400-500 years ago is the position of the outer stone face of the perimeter wall that runs along the south edge of the Dùn, on the cliff top. Captain Thomas' description of the site in the 1860s suggests that the wall was on the edge of the island 150 years ago (Thomas 1878, 516), suggesting that there has been little erosion of the island cliff line since then, and given the description of Dùn Èistean in local oral tradition dating to only a century or so after the Dùn was occupied, it seems most likely that Dùn Èistean was a tidal island accessible only at low tide, even in the 1500s and 1600s AD.

From our modern standpoint it can seem so dangerous and above all such hard work to be clambering on and off the island with peats, food and other supplies and even building materials. The relationship between the Ness inhabitants and their landscape 400 years ago and their notion of accessibility was very different to ours however. What is considered an inconvenience, or a danger, or a barrier to us today, was probably simply a part of the landscape to them, a potential route to a resource, a challenging but not impossible environment. A large part of the wild food resource available to Nisich in the past was to be found in these 'dangerous' places – sea bird colonies on cliffs, fish in shallow rocky inshore waters to be caught from slippery rock ledges, even wild plants growing on cliff tops. The safe navigation and knowledge of these dangerous places had by necessity to be second nature to the Ness inhabitants then – a knowledge acquired in childhood, presumably handed down, generation to generation. Similarly, it can seem incredibly hard work to us to have to bring all necessary food and fuel supplies across and on to the island, and indeed it must have been, but this hard work was as much part of everyday life then as sitting at a computer all day (and then in front of a TV screen at night) is part of life today. It was hard work to carry a creel of peats all the way back to the township from the moor, it was hard work carrying a creel of peats down to the Dùn to be hauled up the cliffs to the site, but this does not mean it wasn't done.

The lack of an obvious landing place on the Dùn was also a frequently discussed topic amongst visitors to the site – made more so by the BBC Time Fliers programme filmed in 2003, which attempted to land a boat on, or even draw near to, the base of the rocky ledges at *Palla na Birlinn* on the east side of the island where the Morrisons were said to have hauled up their boats. Many of these ledges are easily reached by a short scramble down the rocks and they

Illus 14.20 The gap between Dùn Èistean and the Ness mainland from the west, Illus 14.21 Rock falls at Luchruban and Illus 14.22 Fulmar nesting on the cliff at Dùn Èistean

are all named locally, eg *Palla Borgh, Leac Crotach, Palla Ruadh* and *Ruighebhal* (see Chapter 2, Illus 2.9, above; Cox 2006). *Palla* is used locally to mean a ledge on a steep cliff (Fraser 1978, 246) of which there are many in Ness. Pulling a boat alongside the ledges around Dùn Èistean is a similar operation to that undertaken by ten men from Ness who still put out 40 miles to sea to the rocky stack of *Sula Sgeir* every year for the annual *guga* (young gannet) hunt, and manage perfectly well (though not without a little difficulty, good sea knowledge and plenty hard work) to off-load enough supplies for two weeks on to the island in what is often inclement weather and swell (Beatty 1992; MacGeoch et al 2010). There are many photographs held in the Comunn Eachdraidh Nis of the annual Sula Sgeir trip over the years – including photographs of the crew in the 1930s pulling their boat right out of the water and on to the rocks. These things were hard work and risky undertakings, and the high numbers of lives lost at sea generally from sea fishing in Ness is testament to that, but they were still done. Necessity is the mother of invention, not to say bravery and sheer determination.

Local resources, economy and diet
Fresh water and food
Although there is no natural spring on Dùn Èistean, it had its own supply of freshwater from a pond (Structure E) dug specifically for that purpose. Radiocarbon dating of the basal deposits from the pond produced a date range of AD1440-1640, showing that it is contemporary with the main occupation of Dùn Èistean. The original size of the pond may have been around 7m x 20m, and a channel had been dug through the east edge to allow excess water to drain away where overspill formed irregular terraces and a marshier area below. As well as the main source for drinking and cooking, the water in Structure E would have been collected and used in the production of pottery, cleaning of tools and utensils, washing and other domestic uses.

Pollen analysis of a core of sediment taken from the basal deposits of the pond is analysed by Ramsay in Chapter 11 above and she is able to say that the environment at the time of the main phase of occupation on Dùn Èistean was grassland, with only one occurrence of a cereal grain and very low counts of heather pollen, demonstrating that there was no heath land nearby. In her analysis of the assemblage of carbonised plant remains from the site in the same chapter, Ramsay identifies 17,000 carbonised oat and barley grains, plus chaff and weed seeds, at present a rare assemblage of such size and date in the Western Isles. The lack of cereals in the pollen core from the pond suggests that the oats and barley found on the site were not grown on Dùn Èistean itself, but some distance away on the Ness mainland. Evidence for agriculture is seen in the extensive system of *feannagan* or 'lazy beds' on the Ness mainland opposite the site, stretching from Knockaird to the Butt of Lewis, although these probably date to the early nineteenth century (see below). Harvesting would take place in September before the gales, and the barley and oats would be cut with a sickle or the plants pulled up by the roots, then dried in stacks before the sheaves were then cut into two – the heads for drying and grinding and the straw for byre bedding, fodder and thatching (Shaw 1980, 101-3; Emery 1996, 138; MacLeod 2009, 14). In the late medieval/early post-medieval period the land around the townships was unenclosed and open, and worked by common practices maintained throughout the farming calendar (Dodgshon 1993). This also preserved a common interest in the land, something that mattered a great deal in the troubled fifteenth to seventeenth centuries (Shaw 1980, 86).

Ramsay's analysis of the carbonised plant remains demonstrates that the production, drying and processing of oats and barley was a major part of life for the inhabitants of Ness who used Dùn Èistean in the late medieval/early post-medieval period. Burnt oat and barley grains found from the site show that these were the main cereal crops grown and the main food staple. Most of the grain deposits were clean, suggesting that the grain had come to site already beaten out of the sheaf and winnowed. However, some had evidence for chaff fragments, straw-like material, and carbonised weed seeds. This uncleaned grain was probably burnt during parching or gradaning, where sheaves were set alight and the roasted grain was shaken off with a knocking stick and ground into flour or meal for immediate use (MacLeod 2009, 35). A fragment of a quern found re-used in a wall in Structure D16 is evidence for this grinding of grain. Grain would have needed drying after any period of storage in the cool, damper Lewis climate. Grain, chaff, weed seeds and carbonised straw found together in larger quantities is most likely to have resulted from the drying of a larger amount of uncleaned grain over the hearth on a mat or layer of straw. MacLeod refers to accounts from Uist of the drying of barley sheaves placed on marram sacks on a frame called the *tarran* which was then placed over the open fire (MacLeod 2009, 35), and the burnt grain and straw deposits found below the walls of Structures B1, and D10 and D8 were probably the result of a similar process of drying that had presumably caught fire (or the sheaves and grain had fallen into the fire and burnt). The thick deposit of grain and burnt straw found under wall D10 in particular appeared during excavation to include a textile or mat of straw in

Illus 14.24 Taking a pollen core from the pond on Dùn Èistean and Illus 14.25 Oat straw

amongst the burnt grain, and the large deposit of burnt grain and straw found below D8 contained ash and willow charcoal, leading Ramsay to suggest this may indicate a basket or wicker container. It is perhaps not so surprising that a corn-drying kiln barn should have been built on the site when the small-scale domestic methods of drying grain seems to have been rather unpredictable, especially if there were increasing numbers of mouths to feed on the Dùn and there was a need to store and dry large amounts.

The kiln barn on Dùn Èistean is a conundrum however. Whilst it is comparable to late medieval/post-medieval examples that have been excavated to the south in the Uists (Sharples 2000, 91; Symonds et al 2001) and Harris[5] and is very similar to other, later nineteenth/twentieth century Hebridean examples, such as the kilns excavated on Hirta, St Kilda (Emery 1996, 14-17; plates 16-18, figs 64 and 65), noted at Galson, Ness (Scott 1951, 200; fig 5) and surveyed throughout the Ness township by the NALS project (eg in Eoropie, Skigersta, Eorodale and Aird Dell; Barrowman C S 2015, 270), very little carbonised grain was recovered from the kiln bowl, and the burning event evidenced in the flue was hardly substantial. However, this may be due to several factors, not least the considerable disturbance, robbing of stone and modification of the ruins of the kiln bowl, flue and platform to build rough shelters into the ruins of the kiln barn in the eighteenth century. As outlined above, small amounts of carbonised grain *were* recovered, together with charcoal and peat ash at the end of the flue and soils evidence for exposure to heat, and the lack of extensive burnt grain may simply indicate that the use of the kiln was cut short.

As with 'Norse' (horizontal) mills, the form of the Lewis kiln has been maintained over many generations (MacLeod 2009, 35), and it is probable that the workings of the Dùn Èistean kiln would not have differed that greatly from its more recent successors as described by MacLeod:

'There was a raised platform at the upper end, with a deep, round recess in its centre: the *surrag* or *sòrn* in Gaelic...the interior of the platform was filled with clay so as to retain heat once the kiln was fired...In preparing the kiln for firing, a 'roofing' structure was erected over the recess. Two boulders were placed opposite each other across the recess and a wooden beam was placed on top of them. Small lengths of timber were laid against the sides of the beam resembling a miniature timber roof on a blackhouse. These small timbers, the *maidean sùirn* or *cleithean* in Gaelic, sat at an angle of 30° from the horizontal. The wooden frame was then covered with straw; the *streaghaig* in Gaelic – and the grain was laid out on top of the straw to a depth of 3" or so. In some areas sheaves, the *balt* in Gaelic, were laid across the bottom of the straw to keep the grain in place, but this was not done in all areas. With this structure in place over the recess there was still room to move around on the platform.'

(MacLeod 2009, 35-6)

Illus 14.26 Corn drying kiln, Knockaird and Illus 14.27 Close-up of the excavated kiln bowl and flue in Structure C

As well as grain, Ramsay also identifies seeds of cultivated flax in three contexts dating to the Episode I occupation on the site (deposits below wall D010 in Structure D). Flax may have been grown as a crop in its own right, or may have occurred as a weed within the cereal crop but Ramsay is of the opinion that it is unlikely to have grown naturally in this locality and is more likely to be the remnants of a crop, either grown for fibre (linen) or for oil from the seeds (linseed). The low numbers of flax seeds recorded from the site may be because flax does not usually require drying as part of its processing and so there is a much lower chance of it being preserved through carbonization than there is for cereal grain. There is certainly place-name evidence from Ness for the growing of flax. The village of Lionel (*Lìonal*) just a mile or so from Dùn Èistean gets its name from the Norse for 'flax field' (Oftedal 1954, 372), and Cox suggests that nearby Loch Stìapabhat, which divides the village of Knockaird from Lionel, may derive its name from the Norse for 'loch of the steeping' (Cox 2006, 24), a place where the flax was soaked so as to soften the fibres ready for processing.

Meat was also an important part of the diet of the inhabitants of Dùn Èistean, as indicated by the assemblage of burnt animal bone found. Due to the acidic soils on the island the survival rate of unburnt bone is very low, and the burnt bones tended to be smaller fragments retrieved from the hearth. This means unfortunately that many of the bone fragments were not identifiable to species, and Masson-MacLean in his analysis in Chapter 11 is limited in what he can conclude from the assemblage. However, he is able to say that mammal bones are most numerous, with cattle and sheep dominating as a source of meat and probably dairy products. Other sources of food would probably have included domestic fowl, birds, fish, molluscs and crustacean (see Cerón-Carrasco in Chapter 11), as these species are all present in the assemblage. Most bone fragments were recovered from Area D, which is not surprising given that this is the largest area of occupation on the site, and in deposits that are associated with the burning of animal bone in the hearth, either as a way of rubbish disposal or as a fuel. Masson-MacLean is able to identify that butchery did take place on the site, and given the difficulty of access he concludes that animal carcasses were probably at least partially split before being taken there. It is possible that animals were taken live on to the site for short periods for protection, although unfortunately there was no evidence found to either support or refute this amongst the excavated deposits. It was suggested prior to excavation that house A2 may have been a byre, but the finding of a hearth in the centre of the building suggests that, in its final use at least, this building was for human occupation.

Gull and domestic fowl bones were identified amongst the bird bone, but there is no evidence that sea birds were caught for food. Ferguson in Chapter 10 points out that although muskets could have been used for hunting, this is unlikely to have been the case on Dùn Èistean. The only likely hunting to be had on the Dùn would have been sea birds in and around the cliffs, and it seems unlikely that muskets or pistols would be used for this. The hunting of sea birds in Lewis, and Ness in particular, has traditionally been done with nets and nooses, as it is during the annual trip to Sula Sgeir to hunt the *guga* (young

Illus 14.28 Loch Stiapabhat and Illus 14.29 Pieces of bone and iron in situ in layer D036 in Trench D

gannets), a prized local delicacy still eaten in Ness and the wider diaspora (see above; Islands Books Trust 2005). Hunting with guns a century later in the eighteenth century seems to have been reserved for hunting deer in the forests of Pairc and Lochs, and the west coast mainland (Thomas 1878, 538).

Cerón-Carrasco in Chapter 11 identifies from the fish bones found on Dùn Èistean that fishing was mainly an inshore activity that took place throughout the year from the rocky shore and from small boats close inshore using baited lines, with fish eaten fresh or preserved for later consumption. She identifies saithe, cod, haddock, thornback ray and herring bones which, like the animal bone, had mostly been burnt in the fire and then turned up in occupation material, or re-deposited in wall cores where old midden material had been used. Marine shellfish such as limpet, periwinkle and mussel, as well as crab, were also found collected for food and for bait. A rich vocabulary associated with fishing, and words describing the state of the sea, wind, weather and tides, has been preserved in the Gaelic language in more recent centuries in Lewis (see MacLeod 2005) and is testament to the importance of the sea to the lives of the Ness inhabitants. *Creagach* (fishing from the rocks) took place using the *slat-chreagaich* (rock-fishing rod) and *tàbh* (poke-net), (MacLeod 2005, 35, 42, 55). Larger fish such as adult cod and haddock were caught from boats using the baited *lion-beag* (small line) from boats in shallow water (ibid, 42, 54). The dun is still used today for fishing, and there are local place-names for all the ledges, inlets, skerries and cliffs around the coast at Knockaird and Fivepenny, most incorporating Norse elements (Fraser 1984). As discussed above, the Gaelic word '*palla*' for a rocky ledge, usually today associated with a ledge used for fishing, is found on the east and north sides of Dùn Èistean at *Palla na Birlinn* and '*Palla Borgh*' (Ledge of the Fort), and the name *Poll Èistean* is given on Angus MacLean's map (see Illus 2.9) to the waters immediately south-east of the Dùn, with *poll* having the meaning of a 'fishing ground'. This detailed naming is a reflection of the familiarity with and reliance upon the coastal waters and the marine resources around Ness to its inhabitants until a generation or two ago. As Fraser points out, these place-names survived because of their frequency of use and descriptive nature (Fraser 1984, 38-9). For instance, Ness men were renowned for their seamanship in the nineteenth century when Jens Jacob Asmussen Worsaae, a Danish antiquarian who visited Lewis in 1846, records "It is said on the island that the inhabitants of Ness are more skillful fishermen and better sailors than the rest of the men of Lewis" (cited in Stummann Hansen 2000, 89).

Fuel

The main fuel used on Dùn Èistean was peat. Peat ash and pieces of burnt peat are found right across the site, in occupation material, in hearths and in the walls and floors of the buildings. There was also evidence for a peat stack found on the old ground surfaces near Structure D. Peat would have been cut from the moorland interior of Ness as it still is today.[6] The peat is traditionally cut in the late spring from peat banks, using the *tairsgeir*, or peat cutting iron, and then left to dry flat on the top of the banks until it is dry enough to be lifted (put

Illus 14.30 Rocky ledges around Dùn Èistean and Illus 14.31 Peat bank

Illus 14.32 Am Palla Ruadh at the back of (north side of) Dùn Èistean

on end). After a further period of drying, and sometimes further sorting and pulling together of the peats into small stacks, the peat is brought in towards the end of the summer before the moor is too wet. On Dùn Èistean, because all fuel had to be brought up the cliffs to the site, there would certainly have been expedient burning of waste and materials found near the site itself, such as bone (food waste) and driftwood. Ramsay identifies that heather was used as the main fuel in the primary hearth deposit in house A1 for instance, and the hearth in the courtyard D16 had evidence from the soils analysis for the burning of bone mixed with other fuels. Several fragments of burnt animal bone were also recovered from the kiln flue fire spot, and in the pottery clamp kiln. Ramsay also identifies an extremely diverse wood charcoal assemblage, with sixteen tree genera recorded, and suggests that the range of species found on the site reflects a general collection of whatever wood could be found for fuel. She identifies that most of the wood would have had to have been imported or collected as driftwood, (spruce, Scots pine, larch, fir, oak, ash) although species such as willow, alder, hazel and birch would have grown in the peat moor, and preserved birch branches and logs would have been found in the peat when cutting for fuel.

Pottery, metal-working and everyday objects

The assemblage of over 3500 sherds of locally hand-made coarse pottery from the site is the largest excavated from a late/post-medieval site in the Hebrides, is the first large stratified and radiocarbon dated assemblage of this date to be published and as such is of considerable importance. Campbell in Chapter 10 suggests that in the case of Dùn Èistean some pots were probably brought to site intact as containers for cooking and storage, such as for ale, milk, butter or fish oil. He identifies the fingernail impression decoration on a proportion of the sherds as a local characteristic that may have been a particular local or family pattern handed down from mother to daughter. A small collection of cups found in the houses A1 and A2, and in Structure D, are decorated with this fingernail decoration, which is unique to Dùn Èistean.[7] The almost complete smashed pot found on the original ground surface next to the clamp kiln has been reconstructed (see Cat 28 in Campbell, Chapter 10) and shown to be a large globular jar with an upright and slightly out-turned neck was also decorated with closely-spaced fingernail impressions on the interior of the rim. The neck of the craggan jars were shaped this way so that a leather skin could be tied over the out-turned rim and then secured by a cord tied around the neck. Campbell identifies that craggans are not, as previously thought, a late form of earlier Iron Age pottery traditions, but a unique local development of a construction technique widespread in the Hebrides. The globular jar with narrow neck fulfilled a functional niche, and Campbell emphasises that it has not been properly appreciated what an innovation this form was, given the flat-based wares of the preceding Norse period. Traditionally, this locally-made pottery was simply made and fired on the domestic hearth, although a proportion of the pottery from Dùn Èistean may have been fired in the clamp kiln. Campbell confirms that the clay used to make the pots is of immediate local origin, derived from glacial tills,

Illus 14.33 Excavating a pottery rim sherd in Trench D

in turn derived from the underlying Lewisian gneisses, and is full of coarse rock fragments and minerals derived from the breakdown of these rocks.

A small amount of slag and vitrified fuel ash, including a lump of slag from the base of a hearth (or small furnace), is identified by Sneddon in Chapter 10 from Episodes I and II as evidence of small-scale metal-working on the site, probably on an ad hoc basis. There are also indications from the finding of lead scrap that lead projectiles were cast on site, as suggested by Ferguson in Chapter 10. The metal finds from the site identified by Batey comprise mainly iron nails and roves derived from the burning or re-use of driftwood, although there are also fragments of a metal binding strip from a bucket or barrel, which provides a glimpse of the domestic utensils and other objects made out of leather, bone and wood that would have been in use on this site, the evidence for which has decayed away in the acidic soils. Batey's report on the stone artefacts identifies weights, spindle whorls, whetstones, hammer stones and pot lids, all indirect evidence for everyday subsistence activities such as spinning, fishing and processing and storage of food.

The wider landscape of Ness

As evidenced in the archaeology of the site, the stronghold of Dùn Èistean in Episodes I and II was only occupied for short periods of time, as and when needed. For the most part the inhabitants of Ness in the late fifteenth to early seventeenth centuries AD would have lived in small farmsteads around the fertile coastal areas (Dodgshon 1993), as indicated in Ness by the work of the Ness Archaeological Landscape Survey (NALS) undertaken as part of the DEAP (Barrowman, C S 2015, 246-50). The survey has identified traces of medieval pottery eroding from coastal areas and on the edges of eroding settlement mounds along the west coast machair at Cross, Swainbost and Habost, and post-medieval smithy sites eroding from the Eoropie and Swainbost machairs (Barrowman 2007a; 2007b). The site at Swainbost is particularly extensive, consisting of three conjoined eroding settlement mounds containing occupation material as well as remnants of a stone structure and dense scatterings of slag and ironworking debris, including whole furnace bases. However, other than these mounds and other general but elusive scatters of medieval pottery, few remains have been located of the vernacular buildings of what could be termed 'everyday' settlement in Ness at this time. This is due mainly to the building materials that were used (turf walls, with stone footings), which has meant that very little survives in the landscape today. Such dwellings were relatively quick to build and used the raw materials available in the local environment. To some extent they were also a reflection of the seasonal movements of the population. At Bragar, for instance, on the west coast of Lewis south of Ness, Dodgshon demonstrates that during the post-medieval period not all the houses in a settlement would be occupied at any one point as they cycled between phases of use, disuse and reuse (Dodgshon 1993, 434; see also Campbell 2010, 320-1). The evidence from Dùn Èistean confirms that this cycle of building, repair, re-occupation and re-building was an integral feature of rural settlement in the

Illus 14.34 View of Swainbost machair showing settlement mounds

region at this time, even on a nominally higher-status site.

The remains of the agricultural landscape contemporary with this settlement are lost to us today. The extensive system of upstanding lazybeds and enclosures that can still be seen on the Ness mainland immediately opposite and north of Dùn Èistean (see Illus 2.8 and 2.25 above; Barrowman and Driscoll 2000) date to a later period of agricultural improvements in the eighteenth century and into the nineteenth, when they were probably worked by the inhabitants of the new crofting township of Knockaird, rather than being contemporary with the occupation on Dùn Èistean (eg see Halliday 2001, 17; also see above and Barrowman, C S 2015, 167-8). Later settlement and cultivation, and the routine re-use of building stone, and dismantling and rebuilding of turf structures (see Campbell 2010), have largely wiped out such contemporary settlement or agricultural remains from across the landscape in Ness. Also, very few medieval and later rural settlements have been excavated and published in the Western Isles with which to compare. Recent archaeological work has begun to address the lack of study, identification, excavation and dating of this kind of late medieval/post-medieval settlement of turf and stone buildings and their surrounding agricultural landscapes on Lewis (Armit 1997; Armit et al 2008; see also Atkinson et al 2000; Dalglish 2002; Hingley 1993; Dodgshon 1993; 1996). Armit's excavations on the shores of Loch Olabhat in North Uist at Druim nan Dearcag and Eilean Olabhat have identified late medieval/post-medieval settlement and re-use and are one of the few areas of this date to have been excavated and published in the Western Isles (Armit 1997; Armit et al 2008). At Druim nan Dearcag the same pattern is seen as at Dùn Èistean, with the sixteenth/seventeenth century turf and stone buildings pre-dating the ridge-and-furrow cultivation associated with the nearby cleared township of Foshigarry (Armit 1997, 900-1). At Eilean Olabhat, which includes a period of re-occupation during the late medieval period, Armit suggests that small, dispersed settlements like Eilean Olabhat and Druim nan Dearcag represent a tidemark of medieval and later settlement preserved only at the margins of the settled landscape where their remains survived obliteration by later field systems (Armit et al 2008, 100). Certainly the late medieval buildings at Dùn Èistean have survived due to their remote location away from arable land. In addition, the Episode III building of small shelters into the ruins of the medieval stronghold between the late seventeenth and early nineteenth centuries is connected with the seasonal use of the Dun for grazing and fishing purposes by the inhabitants of the contemporary settlements and farmsteads on the Ness mainland (see Episode III, above).

Illus 14.35 Remains of a turf building in Ness

Dùn Èistean, the Morrisons and the MacLeod lordship
Setting the scene: the historical and antiquarian background
MacCoinnich and Stiùbhart's accounts in Chapter 3 provide an historical context for the short bursts of sporadic occupation, activity and conflict evidenced on Dùn Èistean in the sixteenth/seventeenth centuries in the archaeological record. Both historians confirm that the 'brieve' kindred as they were known

prior to becoming known as 'Morison' or 'Morrison', first appeared as a family of hereditary *britheamhan* or judges in the historical record in the later sixteenth century, and they explore the tradition that the site was the stronghold of the Clan Morrison. At this time the *britheamhan* had a 'kindly' right to the lands of Ness, and a stronghold and a large house there (an *Taigh Mòr*, Habost). In addition to this, Stiùbhart discusses the nineteenth century tradition that 'MacLeod of Eoropaidh', had a mansion or castle with an iron gate, and that *Teampall Mholuaidh*, St Moluag's church (also in Eoropie), is described as 'the Laird's Church'. He suggests that both the Morrisons and the MacLeods possessed power bases in the district of Ness in the late medieval period, the Morrisons in Habost, the MacLeods in Eoropie. At this time there is also a tradition that the whole north end of Ness was considered a sanctuary wherein the brieves operated under the jurisdiction of the MacLeods in what Stiùbhart describes as a 'relatively flexible and less adversarial justice system' which was part of 'a patchwork of local customary judicatures' in the late medieval *Gàidhealtachd*, and it is within this context that we should view Dùn Èistean.

MacCoinnich sets forth the history of this turbulent period, described as the '*Linn nan Creach*', or Age of Raids, from the forfeiture of the MacDonald Lords of the Isles in 1493 to the MacKenzie takeover of Lewis in 1610. He details the 'spasmodic, often ineffective, royal attempts' to control the western seaboard, with the MacLeods of Lewis in particular in frequent rebellion right from the start, and describes the events which led to the *britheamhan* becoming embroiled in this conflict. This included when Niall Odhar MacLeod sought revenge for the capture, betrayal and murder of his brother Torcall Dubh (the MacLeod chief) at the hands of the MacKenzies, whom the *britheamhan* handed him over to in 1597. Niall Odhar pursued the brieve and his kin to their stronghold in Ness (probably Dùn Èistean), where he besieged them and then forced them to leave. Stiùbhart considers this besieging and slighting of Dùn Èistean as underscoring the final destruction of the sanctuary system in Lewis, and he suggests that the collapse of the local justice system at the end of the sixteenth century was exacerbated by the collapse of local ecclesiastical structure after the Reformation. MacCoinnich describes how no more is then seen of the brieves in the documentary record until after the turn of the sixteenth century when the *britheamhan* kindred changed their name to Morrison, at the same time as changing their profession from lawmen to ministers, and making terms with the incoming MacKenzie regime.

As followers of the MacLeods of Lewis, who had outright title to the whole of Lewis, MacCoinnich suggests that the Morrisons probably appeared in other parts of the MacLeod lordship in the sixteenth and early seventeenth centuries. Both historians draw attention to the strategic position of Dùn Èistean on the edge of these territories with a vista onto the busy seaways surrounding Ness, and the archaeological evidence from Dùn Èistean should be seen in this context. Northwards, these waters were also the scene of piracy and raiding between the Northern Isles and Lewismen at this time, and southwards to journeys between Lewis and Ulster, where bands of armed

Illus 14.36 Site of Taigh Mòr, Habost and Illus 14.37 Teampall Mholuaidh (St Moluag's church) in Eoropie, Ness

Lewismen were involved in the Irish wars. MacCoinnich's fascinating outline of some of the documentary evidence for the use of firearms in the area during this period demonstrates that it was the norm for the MacLeod leaders and presumably their followers (such as the *britheamhan*), to be armed and trained for war, an observation that renders less unusual the finding of gunflints and lead projectiles on a stronghold such as Dùn Èistean. In particular he highlights his own research into the routes to and from the rich fishing grounds around north Scotland, which were the cause of much conflict and tension between the Lewis MacLeods, the Scottish Crown and continental merchants (MacCoinnich forthcoming). An attempt by King James VI to establish a plantation of merchants and noblemen from Fife in 1598 (the 'Fife Adventurers') to bring stability to the area and exploit the lucrative fishery in the waters around Lewis was faced with violent opposition from the MacLeods, and MacCoinnich quotes from documents that describe that the Fife Adventurers pursued (and slew) any natives that resisted them, back to their home communities. He suggests that whilst no documents mention Dùn Èistean, 'it is almost certain that the colonists' soldiers would have paid such a structure close attention if it were intact at this time (1605)'. Both historians conclude that it would be unlikely that the stronghold on Dùn Èistean survived the chaotic conditions of 1598-1610.

The historical background and traditions relating to the Morrison brieves, the MacLeod lordship and the unrest and skirmishes in Lewis in the sixteenth and early seventeenth centuries, are all entirely consistent with the archaeology on Dùn Èistean. In particular the documentary evidence for the busy seaways, the internecine conflicts within the MacLeod lordship fuelled by the intervention of the Scottish Crown and its attempts at plantation, and the eventual demise of the Morrison judges in the early seventeenth century are all compatible with the excavated evidence. Whilst it is not the author's intention to accept "general historical conceptions at the cost of relegating the field evidence to a supporting chorus" (Campbell 2010, 318), the historical background adds a depth to the material evidence that is not possible from the archaeological remains alone.

Stiùbhart's exploration of the nineteenth century oral tradition that the whole of the northern part of the Ness district was considered a sanctuary in the late medieval period, identifies supporting historical evidence not only in Martin Martin's accounts of other sanctuaries throughout the Isles, but more importantly in the designation of the north end of Ness as 'Ard Chombrick' (Gaelic: *Àird Chomraich,* the peninsula of the sanctuary, see Stiùbhart in Chapter 3, above) on Joan Blaeu's 1654 map (see Illus 3.9, above). He emphasises that it was no coincidence that the Morrison's *Taigh Mòr* was situated immediately adjacent to the boundary of this sanctuary, and stresses that the Morrisons were thus ideally placed to act as 'legal brokers, employing their legal knowledge in order to negotiate agreements between fugitives and would-be avengers' (see above). Also located in this area are sites associated with the MacLeods in oral tradition; *Cnoc a' Chaisteal* (Hill of the Castle), also known as *Caisteal Olghair* (Olaus' Castle), and *An Teampall Mholuaidh* (*Teampall Mholuaidh*; St Moluag's church in Eoropie). Dùn Èistean was therefore placed in a landscape of powerful interplay between the

Morrisons, MacLeods and the mainland authorities, with the Church playing an important role. Stiùbhart concludes that the violence and unrest amongst the competing MacLeod factions at the end of the sixteenth century/beginning of the seventeenth may have been exacerbated by the collapse of local ecclesiastical structure and the breakdown of the sanctuary system after the Reformation. MacCoinnich, in his discussion 'From judges to ministers' in Chapter 3, above, identifies that at this time, from the mid-seventeenth century, the Morrisons switched from being 'brieves' to ministers, with an accompanying name change from mac *a'Bhritheimh* (son of the Brieve) or *MacGilleMhoire* (son of the servant of Mary) to the more acceptable-sounding 'Morrison'/'Morison'.

A place of refuge: Sieges, skirmishes and short-lived occupation

The archaeology on Dùn Èistean in Episodes I and II is characterized by several short-lived occupations of buildings, and evidence for small-scale conflict and destruction. The excavations failed to find any evidence for large accumulation of midden material (rubbish), as would be expected on a site occupied for any length of time. Midden was found instead thrown out of doorways outside buildings, for example at A1, B6 and F1. The method of construction of the tower also indicates a rapid response to an imminent threat or attack: It has the appearance of having been thrown up quickly, to such an extent that it fell down half way through construction, and was then repaired in haste, with the tower base walls simply rebuilt around the failed first attempt, and the upper tower built on top. Traces of successive use/abandonment/re-use in all the remaining structure groups, A–D, F and H within Episodes I and II were also found, and Outram and Batt's conclusions in Chapter 13 that the radiocarbon dating results present an image of a site in repeated use support this.

Within this picture of temporary, short-lived use and hurried response, there may also be evidence for the deliberate destruction of two buildings on the site. When the tower went out of use the upper storey collapsed, resulting in a huge mound of stone rubble falling over and around the lower basal part of the tower. However, when this rubble mound was excavated it was found that it contained two distinct layers of collapsed stone, rather than a gradual slump and accumulation of rubble. Instead it appears that the upper stone tower had suffered a rapid and catastrophic collapse, suggestive of a deliberate slighting or demolition. We also know from the soils analysis by MacKenna and Simpson in Chapter 12 that F1, the small hut on the east side of the island, collapsed relatively suddenly at the end of Episode II as the boundary between the collapse layers and the floor layer is very sharp, suggesting that the turf roof and/or upper turf walls collapsed whilst the structure was in use, or only just abandoned. This may indicate that this structure was also deliberately destroyed. It was certainly never re-occupied.

The artefactual evidence for small-scale sporadic conflict is significant in this context. Ferguson in Chapter 10 suggests that the pistol shot and musket balls found on the site are most likely to represent the debris of multiple events of conflict as some were found in collapsed wall deposits, others were found

Illus 14.38 Collapsed walling of first tower build within second, outer wall, from the north

in hearths and floors where they were discarded unused, some in the process of being manufactured. Ferguson describes how lead projectiles were relatively easy to manufacture and did not require any specialist knowledge except for some basic skills in smelting and a hand held mould, and suggests they were therefore probably made on site. Ballin, in his analysis of the unique gunflint assemblage (see Chapter 10), identifies that gunflints were not only used but also manufactured on site. His study of the distribution of the flints across the site demonstrates that most gunflint production took place in the main areas of settlement, with speedy production of gunflints mostly in sizes associated with smaller firearms, from a limited supply of raw material. He is in no doubt that guns were discharged on the site, and suggests that there were one or more sieges on Dùn Èistean. This nationally-important gunflint assemblage is unique not only due to its age (the oldest known excavated assemblage in Britain), but also the evidence for local adaptation to scarce raw materials and the ad hoc adaptation to a specific stress scenario, such as a siege and is discussed by Ballin elsewhere (Ballin 2012). MacCoinnich's research in Chapter 3, above, suggests it was the norm for clan leaders and presumably their followers to be armed and trained for war. Given the troubled political situation in the Isles in the sixteenth and early seventeenth centuries, we should not be seeing sites such as Dùn Èistean and the material recovered from it as an exception or a rarity — we should be expecting to find them elsewhere in north and west Scotland.

Illus 14.39 Lower collapse layer on west side of tower Structure G

A place of power: Monitoring and controlling access to the seaways

Due to its strategic location, Dùn Èistean would have been ideally placed to monitor the seaways around Ness, especially the trade routes and rich fishing grounds there. This aspect is hard to investigate from the archaeological remains alone. We may however look for comparisons to Gaelic Ireland where tower houses and defensive sites found around the coasts, are thought to have been used to control access to fishing grounds and collect taxes and levies for landing or supply of victuals from those fishing in the jurisdiction of a Gaelic lord's territory (Breen 2001, 423). Like Dùn Èistean, such sites were only occupied for short periods of time. They were by definition seasonal because the work of foreign fishing fleets was confined to the summer months, the winter months not being suitable for working off the Atlantic coast or for journeying between Ireland and the continent (ibid, 425). It is being increasingly recognised that the coastal tower houses of Ireland were also not only defensive, but like Dùn Èistean, located at key control and entry points to the Gaelic lordships in which they were built, including the control of sea resources, and for this they

Illus 14.40 View across the Minch to Sutherland and Assynt on the Scottish mainland

had to be, like Dùn Èistean, effective watchtowers (Naessens 2007, 226; 235; and references therein).[8] Many similarities are seen between the castles found on the west coast of the Highlands and Islands and those on the north Irish coasts. The Scots began to settle in Ulster in the sixteenth century, and regional styles emerged in places such as Co Antrim, for instance, where the MacDonnells built castles in the second half of the sixteenth century of the same type as those found on the coasts of the Scottish Highlands (Loeber 2001, 296, 298). The historical background for the MacLeods of Lewis' involvement in the Irish wars in the final decades of the sixteenth century outlined by MacCoinnich in Chapter 3, above, provides an historical context for this and highlights the importance of the beginnings of multi-disciplinary and cross-cultural research that has begun to take place into the links between the two areas in the late medieval/early post-medieval period.

A very small assemblage of finds from the site indicate that the occupants of Dùn Èistean were also in touch with the wider European trading routes in the 1500s and early 1600s. The rim and neck sherds found on the site from a small bottle or bellarmine (*Bartmanmkruig*) from Cologne dating to between 1525-1575 AD are identified by Will in Chapter 10 above as originating from a bottle of wine and were possibly traded from merchants using the sea routes up and down the Minch between Europe, the Northern Isles and Ireland. He also reports that this is the first example of this type of decoration recovered from Scotland, and that although this type of ceramic is relatively common on urban and east coast excavations, few sherds have been recovered from the north or west of Scotland although wine was one the main imports into the Western Isles in the early seventeenth century (see MacCoinnich in Chapter 3, above; Shaw 1980, 161). A shard tentatively identified by Murdoch in Chapter 10 as being from a sixteenth century Venetian or *Facon de Venise* glass and similar to cold colour decorated glass from other sixteenth century contexts may also be evidence of contact, if indirect, with a wider world of commerce.

In addition to the imports are the two coins found on the site; a billon plack of James VI described by Bateson in Chapter 10 as comparable to coins found at Castle Maol, Skye that were deposited shortly after 1601 (Stevenson 1952), and an English sixpence, a commonly-found coin struck in large numbers by Elizabeth I from 1561 until 1602. Bateson suggests that the English sixpence was probably lost on the site some time in the early 1600s, and whilst we do not know how or why it came to be on Dùn Èistean, it is nevertheless a clear link to the wider political scene of the time and reminds us that Lewis became embroiled in a wider 'British' world following the Union of the Crowns. The James VI billon plack is a particularly interesting find. Bateson describes how it is part of an issue authorised in July 1588 by the Privy Council to fund a proposed expedition led by Francis Stewart, first Earl of Bothwell, to the Outer Hebrides in order to restore order there. The coin issue was to have been used to purchase artillery and other provisions for the expedition, but the expedition never took place. These two small coins therefore are a small indication of how control of what is considered today to be a remote part of Scotland was, at the end of the sixteenth century, a crucial consideration in the machinations of political struggle in the power centres on the mainland. As both historians MacCoinnich and Stiùbhart highlight in Chapter 3 above, the position of the Outer Hebrides on the busy trade and shipping routes around the north of Britain and across to northern Europe meant that they played a crucial part in any fight for control of the maritime trade and resources at the end of the sixteenth and early seventeenth centuries.

Dùn Èistean and the castle tradition

As a defended site Dùn Èistean stands at the end of a long tradition of clan strongholds and stone-built castles that appeared along the western seaboard and islands after the thirteenth century, the most important being Finlaggan, Islay, the centre of the Lords of the Isles (Caldwell 1990; 1991; 1992; 1993; 1994; 1997; 2010; Caldwell and Ewart 1993; Dodgshon 2002, 9-10; 18-19; Miket and Roberts 1990). Excavations at Finlaggan led by David Caldwell uncovered a fantastic group of finds and buildings on two of the islands in Loch Finlaggan, *Eilean Mòr*, and the smaller, *Eilean na Comhairle*, all spanning the period from the thirteenth to the sixteenth centuries. His work identified that Finlaggan in the Middle Ages comprised a castle on *Eilean na Comhairle*, with over twenty buildings, including a hall and a chapel, within timberwork defences, on the adjacent *Eilean Mòr*. Whilst Dùn Èistean post-dates Finlaggan, being associated instead with the period following the demise of the Lords of the Isles, it is similar in that it functioned both as a place of refuge and a symbol of power and prestige within its territory, although of a lower status than Finlaggan. Unlike Finlaggan and other, older, strongholds in the Lordship, however, Dùn Èistean had in outward appearance and building techniques used, more in common with the local settlements lived in by the poorer Ness inhabitants at the time, than with the high status castles of the Lordship. Being largely built from turf, stone and earth walls Dùn Èistean is a unique local interpretation of the concept of a castle, built with materials that were to hand and using tried and tested local methods. As such it differs in appearance to most of the lime-mortared masonry castles and tower houses found along the north-west seaboard. However, Miket and Roberts in their study of the castles of Skye and Lochalsh describe a castle as follows:

> 'Where the area available permitted, a curtain wall with a parapet walk and gateway enclosed both the tower and courtyard area. Within this would have stood the subsidiary buildings necessary to the functioning of a household, such as stores for food, fuel and household goods, stables, sheds and perhaps accommodation for retainers and visitors'

> (Miket and Roberts 1990, 5)

Illus 14.41 Castle Maol, Skye (copyright Historic Scotland)

By this measure Dùn Èistean could be classed as a castle, and certainly functioned as such, with its perimeter wall, lookout tower and ancillary buildings.

When MacPhail first investigated the remains of the ruined tower on Dùn Èistean in 1866 (see Chapter 2, above), Thomas described it as having the appearance of "an incipient peel", probably from the twelfth century by comparison with Cubbie Roo's castle in Orkney (Thomas 1890, 366). It can be seen why Thomas chose this particular castle as a comparison. All that remains of Cubbie Roo is the basement of a 7m square tower, built from walls up to 2m thick, with no ground floor entrance (something which MacPhail specifically searched for in his investigations on Dùn Èistean) and a central water tank in the form of a hollow in the centre of the floor. As such, in plan, it looks very similar to the small tower on Dùn Èistean. One hundred years after Thomas' work however, we now know that the Dùn Èistean tower was built up to 400 years later than Cubbie Roo. There may be a Northern Isles connexion however, given the historical references to raiding and piracy between Lewis and Orkney and Shetland in the sixteenth and early seventeenth centuries (see Chapter 3, above). A re-evaluation of some of the coastal settlements found on offshore stacks and precipitous headlands in the Northern Isles and nominally dated to the early medieval/Norse period is in this context perhaps overdue. It is not beyond the realms of possibility that, like Dùn Èistean, some may have been occupied if not built in the 1500s and early 1600s AD to control and defend the maritime routes around the north of Scotland (indeed far from being linked to good agricultural land, it is noted that many have an immediate view only of the sea; Lamb 1973, 81).

Given the local techniques employed in the buildings on Dùn Èistean, it is most likely that we are to find comparisons for the small tower within the MacLeod territories of the Western Isles and western seaboard of north and west Scotland. The walls of the base of the tower on Dùn Èistean were built with a slight inwards batter, a feature more usually seen in nineteenth century blackhouses in Lewis (Fenton 1985, 70) that would have provided stability by spreading the load of the tower walls across a wider area (James Crawford, pers comm). This feature is also seen at *Teampall Mholuaidh* (St Moluag's), just across from Dùn Èistean and traditionally considered to be the MacLeod's church (see Stiùbhart, Chapter 3 above). A small-scale excavation around the outside of the church in 1977 revealed that it had been built onto the undisturbed clay subsoil without formal foundations, despite its massive size, and the lower courses of the walls were strengthened with a battered plinth to spread the load of the gable walls and prevent subsidence (Barber 1981; Barrowman 2005, 10-13). Barber notes that this is also a feature seen at St Clement's Church in Rodel, Harris (also linked to the MacLeods), and suggests that it may be a Hebridean tradition, saying that whilst there is not direct evidence to support it, "the possibility that Teampull Mholuaidh was, like St Clement's, built in the sixteenth century cannot be ruled out." (Barber 1981, 532). The tower on Dùn Èistean is not of the same monumental size as either St Moluag's or St Clement's churches, and although it is battered, it does not require a plinth as it is built onto rock not clay. However, it is a high status building, and it is possible that the use of battered walls was a particular local technique used in the MacLeod territories, where it is also seen

Illus 14.42 Teampall Mholuaidh (St Moluag's church) in Eoropie, Ness showing batter at base of wall

in castles such as Castle Maol in Skye, a simple four-storey rectangular tower, 10m x 5m internally, which guards the straits of Kyleakin between Skye from the mainland (Miket and Roberts 1990, 32-37).

The Dùn Èistean tower also fits loosely into the tradition of small towers or keeps found throughout the Western Isles, often on small islet duns in inshore lochs in the Uists and Barra in particular (see Raven 2005, 336-361 for full discussion of these sites, who suggests that their inland distribution may reflect a proximity to pastoral resources, and overland routes between both high status Lordship sites, and lower status settlements; ibid, 348-350). Examples of these sites include *Caisteal Calabhaigh* (Castle Calvay) on the east side of South Uist at the mouth of Loch Boisdale, *Caisteal Bheagram* (Castle Beagram) in an inland loch in Drimsdale, South Uist, *Caisteal a' Bhreabhair* on a stack to the south of Eriskay and *Dùn MhicLeòid* (Sinclair's Castle, or MacLeod's Castle) on an artificial island in Loch Tangusdale, Barra. All include small, two to three-storey rectangular towers of around 6m x 5m. *Caisteal Calabhaigh* and *Caisteal Bheagram* are stone-built medieval castles, with a hall and other buildings built within a curtain wall with gun slits on the seaward side (Raven 2005, 339, 341; Salter 1995, 151; Barrowman, C pers comm; Raven 2005, 341-4; Salter 1995, 148). *Caisteal a' Bhreabhair* has turf and stone outbuildings surrounding the tower and was traditionally the haven of a pirate (Raven 2005, 340-2). Dùn MhicLeòid comprises only a rectangular tower 5.4m x 5.5m with walls 1.4m thick standing to 4.5 m high on a small island in the loch (Salter 1995, 151).

These sites are attributed to the MacNeils and the Clanranald, and like Dùn Èistean, date to the sixteenth and seventeenth centuries (see Raven 2005, 346-7). However, they are all built from lime-mortared stonework, none having the same almost solid earth lower storey or earthen wall cores and use of turf seen in the Dùn Èistean tower. This implies that at Dùn Èistean we are seeing a predominantly local response to the unique environment of Ness, or to a specific threat, with little evidence for imported building techniques or materials. Dùn Èistean is a coastal rather than inland site, and Ness is an exposed peninsula jutting right out into the Atlantic and the North Sea, away from the mainland and unprotected from sea gales and storms, and this harsh environment in itself would have necessitated a solid building. Perhaps the solid earthen base is a response to the threat of canon fire. Dùn Èistean was situated in the thick of the shipping routes around north Scotland and Europe and therefore open to the threat from hostile sea traffic. The building of an almost solid earthen base to the tower was wise on a site in danger of attack, including from cannon fire by ships out at sea, which we know were used against fortified coastal sites in Lewis during the sixteenth/seventeenth century period (see MacCoinnich in Chapter 3, above).

Lordship sites in Ness

There are sites within Ness that are traditionally associated with the former MacLeod Lordship of the late medieval period. They are both still visible in the landscape, and this is partly what has ensured the survival of the tradition

Illus 14.43 Dun Mhic Leòid, Loch Tungasdale, Barra

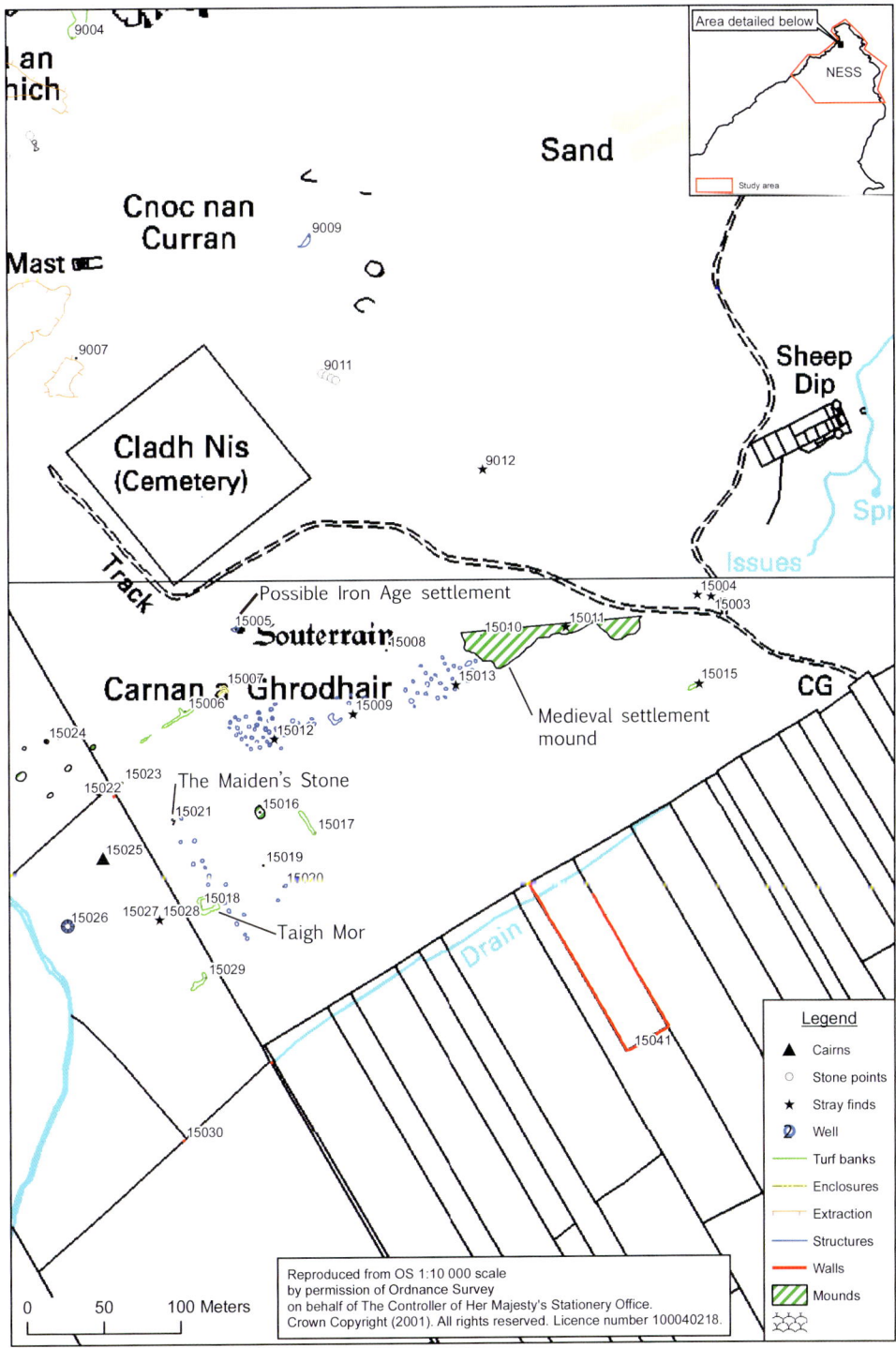

Illus 14.44 NALS survey of Taigh Mor area

attached to them (ie there is a tangible thing in the landscape that can be referred to when the story is passed on, so locating it and facilitating the retention of the story). As discussed by Stiùbhart in Chapter 3 above, *An Taigh Mòr* (the Big House) is traditionally considered to be the *'Taigh a' Bhritheimh'* or Brieve's House, the place from which the *britheamhan*, later Morrisons, would dispense justice. Geophysical survey by the NALS in 2007 recorded a large rectangular building at the site of *An Taigh Mòr*, still just visible on the ground as low banks, possibly divided into three rooms and with a small compartment joined on to the building to the east. The building measures internally at least 8m x 6.5m, with walls up to 2m thick and stone-lined with an earthen core. The survey also picked up evidence for a complicated system of enclosures and cultivation around the area, and identified extensive settlement mounds and scatters of pottery across the machair to the north (Barrowman, C S 2015, 180-3; Barrowman C 2007b, 35-7; Poller 2007b, 38; Poller 2015a).

The site of *Cnoc a' Chaisteal* (Hill of the Castle), also known as *Caisteal Olghair* (Olaus' Castle) in local tradition is found to the north and considered to have been built by the first MacLeods of Lewis (Stiùbhart above; Stiùbhart 2006b, 3). It was surveyed by the NALS field survey, identified at the heart of an extensive medieval landscape which included *An Taigh Mòr, Teampall Mholuaidh* and of course Dùn Èistean (Barrowman, C S 2015, 180-3; 2007, 25). Geophysical survey over the site of *Cnoc a' Chaisteal*, a mound 32 x 25m up to 3m in height, identified evidence for metal-working (as also shown by surface finds of slag and furnace lining from erosion scars on the mound) and three sides of a possible rectangular building (Poller 2015b; Poller 2007a, 28-30).

Other than these two sites so well-known in local tradition, there is possible archaeological evidence for the re-use during the late medieval period of *Dun Mara*, a ruinous Iron Age broch or dun standing on a promontory to the south of An Taigh Mòr on the west coast of Ness, although there are no local traditions specifically linking it to the Lordship. The promontory is defended by what would have been a massive double wall and ditch, and two rectilinear buildings are set into the centre of it which are presumably later in date. Dùn Mara is very similar in plan to *Dùn Ringill* in Skye (Miket and Roberts 1990, 45-48), an Iron Age circular double-walled structure which was re-used and re-fortified by the chief of the MacKinnons and contains two sub-rectangular buildings set into it (ibid, 48).

Unfortunately, without excavation, little more can be said concerning these potential Lordship sites in Ness, but through collaboration during the Dùn Èistean Archaeology Project with the Estates, Residences and Schools of Gaelic Learned Families *c* 1300-1650 project, led by Elizabeth FitzPatrick of NUI Galway in 2005/6, discussions and exchanges concerning the similarities, and differences, between the *Uí Dhábhoireann* (O'Davorens) brehons in the relatively uncultivated area of *Cathair Mhic Nechtain* (Cahermacnaghten), Burren, Co Clare and the Morrison *britheamhan* in Ness provide us with a glimpse of what may once have existed in the Ness landscape before the development of the later crofting agricultural landscape. The O'Davorens were a legal family to the Ó Lochlainn lordship of Burren, as the Morrisons were to the MacLeods of Lewis. FitzPatrick excavated 'Cabhail Tighe Breac', the upstanding ruins of a large house thought to be possibly the *sgoilteagh* (schoolhouse) in classical Gaelic tradition where the law would be taught and texts compiled and copied. During the excavations a slate with a single inscribed character was found amongst the primary occupation layer of the building, of which FitzPatrick is of the

Illus 14.45 View of Cabhail Tighe Breac, Cahermachnaghtan, Co Clare

opinion is potentially diagnostic of school activity (FitzPatrick 2010). Perhaps by comparison with this Irish *brehon* family we get a glimpse of the importance that *An Taigh Mòr*, Habost may once have held. However, unlike the estates of the Gaelic learned families in Ireland, no documents survive detailing the judgements or law meted out by the Morrison *britheamhan*, and in contrast, local tradition holds that the presence of the *britheamh*:

> 'whether in house or field, on horseback or on foot, constituted a court; his decisions were guided either by what he could remember of like cases, or by his sense of justice, and this *lex non scripta* was called 'breast law'. On assuming office he swore he would administer justice between man and man, as evenly as the backbone of the herring lies between the two sides of the fish.'

(MacDonald 1967 (2004), 44)

A chain of defended sites in the MacLeod territories along the east coast of Ness and north Lewis?

As suggested above, we should expect to find late medieval sites like Dùn Èistean elsewhere in the Western Isles, the north-west coast of mainland Scotland, Skye and the Inner Hebrides. This period of historical archaeology has been poorly served in the Western Isles, and has only in the last 20 years or so begun to see a growth in archaeological research. Raven, in his survey of the medieval duns in South Uist for instance, draws attention to two of the unexcavated island duns (*Caisteal Bheagram* and *Dùn Raghnaill*), for which there is no evidence for a prehistoric predecessor, and suggests that they may have been built in the medieval period on 'virginal territory' (Raven 2005, 348-9). Within Lewis, *Dùn Othail* and *Dùn Eòradail* (Dun Eorodale) on the east coast and *Stac Dhòmhnaill Chaim* on the west coast in Uig have been surveyed by the STAC project are all suggested as late medieval defended sites (see McHardy et al 2009; 71-76; 63-67; 17-20, and discussion below). Historical associations lead historian MacCoinnich to also highlight *Dùn Bearasaigh* (Dun Berisay) in Loch Roag, Lewis, *Dùn Ringill* in Skye, associated with the Mackinnon clan (see Dun Mara, above), *Dùn Raghnaill* in South Uist associated with Clanranald clan, and *An Dùn*, Clashnessie, Assynt, probably associated with the MacLeods of Lewis and Assynt (see Chapter 3, above).

Closer to home, there are several duns on the west coast of Ness, but there is evidence that, with the exception of the later re-use at Dun Mara (see above), they are all of Late Iron Age or prehistoric date (Barrowman, C S 2015, 146). Survey and excavation by the STAC project (see McHardy et al 2009) has identified archaeological evidence for Late Iron Age/Norse pottery from past excavations on *Dùn Arnaistean* (Dun Arnistean) in North Dell and Neolithic and Iron Age pottery on *Luchruban* on the west coast of the Butt of Lewis (McHardy et al 2009, 47-55; 57-61). Radiocarbon dating of excavated deposits on *Dunasbroc*, south of Dell on the west coast of Ness has produced Neolithic and Iron Age

Illus 14.46 Dun Arnistean

dates (McHardy et al 2009, 39-46; 87-98). Geophysical survey by NALS of *Dùn Slèibhe*, an inland dun on the west side of Ness at Cross, Ness, suggests that this site is possibly an Iron Age broch similar to the inland lochan dun sites of *Dùn Shiabhat* and *Dùn Barabhat* further south on the west side of Ness (although the former may be Neolithic or medieval, see Barrowman, C S 2015, 146-7; 139).

In contrast to this, there is growing evidence to support a hypothesis that the dùn sites on the *east* coast of north Lewis date not to the Iron Age but to the late medieval period.[9] As the Dùn Èistean project progressed and the excavations began to unearth features dating to this later period, it became clear that there was evidence to support this hypothesis (Barrowman 2008, 108-9). Whilst there is historical and archaeological evidence for the *re-use* of Iron Age dùn sites in Lewis and further afield in the Western Isles in the late medieval period (eg Miket and Roberts 1990, 7-8; Armit 1996, 217-8), at Dùn Èistean there was evidence that the stronghold had been built from scratch in the late fifteenth to sixteenth centuries AD, and for a specific purpose. At the same time, survey work by the STAC and NALS surveys on the east coast dùn sites (Barrowman, C S et al 2004; Barrowman, C S 2006a; 2006b; 2007a; 2007b; McHardy et al 2009) identified a shift of strategic importance from the west to the east coast during the late medieval period.

As a result, along the east coast of north Lewis (ie the west seaboard of the MacLeod territories) a chain of defended sites can now be identified of which Dùn Èistean is the furthest north. At 2km south of Dùn Èistean along the coast lies *Dùn Eòrodail* which has been surveyed by the STAC project (Barrowman, C et al 2004; McHardy et al 2009, 63-67), and is almost identical in its physical characteristics to Dùn Èistean, with which it was first compared by the Ordnance Survey in the 1960s (McHardy et al 2009, 66). The site is only accessible at low tide and is protected by a perimeter turf and stone wall on its landward side, enclosing the remains of up to 12 small circular buildings, a freshwater spring and a large stone rectangular building on the summit. Although these buildings are not as well preserved as the buildings on Dùn Èistean, and the site has no history or local oral tradition attached to it, its similarity to Dùn Èistean is startling, and strongly suggests that it is of similar date and function. It should be noted that an additional similarity to Dùn Èistean lies in the position of one small rectangular building situated at the top of the access route on to the island - a feature also seen on Dùn Èistean where the access routes were guarded by Structures A and B (see Structure M on McHardy et al 2009, 65, illus 44). It has already been suggested (Stiùbhart, above; Barrowman, C S 2015, 247-8) that *Dùn Eòrodail* may have been paired with the promontory of *Beirghe* on the north side of the beach at Port of Ness, and had a role defending the landing there. This pairing may not just be a defensive one either, but one that looked outwards to the sea and the control of marine resources, as suggested for similar sites in Ireland (see discussion above; Breen 2001, 422). 5km south from *Dùn Eòrodail* along the east coast lies *Dùn Bhiliscleitir* (Dun Filisclietir), also identified by the NALS survey as being of possible medieval date. Little of the site remains as the stones were used in the early twentieth century to build a summer retreat

Illus 14.47 Dun Eorodale and Illus 14.48 View of site of Dun Bhiliscleitir

on the cliffs there, but the site is described in the 1850 OS Name Book as 'a small oblong ruin, with no part of the walls standing', which is an unlikely description for an Iron Age site. There is also an enclosure wall cutting across the neck of the promontory on which *Dùn Bhiliscleitir* was situated, on the top of breathtakingly sheer, high cliffs with a clear view across to Sutherland and Assynt and up and down the Minch.

Further south along the east coast stretching down to Stornoway, three further defensive sites can be identified that are comparable to Dùn Èistean. 6km south of *Dùn Bhiliscleitir* on the east coast lies *Dùn Othail*, linked in local tradition to Niall Odhar and the *britheamhan* (see Chapter 2; McHardy et al 2009, 73). This pinnacle of rock with a vertical cliff on its landward side was surveyed by the STAC project (Barrowman 2004b, 133-134; McHardy et al 2009, 71-76) which recorded five structures (Structures A, C, D, E and I) on a series of three terraces covering an area of 20 x 20m on its seaward side protected by a defensive wall (Structure B). The five structures comprised a rectangular building and a semi-circular wall abutting a rock outcrop on the middle terrace, and three sub-rectangular buildings on the lower terrace. McHardy et al are of the opinion that the site is comparable to other defended sites, such as Dùn Èistean, due to its situation overlooking the Minch, its defendable position, and its location in local tradition to the troubled times of the sixteenth and early seventeenth centuries.

Just 1.5km south of Dùn Othail, at the south end of *Traigh Ghearadha* (Garry beach) lies the site of *Caisteal a' Mhorair* (Castle of the Earl, or Nobleman), also surveyed by the STAC project, and considered to be one of the few potential medieval castles in Lewis (McHardy et al 2009, 77-81). This site is situated on the most substantial of three rock pillars on *Traigh Ghearadha*, and excavations there in the nineteenth century found sherds of craggan vessels and hammerstones (Liddel 1874, cited in McHardy et al 2009, 79). The whole of the summit of the rock is taken up with one building, accessed by a cliff path winding steeply up the west face of the stack to the entrance. The building is divided into three parts - a large sub-rectangular area, 9 x 5m internally with two possible entrances, a small adjoining rectilinear room, and a smaller chamber adjoining the room. It is suggested via comparison with Dùn Èistean, that the rectilinear room may have been a small tower, and the large sub-rectangular area a hall or enclosed courtyard (ibid, 81). Once again, this site is situated on an ideal landing beach, with views out across the Minch.

The MacLeods had their own stronghold at Stornoway castle (Salter 1995, 162), which was similar in appearance to the tower on Dùn Èistean but larger and entirely stone built.[10] South of this, on the south coast of Holm lies *Rubha Shildinish*, situated on the approach to *Cala Steòrnabhaigh* (Anchor Bay). This site is situated on a peninsula (Atkinson et al 2005, 8) and is described in the Scheduling register as a promontory fort and homestead. It includes the low turf and stone walls of five main sets of buildings, enclosed by the remains of a turf and stone perimeter wall. It was obviously at one time a well-defended site, although the remains of any tower or larger building (possibly the structure to

Illus 14.49 Caisteal a' Mhorair and Illus 14.50 Rubha Shildinis (both copyright Historic Scotland)

the far south-east) are hard to recognize, and whilst it is blocked from view from the east coast 'chain' of sites (which in any case aren't all visible from each other) it lies in an ideal location to guard the MacLeod waters in and around Stornoway, and may rather than being Iron Age, be medieval in date.

Conclusion

Whilst it is probable that these sites may be late medieval in date and linked to the demise of the MacLeod lordship, the excavated evidence from Dùn Èistean is at present unique, and gives us a detailed picture of life on a late medieval stronghold in the Western Isles in the late fifteenth to early seventeenth centuries AD. It stands at the end of a long tradition of castles seen throughout the Lordship of the Isles, and yet the excavations have shown that it was a distinctive local response to a wider threat. The nationally significant assemblages of gunflints, local pottery, environmental material and radiocarbon dates demonstrate that the site was the scene of several phases of short bursts of intensive occupation and conflict, and was used intermittently in a hurried and rapid response to a conflict situation. The provision of a strategically-placed watchtower on the highest point of the island with an uninterrupted view north and south along the coast and across to the Scottish mainland and beyond, demonstrate that threats and contacts from the sea were as important as, if not more important than, those from the land. The provision of extensive accommodation and storage buildings indicate that the site was occupied by a considerable population at times, and the artefactual and environmental finds from the site reveal that the community on the stronghold were able to be self-sufficient, bringing all necessary supplies up the steep cliffs to the island, or by boat, including peat for fuel, and foodstuffs such as oats, barley, meat and milk in pottery vessels. In addition to this a pond was dug out on the island to collect rainwater, driftwood was collected for fuel, and fish were caught off the rocks or in the shallow waters surrounding the site. Turf and stone were cut from the immediate area for new buildings, clay collected for bonding the walls, and driftwood salvaged for roofing. The corn-drying kiln provided the means to dry oats and barley stored on the site, and pots were fired in a clamp kiln on the island.

The evidence from dated deposits for small-scale conflict and use of weapons on the site confirm that it was the scene of several sieges or skirmishes in the sixteenth and early seventeenth centuries, and although we will never be able to tie the archaeological evidence to one specific event, it would seem almost churlish not to argue that Dùn Èistean is the 'fort in Ness' wherein the brieve kindred, later Morrisons, took refuge, despite it not being named as such in the historical accounts. In local tradition the site was part of the local lordship landscape of Ness, which functioned as a sanctuary where the Morrison brieves dispensed justice from their base at *An Taigh Mòr* in Habost. The site would have played a significant role within the MacLeod lordship, part of a suite of late medieval strongholds along the east coast of north Lewis that were intimately bound up with the troubled times after the collapse of the Lord of the Isles.

In form and function it may be compared to other defended late medieval sites and earlier castles found elsewhere in Lewis, and further south in other lordship territories, and was ideally placed on the edge of the busy sea routes around the north and west coasts of north Scotland and Ireland.

At the same time however Dùn Èistean is a unique site, built on a previously unoccupied island as a local response to a specific threat. The building traditions, the materials and the construction techniques used, the distinctive pottery decoration, the adaptation to available local materials seen in the gunflint assemblage and the manufacture of lead projectiles on the site, and the exploitation of the local environment for everyday subsistence demonstrates the self-sufficiency of a people with a strong local identity in the late medieval/early post-medieval period. After the stronghold was abandoned with the MacKenzie takeover and the changing political situation on Lewis, Dùn Èistean became part of the distinctive agricultural, and later crofting, landscape of Ness. The district still has this distinctiveness, perhaps an echo of those troubled centuries when Ness maintained its independence at the centre of a busy maritime world of conflicting interests and political turmoil.

Endnotes

[1] I am grateful to Dòmhnall Uilleam Stiùbhart for drawing my attention to this paper.

[2] Robson in his book on the duns of Northern Lewis reproduces MacPhail's notes on the local traditions concerning the duns, in which he describes 'The manner in which the stones were collected for them, was by a line of men reaching from the site of the dun to the seashore, from whence the stones were usually taken, and handed from man to man, without touching the ground till it reached the building.' (Robson 2004, 54).

[3] Clay pits can still be seen today in the townships at the north end of Ness, where clay was dug to bond the walls of whitehouses constructed in the 1920s and 30s (see Barrowman, C S 2015, 279-84).

[4] I am indebted to Finlay MacLeod for first drawing my attention to Catriona Mackie's research, and to Catriona for discussing these points with me.

[5] http://www.birmingham.ac.uk/facilities/ba/projects/archaeology/harris.aspx. I am grateful to Mary MacLeod for drawing my attention to this site.

[6] In the 16th and 17th centuries, peat coverage would also have been more extensive than it is today. In Eorodale for instance, just a mile south of Dùn Èistean, old peat banks that were last worked in the mid-20th century can be seen on Àrd Sginis, now grassland and rough grazing. Also on our croft in Eorodale the peaty heath was stripped and used for fuel when the house was first occupied in the 1920s and 30s.

[7] Similar decoration is found on loose finds from *Cnoc Mòr*, Barvas (Mary MacLeod pers comm. Dec 2011).

[8] I am grateful to Elizabeth FitzPatrick for discussing this point with me and bringing this paper to my attention.

[9] As has been variously put forward throughout the DEAP project by the author, Stiùbhart and MacCoinnich (see Chapter 3 above), C Barrowman, (see Barrowman, C S 2015, 247-8) and MacLeod and members of the STAC project (see McHardy et al 2009, 66) during the course of research into these sites.

[10] The original Stornoway Castle was destroyed by Cromwell's troops in 1653 and its ruins of the tower are now found underneath Pier 1 at Stornoway ferry terminal. I am grateful to both Aonghas MacCoinnich and James Crawford for alerting me to the similarities between the tower on Dùn Èistean and the descriptions of Stornoway Castle.

Abernethy, J 2004 'The genetics of Clan MacLeod', *Clan MacLeod Magazine* 98 (2004), 760-4.

Adam, R (ed) 1991 *The calendar of Fearn: Text and additions, 1471-1667*. Edinburgh: Scottish History Society.

Albarella, U and Davis, S J M 1996 'Mammals and birds from Launceston Castle, Cornwall: decline in status and the rise of agriculture', *Circaea, The Journal of the Association for Environmental Archaeology* 12 (1), 1-156.

Anderson, J M (ed) 1926 *Records of the University of St Andrews, 1413-1579*. Edinburgh: Scottish History Society.

Anderson, P D 1982 *Robert Stewart, Earl of Orkney, Lord of Shetland, 1533-1593*. Edinburgh: John Donald.

Angus, S 1997 *The Outer Hebrides: The shaping of the islands*. Strond: White Horse Press.

Armit, I 1996 *The archaeology of Skye and the Western Isles*. Edinburgh: Edinburgh University Press.

Armit, I 1997 'Excavation of a post-medieval settlement at Druim nan Dearcag, and related sites around Loch Olabhat, North Uist', *Proceedings of the Society of Antiquaries of Scotland* 127, 899-919.

Armit, I 2006 *Anatomy of an Iron Age roundhouse The Cnip wheelhouse excavations, Lewis*. Edinburgh: Society of Antiquaries of Scotland.

Armit, I, Campbell, E and Dunwell, A 2008 'Excavation of an Iron Age, early historic and medieval settlement and metalworking site at Eilean Olabhat, North Uist', *Proceedings of the Society of Antiquaries of Scotland* 138, 27-104.

Ashton, N, Dean, P and McNabb, J 1991 'Flaked flakes: what, when and why?', *Lithics* 12, 1-11.

Atkinson, J A, Banks, I and MacGregor, G (eds) 2000 *Townships to farmsteads. Rural settlement studies in Scotland, England and Wales*. British Archaeological Reports, British Series 293. Oxford: Archaeopress.

Atkinson, J, Barrowman, C and Barrowman, R 2005 *Dùn Èistean Archaeology Project (DEAP). Project 2000: A project design*. University of Glasgow, unpublished GUARD report.

Ball, D F 1964 'Loss-on-ignition as an estimate of organic matter and organic carbon in non-calcareous soils', *Journal of Soil Science* 15, 84-92.

Ballantyne, J H and Smith, B 1994 *Shetland documents 1580-1611*. Lerwick: Shetland Times Ltd.

Ballin, T B 1999 'Bipolar cores in southern Norway - classification, chronology and geography', *Lithics* 20, 13-22.

Ballin, T B 2005 'Lithic artefacts and pottery from Townparks, Antrim Town', *Ulster Archaeological Journal* 64, 12-25.

Ballin, T B 2009 *Quartz technology in Scottish prehistory*. Scottish Archaeological Internet Reports 26, http://www.sair.org.uk/sair26/index.html

Ballin, T B 2011 *Overhowden and Airhouse, Scottish Boarders: characterization and interpretation of two spectacular lithic assemblages from sites near the Overhowden henge*. British Archaeological Reports, British Series 539. Oxford: Archaeopress.

Ballin, T B 2012 "State of the art' of British gunflint research, with special focus on the early gunflint workshop at Dun Eistean, Lewis', *Post Medieval Archaeology* 46 (1), 116-42.

Ballin, T B forthcoming(a) 'The lithic assemblage', in Cameron, A Excavations at the Green, Aberdeen: a medieval Carmelite house revealed, *Internet Archaeology*.

Ballin, T B forthcoming(b) 'Lundevågen 31, Vest-Agder, SW Norway. The spatial organization of small hunter-gatherer sites - a case study (or: Binford in Practice)', in Bond, C *Lithic technology: Reduction and replication*. Occasional paper for the Lithic Studies Society. Oxford: Oxbow Books.

Bannerman, J 1980 'Gaelic endorsements of early 17th century legal documents', *Studia Celtica* 14/15 (1979-80), 18-33.

Bannerman, J 1988 'The Scots language and kin based Society', in Thomson, D S (ed), *Gaelic and Scots in harmony*, *Proceedings of the Second International Conference on the Languages of Scotland,* 1-19. Glasgow: Department of Celtic, University of Glasgow.

Bannerman, J 1998 *The Beatons: a Medical kindred in the classical tradition*. Edinburgh: John Donald.

Barber, J W A 1981 'Excavations at Teampull Mholuaidh, Eoropie, Port of Ness, Lewis, 1977', *Proceedings of the Society of Antiquaries of Scotland* 110 (1978-80), 530-3.

Barber, M, Field, D and Topping, P 1999 *The Neolithic flint mines of England*. London: English Heritage.

Barker, D 2005 'Pottery usage in a crofting community: an overview', in Branigan, K, *From Clan to Clearance: History and archaeology on the Isle of Barra c. 850-1850 AD*, 111-22. Oxford: Oxbow Books.

Barnes, M 2004 'Gunflints', *The Lavase River archaeology project,* http://www.city.north-bay.on.ca/

lavase/97FRS626.HTM accessed 23 September 2011.

Barrell, A D M 2000 *Medieval Scotland*. Cambridge: Cambridge University Press.

Barrett, J H, Nicholson R A and Cerón-Carrasco, R 1999 'Archaeo-icthyological evidence for long-term economic trends in Northern Scotland: 3500 BC to 1500 AD', *Journal of Archaeological Science* 26 (4), 353-88.

Barrowman, C S 2002 *Dùn Èistean, Lewis: Geophysical survey and trial excavation - description of the archaeological structures, with contributions from D Maguire*. GUARD 716.2 and 716.3 interim report. University of Glasgow, unpublished GUARD report.

Barrowman, C S 2004(a) *Dùn Èistean, Lewis*. GUARD 716.4 interim report. University of Glasgow, unpublished GUARD report.

Barrowman, C S 2004(b) 'Sea stack survey, Lewis (Barvas; Uig parishes), survey', *Discovery* and *Excavation Scotland* 5, 133-4.

Barrowman, C S 2006(a) *Ness Archaeological Landscape Survey desk-based assessment*. GUARD 2000 interim report. University of Glasgow, unpublished GUARD report.

Barrowman, C S 2006(b) *Ness Archaeological Landscape Survey data structure report*. GUARD 2000 interim report. University of Glasgow, unpublished GUARD report.

Barrowman, C S 2007(a) *Ness Archaeological Landscape Survey field survey 2006* GUARD 2217 interim report. University of Glasgow, unpublished GUARD report.

Barrowman, C S 2007(b) *Ness Archaeological Landscape Survey field survey 2007* GUARD 2378 interim report. University of Glasgow, unpublished GUARD report.

Barrowman, C S 2015 *The Archaeology of Ness: The results of the Ness Archaeological Landscape Survey*. Stornoway: Acair Ltd.

Barrowman, C S and Driscoll S T 2000 *Dùn Èistean, Lewis: Archaeological and topographical survey*. GUARD 716.1 interim report. University of Glasgow, unpublished GUARD report.

Barrowman, C S, McHardy, I and MacLeod, M A 2004 *Severe Terrain Archaeological Campaign (STAC): Rope access and topographical survey*. Stornoway, Comhairle nan Eilean Siar, unpublished report.

Barrowman, R C 2005 *Lewis Coastal Chapel-sites Survey 2004/5*. University of Glasgow, unpublished Viking and Early Settlement Archaeological Research Project report.

Barrowman, R C 2006a *Dùn Èistean Archaeological Project excavations 2005 data structure report*. GUARD 2000 interim report. University of Glasgow, unpublished GUARD report.

Barrowman, R C with Hooper, J 2006b Lewis Coastal Chapel-sites Survey: Topographic Survey 2005.

University of Glasgow, unpublished Viking and Early Settlement Archaeological Research Project report. http://eprints.gla.ac.uk/96357/

Barrowman, R C 2007 *Dùn Èistean Archaeology Project excavations 2007 data structure report*. GUARD 2378 interim report. University of Glasgow, unpublished GUARD report.

Barrowman, R C 2008 'Splendid Isolation: changing perceptions of Dùn Èistean, an island on the north coast of the Isle of Lewis', in Noble, G, Poller, T, Raven, J and Verrill, L (eds), *Scottish odysseys: The archaeology of islands*, 95-111. Stroud: Tempus Publishing Ltd.

Barrowman, R C, Batey, C E and Morris, C D, 1997 *Excavations at Tintagel Castle, Cornwall, 1990-1999*. Society of Antiquaries Monograph 74. London: Society of Antiquaries.

Barrowman, R C, Becket, A, Dalglish, C and McHardy, I 2007 *Dùn Èistean Archaeology Project excavations 2006 data structure report*. GUARD 2217 interim report. University of Glasgow, unpublished GUARD report.

Bascomb, C L 1974 'Physical and chemical analyses of <2mm samples', in Avery, B W and Bascomb, C L (eds), *Soil Survey laboratory methods*, 14-41. Harpenden: Soil Survey of England and Wales.

Batey, C E 1989 'Excavations beside the Brough Road, Birsay: the artefact assemblage', in Morris, C D, *The Birsay Bay Project Vol 1: Brough Road excavations 1976-1982*, 191-229. Durham: University of Durham, Department of Archaeology Monograph Ser No 1.

Batey, C E 1997 'Stone', in Barrowman et al 1997, 200-16.

Beatty, J 1992 *Sula: The seabird-hunters of Lewis*. London: Michael Joseph.

Beijerinck, W 1947 *Zadenatlas der Nederlandsche flora*. Wageningen: Veenman and Zonen.

Bennett, K D, Bunting, M J and Fossitt, J A 1997 'Long term vegetation change in the Western and Northern Isles, Scotland', *Botanical Journal of Scotland* 49, 127-40.

Beveridge, E 1903 (reprinted 2000) *Coll and Tiree*. Edinburgh: Birlinn Ltd.

Binford, L R 1983 *In pursuit of the past: Decoding the archaeological record*. London: Thames and Hudson.

Bingeman, J M 2004 'Gunlocks: Their introduction to the navy', *The Royal Navy's First Invincible*. http://www.invincible1758.co.uk/gun_flints.htm accessed 23 September 2011.

Birks, H J B and Madsen, B J 1979 'Flandrian vegetational history of Little Loch Roag, Isle of Lewis, Scotland', *The Journal of Ecology,* 67(3), 825-42.

Black, G F 1946 (reprinted 1993) *The surnames of Scotland*. Edinburgh: Birlinn Ltd.

Black, R I B 1994 'Ó Muirgheasáin family', in Thomson, D S (ed) *The companion to Gaelic Scotland* (2nd edition), 219-220. Glasgow: Gairm.

Blaeu, W J 1635 *Scotia Regnum*. Amsterdam. http://maps.nls.uk/scotland/detail.cfm?id=135 accessed 23 September 2011.

Boardman, S 2006 *The Campbells, 1250-1513*. Edinburgh: John Donald.

Boessneck, J 1969 'Osteological differences between Sheep (Ovis aries Linné) and Goat (Capra hircus Linné)', in Brothwell, D R and Higgs, E S (eds), *Science in archaeology: A comprehensive survey of progress and research*, 331-58. London: Thames and Hudson Ltd.

Bohncke, S J P 1988 'Vegetation and habitation history of the Callanish area', in Birks, H J B, Kaland, P E and Moe, D (eds), *The cultural landscape - past, present and future*, 445-61. Cambridge: Cambridge University Press.

Bond, J M and Hunter, J R 1987 'Flax-growing in Orkney from the Norse Period to the 18th century', *Proceedings of the Society of Antiquaries of Scotland* 117, 175-81.

Branch, G M 1985 'Limpets: their role in littoral and sublittoral community dynamics', in, Moore, P G and Seed, R, *The ecology of rocky coasts,* 97-116. London: Hodder and Stoughton.

Breen, C 2001 'The maritime cultural landscape of medieval Gaelic Ireland', in Duffy, P J, Edwards, D and Fitzpatrick, F (eds), *Gaelic Ireland c.1250-c.1650, Land, lordship and settlement*, 418-436. Dublin: Four Courts Press.

Bronk Ramsey, C 1995 'Radiocarbon calibration and analyses of stratigraphy: the OxCal programme', *Radiocarbon* 37(2), 425-30.

Bronk Ramsey, C 2000 'Comment on the use of Bayesian statistics for ^{14}C dates of chronologically ordered samples: a critical review', *Radiocarbon* 42 (2), 199-202.

Bronk Ramsey, C 2009 'Bayesian analysis of radiocarbon dates', *Radiocarbon* 51 (1), 337-60.

Bronk Ramsey C 2010 *OxCal 4.1 manual*. Oxford: Oxford Radiocarbon Accelerator Unit. http://c14.arch.ox.ac.uk/oxcalhelp/hlp_contents.html accessed 21 April 2010.

Buck, C E, Christen, J A, Kenworthy, J B and Litton, C D 1994 'Estimating the duration of archaeological activity using ^{14}C determinations', *Oxford Journal of Archaeology* 3 (2), 229-40.

Buck, C E, Kenworthy, J B, Litton, C D and Smith, A F M 1991 'Combining archaeological and radiocarbon information: a Bayesian approach to calibration', *Antiquity* 65, 808-21.

Bullock, P, Federoff, N, Jongerius, A, Stoops, G, Tursina, T and Babel, U 1985 *Handbook for soil thin section description*. Wolverhampton: Waine Research Publications.

Burgess, C 2003 'Martin - an archaeological perspective', in The Islands Book Trust (eds) *Martin Martin - 300 years on. Proceedings of a major 3-day event to mark the tercentenary of the publication of Martin Martin's book on the Western Isles*, 40-55. Callicvol: Islands Books Trust.

Burgess, C and Church, M 1997 *Coastal erosion assessment, Lewis: A report for Historic Scotland*, 2 vols. University of Edinburgh: unpublished report.

Burns, E 1887 *The coinage of Scotland*. Edinburgh: A and C Black.

Calderwood = Thomson, T and Laing, D (eds) 1849 *The history of the Kirk of Scotland, by Mr David Calderwood some time minister of Crailing*. 8 vols (1842-9). Edinburgh: The Wodrow Society.

Caldwell, D H 1990 'Eilean Mor, Loch Finlaggan (Kilarow and Kilmeny parish), medieval residential complex and chapel', *Discovery and Excavation in Scotland*, 31-2.

Caldwell, D H 1991 'Eilean Mor, Loch Finlaggan, Islay (Killarow and Kilmeny parish): medieval residential complex and chapel', *Discovery and Excavation in Scotland*, 52.

Caldwell, D H 1992 'Eilean Mor, Loch Finlaggan, Islay (Killarow and Kilmeny parish): medieval residential complex and chapel', *Discovery and Excavation in Scotland*, 55-6.

Caldwell, D H 1993 'Finlaggan (Killarow and Kilmeny parish): medieval residential complex', *Discovery and Excavation in Scotland*, 64-5.

Caldwell, D H 1994 'The Finlaggan Project (Killarow and Kilmeny parish): Eilean Mor: medieval and later occupation', *Discovery and Excavation in Scotland*, 53.

Caldwell, D H 1997 'The Finlaggan Project (Killarow and Kilmeny parish), prehistoric artefacts and features; medieval structures', *Discovery and Excavation in Scotland*, 19.

Caldwell, D H 2007 'Having the right kit: West highlanders fighting in Ireland', in Duffy, S (ed), *The world of the Galloglass. Kings, warlords and warriors in Ireland and Scotland, 1200-1600*, 144-168. Dublin: Four Courts Press.

Caldwell, D H 2010 *Finlaggan report 1: introduction and background*. National Museums Scotland unpublished report. Deposited on: 26 November 2010. http://repository.nms.ac.uk/214/2/Finlaggan_report_1_-_introduction_and_background.pdf

Caldwell, D H and Ewart, G 1993 "Finlaggan and the Lordship of the Isles: an archaeological approach", *Scottish Historical Review* 72, 148-65.

CSP Domestic = Everett-Green M A (ed) 1857-1859 *Calendar of state papers, domestic series preserved in the State Paper Department, of Her Majesty's Public Record Office. James I 1603-1625*. 4 vols. London: Longmans, Green, Reader and Dyer.

CSP Ireland = Hamilton, H C, Atkinson, E G and Mahaffy, R P (eds) 1860-1911 *Calendar of the state papers relating to Ireland,* 24 vols. London: Public Record Office.

CSP Scotland = Bain J et al (eds) 1898-1969 *Calendar of state papers relating to Scotland and Mary Queen of Scots, 1547-1603*, 13 vols. Edinburgh: H M General Register House.

Cameron, J 1937 *Celtic law. The Senchus Mór and the Book of Aicill and the traces of an early Gaelic system of law in Scotland.* London: W Hodge and Co. Ltd.

Campbell, A C and Nicholls, J 1989 *Seashores* and *shallow seas of Britain and Europe.* London: Hamlyn Guides.

Campbell, E 1991 'Excavations of a wheelhouse and other Iron Age structures at Sollas, North Uist, by R J C Atkinson in 1957', *Proceedings of the Society of Antiquaries of Scotland* 121, 117-73.

Campbell E 1997 'Pottery', in Armit 1997, 909-13.

Campbell, E 2002 'The Western Isles pottery sequence', in Ballin Smith, B and Banks, I (eds), *In the shadow of the brochs: the Iron Age in Scotland,* 139-44. Stroud: Tempus Publishing Ltd.

Campbell, Rev J G (ed Ronald Black) 2003 *The Gaelic otherworld.* Edinburgh: Birlinn Ltd.

Campbell, R 1901 *The father of St Kilda. Twenty years in isolation in the sub-Arctic territory of the Hudson's Bay Company.* London: Russell. http://www.archive.org/details/fatherofstkildat00campuoft accessed 23 September 2011.

Campbell, S D 2010 'Post-medieval settlement in the Isle of Lewis: a study of adaptability or change?', *Proceedings of the Society of Antiquaries of Scotland* 139 (2009), 315-332

Canti, M 2009 'Geoarchaeological studies associated with remedial measures at Silbury Hill, Wiltshire, UK', *Catena* 78, 301-9.

Cappers, R T J, Bekker, R M and Jans, J E A 2006 *Digital seed atlas of the Netherlands,* Groningen Archaeological Studies 4. Eelde, The Netherlands: Barkhuis Publishing.

Carmichael, A (ed) 1900-71 *Carmina Gadelica* (6 vols). Edinburgh: Oliver and Boyd/T and A Constable.

Carovillano, J R 2002 *Worked ballast flint at Den Rock.* http://www.schtick.net/2002/5/03strikealight.htm.

Cathcart, A 2009 'The statutes of Iona: the archipelagic context', *The Journal of British Studies,* 49 (1), 4-29. http://strathprints.strath.ac.uk/26412/1/strathprints026412.pdf accessed 23 September 2011.

Cerón-Carrasco R 1994 'Investigation of the fish remains from an Orkney farm mound', in Van Neer, W (ed) *Fish Exploitation in the past, Tervuren: Annales del Musée Royal de l'Afrique Centrale, Sciences Zoologiques* 274, 122-55.

Cerón-Carrasco R 1998(a) 'The fish bone assemblage from St. Boniface, Papa Westray, Orkney', in Lowe, C, *St. Boniface church, Orkney: Coastal erosion and archaeological assessment*, 149-55. Stroud: Sutton Publications/ Historic Scotland.

Cerón-Carrasco R 1998(b) 'Fishing: evidence for seasonality and processing of fish for preservation in the Northern Isles of Scotland during the Iron Age and Norse times', *Environmental Archaeology* 3, 73-80.

Cerón-Carrasco R 2005 *Of fish and men (De iasg agus dhaoine): Aspects of the utilization of marine resources as recovered from selected Hebridean archaeological sites*. British Archaeological Reports, British Series 400. Oxford: Archaeopress.

Chandler, R H 1917 'Some supposed gun flint sites', *Proceedings of the Prehistoric Society of East Anglia* 2 (1916-17), 360-65.

Cheape, H 1988 'Food and liquid containers in the Hebrides: a window on the Iron Age', in Fenton, A and Myrdal, J (eds), *Food and Drink and travelling accessories. Essays in honour of Gosta Berg*, 6-27. Edinburgh: John Donald/National Museums of Scotland/ Skansen/ Nordiska Museet.

Cheape, H 1993 'Crogans and Barvas ware: handmade pottery in the Hebrides', *Scottish Studies* 31 (1992-3), 109-27.

Christison, D 1883 'On the grated iron doors of Scottish castles and towers', *Proceedings of the Society of Antiquaries of Scotland* 17 (1882–3), 98-135.

Christison, D 1888 'Additional notices of yetts, or grated iron doors, of Scottish castles and towers', *Proceedings of the Society of Antiquaries of Scotland* 23 (1887-8), 286-320.

Clanchy, M T 1970 'Remembering the past and the good old law,' *History* 55 (184), 165-76.

Clancy, T O 2003 'Magpie historiography in twelfth-century Scotland: the case of *Libellus de nativitate Sancti Cuthberti*', in Cartwright, J (ed), *Celtic hagiography and saints' cults*, 216-31. Cardiff: University of Wales Press.

Clancy, T O 2010 'A fond farewell to last night's literary criticism: Reading Niall Mór Macmhuirich', in Munro, G and Cox, R A V (eds), *Cànan & cultur / Language and culture. Rannsachadh na Gàidhlig 4*, 109-26. Edinburgh: Dunedin Academic Press.

Clapham, A R, Tutin, T G and Moore, D M 1987 (3rd edition) *Flora of the British Isles*. Cambridge: Cambridge University Press.

Clarke, A 2006 *Stone tools and the prehistory of the Northern Isles*. British Archaeological Reports, British Series 406. Oxford: Archaeopress.

Clarke, A 2007 'Coarse stone', in Hunter, J (with Bond J M and Smith A N), *Vol 1, Investigatons in Sanday, Orkney: Excavations at Pool, Sanday. A multi-period settlement from Neolithic to Late Norse times*, 353-88. Kirkwall: The Orcadian Ltd/Historic Scotland.

Clydesdale, A 2007 *Dun Eistean, Ness, Isle of Lewis. Conservation of selected finds from the 2006-2006 excavations*. Edinburgh: AOC Project no 20285.

Collectanea de Rebus Albanicis. 1847 Edinburgh: Iona Club.

Courty, M A, Goldberg, P and Macphail, R I 1989 *Soils and micromorphology in archaeology*. Cambridge: Cambridge University Press.

Coutts, W 2003 *The business of the College of Justice, in 1600. How it reflects the economic and social life of Scots men and women*. Edinburgh: Stair society.

Cox, R A V 2002 *The Gaelic place-names of Carloway, Isle of Lewis: their structure and significance*. Dublin: School of Celtic Studies, Dublin Institute for Advanced Studies.

Cox, R 2006 *The Norse element in the place-names of Ness*. Unpublished report. Prepared for the Dùn Èistean History Project.

Crompton, A 2004 '17th century gunflints found at Le Vieux Fort, Placentia'. The web site of *Placentia Area Historical Society*. http://www.mun.ca/archaeology/outreach/image_pages/Gunflints.html accessed 23 September 2011.

Dalglish, C 2002 'Highland rural settlement studies. A critical history', *Proceedings of the Society of Antiquaries of Scotland* 132, 475-95.

Daniell, W 1820 *A voyage round Great Britain*. London: Longman, Hurst, Rees, Orme and Brown.

Davis, R S 1997 *Technology in Stone. Notes*. http://www.brynmawr.edu/Acads/Anthro/anth240/chipped_stone.pdf accessed 23 September 2011.

Dean, V 2007 'Ceramic vessels associated with late 13th to 18th century coin hoards', *Proceedings of the Society of Antiquaries of Scotland* 137, 433-60.

Dearing, J A 1994 *Environmental magnetic susceptibility: Using the Bartington MS2 System*, Kenilworth: Chi Publishing.

Dennistoun, J (ed) 1830 *Memoirs of the affairs of Scotland by David Moysie, from the year MDLXXVII-MDCIII*. Edinburgh: Bannatyne Club.

Dickson, C A and Dickson, J H 2000 *Plants and people in ancient Scotland*. Stroud: Tempus Publishing Ltd.

Dickson, J H 1992 'North American driftwood, especially *Picea* (spruce), from archaeological sites in the Hebrides and Northern Isles of Scotland', *Review of Palaeobotany and Palynology* 73, 49-56.

Dobney, K, Jacques, D and Irving, B 1996 *Of butchers and breeds: report on vertebrate remains from various sites in the city of Lincoln*. Lincoln: Lincoln Archaeological Unit.

Dockrill, S J, Bond, J M, Turner, V E and Brown, L D 2007 *Old Scatness excavation manual: a case study in archaeological recording*. Lerwick: Shetland Heritage Publications.

Dodgshon, R A 1993 'West Highland and Hebridean settlement prior to crofting and the Clearances: a case study in stability and change', *Proceedings of the Society of Antiquaries of Scotland* 123 (1993), 419-38.

Dodgshon, R A 1996 'Hebridean farming townships prior to crofting and the clearances: a documentary perspective', in Gilbertson, D, Kent, M and Grattan, J (eds), *The Outer Hebrides: the last 14,000 years*, 185-94. Sheffield Environmental and Archaeological Research Campaign in the Hebrides vol 2. Sheffield: Sheffield Academic Press Ltd.

Dodgshon, R A 2002 *The age of the clans. The Highlands from Somerled to the Clearances*. Edinburgh: Birlinn/Historic Scotland.

Donaldson, G 1984 'Problems of sovereignty and law in Orkney and Shetland', in Sellar, D (ed), *Miscellany two of the Stair Society*, 13-40. Edinburgh: Stair Society.

Dransart, P 2003 'Saints, stones and shrines: the cults of Sts Moluag and Gerardine in Pictland', in Cartwright, J (ed), *Celtic hagiography and saints' cults*, 232-48. Cardiff: University of Wales Press.

Dumbrell, R 1992 *Understanding antique wine bottles*. Suffolk: Antique Collector's Club.

Dunthorne, H 2004 'Stewart, Sir William (*d.* 1602x4)', in Goldman, L (ed), *Oxford Dictionary of National Biography*. Oxford: Oxford University Press.

Egan, G 1998 *The medieval household. Daily living c 1150-c1450. Medieval finds from excavations in London 6*. London: Museum of London.

Emery, N 1996 *Excavations on Hirta 1986-90*. Edinburgh: NTS/HMSO.

Entwhistle, J A, Dodgshon, R A and Abrahams, P W 2000 'An investigation of former land-use activity through the physical and chemical analysis of soils from the Isle of Lewis, Outer Hebrides', *Archaeological Prospection* 7, 171-88.

FES = Scott, H (ed) 1928. *Fasti Ecclesiae Scoticanae. The succession of ministers in the Church of Scotland from the Reformation. Vol VII. The Synods of Ross, Sutherland and Caithness, Glenelg, Orkney and of Shetland. The Church in England, Ireland and Overseas*. Edinburgh: Oliver and Boyd.

Fenton, A 1978 *The Northern Isles: Orkney and Shetland*. Edinburgh: John Donald.

Fenton, A 1982 'Net-drying, pot-drying and graddening: smallscale grain drying and processing techniques', *Saga och sed* (Yearbook of the Royal Gustavus Adolfus Academy), 86-306.

Fenton, A 1985 *The shape of the past 1: Essays in Scottish ethnology*. Edinburgh: John Donald Publishers Ltd.

Fenton, A 1997 (reprint) *The Northern Isles: Orkney and Shetland*. East Linton: Tuckwell Press.

Fettes, D J, Mendu, J R, Smith, D I and Watson, J V 1992 *Geology of the Outer Hebrides*. London: HMSO British Geological Survey.

FitzPatrick, E A 1993 *Soil microscopy and micromorphology*. Chichester: John Wiley and Sons.

FitzPatrick, E 2010 *Excavations in the Law School settlement of the O'Davoren Brehons, Cahermacnaghten, Co Clare*, unpublished report to the Royal Irish Academy, Dublin, August 2010.

Forsyth, K, Broun, D and Clancy, T 2008 'The property records: Text and translation', in Forsyth, K (ed) *Studies on the Book of Deer*, 131-44. Dublin: Four Courts Press.

Fossitt, J A 1996 'Late Quaternary vegetation history of the Western Isles of Scotland', *New Phytologist* 1323, 171-96.

Fraser, I A 1978 'Gaelic and Norse elements in coastal place-names in the Western Isles', *Transactions of the Gaelic Society of Inverness* 50 (1976-8), 237-55.

Fraser, I A 1984 'Some further thoughts on Scandinavian place-names in Lewis', *Northern Studies* 21, 34-41.

Gale, R and Cutler, D 2000 *Plants in Archaeology*. Otley: Westbury Publishing.

Geddes, G F 2006 'Vernacular buildings in the Outer Hebrides 300 BC - AD1930: Temporal comparison using archaeological analysis', *Internet Archaeology* 19. http://intarch.ac.uk/journal/issue19/4/toc.html Accessed 23rd September 2011.

Goodare, J 1998 'The Statutes of Iona in context', *Scottish Historical Review* 77, 31-57.

Goodman-Elgar, M 2008 'Evaluating soil resilience in long-term cultivation: a study of pre-Columbian terraces from the Paca Valley, Peru', *Journal of Archaeological Science* 35 (12), 3072-86.

Gordon, Sir Robert = Weber, H (ed) 1813 *Gordon's genealogical history of the earldom of Sutherland*. Edinburgh: G Ramsay and Co.

Gregory, D 1881 (reprinted 1975) *History of the Western Highlands and Isles of Scotland from AD 1493 to AD 1625*. Edinburgh: John Donald.

Grimble, I 1965 (reprinted 1993) *Chief of Mackay*. Edinburgh: Routledge and K. Paul.

Grimm, E 1991 *TILIA and TILIA.GRAPH*. Illinois: Illinois State Museum.

Gunn, A 1897 'History, Part II (AD 1560-1800)', in Gunn, A and Mackay, J (eds) 1897 *Sutherland and the Reay Country*, 43-77. Glasgow: J Mackay.

Guttmann, E B, Simpson, I A, Davidson, DA and Dockrill, S J 2006 'The management of arable land from prehistory to the present: case studies from the Northern Isles of Scotland', *Geoarchaeology* 21 (1), 61-92.

Halford-MacLeod, A 1994 'The MacLeods of Lewis …and of Assynt, Coigach and Gairloch', in Baldwin J R (ed), *Peoples and settlements in north-west Ross*, 193-213. Edinburgh: Scottish Society for Northern Studies.

Halliday S 2001 'Appendix 1 rig and furrow in Scotland', in Barber, J, *Guidelines for the presentation of areas of rig and furrow in Scotland*, 10-20. Scottish Trust for Archaeological Research. Edinburgh: AOC Archaeology Group.

Hamilton, J R C 1956 *Excavations at Jarlshof, Shetland*. Edinburgh: HMSO.

Hanson, M and Cain, C R 2007 'Examining histology to identify burned bone', *Journal of Archaeological Science* 34, 1902-13.

Harris, D R 1987 'The impact on archaeology of radiocarbon dating by accelerator mass spectrometry', *Philosophical Transactions of the Royal Society of London (Series A)* 323, 23-43.

Hillman, G C 1981 'Reconstructing crop husbandry practices from charred remains of crops', in Mercer, R (ed), *Farming practice in British prehistory*, 1123-62. Edinburgh: Edinburgh University Press.

Hingley, R (ed) 1993 *Medieval or later rural settlement in Scotland – management and preservation*. Occasional Paper No. 1. Edinburgh: Historic Scotland.

Holleyman, G A 1947 'Tiree craggans', *Antiquity* 21 (84), 205-11.

Homer, R F 1991 'Tin, lead and pewter', in Blair, J and Ramsay, N (eds), *English Medieval industries: Craftsmen, techniques, products*, 57-80. London: The Hambleden Press.

Horsburgh, D 2002 'When was Gaelic Scottish? The origins, emergence and development of a Scottish Gaelic identity, 1400-1750', in Ó Baoill, C and McGuire, N (ed), *Rannsachadh na Gàidhlig 2000. Papers read at the conference Scottish Gaelic Studies 2000, held at the University of Aberdeen, 2-4 August 2000*, 231-42. Aberdeen: Department of Celtic, University of Aberdeen.

Hume, I N 1982 *A Guide to artifacts of colonial America*. New York: Alfred A. Knopf.

Hunter, J R 2005 'Isle of Harris survey, Western Isles: survey and trial excavation', *Discovery and Excavation in Scotland* 6, 144-5.

Hutton, R 1996 *The stations of the sun*. Oxford: Oxford University Press.

Hyams, P 2001 'Feud and the state in late Anglo-Saxon England', *Journal of British Studies* 40, 1-43.

Hylleberg, J and Christensen, J T 1977 'Phenotypic variation and fitness of periwinkles (Gastropoda:

Littorinidae) in relation to exposure', *Journal of Molluscan Studies* 43, 192-9.

Ingrem C 2005 'The fish remains', in, Sharples, N, *A Norse farmstead in the Outer Hebrides: Excavations at Mound 3, Bornais, South Uist*, 41-9. Oxford: Oxbow Books.

Inizan, M-L, Roche, H and Tixier, J 1992 *Technology of knapped stone*, Préhistoire de la Pierre Taillée, 3. Meudon: Cercle de Recherches et d'Etudes Préhistoriques.

Innes, C (ed) 1867 *The ledger of Andrew Halyburton, Conservator of the Privileges of the Scots nation in the Netherlands, 1492-1503, together with the book of customs and valuation of merchandises in Scotland, 1612.* Edinburgh: H M General Register House.

Islands Books Trust 2005 *Traditions of sea-bird fowling in the North Atlantic region.* Callicvol, Isle of Lewis: Islands Books Trust.

Jacomet, S 1987 *Prähistorische Getreidefunde, Eine Anleitung zur Bestimmung Prähistorischer Gersten und Weizen Funde.* Basel: Herausgegeben im Eigenverlag.

Johnston, M 2006 'Medieval/post-medieval pottery', in Simpson, D D A, Murphy, E M and Gregory, R A, *Excavations at Northton, Isle of Harris.* British Archaeological Reports, British Series 408, 168-9. Oxford: Archaeopress.

Jordan, W C 2008 'A fresh look at medieval sanctuary', in Mazo Karras, R, Kaye, J and Matter, E A (eds), *Law and the illicit in Medieval Europe*, 17-32. Philadelphia: University of Pennsylvania Press.

Kelleher, C, 2007 'The Gaelic O' Driscoll Lords of Baltimore, Co. Cork: settlement, economy and conflict in a maritime cultural landscape', in Doran, L and Lyttleton, J (eds), *Lordship in Medieval Ireland: Image and reality*, 130-59. Dublin: Four Courts Press.

Kelly, F 1988 *A guide to early Irish Law.* Dublin: Dublin Institute for Advanced Studies.

Kelly, F 2005 'Law schools, learned families' and 'Law texts', in Duffy 2005, 263-66.

Kirk, J (ed) 1995 *The Books of Assumption of the thirds of benefices: Scottish Ecclesiastical Rentals at the Reformation.* Oxford: Oxford University Press.

Knapp, W R 1996 'Making your own gunflints', in *The History and Primitive Technology Page.* http://www.onagocag.com/gunflnt.html accessed 23 September 2011.

Koch, E 1990 'Fire', *Skalk* 5, 16-17.

Lamb, R G 1973 'Coastal settlements of the North', *Scottish Archaeological Forum* 5, 76-98.

Lane, A 1983 *Dark-age and Viking-age pottery in the Hebrides, with special reference to the Udal, North Uist.* University College, London: unpublished PhD thesis.

Lane, A 1990 'Hebridean pottery: problems of definition, chronology, presence and absence', *in* Armit, I (ed) *Beyond the brochs*, 108-30. Edinburgh: Edinburgh University Press.

Lane, A 2005 'Pottery', in Sharples, N, *A Norse farmstead in the Outer Hebrides: Excavations at Mound 3, Bornais, South Uist*, 194-5. Oxford: Oxbow Books.

Lane, A 2007 *Ceramic and cultural change in the Hebrides AD 500-1300*. Cardiff: Cardiff Studies in Archaeology Specialist Report No 29.

Lawrence, M 1990 *The Yachtsman's pilot to the west coast of Scotland: Castle Bay to Cape Wrath*. St. Ives, Cambridgeshire: Imray, Laurie, Norie and Wilson.

Lawson, B 1994 *The teampull on the Isle of Pabbay: a Harris church in its historical setting,* Northton, Isle of Harris: Bill Lawson.

Lawson, B 2004 *North Uist in history and legend*. Edinburgh: John Donald.

Lawson, B 2008 *Lewis in history and legend: The West Coast*. Edinburgh: Birlinn Ltd.

Loeber, R 2001 'An architectural history of Gaelic castles and settlements, 1370-1600', in Duffy, R J, Edwards, D and FitzPatrick, E (eds) *Gaelic Ireland c 1250 - c 1650: Land, lordship and settlement*, 271-314. Dublin: Four Courts Press.

Logan J 1972 'The operation of a glassworks in the Industrial Revolution', *Industrial Archaeology* 9 (20) 177-87.

de Lotbiniere, S 1977 'The story of the English gunflint', *Arms and Armour Society Journal* 9 (1), 18-53.

Low, G 1813 *Fauna Orcadensis or The natural history of the quadruplets, birds, reptiles, and fishes of Orkney and Shetland*. Edinburgh: George Ramsay and Co.

Lyman, R Lee 1994 *Vertebrate taphonomy*. Cambridge: Cambridge University Press.

MacCoinnich, A 2002 "His spirit was given only to warre': Conflict and identity in the Scottish Gàidhhealtachd c.1580-c.1630', in Murdoch, S and MacKillop, A (eds) *Fighting for identity: Scottish military experience, c. 1550-1900,* 133-62. Leiden, Boston, Köln: Brill.

MacCoinnich, A 2004 *Tùs gu iarlachd, eachdraidh Chlann Choinnich, c. 1466-1637*. University of Aberdeen, unpublished PhD thesis.

MacCoinnich, A. 2006(a) 'Mar phòr san uisge: Ìomhaigh Sìol Torcail ann an eachdraidh', in Byrne, M, Clancy T O and Kidd, S (eds), *Litreachas* and *eachdraidh, rannsachadh na Gàidhlig 2, 2002*, 214-231. Glasgow: University of Glasgow.

MacCoinnich, A 2006(b) "Cleiffis of Irne': Clann Choinnich agus gnìomhachas iarainn, c. 1569-1630', in: McLeod, W, Fraser, J E and Gunderloch, A (eds), *Cànan & cultar: rannsachadh na Gàidhlig 3*, 137-152. Edinburgh: Dunedin Academic Press.

MacCoinnich, A, 2007 'Siol Torcail and their lordship in the sixteenth century', in *Crossing the Minch: Exploring the links between Skye and the Outer Hebrides*, 7-32. Callicvol, Isle of Lewis: The Islands Book Trust.

MacCoinnich, A. 2008 'Where was Gaelic written in late medieval and Early Modern Scotland? Orthographic practices and cultural identities', in Ó Baoill, C and McGuire N (eds), *Caindel Alban. Fèill sgrìobhainn do Dhòmhnall E. Meek. = Scottish Gaelic Studies 24*, 305-356.

MacCoinnich, A forthcoming *Native and stranger. Plantation and civility in the North Atlantic world. The case of the northern Hebrides, 1570-1637*. Leiden: Brill.

Macdonald, Rev. D 1797 Parish of Barvas, *Old Statistical Account of Scotland (1795-7)*. Vol 19, 263-73.

Macdonald, D 1967 (reprinted 2004) *Tales and traditions of the Lews*. Edinburgh: Birlinn Ltd.

MacDonald, D F M (ed) 1981 *Fasti ecclesiæ Scoticanæ* (vol 10). Edinburgh: Oliver and Boyd.

Macdonald, N 1975 (ed) *[The] Morrison manuscript: Traditions of the Western Isles, by Donald Morison Cooper, Stornoway*, Stornoway: Stornoway Public Library.

McDonald, R A 1997 *The kingdom of the Isles. Scotland's western seaboard, c.1100-c.1336* East Linton: Tuckwell Press.

Macfarlane, N C 1924 *The 'Men' of the Lews*. Stornoway: Stornoway Gazette Office.

MacGeoch, C, Love, J, MacLeod F and MacGeoch, J 2010 *Sulaisgeir: Photographs by James MacGeoch*. Stornoway: Acair Ltd.

MacGilliosa, D 1981 *An Eaglais Shaor ann an Leódhas 1843-1900*. Edinburgh: Knox Press.

MacGregor, M 2002 'The genealogical histories of Gaelic Scotland', in Fox, A and Woolf, D (ed), *The spoken word. Oral culture in Britain, 1500-1850*, 196-139. Manchester: Manchester University Press.

MacGregor, M. 2006 'The Statutes of Iona, text and context', *The Innes Review* 57 (2), 111-181.

MacGregor, M 2008 'Writing the history of Gaelic Scotland: A provisional checklist of 'Gaelic' genealogical histories', in Ó Baoill, C and McGuire N (eds), *Caindel Alban. Fèill sgrìobhainn do Dhòmhnall E. Meek. = Scottish Gaelic Studies* 24, 357-380.

McGurk, F (ed) 1976 *Papal letters to Scotland of Benedict XIII of Avignon 1394-1419*. Scottish History Society, Edinburgh: T and A Constable. Fourth Series, Vol 13.

McHardy, I, Barrowman, C S and MacLeod, M 2009 *STAC: the Severe Terrain Archaeological Campaign -*

investigation of stack sites of the Isle of Lewis 2003-2005. Scottish Archaeological Internet Report 36. http://www.sair.org.uk/sair36/index.html

Macinnes, A I 1993 'Crown clans and fine: the 'Civilising' of Scottish Gaeldom, 1587-1638', *Northern Scotland* 13, 31-55.

Macinnes, A I 1996 *Clanship, commerce and the House of Stewart, 1603-1788*. East Linton: Tuckwell Press.

MacInnes, C T (ed) 1940 *Calendar of writs of Munros of Foulis, 1299-1823*. Edinburgh: Scottish Record Society.

Macinnes , J 2006 'Clan sagas and historical legends', in M Newton (ed), *Dùthchas nan Gaidheal. Selected essays of John Macinnes*, 48-63. Edinburgh: Birlinn Ltd.

Maciver, I 2003 'Martin, Sibbald and the 'indweller', John Morison', in J Randall (ed), *Martin Martin – 300 years on. Proceedings of a major 3-day event to mark the tercentenary of the publication of Martin Martin's book on the western Isles, 11-13 September 2003 in Ness, Isle of Lewis*, 56-64. Callicvol, Isle of Lewis: Islands Book Trust.

Mackay, A 1906 (reprinted 2009) *The book of Mackay*. Salem, Massachusetts: Higginson Book Co.

Mackay, J 1897 'Sutherland and the Reay country. History, Part I', in Gunn, A and Mackay, J (eds), *Sutherland and the Reay country*, 1-42. Glasgow: J Mackay.

Mackay, W (ed) 1905 *Chronicles of the Frasers, The Wardlaw manuscript entitled 'Polichronicon seu policratica temporum, or the True genealogy of the Frasers, 916-1674, by Master James Fraser minister of the parish of Wardlaw (now Kirkhill), Inverness*. Edinburgh: Scottish History Society.

Mackenzie, C 1792 'An account of some remains of antiquity in the Island of Lewis, one of the Hebrides', *Archaeologia Scotica* i, 282-92.

Mackenzie, A 1898 *History of the Munros of Fowlis*. Inverness: A and W McKenzie.

McKenzie, J 2008 'Soil micromorphology and bulk soil analyses', in Birch, S, Wildgoose, M and Kozikowski, G, *Uamh An Ard Achadh (High Pasture Cave): the preliminary assessment and analysis of late prehistoric cultural deposits from a limestone cave and associated surface features*. Data Structure Report HPC004.

Mackenzie, W C 1903 *History of the Outer Hebrides*. Edinburgh: Alex Gardner.

Mackenzie, W C 1905 'Notes on the Pigmies Isle, at the Butt of Lewis, with results of the recent exploration of the 'Pigmies Chapel' there', *Proceedings of the Society of Antiquaries of Scotland* 39 (1904-5), 248-58.

Mackenzie, W C 1919 *The Book of the Lews: the story of a Hebridean isle*. Edinburgh: Alex Gardner.

Mackie, C 2006a *The development of the Lewis house in the nineteenth and twentieth centuries, with particular emphasis on the Bragar township*. Phd thesis, University of Edinburgh.

Mackie, C 2006b 'The development of traditional housing in the Isle of Lewis: Social and Cultural influences on vernacular architecture', *Béaloideas* 74, 65-102.

Mackie, C 2013 'The bed-alcove tradition in Ireland and Scotland: reappraising the evidence', *Proceedings of the Royal Irish Academy* 113C, 1-32.

Mackie, C forthcoming 'Crossing the threshold: Negotiating space in the vernacular houses of the Isle of Lewis', *Archaeological Journal*, accepted for publication.

MacLean, G and MacLeod, F 1989 'Captain Otter and Captain Thomas', in MacLeod, F (ed) 1989, 117-121.

MacLeod, A P 2000 'The ancestry of Leod', *Clan MacLeod Magazine* 91, 262-70.

MacLeod, F (ed) 1989 *Togail tir. Marking time. The map of the Western Isles*, Stornoway: Acair Ltd and An Lanntair Gallery.

MacLeod, F 2009 *The Norse mills of Lewis*. Stornoway: Acair Ltd.

MacLeod, G 2005 *Muir is tìr*. Stornoway: Acair Ltd.

Macleod, J 1965 *By-paths of Highland church history*. Edinburgh: Knox Press.

MacLeod, J 2008 *Banner in the west: A spiritual history of Lewis and Harris*. Edinburgh: Birlinn Ltd.

MacLeod, R C (ed) 1938 *The Book of Dunvegan, being documents from the muniments room of the Macleods, 1340-1700, Vol. 1*. Aberdeen: Third Spalding Club.

McLeod, W and Bateman, M 2007 *Duanaire na Sracaire. Songbook of the Pillagers. Anthology of medieval Gaelic poetry*. Edinburgh: Birlinn Ltd.

McNabb, J and Ashton, N 1990 'Clactonian gunflints', *Lithics* 11, 44-7.

Mac-Neacail, N. 1894 *An t-Urramach Iain Mac-Rath ('Mac-Rath Mór')*. Inverness: A MacLabhruinn.

Macphail, J R N (ed) 1914 *Highland Papers Vol. I*. Edinburgh: Scottish History Society, Second Series, 5.

Macphail, J R N (ed) 1916 *Highland Papers Vol. II*. Edinburgh: Scottish History Society, Second Series, 12.

Macphail, Rev. M 1895 'Traditions, customs and superstitions of the Lewis', *Folk-Lore* 6, 162-70.

Macphail, Rev. M 1898 'Teampull-Eoropie, Lewis', *Oban Times*, 5 November 1898.

MacPhàrlainn, C, deas. 1923 *Dòrlach Laoighean do Sgrìobhadh le Donnchadh MacRath, 1688* (Làmh-sgrìobhainn Mhic Rath / Fernaig Manuscript). Dundee: MacLeoid.

MacQueen, H L 1995 'Scots law and national identity', *Scottish Historical Review* 74, 1-25.

McSheffrey, S 2009 'Sanctuary and the legal topography of pre-Reformation London', *Law and History Review* 27, 483-514.

MacTavish, D C (ed) 1943 *Minutes of the Synod of Argyll, 1639-1651*. Edinburgh: Scottish History Society.
Maguire, D 2002 'Geophysical survey', in Barrowman 2002, 11-15.

Mann, L 1908 'Report on a pottery churn from the island of Coll, and remarks on Hebridean pottery', *Proceedings of the Society of Antiquaries of Scotland* 44, 326-8.

Martin, Martin 1703 *A description of the Western Isles of Scotland*. London: A. Bell.

Martin, Martin 1999 *A description of the Western Islands of Scotland circa 1695*. Edinburgh: Birlinn Ltd.

Martingell, H E 2003 'Later prehistoric and historic use of flint in England', in Moloney, N and Shott, M J (eds), *Lithic analysis at the Millennium*, 91-7. London: Institute of Archaeology, University College London.

Marwick, J D (ed) 1876 *Extracts from the Records of the Burgh of Glasgow, A D 1573-1642*. Glasgow: Scottish Burgh Records Society.

Matheson, W 1970 *An Clàrsair Dall. Orain Ruaidhri Mhic Mhuirich agus a chuid ciùil. The Blind Harper. The Songs of Roderick Morison and his Music*. Edinburgh: Scottish Gaelic Texts Society.

Matheson, W 1974 'The Pape Riot and its sequel in Lewis', *Transactions of the Gaelic Society of Inverness* 48 (1972-4), 395-434.

Matheson, W 1979 'The Morrisons of Ness', *Transactions of the Gaelic Society of Inverness* 50, 60-80.

Matheson, W 1980(a) 'The ancestry of the MacLeods', *Transactions of the Gaelic Society of Inverness* 51 (1978-80), 68-80.

Matheson, W 1980(b) 'The MacLeods of Lewis', *Transactions of the Gaelic Society of Inverness* 51 (1978-80), 320-37.

Maxwell-Irving, A M T 1971 'Early firearms and their influence on the military and domestic architecture of the Borders', *Proceedings of the Society of Antiquaries of Scotland* 103 (1970-1), 199-224.

Meaden, H Anderson 1921 'Eorrapaidh in the Lews: an ancient church restored', *Transactions of the Scottish Ecclesiological Society* 6 (3, 1920-1), 170-3.

Medieval Pottery Research Group 1998 *A guide to the classification of medieval ceramic forms* (Occasional Paper

1), MPRG.

Medieval Pottery Research Group 2001 *Minimum standards for the processing, recording, analysis and publication of Post-Roman ceramics* (Occasional Paper 2), MPRG.

Mijers, E 2006 'A natural partnership? Scotland and Zeeland in the early seventeenth century', in Macinnes A I and Williamson, A H (eds), *Shaping the Stuart world, 1603-1714: The Atlantic connection*, 233-60. Leiden: Brill.

Miket, R and Roberts, D L 1990 *The mediaeval castles of Skye and Lochalsh*, Portree: MacLean Press.

Mikkelsen, E 1991 'Flintmaterialet', in Schia E and Molaug P B (eds) *De arkeologiske utgravninger i Gamlebyen, Oslo 8. Dagliglivets gjenstander - Del II*, 251-71. Øvre Ervik: Alvheim and Eide/Akademisk Forlag.

Mikkelsen, E 1994 *Fangstprodukter i vikingtidens og middelalderens økonomi: Organiseringen av massefangst av villrein i Dovre.* Universitetets Oldsaksamlings Skrifter, Ny rekke 18. Oslo: Universitetets Oldsaksamling.

Miles, A 1989 *An early Christian chapel and burial ground on the Isle of Ensay, Outer Hebrides, Scotland with a study of the skeletal remains.* British Archaeological Reports, British Series 212. Oxford: Archaeopress.

Mitchell, A 1862 'On various superstitions in the north-west Highlands and Islands of Scotland, especially in relation to lunacy', *Proceedings of the Society of Antiquaries of Scotland* 4 (1860-2), 251-88.

Mitchell, A 1880 *The past in the present: what is civilisation?* Edinburgh: David Douglas.

Mitchell, A and Clark, A T (eds) 1908. *Geographical collections relating to Scotland made by Walter MacFarlane. Edited from MacFarlane's manuscript in the Advocates Library by Sir Arthur Mitchell.* (3 vols, 1906-8). Edinburgh: Scottish History Society.

Mitchell K L, Murdoch K R and Ward, J R 2001 *Fast Castle, excavations 1971-86.* Edinburgh: Edinburgh Archaeological Field Society.

Monro, D 1549 (reprinted 1999) *Description of the Occidental, i.e. Western Islands of Scotland by Mr Donald Monro who travelled through many of them in Anno 1549*, appendix in Martin Martin: *A Description of the Western Islands of Scotland circa 1695*, 299-334. Edinburgh, Birlinn Ltd.

Moore, P D, Webb, J A and Collinson, M E 1991 (2nd edition) *Pollen analysis.* Oxford: Blackwell Scientific Publications.

Moreno-Nuño, M R 1994a *Arqueomalacología. Identificación de moluscos.* Informe no. 1994/18. Madrid: Laboratorio de Arqueozoologia. Madrid: Universidad Autónoma de Madrid.

Moreno- Nuño, M R 1994b *Arqueomalacologia: Cuantificacion de moluscos.* Informe no. 1994/19. Madrid: Laboratorio de Arqueozoologia. Madrid: Universidad Autonoma de Madrid.

Morris, C D; Batey, C E and Rackham, D J 1995 *Freswick Links, Caithness excavation and survey of a Norse settlement*. Inverness and New York: Highland Libraries/NABO.

Morrison, A and Mackinnon, D 1968-1976 *The Macleods - The genealogy of a clan* (Five parts), Edinburgh: Clan Macleod Societies.

Morrison, A 1986 *The chiefs of Clan MacLeod*. East Kilbride: Associated Clan MacLeod Societies.

Morrison, D 1997 *Nis Aosmhor. The photographs of Dan Morrison*, Stornoway: Acair Ltd

Mould, D D C Pochin 1953 *West-over-sea*. Edinburgh: Oliver and Boyd.

Munro, R W (ed) 1978 *The Munro Tree: a genealogy and chronology of the Munros of Foulis and other families of the clan: a manuscript compiled in 1734*. Edinburgh: Munro.

Munro, R W and Munro, J (eds) 1986 *Acts of the Lords of the Isles, 1336-1493*. Edinburgh: Scottish History Society.

Naessens, P 2007 'Gaelic Lords of the Sea: the coastal tower houses of south Connemara', in Doran, L and Lyttleton, J (eds), *Lordship in medieval Ireland: Image and reality*, 217-35. Dublin: Four Courts Press.

Nelson, W 2004 'Notes on flints and flintlocks'. The web site of *The New Zealand Society of Gunsmiths Incorporated*. http://www.gunsmithsociety.com/technical-flints-print.htm accessed 23 September 2011.

NicAoidh, C 2000 *Mullaichean Taighean nan Eilean Siar (a'toirt a-steach Hiort agus Tiriodh)*. Unpublished MSc thesis, Department of Celtic. University of Edinburgh: Edinburgh.

Nicolson, A 1995 (2nd edition) *The history of Skye*. Portree: Maclean Press.

Nicholson, R A 1991 *An investigation into variability within archaeologically recovered assemblages of faunal remains: The influence of pre-depositional taphonomic processes*. University of York: unpublished PhD thesis.

Nixon M and Whiteley D 1972 *The Oxford book of vertebrates*. Oxford: Oxford University Press.

North, J J 1991-6 *English hammered coinage Vol 2, 1272-1662*. London: Spink.

Ó Baoill, C and Bateman, M 1994 *Gàir nan clàrsach. The harps' cry. An anthology of seventeenth century Gaelic poetry*. Edinburgh: Birlinn Ltd.

O'Dowd, M (ed) 2000 *Calendar of state papers Ireland: Tudor period, 1571-1575*. Dublin: Public Record Office.

Oftedal, M 1954 'The village names of Lewis in the Outer Hebrides', *Norsk tidsskrift for sprogvidenskap* 17, 363-409.

Ottaway, P 1992 *Anglo-Scandinavian ironwork from Coppergate. The archaeology of York. The small finds 17/6*.

York: Council for British Archaeology.

Parker-Pearson, M and Sharples, N 1999 *Between land and sea: excavations at Dun Vulan*. Sheffield Environmental and Archaeological Research Campaign in the Hebrides vol 3. Sheffield: Sheffield Academic Press Ltd.

Parr, J F and Boyd, W E 2002 'The probable industrial origin of archaeological daub at an Iron Age site in Northeast Thailand', *Geoarchaeology* 17 (3), 285-303.

Phillips E 2006 'Pottery petrology', in Simpson, D D A, Murphy, E M and Gregory, R A, *Excavations at Northton, Isle of Harris*, British Archaeological Reports, British Series 408, 208-226. Oxford: Archaeopress.

Pitcairn, R (ed) 1833 *Ancient criminal trials of Scotland, compiled from original records and mss, with historical illustrations, etc.* (3 vols in 7 parts). Edinburgh: Bannatyne Club.

Pitcairn, R (ed) 1862 *The autobiography and diary of Mr James Melville, minister of Kilrenny in Fife and Professor of Theology in the University of St Andrews. With a continuation of the diary*. Edinburgh: Wodrow Society.

Poller, T 2007(a) 'Area 4 Carnan a Ghrodhair: Geophysical survey', in Barrowman 2007, 28-35.

Poller, T 2007(b) 'Area 6 Teampull Thòmais short cist: Geophysical survey', in Barrowman 2007, 38-41.

PoMS 2012 Beam, A, Bradley, J, Broun, D, Davies, J R, Hammond, M, Pasin, M (with others), *The people of medieval Scotland, 1093 – 1314*. Glasgow and London: www.poms.ac.uk.

Poller, T 2015a 'Taigh Mòr: Geophysics report', in Barrowman, C S 2015.

Poller, T 2015b 'Cnoc a'Chasteil: Geophysical survey results', in Barrowman, C S 2015.

Prummel, W and Frishch, H-J 1986 'A guide for the distinction of species, sex and body side in bones of sheep and goat', *Journal of Archaeological Science* 13, 567-77.

Punt, W 1976-91 *The northwest European pollen Flora*. Vol.1-6. Amsterdam: Elsevier.

Quine, D A (ed) 2001 *Expeditions to the Hebrides by George Clayton Atkinson in 1831 and 1833*. Waternish: Lusta.

Raven, J A 2005 *Medieval landscapes and lordship in South Uist*. University of Glasgow, unpublished PhD thesis.

RCRBS = Marwick, J D (ed) 1870-1890 *Records of the Convention of the Royal Burghs of Scotland 1295-1738* (6 vols). Edinburgh: William Paterson.

RPS = Brown, K M, Macintosh, G H, Mann, A J, Ritchie, P E and Tanner, R J (eds) 2007-2011 *Records of the Parliaments of Scotland to 1707*. St Andrews: The University of St Andrews. http://www.rps.ac.uk/

accessed 23 September 2011.

RPCS = Masson, D and Burton J H (eds) 1877-1898 *Register of the Privy Council of Scotland, 1545-1625.* (First Series, Vols. 1-14) Edinburgh: H. M. General Register House.

RPCS = Masson, D and Hume Brown P (eds) 1899-1906 *Register of the Privy Council of Scotland 1625-1643.* (Second Series, Vols 1-7) Edinburgh: H. M. General Register House.

RSS = *Registrum Secreti Sigilli regum Scotorum.* Livingstone, M et al (eds) 1948-1982 *Register of the Privy Seal of Scotland 1488-1580.* (8 vols) Edinburgh: H.M. General Register House.

Reimer, P J, Baillie, M G L, Bard, E, Bayliss, A, Beck, J W, Blackwell, P G, Bronk Ramsey, C, Buck, C E, Burr, G S, Edwards, R L, Friedrich, M, Grootes, P M, Guilderson, T P, Hajdas, I, Heaton, T J, Hogg, A G, Hughen, K A, Kaiser, K F, Kromer, B, McCormac, F G, Manning, S W, Reimer, R W, Richards, D A, Southon, J R, Talamo, S, Turney, C S M, van der Plicht, J, and Weyhenmeyer, C E 2009 'IntCal09 and Marine09 radiocarbon age calibration curves, 0-50,000 years cal BP', *Radiocarbon* 51 (4), 1111-50.

Reis, B 2004 'Certificate of authenticity. Musket flint from Earl of Abergavenny (Wrecked 1805)', The web site of *Anything Anywhere - Militaria, civicalia, politicalia, religialia.* http://www.anythinganywhere.com/commerce/military/brgunfltenl.htm accessed 23 September 2011.

Richards, M P, Fuller, B T, Molleson, T 2006 'Stable isotope palaeodietary study of humans and fauna from the multiperiod (Iron Age, Viking and Late Medieval) site of Newark Bay, Orkney', *Journal of Archaeological Science* 33, 122-31.

Robertson, H 1976 'Studies in Carmichael's Carmina Gadelica', *Scottish Gaelic Studies* 12 (2), 220-65.

Robson, M 1991 *Rona: the distant island.* Stornoway: Acair Ltd.

Robson, M 1997 *A desert place in the Sea. The early churches of Northern Lewis.* Habost, Ness: Comunn Eachdraidh Nis.

Robson, M 2004 *Forts and fallen walls. The duns of northern Lewis.* Port of Ness: Islands Book Trust.

Robson, M (ed) 2008 *People of Ness. Some earlier records – Galson to Eoropie,* 10 Callicvol, Ness: Michael Robson.

RCAHMS 1928 *The Royal Commission on the Ancient and Historical Monuments of Scotland. Ninth report with inventory of monuments and constructions in the Outer Hebrides, Skye and the Small Isles.* Edinburgh: HMSO.

Salter, M 1995 *The castles of western and northern Scotland.* Malvern: Folly Publications.

Sanderson, M H B 1982 *Scottish rural society in the sixteenth century.* Edinburgh: John Donald.

Sanderson, M H B 2002 *A kindly place? Living in sixteenth century Scotland.* East Linton: Tuckwell Press.

Schiegl, S, Goldberg, P, Bar-Yosef, O. and Weiner, S 1996 'Ash deposits in Hayonim and Kebara Caves, Israel: Macroscopic, microscopic and mineralogical observations, and their archaeological implications', *Journal of Archaeological Science* 23, 763-781.

Schiffer, M B 1986 'Radiocarbon dating and the "old wood" problem: the case of the Hohokam chronology', *Journal of Archaeological Science* 13, 13-30.

Schiffer, M B 1987 *Formation processes of the archaeological record.* Albuquerque: University of New Mexico Press.

Schmid, E 1972 *Atlas of animal bones for prehistorians, archaeologists and quaternary geologists.* Amsterdam and London: Elsevier.

Schweingruber, F H 1990 *Anatomy of European woods.* Berne and Stuttgart: Haupt.

Scott, AW 2007 'Thatching in the Outer Hebrides', *Structural Survey* 25, 127-47.

Scott, L 1951 'Corn-drying kilns', *Antiquity* 25:100, 196-208.

Sellar, W D H 1981 'Highland family origins, pedigree making and pedigree faking', in MacLean, L (ed) *The Middle Ages in the Highlands*, 103-16. Inverness: Inverness Field Club.

Sellar, W D H 1989 'O'Donnell Lecture 1985. Celtic law and Scots law: Survival and integration', *Scottish Studies* 29, 1-28.

Sellar, W D H 1998 'The ancestry of the Macleods reconsidered', *Transactions of the Gaelic Society of Inverness* 60 (1997-8), 233-58.

Sellar, W D H, Maclean A and Harman-Nicolson, C B 1999 *The Highland Clan MacNeacail or MacNicol. A history of the Nicolsons of Scorrybreac.* Waternish: Maclean Press.

Sharples, N 2000 'Bornais (South Uist parish) Late Iron Age to Norse houses and settlement', *Discovery and Excavation in Scotland* 1999, 90.

Shaw, F J 1980 *The Northern and Western Isles of Scotland: Their economy and society in the seventeenth century.* Edinburgh: John Donald Publishers Ltd.

Silver, I A 1969 'The ageing of domestic animals', in Brothwell, D R and Higgs, E S (eds), *Science in archaeology: A comprehensive survey of progress and research*, 283-302. London: Thames and Hudson Ltd.

Simms, K 1990 'The Brehons of medieval Ireland', in Hogan D and Osborough, W N (eds), *Brehons, Serjeants and Attorneys, studies in the history of the Irish legal profession*, 67-70. Dublin: Irish Academic Press.

Simpson, IA, Milek, K B and Guðmundsson, G 1999 'A reinterpretation of the great pit at Hofstaðir, Iceland using sediment thin section micromorphology', *Geoarchaeology* 14 (6), 511-30.

Simpson, I A, Vesteinsson, O, Adderley, W P and McGovern T H 2003 'Fuel resource utilisation in landscapes of settlement', *Journal of Archaeological Science* 30 (11), 1401-20.

Skertchley, S B J 1879 *On the manufacture of gunflints, the methods of excavating for flint, the age of Palaeolithic man, and the connection (sic) between Neolithic art and the gunflint trade*. Memoirs of the Geological Survey of England and Wales. London: HMSO.

Smith, B F and Bain, D C 1982 'A sodium hydroxide fusion method for the determination of total phosphate in soils', *Communications in soil science and plant analysis* 13 (3), 185-90.

Smith, A N and Forster, A 2007 'Steatite', in Hunter, J (with J M Bond and A N Smith) *Vol 1: Excavations at Pool, Sanday. A multi-period settlement from Neolithic to Late Norse times. Investigatons in Sanday, Orkney*, 412-433. Kirkwall: The Orcadian Ltd/Historic Scotland.

Stace, C 1997 (2nd edition) *New flora of the British Isles*. Cambridge: Cambridge University Press.

Stapert, D and Johansen, L 1999 'Flint and pyrite: making fire in the Stone Age', *Antiquity* 73 (282), 765-77.

Steier, P and Rom, W 2000 'The use of Bayesian statistics for ^{14}C dates of chronologically ordered samples: a critical analysis', *Radiocarbon* 42 (2), 183-198.

Steier, P, Rom, W and Puchegger, S 2001 'New methods and critical aspects in Bayesian mathematics for ^{14}C calibration', *Radiocarbon* 43 (2A), 373-80.

Stevenson, R B K 1952 'Coin hoard, Castle Maol, Skye', *Proceedings of the Society of Antiquaries of Scotland* 85, 1950-51, 158-9.

Stiùbhart, D U 2006(a) 'Some heathenish and superstitious rites: A letter from Lewis, 1700', *Scottish Studies* 34, 205-26.

Stiùbhart, D U 2006(b) 'The early history of Ness - an interpretation', in *Island Notes* 23. Coll/ Isle of Lewis: The Islands Book Trust.

Stiùbhart, D U 2007 'Uses of historical traditions in Scottish Gaelic', in Beech J, Hand, O, Mulhern, M and Weston, J (eds), *Oral literature and performance culture* (*Compendium of Scottish Ethnology* Vol. 10), 124-52. Edinburgh: John Donald/European Ethnological Research Centre.

Stone, L M 1974 *Fort Michilimackinac 1715-1781. An archaeological perspective on the revolutionary frontier*. Anthropological series. East Lansing: Publications of the Museum, Michigan State University.

Stoops, G 2003 *Guidelines for the analysis and description of soil and regolith thin sections*. Madison, Wisconsin: Soil Science Society of America.Storer-Clouston, J (ed) 1914 *Records of the earldom of Orkney, 1299-1614*. Edinburgh: Scottish History Society.

Stummann Hansen, S 2000 'A wealth of archaic building customs: Gudmund Hatt's journey to the Hebrides in 1936', *Review of Scottish Culture* 13 (2000), 87-105.

Symonds, J, Badcock, A, Parsons, V and Brighton, S 2001 'Airigh Mhuilinn', *Discovery and Excavation in Scotland*, New Series Vol 1(2000), 96.

TA = Dickson, T, Paul, J B and Macinnes, C T 1877-1978 *Accounts of the Lord High Treasurer of Scotland 1473-1580: Compota Thesaurariorum Regum Scotorum 1473-1580.* (13 vols). Edinburgh: HM General Register House.

Thomas F W L 1862 'Notice of beehive houses in Harris and Lewis; with traditions of the Each-uisge,' or Water-horse, connected therewith', *Proceedings of the Society of Antiquaries of Scotland* 3 (1857-9), 127-44.

Thomas, F W L 1863 'Observations respecting articles collected in the Outer Hebrides, and now presented to the museum', *Proceedings of the Society of Antiquaries of Scotland* 4 (1860-2), 115-19.

Thomas, F W L 1870 'On the primitive dwellings and Hypogea of the outer Hebrides', *Proceedings of the Society of Antiquaries of Scotland* 7 (1866-8), 153-95.

Thomas, F W L 1878 'Traditions of the Morrisons (Clan MacGhillemhuire), hereditary judges of Lewis', *Proceedings of the Society of Antiquaries of Scotland* 12 (1876-8), 503-56.

Thomas, F W L 1880 'Traditions of the Macaulays of Lewis', *Proceedings of the Society of Antiquaries of Scotland* 14, 363-431.

Thomas, F W L 1890 'On the duns of the Outer Hebrides', *Archaeologia Scotica* 5, 365-415.

Tipping, R 1995 'Holocene landscape change at Carn Dubh, near Pitlochry, Perthshire, Scotland', *Journal of Quaternary Science* 10, 59-75.

Turnbull J 2001 *The Scottish glass industry 1610-1750.* Edinburgh: Society of Antiquaries of Scotland, Monograph No 18.

Turner, D J and Dunbar, J G 1970 'Breachacha Castle, Coll: excavation and field survey 1965-71', *Proceedings of the Society of Antiquaries of Scotland* 102, 155-87.

Umbanhower, C E and McGrath, M 1998 'Experimental production and analysis of microscopic charcoal from wood, leaves and grasses', *The Holocene* 8, 341-6.

Van den Bossche, W 2001 *Antique wine bottles, their history and evolution 1500-1850.* Suffolk: Antique Collectors' Club.

van der Veen, M 1992 *Crop husbandry regimes.* University of Sheffield Archaeological Monographs 3. Sheffield: Sheffield Academic Press Ltd.

Von Den Driesch, A E 1976 *A guide to the measurement of animal bones from archaeological sites.* Cambridge, Massachusetts: Peabody Museum of Archaeology and Ethnology, Harvard University Bulletin 1.

Walker, B and MacGregor, C 1996 *The Hebridean blackhouse. A guide to materials, construction and maintenance.* Edinburgh: Historic Scotland Technical Advice Note 5.

Walton Rogers, P 1997 *Textile production at 16-22 Coppergate*. The archaeology of York The small finds 17/11. York: Council for British Archaeology.

Watkins, C 2004 "Folklore' and 'Popular Religion' in Britain during the Middle Ages', *Folklore* 115, 140-50.

Watson, W J 1926 *The history of the Celtic place-names of Scotland*. Edinburgh: W. Blackwood and Sons Ltd.

Watt, J, Pierce, G J and Boyle, P R 1997 *Guide to the identification of North Sea fish using Premaxilla and vertebra*. Denmark: ICES Cooperative Research Report No. 220.

Weber, H, (ed) = Gordon, Sir Robert 1813 *Genealogical history of the Earldom of Sutherland from its origin to the year 1630 with a continuation to the year 1651*. Edinburgh: A Constable.

Wheeler, A 1969 *The fishes of the British Isles and north-west Europe*. London: Macmillan.

Wheeler, A 1978 *Key to the fishes of northern Europe*. London: Frederick Warne.

Wheeler, A and Jones, A K J 1989 *Fishes*. Cambridge Manuals in Archaeology. Cambridge: Cambridge University Press.

Whittaker, J C 2001 'The oldest British industry: continuity and obsolescence in a flintknapper's sample set', *Antiquity* 75, 382-90.

Wood, M (ed) 1936 *Extracts from the records of the burgh of Edinburgh, 1626 to 1641*. Edinburgh: Oliver and Boyd.

Wordsworth, J 1982 'Excavation of the settlement at 13-21 Castle Street, Inverness, 1979', *Proceedings of the Society of Antiquaries of Scotland* 112 (1982), 322-91.

Wormald, J 1985 *Lords and men in Scotland: Bonds of Manrent, 1442-1603*. Edinburgh: John Donald.

Yeoman, L (ed) 2004 *Witchcraft cases from the register of Commissions of the Privy Council of Scotland, 1630-1642*. Edinburgh: Scottish History Society (Miscellany III), 223-65.

Young, A l956 'Excavations at Dun Cuier, Isle of Barra, Outer Hebrides', *Proceedings of the Society of Antiquaries of Scotland* 89 (1955-6), 290-328.

Young, M D 1993 *The Parliaments of Scotland. Burgh and Shire Commissioners*. Edinburgh: Scottish Academic Press.

Zohary, D and Hopf, M 2000 (3rd edition) *Domestication of plants in the Old World*. Oxford: Oxford University Press.